CRM at the Speed of Light, Fourth Edition:
Social CRM Strategies, Tools, and Techniques for Engaging Your Customers

Paul Greenberg

New York Chicago San Francisco Lisbon London Madrid Mexico City
Milan New Delhi San Juan Seoul Singapore Sydney Toronto

The *McGraw·Hill* Companies

Library of Congress Cataloging-in-Publication Data

Greenberg, Paul.
  CRM at the speed of light : social CRM strategies, tools, and techniques
for engaging your customers / Paul Greenberg.—4th ed.
      p.   cm.
  ISBN 978-0-07-159045-7 (alk. paper)
  1. Customer relations—Management.   2. Electronic commerce.   I. Title.
  HF5415.5.G743   2009
  658.8'12—dc22   2009038435

McGraw-Hill books are available at special quantity discounts to use as premiums and sales promotions, or for use in corporate training programs. To contact a representative, please e-mail us at bulksales@mcgraw-hill.com.

CRM at the Speed of Light, Fourth Edition: Social CRM Strategies, Tools, and Techniques for Engaging Your Customers

1 2 3 4 5 6 7 8 9 0   FGR FGR   0 1 9

ISBN   978-0-07-159045-7
MHID   0-07-159045-5

Sponsoring Editor Roger Stewart	**Indexer** Karin Arrigoni
Project Editor Patty Mon	**Production Supervisor** Jean Bodeaux
Acquisitions Coordinator Joya Anthony	**Composition** Glyph International
Copy Editor Lunaea Weatherstone	**Illustration** Glyph International
Proofreader Paul Tyler	**Art Director, Cover** Jeff Weeks

··

In January 2008, I lost my father, Abraham, at the age of 93. Many people say to me, "He lived a long life." But I will always think it wasn't long enough. Dad, I think about you every day and miss you all of them. You were and are a great father and for that I give you, not just this book, but my heart.

About the Author

Paul Greenberg is president of The 56 Group, LLC, a customer strategy consulting firm, focused on cutting-edge CRM strategic services, and a founding partner of the CRM training company BPT Partners, LLC, a training and consulting venture composed of a number of CRM luminaries that has quickly become the certification authority for the CRM industry.

CRM at the Speed of Light: Essential Customer Strategies for the 21st Century has been published in eight languages and called "the bible of the CRM industry." It is used by more than 70 universities as a primary text. It was named "the number one CRM book" by SearchCRM.com in 2002 and is one of two books recommended by CustomerThink. The Asian edition of *CIO Magazine* named it one of the 12 most important books an Asian CEO will ever read. Paul has also authored two other books, *Special Edition: Using PeopleSoft* (Que, 1999) and *E-Government for Public Officials* (Thompson Publishing, 2003).

Paul is the co-chairman of Rutgers University's CRM Research Center and the executive vice president of the CRM Association. He is a board of advisors member of the Baylor University MBA program for CRM majors, a unique national program.

Paul is considered a thought-leader in CRM, having been published in numerous industry and business publications over the years and having traveled the world speaking on cutting-edge CRM topics geared to the contemporary social customer. He has been called "the dean of CRM," "the godfather of CRM," and even the "Walt Whitman of CRM" by analysts and organizations throughout the industry. In fact, at the end of 2007, he was the number one nonvendor influencer, named by InsideCRM in their annual "25 Most Influential CRM People" announcement. He was also named one of the most influential CRM leaders in 2008 by *CRM Magazine*. Paul is known particularly for his work on the use of social media, such as blogs, podcasts, and wikis, and social networks in CRM as tools for customer collaboration with a company. He is often seen as the "voice of the customer" and is well known within the CRM industry for this work. His blog, PGreenblog (the56group .typepad.com), was named the winner of the first annual CRM Blog of the Year in 2005 by SearchCRM and the 2007 "Whatis" Award for CRM blogs, by their parent company, TechTarget. He also received the Number One CRM Blog award from InsideCRM at the end of 2007 and in 2008. The blog is also the central focus of KnowledgeStorm's CRM Blog community. He now also writes the CRM blog for high profile technology media property, ZDNet (blogs.zdnet.com/crm).

Paul is a member of the Destination CRM Board of Experts and the SearchCRM Expert Advisory Panel and a member of the board of advisors for GreaterChinaCRM, for many years among many others.

Paul lives in Manassas, Virginia, with his wife and five (yes, five!) cats. To reach Paul, please e-mail him at paul-greenberg3@comcast.net. You can follow him on Twitter at www.twitter.com/pgreenbe or join up with him on LinkedIn or Facebook.

Contents

Foreword

I have a saying that one always overestimates what can be done in one year and underestimate what can be done in ten years. We see this over and over in the technology industry, and we see it in other areas as well, including politics and the various industries with which we work every day.

But we have especially seen it in CRM. Most people would never have guessed ten years ago that our company would be where it is today. Who would have guessed that on-demand and software as a service would be key parts of our CRM vocabulary? The last decade has certainly been a fascinating and exciting time, and I am thrilled to be a part of it.

For another perspective, you can look back and see that it was not that long ago that CRM did not exist. There was also a time when software was designed for hobbyists—not business professionals—who used desktop computers, which looked radically different than they look now. And just before that era, there was no such thing as information technologists, the IT industry did not exist, and the stuff that ran enterprises was named after an age that had passed long ago—big iron. This was the time when mainframes were scary and movies had computer villains named suspiciously close to venerable companies (although offset by one letter). Yes, HAL was a villain in *2001*, but HAL knew things and people interacted with HAL in very interesting ways. They asked questions and they received answers, albeit those answers might not be the ones the people were looking for.

Why did HAL exist as a figment of Stanley Kubrick's and Arthur C. Clarke's imaginations? It was because *2001* was born at a precarious time in history. In 1968, there was immense distrust for organized entities and an immense feeling of individual freedom. Between the two, the twain might never meet! Individual empowerment was more of an emotion—something aspirational more than practical.

Individuals may have been slightly more empowered 40 years ago than they were a decade ago, but not much more. The reason is that they did not have the same level of access to knowledge as they do now. My, how times have changed. Just ten years ago, when CRM was emerging from its infancy, it was all about control and the management of people. I know—I spent 13 years in the enterprise software industry before I founded salesforce.com.

I did not bring up HAL as an example of how humans should interact with computers. I bring it up as an example of what the expectation of the future was at different eras. We are entering a new era now and as you would expect, the concept of CRM elicits new expectations. People interact with their CRM service—hopefully it is ours—and they get information back. The better the information that they put in, the better the system works, and the service can help them—as individuals and companies—make better decisions. That is the expectation of today and it has been remarkably effective.

If we stopped doing what we are doing right now, though, the world would still change. It is no longer the vendors that are driving what is needed in the industry. It is the consumers and individuals. It is you, the reader. You have always been ahead of the game; you have always known what is innovative and what is not.

I feel that, as a CEO of a major public company, I have always listened to you, via e-mail, via blogs, via phone calls and live conversations. And in listening to you, I think CRM should be able to help you even more. It should not be just about sales or service and support or marketing campaigns—three of the original core components of CRM. Those days are not gone. But they are evolving—rapidly—and it is at your request.

And the number one thing I am hearing is that CRM is ultimately about creating better relationships. It is a technology for sure—and that is how my company's service can help. It is also about process and, of course, people! We can help there as well. But first we all need to change the game—and we have to do it collaboratively. We have to work with you and make sure you are involved in the decision every step of the way.

Of course, you will always have issues about technology—what devices work with the system; how you can handle governance; how you can ensure that your systems are secure and safe; and how you can be more productive using our tools. We as an industry will continue to make gains there.

It is the way you interact with the system—whether it is ours or someone else's—that you will dictate. You will do it through something like our Ideas technology, which is now in use at salesforce.com as well as Starbucks and Dell. You will do it through portals, and you will provide your ideas directly into the CRM system, in effect changing the system from a tool to a collaborative engine.

I am extremely excited about this technology and the changes that are coming, and I am confident that these next few years will see the most incredible things happen in our industry.

This brings me to Paul Greenberg. If there is any one as excited about CRM as I am, it is Paul. But more than that, Paul has been talking about the age of collaboration and individual empowerment for years! If there is anyone who has set the tone for industry expectations or demand, it is Paul.

He has been incredibly right on about the state of the CRM industry. In fact, he has been leading the charge and setting the agenda. In other words, he is the one who has given some companies those aspirational goals that they cannot possibly hit in a year but could hit if they stuck it out a decade. I think it deeply saddens Paul when those companies do not execute. He takes it very personally. But one can imagine how thrilled he is when they do!

Paul has been an integral part of this industry for a long time. Before he was writing about CRM, he was a political radical fighting for individual rights, not knowing there would come a time when he would bring his experience to an industry that was as much about human empowerment as CRM is. It is hard to believe, but there may have been a time when Paul would not have guessed how much he was needed by that industry.

But things change. Now Paul is involved with consultancies, his blog, online publications, his speaking engagements around the world, and, of course, this incredible book. As Paul writes, software as a service has become mainstream. Venture capital companies on Sand Hill Road just south of our headquarters in San Francisco are not funding on-premise software companies anymore. They know that the next big thing is not going to be a company offering its software on CDs or DVDs. They know what the consumers already know—that it is the Internet that matters. And services should be delivered over the Internet. Paul was right there talking about it. But it is not just any service—it has to have something to do with collaboration.

I had an eye opening experience a while ago on a trip to Europe for our Dreamforce conference. Our team was showing me an example of collaboration between Facebook and salesforce.com, and I was accessing it on my iPod. There was no special software for the iPod—it was all handled on the Internet. You see this through Apple's App Store, too. There are thousands of applications, games, and productivity tools on the iPhone.

Everyone is connecting to different devices. The kids today who will be using services in business in the next few years do not interact with antiquated e-mail systems. They use Facebook. They expect collaboration and if they do not get it from their business applications, they will be frustrated and unproductive.

Paul has seen that already.

The best companies have been thinking of how they could manage these changes. Our company has seen this. We have been following Paul for a long time. Paul has always taken the voice of the customer and merging that with the most interesting technology trends, like Web 2.0, platform as a service, and an engine that absolutely fuels the customer/vendor relationship. Paul has been talking about this with the very first edition of *CRM at the Speed of Light.*

But he did not stop there. He rewrote the book from scratch, and then he did it again for the third edition. And now he is doing it again for the fourth edition. And guess what—he is on to something, and it is something I passionately believe in too.

This book is ultimately about collaboration. In fact, it is so deeply about collaboration that Paul has taken a collaborative effort in creating it. There are multiple contributors shepherded by Paul to create this fascinating and insightful analysis, not of what CRM is, but where it is going. It is not moving slowly. It is in fact moving at the speed of light. Get on board now, or you will be light years behind tomorrow.

—Marc Benioff,
Chairman and CEO, salesforce.com

Acknowledgments

Ordinarily, I spend an incredible amount of time on acknowledgments. But two things limit me in this particular case. First, to thank everyone who helped me would be the equivalent of thanking a small country, name by name. Everyone whose name appears in this book has my deepest, undying, and permanent gratitude. Without any question. Please, when you read their names, think of Steve Martin: "I'd like to thank each and every one of you for being here tonight. Thankyou Thankyou Thankyou Thankyou Thankyou Thankyou Thankyou Thankyou Thankyou Thankyou Thankyou Thankyou . . ." you get the idea. Each of the contributors did not have to do what they did, but they did it out of the goodness of their hearts. Their contributions and their goodness kept me going.

The people I do want to thank here by name are the ones who are not in the book by name. There are a few.

First, I would be remiss and probably beaten up if I did not thank my long-time McGraw-Hill editor bossman and real friend, Roger Stewart, whom I have worked with for a decade now. I think he's da bomb as an editor (that is a good thing) and a wonderful friend who will be so long after my relationship with McGraw-Hill ends. Thanks also to Joya Anthony and Patty Mon, who have been the overseers of my lazy self, making sure that I got in the chapters and that they got edited, too. I have never seen Joya and Patty, and do not even talk to them that much, but I sure appreciate them. I cannot forget my copy editor, the one who actually knows my voice and makes sure I do not sound like I am gargling when I write. That is Lunaea Weatherstone, easily the best copy editor I have ever run across in my long and not so illustrious life. Each and every edition of this book, she has been there. She makes my writing tone dulcet.

I also owe a crew that I have never met. That would be S. J. Perelman, Woody Allen, Steve Martin, the Marx Brothers and the cast of *Saturday Night Live*. They are funny, ironic, and my icons for NY-style humor which I try, oh how I try, to emulate. S. J. Perelman in particular, a humorist who ruled literary circles in the 1930s and 1940s, used the English language as a weapon for sardonic literary humor in a way that I can only worship from afar. Don't condemn me for my results. Respect me for my attempts. Please.

Are there others who are not in the book who trigger my intelligence? You bet. I am inspired by my intellectual buds like Graham Hill, who has one of the finest minds I have encountered in CRM and is one of the best-read people I have ever met.

Normally, I'm a do it yourself kind of person—a lone wolf. Weirdly, I also love to collaborate. This is the first time I ever worked with researchers who weren't named Paul Greenberg, and am I glad of that. I had two absolutely wonderful friends who did research for me. One was Anita Soni, a multitalented, humane, good person who did some extraordinary research on enterprise social networking sites that just blew me away. The other was Bill Howell, who not only knows how to do outstanding research, I think he knows how to do everything. He is smart, experienced, and just simply a very kind human being who has been a glue for me and many others over many years. Thank goodness for these two. Makes me want to retire my lone wolf-dom.

There are a few besides my family who are in the book, but I want to thank them here anyway. Guys like Bruce Culbert, who is not only a business mentor to me but a brother. He has an incredible business sense, a wonderful family, and a deeply charitable heart. Also, Brent Leary, my CRM Playaz pal, who is a constant source of knowledge and a blast to hang out with and has been a huge encouragement for me all the time.

Some people went above and beyond encouraging me via e-mail, Twitter, LinkedIn, Facebook, and phone calls. A few truly stand out. My college buddy, Steve LeMay, now a professor of marketing at Dalton State College down in Georgia. Our freshman year at Northwestern University I was his wingman (long story). He was mine throughout this effort—always encouraging, always supportive. Louis Columbus, analyst, manager, and human being par excellence, whose kindness knows no bounds—a champion of the actual downtrodden and those feeling that way on occasion—a selfless man.

Finally, of course, I am nothing without my family. What makes them special is that they are *my* family, not someone else's.

My brother Bob, a contributor to this book, is one of the smartest guys I have ever run across. He built a business in a field where businesses do not get built and is numero uno in that field. He decided a few years ago that women's professional soccer needed a second chance in the United States, and we now have the Women's Professional Soccer League because of him. He is my rock and the bestest brother in the whole wide world. He keeps me sane.

My sister-in-law Freyda always amazes me and I love her for that. She went from being a Sybase guru to being a paramedic and ambulance driver and a successful and even ranked marathon runner, all as she turned 60—and did it because she wanted to. Wow is pretty much what I always say because she is that remarkable.

My mom, Helen, is 93 years old and still has the mind that led her to skip a zillion grades in school, go to college at 14, and become the captain of CCNY's girls' basketball team at 5'1". Her mind and humor are not only intact, they are sharp as tacks. I hope I am like her at 92. She was and is a great mom, even though I am still her child at 59. How lucky am I?

My niece Sara has been away at college, but if we had kids, we would wish that our child was just like her. She is beautiful, smart, infinitely cool, and a great person with a bright future. Yvonne and I are blessed to have her in our lives.

Ahh, Yvonne. She is what my life means. I see her and realize that I may have a lot more than just her, but if I only had her I would have all I need. Why say any more?

Introduction

HEY! You HAVE to Read this Introduction

I lied.

Yep, I did. In the third edition, which I am sure all of you read, I know you remember these absolutely memorable words, the ones branded into your cerebrum right from the first paragraphs of the introduction:

This is going to be the final edition of CRM at the Speed of Light. *And please, I'm not coming out of* CRM at the Speed of Light *retirement to write it after the public clamor for the fourth edition gets so great that I can't ignore it. First, I can ignore it. Second, it's easy to ignore when there is neither hue nor cry.*

Well, it turns out to be pretty rough to ignore, despite no hue and cry. Well, maybe a little cry. Mostly me doing that, though. Hold on! There is no crying in CRM—or, wait, that's baseball.

But there is a reason why I (inadvertently) lied. I really had no intention of writing a fourth edition because things in CRM had matured, other things had dramatically changed, and all in all, I felt that I had a different book in me. I thought it was going to be a novel on baseball and the Negro Leagues, but as it turns out, this is the different book.

When I wrote the third edition, I underestimated the social transformation that was going to take place, largely spurred by the political and economic environment that was beginning to roil right around the time the third edition came out. I thought that CRM itself was probably going to be transformed by something, thus the title of the last chapter of the book, "Bye Bye, CRM, Sort Of. . ." What I didn't realize is that many of the world's social, political, government, economic, and business institutions were going to be irrevocably changed, that the way we communicate would undergo a dramatic transformation, and the expectations we had of both individuals and institutions would be altered in ways that were unimaginable five years before.

Do you remember that *Saturday Night Live* skit with Chris Farley where he was the host of a TV show and interviewed celebrities like Paul McCartney and said things like, "Hey Paul, 'member when you were, um, in the Beatles? Remember that?" Then he would hit himself on the head and go "IDIOT!! STUPID!! IDIOT!!"

I'm that kind of idiot. I *really* thought I wouldn't be writing this book, but the changes in the world dictated it and here I am, like it or not. (Of course, I like it. If I didn't, I doubt I would have written this anyway. Writing a book just isn't that easy.)

Want some proof of those changes, oh pragmatic skeptical one? Let's look at the research methodologies I used for the third edition in 2004 and then in 2008–2009 to cure you of your cynical streak.

Third Edition Research, 2004

I did several kinds of primary and secondary research. If you were to categorize it (and, take my word, you should categorize it), it would fall into place something like this.

The primary research consisted of e-mail and phone interviews and some face-to-face interviews with key industry leaders or practitioners who were doing intelligent things with CRM and with thought-leaders in the field. It also involved reviews of hundreds of software applications over time through either visits (physical ones—yes, that primitive method) or, more frequently, demos on WebEx or other collaborative sites and live demos on the Web. My direct consulting experience and other people's consulting or vendor-related or writing experiences played a significant part.

Secondary sources consisted of books, magazines, and websites with some visibility into user groups and discussion areas for specific things, like the investor discussions on Yahoo Finance about Siebel or something like that. I used Google search to find multiple sources and links from those sources to do further resource. I read the standard CRM sites like CustomerThink or SearchCRM and would "locally" search them to find out what I needed.

That's about it.

Fourth Edition Research, 2008

All of the above played a part without a doubt. None of it went away. But what is different is what makes this incredible. I used social media, crowd sourcing, and peer-to-peer communication in digital real time.

Before I get into it, you know what just occurred to me?

A Momentary Digression

The first two editions of *CRM at the Speed of Light* were subtitled "Capturing and Keeping Customers in Internet Real Time." Then for the third edition we changed it to "Essential Customer Strategies for the 21st Century." The irony is that the original subtitle is more appropriate now than when we named it for the first two versions. Weird.

Back to the Subject at Hand

In addition to all of the above, I used social networks—particularly LinkedIn and Plaxo—to ask questions of the communities in general and specific groups within the communities, such as the CRM Experts Group within the cyberwalls of Plaxo's communities. I asked questions of the people I follow or who follow me on Twitter—all in 140 characters or less. I did the same through groups and in general on FriendFeed and on Facebook. I set up a wiki to get input on the book using the hosted wiki service called PBwiki (which stands for peanut butter wiki, by the way). I was able to use research that I had done and written on for my blog, *PGreenblog* (the56group.typepad.com), which has won all the awards ever given to CRM blogs in the course of all the years since 2005, which is when I started writing it. That would be three of them. Ahem.

I used the valuable intel provided by the commenters on my ZDNet blog *Social CRM: The Conversation* to identify products I didn't know of, or spark a thought or two I wouldn't have had otherwise.

But it goes so much further than that. I was able to draw on intelligence from a significant number of well-respected blogs that are being produced not just on CRM but on the social customer. I have been able to use Wikipedia for a knowledge base drawn up by us common folk (as we'll see it's called crowd-sourcing) that is as accurate as any that the planet has produced since Encyclopedia Britannica. I was able to use not just the search engines of Google, which found web archived information, but also search engines that grabbed unstructured information from social networks and communities. I had a much higher degree of participation from that abstract yet real community of CRM-interested folks out there who gave me great suggestions via e-mail, phone calls, wiki participation, blog commentary, Twitter responses, survey results, community conversation threads—in fact, in all means of contemporary communication but a snail mail letter—that are attributed in the book in various ways.

It didn't stop anywhere near just that. Well into writing this, I found a very good social bookmarking tool called Diigo (www.diigo.com) that allowed me to annotate and bookmark specific Web content and then share it with my friends and/or with any groups I created—like the one I created for this book. The members then would provide their bookmarks to me and the other members—related to my research—so I had a powerful team of disconnected but highly interactive helpers for this.

Plus I had much more access, partially because of my increased "status" and reputation within the CRM community (I was named the number one non-vendor influencer in CRM by InsideCRM in 2007–2008 and one of the top influencers by *CRM Magazine* for 2008), but even more so because the social barriers that were in the way of direct communications four years ago are no longer there and access is easier than ever. In fact, it's seen as "good business" to be more accessible.

Oh yeah, just to show you the evolution of all this even more—the third edition of this book is now in the Amazon Kindle format. For those of you who don't know what the Kindle is, shame on you. It's a wildly popular, though sort of ugly, e-book reader released by Amazon that has a high-speed free EV-DO wireless connection so you can literally download books on the fly right to the Kindle. *CRM at the Speed of Light* third edition is one of those. The downside is that I had to pay for my own book to get the Kindle edition—and pay twice as much as the normal Kindle book price, for some reason. Nothing is free. Actually, as we're going to see, that's not true, but it helped the section's drama to say that.

So you can see why I needed to write the book just due to the startling difference in research methods and available knowledge. The difference in CRM community participation in this book was staggering. Or maybe I'm the one staggering . . .

The Book? Ah, the Changes in the Book

The emphasis of this book is *vastly* different than the last three. Despite my protestations about the definition of CRM, there was a huge technology focus on that book because traditional CRM was primarily operational. Operational excellence needs systems. Systems usually need automation. Automation needs software. So it fell to technology despite my best intentions.

While the technologies will be an important part of this edition too, you will be getting much more strategic information, socioeconomic and business data, and a clearer look at the experiential and emotional than last time because the changes have been significantly right-brained and if I can't respond to the nature of the changes, then why write a fourth edition?

I keep asking myself that.

Most importantly, you'll hear more customer stories than last time and have conversations with a lot more people than just me. The strategies will be based on customer engagement more than systems and customer management. Management is still part but a smaller part of the book than the last time.

Also, there will be a lot less technical detail, though still enough to drive a sane man mad or a madman sane. You didn't need that much anyway. Proof? If you read the third edition, how many of you got really excited over my description of the processes that went into scoring data gathered by business intelligence applications? You? How about you? Maybe you? I thought not.

Six Feet Under(lying)

All these social changes have a material effect on how the book is being done too. While the past efforts have been clearly in my voice (as grating as that may have been), and this one will be for the most part in my voice, I'm going to start a few substantial conversations and many mini-conversations between some seriously smart people and y'all (my concession to Virginia). You can get the benefits of their wisdom, and you'll see places to go to share your own cranial contributions. Some of the highlights:

▶ At the end of the appropriate chapters there will be mini-conversations with a known thought-leader in some specific areas of the industry—analysts, commentators, subject matter experts, and others. So, for example, you'll find Shel Israel, one of the leading authors on blogging, giving you three things you should concentrate on when setting up a business blog, or Michael Maoz of the Gartner Group on how to handle the intent-driven enterprise. These could be a group of ideas, best practices, hints, or tips on how to take the subject of that chapter and do something practical with it.

▶ There will be a series of initiated conversations—longer than the mini-conversations—with experts like major league CRM analyst Denis Pombriant, star small-business guru Brent Leary, social media champ Chris Carfi, government 2.0 expert Bob Greenberg (yes, he's related—he's my bro), and the man who closes the big deals, Bruce Culbert, among others.

▶ There will be occasional links listed to sites you need to go to and these will be interactive with some of the content of the book—though there won't be a lot of that because it can be damned annoying if you're leafing through pages and then have to cycle away to the Web and then back to the book, back to the Web, back to the book . . . you get the idea.

▶ Most of the chapters are dense. This isn't to give you vertigo or make you think you're in some weird dreamlike state. Rather than trying to have small bites, the level of importance and explanation that I think the different segments of this new subject, Social CRM, needs is reflected in the chapter size. If you are looking for technology or heavy process detail, just reread the third edition—it's all in there and all valid. The emphasis here is on the new ground that has to be covered, which is quite extensive.

Coolness

One final thing. Coolness will matter in this edition. Style is going to be important. For those of you who expect only a traditional book on business and/or technology with all the right buzz words, you ain't gonna get it.

The fact is that style is a facet of business that people actually care about, and it will count in how this book is constructed and how this book "thinks." We are conversing, and your absolutely drop-dead coolness matters to me. Know why?

Forget that. You'll hear about it in Chapter 3.

Changes in the Book + Coolness = New Format

One final thing. Since transparency is something we all need to keep practicing, I have to be straight with you. I have 600 plus printed pages to mess around with. That's it. The publisher's bottom line limits me to that. But the book, as you can't see but have to trust me to tell you, is much more than 600 plus pages. Consequently, we are going 21st century and becoming very cool, throwing in some hip thinking that was the result of Twitter and blog conversations with followers and readers. We (McGraw-Hill and me) are using some of their suggestions to deal with what is actually a publishing reality—cost control. More than 40 people suggested different approaches, though I have to say my LOL moment was from Tien Tzuo, the CEO of Zuora, who just said "8 point font."

I do want to thank all 40 of the contributors for their suggestions and particularly (in alphabetical order) Gay Bitter, Louis Columbus, Pierre Hulsebus, Steve LeMay, Logotrope, Karl Wabst, and Dik Whitten, all of whom suggested parts of the ultimate solution. No one had the whole thing, but then, that's what the wisdom of the crowd is for.

So here's what we're going to do. We will offer up content to you and anyone who wants it—free of charge. That content will be several chapters of the book that will be strictly electronic and not in the printed tome. There is a site—www.mhprofessional.com/greenberg/—that will provide you with those chapters without registration. If you register, however, you will get special registration-only content that I'm going to provide. I'm not telling what it is, so I know something you don't know, nyah, nyah—unless you register.

The site will also serve as a place where you can go to ask questions on things that I've left unclear in the book and get the answers, though you have to cut me some slack on the time it takes me to answer. If I notice a significant pattern of similar questions, it will foster a book supplement of a page or two or three that will be made available to you free of charge. I have zero issues with those who want to take issue either with their comments—which will be organized by chapter. So what is basically a recessionary move can now be pretty cool if you help me make it that.

The Previous Three vs. the Fourth

If you're a business person looking for what the first three editions gave you, don't read this book. This is the fourth edition of *CRM at the Speed of Light*, but it might also be considered the first edition of *Social CRM at the Speed of Light* and is a radically different book than the last three. This one is more focused on the conversation that is now going on between company and customer and the collaborative models that cutting-edge companies are carrying out for customer engagement. There is less on management of internal process and technology and more on the types of models and practices that encourage customers to become advocates. There are more stories and less (though still a lot) data and it encompasses CRM more richly than before. It is not as technically detailed but more important to your business directly. After all, business models can be important to business, can they not?

To Reach Me

I'm going to give you a lot of ways to reach me. Any reader of this book is a friend of mine, and the transformation going on out there doesn't stop with the publication of this book. So I'd like to continue with you. Is there anything faster than the speed of light you can clue me into?

▶ My cell phone: 703-338-0232

▶ My office phone: 703-551-2337

▶ My e-mail: paul-greenberg3@comcast.net

▶ My Twitter ID: pgreenbe

▶ My Blog: *PGreenblog* (the56group.typepad.com)

▶ My ZDNet Blog: *Social CRM: The Conversation* (blogs.zdnet
.com/crm)

▶ My Facebook page: www.facebook.com/pgreenbe

▶ My Podcast: CRM Playaz, co-hosted with Brent Leary (currently
on posted on my ZDNet blog). We riff on everything CRM
related. Everything and everyone.

▶ To Google me: Enter the words "Paul Greenberg" and CRM (that
filters out the other Paul Greenbergs). Use the quotes around my
name.

▶ Want to work with me on new concepts? Sign up and befriend
me on Diigo (www.diigo.com), the social bookmarking social
network I mentioned earlier.

▶ Want to work on the Social CRM definition? Go to the CRM 2.0
wiki, which I run at http://crm20.wetpaint.com and, the older
version (for reasons of history), at http://crm20.pbwiki.com.

▶ In addition to Facebook, I'm also on LinkedIn, Plaxo, and dozens
of other social networks. Want me as a friend or connection? You
got it. Feel free to go to your favorite, or if you're a newbie, join
one, and hook up to me as a friend—even as your first friend, or
whatever their unique cute social lingos call them. I'm yours. Just
let me know you're a fourth edition reader so I know from
whence you came. Also, you need to know that I'm the Paul
Greenberg from The 56 Group, LLC or Manassas, Virginia, etc.,
so you can pick me out of a crowd.

The Traveling Wilburys

The Traveling Wilburys were an "accidental" mash-up band that was
the brainstorm of George Harrison in 1988. I won't go into their history, but they were one of the greatest collections of artists in the history of music. Think about George Harrison, Roy Orbison, Tom Petty,
Bob Dylan, and Jeff Lynne (ELO). I'm in love with them—in a strictly
platonic way. I've been listening to them while working out, while on
airplanes, and when resting in my house or in hotel rooms—for weeks
on end.

They capture the spirit of this book well in a song called "End of the
Line." Go check out the lyrics online, since I can't reprint them here

without completely wiping out my royalty stream. Get the album too. In the spirit of the lyrics, though, my gray-haired self has a lot to say and all I ask of you, for god sakes, is let me live. Look it up if you're confused.

This time, the fourth edition is the end of the line for me. Check out the last pages of this book when you get to them. You'll see I mean it.

Here . . . we . . . GO.

PART I

The Era of the Social Customer

1

. . . .

OMG! Your Customer Really Is Your BFF!

I want to poke you.

Yes, you heard me right. I want to poke you. In fact, I want to SuperPoke you.

So there.

Before you go contacting your attorney to find out how to sue me for sexual harassment, hold up a minute and listen.

"I want to poke you" goes to the heart of why I wrote this fourth edition of *CRM at the Speed of Light*. It is a reflection of the evolving Social CRM, which is markedly different from CRM 1.0—or CRM as you knew it and as I wrote about in all three prior editions. It is an indication of why Social CRM is not just the purely operational CRM that you knew and loved (or hated). Before you pick up the phone and make that call to your attorney, hear me out. It shouldn't take long. A few hundred pages or so. By the end, you'll know why me wanting to poke you is a good thing (for the most part). Not only is it good for you, it's meaningful to your customers. Much better than a megabucks lawsuit—think of the time you'd have to spend in court, when you could be spending it reading this book instead.

Bursting the New Mythology: Zeus Drops to Earth

Before we get into the guts of how this book is organized, I have to start out by dispelling some myths because....well, I have to. Trust me.

Myth #1

There is a business transformation going on that is forcing the make-over of CRM 1.0 (or even 1.5) to Social CRM.

Reality: FALSE

The change is a *social* change that impacts all institutions including business (this chapter and Chapter 12 explain all). Unlike the past, business has no substantial or even marginal advantage over any social, political, economic, government, or other form of institution. It is a revolution in how we communicate, not how we do business.

Myth #2

Web 2.0 is going to go the way of Web 1.0. Things like social networking are fads that will pass and investments in them will fail as did the Web 1.0 investments.

Reality: FALSE

Web 1.0 was a technology-based fantasy that operated on the premise that the Web would be able to provide a way to overcome all sorts of business problems through automation and cool apps. The cooler or more efficient the technology, the more money there was to be made. But there were no social conditions to support Web 1.0. It was driven by investments in the technology du jour and a bit o' buzz created around it, not the actual value it had.

Web 2.0, which plays a significant part in the Social CRM transition, is not based on making money from technology investments that may or may not have some utility. In fact, from the standpoint of technology, much of the technology that underlies Web 2.0 is technology made freely available in one incarnation or another to anyone who wants it. Often, it's been developed as open source, which means there is a community of developers who have been given easy access to the source code. In return, they develop features, functions, and entirely new applications based on collaboration with other developers and the providers of the source code. Typically, the Web 2.0 tools facilitate peer-to-peer collaboration and easy access to real-time communication. That, my friends, is the core of the social change we've been seeing in dramatic fashion since 2006.

Because much of the communications transition is organized around Web-based technologies, it's called Web 2.0, but its relationship to Web 1.0 is specious at best.

You dispute the drama? You say, yo, Greenie, you're overstating the case. Ask Barack Obama about that. One of the primary reasons that Barack Obama was able to become the President of the United States was because of the social presence he had *online*, which I will examine in some detail in Chapter 14.

Unlike Web 1.0 and the collapsed bubble of 2000–2001, this one is here for good. The technology drives it and supports it, but doesn't own it. It's owned by the customers themselves—the human beings involved.

Myth #3

Social CRM means that the "old style" of CRM—the operational stuff that's based on sales, marketing, support processes, and automation through technology—is no longer viable.

Reality: FALSE

In fact, the operational is still as necessary today as it was five years ago and even three years ago. But the requirements of customers, their expectations, and who they trust have dramatically changed. Consequently, for a business to get the attention of customers, much less retain them or turn them into advocates, it's become necessary to provide new means of developing and sustaining relationships in response to changed customer expectations. The baby remains, even as the bathwater drains.

How the Book Is Organized

I've tried to be rational about how this book is organized, but I have to say, this is one daunting subject. CRM is much more complex than it used to be, which I'm sure thrills you all, given that it never was terribly simple. The model for enterprise-customer relationships has been turned on its head to a large degree, which means there are new ways that businesses need to act and new ways that customers are demanding to interact.

I've organized the book accordingly. There are five parts in this book, each of which has several chapters. Most of the book is the printed edition you have in your hands, but there are several digital chapters available at www.mhprofessional.com.

Part I: The Era of the Social Customer

This section is devoted to giving you the big picture—what the change is, why it's occurred, and what it means for business, customers, and CRM as a discipline. While I'd love to do an entire socioeconomic treatise on what's going on, I can't. First, I'm neither a sociologist nor an economist. Second, because this is a book on how to define and apply CRM as it needs to be defined and applied in 2009 and beyond. However, Part I does cover social, economic, and psychological elements of the change because they are necessary to understand business as the customer is reconstructing it. The chapters are organized around the biggest picture you can get—the definition of CRM as seen by industry leaders. We'll cover the new business models and how they are assembled, the permutations of CRM and the disciplines that are becoming prominent in parallel with CRM, such as customer experience management—a rotten name if I ever heard one—and the also ineptly named but important vendor relationship management (VRM).

Part II: So Happy Together—Collaborating with Your Customer

The customer's ownership of their personal experience with a company means that the company has to accommodate it. But how? This section will highlight the strategies for customer engagement and collaboration and the tools that are of value in realizing the programs. As in all past editions, there will be a group of tools and vendors that will be highlighted if merited, and the actual technology, processes, and methodologies will be covered, describing how the company needs to collaborate with their customers, not just manage relationships with them. This time around it's called "Superstah!"—for all you Molly Shannon fans out there.

This section is where you get to see all the cool stuff—the user-generated content, the social networks, blogs, wikis, podcasts, social software, the mobile life we are now leading, the way to view the generations involved—and how this should be integrated into contemporary CRM strategies.

Part III: Baby Stays, Bathwater Goes— CRM Still Needs the Operational

This is the old-fashioned stuff. This entire section is devoted to the developments and evolution of the operational side of CRM that we're all so familiar with. That means how it impacts sales, marketing, and customer support, and also how it extends to the back office, especially the supply chain, whether you think of it that way or not.

Part IV: Different Strokes for Different Folks—CRM Goes Vertical

Not only has CRM incorporated collaborative features, it also has become increasingly specialized. Vertical applications are particularly hot and becoming more important as company after company realizes that their industry has some very specific ways they do things. Particularly exciting sectors for vertical CRM are health care, financial services, and entertainment (including sports), where the customer engagement is highly emotional. Most important for CRM's vertical stripe is the public sector, both on the agency/administrative side and in the political realm. Public servants and candidates are realizing that their constituents increasingly demand participation in their destinies. The institutional trust that's necessary for these public service groups to survive is based on their constituents' willingness to grant that participation.

Additionally, even though I'd be hard pressed to look at the small and medium business market as a "vertical," I do look at it here because it fits best in the scheme of things. But rather than the standard junk you'll get from most CRM tomes about the "SMB market," I'm going to do something that is sacrilegious when it comes to acronyms. I'm going to distinguish between "small" and "medium." There will be no more lumping them together, no sir.

Much of this section will be digital with the exception of the public sector chapter. Go get 'em.

Part V: Looking at the Framework

There's a lot to making CRM decisions and there are a lot of ways to implement CRM programs. This is the most extensive part of the book, covering the transactional and interaction sides of the story. You're going to be treated to looking at strategies, programs, customer experience mapping, mission and vision statements, organizational change, process development and mapping, privacy, compliance, governance, metrics and analytics, and the technologies that support all that.

Then, briefly, we're going to lightly trip through how to implement CRM, including picking the right vendor and the right technology, from the software and services to the architecture and delivery models to the data models.

Ugggggghhhh.

What does that mean to you? Before I tell you what it should mean, a brief story.

I went to Northwestern University back in . . . err . . . a while ago. My inclination has always been literary, so needless to say, I was *not* a stellar science student. I majored in journalism, and my science courses were somewhat elementary, though required. One that I took was called "Physics for Poets." Even though I admit this grudgingly, I kind of liked the course and thought, hey, there's nothing wrong with learning science this way.

That is the way I am going to present that always-confusing subject of technology. There will be no geekspeak. None. I'm covering only the subjects that you need to know because (1) you need to know them, (2) they will affect the cost of your CRM deployment, and (3) it's actually interesting stuff when the language used is not programming (or Latin).

For example, there is a chapter entitled *SOA for Poets* (SOA is service-oriented architecture), which is of course an homage to my college course and should give you just enough to understand what SOAs are.

That's how the book is organized. Now let the games begin.

Starting with a Test

We're going to start this book with a test. Get out your laptops or cellphones (or your pen and paper, if you use such primitive tools), and tell me how many of the terms in Table 1-1 you can define well.

I venture to guess you only know a few. Yet, each and every one of those terms has real importance to your contemporary CRM strategy, like it or not.

Let me make something clear. What you're going to see in this book is a significant change in how CRM strategies are determined and what tools are used. The conventional ones that you know of and that give you comfort—the pure and clean version: people, process, technology—aren't sufficient any longer. I'm not saying they aren't useful. I'm saying they aren't sufficient, and you have to get your arms around that right away, because the customers aren't waiting for you.

Table 1-1: Social CRM Related Terms You Most Likely Don't Know

Enterprise 2.0	Web 2.0
Customer-managed experiences	Experience economy
Customer-managed experiences	Social networks/user communities
Social customer	Social media
Wikis	Podcasting
Blogs	User-generated content
Experience mapping and design	Social bookmarking
Unified communication	Customer experience management
Voice of the customer	Return on customer
Customer value	Customer ecosystem
Customer advocacy	Service-oriented architecture
On demand	Twitter & micro-blogging
Transparency	Authenticity
Marketing as conversation	Personalization
Mashups	Cloud computing

When you have your customer hat on, especially if you're under 40 or so, you aren't waiting for the companies you want to interact with. What makes you think you're getting a pass from your peers?

You're not. This is the "era of the social customer" and it calls for a new approach to CRM strategy that is undeniable—whether or not you want to deny it. You have the right to throw this book into the trash after you read it. You paid for it or got it at a conference or from me or stole it or something. I actually don't care how you got it. What I do care about is that you conclude that your company needs to change the way you deal with customers now—because the customer has already changed the way they deal with you.

By the end of this book, you're going to know about not only the more traditional CRM terms, strategies, and tools, but also the contemporary Social CRM thinking, approaches, practices, and stories. If I've done that, I've done my job. Then you have to go and do yours.

Welcome to the Era of the Social Customer

Here are a few declarations in bold and italics.

We are now living in the era of the social customer.

The traditional customer is the one we all were as recently as a decade ago. We bought products and services and based our decisions a great deal on utility and price. We communicated with the companies we were dealing with by letter, phone call, and occasional e-mail, if they had the facility to do that.

But that customer changed because of a social change in the early part of this millennium. The customer seized control of the business ecosystem and it was never the same.

We now live in a customer ecosystem.

To begin this discussion, I want to introduce you to someone who is not only a major thinker in the CRM space but a great friend and colleague. Readers, meet Denis Pombriant. Denis, meet the readers. To begin this roundtable of a book, Denis is going to give you his take on the social customer and then I'm going to get into mine. You're going to see a lot of this throughout the book. Experts who have insights that I might not have will share them with you. That way, you can get a well-rounded look at the strategies you have to consider and the practical efforts you should think about making. This book is more community driven than in the past, though hopefully, my edgy tones will still emanate throughout. Denis will also be heard in other places in the book.

Okay, now for your formal introduction.

Denis Pombriant is the managing principal at Beagle Research Group, which is not only a significant analyst force in the CRM community but has one of the best company names I've heard. When Denis headed up the CRM practice at Aberdeen Group in the early part of this millennium, he identified salesforce.com and the on-demand model as a "disruptive innovation" and it has since proven to be exactly that. Denis has since become *the* go-to consultant and analyst in on-demand, as well as one of the foremost writers about identifying the larger economic and social conditions that lead to change in the business world, especially when it comes to customer-driven change.

Listen to this man. He gets it.

Denis Pombriant on Why the Social Customer

As they used to say in old movies, the jig is up. Whether your definition of jig is a dance, a practical joke, or a trick, the upshot is the same in CRM today—customers are in control of their relationships with vendors a lot more than they were just a few years ago. The power center has moved and the reasons range from the elementary to the sophisticated.

The short story is that the marketplace has been struck by a tsunami called high-tech at the same time that customers have gained new levels of education and wealth. During that time, a whole host of new products and services have become available based on the availability of cheap, fast computing power. More than just computers themselves, this rising tide has brought in consumer products and services. It has also enabled enterprise business processes based on information availability and just-in-time materials delivery.

Beyond the obvious new inventions, just about every "old fashioned" product has undergone a makeover to install cheap computing power that results in better functioning products. Everything from cars to kitchen trash cans now have some kind of embedded silicon that improves functionality and usability. That's the good news. Now the bad.

Customers have learned a lot in the last few decades. While we generally like our iPods, cellphones, GPS systems, air bags, computers, the Internet, and a lot more, we have also become wise in the ways of buying these things. The decades have made us smart consumers of products and services and, just as the high-tech era has paused to catch its breath, we have formed ideas and opinions about what we want the next time we enter the market to buy a gizmo. Most importantly, vendors need to know what we know, but for the most part, they are inept at it so far.

There's nothing remarkable about any of this; it is the way markets behave. Some days you are the pigeon and some days you are the statue. What is remarkable, though, is that because it has been such a long time since consumers last had the upper hand, there is a whole generation of people in business who have never seen the phenomenon. They are used to selling version one-dot-oh—make an appointment, take an order. Simple. But in a world that sprouts 2.0 signs faster than a real estate agent staking out a subdivision, things are different.

Today's smart, well-educated, and wealthy consumers want their needs met, and successful vendors have to be aware of those needs. Relatively superficial needs development and analysis result in the same old same old. It's a simple process: make a product and see if someone buys it. It's also expensive and prone to failure. One study I read said that 80 percent of new products introduced this way failed. It doesn't take a high IQ to see that this approach to needs analysis could use refinement.

Real needs analysis makes few assumptions and asks more broadly about needs as well as biases, lifestyles, and a lot more—the kinds of things that a real BFF would know. Real or modern needs analysis also starts earlier in the relationship and in the product development cycle. Your BFF and you go back a long way and the reason your BFF is so attuned to you is because he or she has been studying you for a long time—certainly longer than it takes to analyze a log file.

Getting that level of information can be a challenge. Earlier generations relied on massive and expensive surveys and focus groups to gather some of that information, but the cost and complexity made it difficult. Today we have the Internet and social networking ideas to help us. But like the proverbial man with a hammer, each company employing social networking techniques typically tries to solve all of the world's problems with a single solution.

It is actually a fun time to be in this business. If you watch carefully, you see point solutions emerging and becoming successful. Most will fail, but some will survive and prosper by merging with others to form better and better solutions for the end-to-end problem of knowing a customer.

It's also a fun time to be a customer. Like any relationship, those between individuals and vendors will have their ups and downs. But armed with the simple knowledge that customers have power and a willingness to express themselves, most vendors will happily engage them and the customers will likewise be happy to be asked.

Okay, back to me.

What's a Customer Ecosystem?

Wikipedia defines an ecosystem as

> *The interactive system established between a group of living creatures and the environment in which they live. The centerpiece of this definition is the idea that living organisms are continually engaged in a set of relationships with every other element constituting the environment in which they exist.*

A customer ecosystem is simply the totality of interactions centered around customers that takes place over time. The customer sits at the hub, rather than just being a spoke in the corporate wheel. The relationship changes from one where the customer is the object of a sale to one in which the customer is the subject of an experience that he or she controls with businesses. How'd that happen? I'm so glad you asked. Gather 'round the campfire.

Once upon a time in a land not so far away . . .

The Product-Focused Corporate Ecosystem

If you tool back to the 1950s and 1960s, it was a different world. Madison Avenue advertising agencies created markets and market demand, manufacturing ruled the universe, and the way information was captured was, shall we say, primitive.

Typically, you would read a magazine or watch TV (in black and white) and see something of interest to you. If you were reading *Life* magazine, for example, you would find an ad, clip out the coupon, identified by a cute little pair of scissors, fill it out, put it in an addressed envelope with a 3-cent stamp, and send it off to the producer of the "item of interest." Then you would wait two weeks or more to get a brochure from the manufacturer, read it, decide based on the manufacturer's information whether you want the product, go to a store that sold it, listen to a salesperson's pitch, and then you would buy it and hope for the best. You had no control over the information and no access to knowledge of the product beyond that given to you by the manufacturer, unless you maybe had the benefit of a neighbor who owned it.

According to a 2004 *Business Week* article, during the 1960s an advertiser could reach 80 percent of U.S. women with a single ad aired simultaneously on CBS, NBC, and ABC—the only three TV networks that existed. To reach that same 80 percent in 2008 it would take at least a parallel airing on a minimum of 100 channels, and that's only if that many women were watching TV at some time.

Additionally, during this era and through the 1980s, newspapers were the only other real source of media that was mass consumed. A well-placed ad in a local or national publication would reach the specific groups that were being targeted. We now have a major decline in the number of print media readers as more and more get their content pushed to them via the Internet or at least scroll to CNN or ESPN or even the *New York Times* online before they touch a TV set or newspaper.

But back then, that wasn't the case, folks. Because the products were standardized, and aimed at broad consumption—not at all focused on individuals—the product manufacturer was in control of supply. The retailers owned the market. And they all owned the knowledge flow in conjunction with the advertising agencies that manufactured that information. Because the post–World War II period (at least in the United States) generated wealth unheard of until then, the demand outstripped the supply, making the producers and retailers happy.

These consumable products were mostly generic, for one reason: customers were perfectly willing to buy them. The expectations of the customers were low. As described in a *CBS Marketwatch* article in June 2008:

> *Customers 1.0 were dutiful consumers of mainstream messaging and one-size-fits-all goods. They would gladly drive miles out of their way to visit retail outlets, they readily leaned heavily on advice from retail clerks in making their selections, and they happily bought goods from among arrays of pretty generic offerings. They put up with long lines and poor service, because retailers had the power and their customers were just grateful to get the goods.*

The corporate ecosystem was in the hands of those who manufactured products and they dictated the terms to customers with low expectations.

CRM as a science didn't exist. It seemed to be there in the often abused and not really believed term "the customer is king." But with the limited tools the customers had and the limited availability of information, if the customer was king, the manufacturer was a god.

The Customer-Focused Corporate Ecosystem

From the late 1980s through the early part of the millennium, technology was developed that made the delivery of more customized goods at lower prices feasible. The Internet was available to the potential buyer so that they could get vast amounts of information on the products they were considering from other users, not the manufacturer. The availability of courier services like Federal Express (FedEx) and United Parcel Service (UPS) meant that any manufacturer could deliver products at reasonable cost and with lightning speed. The size of an enterprise or its ability to shave cents off of a price was no longer the game changer it once was. Customer demands changed because customers felt empowered by the copious amounts of information that became available to them. Retail began to change to meet the needs of those newly demanding customers. Retail moved to niche products that customers wanted and were willing to spend money for. But at the same time, we saw the rise of Costco and Sam's Club where high volume purchases brought significant price discounts. If you shopped in the middle, you could shop online. Even that changed as the millennium hit. Those ultra-niche products became available online at sites like eLuxury.com. The price or availability advantages the stores had were eliminated leaving the caché of the shopping experience in the Prada store in Manhattan. But as we will see throughout this book, great experiences trump the availability and price of goods, more often than not.

There were wrinkles at the lower end of the equation too. Stores like Walmart.com gave even greater discounts online and sites like Overstock.com were able to make high volume purchases and then sell single items to consumers at a high volume price. This gave them a margin of advantage over Costco and BJ's Warehouse, where the high volume purchase was required. Game, but not set or match, to Overstock.com. That's because the set and soon the entire match was being won by the customers and on a new court.

That court was the Internet.

The power of the Internet for both customers and businesses became apparent in the mid-1990s when both e-commerce and online review sites became increasingly popular ways to do business and communicate. It made information easily available directly from the manufacturer or retailer via their websites. It also gave, for the first time, an independent voice to the users of the products and services being bought, who were often far more knowledgeable than the actual producers.

Retailers began to see the value of this too. They started allowing customers to order online and pick up in stores or get the products shipped. The 1995 growth of Amazon.com drove the creation of BarnesandNoble.com. Amazon's success showed Barnes and Noble that they were going to have to allow customers to order books online too. Their advantage, they thought, was to allow customers to pick up the books at their retail stores. Once again, though, Amazon's vastly superior customer experience trumped Barnes and Noble's convenience.

Over time, the digital and physical business worlds began to intertwine. Retailers let you order online and pick up in stores (such as Best Buy), travelers could get their tickets online and then print out their boarding passes from their PCs (such as United Airlines); you could buy your clothing online and return it to a brick-and-mortar store anywhere (such as Nordstrom's). This signaled a shift to the customer's unique capabilities to command how he or she purchases. Along with the leveling of the playing field by the courier services, increasing Internet use, better web security protocols, and the evolution of Google search also translated to the customer being able to more safely find other providers of the products and services they wanted anywhere around the world with equal alacrity. They didn't have to be limited to their neighborhood stores anymore. All avenues were opening up for e-commerce. As they said in New York in the 1930s "the world was their [customers'] erster." That would be "oyster" for those of you unacquainted with Brooklyn's regional dialect.

Obviously, given the choices that customers now had, businesses at every level had to widen the choices that customers were being given, whether those customers were consumers or other businesses. Products and services were no longer the differentiators they had been. Price and availability were no longer the way to a customer's wallet share.

Experiences became the thing.

This wasn't a big surprise to some. In 1998, Joe Pine II, who you'll meet in the first digital chapter (see the web chapter, "CRM 2.0 Leaders Speak from Out There"), and his business partner at Strategic Horizons, LLC, James Gilmore, wrote a groundbreaking book called *The Experience Economy*, which discussed not just the desire of customers to have an experience with the company but the approaches that a company could take to commoditize that experience in ways the customer would be willing to pay for. As we'll see, no customer is concerned about paying premiums for things. They just have to want them enough to make the purchase. The most famous example of that is, of course, Starbucks. Five bucks for a cup of coffee that costs about 45 cents to produce including overhead. Hmmmm. That would be more than 1,000 percent margin. What for? Not just the coffee but the Starbucks experience. You know what it is—or at least was. You felt cool going to Starbucks and working on your laptop with then-free wireless connectivity, sitting on a couch gabbing with your friends. You weren't drinking *coffee*; you were sipping something called *vente mocha cappuccino skim latte*. Guilty pleasure. Five bucks.

This was a significant transition point in how companies treated customers. Because, as we will see, the business model began to shift for how customers interacted with companies. But even with this transition, it was still an ecosystem governed by the company, no matter how customer friendly it was (see Figure 1-1).

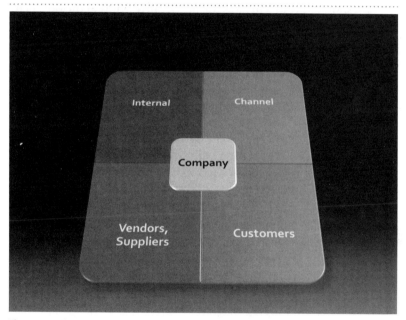

Figure 1-1: The customer-focused corporate ecosystem

CRM grew up in this era. The idea of how you were going to manage your customers in ways that retained them—or in more lucrative periods, acquired them—became of paramount importance as the playing field in the competition for customers became more level. CRM 1.0 promised efficiencies in your operations, especially with customer-facing activities like marketing, sales, and customer service, that would free up your representatives to spend more time with customers doing what they did best—selling to them, solving customer service problems. Sales force automation (SFA) was the lead application and sales effectiveness the primary strategy. For the simple purposes of this discussion, the questions that CRM was supposed to answer during this time were:

▶ How do you manage the relationships you have with customers in such a way that you can increase your revenue opportunities with them?

▶ How do you capture and aggregate enough customer data to give you a well-rounded record of customer information to help you make better decisions on how your customers would respond to you? This was the holy grail of CRM at the time. The consistent 360-degree view of the customer, available to who needed it, when they needed it.

Things didn't stop here. More consumers were becoming aware that they were empowered in ways that had been previously unavailable to them—largely thanks to their ability to communicate via the Internet with complete strangers. It was apparent that the users of the products not only knew more about those products than the manufacturers who made them or the retailers who sold them, but they could communicate that knowledge to others easily, at their leisure. The result was the Cro-Magnon version of user-generated content (UGC): the review site.

Do not underestimate the power of this. We'll take a look at that power in later chapters. Just trust me here. Study after study shows that people trust their peers or supposed peers more than any of the corporate declarations of quality and value that are issued about products. Their decision-making process is complex and never a matter of just good review versus bad review.

But this was just the harbinger of something much more important and deeply affecting.

Customer Ecosystem

We are now living in a customer ecosystem. I'm not saying a customer-centered corporate ecosystem. The customer now is at the hub of the business ecosystem (see Figure 1-2). This has vast implicit and explicit effects on how you craft your business strategies, how you manage your processes, the business models you use, the technologies you choose, the programs you create, and the way you engage with your customers. They've changed the way they deal with you.

CRM 1.0 is, by itself, inadequate to grow businesses in the way that it traditionally did. But the incorporation of the operational capabilities of "historic" CRM with the new social capabilities of social media and social networks provides a set of powerful new approaches and tools to actually succeed more effectively than CRM traditionally ever did.

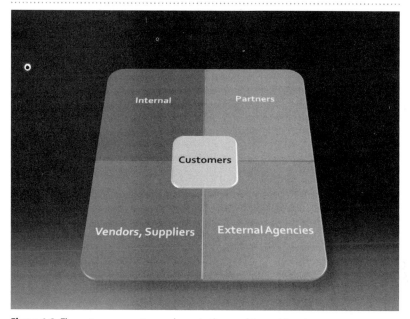

Figure 1-2: The customer ecosystem: welcome to the era of the social customer

What exactly do I mean by a customer ecosystem?

There are entire generations of people who are now part of the workforce who not only grew up to be multitasking Internet-savvy adults, but who also have a different set of demands and expectations. Social, political, and business institutions are all recognizing that they have to meet these demands because the conditions to even get the attention of these people is a dramatically different process, and much more competitive than ever before. Competition is no longer driven by the purveyors of similar products and services, but also by the thousands of messages that each person gets each day via their chosen means of communication and knowledge access.

Once again, *CBS Marketwatch,* June 2008:

Now, customers dictate how they will purchase and consume—where, when, and how much—using a variety of channels largely, if not exclusively, configured by them: They are using community-based online tools (social networking, social book-marking, and social shopping) to guide one another, which has made dot-com darlings like Amazon.com look almost quaint compared with media-meets-commerce-meets-community start-ups like Glam.com.

They are populating social networks, composed of the people they trust, and their networks—their social ties—are rapidly becoming key distribution channels for retailers' marketing and promotion. They populate the online world with ratings and reviews, videos of what they've bought or consumed, and comments on corporate reputations and consumer brands, making Shopzilla or PriceGrabber more valuable than Consumer Reports or J.D. Power.

This is the social customer that drives the customer ecosystem. All institutions, social, political, and business, are affected; all generations impacted. Since this is a book on CRM, needless to say we're going to concentrate on the strategies, tools, and programs that can engage these already empowered social customers who know that they can ally with each other if they must, to get business to do what they want it to do.

The Social Customer Needs Your Attention to Get Theirs

Okay, so we have the customer ecosystem and we know that the customer is firmly in command of the conversation. What does that mean? Who is the customer firmly in command of the conversation? How did we get to this point?

Coming of Age

In 2006, Forrester released its annual North American Consumer Technology Assessment Survey. They found something that was interesting, to say the least, and profound for anyone who needed to acquire or retain customers: Generation Y is the first generation to spend more time on the Net than watching TV, with 10.6 hours per week watching TV and 12.2 hours surfing the Web.

The implied significance of that is nothing less than mission-critical when it comes to how you begin to think about the future of your business. The generation it's talking about—those born, depending on who you believe, between 1977 and 1994—thinks of things differently and acts differently when it communicates. It also expects differently than either its immediate predecessor, Gen X, or Gen X's parents, the baby boomers. Gen Yers are called by Sarah Perez of Read-WriteWeb (www.readwriteweb.com) "digital natives" because of their comfort levels in multitasking among their laptops, cellphones, and multiple other communications media. They routinely time shift and place shift. That routine actually impacts your business.

Do you even know what that means?

Time shifting and place shifting in combination would be downloading something to your iPod or other media player (place shifting) and listening to it whenever you want to (time shifting). It means you're not tethered to what you listen to, how you listen to it, or when you listen to it.

Is that a really important characteristic of Gen Y and those driven by the change? It is to the entertainment media.

Beth Comstock, then-president of Integrated Media at NBC, said the following in a *Fast Company* interview in May 2007:

Fast Company: How are viewing habits changing?

Beth Comstock: We've had 60 million streams [of TV shows] at NBC.com. A lot of those are repeat viewers. Others are time-shifting. They're place-shifting, too, with iTunes or on phones.

Fast Company: And does that work for you?

Beth Comstock: It has to. If consumers are in control, they're going to figure out how they want to watch. We have to find the right solution.

Her key phrase: If consumers are in control. The consumers, a.k.a. the social customers.

The entire premise of Social CRM is that these very same social customers are now in control of the business ecosystem because of the choices they have in their relationships to institutions and the intensity and sheer numbers of their relationships to their peers. Social customers have one other important characteristic: they are willing to mobilize into action.

Gen Y drives this. Gen X participates. Baby boomers are coming along.

Why Y?

If you accept the rough birth dates for Gen Y, their numbers come to 76 million, even more than the previously largest generation, baby boomers. Poor Gen X is only about 45 million strong. What makes Gen Y important to a book on Social CRM is as much what they reflect as what they drive. They are the first generation old enough to have an economic and social impact who grew up with the expectations that the ways they communicate and gather knowledge and then use that knowledge will simply be accommodated.

They are not just technology-savvy, which is often touted as one of their key traits. They actively use technology for their communication and personal productivity and they do it as highly mobile, though still sentient, beings.

Here are a few numbers from the younger Gen Yers, those still in college:

▶ 97 percent own a computer.

▶ 94 percent own a cellphone.

▶ 76 percent use instant messaging (IM).

▶ 15 percent of IM users are logged on 24 hours a day/7 days a week.

▶ 34 percent use websites as their primary source of news.

▶ 28 percent author a blog and 44 percent read blogs.

▶ 49 percent download music using peer-to-peer file sharing.

▶ 75 percent have a Facebook account.

▶ 60 percent own some type of portable music and/or video device such as an iPod.

Source: *Connecting to the Net.Generation: What Higher Education Professionals Need to Know about Today's Students*, by Reynol Junco and Jeanna Mastrodicasa (Washington, D.C.: NASPA, 2007).

This isn't just savvy. This is active participation with technology, a tool in their lives that allows them to communicate with their "trusted sources," a.k.a. their BFFs. (If you need to know what BFF means at this point, it means "best friend forever." That means "trusted source" in the far less colorful language that we older folks speak. For the purposes of this book, I may use them interchangeably.)

This active, untethered use of technology doesn't mean it's the only way they communicate, despite what you see your teen kids doing all day. When you're thinking about your business strategy, you'd better be considerably less anecdotal, because the data is a little different than what you think you're seeing.

A study done by eMarketer in July 2008 found that 60 percent of younger Gen Yers are purchasing online—the majority of them buying clothes, shoes and, of course, accessories. But 82 percent of them *prefer* to shop in stores, not online. Got that?

Why? Here's what Mandy Putnam, vice president of TNS Retail Forward, said in the June 2008 *Stores* magazine: "…young people prefer the sensory stimulation that accompanies shopping with friends at stores." If I had to interpret that, and I do, I'd offer a business translation that went something like this: The younger Gen Yers prefer the experience to the purchase itself. They are actively shopping online and that tells you about their comfort with technology, but the reason for that online purchase is primarily because it's a more convenient way of trolling for good prices and value. Their online shopping is more for parsimony, not for reveling in experience. The social side of shopping with friends in a cool environment is where the experience is for them.

This is the first trump card to play when planning your customer strategy. Experience trumps utility. Note, though, I didn't say offline or online—just *experience*, without modifiers. More on all that in Chapter 3.

This is also a generation with different expectations. They expect to get what they need. They've been raised to think they will. More often than not, they do.

Bruce Tulgan, author of *Managing Generation Y*, put it well in an interview with *USA Today* on Gen Y's expectations at the workplace:

> *This is a generation of multitaskers, and they can juggle e-mail on their BlackBerrys while talking on cell phones while trolling online. And they believe in their own self worth and value enough that they're not shy about trying to change the companies they work for. That compares somewhat with Gen X, a generation born from the mid-1960s to the late-1970s, known for its independent thinking, addiction to change, and emphasis on family. They're like Generation X on steroids. They walk in with high expectations for themselves, their employer, their boss. If you thought you saw a clash when Generation X came into the workplace—that was the fake punch. The haymaker is coming now.*

I'm not going to dwell on this, because that would be beyond the scope of the book, but that haymaker has been thrown and it landed. The combinations that followed were heavy. The impact of Gen Y on other generations that were inclined to be like them to some degree (Gen X) or inclined toward change at one point in their lives (boomers) was powerful. In fact, it created what Springwise (www .springwise.com), a site that covers long-tail business trends, and I call Generation C—a cross-generational grouping that is exactly those customers you have to deal with now. Those social customers.

Generation C: From la Vita Contemplativa to la Vita Attiva

In his most overtly political work, *Convivio*, Dante Alighieri identified two states of life that most people desire and some attain: *vita contemplativa*, the thoughtful, pure intellectual life, and *vita attiva*, the active life. Dante saw them both as righteous paths to a good existence. Though the contemplative life is the optimal state in Dante's view, *vita attiva* is the state of social customers. Let's take a look at how they got there.

Gen C: The Early Years

In the earliest part of the 21st century, social and cultural shifts in combination with the beginning of the Web 2.0 technology developments began to change how people thought and what they expected of the institutions they had to deal with. To just give you a flavor, not an extended sociological analysis, here are some of the reasons worth mentioning:

▶ Gen Y's entrance into the workforce and their demands for what they needed in order to work and communicate

▶ The development of the over-the-air infrastructure, allowing much higher speed data transfer and better quality communications

▶ The easy availability of inexpensive or free hardware devices and software that could utilize those higher speeds, available bandwidth, and improved communications

▶ The decrease in the cost of storage, making the archiving of large files for photos and videos reasonable for the first time

▶ The fact that baby boomers did not retire due to both the early millennium economic downturn and their continued interest in working

▶ The increasingly easy and inexpensive availability of Internet access through wired and wireless sources

But the most important inflection point came when who and what trusted sources were began to change. In 2003, according to the Edelman Trust Barometer, "a person like me" (more on that later) was the most trusted source for only 22 percent of the population in North America and 33 percent in Europe. By 2005, that had shifted to an incredible 56 percent in North America and 53 percent in Europe, and it has never looked back since. Now trust was based on someone who had the interests and/or political beliefs that you had, not institutions that had been providing self-aggrandizing literature to convince you to buy products, or even industry experts who had the subject matter knowledge, or nonprofits that were pure of heart and motive with their social agendas. You and your social doppelgangers were the ones you went to for get advice or share beliefs.

Gen C: Technology Transformation and Lifestyle

Technology plays an important part in the social changes that have driven the growth of Gen C. It has been an enabler and even something of a driver in the confidence that social customers have in their decisions about how they want to do business and with whom they care to continue doing it.

From the corporate side, some of this was precipitated by the evolution of the on-demand model for software services (see Chapter 16). In the olden days of 2003, it was called the application service provider (ASP) market or "net native" services companies. Salesforce.com led the charge to this new way of delivering technology services. Denis Pombriant, whom you've already met, was the first in calling it "disruptive" and it was. For businesses, CRM-related services—sales force automation in particular—became a manageable cost with flexible, multichannel access. This revolutionized the delivery of CRM to companies, making them considerably more aware of what it was, precisely at the time when the world was changing

There was one other important change. Lifestyle and business started to become inextricably linked (see Chapter 3). Consumer thinking began to mesh with business strategy and activity. Companies like Research in Motion (RIM), creators and manufacturers of the ever-popular BlackBerry, began to consider style as something that was a true feature of their business offering. The old clunker 7200 series was replaced by the very cool BlackBerry Pearl.

Additionally, people began to use the Internet not just for e-commerce, which was the first true business activity on the Internet, but also for research on the products and services that they were interested in using. This was reflected in the exponential growth of Internet search, especially Google, which reached to nearly 500 million unique visitors in the month of November 2007 alone. Getting information in less than a second became standard. Search software, which often cost thousands of dollars, was no longer necessary. The minutes it took to do an unstructured search turned into nanoseconds. The world changed. Google is free and so ubiquitous that *to Google something* is now a verb. In fact if you Google "Google," there are 2.78 *billion* results (which I found in 0.22 seconds).

Because of the shift in who you trusted and the easy availability of tools like Google, how you investigated information and what you believed became very different from what it had been when the millennium dawned (that's 2000 or 2001, depending on how literal you want to be). The social customers, younger or older, didn't have to rely on corporate literature and self-interested salespeople any longer. They could rely on each other for information on their potential purchases and for deeper knowledge about their common interests—work or play.

This gave rise to simple review sites. These sites were available to the users of products, services, or visitors to institutions. They provided a means to rate (usually with 1 to 5 stars) and comment on the products they used. This resulted in unvarnished information such as:

▶ How good was the product?

▶ Did it meet the expectations the buyers had of it?

▶ What did it do right? Wrong?

▶ Did the manufacturer or retailer product provide appropriate service around the product?

▶ How did the company handle the order, shipping, and customer service?

All with a healthy dose of informality and conversational language. Certainly there were agendas being met by some of the reviewers. Some were shills for the companies that made or sold the products; others had a personal agenda. But when taken as a whole and read granularly, each of the product reviews and the picture painted overall of the product affected whether the review readers would purchase the product. A study done by BigResearch in 2007 found that the most powerful form of influence is word of mouth from trusted sources. The review sites were word of mouth online.

For example, Figure 1-3 is a page from Epinions (www.epinions .com). Take a good look, commit it to memory, because we're now going to begin the ride for real.

Gen C Arrives Ready for Action

But review sites tend to be passive. You read and you judge the product based on opinions that are on the website. The experience is unidirectional. By 2006, the social customer was operating in a brand new sphere. They weren't just reviewing and presenting. They were engaged in proactive broadcasting of their opinions, ideas, and innovations. They were interested in others hearing what they had to say and interested in mobilizing for actions or being mobilized for action.

The insane growth of the blogosphere was a prime indication of this. While you'll be hearing a lot more on how this worked in Chapter 7, suffice it to say that the blogosphere, now part of the mainstream on both the personal and business sides, is still growing exponentially with roughly 120,000 new blogs per day showing up throughout the world. Blogs have had an impact on political campaigns, social agendas (TechPresident, Daily Kos, etc.), and business. Just take a look at what I describe in Chapter 7 about Dell Hell. Bloggers are credentialed as journalists at major events and conferences because of the power they have to influence thinking. The ability of a single person to affect thousands and even millions of others has never been more prevalent than it is today. All because of links and RSS feeds associated with blogs.

Want proof of how powerful it is? Check out what I say about MyBarackObama.com in Chapter 14. He is the President of the United States because he understood the desire for action and the power of the Internet in effecting change and affecting thinking.

The business value of this active customer is greater than ever before. There are indicators everywhere that the one thing customers

Figure 1-3: Epinions reviews: do you trust them?

demand of companies now is the products, services, and tools that craft highly personalized experiences with those companies. That means they need transparency into and knowledge of those companies. These are factors that dramatically impact the business models the companies need to develop (Chapter 5).

But it goes even further than that. The trusted sources have been organizing themselves into social networks. You've seen them on Facebook (230+ million members), LinkedIn, and Plaxo when it comes to those most frequented for business purposes. You've seen the highly revealing social profiles. What were embarrassing revelations in 2005 are just run of the mill now. In late 2007, *New York* magazine ran an article on teenagers today that found they were involved in an average of 14 social networks and had no problem revealing intimate details that would have sent their female ancestors to a fatal dunking in Salem three and a half centuries ago.

The social customer is organized to take action through social networks and to provide proactive thinking on subjects germane to the networks they are a part of. The people like them are on that network. In social networking terms, these are communities of practice or interest.

As scary as this active, organized, gigantic mob seems, it has huge benefits to business if you're willing to cede control to customers as NBC Interactive Media did. This is a generation driven by Y but called Gen C for its six interests:

▶ **Content**   They want information so they can make intelligent decisions about how and where they do their business.

▶ **Connected**   They are intermeshed with each other at a peer-to-peer level, and they are mobile and untethered about how they are connected.

▶ **Creative**   They are willing to present new ideas, often for free, if they find it's in their interest to do so.

▶ **Collaborative**   As customers, they are willing to engage with companies and partners to come up with solutions that benefit all of the parties involved.

▶ **Contextual**   Knowledge and ideas are meaningful to them—if they see the reason for that meaning and the benefit of that meaning under the circumstances they are in.

▶ **Communicative**   They are going to talk to others about you, for good or ill. Which way is up to you.

This is just the overview. The fun (or fear) is just beginning. Let's dig in. Before I tell you what you have to do to engage these social customers with Social CRM strategies, we need to define Social CRM. I'm going to take you to a cybersalon where you'll hear from some of the leading luminaries on what they think it is. Go download and read what they are thinking. Otherwise, you have mostly me for a while. You *know* I have an opinion.

2

. . . .

CRM, CMR, VRM or . . . Who Cares?

The leaders in the web chapter, "CRM 2.0 Leaders Speak from Out There," did a great job, didn't they? Give 'em a hand! Come on, let's hear it! Oh, you didn't download it yet? Whaaaa? Go do it now. I can wait.

Okay. We're going to start with three-letter acronyms. In order, they are: CRM, CMR, Social CRM, VRM.

As astounding as the number of acronyms is and as befuddling as they are to the thinking around CRM, with their ability to further muddy already muddy waters, each of these acronyms needs to be understood if you want to develop a customer engagement model.

Defining your terms is an important first step—and one you cannot, I repeat, cannot, skip no matter how trivial you think the exercise might be. Don't think so? Marc Benioff once told me, "I love convincing skeptics." Me, too.

One client of mine, when I first began my assignment with them, insisted they already had CRM—which of course was a little perplexing because I had to wonder why, then, did they hire me? In the course of my initial work, I went to spend time at one of their retail stores. While I was there, the store manager showed me this big paper mass with records of customer transactions, mostly orders, that was sitting in a gargantuan binder. I was told that this was their "CRM" book. A-ha! And uh-oh.

It took months to overcome their existing definition of CRM so they could understand what I was talking about. Defining CRM would have been relatively simple if it hadn't been poorly defined before I got there. But because their definition was wrong and the company had incorporated that incorrect definition into routine use, I had to embark on a lengthy education process to get the term right. In the long run, it paid off.

What you never want to hear at a company is "Oh, *that's* what you meant by CRM."

So let's start with the 10,000 foot view of CRM. There will be a lot more detail later on.

"Traditional" CRM

CRM is a philosophy and a business strategy supported by a system and a technology designed to improve human interactions in a business environment.

—Paul Greenberg, *CRM* Magazine, October 2003

When I created that global definition of CRM 1.0 in 2003, I had no idea that the social dynamics of the era and the technology transformation to Web 2.0 would require a change to it within roughly four years. This particular definition, as broad as it may seem, is defined primarily by traditional CRM—an operational, transactional approach to customer management that was focused around the customer-facing departments—sales, marketing, and customer service. The entirety of the first three editions of this book was based on that premise. How do process modification, culture change, automation through technology, and the use of data for customer insight support the management of customers so that it can meet a corporate objective? Those objectives might have included increases in revenue, higher margins, increase in "selling time" or campaign effectiveness, reduction in call queuing time, or really hundreds of other metrics. The core value proposition was a potential increase in customer acquisition or higher rates of customer retention, with loyalty a bonus.

CRM has been a program for externally facing operational excellence. Once you developed a strategy and were able to plan appropriate programs, applying the newly defined or redefined processes and a well-chosen technology would support your ability to manage those relationships. The customer's benefit, theoretically, was better service, attention, and support from the company—and, if the company used a sophisticated enough system, optimized deals that were personalized to the customer's likes, which of course, led to more and higher value purchases by the customer.

In theory, it was great. In practice, despite notable failures, as it matured and the thinking about it became clearer and the tools better, the success rates increased. The numbers supported that. But it didn't start out that way. In 2002, when CRM was immature and still trying to find its legs, Gartner found that failure rates were apparently between 55 and 70 percent. This was a shocker that became a buzz that became a constant noise. It was the industry naysayer's mantra. The irony, of course, is that CRM was in its toddlerhood and as far as I know, you don't ask a two-year-old why he doesn't have a $75,000 job yet.

There were reasons for the failures; they didn't occur in a vacuum. User adoption was always difficult, accounting for 47 percent of the reasons given for failure, according to an IDC study in 2004. The earlier CRM applications and programs, while customer friendly, were not employee friendly. For example, the sales tools were typically aimed at opportunity management or pipeline visibility across a company. What did this do for a salesperson? Not a lot. For a sales manager it was great—they could more accurately forecast revenue, provide a clearer analysis of lead-to-close rates, etc. But there was little to no benefit for the salesperson. What it did more frequently than not was to take away the one leverage point the salesperson felt he had in his dog-eat-dog, high pressure environment—his relationships.

Think about this. ACT!, the contact management application, was wildly popular with over 2.5 million users in 2005 and yet, SalesLogix, the SFA application designed by the very same creators of ACT!, had serious adoption issues. Why? Because ACT! had a flat file database and wasn't network friendly. What that means, practically, is that an individual copy resided on the desktop and was only visible to the "owner" of the desktop—the salesperson. Their managers didn't have access to the contact/account databases. With SalesLogix, this was not the case. The database was relational and, back then, a client/server network made it available to sales managers at their leisure. SalesLogix could accumulate the data the managers needed to compare one salesperson's performance against others. Why in the world would a salesperson be interested in that? The short answer was (and still is), they wouldn't and weren't. Thus the 47 percent.

But by 2004, CRM strategies began to mature and the tools got better. The perception of CRM changed so that it was seen as a key tool for administering the connections with customers and the performance of the customer-facing staff. The tools were improved so that, for example, in the case of sales force automation (SFA), the sales component of CRM, tools that would aid the salesperson were added, such as Oracle's 2004 addition of a quoting tool for salespeople who were on the road with their customers. There were more tools to support the staff in their never-ending effort to sell to customers.

That's led to a remarkably robust industry despite the economic downturn. CRM is still projected by analysts to continue to grow, maybe even be recession-proof. Even recession-inspired. What is the most important thing you can do in a recession? Keep your existing customers and encourage them to continue to buy from you.

This translates to some staggering numbers for what is primarily the CRM 1.0 applications and services market. In July 2008, the noted analyst firm AMR Research released their "Customer Management Market Sizing Report, 2007–2012." Their estimate for the CRM software revenues in 2007 alone topped $14 billion, a 12 percent jump over 2006 revenues. They didn't have the final numbers at the time they released the report. More amazing was the prospectus—again this is just for software. They projected a market size of more than $22 billion in 2012, a 36 percent growth rate—with a poor economic outlook floating everywhere. If nothing else, this shows you the enthusiasm that CRM engenders—even the traditional operational side. Slightly less optimistic but still staggering were the Gartner July 2008 numbers, which said that the 2007 CRM software license revenues were $8.8 billion and projected to be $13.3 billion by 2012. Either number is very large, n'est ce pas?

Throughout this book will be discussions of the core of CRM 1.0 as it is included in a Social CRM context. If you want a big and pure CRM 1.0 book, look at the third edition of *CRM at the Speed of Light*—it is 671 pages of CRM 1.0 goodness. The concepts, as we will see, remain intact. Some of the data is clearly outdated, since it came out in 2004. But it will give you a comprehensive look at CRM 1.0 probably well beyond where you want to see it. This fourth edition is all about Social CRM. But let's continue on to see how we got to Social CRM in the first place.

From CRM to CMR

In 2006, Seth Godin reported on his blog that Disney Destinations, the travel and vacation arm of Disney, had changed their acronym from CRM to CMR—from customer relationship management to customer-managed relationships. Here's a bit of the blog entry "CRM Is Dead":

> *It might be more than just semantics. Disney Destinations Marketing has a new department:*

Customer-Managed Relationships

Here's the quote from them that Tim shared with me, "CMR is our version of CRM—just a slight nuance regarding our philosophy that our guests invite us into their lives and ultimately manage our presence/relationship with them."

Disney Destinations characterized this as "just a slight nuance." As much as I love Mickey and Goofy, I beg to differ with Disney here. This was by no means trivial. It was a big deal because it was a reflection of the sea change going on in CRM, the recognition that the customer was looking for something quite different than in the past several years. In fact, this is a major company showing some foresight in the knowledge that the business ecosystem has the customer at its hub. And they aren't the only ones.

In August 2007, George Colony, CEO of Forrester Research, put it as succinctly as one can:

It's now a two-way conversation. Listen, respond and talk intelligently. Stop dictating to customers. It's your customers, not you, who have the power.

None of these are trivial and all of them have had real-world impact or been driven by real-world actions that forced the companies to think about how to handle themselves in this new business environment.

Remember back in Chapter 1, I mentioned Beth Comstock, president of NBC Interactive Media? Why she agrees with George Colony was made very clear in the *Washington Post* article on October 21, 2006:

NBC Universal announced sweeping cuts to its television operations yesterday, demonstrating just how far a once-unrivaled network must now go to stay competitive with YouTube, social networks, video games and other upstart media.

NBC wasn't doing this out of their love for customers or an attempt to pander to youth particularly. They were slammed with the changing business environment and had come face to face with the forces that were driving that change and it damaged them. Their losses were material. They made budget cuts of $750 million and 750 staff cuts directly attributable to "YouTube, social networks, video games and other upstart media."

This social change is not a joke, nor is it a trivial matter for any institution—and business is going to be particularly impacted by it.

What Disney Destinations was doing was making decisions to provide their customers and those just interested in testing their services the means to control their own experience with Disney Destinations. The idea was simple. Provide online tools such as a trip planner so a family can plan its trip to a Disney property or through a Disney agency down to the details. They can identify the locations, length of stay, prices, extras, and means of travel, all in their own time, under their aegis. This would enhance the experience the customers had with Disney, making travel planning simple and not stressful—which as you know is a huge issue in travel planning. You know it, because you know how stressed *you* get.

But this was just a harbinger of things to come less than a year later. Customers managing their own relationships was a step in the personalization of the customer's experience with a company. But personalization of the experience was still insufficient, however important it can be. It was only a first step in what is now . . .

Social CRM

Social CRM. The reason this book is being written. This is the time for your adoption of these new strategies. The sooner you can acknowledge that the customers are running the show, the sooner you can execute an appropriate Social CRM program and strategy that will engage those very empowered customers. I'll begin by providing you with the first definition of Social CRM, largely shaped by the CRM community on a wiki that has around 300 participants. The purpose of the wiki is to come up with a definition of Social CRM that is acceptable to the overall industry and its practitioners so that the self-aggrandizing definitions of CRM 1.0 will be a thing of the past—and we can commonly agree on something. A standard, if you will—the 1.0 definition of Social CRM:

> *Social CRM is a philosophy and a business strategy, supported by a technology platform, business rules, processes, and social characteristics, designed to engage the customer in a collaborative conversation in order to provide mutually beneficial value in a trusted and transparent business environment. It's the company's response to the customer's ownership of the conversation.*

You'll note there is a difference between the definition of CRM 1.0 and Social CRM in this chapter. That difference actually implies an entirely different set of strategies, models, technology use, and process conception.

Differences Between Traditional CRM and Social CRM

The underlying principle for Social CRM's success is very different from its predecessor. As I've already established, traditional CRM is based on an internal operational approach to manage customer relationships effectively. But Social CRM is based on the ability of a company to meet the personal agendas of their customers while at the same time meeting the objectives of their own business plan. It's aimed at customer *engagement* rather than customer management.

In fact, my contention is that the CRM technologies we have been used to, such as sales, marketing, and support applications, even the on-demand versions of those, are not the technical capital of the 21st century's "era of the social customer." The customer is not just becoming the central repository for value, but wants to actively participate in value creation with business. Therefore the consumer technologies and service offerings adopted as platforms for individually meaningful "life choices" are where CRM technology needs to be. This doesn't mean I'm saying goodbye to Siebel, Sage, Oracle, SAP, or any of the on-demand vendors. However, their technologies will have to evolve and not just associate with some reorganized contemporary set of business processes. They will have to integrate the features of newer technologies that facilitate market conversations, social networking, user communities, and the like—in other words, that exist to transform and operate businesses not just as process-pushing producers but as aggregators for and partners in the customer value chain (more on that later). That will probably come later than sooner—we may be a few years away from that. But there are some things that are both happening now and need to happen now. Even though the on-demand "software as a service" (SaaS) paradigm has become popular, we also now have to consider moving to an additional paradigm of "platform as a service" (PaaS). So that when you as a customer buy a laptop or a cellphone, whatever your specific purposes, you are choosing a piece that will fit into the platform you use for the services and associated goods you need to conduct your life—which among other things, consists of business services, in that there are businesses associated with them.

The differences are deep, though all the differences are permeated with either the principles or practices of managing customers or involving them in the activities of the company in a mutually beneficial way. Table 2-1 shows the differences as defined by a community of 300 CRM professionals on the wiki I mentioned above.

Spend some time investigating here because the rest of the book is going to be spent in explaining all the things in this table—with the experts who are involved chiming in to help.

Table 2-1: Differences between CRM 1.0 and Social CRM (Source: CRM 2.0 Wiki)

CRM 1.0 Features/Functions	Social CRM Features/Functions
Customer-facing features—sales, marketing, and support; still isolated from back office, supply chain	Fully integrated into an enterprise value chain that includes the customer as part of it
Tools are associated with automating functions	Integrates social media tools into apps/services: blogs, wikis, podcasts, social networking tools, user communities
Encourages friendly, institutional relationships with customers	Encourages authenticity and transparency in customer interactions
	Utilizes knowledge in context to create meaningful conversations
Models customer processes from the company point of view	Models company processes from the customer point of view
	Recognizes that the customer relationship encompasses information-seeking and information-contributing behavior
Resides in a customer-focused corporate business ecosystem	Resides in a customer ecosystem
Utilitarian, functional, operational	All those plus style and design matter
Marketing focuses on processes that send improved, targeted, highly specific corporate messages to customer	Marketing is front line for creating conversation with customer—engaging customer in activity and discussion—observing and redirecting conversations among customers
Business produces products and creates services for customer	Business is an aggregator of experiences, products, services, tools, and knowledge for the customer
Intellectual property protected with all legal might available	Intellectual property created and owned together with the customer, partner, supplier, problem solver
Business focus on products and services that satisfy customers	Business focus on environments and experiences that engage customer
Tactical and operational	Strategic

Table 2-1: Differences between CRM 1.0 and Social CRM (Source: CRM 2.0 Wiki) *(continued)*

CRM 1.0 Features/Functions	Social CRM Features/Functions
Customer strategy is part of corporate strategy	Customer strategy *is* corporate strategy
Innovation from the designated	Innovation from both internal and external sources
Focus on company customer relationship	Focus on all iterations of the relationships (among company, partners, customers) and specifically on identifying, engaging, and enabling the "influential" nodes
Company manages the relationship with the customer	Customer collaborates with the company
Technology focused around operational aspects of sales, marketing, support	Technology focuses on both the operational and the social/collaborative and integrates the customer into the entire enterprise value chain
Relationship between the company and the customer is seen as enterprise managing customer—parent to child to a large extent	Relationship between the company and the customer must be peer to peer (C2P or P2C, so to speak) and yet the company must still be an enterprise in all other aspects

Social CRM Technology: Features, Functions, Characteristics

The differences don't stop there. Even the technology and the approaches to the technology are different.

Traditional CRM technologies have always been defined by features and functions. What are the technology tools and available automation that can make a company's operations more effective when it comes to managing customers' interactions with the company—or, as CRM got increasingly sophisticated, optimizing the customers' experiences with the company?

For example, here's how the data sheet reads for Maximizer CRM 10 for Sales:

▶ Features

▶ Account and contact management

▶ Time management

▶ Task management and automation

► Sales force automation

► Sales forecasting

► Marketing automation

► Email marketing

► Customer service management

► Microsoft Office integration

► Outlook and Exchange synchronization

► Accounting integration

► Business Intelligence

► Workflow automation

► Partner relationship management

► eBusiness

► Access options: Windows desktop, Web, mobile devices, remote synchronization

This is an entirely straightforward listing of what is generally included in the CRM 10 for Sales application—one which, incidentally, is well suited for small and the low end of medium businesses. These features are also representative of those offered by most small and medium business (SMB)–focused CRM suites.

But Maximizer CRM 10 for Sales is not a Social CRM application by any stretch of the imagination. The closest "feature" that fits a Social CRM technology profile is mobile device access. The rest is the historical and traditional CRM—"Not that there's anything wrong with that," as Jerry Seinfeld says. But it isn't enough when it comes to customers whose trust lies in their peers, and the personal interactions with those peers are the bonds that strengthen the trust.

The 360° View Isn't Enough

But why isn't the Holy Grail of traditional CRM, the 360-degree view of the customer with a single customer record, enough to monitor the interactions and provide the insights? After all, if you could achieve that complete customer record and make it available consistently across departments, you'd have what you needed, right?

You'd think so if you heard these quotes:

When running a multichannel retail operation, the most valuable resource is having a single view of leads, prospects, and customers across different channels. (DM News, March 2007)

Nationwide Gains a "360-Degree" View of the Customer to Advance Its "On Your Side" Promise (Tech Republic White Paper)

You and everyone else in your organization want to know everything possible about your customers. You want a single view of the customer that everyone across the enterprise can use. There's nothing new about this. Businesses have been trying to get a single view of their customers and prospects for years. (Informatica Marketing Collateral)

In fact, if you Google "single view of the customer" there are between 32,000 and 107,000 references to that exact phrase on any given day and with any given algorithm.

Yet, while certainly valuable, it is *data*—not insight, not behavior, not a substitute for judgment, not a way to engage customers. It is a state devoutly to be wished when the ecosystem is owned by the company, not the customer, because when the ecosystem is owned by the customer, the customer is carrying on important parts of the business conversation well beyond the company's walls and out of the company's immediate earshot. Certainly the 360-degree view is valuable because it can provide you with a customer's transaction histories and interactions with different departments, which gives you some knowledge to begin to develop an increased understanding of your customer. But this former Holy Grail is now just a prerequisite for customer insight, not a state of grace to be achieved.

Doing More to Get Their Attention

Why is so much knowledge needed and why a great depth of insight? Why not just basic patterns of activity or a reasonable but not deep knowledge of the customer's other interests?

Because, my future and current colleagues and friends, the competition for that customer has left the halls of similar product offerings from competitive companies. Your competition is no longer Coca-Cola vs. PepsiCo. It's Coca-Cola vs. PepsiCo and every single message that a single customer gets in a single day. You aren't competing for their purchase at this stage. Because of the incredible proliferation of information, available 24 hours a day, 7 days a week from multiple channels, you are competing for the *attention* of the customer. While we're going to cover that in a later chapter (Chapter 12), the level of personal knowledge and insight you need for a customer is of a magnitude that is affected by the 3,000 messages that each customer gets each day—a lot of noise that they may not answer, but they also may not differentiate between you and that noise. Again, more later.

Before we take this to the deepest part of center field, let's look at what's getting pitched. There is a combination of components that are critical for deep insight that are not the same components you might be used to—or at least, most of them aren't.

▶ **Data**   This includes the information the company can gather through the activities of the customer. That means purchase histories, returns, visits to e-commerce websites and time spent on different pages, marketing response to campaigns, and customer service inquiries and problems, among many others.

▶ **Profiles**   This is the "personal" information that is now so important in gaining insights into how a customer wants to interact with the company. This could be their movie and literary interests, their hobbies, their "style" likes and dislikes, their unstructured text comments in a community or social network that is either owned by you or deals with your company's interests, such as Yelp for a restaurant or a geographically based retailer. Profiles become essential with the growing interest in micro-targeting—the deep dive into the customers' lives (hopefully, without being intrusive) to understand their style and selection choices for predicting future, sometimes apparently unrelated, behaviors.

▶ **Customer participation**   This is their active involvement in supporting the development of your insight into their interests, including interactions through mapping experiences and the customer's individual interest in fostering a relationship with the company. It's the difference between marketing presuming they know what the customer is thinking (which, take my word and check out Chapter 12 on sales and marketing, they almost always do) and actually asking the customer what they're thinking and expecting. Customer mapping (see Chapter 18) is one method of finding that out.

Okay, components understood. What's the rest?

The Social Stack

Features and functions are no longer the ne plus ultra for Social CRM technology. Interestingly, what had been historically considered "right-brained" functions—the emotional and behavioral characteristics of human interactions—are now creeping into the more left-brained sectors of CRM, the technology. That means we are looking at social characteristics.

Unlike features and functions, social characteristics are based on the profiles of individuals who are participating in web-based interactions among peers and, for our purposes, between customers and companies. Rather than focusing on what the software can do, we're looking at the distinctions between software users, the impact these distinctions will have on customer activities with the company, and the levels of additional insight the profiles can provide to the company.

Thomas Vander Wal, whom you will meet in Chapter 6, is the creator of social tagging and folksonomies—a legend in the Web 2.0 world. He has developed an approach to the way that human profiles on the Web are affected by their actions on each other and the implications of that for business and for web activity. He calls it the social stack. I've modified it a little to make it practically applicable to a contemporary CRM strategy.

Identity and Objects

The core components of the social stack are what Vander Wal calls "identity" and "objects." Identity is just what it seems to be—who you are and how you present yourself. The simplest form is your personal profile. Objects are those things that you use to enhance your identity—photos, videos, comments, social tags, ratings, and bookmarks. They are often called user generated content (UGC). They are typically digital, but don't have to be. In a business setting they can be assets, but don't have to be. For our purposes, they are digital and potential assets. Central to their very nature is that objects more often than not are shared—and that is a critical difference between a valueless object and a valuable object. Also of Social CRM importance, collaboration can alter the nature of an object.

While there are two core components, each of them is affected by a separate group of characteristics that affect the way they interact. These are active elements (see Figure 2-1). I'll explain each and then apply them in a way that shows how they work in the real world.

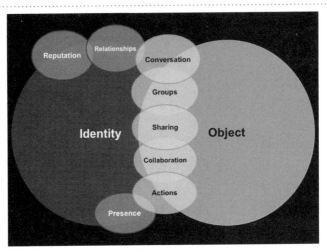

Figure 2-1: The elements of the social stack

▶ **Presence**   This is most commonly seen through instant messaging. You probably don't think twice about it, you're so used to seeing it. When one of your instant messaging buddies is online, you're notified and you know they are online. Presence also lets you know how they want to be contacted when they are online. That's why you see "away," "not available," and so on as options in IM. This is presence, pure and simple. When location becomes a factor, it gets considerably more complex, but also eminently more interesting. For example, Concordia University (Montreal, Quebec) uses a presence-based routing system at their helpdesk. Based on a caller's profile attributes such as role, language, current or historic activity, the call is routed to the appropriate person automatically without a lot of major expenditure on call center applications. (See "Context" below as another active element in this sequence.)

▶ **Actions**   This is straightforward. You upload a photo, comment on a video, send a message—pretty much anything you can do with a verb that's related to the objects and the identity.

▶ **Sharing**   This is the singular element. A private object, one not shared, is one that has little value. For example, shooting a video is not unique, new, or even evolutionary. Home videos have been shot ever since families acquired analog cameras to shoot them.

I still remember the home movies that my family took, which we played on a reel projector. They fit the definition of an object. But there was no real extant value to that object. Sentimental value, sure. But it didn't and doesn't have the impact of a shared video on YouTube that materially affects the world in some concrete way. For example, take a look at the Obama Girl video on YouTube. It has been seen by nearly 15 million people at the time I wrote this chapter. Articles have appeared on the value this video spoof with a gorgeous female had for the Obama campaign because of the increase in interest and visibility the viral nature of the video allowed. The social action around sharing the object makes the difference. Digital formats and devices that can handle videos have made producing them an easier task. But it is uploading them to YouTube that begins the social act. You are "licensing" them to be shared so that actions (the video is viewed; someone comments) can be taken with your permission. The act of uploading is the agreement to share.

▶ **Reputation**   Reputation is best understood by the following question: "Do I trust the action that this person is taking or the object that this person is providing?" Your level of trust is based on this person's shared reputation or perhaps their reputation with you individually. Reputation is one of the most complex characteristics you're going to have to consider with your customers. It is not identifiable through a tool or an application, yet how you interact with that customer and they with their community is affected by the reputation of whom you are interacting with. For example, if an expert in CRM whom you don't personally know recommends that you subscribe to a blog, how much more likely is it that you will than if a stranger who is an expert in animal husbandry or a friend who may or may not be a CRM savant suggests the same thing? Reputation can be enhanced by the participation of individuals in collaborative environments, like wikis or communities. In a joint study done by faculty from USC and City University of Hong Kong on the sustainability and benefits of wikis, between 23 and 29 percent of the respondents found that wiki participation enhanced their reputations by earning the respect of others (28 percent); improved their professional standing (23 percent); and improved their reputation within the company (29 percent).

▶ **Relationships**   These are the interactions between people who choose to engage based on reputations. This is an obviously important characteristic because it is how people trust the results of the actions—if the reputation and relationship work, the collaboration or interaction result is all the more trustworthy.

▶ **Conversation**   As I've stated about a million times already, one of the most important mantras of the 21st century is that the relationship between the company and the customer has shifted from the company pushing "stuff" at the customer to a conversation between the company and the customer. That means that the customer collaborates with the company to create the appropriate experiences that are valued by the customer and the company is rewarded in return. How these conversations are structured, what modes for carrying them out are provided, and what information is captured are dependent on what kind of strategies you are building to enhance peer-to-peer and peer-to-company communications. The conversation between any two communicators is very much built along the same lines and can be done via synchronous (e.g., IM) or asynchronous (e.g., e-mail) methods. Conversations can be structured so they occur in user communities or forums. They can be around a specific topic or they can be outcome based—a specific community or group formed to accomplish a specific task. But the conversation needs to be fostered as a major characteristic of the new CRM strategy and program.

▶ **Groups**   These are organized most frequently as communities of interest or practice that consist of those who care to interact around a specific domain. They are created by the practitioners of the common interest—a self-organized, member-created group—or by the owners of the real estate in which the group resides, such as a club that does business in California, created by JetBlue.

▶ **Collaboration**   As you'll see in Chapter 11 on the collaborative value chain, this is one of the characteristics with the most measurable and valuable benefits. It is typically represented by a central location that provides the tools, experiences, products (applications), and services (experts) to collaborate around building specific objects. This could mean a wiki on developing a SugarCRM module or a body of knowledge around business travel or business practices in China.

There's one more element I added to the stack—an important characteristic that underlies several of these:

▶ **Context**   This is how the profile you create is used to define what you want and what you see and when you see it. So you will see a business car rental price based on your requirements which you don't have to search for—it is there because you have logged in and given permission for the car rental company to access your profile. It is also which friends you are automatically engaged with when you log in and which ones you aren't. In effect, it is all you need to have at your fingertips during the appropriate times so you can take actions that make sense to you.

Social CRM and VRM

We've established quite a bit here:

1. The customer has taken ownership of the conversation.

2. This has created the need for a new approach to CRM strategy because the customer's demands and expectations have changed and whom they trust has changed.

3. Consequently we have to take a considerably deeper approach to CRM than in the past, not only accounting for the operational CRM of process, technology, metrics, and culture change programs, but also a social CRM strategy that actually involves deep knowledge of the customer, some of which is derived from the customer's actual thinking and some from the customer's transactional history.

4. To do that, we have to provide the institutional facilities to the customer so that on the one hand we satisfy their social and business requirements and on the other we are able to gain deeper insight into the customer and deeper commitments from the customer—a necessity because of the much deeper difficulties in just getting the attention of customers, much less getting them to stay customers.

But there is more to it. There is a increasingly important methodology and approach that has to not only be taken into account but understood if you are going to understand Social CRM. It's called vendor relationship management (VRM) and, after I tell you a little about it, I want you to shake the hand of someone I think you need to go have a cup of coffee with while he explains VRM.

Vendor Relationship Management (VRM)

VRM has a heck of a pedigree. It has landed a wiki at Harvard University called Project VRM and is the product of the fertile mind of Doc Searls (though he didn't name the technology—Mike Vizard did). Searls is one of the authors of *The Cluetrain Manifesto*, which is perhaps the best book (if a bit dramatic) on the thinking of the new customer that has been written to date (see Chapter 12).

VRM is not hard to understand: It is the actions taken by the customer to control the business environment that they are apparently in control of. The name is unfortunate and a bit boring, but the concept is fortunate and anything but boring. The idea is that customers have the means to sculpt their own experience and determine their own fate when it comes to how they deal with businesses of interest. The (abbreviated version of the) definition given to the technology by Project VRM, which is run by Doc Searls and Harvard University, is:

> *VRM, or Vendor Relationship Management, is the reciprocal of CRM or Customer Relationship Management. It provides customers with tools for engaging with vendors in ways that work for both parties. . . . VRM immodestly intends to improve markets and their mechanisms by equipping customers to be independent leaders and not just captive followers in their relationships with vendors and other parties on the supply side of the marketplace.*

It is the equivalent of the labor side of the labor/capital equation of old. VRM provides customers with the tools and strategies to control the ecosystem that businesses now seem willing to cede to them.

Now it's time for that handshake and the large café mocha with nonfat milk. Readers, this is Chris Carfi, the CEO of Cerado, a social networking software company and the guy who writes the amazing (and funny) "Social Customer Blog." As one of the foremost experts in the field, Chris can tell you considerably more about VRM than I can. That's why he's hanging out with us. Hey Chris. This is the reader. Reader, Chris. Dude, tell them about VRM. You two enjoy your coffee. I'm going to keep writing.

CONVERSATIONS WITH A REGULAR EXPERT, CHRIS CARFI

As of this writing, vendor relationship management (VRM) is an emerging initiative that is creating tools for individuals to manage their relationships with vendors. Now, think about that for a second. VRM is about giving *individuals* tools to manage their relationships with *their* vendors! (This is in marked contrast to the traditional role of CRM systems, which gave vendors tools with which they could manage, manipulate, and extract value from customer data and information.) Initially conceived by Doc Searls as the reciprocal of traditional CRM, VRM starts with the individual and seeks to build mutually beneficial relationships between buyers and sellers. Project VRM is an initiative sponsored by the Berkman Center for Internet and Society at Harvard University.

As CRM systems have evolved, organizations have created myriad methods to store, manage, and mine information about their customers. However, these interactions are historically very one-sided; the vendor keeps all the information, and the customer is a passive participant in the transaction, merely exchanging cash for product. But something has changed, and this change affects both sides of the interaction.

On one side, customers are beginning to realize that they are powerful, far more powerful than they have ever been in the past. Through the opportunities to publish their experiences for the world to read (and more importantly, find via search engines), customers are sharing their firsthand accounts of their interactions with vendors. They are not only publishing their thoughts on their personal spaces such as blogs, but they are also banding together in online communities such as Yelp, an online review site, in order to proactively praise vendors or warn others away based on a subpar experience.

On the other side, for a vendor that traditionally held all the cards, this increase in customer power is a frightening proposition. Correspondingly, a vendor today can choose to go in one of two directions, either moving toward a direction of maintaining the status quo in an attempt to control all aspects of the customer experience, or lowering the drawbridge to give customers access to the information, the processes, and, most importantly, the people who comprise the vendor organization.

With these changes comes a revelation and a requirement: customers (that is, "we") need to have tools that allow us, as individuals, to manage our information and relationships, tools that are *independent* of the CRM systems that vendors have in place. VRM is about the creation of those tools.

So, What Do You Mean by Tools?

Let's take a simple example, that of a customer's address. In today's world, every vendor with which a customer does business has a copy of that customer's address in its CRM system. Every credit card company, every hardware store, every online catalog, Amazon, the iTunes store, you name it . . . every one has its "version" of the address, with varying levels of accuracy in the data.

Now, the customer moves to a new apartment across town.

The way things are today with traditional CRM systems, the customer must enter into an arduous, perhaps months-long process to contact every one of those vendors in order to attempt to change her address. Dozens of phone calls, innumerable postcards, hours on hold in vendors' call centers, and hundreds of mouse clicks, just to change an address! It is in some ways both humorous and tragic that this is an instance where a physical move of every *atom* in an individual's possession only takes a weekend, yet changing a few *bits* of digital information about that individual might take many months.

VRM proposes a better way for all parties involved and proposes that the *customer* is in true, independent control of her own information. The customer then selectively grants access to that information to the vendors she chooses.

So how would the scenario above work in practice? While there are myriad implementation options, there are a few fundamental concepts that are illustrative, all of which center around this idea of a *personal data store* where an individual can collect, store, and selectively grant access to information.

By way of a partial analogy, think about how photo-sharing sites such as Flickr work today. Let's say your name is John Jones. Flickr gives each individual a unique URL such as www.flickr.com/johnjones, which can then be shared with others with varying levels of privacy (typical privacy levels would be "everyone," "friend," and "family"). Instead of giving everyone his photos, John Jones instead keeps his photos in one place and gives others his URL, to which he grants selective access to various photos to various individuals.

Now, the one place where the analogy above admittedly breaks down is that John Jones is still delegating all responsibility to Flickr to keep his photos safe and accessible. But what if he had his own domain, such as http://johnjones.com, where he could store all his digital information? He could set up a directory, such as http://johnjones.com/address/, where he could store his address information in an open format such as hCard or vCard. Now we're getting somewhere! With this setup, when John moves, he simply needs to let all his vendors know simultaneously that they can get his new apartment address at http://johnjones.com/address/johnjones.vcf and voilà, problem solved.

A more pressing case of the need for VRM comes in the health care arena. Currently, every doctor, every hospital, and every health care system has its own "version of truth" with respect to information on a specific patient. Although (in the U.S., anyway) doctors will give you your health care records upon request, that information is in either printed or fax form, and every doctor you've ever visited has a different set of information about your history, based solely on the tests and procedures that she may have performed on you. In the *best* case scenario, you can walk into a new doctor with a footlocker filled with every bit of medical information on your case history, written in a number of different scrawls. Now, realize that doctor has only allotted 10 minutes to see you. Will that doctor be able to find the needle in the haystack that might enable her to give you the best care? Not likely.

What is more likely is that you're handed a clipboard upon walking into the office, asking if you know if you have one of dozens of different (and possibly serious) conditions or if you have any known allergies. What if you forget one? What if you spell the name of something wrong? In today's world, your health and well-being, your possibility of becoming another statistic listed under the euphemistic heading of "negative outcome" on a report, might be based on something as mundane as a typo or a momentary memory lapse.

In a VRM scenario, the situation is quite different. With a VRM model in place, our protagonist would be able to set up http://johnjones.com/health/, into which he could store his medical records. In this personal "health vault," John would be able to store the information of all his tests, both common and obscure, past MRIs and x-rays, as well as an ongoing record of any medications he is (or had been) taking. And, when he goes to his new doctor, he can grant his doctor access to http://johnjones.com/health/ and give his doctor the information she needs in order to provide him the best care available.

This idea of a VRM-centric personal data store also can be applied to the more common interactions we have with vendors of all stripes on a regular basis. Let's say you have a personal blog up at http://mypersonalblog.typepad.com. One can, today, publish a "feed" of relevant information to which the *smart* vendors will be paying attention. To that end, let's use a VRM-based model to purchase a car. Here's what we want:

▶ Looking to: Buy

▶ Make: Toyota

▶ Model: Prius

▶ Model year: 2006 or later

▶ Trim package: GS

▶ Zip code for delivery: 94063

▶ Contact URL: http://johnjones.com/contact/

By simply creating a blog post with this information, John Jones has *placed a demand signal into the marketplace.* Now, the smart vendors out there should already be setting up alerts that are looking for blog posts or web pages that contain phrases like "looking to buy" and the name of their product or service. Upon seeing this information in John's feed, vendors who are interested in creating a business relationship should be reaching out to him with further information about how they might be able to fulfill his needs.

VRM: The Reciprocal of CRM

Traditional CRM systems typically address three touchpoints with customers: marketing (Chapter 12), sales (Chapter 12), and support (Chapter 13). So, if VRM is about creating mutually beneficial relationships between customers and vendors, what are the customer-side analogues to marketing, sales, and support?

Happily, the answers are intuitive. If marketing is what a vendor does before a sales transaction occurs between itself and a customer, then the customer-side analogue to "what happens before a transaction" is *search*. So, the VRM model must support search, where a customer can look for as well as store and collect information about vendors and/or products that she in interested in learning more about.

Similarly, when a customer is ready to engage in a transaction, she should be able to place a demand signal into the market, as was exhibited earlier with the auto purchase example. This can be thought of as the case where a customer engages in *shop* activity to engage in a transaction with a vendor.

To round out the model, a customer needs to be able to get support from vendors with whom she has a business relationship. But instead of navigating through a morass of phone trees or less-than-stellar FAQ (frequently asked question) lists on a vendor's site, the customer needs to be able to put a description of the problem into her personal data store, to which the vendor (or, perhaps more interestingly, a member of the community at large) can proffer a solution.

Transaction—Conversation—Relationship

The other major difference between VRM and CRM is one of central focus. Perhaps cynically, the implicit question answered by CRM systems has historically been "what can we do to leverage the information we have about this customer to get the customer to engage in (another) transaction?" The driver behind VRM is very different; VRM is about how a customer manages his own information, independent of any vendor's silo, in such a way that he is able to engage in the types of business relationships that he desires.

A stellar model for this point of view was put forth by Doc Searls in a December 26, 2007, blog entry. In this post, he notes that there are three levels of interaction:

▶ Transaction

▶ Conversation

▶ Relationship

This perspective is one that is quite different from one that is being myopically driven through quarter-by-quarter financials. Instead, this model notes that the conversation (that is, the interaction of human beings exchanging information and growing increased context) is the cornerstone of customer-vendor interaction. This also implies that, as conversations progress, a (true) relationship develops between a customer and one or more individuals in a vendor organization.

It also means that the transaction is not the paramount artifact of the interaction. Instead, a transaction becomes a "side effect" of rich relationships that are built on conversation.

This notion is fundamental, and is a radical switch in priorities for the interaction between customer and vendor. Instead of the transaction being the goal of the interaction, it instead becomes a side effect.

There are both pragmatic and strategic reasons for an organization to care about VRM. On the practical side, the best person to manage data about an individual is . . . the individual herself! This is the one person who wants to make sure that all information about her is correct, especially when dealing with vendors of high importance (phone, gas, electric, credit cards, etc.) or high value (providers of goods or services that she greatly likes). In fact, enabling the individual to manage her own information could make a dent in the data quality problems that the Data Warehousing Institute estimates costs businesses $600 billion a year. Similarly, a VRM approach where customers explicitly grant access to their information to trusted vendors ensures adherence to privacy laws such as CAN-SPAM.

More interesting, however, is the strategic benefit to vendors that is inherent in a VRM-based interaction with customers. For example, when a customer is searching for information, that is the perfect time for a vendor to get in front of him with information about how that vendor might be able to meet a need. (This was the genius behind Google AdWords.) When a customer puts a "personal RFP" out into the marketplace (ref: "Sell This Man a Car!" www.socialcustomer .com/2008/03/sell-this-man-a.html), it is the perfect time to begin a new relationship with a customer. When a customer notes that she needs assistance with an existing product, the vendor who can ride to the rescue and make a virtual house call to solve the problem is the one the customer will tell her friends about.

The benefits are clear to the vendors who are engaged.

Where VRM Goes from Here

One thing that can not be overemphasized is that, at the present time, the VRM movement is extremely nascent. The concepts offered in this section are the state of the art as of this writing, in mid-2008. However, as with all organic, community-based efforts, its exact endpoints are nearly impossible to predict. Will we end up with tools that grant customers the power and independence to interact on a peer-level with vendors? This outcome is likely, and perhaps inevitable. Can we predict with any credible certainty a date by which this transition will take place, or what it will exactly look like in its final form? Those answers, on the other hand, are less clear. What we do know, however, is that these changes are afoot, the customer is in (increasing) control, and the direction of movement toward increasing customer power is clear.

Now Do You See CRM, Social CRM, and VRM?

As you probably have figured out by now, none of this is going to be easy, though I'll do what I can to make it easier for you. There is a clear difference between CRM and Social CRM, and VRM is in the mix. But the fundamental statement that will be drilled into this book everywhere is that the customer has already altered the way they're dealing with you and it's time for you and your brethren in the enterprise, medium, and small business world to change the way that you deal with them. If you're not interested in doing that, here's the game plan:

1. Return this book.

2. Go to sleep. It's going to be a long century.

The next question I know you're asking is what kind of interactions with the customer are we talking about? That, my fellow CRMians, is the subject of the next chapter on customer experience. Let's boogie or if you're a little older, move to the groove, and head over to Chapter 3.

3

The Customer Owns the Experience

There's a store in Beverly Hills called Fashionology LA (www
.fashionologyla.com) that has female tweeners (girls between 8 and 14)
designing and creating their own clothes right in the store. The basic theme
for the store is "Dream It! Make It! Wear It!" Even before the kids start
designing, they are working from what the store's creators, Jamie Tisch and
Elizabeth Wiatt, call "fashion moods," which are seasonal. The first season
of the store's opening, summer 2008, they had moods called Rock and Roll,
Pop Princess, Malibu, Juku, and Peace, which are in the form of a character.
I'm presuming that Juku is modeled after the style-setting Japanese Harajuku
Girls that Gwen Stefani lauds in her music. If you don't like the styles offered,
you can create your own.

Figure 3-1 shows a few Harajuku trendsetters for those of you who spend
their nights wondering about Gwen Stefani's fashion faves.

The kids come in and go to a huge kiosk-like design station, all very
colorful, highly interactive, and functional. They choose the seasonal style.
They then choose what they'd like to design—a dress, pants, or shirt. The
big picture. Then they start accessorizing right away with "Thingalings."
(A little too cutesy for me, and maybe even for an 8- to 14-year-old too.)
These can be bling or charms that are hung onto the apparel, a thing that's
sewed on or clipped on. It can be as much or as little as you want. Here's
a description from *Mami* magazine on what happens next that's probably
better than anything I could write, given that I'm not particularly fashion
smart, nor am I a tweener girl, despite the way I throw a fastball:

> *Once the girl completes her design, she proceeds to the U-Bar, where a*
> *friendly Fashionologist, who could be likened to the coolest babysitter or big*
> *sister a girl could have, uses a heat press to add the key design element to*

her new look and gives her a tray of embellishments to take to a customized Make It! table. The girl settles in to sew, bling, pin and clip to create what will soon become her favorite piece of clothing. Once her garment is ready to wear, the girl steps onto the Fashionology LA stage where she proudly displays her creation for the camera. With her approval, the picture and her unique design will beam through the store on a 70-inch LCD screen and will be emailed to her so she can share her new look with her friends that very day.

Figure 3-1: Harajuku Girl fashions are cool for tweeners. (Source: istockphoto.com)

I know that all sounds oh-so-very-hip-girlfriendly, and you may wonder what the importance is of something that appeals to kids whose families can afford a store in Beverly Hills. Don't be so dismissive.

This is an important example of the most significant customer value in a Social CRM model—the immersion into an experience that meets the "provision of value" needs of the customer.

Regardless of your feelings on crass materialism, the Fashionology LA business model is interesting and represents what we'll see more in both young and adult environments. While the model in this case is hands-on and that's not what we'll necessary see in other permutations, what makes this invaluable is the sense of "I did that" that comes from the experience.

Here's a test. What's more appealing? A shirt you bought at Prada (or at Wal-Mart) that you wear, or a shirt that looks exactly like the one you might have bought at either of those stores, but you yourself dream it, make it, wear it? Of course the latter, unless accomplishment isn't one of the values that means something to you. The do-it-yourself (DIY) aspect of the outfit is substantive and satisfying because *you* participated in its creation. It is something *you* crafted to the way *you* wanted and then *you* built it using *your* hands.

Human beings love to participate and create. Co-creation and collaboration-based business models are showing up everywhere, from the writings of academic core thinkers like C. K. Prahalad in his *The Future of Competition* to stories of those business models as outlined in thought-leader Patricia Seybold's *Outside Innovation*. Salesforce.com is doing the same with its IdeaExchange, where customers not only create ideas but can vote them on or off the feature-function island. You'll hear more about this kind of collaboration in Chapter 11.

Here, I want to concentrate on the DIY element. We're not talking about a set of verbal or written directions being handed out or read. We are talking about the tweeners directly participating in the design and creation of their apparel. They feel fully engaged in something they had not previously thought they had the skills or the tools or the time or the talent or any form of wherewithal to do. But here's this store saying, hey, kid (or in other circumstances, a company saying, hey, old enterprise guy), don't just buy a product. Design, showcase, and wear your creation—the one you made with the products, services, tools, and experience in this fab store we've provided for you. Everyone is happy with the result. Mom and/or Dad are happy to pay a premium price for the experience their child had in creating something they could keep and use. Thus, the store is happy. The tweener is happy because not only can she wear the product, but she'll remember how she got it, and that's something she can tell her friends about.

This model doesn't just work for pre-teen and teen girls. It works for Boomers, it works for Gen X, it works for Gen Y, and it works for seniors. It works for the crassly commercial. It works for the minimalists who spend $2 million on a loft in Manhattan so they have a place to not furnish. All in all, a model that engages you in an unparalleled experience is a model that works for everyone. It is also a central premise of success in a Social CRM strategy. This is a highly personalized experience that is sculpted by the customers themselves, using the products, services, tools, and environments made available by the company engaging them.

Fashionology LA is just one example of an interesting model for business that is based on something I care about greatly—and hopefully, so do you: customers owning more of their experience than they ever have been able to in the past.

The Transition from Management to Engagement Through Experience

Companies used to focus on making new, better, or cheaper products and services. . . . Now the game is to create wonderful and emotional experiences for consumers around whatever is being sold. It's the experience that counts, not the product. . . . People . . . want capabilities and options, not uniform products. . . . business is there to provide the tools.

—Business Week, *December 19, 2005*

We have to create a great experience every time you touch the brand, and the design is a really big part of creating the experience and the emotion. We try to make a customer's experience better, but better in her terms.

—A. G. Lafley, CEO, Proctor & Gamble

Why should customer experience supersede customer management as the operating paradigm for a successful CRM strategy? Simply, customers are demanding it, and customers are human beings like you, who I presume remember that you are a customer too.

This is more than just a nice homily to the personal side of human beings. This is a foundation for CRM if it's to be done successfully. The premises are not too complex:

▶ If a customer likes you, he will stay with you.

▶ If a customer doesn't like you, in time, he will leave you.

▶ People are looking to control their own lives.

▶ People are looking to fulfill their own agendas. They are self-interested.

▶ If you help them control their lives and fulfill their agendas in valuable and unobtrusive but memorable ways, they will like you.

▶ If you fail to help them, they won't like you and won't continue with you because someone else will help them.

Those premises are the entire practical foundation for Social CRM. Simple, but the rest can be complex. I'll simplify the complex for you throughout this book. I promise.

The Experience Economy Realized

In 1998, Joe Pine (whom you met in "Social CRM Leaders Speak from Out There") and James Gilmore wrote what has since become a classic, *The Experience Economy: Work Is Theater and Every Business a Stage.* Their central premise was that customers were looking to businesses to provide them not with products and services, but with experiences. Products and services, the backbone of the old business model, were created to be in service of the experience. They also made the point that customers would pay premiums for those experiences.

What Pine and Gilmore make clear is that these experiences are the foundation for how the company constructs its business model (see Chapter 5). Products become the props and services the stage for the experience. The enterprise is able to charge for the experience, which is both personal and memorable. I would add sharable to their equation.

This is perhaps the most important aspect of Social CRM. A personalized experience that is shared—or at least can be shared—is what differentiates one company from another and engages the customer in ways that are unique and immersing.

The way that Pine and Gilmore put it was that this could be a *commoditized experience*. Put more simply, if the customers find it valuable, they'll pay for it.

How do you pay for an experience? Easy. With money.

Let's get real for a second. No one is talking about those who are having difficulties meeting bills or who have to scrape by each paycheck or have no way of earning a living. These experiences are for those people who can afford it. This is a business strategy, not a social strategy. Many businesses, like salesforce.com, have strong philanthropic programs that aren't just for PR purposes. But what we are talking about now is something that people pay for, like any other commodity. This is not to be confused with their deeply personal and organic experiences that happen spontaneously. These are created experiences designed to delight and be memorable. They are authentic only in the sense that they are what they are openly intended to be. Please don't confuse authenticity with spontaneity or natural growth.

Pine and Gilmore knocked it out of the park with their notion of how business experiences work. As the millennial divide was crossed, customers demanded personalized experiences as part of the way they were engaged and treated by the companies they were choosing to deal with.

Starbucks, now in trouble, is the classic experience that, since Pine and Gilmore, has been used by the rest of the known universe. But the experience economy is best reflected by one even more calculatedly encompassing experience: Mattel's American Girl dolls and the world that has been built around them.

American Girl: A Cup of Tea and $200

The average cost of a pair of Fisher Price dolls is $38. The average cost of a Mattel American Girl doll duo is $205. Yikes.

Why is that? Because American Girl has been intelligent enough to understand that their market is the mothers and grandmothers of the little girls whose imaginations they intend to capture. Rather than just sell a product, they are selling a *story*. This is an experience, not just a plastic object. Here's how it works.

AMERICAN GIRL: THE COMPANY

Whereas Fashionology LA is new, American Girl is an iconic company to both young girls and businesses looking for a model of success. It was founded in 1986 and became a wholly owned subsidiary of Mattel, Inc., in 1998. The numbers of staff are between 1,800 and 4,700 (during the holiday rush). They have their headquarters in Middleton, Wisconsin, with 560,000 square feet of doll brainpower. More than a million people a year visit their American Girl Place stores, and 650,000 subscribe to *American Girl* magazine, making it among the top 10 children's magazines in the United States. All in all, the numbers are big, but as you'll see, the customer experience is even bigger, which makes for an even bigger return on investment (ROI).

AMERICAN GIRL: THE MOVIE

In July 2008, a movie starring in-demand kid actress Abigail Breslin, Chris O'Donnell, and Julia Ormond hit the theaters, to primarily positive (81 percent) reviews. It was called *Kit Kittredge: An American Girl*. Note the title. Yes, this movie was based on the American Girl doll character Kit Kittredge, a doll with a life history in the 1930s U.S. Depression era.

The plot in a nutshell: Kit Kittredge, daughter of a dad with a failed car dealership and a mom taking in boarders to make ends meet, writes articles on a typewriter in a tree house. She writes an article on a hobo camp that she tries to get a mean newspaper editor to publish. He refuses. In the meantime, her mom buys chickens and Kit goes around selling the eggs. Her mom's locked-up treasures are stolen, and all signs (a footprint) point to a hobo boy named Will. Kit and her friends Zach and Ruthie (another actual doll) investigate to prove Will innocent.

What makes this truly amazing is that this is the fourth film production for American Girl; the first three were made-for-TV movies. Even more amazing is the web page shown in Figure 3-2.

Look at the prices for the various products. Kit and Ruthie are $205 for the pair plus a few accessories, though you can buy them separately. Then there are coordinating items like Kit's dog, Grace (adopted in the movie), for $18 or her tree house for $250. Plus there are the "you might also like" items like Kit's bedroom collection ($135) or Kit's bed and quilt set ($80). This might seem insane to you if you're a guy without a daughter, but there are parents and grandparents paying for this without reservation—even if a large gulp precedes the unreserved payment.

But the experience doesn't stop with American Girl movies. That's just a small part of this.

AMERICAN GIRL: THE STORE EXPERIENCE

Four hundred dollars for a visit to an American Girl store is *de rigueur*. When you go to the store, you can have lunch with your doll

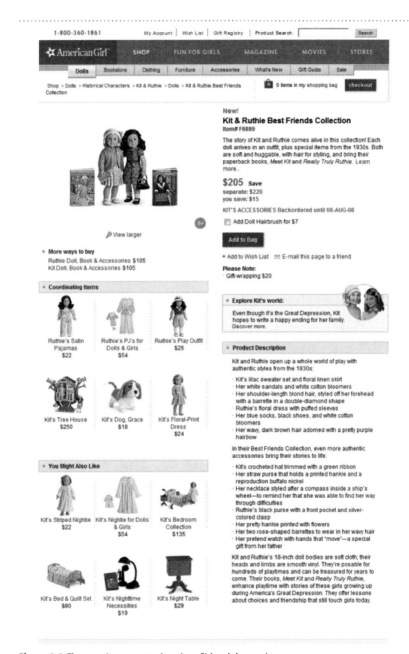

Figure 3-2: The experience counts: American Girl and the movies

in the café—mom and youngster enjoying hot dogs, lemonade, and dessert while their dolls sit next to them in special doll chairs attached to the table. Of course, in keeping with what you will see is their model, the chairs are also for sale. Now look at what varying permutations of the hot dogs and lemonade will cost you in the American Girl Place (one of two types of experience) store at Chicago's high-end Water Tower Place:

▶ Brunch is $18 per person.

▶ Lunch is $20 per person.

▶ Afternoon tea is $17 per person.

▶ Dinner is $22 per person.

It doesn't stop with just food. There is a theater where you, your child, and her doll can watch *The American Girls Revue* for $28 per person. In case you were wondering, the doll is not a "person" as far as the price goes. There is also always *Bitty Bear's Matinee: The Family Tree*, for a mere $15 per person.

In preparation for that big matinee, you can get your doll's hair styled for between $10 and $20. If your doll is in need of further pampering, how about a facial, an ear-piercing, or some nail decals? For an additional price, you can get a photo taken of you and your doll that is placed on the cover of a souvenir copy of *American Girl* magazine (only $22.95 for six issues of the real deal). Needless to say, each store has books with the stories of the dolls, and clothing and accessories for the dolls to buy. There are special services such as birthday parties, personalized tours, and activities and . . .

Then there's the dolls themselves.

AMERICAN GIRL: THE DOLLS

The American Girl experience is of course organized around the dolls themselves. There is an almost scary brilliance about how the dolls are used. They are not just products; the dolls are the centerpiece of the new business model that drives Social CRM—which is, as we will see in detail in Chapter 5, an aggregation of products, services, tools, and crafted experiences that are made available to customers to fulfill their own agendas and personalize their own experiences.

There are multiple lines of American Girl dolls, but two are significant for us. The most famous line is the American Girl Collection line.

The dolls each represent a period in history that contains a story for the dolls themselves. For some reason, the years that they represent all end in 4 (1934, 1944, and so on). Each doll has a book that tells her story and a line of accessories and clothing that reflects her heritage and history. For example, here is the Kit Kittredge story according to Wikipedia: "Kit Kittredge is growing up in the early years of the Great Depression in Cincinnati, Ohio. Her family struggles to adjust to the realities of the economy after Kit's father loses his job. Although referred to as 'Kit' in almost all books and promotional material, Kit's full name is Margaret Mildred Kittredge. She got this name when her father kept singing her the song, 'Put All Your Troubles In Your Old Kit Bag,' after he learned it when fighting in World War I. It should be noted that although the year 1934 appears on the cover of the book, 'Meet Kit' is actually set in 1932. The Kit books were illustrated by Walter Rane."

There is also a line of contemporary dolls that becomes significant (more or less) if you remember the Edelman Trust Barometer. They were called "American Girl Today" but in December 2005, the name changed to "Just Like You" dolls. 2005 was a year after "someone like me" became the most trusted source. I'm not sure they are directly related, but this reinforces the trend that occurred around that time—a nodal shift toward a customer ecosystem dominated by peer trust and moving away from corporate trust.

The way the Just Like You doll works is that you get 28 options, each with a unique combination of face mold, skin, hair, and eye color. This is directly in line with Pine and Gilmore's concept of the commoditization of experiences. You provide the customer with choices that are substantial and flexible, and they pick and choose according to their personal desire. That's exactly what the story is with the Just Like You dolls.

WHY IT WORKS

American Girl seems to be pretty money hungry, exceptionally pricey, and yet, parents I've spoken to who can afford to provide their children with this experience have no problem with the cost because of the incredible thrill that their kids get from the visit, the stories being told, and the totality of the experience. What you are paying for here are not dolls but tools for the child's imagination and the memory of it all. The child is engrossed in the story of her doll. It has a specifically imagined personality and also an actual written story to go with that personality. That story is supported by the accessories, the clothes, the furniture, and then the ambiance and attention that they and the doll get when they go to the store.

Yet, the target market is the parents and grandparents who can pay for it. People are willing to pay for a premium if they see the value in paying for it. They are willing to pay the extra if there is a memorable and sharable experience associated with the purchased goods. Social CRM aims at that experience squarely because it is the experience that binds the customer to the company in ways that a product sale alone never can.

Think of it this way. The memory of the experience will be there when the dolls have long turned to whatever it is plastic degrades to.

Want some numbers? While Barbie sales in 2008 were down 9 percent, American Girl sales were up 7 percent to $463,000,000. That represented 8 percent of Mattel's gross sales and about 15 percent of their operating profit. To continue this string of left-brained return, there were more than a million store visitors in 2006 and their revenue per square foot topped $500, which outside of Apple stores, at an insane $2,800 per square foot, is the highest rate in the world.

Not too shabby for dolls.

Voice of the Customer vs. Corporate Calculations

What does this mean for you? How do you create this kind of experience and then generate the numbers that something like American Girl does? The first maxim I'll give you to memorize is "Know thy customers." Rather than do what most marketing departments do, which is to assume that you know your customers, actually listen to real customers. That's what they call "the voice of the customer."

Far too often, companies make assumptions on behalf of their customers. For example, I had a client who developed a campaign to make sure that a consistent marketing message was transmitted across all channels. The words "multichannel message" resonated through the proposed program planning document. This client asked me to check out the document to make sure it could be deemed "customer-centric." Their assumption was that because the message was consistent and being delivered through eight different channels, that it *must* be customer-centric.

I asked them a simple question: "Did you ask the customers if they wanted that many messages?" "No." "Then it isn't customer-centric."

The principle is simple. *To provide the customers with an optimal experience, ask them what they want.* We'll cover how to do that in the chapter on strategy (Chapter 17) and on mapping the customer experience (Chapter 18). Suffice it to say, while you have business imperatives, understanding the customer's experiences with you and listening to their voice are the most important things you can do. That means their real voice, not the voice echoing in your head.

It's Really Very Personal

I'm not sure how many of you reading this book have metrics that characterize the lifetime value of your customers and, if you're more advanced than most, of their households. Customer lifetime value (CLV) can be important because it can help you determine how to allocate what are most likely limited resources. Clearly, if you determine, using CLV assessments, that this customer group is highly profitable and low maintenance or that this is a profitable but very high maintenance group or that this group is losing you dollars, then you can make some decisions on where to invest time and money to optimize the use of the resources and the return on the investment of those resources.

But there is a problem when you rely on assessments as a substitute for judgment, which is, unfortunately, the usual way. A story to illustrate: Orbitel, a Colombian telco, had an interesting policy. Anyone who was a CTO who had Orbitel's residential service was considered a high value customer, even if they didn't spend more than the monthly absolute minimum needed to make them a customer.

With a classic CLV analysis, this kind of person would be low value, barely worthy of the expenditure of a breath, much less resources of some magnitude. But Orbitel was smart enough to recognize that context mattered. While these were residential customers, it was in their business environment that they could be a potentially viable high value customer, if they were treated like that in their residential environment.

Nothing that algorithms do can substitute for judgment.

There is a much bigger issue than that. There is also no substituting algorithm for reality. As a business, there is definitely some value in running CLV assessments on your customers and their households. The results give you the ability to make judgments as to who is going to be high value or low value to you. But jump into your customer shoes (ordered from Zappos, of course) for a second. As a customer, is there *any* company you deal with regularly where you think of yourself as a low value customer?

Do you honestly think, when the world is controlled by customers like you, that there is a customer—even one—who will say, "Well, yes, I'm low value and I appreciate being treated that way with degraded service, or lower priority, or fewer discounts, because, hey, company, the numbers I provide just bear that out"? Are you that gracious and understanding as a customer? Is there a single customer who thinks of himself or herself as low value and expects to be treated as such? If there is, lock me up.

Of course there isn't. You wouldn't think that way.

But, you say, then I'll just do what Sprint/Nextel did with their low value nuisance customers: I'll fire them. Cut them from the rolls of my corporate benevolence.

You could do that. Before you do, check out Chapter 7 of this book, on blogging. Because it isn't those particular low value customers I would be concerned with. It's all those trusted peers who listen to them complain. They could do far more damage to you than the cost of keeping them on the rolls as a reasonably satisfied low value customer.

It's not the same cut and dried world it was. Corporate expectations that were in vogue just three or four years ago are as extinct as a passenger pigeon. So here are some rules of thumb:

▶ CLV and other analytics related to customer valuations are only useful to make judgments. They don't substitute for judgment.

▶ No one thinks of him- or herself as a low value customer.

▶ The low value customer whom you make to *feel* low value could hurt you far more than in the past—and they will if they can. So, if possible, figure out a way to accommodate them.

Customer Experience Management (CEM): Different from CRM?

About three years ago, there was a discussion going on in the CRM community about how customer experience management (CEM) "fit in" with CRM. Was it a subset? Was CRM a subset of it? Was it a superset? Was it a superset of a subset?

The discussion was even more ridiculous than it appears—which is pretty lame. There has been a CEM discipline for about 60 years, with the mainline company Cheskin and Associates leading the charge. But to make the argument/discussion even sillier, the CEM guys thought that CRM was useless or next to useless.

While there is certainly a difference in approaches and methodology, both disciplines are attempting to do the same thing: attract customers in ways that are sticky. Sticky means keeping customers around once they sign up.

However, there are some differences in approach between CEM and CRM 1.0 in particular that surfaced in the discussion (see Table 3-1).

Table 3-1: Some High Level Differences Between CRM and CEM

CRM	CEM
Focused internally operates from the perspective of the company out to the customer—inside out (company or data or process-centric)	Focused externally operates from the perspective of the customer to the company—outside in (customer-centric)
Management of customer relationships to optimize corporate return	Management of customer interactions to optimize their experience across all touchpoints
Data and process driven	Interaction and experience driven
Uses algorithms to aid customer insight	Does granular mapping of the customer's actual experience to aid customer insight
Purpose is to create effective processes, programs, and internal environment to improve business–customer relationships	Purpose is to provide the best possible experience for each customer with the company

Social CRM and Knowing the Customer the Right Way

How does this apply to Social CRM? Because Social CRM is focused on customer engagement, and the acknowledgment that the customer controls the conversation, then the purely "inside out" (a.k.a. internal) approach of CRM is now null and void. Social CRM is an outside-in program and methodology for intelligent customer interactions with a company, and the company's response to the customer's control. That means that we've taken the concepts of CRM 1.0 and CEM and effectively merged them.

IBM certainly agrees. Look at this quote from *Computer Zeitung* on July 15, 2008, in "IBM: Next Generation CRM Will Be a Customer Experience Engineering":

> *According to IBM's most recent CEO survey, company leaders expect massive changes for their businesses by a new category of so-called inquisitive consumers. More than 22% of CEOs feel the need to better service this demanding clientele, planning to raise their investments*

in modern CRM systems, analysis tools, Web 2.0 and information on demand over the next three years. "There will be a next generation CRM, which we call Customer Experience Engineering," said Michael Bauer, head of IBM Global Business Services, which consults clients on CRM. "Customer Experience Engineering will include an active and consistent management of all contacts, to improve interaction and experience of customers. This also covers functional aspects such as products, services and distribution channels," Bauer added. Modern, open infrastructures for collaboration, called "Enterprise 2.0," would also play a crucial role.

Okay, the debate is now over and done, though traditional CRMers and CEM mavens will continue it despite the rest of the world not caring. The question becomes, how do you begin to provide that highly personalized experience we've spoken of throughout this chapter to the potentially millions of customers that your large enterprise might have? Or even the thousands that your midsized business or hundreds that your small business interacts with all the time?

The answer is: you don't. You provide them with what they need to interact with you on their time, with their specific needs, and then you meet their specific expectations. You do not have to hug and kiss each of them. If that were the case, Chapstick sales would be over the top.

We'll get into the methodology specifically in Chapter 18, but for now, realize that to truly understand the requirements, the customer has to be engaged with you, you need a granular map of every customer interaction at each touchpoint. The web experience as well as the store experience as well as the phone experience, etc., have to be discovered from the standpoint of the customer, not the company. That involves interviews with those customers that will take time, and yet, the results are extraordinary.

Your purpose for this granular look at the customer's specific experience is to find out what you need to provide them with that is actually important to them. It allows you to understand what it will take to reinforce the positive, reduce or eliminate the negative, and meet or exceed customer expectations. You can't ask for more than that.

What happens once you find out what the customer experience is? How do you create it? How do you design it? How do you measure it, when experiences are so emotional? Do you measure the delight of the little one who goes to American Girl? Or what their parents spend? But is the money spent a measurement of the experience that's reflective of what happened—a true measure?

Quantifying the Customer Experience: An Oxymoron?

Two more questions: Can you quantify the customer experience? Is it an oxymoron?

Not exactly, but correlation can be a bitch.

In a March 2008 study, Forrester Group senior analyst Megan Burns found that more than 80 percent of the respondents said they were increasingly concerned (more than in the past several years) with improvements of the online experience—particularly when it comes to enjoyment, usability, and usefulness. Their top two Web spending priorities were Web analytics—good—and customer satisfaction surveys—bad, very bad.

Burns says that there is a growing focus on measurement of core components of customer experience and that seems to be a good thing. I would agree there. So would Burns's colleague, Bruce Temkin, a highly respected Forrester principal analyst in customer experience, who echoed Burns's thinking in his report released in 2008, "The Business Impact of Customer Experience," in which he identified the correlation between customer experience and customer loyalty.

What bothers me is not the Burns finding, which is right on, but the spending priorities that the respondent companies are giving to the so-called CEM online efforts. To type customer satisfaction as a core component should be a cause of concern, given the escalation of customer demands and the generally diminishing value that customer satisfaction has as a metric. Companies are apparently aware of the importance of improving the emotional connection of the customers to them, but are misplacing what to discover about that connection.

Temkin's study was a little more calming. It showed the strong correlation between customer experience and customer loyalty, not satisfaction. What was surprising to him, though not to me, was that bank customers showed the strongest relationship between experience and loyalty. "Banking relationships have a little bit of an emotional factor to it," he says. "Customers are influenced by the trust in the institution, which is influenced by how they're treated. The experience plays into perception of trust, which plays into their loyalty with the institution."

In fact, what could be more emotional than the relationship of a household to their future, often determined by their ability to save for when they can no longer, willingly or unwillingly, work? To put it another way, how emotional have you been in the midst of the incredible up and down vagaries of the stock market, throughout 2009?

Really, really upset, is what I think. But if I trusted the company I was dealing with to do the right thing with my dollars—my most sacred nest egg—as a customer I'd be intensely loyal, because my experience with the company was one that allowed me to trust it.

Customer Value Just Ain't the Same

One of the reasons this is all so difficult to understand is that what the enterprise thinks of value is entirely different from what the customer finds is value. Check out Table 3-2 and you can see what I mean.

Table 3-2: Company and Customer Differences in Value

Company: Left-Brained	Customer: Right-Brained
Revenue	Validation
Profitability	Coolness
Cost savings	Reputation
Effective process (from lead to close)	Empowerment
Marketing campaign response rate	Accomplishment
Percentage of gross margin	Community
Customer satisfaction scores	Justice/fairness

It's easy to see from the table that there is a distinct difference in what constitutes value to a company and to a customer. Corporate values are often based on the components of shareholder value—what returns shareholders are looking for. The metrics are very much left-brained. Customer values are quite different. The ones that are measurable are typically what the companies are looking for from the customer—such as repurchase rates—rather than what the customer is looking to get from the company. The customer is looking for emotional satisfaction, something that allows them to say—always with differing criteria and differing levels of importance of that criteria—I like these guys. They are a *great* company.

When I speak in public, I often ask people if they can tell me about a company they think is fantastic. *Everyone* has at least one they can tell me about, and when I ask them to talk about it they wax rhapsodic, meaning they go wild and talk it up. That is customer value—a memory and set of relationships in combination with a valid consumer experience that turns the customer into an advocate.

The Importance of Style, or a String of Pearls for BlackBerry

"Life imitates art." Well, every now and then life doesn't imitate anything you could ever imagine from any recent experience you've had with art or your most fevered dreams. It's usually when style is involved. Take my word for it, style plays a big part in Social CRM, the customer experience, and customer value.

In 2005, I was reading *CPU* magazine and I ran across a blurb that said that Intel and Toray Ultrasuede (I swear) were going to produce a "concept" high-end laptop that would use microfiber for a cover. Specifically, folks, that means creating an *ultrasuede laptop*. The soft, leathery microfibers would be in blocks of color that would look something like a Mondrian painting. This mutant alliance even went to the point of getting a quote from the totally hilarious Steven Cojocaru, an over-the-top fashion analyst who makes cogent and catty remarks at most of the awards ceremonies. Here's his comment:

> For many people, a laptop may be just as much an everyday accessory as a hip belt or skyscraper stilettos, so we're seeing an image-conscious culture demanding that their laptop looks as great as it performs. The ultrafashionable concept is a very forward illustration of what can happen when unlikely partners shake up the status quo. This laptop is so eye-catchingly stunning, I'm trying to find a way to wear it as a necklace to the Golden Globe Awards.

When I read that quote I thought, "Is someone putting me on here, or what?" Cojocaru is actually a funny guy so maybe this is a joke. A laptop and stilettos?

As nuts as this whole thing seems, there are underlying reasons for this strange example of accessorized technology. A study done in September 2005 by Harris Interactive called (naturally) "The Intel/Ultrasuede Laptop Style Study" came up with a number of very interesting insights. Here's a few:

▶ 73 percent of U.S. adult computer users want to buy technology products that reflect their personal style.

▶ 76 percent of those computer users who admit to glancing at someone else's laptop PC are checking out its style or design.

▶ 40 percent of U.S. adult computer users find their laptop to be generic, boring, dull, sterile, or lackluster.

▶ 60 percent would like to be able to customize their laptop with options such as color, patterns, and fabric.

While it's likely there is some fluff in this thing, what it shows is the laptop, a technology that has primarily been associated with business and road warriors, is now seen by the general population as more than just something whose value proposition is utilitarian. In fact, it has meaningful value as a lifestyle choice.

Style matters. And you're willing to pay for it. Unless, of course, it's an ultrasuede laptop.

So, Style Does Matter

Everything you consume or use, everything associated with whatever it is you *do*, has been purchased by you or by someone who gave it to you. Everything you use to make your life "feel good" or to have a "wonderful moment" is purchased somewhere.

"No! You unromantic SOB," you say. "What about love?" What about it? While ideals, romance, beauty, and love aren't tangible items, there is a commerce decision somewhere in there. The commerce isn't what makes you happy, but it provides you with what you need on the journey to being happy. If you are in love, odds are you are doing things that involve purchases. Even if it's just a romantic walk in the park, you're wearing clothes and shoes. You may have chosen *just the right clothes* to impress this person you are walking with. Which means you chose from multiple combinations of outfits you own—that you bought or were bought for you. Did you take a shower before you went out? Did you make the soap out of thin air? You get my point. I'm not trying to take the romance or beauty out of that simple walk. Anyone who knows me knows I'm a romantic who prefers love and humor to CRM any day. I'm just pointing out that commerce, the purchase activities of consumers, and their relationships to businesses are a part of life, not something separate and not something you can ignore—either as the consumer in question or the business providing the services. But how the things you buy make you feel when you use them is almost as important as the use you expect from them. Style, not just utility, is a part of your life.

For example, if I say "priceless." What do you think? Unless you watch no TV at all, the first thing that came to your mind was "MasterCard."

What do you think makes that MasterCard commercial so memorable and timeless and provides endless possibilities for its future? Because it is conceived around exactly what I'm saying. "Your journey through life is intangible and meaningful (priceless), but we give you the instrument to buy those things that aid you in the transport along that priceless, beautiful journey of life. We can't be your life, we can only give you an instrument that supports your chosen lifestyle and selected style choices." Compare that to the totally lame and clueless "Life Takes Visa," which I trust someday will be changed to "Life Takes Visa Away from Us" so we no longer have to endure the torture of its incomprehensible message. MasterCard gets the idea of the "era of the social customer." Visa doesn't.

There is incredible depth in every decision you make in your life, even a purchasing decision. For example, when you make the decision to choose that laptop or cellphone, you are also choosing, although opaquely here, the web services architecture it will run on, and then, more consciously, the specific services you need or want. You are also choosing features that are not just functional and utilitarian but are cool and make you feel good using them. The service-oriented architecture doesn't make you feel good. The services you need are practical. The services you pay a premium for and want are both practical and make you feel good. And the style—oh baby, the style—is *valued* for its coolness and how that makes you feel with your peers, or even just for yourself. That coolness, that style, is responsible for 1 million 3G iPhones sold between July 11–13, 2008—the first three days on the market and the additional 1 million 3G S iPhones sold the last weekend of June 2009. That would be totaling about 21 million iPhones sold since their inception.

One final test. Take a look at the following figures. Given that these two BlackBerrys do the same thing, which one would you buy?

This one?

Or this one?

Sure. The cool one.

Stylish choice.

Superstah! ResponseTek

About two years ago, I ran into ResponseTek, run by the always intel-lectually engaging and extremely nice Syed Hasan. I got interested in them because they had what seemed to be a serious engine for measur-ing customer response when related to experience, rather than pur-chases or service tickets. A solid engine, nothing frivolous, very fast, and also visual enough to be readable by human beings who didn't have cranial chip implants.

After due deliberation, they easily represent the Superstah! for cus-tomer experience management because they've been doing this all well since 1999.

The Company

Before I get into their mission and applications, I'm going to give you a brief picture of the approach of the company.

I like these guys—always have, probably always will. They have a friendly, responsive culture that is reflected in their thinking and their actions.

For example, much of their deployment methodology is fairly traditional in how it approaches their customers: setting the scope of a project, finding out the company's internal business rules that drive customer service delivery, and reporting and then implementing the solution with training, following it up with support. But what they add, which is perhaps the most important part of a customer-related engagement, is doing a granular mapping of the entire customer experience. They call it the "customer lifecycle," and it's how that customer interacts with the company in relationship to the key processes that the company utilizes. In Chapter 18, you'll learn a different method for this mapping, but the mapping itself is both key and unusual for a technology vendor.

By the way, it takes anywhere from a month to three months to deploy their solution—depending on how complex your requirements are.

Mission 21st Century

Syed Hasan on their mission and vision for 2009 and beyond:

> In the future, CEM solutions will become standard-issue enterprise software for most corporations, and voice of the customer information will be recognized in much the same way that financial data is today—as high-value, high-impact, predictive and strategic.
>
> The world is changing, both for businesses and consumers. In our vision, change can actually draw the two closer together, rather than further apart. When provided the channels to tell companies about their experiences, consumers are empowered, engaged, and can resolve their issues. When provided the processes and technologies to manage customer experiences, companies drive customer advocacy, understand its value, and see its effects on their bottom lines. The future of CEM includes customer-driven social networking tools that will inform strategic planning and service delivery in the business world, and ResponseTek will continue to innovate in the space, with ongoing expansion of ResponseTek:CEM applications, and unique offerings like Zoykes.

Zoykes?

Yes, Zoykes. ResponseTek, aside from clearly being Scooby-Doo fans, also have a perception, which is certainly accurate enough, that some companies just aren't getting this whole transformation, withdrawing rather than reaching out to the customers. To combat that, they've launched Zoykes, a social networking application that applies user-generated content such as ratings, rankings, and comments to bridge the customer–company gap and share customer experiences. It is peer-to-peer-to-company and any permutation thereof. What makes Zoykes different from a typical social network is that this isn't a company hosted peer-to-peer network but a social network that is peer-to-peer-to-company—meaning that the company is part of the conversation about the experiences the customers are having. Zoykes is organized to drive improvements based on that P2P2C model. This model can incorporate partners, suppliers, and vendors as well. They call it, rather than point-in-time market research, "a continuous pulse on what the customer thinks and feels."

The Application

But Zoykes is ResponseTek's new stuff. They have a long history with customer experience applications that have a powerful and valuable analytics engine. Here's a look at their flagship product ResponseTek:CEM analytics capabilities.

▶ **Roll-up/drill-down**   The entire organization can be mapped into the reporting tools, allowing real-time analysis of how every part of the organization is delivering the customer experience, including roll-ups to divisional or regional levels, and drill-downs to the individual agent level. That's invaluable for customizing what you need for insights.

▶ **Ownership**   Accountability for the customer experience is integrated within ResponseTek:CEM, ensuring all employees have direct and transparent ownership of issues that relate to their part of the business. The employees may not love that feature, but, hey, it may get them a bonus.

▶ **Customer segmentation**   Segmentation and analysis by custom, client-driven criteria, through in-depth knowledge of how customer experience varies by customer segment or by complex multisegment scenarios, are all possible to a granular level.

▶ **Multiple measures**   Key indicators such as advocacy can be analyzed against every measure available to determine the factors that influence loyalty in every customer segment. You can measure satisfaction too, but I don't know why you'd want to.

▶ **Real-time alerts** Integrated alerting rules scan every single conversation against any number of rules to identify critical issues and at-risk customers for immediate escalation and resolution. This is an invaluable feature and also one place where analytics and business rules do mix well.

One picture to get an idea of what they have—Figure 3-3.

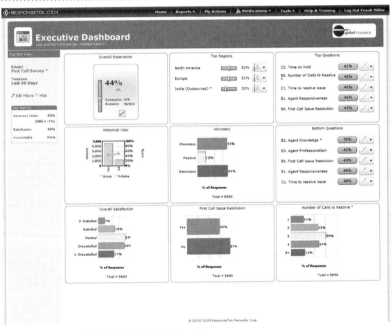

Figure 3-3: ResponseTek:CEM solution dashboard

A Guiding Principle for Crafting Experiences

I've spent a lot of time in this chapter talking about experiences that are affordable for the well-heeled, not the ordinary citizen. This luxe market is not the bulk of the population, but it does reflect something that is a bit counterintuitive—a principle that I religiously follow when working with my clients—and when buying stuff for myself too. Remember this if you only have room to remember one more thing on a crowded brain-matter day:

You don't have to have luxury. You just have to feel luxurious.

This is something to always remember when it comes to Social CRM. Each of us has different ideas of what makes us feel really good. Make me feel good and I will love you. You have to figure me, the customer, out, what makes me stretch out and purr, and then figure out the best way to provide me with that within the context of your own plans and budgets. That doesn't have to be a Vertu diamond cellphone or a Hermes handbag. It can be a very cool T-shirt or an opportunity to meet your CEO or attend a baseball game at your expense. It can even be a game on your website that I love or a 20 percent discount on all items for a week. All you need to do is make me feel luxurious. With or without Prada.

I'll personally take two tickets to the next Yankees World Series, please.

Before I go to watch the Yankees in the Series, I want to introduce you to someone who has something to say about customer experiences and how to go about planning your thinking when it comes to evoking them.

Welcome David Boulanger, senior analyst at Frost and Sullivan.

Mini-Conversation with David Boulanger

David's been around the block, to say the least. He has been involved in developing the strategies and techniques and identifying the trends for C- and D-level audiences in customer management, sales and marketing automation, call center, CRM analytics, and CRM software-as-a-service. He's spent time with a number of industry giants, getting his street cred at Dun & Bradstreet Software, PricewaterhouseCoopers, IBM Global Services, SAP America, AMR Research, and Tata Consultancy Services. His current focus is a deep understanding of end-user business processes and practices, the application of enterprise software to achieve customer-related goals, and the trends and strategies of related software vendors.

Looking at Delighting the Customer Requires a New Mindset

There is a serious transformation underway in the way that many best-in-class businesses are looking at the customer experience—not from the inside-out, but from the outside-in. This outside-in approach—called Customer Experience Management by many—carries a simple, straightforward goal: "right touch/right customer/first time/every time."

These best-in-class companies are increasingly focusing on customer experience—and the role that customer service plays in a company's competitiveness—as the direct link to greater customer intimacy, greater brand loyalty, and faster brand growth. CEM benefits drop directly to the top and bottom lines: more revenue, more profit, more profitable brand expansion. These are all great goals.

Now for the tough news: successfully implementing a CEM program requires a change in mindset that starts at the executive level as not a point-in-time change but rather a continuous-improvement multiyear journey where people, process, organization, key performance indicators, and supporting technology have had to be aligned to provide this "right touch/right customer/first time/ every time" experience.

Right Environment/Right Attitude

CEM requires that there be an executive champion—ideally the CEO—able to support making some tough choices. There needs to be a team of empowered D-level business unit executives who are trusted and respected and who won't mind getting into the details and defending a position with their peers.

It requires patience on the part of these team leaders to see changes through to completion, yet they need to empower employees to make decisions faster. It requires cooperation across business units and across the organization where up until now problems have been shifted upstream and downstream. Business processes will have to be rethought and reassembled to ensure that a positive customer experience is paramount.

This rethinking of the business plays out in thousands of ways. For instance:

▶ *For the sales executive planning his monthly schedule, how often does he schedule customer visits?*

▶ *For the contact center manager incenting agents, how will he or she be compensated—based on number of calls closed in an hour, or based on satisfaction per call even if the call takes longer?*

▶ *For the manufacturing vice president who can tune a factory for long runs of one product or for shorter runs of critical products, how should he plan?*

▶ *And if he or she is producing consumer electronic components in August for Christmas for a major North American retailer, should excess production be scheduled in anticipation of increased November orders?*

CEM also can't be successful without the critical cooperation of respected company frontline employees. They need to be engaged and empowered to make decisions.

CEM is also not a one-time event; the empowered team needs to assemble a "continuous-improvement mindset" and a three-year plan. CEM takes patience and persistence to implement.

Lastly, best-in-class companies have identified a new role, chief experience officer, on a par with other C-levels to be a champion and executive sponsor for this effort.

Right Measures

Commonly agreed-to metrics and key performance indicators become an essential component of measuring customer experience and satisfaction. Best-in-class customers have also settled on a small number of well-defined and commonly understood metrics to declare success; year-over-year retention rates, sales growth and loss, sales growth from existing and new customers, year-over-year brand loyalty metrics and "top five in the industry" metrics are commonly used. But each industry and each company within the industry will settle on a small number of critical indicators, and CEM will require constant measure against these.

Right Technology

CEM also requires an integrated platform consisting of multimode customer relationship management suites, analytics, unified communications and contact center, Web 2.0/Social CRM social media and collaborative, enterprise feedback, predictive analytics, and wireless capabilities to be effective in measuring, analyzing, and predicting a 360-degree view of the customer.

Best-in-class customers start with multimode CRM able to record transactions but have added additional collaborative technologies—social media and collaborative technologies. These complement baseline CRM, analytics, contact center, enterprise feedback, and wireless capabilities.

These best-in-class customers have pegged the ROI from these specific technology investments to specific improvements in customer KPIs and metrics and to improvements or expansions in specific brand, campaign, or other sales or service activities.

Like the rest of the three-year CEM plan, best-in-class has adopted a phased approach for these technologies matching the overall plan.

CEM: successfully implemented, a great program, great results, lots of work. ❧

Okay, we've spent a lot of pages talking about CRM, CEM, VRM, and, most importantly, what Social CRM is. Now we move on to one more social business category—Enterprise 2.0 in Chapter 4—that has to go on behind the company scene. Let's move.

4

Enterprise 2.0: Not Exactly What You Think

Wow. The customer experience is pretty intense—especially when it's with customers who trust their peers more than they trust your company. That's a lot to take in for a businessperson like you, isn't it?

Speaking of business, how is a business supposed to respond to all this? The experience of the customer is highly individual and interaction-focused, but business is typically process driven, transaction directed, and operationally focused—the paradigmatic opposite of the customer. The business is inside-out, and the customer sees the company outside-in. To start thinking about this, Enterprise 2.0 is worth taking a peek at, if only to understand the dynamics of how customers need to engage a company that is transforming its workplace culture because of the influx of younger workers and the penetration of consumer thinking into its pores. When we get to Chapter 9 on social networks and communities, we'll see how to deal with customers from the outside in. For this chapter, it's inside-out, in a fashion suitable for the 21st century "company like me."

Defining Enterprise 2.0

While I'd love to say that I was the creator of the Enterprise 2.0 definition, I was not. It was Andrew McAfee, an associate professor of business at Harvard Business School (and, much to my New York Yankees–loving chagrin, an ardent Boston Red Sox fan). He wrote a seminal article in the *MIT Sloan Management Review* entitled "Enterprise 2.0: The Dawn of Emergent Collaboration" (freely available at http://sloanreview.mit.edu/the-magazine/articles/2006/spring/47306/enterprise-the-dawn-of-emergent-collaboration/), which defined the use of new tools and a new business culture that could transform business.

His definition was simple: "Enterprise 2.0 is the use of emergent social software platforms within companies, or between companies and their partners or customers." However, what composes the Enterprise 2.0 character and function map is anything but simple.

McAfee identifies the characteristics of Enterprise 2.0 as SLATES. Table 4-1 describes what SLATES stands for. The table definitions are my own, the acronym breakdown is Andrew McAfee's. SLATES is what differentiates an Enterprise 2.0 workplace *toolset* from a more traditional Enterprise 2.0 workplace *toolbox*.

Table 4-1: Definitions for the McAfee Enterprise 2.0 Characteristics (Source: "Enterprise 2.0: The Dawn of Emergent Collaboration," *MIT Sloan Management Review*, 2006)

Term	Definition
Search	The ability to find information easily using tools that can organize structured and unstructured data, typically through the use of keywords.
Links	The means to be able to "hook up" to web pages and other areas internally through the use of hyperlink technology. The "best" links are those most frequently clicked on.
Authoring	Writing for a broad audience using tools and spaces that make the content available to that broad audience, such as a wiki or blog.
Tags	The organic categorization of content using one or two word tags. This isn't the same as being asked to fit the content description into a set of preformed categories. The categorization is done by individuals. So rather than just being given categories as with Web 2.0, or with CRM to try to fit the new CRM models into, the content provider can create a tag of Social CRM or Social CRM. It's a bottom-up rather than a top-down approach.
Extensions	Tools that provide some automated form of analysis that enriches the productivity of their users. For example, if you tag something Social CRM, you might get a series of links fed back automatically that provides you with articles on Social CRM or even a set of other associated tags based on your preferences, like Sales 2.0, sales optimization, community retailing, and so on.
Signals	Tools like RSS that inform you when new content is available or relevant content is available elsewhere.

The old-school models of the enterprise were operational and process driven, based on the efficiencies that lead to productivity. The new school is an interaction-based collaborative social model that emphasizes effectiveness and knowledge exchange, which lead to increased productivity.

While all these are the technological characteristics of a company with the chops to implement an Enterprise 2.0 strategy, this isn't necessarily the be all and end all of Enterprise 2.0 as it should be viewed. Before we take a deeper dive, there has to be the "why in the world?" question going through your heads. What would be the purpose and the benefit of using the Enterprise 2.0 tools and establishing an appropriate culture? Besides the obvious answer, "increased productivity."

It's important to see that Enterprise 2.0 is not defined strictly by the technology it uses to incorporate communication and collaboration into an enterprise. The technology used is a function of a successful Enterprise 2.0 culture—a subject that rarely gets discussed but has as much or more of an impact as the technology itself.

In fact, here's how I would extend the definition of Enterprise 2.0, with a hat tip to Andrew McAfee: "Enterprise 2.0 is the use of emergent social software platforms within companies, or between companies and their partners or customers, to support and foster a culture of collaboration and trust that extends beyond the doors of the company itself."

If you don't like that definition, sue me. Otherwise, let me explain how this works with Social CRM in perspective.

Enterprise 2.0: Here's Why You Need It

The contemporary workforce has a different outlook than the traditional workforce, which leads to a different kind of thinking. Those same people who are likely your customers are also employees of the company whose expectations are not what they used to be.

The use of Enterprise 2.0 tools fosters a culture of collaboration and outreach which can only benefit the transformation of a company to a customer-centered culture that's defined by how it administers the customer experience and engages customers in a continuous fashion. The culture is egalitarian and informally iterative by nature. The successful use of those tools reduces cost and increases productivity. Familiarity with their use helps in the implementation of the same or similar tools with the customers.

The Transformation of the Workforce

In Chapter 1, we found that the 76,000,000 Gen Yers are the first generation to spend more time on the Internet than watching TV. It is a multitasking generation that grew up with the idea it could have what it wanted and have it now.

An anecdote from a Wisconsin Technology Network story on Gen Y:

As CEO of Madison-based CDW Berbee, formerly Berbee Informa-tion Networks Corp., Paul Shain is familiar with the challenges asso-ciated with managing the next generation of IT workers.

On the day the iPhone first became available, Shain said Berbee received no less than 125 requests from staff members who asserted that they required the devices "immediately" in order to effectively perform their jobs.

The Gen Yers need to communicate *right now*, and in the way they want to communicate. This has had a dramatic impact on the work-place. But the differences in expectations go beyond just constant and immediate communication. They can be:

▶ Work to live, not live to work

▶ Desire to have fun in the workplace

▶ Increased involvement of parents in their workplace decisions

▶ Desire to collaborate (which extends to Gen X also)

▶ Not a lot of respect for formal authority via titles

▶ Expectation that the tools they need to work will be available to them—at least as available as they are outside of work

Ignoring the differences between the expectations of Gen Y and other generations is at your own peril, with anecdotal evidence that "at your own peril" is more than just a metaphorical expression.

For example, Penelope Trunk, Gen Y human resources influencer and popular writer of the *Brazen Careerist* blog, wrote in a 2007 *Time* magazine article of a study done by Deloitte consultant Stan Smith on the high Gen Y attrition rate at the firm. What Smith found out was not all that surprising.

People would rather stay at one company and grow, but they don't think they can do that. . . . Two-thirds of the people who left Deloitte left to do something they could have done with us, but we made it difficult for them to transition.

What kind of Enterprise 2.0 culture would have made it easy?

Cultural Change: We Trust You—Really

While communications and technology tools are certainly part of the necessary internal workings of an enterprise, the culture change is even more critical. You can see the most visible exhibition of the kind of culture a company has in how it invests in and manifests its customer service—and we will see that in Chapter 13. Empowered, happy employees, and their associates such as contractors, business partners, or vendors, make for very loyal customers.

What makes the Enterprise 2.0 culture particularly effective is that the employee is valued. While this sounds like standard operating procedure, it is actually rarely seen. But there are companies like Zappos, the online merchandise store, and Best Buy, the consumer electronics and appliances retailer, who have established cultures that work in a contemporary environment, allowing for the nature of new employees, and also offer advantages to the other generations of employees still at the companies.

We'll look at Zappos. Sorry, Best Buy, maybe another time.

Zappos: The Company

The best way to describe what Zappos does is to call it a shoe store. But that's not all it does. It also sells clothing, handbags, watches, and other accessories in an incredibly wide array of brands and styles.

My (fake) disclaimer: I'm a diehard Zappos fan and have ordered New Balance sneakers and Mephisto brand shoes from their online premises over the past year. I've also ordered shoes from little-known Israeli brand Naot for my 92-year-old mom. I've had every single pair delivered to me within one to two days of when I ordered, with clear instructions on returning them at no charge at any time in the next 365 days.

Zappos has over 1,200 brands, 200,000 styles, and more than 900,000 unique UPCs. They have 4 million items in their warehouse with every single item in their catalog inventoried. They don't believe in drop shipping because of the extra layer of "something could go wrong" that drop shipments imply.

The success of their business is measured by multiple numbers (see "Zappos: The Results" later), but one telling statistic. They have 9.7 million customers. That is almost 3.5 percent of the U.S. population. Yet, even with the recession and a 10 percent cutback in their workforce, they continue to provide sterling service to that large customer base, including free upgraded overnight shipping to repeat customers or VIP Club members. (Even that level of service was a cutback concession to the recession: new customers were often upgraded by surprise to overnight shipping. No longer.)

What distinguishes them from almost any company on the planet, much less in the United States, is that even with the scale they operate on, they have a truly remarkable culture.

Zappos: The Culture

The culture is premised on 10 core values. They are:

1. Deliver WOW Through Service

2. Embrace and Drive Change

3. Create Fun and a Little Weirdness

4. Be Adventurous, Creative, and Open-Minded

5. Pursue Growth and Learning

6. Build Open and Honest Relationships with Communication

7. Build a Positive Team and Family Spirit

8. Do More with Less

9. Be Passionate and Determined

10. Be Humble

These are so much more than just verbiage. To reinforce them, the performance objectives are not based on measuring call time, so CSRs can focus on the quality of the call, rather than the call efficiency—the time spent on the call and the call volume. There are no sales-based performance goals, so concentration on service is the core value of the culture. Performance reviews are 50 percent based on the 10 core values.

But wait. There's more. There are five weeks of customer service and core value training for every single employee. In the course of those five weeks, they offer you first $1,000 and then later $2,000 to quit before the training is over, if you don't feel you're fitting in. They used to offer less than $2,000, but they felt that not enough of the trainees were taking the offer, so they sweetened the pot.

Tony Hsieh, the CEO and founder (and plurality but not majority shareholder), also walks the walk. In an era when bank CEOs getting federal bailout funds take millions of dollars in salaries and bonuses despite their failures, this highly successful fella takes a salary of $36,000 a year, success or not.

One other salient feature of the culture. *Any* employee is empowered to give any other employee a $50 bonus for whatever reason
makes sense. Not just managers, *any* employee.

All of this is annually captured in a "culture book," which is the
unedited, raw commentary by Zappos employees and senior management on the anecdotal success of the company's culture over the year.
The 2008 culture book, a whopping 480 pages, is available to anyone
who wants a copy.

This isn't altruism or appeasement to Gen Y. Zappos understands
the nature of an Enterprise 2.0 culture, even if they don't think of it
using that phrase. This means that anyone who doesn't take the $2,000
to quit is implicitly agreeing to the core values and the standard of
service that has to be provided to each and every customer and internally among the employees. By no means is this an informal or trivial
matter. That standard has to be adhered to by all the newbie employees
for the life of their employment with Zappos.

The 1,300-plus current "survivors" of the five-week $2K "take it or
leave it" marathon training are trusted—which is perhaps the most
important part of the Zappos culture. As Alfred Lin, the COO/CFO
(yes, he's both) of Zappos made clear in a February 2009 online presentation, one of the most important items in building a brand that
matters is "Be real and you have nothing to fear"—a.k.a. authenticity.
That goes for all relationships and the way the corporate left brain is
exposed—meaning the data that this private company shares—which
is refreshingly extensive.

Zappos: The Tools

Zappos knows that they need to build a cohesive set of standards that
can be institutionalized and thus don't depend on any specific employees. To do that, they need to communicate with the employees internally and provide the tools for the employees to communicate with
the customers.

They use social media tools to externalize their culture and to
inspire the culture internally. They not only have outreach to Facebook, LinkedIn, and Twitter, but they use blogs and a Zappos TV presence for both internal and external broadcasting.

Twitter has perhaps been their most successful effort in both outreach and internal communications. In November 2008, Zappos,
which still ultimately hit over a billion dollars in revenue that year, had

to lay off roughly 125 employees due to the downturn. They chose the unfortunates based on performance, reliability, and attendance. The severance package, given everything it could have been, was very strong—salaries paid until end of the year for those with under two years of service; for more senior employees, a month's severance pay for every year worked; six months' extension on health insurance; and counseling for stress created by the layoffs. At the request of the laid-off employees, Zappos allowed them to keep their 40 percent employee discount through Christmas.

But it wasn't just the package alone. It was how the adversity was communicated. For example, after each of the employees was informed by their respective managers of the layoff, an e-mail explaining why the layoffs occurred was both sent out and posted on Twitter. Keep in mind, CEO Hsieh has almost 960,000 followers on Twitter as of July 2009. Why exposed that way? Core value #6 is "Build Open and Honest Relationships with Communication." That's why.

They don't just work with Twitter. They have a number of blogs that are highly transparent and very useful. For example, the CEO blogs but so does the full-time life coach. The CEO's blog entries are on things like, "How Twitter can make you a better (and happier) person," while the life coach blogs with a daily hint or tip—as of mid-July 2009 there were 805 of those. Other blogs cover running, family, couture, and Zappos internal events.

But they don't stop there. There is Zappos TV that offers a whacked-out look at things like "Brett sets fire to Melissa's car" or a video of the Zappos internal ping-pong tourney or annual head-shaving day.

All in all, they understand how to utilize social media tools to improve culture, not just simply define the collaboration efforts at the company—as most other companies who are Enterprise 2.0–focused do. They get results that are phenomenal because of this approach.

Zappos: The Results

In 2000, a year after they were founded, Zappos turned over $1.6 million in revenue. In 2003 it was $32 million, in 2005 it was $370 million, and in 2008 it was just over $1 billion. They not only made money, but even though they are venture backed (Sequoia is a big investor), they are profitable with a 5 percent net margin on 2007 revenues and cash flow positive.

But investment numbers aren't the only measure of success for this remarkable company. They have a repeat buyer customer rate of

75 percent with 9.7 million customers. These repeaters don't only buy once either. They buy 2.5 more times over a given year, and the amount they spend increases as it goes.

Think that's all? Nope.

As with customers, a culture premised on trust and collaboration will end up with the happiest employees—and thus, those best suited to engage customers—because of institutional support, not just individual merit. In 2008, Zappos debuted on *Fortune* magazine's Best Places in America to Work list at number 23—the highest for any rookie company that year. If you think now we're at the end of it, wrong again. In July 2009, Amazon acquired Zappos for $928 million.

Oh, in case you're curious . . . only three now-former employees-in-training took the $2,000 bribe to leave the company in 2008.

Yep.

Enterprise 2.0 Tools—Really Briefly

The tools of Enterprise 2.0—the social software that Bosox-loving Professor McAfee discusses—are explicitly aimed at collaboration. These include the aforementioned blogs, instant messengers like Twitter, and, as importantly and perhaps even more so, wikis.

You're going to hear a lot about these tools and their application to Social CRM in succeeding chapters—Chapters 6 through 9 to be exact. So I don't want to beat them into the ground in this chapter. You've seen a hint of what some of them can do when they are applied to a progressive Enterprise 2.0 culture like Zappos. Now we'll take a brief look at how they are structured inside the contemporary intelligent business.

What you see in Figure 4-1 is a matrix of the most likely tools to be used by the enterprise to bridge the gap both technologically and culturally between the operational side of the company (left column) with the interactions of the customers (right column). That intersection becomes real when the culture of the company supports the use of the tools internally. Not only is productivity improved, but the staff is familiar and comfortable enough with their own collaboration and their subsequent empowerment to work with their customers in the same way. But note the figure's central column. Those are the tools most commonly used to internally collaborate. For example, IBM created its social software product, Lotus Connections (see Chapter 7 for a longer discussion), based on its internal use of wiki-like collaboration spaces called activities, social bookmarks and social tagging, blogs with the capability to rate and comment on the wiki, and community threads thrown in for good measure.

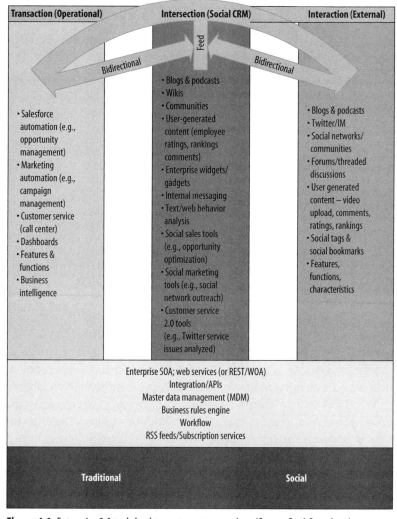

Figure 4-1: Enterprise 2.0 tools lead to customer transactions (Source: Paul Greenberg)

That doesn't tie any given tool down to a single use either. A blog can be used as a means to let employees and senior management communicate. It also can be provided to dispense advice (see the Zappos life coach). It can be something that's also lighthearted such as *The BeeHive* (www.scottishlife.co.uk/scotlife/Web/Site/BeeHive/), the blog of Steve Bee, head of pension strategy at Royal London Group. Bee is known for actually living up to his tagline of "Pensions Gobbledygook Explained." He has 28,000 unique visitors per month and was named in 2007 as one of the London *Times'* best business blogs. Do you think pension strategy blogging would draw 28,000 visitors if it wasn't fun?

To further the case, *Future Changes: Grow Your Wiki* (www.ikiw.org), a site devoted to the effective use of wikis in business run by Atlassian evangelist Stewart Mader, did an informal poll of roughly 200 of its readers and found a remarkably diverse spread on how wikis were used at companies (see Figure 4-2).

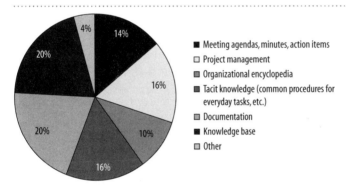

Figure 4-2: The business uses of a wiki (Source: *Grow Your Wiki*, Stewart Mader, 2009)

What is very clear is that social software tools are used according to the needs of those using them. They are malleable and agnostic in their functionality. They are valuable because of their contribution to a new kind of enterprise culture that has to be a foundation for how companies act and think when it comes to the social customer—*their* social customer.

What This Means for CRM

I know this isn't the standard view of Enterprise 2.0, nor do I mean it to be. I'm sure if you've investigated the issue what you typically read is that social software tools are the Enterprise 2.0 thing. But when it comes to how you engage your customers, the primary resource remains what it always has been, 21st century or not, and that's people. The kind of culture that propagates throughout a company is a key determinant in the effort to make that customer engagement fruitful, to the point of creating a customer relationship that is both delightful and extraordinary, à la Zappos.

It's now time to head over to the new business model chapter but not before we hear from Dion Hinchcliffe, who will walk with you over there.

Mini-Conversation with Dion Hinchcliffe

Dion Hinchcliffe, CEO of Hinchcliffe and Company, is an internationally recognized business strategist and enterprise architect who works hands-on with clients in the Fortune 500, federal government, and Internet startup community. He has been a leading thinker when it comes to Web 2.0 in the enterprise with at least two blogs: ZDNet (http://blogs.zdnet.com/Hinchcliffe) and the Web 2.0 Blog (http://web2.wsj2.com). He is extensively published in leading industry periodicals and publications. Dion was founding editor-in-chief of the respected *Web 2.0 Journal* and is current editor-in-chief of *Social Computing* magazine. He has been quoted in *BusinessWeek*, *CNET News*, *Wired* magazine, and *CIO* magazine, among others. He keynotes major conferences including Web 2.0 Expo, Enterprise 2.0 (naturally), and CeBIT, and is founder of the Web 2.0 University (http://web20university.com). He can be reached at dion@hinchcliffeandco.com or http://twitter.com/dhinchcliffe.

The credentials go on and so could I. But enough of me. Take it away, Dion.

Key to Enterprise 2.0 Strategy

As more and more organizations begin to apply social media and emergent collaborative tools to operate more efficiently and effectively, successful best practices and techniques for adoption have started to become clear. Here are three of the most important considerations for an Enterprise 2.0 strategy today. These have been culled from the analysis of a number of Enterprise 2.0 projects in the Fortune 500 and medium-sized businesses:

> ▶ *Engage the organization vertically   The best Enterprise 2.0 initiatives have early engagement at a number of levels in the business from top to bottom, including senior management, middle management, and line staff. One leading success factor is when several high profile managers begin using blogs and wikis publicly within the organization. Another is when line employees receive requests for their work to be delivered in social media form such as reports, project status, and recruiting notes.*

A third is when all workstations in the organization have desktop short-cuts and Start menu items added to their computers, right next to their existing productivity tool links, providing a broad, easily accessible "on-ramp" to the tools. All of these drive the use of their platforms and adoption through viral engagement and distribution. Thus, the end strategy of horizontally engaging the organization seems to begin when a vertical slice through the organization is effective in Enterprise 2.0 uptake and spreads out virally.

▶ ***Use the right platform***   *Many organizations attempt Enterprise 2.0 initiatives using the tools at hand, often older generation IT solutions that are already amortized. The tremendous success of consumer Web 2.0 was driven by very different application models that are much simpler, more open, and have specific design features that have been proven on the World Wide Web to foster high levels of participation. However, consumer tools often lack enterprise context around security, governance, and other considerations. Fortunately, a generation of enterprise-class tools have recently emerged that combine the successful aspects of Web 2.0 with the needs of enterprises today. These tools are particularly potent in effectiveness and are more likely to create the desired outcomes based on the number of successful outcomes so far.*

▶ ***Connect it to the business***   *While Enterprise 2.0 tools are designed to encourage unintended outcomes and can be opportunistically applied to business issues, many successful rollouts begin by focusing on a specific business challenge in some part of the organization. This can be to address knowledge retention in high staff turnover areas of the business, to address business agility around content management, or to create better and closer collaboration between far-flung business units or external partners or customers.*

The full extent of the possibilities and business application of Enterprise 2.0 applications is still just being understood, but the business world can already reap significant benefits by focusing on the key considerations above to ensure good return on their Enterprise 2.0 investments.

The result will be products that are more effective than ever before, customers who are more demanding than ever before, and a software vendor ecosystem that will rise to the occasion—or be passed by.

The software industry is being reborn—yet again. Enterprise 2.0 will bring massive innovation to business computing. I stand by the assertion I wrote last year: in five years, we will look back and not recognize the software company of today.◆

Thanks, Dion, for the talk and walk. Okay, peeps, we're at the door of a very important building—one premised on new Social CRM business models. Up to now, we've looked at the foundation of Social CRM: what it is and what impacts it. Now we're going to start looking at the block and tackling of the "how"—what needs to be adopted. Business models first. I've already knocked. C'mon in. The door is open.

5

A Company Like Me:
New Business Models = Customer Love

To recap the game so far:

CRM 1.0 has been a series of processes, technologies, and methodologies organized around the operational tasks that were designed to institutionalize a way of managing customer–company interaction. Social CRM, while incorporating what CRM 1.0 does, also incorporates the personalization of those customer–company interactions and the integration of the customer into the planning, strategies, and direction of the company through use of tools, products, services, and experiences so the customer feels they are participating in the companies they choose to do business with.

CRM 1.0 concerned itself with the customer as the object of a successful sale. Social CRM concerns itself with the customer as the subject of a valuable experience. In their own ways, they both attempt to institutionalize practices that allow better customer–company interaction. Their respective visions are driven by the expectations of the social forces in command of the contemporary business ecosystem of its era (we are narrowing this conversation to just business here regardless of the broader social implications). In the CRM 1.0 days, that would be the company and the enterprise value chain associated with it. In the Social CRM days, a.k.a. *right this second*, that would be the much-empowered customer and the peer-to-peer social networks associated with it.

Suck some air into your lungs, because we're going deep.

Why? Because We *Like* You and Trust You

Like and trust are a pair of terms not usually associated with the company-customer relationship, now are they? Well, sorry to say (though not really), the social customer says they have to be—and these are requirements that can't be ignored. But neither like and especially not trust are very easy to establish anywhere, especially in an enterprise.

Want proof? Let's start with this list. Tell me, metaphorically of course, who do you trust on it?

▶ Mom and/or Dad and/or siblings?

▶ The press or a part of the press in particular?

▶ The ads you see on TV or hear on the radio?

▶ The pop-up banners you see on the Web?

▶ Google ads?

▶ Your best friend? All the time?

▶ Your not-as-good-a-friend? All the time?

▶ A total stranger you meet on the street whom you ask for instructions on how to get somewhere in their town?

▶ A person you know well whom you ask for instructions on how to get somewhere who has visited the town?

▶ Commentary on Epinions or Amazon about a product from a total stranger named rabiddog@comcast.net who knows you as whatever your handle is?

That's the point. You're as likely to trust the latter as much or more than the former when it comes to a buying decision because of the elements that go into what is considered a trusted relationship. For example, it's highly unlikely that you're going to trust your best friend on what he thinks of a product he never used, because his knowledge of the product isn't direct. But you will trust rabid dog on it, because he used it. Yet, if you think back to the '60s and '70s (see Chapter 1), whom did you *have to* trust when it came to a product?

▶ The ad you read about the product

▶ The company that produced the product

▶ The advertising agencies (a.k.a. Madison Avenue) that produced the ads

► The salesperson who wanted to sell you the product

► The brochure you read about the product

► If you were lucky, a neighbor who used the product

All were concerned with one thing, making sure you buy the product—with the exception perhaps of the neighbor, who actually had a vested interest in making sure you thought their decision to buy it before you did was a smart one. Read the literature of the '50s and '60s, such as the *The Organization Man* by William Whyte, and you'll get an idea of how trusting and not-volatile the customer and employee of the post–World War II era were. Your trusted sources were pretty much those who had every reason to exaggerate the truth if they had no particular moral compunctions or a strong reason for spinning their product perspective.

But obviously, that's changed. One of the most significant studies, done in late 2005/early 2006 by Carnegie Mellon, was on the Facebook member students from Carnegie Mellon. I'm presuming you know what Facebook was before what it is now, but just in case, it was a social networking website where college students hung out to meet each other. As they do now, the members were perfectly willing to provide personal information about themselves and socialize online. Their likes, dislikes, and personal follies and foibles were exposed for the world to see. What's amazing is that the Carnegie Mellon study showed when sampling those college student members back in 2005 that 52 percent of the Carnegie Mellon students registered on Facebook didn't *want their immediate families or dearest friends to know what they posted publicly on the site.*

Think about that for a minute because this really hasn't changed that much. The trusted recipient of this really personal info back then was riverrat@northwestern.edu, not mom, dad, best boyfriend or girlfriend. This tells you that the existing business logic needs to be fixed or replaced fast. The only difference is that BFFs are now allowed to see the information—but still not mom or dad. Trust is at the core of the change we're seeing and that we're all involved in, and the world of trust has turned upside down.

Edelman Trust Barometer: Left-Brained Confirmation

I'm sure you remember the discussion of the Edelman Trust Barometer in Chapter 1. From 2004 to the present, Edelman found that in

North America and most of Europe, the most trusted source was "someone like me."

► In Brazil, Canada, Germany, the Netherlands, Spain, Sweden, and the United States, "a person like me" is the most trusted source. A person like me is someone who shares my interests and my political beliefs.

► In France, India, Ireland, Mexico, Poland, South Korea, and the United Kingdom, a financial or industry expert is the most trusted source.

There are two important inferences here. First, I should move to France or India immediately. Second, if the most trusted source in much of Europe and almost all of North America is "a person like me," that sets a unique standard for all institutions on how to interact with the individual. We will get into that.

But there are three other conclusions that bear strongly on a Social CRM strategy:

► By 2006, "a person like me" was the most credible spokesperson for companies. That year, people trusted employees significantly more than company CEOs. Equally as important, younger opinion elites, who are defined as college-educated, top 25 percent of their age group in income, and who spend time searching out news and politics, actually trust business more than the older elites do. To make that easier to digest, "never trust anyone over 30" is *not* the mantra of Gen Y. That was our (my) generation's mantra, which if you're to believe gray-hair highlight dye commercials, is now "never trust anyone over 90."

► Edelman 2008 added what they called "TrustHolder" profiles, which looked at communication and activity styles. Of the four Trust-Holder profiles, it is social networkers, representing 39 percent of the "global elites," who trust business the most. Their primary trust criteria are marketing practices, financial performance, safety record, and environmental concerns. This is a very important group because they are defined by their interest in peer-to-peer (someone like me, again) conversations and traditional media—that means *both*. Remember that when we get to the sales and marketing chapter (Chapter 12) later. This is the most influential group with friends, family, professional networks, communities, and groups—both physical and online. Sixty-one percent of them trust business.

► The most trusted industry is technology (79 percent). Number 3 is, oddly, banks (67 percent). Least trusted? Media companies, the same traditional media and advertising agencies that are in such tumult now, at 44 percent.

These results have a very strong impact on how you have to craft your Social CRM business model and strategy.

Someone Like Me and Business Liked by Me

Spend some time reading the above and drawing conclusions. Two have serious impact on your Social CRM strategy:

► Customers want to trust the company *the way they trust their peers.*

► They have no problem trusting the company, despite the general distrust that exists for the denizens of the corporate world—if their criteria for trust are met. In fact, the most influential movers and shakers among them are happy to trust the company for the most part.

That means you have to earn their trust and give them reasons to continue to trust you once you do. If you do that, and you're not Enron, they will. But there are a number of changes you're going to have to effect to make sure you can earn and keep their confidence.

One of the most significant comes from the recognition that the most trusted spokesperson is "someone like me." This person is the perceived face of the company and, like it or not, represents the customer's perception of the corporate image, as do the employees in sales and customer service. The spokesperson is also the only person visible to people with little interaction with the company—like future prospects. Their entire interaction with your business might be no more than seeing this spokesperson on TV or via the Web talking about your business and its plans. Maybe it's your CEO being interviewed by Brian Williams of NBC News, or by Chris Brogan of Chrisbrogan.com, or Billy Bush of Access Hollywood. I hope not, because Edelman found that one of the least trusted sources is the CEO. It could be your VP of Marketing or a public relations representative you hired—though given the 44 percent trust rating they have, I wouldn't recommend it.

Customers are not only attempting to personalize their experiences with the company, they are attempting to create a human face for the company, to see if that company fits a model of a "company like me."

The humanization of the company is the new Holy Grail for Social CRM. At this stage, it is achievable only in part most of the time. It has been fully achieved in a very small number of instances.

We know how we act and think as customers, don't we? With businesses we interact with frequently, we usually also have a favorite salesperson, or a friend we've made in customer service, or we can point to great experiences with the company that we speak of warmly—in other words, with emotions that we reserve primarily for other people. But the issue that has to be addressed isn't "Do we have great sales or customer service people?" It's "How do we institutionalize the kinds of practices, culture, and technologies to provide a customer with the kind of experience that makes him or her think of us as the 'company like me'?" Which has a corollary: "When that great customer service person leaves us, how do we institutionalize all those practices, culture, and technologies so that we can easily replicate those capabilities?"

Humanization

That institutionalization has the effect of humanizing the company in ways that were almost unheard of twenty years ago. The interesting thing is that customers may not be thrilled that you're trying to meet these service standards and emotional values, but they *expect* that you will to continue to engage them.

Customers want to and expect to interact with a company the same way they interact with a friend or peer they trust. That means they expect a personal relationship with *the company*, not just with a person in the company, though that may be how the relationship manifests itself most of the time. It also means they expect that the attributes of a deeply personal connection they have to a peer will be part of the way the company interacts with them. Trust and transparency have to permeate the company's DNA. The company has to have something distinct about it. The customer is expecting the company to converse with them, not just push corporate hype. It's why you see contemporary marketing so geared toward buzz, word of mouth, or engaging customers in conversation through use of social media like blogs or wikis. The customers expect it.

It's also why coolness and style (remember Chapter 3?) are now factors in that conversation between customer and company—because they are intimate parts of the conversation between friends.

This level of humanization is important, but not necessarily defining for all companies. While customers have a much more demanding level of expectation, they still simply purchase things in a utilitarian fashion from at least a plurality of companies they deal with, if not a majority. They don't have that level of expectation from every company they interact with. They treat the company as the object of a purchase. Turnabout is fair play because the company treats them as the object of a sale often enough.

Even though most customers don't have an intimate relationship with a company, the company still has to aspire to create not just a repeat purchaser, but an advocate who is going to say, "This company loves me the way I love it." They have to gear their strategies toward getting that kind of customer (whether B2C or B2B) while attending to the customer who merely returns to buy.

Personalization

Customers are unique, and they expect unique interactions that are appropriate to them. Yet to a large degree they are not willing to accept companies as more than institutions. They want to deal with individual humans when necessary, but otherwise be left alone to craft a personal approach to their interactions with you that fits their desires—not yours. They buy your products, services, and experiences to meet that unique need.

I ran across an ad in the August 31, 2008 issue of *Wine Spectator*, for Raymond James Financial Services (whom I use, BTW, in a fit of full disclosure), that I thought encapsulated exactly what personalization is in a relationship between a company and its customers. Here's how it goes:

A picture of an attractive, over-55 smiling woman riding a bike with a *totally* cute Jack Russell terrier in a basket on the front handlebars appears across three quarters of the ad, with some lavender, green, gray, and purple stripes between the picture and the main text:

Single women over 55 who like to cycle	420,196
Who married their college sweetheart	28,347
And are funding a bike trail in his memory	8
Named "Walter's Way"	1

"There is no one exactly like you. Raymond James financial advisors understand that. The interests you have, the people you care about, and the causes you support make you an individual with your own set of goals. By listening to you and understanding your history of giving and plans for the future, your advisor can help guide you through financial planning in a personal way. . . ."

It goes on like that for a bit, but you get the idea. This is a really good representation of the expectation (I'm an individual), the problem (businesses have to personalize how they treat a customer), and the first step in the solution ("By listening to you. . .").

But it also points out the dilemma that companies trying to connect to customers have. How do you humanize a company when a customer is looking for a highly personalized, unique experience with that company *and* what they individually require for "a company like me" is exactly that—different with each individual?

Why a New Business Model Is Necessary

This calls for a new business model that is aimed at customer participation in the commercial life of the company. We talked up a few reasons why this is necessary in Chapter 1, but before we get into the meat of the model, I want you to hear the take of Anthony Lye, the SVP of Oracle CRM (and also a member of online chapter, "Social CRM Leaders Speak from Out There," Social CRM elite). I asked him why he thought a new business model is called for. Here's what he said:

> I think what's happened is a reduction or elimination of the middle class. Markets have had to move to either end. Vendors need to offer more consumer mass offering generic products or high end consumables. Macy's, Sears, Ford—all midmarket brands—had to reply with low cost, low end brand offerings or high end. Ford, for example, has been disintermediated by Toyota on the one end and BMW and Mercedes on the other.
>
> The world has become richer all told and the middle is no longer satisfactory to many. People's requirements have fallen below or gone above the line. What can I get at a low cost at the easiest place? [Author's note: A utilitarian purchase.] Or if I have to spend at a premium, I'm going to research it and try to understand the company at a really detailed level.

*Some companies, like Amazon, have a business model that opti-
mizes the two-minute relationship—in fact, they invented it. Boeing
is the master of the 10-year relationship. They have optimized their
model around build-to-order in small numbers like 10s and 100s.*

*But there is risk inherent in any new business model. For example,
Amazon runs the risk of being superseded by social sites that allow
buyer participation. Amazon is retail with a touch of social. The next
generation is social with a touch of retail.*

Whether or not this resonates with you, Anthony's key premise—
that a new business model is required because of economic and social
changes—is dead on, so pay attention!

The New Business Models Unveiled

We know from Chapter 4 that consumer thinking and new expectations on how one works are all part of the new framework for corporate operations. Good start, if I do say so myself—and I do.

But I'm going to tell you a story about the PC and video game
industry, which is the prototype of the new business model. Based on
that story, I'm going to extract the characteristics so that you can see
what kind of business model has been so successful and, hopefully,
how it applies to you. Then we're going to take a look at what to expect
from it—advocates or at least loyal customers—and the current ways
to measure that.

Get into the Game: PC/Video Games
as a Prototype of the New Model

In his book *The Ambiguity of Play*, Brian Sutton Smith says something
that deserves to be immortal: "The opposite of play isn't work. It's
depression."

The integration of work and play is why we have a game industry
(as opposed to a gaming industry) that raked in $25.4 billion in 2006,
blew that number out with $41.8 billion for combined PC and video
games in 2007, and is expected to do $68.4 billion in 2012 according
to PricewaterhouseCoopers' game industry 2008 annual report.

The growth of high quality consoles like the XBox360, PS3, and Nin-
tendo Wii and the games that go with them is certainly one of the reasons why the industry has skyrocketed to one of the most substantial on

the planet. But there is another major explanation for this vast growth. Participation by the customers—the gamers—in the creation of their own experience. This is not only not trivial, it is perhaps why PC and video games are the cash cow they are. *Everyone* plays them—including 59-year-old me. The best way to understand how this can be is to talk about the mod community and the prototypical new business model.

The Mod Community: Hacking Is a Good Thing

Mod doesn't mean "modern" like it did in the sixties. It means "modification." It applies to a specific way of configuring video or PC games. Rather than accept the product out of the box as is, you can actually alter everything from look to gameplay. The game becomes something you want rather than merely something you bought. There are groups of gamers devoted to nothing more than producing these mods. The experience is multiplied because there are very large global online communities working to sculpt changes to the games, which are then made freely available by the mod creators, often on the sites of the game producers.

This all began in 1996 when John Carmack, then president of ID Software, published his now classic game *Doom*. Prior to *Doom*, he had released another classic first-person shooter, *Wolfenstein*, which was hacked right away and new gameplay, characters, and levels were introduced. Rather than freaking out over the unauthorized hacking of *Wolfenstein*, Carmack decided that this was actually a pretty cool use of the game. As he said in an interview in 1999 on Slashdot:

> Based on that the hacking in Wolfenstein, Doom *was designed from the beginning to be modified by the user community . . . after the official release I did start getting some specs and code out.*
>
> *The original source I released for the bsp tool was in objective-C, which wasn't the most helpful thing in the world, but it didn't take long for people to produce different tools.*
>
> *I still remember the first time I saw the original* Star Wars Doom *mod. Seeing how someone had put the death star into our game felt so amazingly cool. I was so proud of what had been made possible, and I was completely sure that making games that could serve as a canvas for other people to work on was a valid direction.*
>
> *A* Doom/Quake *add-on has become almost an industry standard résumé component, which I think is a Very Good Thing. The best way to sell yourself is to show what you have produced, rather than tell people what you know, what you want to do, or what degrees you have.*

This triggered what has been the largest and most advanced customer company collaboration in any industry. The fans of any particular game are routinely creating modifications so that they—and their own fans in their communities—have a personalized version of the game that suits their style of play.

The idea of customer participation reached a new level in mid-2008 with the release of the *Spore* Creature Creator. *Spore* is a game produced by Will Wright, one of the legendary game designers. The Creature Creator is an authoring tool that lets gamers create their own creatures, using a rich feature set of virtually functional body parts—meaning which hand with claws you choose will affect how the hands are used throughout the game—and a set of social characteristics and behaviors. That creature is then placed in an environment where it can evolve. You can create an infinite number of different creatures or clone an infinite number of the same creatures.

One of the unique features of the game is the *Spore* community catalog, a community repository for all the creatures sculpted by individual gamers. They can be plucked up and put down in each gamers' unique *Spore* universe so you can see how well they adjust to an environment and what effect they will have on the environment over the centuries the game encompasses.

In a brilliant move, Electronic Arts released the Creature Creator months before the full game's September 2008 release date. This allowed the aspiring *Spore* gamers to create their creatures and place them into the community repository (and locally on their own PC) before the game's full environment was available. The Creature Creator retailed at $9.95—which is above and beyond the retail price of $49.95 the full game sold at. The expectation was that there would be a million creatures created by year-end 2008. Here are the real numbers for the first month to July 18, 2008 at 4:00 PM, directly from the *Spore* community site—one month after the release of the Creature Creator:

▶ 1,970,195 total creatures uploaded in the 30 days.

▶ 31,955 creature uploads in the last 24 hours.

▶ 7,604 people joined the *Spore* community in the prior 24 hours.

▶ 691, 242 joined the *Spore* community in that first month.

This is staggering, and it proves the benefit and value of the mod community as a new business model:

▶ The effect of releasing a tool that modifies a game can be viral—nearly 2 million creatures created in a month.

▶ The marketing value? There were 691,242 members of a community anxiously awaiting the game release so they could buy it.

▶ The conversation on this is vibrant and continues to this day—if you Google "Electronic Arts" and "Spore," just short of a year after its release, there are 5,990,000 references that pop up in a nanosecond or two.

▶ The revenue potential was (and is) phenomenal. There is a free version of Creature Creator, but the number of sales of the $9.95 version reached such substantial numbers its first week that it was number one in PC game sales and number six in overall consumer software sales that week and continued that strongly for several weeks after. Keep in mind, this tool was just the teaser for the full game, which was a separate purchase.

▶ The community is participating in the *Spore* "experience" as its members are creating creatures, blogging about it, talking about the individual creatures, and commenting on the creatures that others have created.

If you're interested, here's my first *Spore* creature.

More Mod Please

This is only one example of countless mod community success stories. One of the key factors in that success is that the game production companies are co-participants and active supports of the mod communities. Many game companies host fan sites where the mods are available for download and forums discuss the finer points of anything from coding to the history of the mod. This involves a major effort on the part of the modders themselves. Their participation is passionate and their involvement deep. Yet they are not compensated for their efforts by the game company. What the game company does is provide them with tools to do the modification and visibility into the source code, with resources that will help them publicize the mods—such as forum locations, storage for the mods themselves, and downloading tools. That's pretty much what the modders get for what is often months and even years of work. But remember, this isn't a typically mercenary effort. This is a labor of love and play, which, incidentally, is every bit as much value to a customer as revenue is value to a company.

This all goes back to what customers value, as we discussed in Chapter 4. It isn't necessarily what the companies value. There is value for the game's fans in the actual experience of creating the mod and value in the community participation. There is value in the mod being made available for free. There is value in the input the modders give the company about the tools and the changes in the game that they are looking for, whether as code changes or new features or functions.

One particularly crisp example revolves around a game called *Rome: Total War*, a runaway hit that opened a game franchise when it was released in 2005 by Sega for the PC. In fact, it was so popular that IGN, a gamer rating service and publication, named it number four in the Top 25 PC games of all time.

The game was loosely based on Roman history. You adopted a faction and historical leader and attempted to conquer Rome. A group of committed fans decided that the historical accuracy wasn't sufficient, and in 2006 they began to create a mod that they called *Rome: Total Realism*. What made this remarkable was the level of effort, the team that built it, the remarkable discussions, and the number of downloads. The team that built version 6.0 of this mod consisted of the following positions (some individuals had multiple positions):

▶ Lead programmer

▶ Lead skinning artist, 3D artist, jack of all trades

► Lead graphics artist, video producer, web designer

► Lead 3D artist

► Programmer, 3D artist

► Lead historian, programmer

► Skinning artist

► Music composer

► Assistant programmer

► Graphics artist, programmer

► Campaign map designer

► Forum administrator

► Public relations

Remember, these are unpaid, passionate fans devoting their time to creating this mod, which was downloaded over 800,000 times in its first year of existence. If you didn't know that, you'd think this was a full-blown professional development team working for Sega. The level of detail involved was astounding. Discussions went on in the forums about arcane points of Roman history to make sure that a uniform had the proper color for a barbarian army. Take a look at this one of thousands of changes to the gameplay.

Changed Parthian stables. Now Tier 1 builds Horse archers, tier 2 Huvaka, tier 3 Persian cavalry and tier 4 cataphracts.

Whatever that means.

But there is another case. What happens when you care about your products, but you don't really care much about your customers?

Sony Does It Wrong, Again

This one will be short and sour.

Sony produces excellent hardware. They have an engineering culture that is defined by a view of the customer that says "if we build it, they will come." This means, we'll figure out what we want to produce, produce it, and the customer will buy it. Pretty much like Oracle was until the last couple of years.

Sony builds a product like the Bravia TV or the PSP or a Blu-Ray player and while people attracted to the hardware will buy it, it never seems to sell at the expected level.

Why is this? Because the customer not only has little to say about the development of the product in an era where product development has entered the customer's domain, but Sony actively has discouraged customer participation and stays invisible (or opaque, if you prefer) to their customers when other companies are struggling with how to be more transparent. Sony considers its intellectual property entirely sacred and makes every effort to prevent any encroachments on it, unlike the open source approach taken by the John Carmacks or the Segas of the game world.

A case in point was their handling of the first crack in the PSP firmware. In its earliest days, the Sony PSP (the handheld game unit that Sony has been producing since 2005) was hacked. There was a game called *Wipeout Pure*, which, if you reverse engineered it, would provide an Internet browser, in violation of Sony's agreements. Sony's response? They created an Internet browser for the PSP owners and then closed off the hole by updating the firmware so the product couldn't be hacked. Unlike much of the game community, which releases the source code and even best practices guides on how to modify the games, Sony thinks this is a dangerous thing and remains a closed, somewhat arrogant environment. Their lack of customer involvement is also why as early as 2005, they lost the number one position in consumer electronics to Samsung, who very much involves their customers and external expert networks in their planning, development, and problem solving.

Much of the game industry, even including its multi-billion dollar giants like Electronic Arts, supports the open source approach that has driven much of its success. Their approach supports the contemporary customer's outlook without trying to subvert it. It accepts the peer trust that exists and at the same time is able to institutionalize practices that will both cede control of the environment to their customers and still profit from it, because they give the customers the ability to participate in the creation of a highly personalized experience that also drives sales. This is borne out by data from IDG Consumer Research Report on the game industry which found that, as far back as 2006, even before all the social networking had become prevalent, only 17 percent of gamers actually found official publisher game sites useful, while 70 percent of gamers got game-specific info from forums, game fan sites, and third-party news websites—which were often sponsored or supported by the game companies!

Most important, what kind of business model can be extrapolated from this example?

Characteristics of the New Business Model

Traditional business models are rapidly losing their oomph. The kind of business organization that sees itself as a producer/distributor of products or a service provider and then sees its returns based strictly on products or services sold, is becoming the coelacanth of the 21st century—a weird looking specimen in a fossilized state.

While the game industry has been a great lab for a new business model, it is gaining credence throughout multiple sectors, far beyond just games. The model is intermeshed with contemporary social CRM and customer engagement strategies. You can't have one without the other, though you can build toward either or both incrementally. There are some distinct characteristics that define this model:

▶ **The lines between producer and consumer are blurred.** The effort is cooperative and the interest in making the products "consumable" is mutual. For example, at the 2002 annual Game Developers Conference in San Jose, game company Valve Software founder Gabe Newell unveiled Steam, a distribution network that would offer instant updates to recent Valve games and new titles from Valve and other companies. Among the new titles was *Day of Defeat*, a multiplayer add-on to Valve's best-selling first-person shooter (FPS), *Half-Life*. This wasn't a Valve original product. *Day of Defeat* was a mod and the company supported it by distributing the updates as if it were a company product. The company and the customer were operating in conjunction with each other. This is a collaborative value chain in (my) enterprise jargon. (See Chapter 11.)

▶ **The company moves from being the producer or distributor of goods or the provider of services to the aggregator of products, services, tools, and experiences to allow the customer to meet the needs of their personal agenda, or in bizbuzz, their personal value chain.** This implies that what the company packages is actually a solution set, though not in the classic sense. For example, with the release of *Half Life 2*, not only did

Valve release the game itself, but the source code, the tools to author the modifications, and a page where you could download the best practices that were culled from the hundreds of mods the game had engendered. You had all you needed to tailor your own experience if you were so inclined.

▶ **The users and producers are engaged in the co-creation of value.** The game companies sell millions of copies of the game, and the gamers are able to make the game into something that has value to them—often emotional and always replayable without buying a new game.

▶ **The users have the tools to configure and/or customize their personal experience with the product.** This is part of the core difference with the older business model. The traditional model treats products and services as items for purchase. The new model incorporates configuration tools as something available for the customer's use.

▶ **The users and producers encourage each other and mutually define the future directions of the specific products.** The game industry sponsors conferences for modders, and will typically invite influential modders and other key gamers into corporate strategy sessions. Blizzard, which holds an annual conference attracting as many as 6000 gamers, will wine and dine key gamers at the conference and let them in on future plans, in return for advice. The users and producers take advantage of the most advanced methods of communication within the global matrix (e.g., user communities on the Web). Transparency is the rule, not the exception.

▶ **Even though the users are working on the product changes for their own experience, the changes to the product have universal and commercial value and drive the sales of the product.** Valve Software's *Half Life 2* is one of the most modified games in history. One mod, *Counterstrike*, was so popular that Valve acquired it and by 2006, it had sold over 18 million copies, was being played on 36,000 servers as a multiplayer game 24/7, and had over 4.5 billion minutes a month being played. Not a commercial game—a mod. This game has since been superseded by *World of Warcraft*—you know, the one that you're playing, but the mod was the most successful in gamer history.

▶ **The producer is not just the publisher/manufacturer but operates as an aggregator for the user's creative interactivity.** The company provides the products, services, tools, and experiences that allow the customer to personalize their interactions with the company in the way they want them.

▶ **The user is not just a purchaser but also an advocate of the experience around the product and, by extension, the company.** The existence of multiple communities and sites associated with modders who are constantly chattering is a perfect example of this. Firaxis, the publisher of *Sid Meier's Civilization IV*, has hundreds of mods—some on sites that are for the mods themselves (such as www.civfanatics.com), some that are the subjects of threaded discussions on the main *Civilization IV* website.

▶ **The companies and the customers jointly create and provide the tools to make this collaboration successful.** The customers often create the tools. For example, the *Rome: Total Realism* team developed their own skinning tools to make the uniforms of the varying factions in the game accurate.

▶ **The customization effort itself, not just the result, is part of the experience, thus enhancing the producer/consumer collaboration all the more.** Most of the more complex mods are team efforts, and the collaboration itself and the sharing of the mod with the public is as important as the results of the effort.

▶ **The overall effort involves a corporate culture that is defined by the voice of the customer first.** The difference between John Carmack or Valve Software versus Sony. I rest my case.

▶ **The model uses and provides the most advanced technological tools for these globally matriced communities that are interactive and real time.** Many of the mod teams have never met their fellow developers. They are successful because all tools, code, and communications media are available via the Web in either real time or as threaded discussions accessible on demand, despite the teams being spread across multiple nations.

▶ **The company and the customer each get value in ways that are appropriate and satisfying to them.** As we discussed in Chapter 4, they may have different sets of values, but the company and the customer are participating jointly in creating something mutually beneficial. Revenue or profit for the company; some form of emotional satisfaction for the customer.

▶ **The company's revenues increase accordingly, as does their profitability, given that their customers are doing something freely—and for free.** That remains the most astonishing facet of this business model. The customer has no problem doing this for free because they see it as a benefit to them.

Social CRM Business Model, in Sum

Social CRM's business model is based around one central premise. The company moves from being a producer of products and a provider of services to an aggregator of products, services, tools, and experiences that give the customer the means to meet their own agendas.

Another Model Worth Getting Behind

Gartner's Michael Maoz, one of the most straightforward and insightful analysts I've ever met and one of the nicest people, unveiled a business model for 21st century enterprises at the SAP Sapphire Conference in Orlando in 2008. This model, something quite different from Gartner's historic models, is an exceptionally intelligent and highly useful piece of work—in fact, one of the few models (besides mine, of course) that is aimed squarely at the reality of a customer-dominated business ecosystem.

Michael calls it the intent-driven enterprise. Here's what it consists of, what I think about it, and why you should pay some serious attention to it.

The Intent-Driven Enterprise

During Michael's presentation at Sapphire, he unveiled some Gartner 2008 research that was fascinating. CRM turned out to be 2008's top priority for business as companies realized that, with the economy tanking, retaining customers was most important and was going to be a major problem. The way this panned out was:

▶ The biggest business issue was enhancing and retaining customers (8.1/10).

▶ The second biggest business issue was tracking new customers (8.0/10).

► When just CEOs were queried, they saw sales productivity (36 percent) and customer care (35 percent), the traditional pillars of CRM, as the number one and number two issues.

► When just the IT folks were queried, number one was improving business processes, and number two was attracting and retaining customers. Interestingly, number three was innovation—up from number ten the year before.

All of that is useful information and simply reinforces the need for CRM. It's also an interesting indicator of a market that remains very healthy despite the ill health of the overall economy. But Michael threw a seriously hard-breaking curve at this point: "CRM is the business priority of 2008—but my daughters don't know that." Michael's daughters do their purchasing based on what their friends on Facebook or MySpace tell them. They use aggregators like FriendFeed (www.friendfeed.com) or social sites like Yelp to find out where to go tonight or the best place to get a bargain handbag or how to make a complex purchase. "What the other companies are doing doesn't mean squat to them."

Michael made the point that his kids and many others are moving to control their own experiences outside the channels provided by the company, and this is an inevitable march. These peer-to-peer relationships, the external communities not in the control of the business, are creating a new set of expectations which he identified as:

► The 24/7 availability of services

► The desire by the customer to be needed, recognized

► The need to have access to channels for dialogue with the company, so that the customer feels as if they have some control.

► The customers need to not only know that you have domain expertise, but to have access to it.

The optimal enterprise here would not be the current one, which Michael called the function-driven enterprise, but instead the intent-driven enterprise. This is a company that not only knows what I want, but also knows my intent, the reasons why I want what I want, and what I will be interested in down the road—knowledge they got from me, Señor Customer. In other words, the company understands the context. Michael then identified the top functionality requirements for the intent-driven enterprise:

▶ It is in sync with evolving needs.

▶ It engages community opinions.

▶ It is reliable and trustworthy.

▶ It allows independent ratings.

▶ It uses "like type" comparisons (once again, "someone like me").

Because this is so complex, success can't be defined as good "sub-optimal" results (good marketing, good sales, good service, etc.) but has to be defined as the engagement of an integrated ecosystem made available to the customer.

Michael defined what I would call a perceptual model for the future customer. He said the customer had to have the illusion of free will, of the availability of multiple paths for exploration, and of the means to achieve several goals with the business. The business reality is that the paths are probably predetermined, there is one process that is truly available, and one goal is there for the customer. Michael wasn't advocating this; he was saying that's what the business reality is and probably will continue to be. This is very much the same concept in a somewhat different framework that Joe Pine II advocates in *Authenticity: What Consumers Really Want,* which is fake-real in a manner of speaking. My take on this is more benign since I don't think that fake *anything* is what needs to happen. But, as I said before, you don't need to own luxury, you need to feel luxurious. You know the old saying, "Whatever floats your boat"? That's what I mean, but the business has to see it from the perspective of what it costs them to make the boat the customer wants to float, and no one in their right mind can argue this is wrong. I do think there is an optimal state possible, though. The engagement of the entire ecosystem of the company for the customers opens up options that give them increased degrees of freedom while at the same time allowing the enterprise to execute its business plan successfully—a real-real collaboration, not fake-real. There are a lot of forces involved in an ecosystem, not just one company and one customer, but multiple value chains associated with either the customer or the enterprise. What is abundantly clear with the intent-driven enterprise is that business value and customer value are two very different ideas that have to work in conjunction for both the customer to get what he/she wants and the business to get what it wants. That can get complex, but it can also be as simple as understanding how Michael's daughters listen to their friends on Facebook. Simple. But not easy.

I think we're making progress. Before we wrap this chapter up with a conversation with Michael on his three takeaways for the intent-driven enterprise, let's look back and look ahead.

We're cool with the reasons why Social CRM is necessary, the definition of what it is from key industry leaders and of course from me. We've locked and loaded the customer's reasons for their desire for a new paradigm—which is their personal experience—and briefly explored what the internal guts of an enterprise have to look like to make that experience happen. Now, we have the foundation for a new business model. The only way to characterize this: a methodical rollercoaster. I'll leave you to interpret that.

Now, once Michael and you are done chatting, I'm going to take it to the next level—a look at the social media and social networks and what they mean to CRM engagement strategies. That will keep us busy for several chapters. So, talk to Michael, then go have lunch. I'll see you in about an hour or so.

Mini-Conversation with Michael Maoz

I've already introduced Michael Maoz to you personally. He is a Distinguished Analyst at Gartner Research, with a focus on customer-centric technologies and processes. He was one of the first to write about social networks, beginning in 2004. He has 20 years of international business and technology experience in Asia, Europe, and the United States.

> That is not what I meant at all.
> That is not it, at all.
> —"The Love Song of J. Alfred Prufrock," T. S. Eliot

Business leaders anguish over the question of how to better serve customers, only to find the customer's experience falls far short of expectations. Our analysis of business processes over the past ten years points to two basic problems. The first is a failure to determine and understand the customer's overall intentions in engaging the business or organization. The second is a lack of alignment between IT and the lines of business to identify and act upon the customer's most likely intentions during an interaction. The failure to improve processes and technologies so that an organization can respond to a customer's intentions inhibits business growth. And what may be even worse for the business: the emergence of Internet-based social networks has given customers a way to share their bad experiences with a global community.

Three Takeaways

1. *Businesses exist to serve customers, and usually they are required to do so at the optimal profit level. Yet IT spending does not map directly to this goal, and few organizations can claim to understand a customer's intent during an interaction. To better align IT project selection with the core business value of serving the customer, make IT an embedded part of the business units and functions. That means that IT, sponsored by the CEO and supported by the heads of marketing and sales, will define, measure, and gain alignment between the enterprise's intent and the customer's intent.*

2. *Innovative businesses and other organizations already are moving beyond business intelligence and CRM software, and beginning to provide social networking tools to capture and respond to the customer's intentions and experiences:*

▶ *Providing tools to allow customers and non-customers to "people map"—to find people or businesses with similar interests or skills to solve problems or address opportunities.*

▶ *Encouraging Facebook communities where opinions or notes about the business or a product might be shared.*

▶ *Providing the option for a customer to complete a structured, opt-in, confidential survey of their wants and needs. Such survey information is dynamic and updatable, and provides the business with a way of refining how it supports customers and their evolving needs.*

▶ *Creating managed, permission-based Internet communities where customers can share ideas on how to improve the business, products, and services.*

▶ *Supporting Twitter, outbound SMS messaging, and RSS feeds to stay in touch and in tune with the customer.*

▶ *Providing visualization and analytical tools to view the digital path by which each customer travels to find information, make a purchase, or receive service.*

3. *To be an intent-driven organization, you must clearly understand the strategies and tactics used to engage customers at every level. Organizations must learn to measure the extent to which the brand promise is being upheld across all interaction channels. The best companies already carefully select and reselect metrics for identifying happy/unhappy customers and the tiny details that turn them off. Increasingly, CIOs are refusing to fund projects that cannot demonstrate an improvement to customer-facing processes. They identify critical interaction points, and define the roles and processes best suited to achieve the interaction goals. Keep in mind that vendors don't fully grasp the concept of customer intent or real-time insight, and they do not see it as either a product or a market. It will remain up to the IT and business leaders to push the concept of the intent-driven enterprise.*

Organizations streamlining customer-facing business processes will focus on results, basing efforts on understanding the organization's intentions toward the customer and the customer's likely intentions toward the business. This is particularly true in customer interactions—the moments of truth *where the business either lives up to its promises or fails.* ✱

PART II
So Happy Together:
Collaborating with Your Customers

6

Do You Have the Ring?
Tools for Customer Engagement

*S*ocial CRM is . . . *designed to engage the customer in a collaborative conversation in order to provide mutually beneficial value in a trusted and transparent business environment."*

As interesting as this somewhat abbreviated definition of Social CRM is, it's useless if there is no execution. How do you engage the customer in that conversation? What tools does an enterprise use to make sure there is some way of communicating with the different kinds of people and the different market segments of a company that interest them? Can they handle the customers' drastically altered expectations? What should they do with them once they have them? Who should own them, the company or the customer?

Patience, my pretties, all of that will be answered here.

The Value of Social Media in CRM

Charlene Li, the former Forrester analyst, current President of Altimeter, and co-author (with Josh Bernhoff) of *Groundswell* (well worth reading), defined the use of social computing as "a social structure in which technology puts power in communities, not institutions." Those technologies are the social media applications and the vessels for human participation—the social networks and communities that have begun to redefine the way businesses are looking at working with their customers.

Social media—blogs, podcasts, videocasts, wikis, RSS feeds, social tagging/bookmarking, and to a lesser extent, texting and instant messaging—have been available to consumers for years and they've been using them to communicate with each other. Text messaging has been a staple of communication since 2001. In 2001, there were 17 billion text messages sent; by 2004, there were 500 billion text messages sent; in 2007 it was 1.9 trillion, and that is only going up. According to a research report released in mid-2009 by BuddeComm, the estimate for text messages sent in 2009 is 3 trillion.

But it is only very recently that businesses are beginning to see the value of social media as a means of communicating with customers—and that only because the customers expect that kind of communication. There is a real reluctance to move forward, but the upward pressure of customer demand is pushing IT departments in particular forward to deploy these tools.

Part of the disinclination was simply IT budgetary constraints. For example, as late as June 2008, a Forrester report about the U.S adoption of Web 2.0 technologies found that of 729 IT decision-makers at U.S companies with 500 or more employees, 64 percent of the IT shops wouldn't invest in wikis in 2008 and 69 percent wouldn't invest in blogs; 66 percent had no interest in RSS investment.

The chant keeps getting louder. Statistics are there—Gartner estimated that by early 2009, 50 percent of all corporations will have social software or its components up and running. That hasn't quite happened, but adoption rates are up over last year. But it isn't the numbers that drive it, it is that verbiage which goes, "Customers are going to have the conversation with or without you. Whether or not you give them what they need to have it with you is up to you, fair enterprise."

What Are the Tools?

In this chapter and the next three chapters, we're going to cover the newest and most important tools of Social CRM—the social media and social networks that have been such a hot topic. The more traditional tools and practices will be covered in Part III.

Social Media, Social Networks—I Don't Get It, Do I?

Actually, you do. You're using them, or reading them or commenting on them or even donating through them or seeing them or hearing them or writing on them. A study completed in August 2008 by the Interpublic Universal McCann (UM) unit called "Media in Mind" found that more than half of all adults are relying on at least one of the social media—okay, Web 2.0—platforms for communicating on a regular basis with someone from somewhere. The specific forms of communication are social networks, text messaging, blogging, or some other digital interaction. In fact, in the 18- to 34-year-old bracket, Gen Y, social media is the dominant form of communication according to the study, with—get this—85 percent using Web 2.0 platforms to stay in touch with others. Universal McCann's conclusion, which is correct, is:

> Although age is the driving force behind usage patterns of these technologies, it is clear that a fundamental shift has taken place in all of our lives about what it means to communicate in the 21st century.

This revolution in communication has accelerated at remarkable speed. The same "Media in Mind" report found while in 2007, 5 percent of all Americans were publishing a blog, as of 2008, 10 percent were. The same doubling occurred in the 18- to 34-year-olds, with the rate going from 10 percent to 20 percent. The readership has soared also. We all know that to one degree or another, but what's interesting is the reason that UM figured out:

> We think that's due to the increased use of social networking, and blogs are an integral part of using them. Two years ago, asking people about blogs, people were shaking their heads. I think now it's taking off because social networks are taking off. RSS feeds, which make reading blogs easier, have become an integral part of the way people communicate and exchange content. People may have been doing it before, but may not have realized it. Now they're recognizing it for what it is.

The revolution in customer engagement and Social CRM starts with the revolution in the use of social media.

Social Media . . .

Publishers always want text to fill in the space between headers. I find that a strange and kind of useless convention so consider this minor diatribe as me acceding to the convention. Now to the real stuff.

In General . . .

For starters, what am I calling social media? It varies, really.

Some of the social media are tools, like blogs, wikis, and podcasts. Some of the social media uses are organized around user-generated content (UGC), such as reviews, social tags, social bookmarks, comments, rankings, ratings and photos, and videos. There are even levels of sophistication in the use of particular social media. For example, you can use tags as referenceable categories or you can use them for the creation of folksonomies—organic tag groups, which, oddly, can simplify the tags. In other words, what you can call social media vary widely in both types and the levels of sophistication with which they are applied. That's why it's not so simple.

In early 2008, Forrester Research did a study of 333 interactive marketers of either midsize or large corporations on their interactive spending levels for 2008 despite poor economic conditions. The results are telling:

▶ Increase investment in social networks – 48 percent

▶ Increase investment in user-generated content – 42 percent

▶ Increase investment in e-mail marketing – 41 percent

▶ Increase investment in blogging – 40 percent

▶ Increase investment in search marketing – 38 percent

Yet only 10 percent are increasing spending on display ads and 40 percent will cut back spending on the same.

You could infer from this data that we are in the somewhat early stages of an exodus from the world of traditional marketing—and to some extent you'd be right. But don't fall for the trap here. This doesn't mean much more than companies are becoming aware that they have to change how they are interacting with customers. They aren't necessarily doing it.

In fact, most of them aren't doing it, even if they're considering what their options are. Kathleen Reidy of the technology analyst firm The 451 Group released a study at the end of May 2008 that polled 2,081 IT and business professionals. She found that when it came to the use of social media (which was defined for the purposes of the report as blogs, wikis, and social networks) only 24 percent of the respondents were using the social software needed to build or use those communication media.

But then there's this third study. In February 2008, IDC found that 14 percent of all the enterprises polled already had social networks and by year end that number was expected to be an inverse 41 percent—meaning that white label (private label) social networks (and communities) entered the mainstream.

So whom to believe? All of them and none of them. First, don't be fooled by the 451 Group number. If 24 percent were using social media, that's about 24 percent more than three years ago. If 41 percent had social networks by the end of 2009, that is a 300 percent increase within the year itself. The Forrester Research indicates a willingness to keep spending on it—except for IT departments.

In Brief . . .

I'm going to handhold you through this chapter. These social tools, technologies, and features can be confusing and are not at all clearly a part of a traditional CRM strategy. Of course, we're not talking about a traditional CRM strategy in this book, so that's understandable.

In this section, I'm going to give you brief *business* definitions, just mention some of the best tools available for the specific media and give you a short use case for Social CRM. For each tool, a short list will summarize its upside and downside. The idea is to get acquainted with these tools. The social tools most important for CRM also have their own chapters in the book—blogs, wikis, and social networks—but by the end of this chapter you'll have at least enough acquaintance with them to incorporate them into your engagement strategy.

One reminder before we go on: These are tools. They are not substitutes for engagements with customers; they are not substitutes for strategy. They have their own benefits and problems, and they should be used judiciously and not just because they are there or are cool.

You think that's ridiculous? A little history, maestro. Play that funky music, tech boy.

The biggest battle those of us immersed in the world of CRM have had to fight was with our clients. Why? Because the vast majority, without a scintilla of exaggeration or irony, saw and still see CRM as a technology. Despite the protestations by many that CRM is a strategy enabled by technology, the myth of "CRM the technology" persisted to the point that practitioners would cripple themselves by implementing CRM before they even had a plan for their customers.

In retrospect, part of the problem was that despite all the protestations of the industry, for the most part it consists of software and SaaS vendors—and they wanted to (and still want to) sell their products and services to their customers. As the good old Edelman Trust Barometer for 2008 indicated, they are also in the most trusted industry of all—high tech. So even when the vendors would say, "CRM is not about software; it's all about people," let's just say they weren't trying to sell you people the following morning.

Do you think that mindset has changed much in the past three years? Nope. Not a bit. Realistically, the inclination businesses have is to throw tools and technology at what are human issues and hope they automate the issues out of existence.

Notwithstanding, there is a growing recognition that beneficial customer interactions are governed by trust, transparency, and personalized experiences. Four years ago, the answer was to throw sales, marketing, and customer service applications at the interactions. Now the answer seems to be that you should throw blogs, wikis, and social networks at the interactions—perhaps with some sales, marketing, and customer service applications.

This is, once again, the wrong approach. Take my advice, please. These are tools that are meant to be used as enablers, not drivers, and more to the point, not substitutes for anything at all, except maybe sugar.

The inclination to use the tools is going to be because:

▶ Everyone else is.

▶ They are really cool and fun to play with.

▶ As drivers, they are an apparently easy out for developing a customer engagement strategy. Truly, that thinking will cost you big time.

Pretty much like everything else in life, if the tools have real value, then they are worth using. Not that complicated, really. For example, if your customers are senior citizens over 75, it is likely those tools would be a useless addition to your engagement arsenal, no matter how much fun they might be for you to play with.

Now, grab my hand and let's start walking.

Blogs

Blogs are the most prevalent form of social media and the most mature. They are among the best entry points for an incremental social media plan because they are the easiest to understand and have the most commonly available tools. But that doesn't make them easy to do in a corporate environment. Because they are still viewed somewhat uneasily, there are only 12.2 percent (61) of the Fortune 500 blogging as of April 2009 according to the Fortune 500 Business Blogging wiki (www.socialtext.net/bizblogs/). That's not so good.

Definition

Most simply, a blog is a web-based journal. It is a running account of events or thoughts or ideas that can be authored by one person or sometimes multiple people. Typically it is used by businesses for branding or to reach out to customers or internally to discuss ideas or as a team document. The business blog is defined typically by a specific focus, subject matter expertise, or a particular ongoing message or environment that the company either wants to push or allows to happen. Chapter 7 will cover blogs in a great deal of detail.

Best Tools

There are two companies that are the undisputed leaders of blogging tools—Six Apart and Word Press. Each of them has millions of adherents; each has its own strengths and weaknesses. Word Press is more laser focused on being a platform for blogging, while Six Apart's central products, Movable Type and to a lesser extent its hosted version, Typepad, are more in the vein of a product set built to the center of a community platform—a social publishing platform. Six Apart and Movable Type are my Superstah! choice in Chapter 7. With my criteria being what is most representative of Social CRM and the chapter, Six Apart was the hands-down victor. Check it out. Just come back when you're done. I'll wait.

CRM Use Case

There are multiple uses for blogs in an engagement strategy:

▶ They offer direct access to senior management for customers (such as General Motors FastLane, http://fastlane.gmblogs.com).

▶ They are a place for customers to collaborate on ideas (such as MyStarbucks Ideas, http://mystarbucksideas.com).

▶ They provide a place to deal with customer service issues that invites customers to help solve problems. (For example, Comcast Cares is a Twitter microblogging outreach site, http://twitter.com/comcastcares. More in Chapter 7 on Twitter.)

▶ They offer a way to link to and collaborate with business partners and sales channels (such as Dell Channel, http://direct2dell.com/channel).

Blogs Upside

▶ They encourage conversation with customers and employees.

▶ They break down social/corporate barriers—make the previously inaccessible, accessible.

▶ They provide a relatively nonintrusive place for customers to present ideas without fear.

▶ They become a forum to answer questions within hours that would otherwise take weeks.

▶ They can be a huge plus for the company's brand image.

Blogs Downside

▶ They can inadvertently expose you to liability.

▶ They can be a public relations nightmare if perceived as inauthentic.

▶ They have had issues with IT perceiving it as a security problem—though less than in the past.

▶ They can be perceived as hype if the voice of the blogger(s) doesn't come through clearly.

▶ They can cost quite a bit if you consider labor time.

Podcasts

Podcasts are odd. They can provide a truly viable platform for content delivery and a real opportunity for unique branding. At the same time, while there are millions of podcasts and hundreds of millions of episodes, their adoption as a business tool is erratic.

DEFINITION

A podcast is an audio file that uses RSS (Really Simple Syndication) to distribute the broadcast to subscribers or allow them to download it to computers or portable music devices. The content is usually specific to an interest or some other kind of theme. (More on podcasting in Chapter 7.)

BEST TOOLS

There are no specifically great enterprise-level podcasting creation tools. Any major music editor such as Bias Peak Pro (Mac) or Adobe Audition (PC) will work well with the creation and editing of a podcast. Most of the latest incarnations incorporate podcast publishing tools as well. Good microphones (the Electrovoice RE20 is a popular choice for professional use) and good mixers (such as Mackie mixers) are imperative and it can go up from there.

CRM USE CASE

Podcasts have certain somewhat limited but important advantages:

▶ They are superb learning tools (see MIT OpenCourseWare programs, http://ocw.mit.edu/OcwWeb/web/courses/av/).

▶ They can support a marketing effort that is focused around mindshare and thought leadership (such as Motorola Enterprise Group—see an interview with Eduardo Conrado of Motorola on this subject at www.marketingprofs.com/7/eduardo-conrado-using-thought-leadership-to-position-motorola-dunay.asp).

▶ They are useful for internal education and for do-it-yourself information (such as Cleveland Clinic's Center for Continuing Education, www.clevelandclinicmeded.com/online/podcasts/).

▶ They reach tech-friendly (not even savvy) audiences that might not otherwise be reached. (Just look at iTunes' available podcasts. You'll get the idea.)

PODCASTS UPSIDE

▶ Because they are audio or video files, attention paid to the material is considerably higher—all the standard studies on how much people remember when dynamic rich media presentations are done versus static PowerPoint presentations apply.

► Podcasts (video and audio) encourage different types of learning, and in portable formats so the listener can control their learning experience—thus increasing both information retention and improving brand image and reputation of the company because the company is providing the capabilities.

► The enterprise manages the podcast production process from end to end so that the company has enormous command over the presentation and choice of material they make available and the frequency and length of the episodes.

PODCASTS DOWNSIDE

► Podcasts can be labor intensive and, thus, time sucking.

► Even though podcasts are expected to be informal and authentic, there is an expectation of professional production values—driving up the costs of the effort.

► Inconsistency in length or frequency, not just bad content, is often punished by listeners by leaving the show.

Enterprise Wikis

I'm devoting a short but entire chapter to wikis (Chapter 8), but in the spirit of this chapter, here we go. I'm not dealing with community-based wikis here but only the pertinent type of wiki—the enterprise wiki.

DEFINITION

I'm going to use the Wikipedia definition of wikis, mostly for the tasty irony of doing that:

A wiki is a collection of web pages designed to enable anyone who accesses it to contribute or modify content, using a simplified markup language. Wikis are often used to create collaborative websites and to power community websites. The collaborative encyclopedia, Wikipedia, is one of the best-known wikis. Wikis are used in business to provide intranets and Knowledge Management systems.

This definition is actually pretty lousy on its own. So I'm going to throw in the Wikipedia definition for corporate wiki:

A corporate wiki is a wiki used in a corporate (or organizational) context, especially to enhance internal knowledge sharing. Wikis are increasingly used internally by companies and public sector organizations, some as prominent as Adobe Systems, Intel, Microsoft, and the FBI. Depending on the size of a corporation, they may add to or replace centrally managed content management systems. Their decentralized nature allows them, in theory, to disseminate needed information across an organization faster and cheaper than a centrally controlled knowledge repository. Wikis might also be used for project management (better collaboration) and even marketing purposes (wikis for customers). Better.

Best Tools

There are dozens of free and inexpensive wiki applications available to anyone who cares to use them. Most of them are *not* industrial strength and I would be loath to recommend them. If still interested, there is a wiki on wiki software (once again, striking while the irony is hot) that you can find at www.wikimatrix.org. There are several applications that will be discussed in more detail in Chapter 8. The clear pack chief is Socialtext (www.socialtext.com), which is also my Superstah! winner for Chapter 8. For small businesses, I would recommend PBworks (www.pbworks.com), which went from cheap to expensive in 2009, but is still good, and Wetpaint (www.wetpaint.com), two hosted wiki services. Again, wait until Chapter 8. Patience.

CRM Use Case

▶ Wikis drive collaboration between customers and employees which in turn drives innovation (IBM, Innovation Jams).

▶ They are a uniquely flexible tool for project management (Qlimited, www.socialtext.com/customers/case-studies/qltd/).

▶ They can be a repository for a manageable yet still dynamic knowledge base and even an on-demand content delivery system (ZohoCRM Wiki, http://zohocrm.wiki.zoho.com/).

▶ They allow you to tap external resources for knowledge and insight (SugarCRM's Sugar Developer Wiki, www.sugarcrm.com/wiki/index.php?title=Sugar_Developer_Wiki).

WIKI UPSIDE

▶ There are numerous stories about increased speed of innovation and collaboration from wikis—internal, external, and both.

▶ Wikis constitute a dynamic tool that is controlled by its users.

▶ Technology companies are making serious strides to integrate wikis into the enterprise system and Web 2.0 tools (e.g., social tagging) via standard web services, making it less of a headache for IT.

▶ Enterprise-level wiki technology allows all the necessary security, scalability, and administrative control.

WIKI DOWNSIDE

▶ There are no guarantees about the veracity of the material provided.

▶ Adoption is often slow.

▶ Open editing leaves some susceptibility to serious cyber-attack. Some.

There isn't much else wrong, really.

Social Tagging and Folksonomies

Social tagging is something you see ubiquitously—most often on the social sites that allow you to share content such as YouTube, Facebook, Flickr, or Slideshare. But when it comes to both clear differentiation between it and taxonomies or categories, and when it comes to business value, it often seems to be much murkier. Between this section and the mini-conversation with Thomas Vander Wal late in this chapter, you should be able to not only understand the difference but figure out the business value. If not, I will cry because I will have failed. I hate failing. Don't make me cry.

DEFINITION

A folksonomy—a term coined by Thomas Vander Wal—is a socially constructed classification scheme, unlike a taxonomy, which is a hierarchically constructed one. The difference is that when hierarchically constructed, the constraints of the scheme—the category you are given—is imposed on you and you are forced into choosing the category that's the least of evils. A folksonomy uses social tags—keywords that you as a consumer or producer of content can create. This is not like the categories you are used to and the taxonomies that organize them.

For instance, you're adding an entry to a baseball wiki (what else?) and the category imposed is "NY Yankees." Even though your real subject is the Mickey Mantle 1956 Triple Crown, you are going to have to use "NY Yankees." So all generic information and specific information about the Yankees and players and events are lumped under this one category, which loses any capability to provide rich insights. If it's hyperlinked, it might link you up to someone who has an interest in only Don Mattingly's eight consecutive game home run streak.

However, if you tag it "Yankees," "Mickey Mantle," "1956 Triple Crown," or a string that encompasses all of those elements:

▶ It provides much richer insight into what is of interest to you.

▶ It allows you to find the other Mickey Mantle lovers out there (me and probably the entirety of all living baby boomers from NY).

Best Tools

Social tagging tools may seem like a weird idea, since social tagging is pretty much just an advanced set of hyperlinks, but a Mountain View, California, company, Connectbeam, has an integrated appliance with a sophisticated social tagging engine. On the software side, so does IBM's Lotus Connections (more at the end of this chapter).

Social Tagging Use Case

▶ Tagging fosters the growth of communities organized around common interests and viewpoints (IBM and Oracle has internal communities for this—sorry, no URLs).

▶ Tagging gives you the ability to do highly focused or broad-reaching topical research (Slideshare, www.slideshare.net).

▶ Looking at tags or tag clouds provides valuable insight into how taggers qua customers are thinking.

SOCIAL TAGGING UPSIDE

▶ Tags can be shared—knowledge through aggregation. Clay Shirky (www.shirky.com), author of *Here Comes Everybody*, calls it market logic—"individual motivation, group value."

▶ That aggregation provides information about the specific interests of the individuals doing the tagging and the descriptors they use provide insight into their thinking. This is a rich source of knowledge that no traditional CRM system has ever had at its disposal—nor are they programmed to capture it.

▶ Meaningful concepts for individuals are in their own vernacular and thus highlight what can be important to specific customers in their own metaphor. Once again, out of the scope of traditional customer analytics or business intelligence.

SOCIAL TAGGING DOWNSIDE

▶ The tags can provide inaccurate information because they are perceived as poorly worded or misleading or are at different levels of specificity. So for example someone might tag something "homes" and someone else tag the same thing "neighborhood." Or someone might tag something "old house" and someone might tag it "18th century Georgian mansion."

▶ Traditional indexing doesn't work well with social tagging. Syntax and rules structures are antithetical.

▶ Different behavior on different days can alter the nomenclature used in the social tagging. So if I'm in a good mood, I might tag a photo I'm uploading to Flickr, "sunny day in Barcelona," but if the next day I'm in a bad mood, I might tag the same photo, "Barcelona partially cloudy." The tags are personal but not necessarily precise to someone trying to decipher them.

Social Bookmarking

This is a derivation of social tagging that's focused around sharing and annotating different URLs and content associated with that.

DEFINITION

Social bookmarking is the sharing of information typically through hyperlinked site references. For example, I can use the outstanding social bookmarking tool, Diigo (www.diigo.com), to highlight content on a web page and then tag the URL, the name of the content, and some or all of the content—and annotate the content. Then I can either keep it privately or share it with all my friends, the public, or a specific group that I'm a part of, while inviting comments to the content I tagged or the annotations I wrote.

Best Tools

The best enterprise-level tool for social bookmarking is IBM's Lotus Connection, which I cover in detail below. They call their social bookmarks "dogears." Not my name for it. Don't shoot the messenger.

Social Bookmarking Use Case

▶ It can be used for team collaboration.

▶ It can be used for research.

▶ It can engage communities and special groups in sharing knowledge and best practices.

▶ It can be used for customer service knowledge bases so that the customer's actual knowledge can easily be incorporated into the company's best practices.

Social Bookmarking Upside

▶ The bookmarks can be aggregated and shared and commented on—which provides an organic community of like-interested people who are engaged to create an outcome.

▶ Here's one from social media guru Chris Brogan (his twitter address is http://twitter.com/chrisbrogan): "Social bookmarking means that entire groups can learn of new articles, tools, and other web properties, instead of leaving them all on one machine, one browser, for one human."

Social Bookmarking Downside

▶ The aggregated bookmarks can get cluttered with meaningless or useless detritus without some self-policing and constraint going on.

▶ Can be complex to organize and maintain as the number of bookmarks increases.

Social Search

This is a new area that's been around. That contradiction is actually the reason why there is a lot of promise for social search, but at this stage, the CRM-related use cases are primarily related to sales, though certainly there are going to be many others as it evolves.

DEFINITION

We all know what "search" means, since I doubt that anyone reading this hasn't Googled something, but social search involves more than that. On the one hand, Google search provides a somewhat disorganized but always important useful and fast (a.k.a. down and dirty) way of getting what you need. But social search takes it a step further because, when used appropriately, it can combine corporate structured data with external unstructured data, such as profile information from Facebook or customer feedback from external forums, and make it into useful knowledge.

BEST TOOLS

Please don't confuse the tools. There are enterprise search tools like Coveo (www.coveo.com), which can find CRM data that you have internally and tie it to ERP data so that, for example, you can not only see the sales history of a customer but also the payment history. There are also social search tools that are focused on the consumer side like Retrevo (www.retrevo.com), which finds consumer electronics products and then conveniently breaks out its search results into information buckets like Forums & Blogs, Reviews & Articles, Manufacturer's Info, and Shopping so that you find what you want—and it even has tag clouds.

But those aren't what we're talking about here. Companies like SAP have strong social search engines that can do this. If it's sales-related data, the Oracle Sales Prospector application has serious capabilities (more on this in Chapter 12). On the standalone side, InsideView (www.insideview.com) has a product that combines social search and some analytics called SalesView Team (the enterprise version of SalesView) that provides you with not only the corporate data that you expect from Reuters or Hoovers, but also information like who has moved to another company, who has been promoted, what acquisitions are made—and has integrated it into the respective salesforce .com or SugarCRM dashboards, among others.

Social Search Use Case

▶ It can deliver not only the normal static data from Hoover's and so on, but also business intelligence from social networks and other less standard sites that can decrease the lead to closing cycle time (such as Rearden Commerce using SalesView).

▶ It mines internal and external data that will provide you with the insights you need to decide what the best product mix and approach would be toward a prospective customer (for example, Breg, Inc., using Oracle Sales Prospector).

Social Search Upside

▶ The sales data is dynamic and provides information that gives you insight into a lead, prospect, or existing customer.

▶ The information is integrated into your CRM dashboard and the transactional databases.

▶ The tools are relatively easy to use and take little training to be up and running without a master's degree in information technology.

Social Search Downside

▶ The information is substituted for judgment—a not-infrequent problem with social search.

▶ The search is inaccurate due to the terms defined by the searcher. Wrong decisions made based on the information that was right in the context of the wrong search—if you get what I mean.

Special Notes

There are a few things that bear mentioning—either due to their ubiquity or their importance they are given coverage elsewhere at length, but still need to be noted here.

User-Generated Content (UGC)

When I was developing the outline for this book, up until the final iteration and even while already writing, I had considered a separate chapter on user-generated content (UGC). In case you've only recently been awakened by the kiss of a handsome prince (or gorgeous princess, depending on your inclination), UGC is the actual content being created by the customers/constituents/members—in other words, human beings—who are then sharing that content with others, often through communities, social networks, websites, or even cellphone transmissions.

The forms UGC takes are almost endless. Here is a partial, by no means conclusive, list to give you a taste:

▶ Comments on blogs and social review sites (such as Yelp, www .yelp.com)

▶ Ratings

▶ Rankings

▶ Video

▶ Audio

▶ Social tags

▶ Social bookmarks

▶ Wiki text—original or modification

If you think about it, much of this kind of content has been around since Babylon and Mesopotamia. After all, if you're an over-50 baby boomer, I'm sure you remember 8MM movie reels? No? The ones that show you and your annoying little sister at the beach bouncing beach balls off of each other's heads? Yep. Those.

The key difference between the 1958 analog video and the 2009 user-generated digital video is that the latter is shared with others and can be embedded on others' sites. Sharing is why UGC is so important and so prevalent. For example, there is a site powered by Neighborhood America's enterprise social network engine (see Chapter 9) at Home and Garden TV (HGTV). It's called *Rate Your Room*. The idea is that an interested party can upload photos of their newly refurbished, newly decorated, or recently built kitchen, bedroom, patio, or whatever they care to. They are open to being rated from 1 to 5 stars and commented on by other visitors to the site who have registered. Those that have the highest rank through the ratings are driven to the most visible positions on the site. This has proven to be so popular that page views on the HGTV website went up from thousands prior to the creation of *Rate Your Room* to millions shortly thereafter.

This sharing of content controlled by the creator of the content, and content that can be communicated and created on demand, is the power of UGC and one of the most potent reasons for using that power as part of a Social CRM strategy.

I realized that this is such a ubiquitous phenomenon that it doesn't pay to separate it into a chapter of its own. It permeates everything. In fact, you could make the case that the whole book is UGC. I did write it.

Social CRM = Social CRM Strategy, Not Just Tools

Customer strategies just a few years ago were primarily based around internal factors. What kind of processes do we need to allow us to reach out to the customer more often and with greater effectiveness? What kind of tools do we need to make sure we have an accurate record of our individual customers' activities so we can develop programs or campaigns that will be optimal for varying groups or, if really sophisticated, individuals? What do we do to increase the customer's commitment to us? Transactional strategies ruled the day. But as we will comprehensively see in Chapter 17, the strategies have moved from transactional to interactional. That means the involvement of customers isn't just important—it's vital to how you improve customer commitment and thus improve your acquisition and retention of customers.

All the tools we discussed above can play a role in the execution of your strategy. Note two things, though—they are tools and I said "can" not "will" play a role. Their purpose is to provide communication pipelines with your customers so you can have a conversation with them regularly. But each tool needs to be evaluated the same way you evaluated the internal CRM tools—though if past practices I have to deal with are any indicator, maybe that's not a smart thing for me to say. Actually, first you need a purpose. Then and only then, you select the tools that fulfill that purpose. Don't do what so many traditional CRM implementations did—buy the tools and try to create a purpose (otherwise known as an excuse for using them).

Much more later on this, but now let's look at what I think is the best integrated enterprise social toolset out there. Music, please. Perhaps a little of indie rock band Criteria's "Connections":

And it's rational that it's logical
There is no point in denying
Give yourself a chance, you might like it
We must make connections
We must make connections
We must make connections
We must make connections

Let's hear it for our Superstah! Lotus Connections!

Superstah! Lotus Connections

Years ago, I spent much of my time building Lotus Notes practices. For those of you who don't know what I mean, I mean that I built groups within my company that were Lotus Notes developers, consultants, and so on. For those of you who don't know what Lotus Notes was (and is), in my opinion it was the most misunderstood platform in history and was usually used as either a database tool or an e-mail program. Around 1995, IBM bought Lotus, and Lotus receded into the IBM netherworlds to emerge only about two years ago as the division that ran IBM's collaboration services. But they weren't doing just Lotus Notes on the client side and Lotus Domino on the server side. In 2007, they announced a social software suite called Lotus Connections—the sole social software (not CRM) suite that exists fully integrated. There was a second, short-lived attempt at one called Take 2, which was umbrellaed by Intel but was a group of best-of-breed tools such as Socialtext (see Chapter 8) and Six Apart's Movable Type (see Chapter 7) that were loosely coherent, with integration coming from the web services that they each were built on.

But version 1 had a few problems—a lack of some features and functions not worth going into here because version 2 is out, and it is easily best of class when it comes to integrated social software suites— and not just because it's the only one. This is our Superstah! for this chapter, without question.

Lotus Connections – Mission 21st Century

I had the good fortune to chat with Carol Jones, one of 60 IBM Fellows (out of 38,000 plus employees) and the creator of Lotus Connections. She described to me what they did to determine what to include in the creation of Lotus Connections:

> When we decided [in 2005] that we wanted to develop a social software suite, rather than guess at it, we decided to go somewhere that the tools were being used and the need was there. We went around IBM because we were using these tools all over the company. We wanted to find out what was really popular, and what we found was that there were several tools that were popular because they helped people communicate better. Our observations helped us figure this out.

So going to the source, IBM employees, was the foundation for the creation of this social suite—one that I recommend you take a serious look at if you're looking for a single suite. What is far more fascinating was Carol's view on the purpose of the suite, the mission for its existence:

> *I often think of all this stuff as serendipity. But it's not really. We had people using the tools and it made sense for us to figure out not just what tools but why they were using them. Our perspective has always been that we're trying to engineer accidents. We're trying to create better odds for these knowledge accidents to occur, when just the right people connect. We do that by providing the tools and avenues for those combinations of people to come together.*

Suite Features and Functions

I'm going to spend a bit more time with this suite than a lot of the other applications throughout the book because, aside from its "Super-stah!" status, it is an excellent representation of the kinds of enterprise-level features and functions you have to be looking for (with that notable omission later) when you start thinking through your investment in the social CRM technologies you're going to be playing with. First, a good view of what they have (Figure 6-1).

Figure 6-1: This is a typical business profile, aimed at a professional audience. (Source: IBM)

Profiles

This is one of the core components of the suite. It was originally developed because of the creakiness of the internal IBM application Blue Pages, which tracked employee activities in an HR sort of way. But this is far beyond even the profiles of Facebook or LinkedIn in the way it deals with its profiles. What makes it stand out is that it incorporates an integrated approach to profiles.

Typically, as those of you on Facebook or LinkedIn (and others) might know, you create your own profile, provide basic user information, upload a photo, and then identify your specialized interests and tag them. The end.

The Lotus Connections profile is far richer and designed specifically for enterprises, not consumer-side social networks. Not only does it take all that rich information you've provided, which you control, but it adds some aggregation capabilities that you won't find in standard profiles, such as the accounts/customers you work with and the communities you're engaged with. Even more robust than that, it links the part of the profile you own to your human resources–controlled information—your job description, your availability within the confines of your enterprise, your expertise, your history with the company (such as what you've produced), what projects you're working on, your company-sponsored training. It also covers reporting structure, department, and location (including time zone). The profile is not only richer but vastly more accessible. Plus if you care to, you can create customer membership communities (see below) that use standard profiles à la Facebook.

It's also customizable. For example, you can create personas or types (whatever you want to call them—I don't care nor do the conventions of the application), such as full-time employees who will show their reporting chain or consultants who have no reporting chain.

Imagine this scenario:

I need to find some expertise that's available in a specific domain— say someone to help me develop a new social networking feature set. I can use social tags to not only find the expertise but to find the *available* expertise within the company and to see when and what they are doing. Plus I have the ability to then query them and their manager (who is part of this Lotus Connections profile—but wouldn't be if it were a Facebook clone) and get the time set and the work done.

The initial version's major weakness was the lack of social tagging. The new version includes social tagging. You can tag yourself or someone else. What's very cool here is that you can display the tags as a tag cloud (more on these in Chapter 8) or a list—your coolness quotient choice (guess which is the cooler way?)—on the individual's Profiles page, which means you can be found fast if you are associated with the search topic.

If you tag someone else, these colleagues' (though a tag doesn't necessarily create a collegial situation) tags can be used to have your home page track their feeds with new bookmarks and blog entries.

Communities

These are effectively "group profiles," according to Carol Jones. What you can do with a singular profile you can do with a community—meaning access expertise, find collaborators, tag information, and communicate via e-mail, web browser, or in deference to their own product, Lotus Sametime. As with profiles, you can create your own bookmarks (the Beamers call them "dogears") and carry out activities—more on that later. These are communities of interest and practice, just like others out there—with forums that can use threaded discussion to have conversations on topics of interest. Most important, especially in light of their big whole, the Communities component allows integration with supported wikis so that any wiki operating with web standards will be able to be accessed, shared, and edited through the community it is associated with.

One final cool feature of this component comes when you buy licenses to Lotus Sametime Advanced—their instant messaging client. You can start a real-time chat from within a discussion thread in a user group within a community (you push the first valve down, the music goes round and around . . .) *and* you can capture the chat for viewing later.

Blogs

This is blogging within the corporate firewall. What makes this interesting is that it's not just a tool for outreach to customers, it's often the way that younger employees prefer to communicate. Some, according to Carol Jones, see it as a way to record their career. So this is a strongly customizable tool, that "errs to the geeky side. It's not high on aesthetics." But the administrative features are strong. This is probably the weakest feature of the entire suite, but still can do the job.

Dogears

You know what a dogear is, don't you? That's when you mark a page of a book by bending a corner of it down onto the page. Why do they call it a dogear? I have no idear—I mean, idea. In cyber-parlance, this is a bookmark. This component is actually one of the most interesting and has the best name. The idea is that you can bookmark something interesting, ranging from a piece of web content to an internal memorandum, and then share the bookmark with someone of like interests—which is determined by the profiles and communities that are extant to the company. This opens up the means to discover other bookmarks qualified by those of similar interest. So if I dogear a web page that is about "Loving the New York Yankees" I can then share that and find out that someone who accessed that particular dogear had four of their own dogears on the same topic, right at the point of the bookmark. So not only do I have access to the content, I know from whence it came.

The navigational choices are extensive too—tags, links, individual profiles. Plus I can multitask (oh boy! my favorite thing in the world to do) by adding a single bookmark that will be part of dogears, activities, and communities simultaneously. As new ones come up they can be accessed through an RSS feed.

The key to this component is the ease of tagging that it provides. When you tag something it actually prompts you ("it" being the tagging deity). So for example, if I type "CRM" as a tag, up pops other places that CRM appears as a tag and the other tags that the CRM tagged piece has attached—so context and relationships make this a rich experience.

Activities

In Chapter 9, you're going to see a discussion of what I'm calling "outcome-based social networks" based on a conversation I had with . . . you'll see. These are social networks that exist for a single purpose that, when fulfilled, ends the useful life of the social network. They are tactical in nature since, really, you could define any social network that way if you chose to. What IBM/Lotus Connections does here is exactly that. These are short-term collaborative efforts that are put together for a specific tactical reason—such as a project. Let's say you were writing a journal article with two other authors. The article's subject was privacy, and therefore it had to go through your legal department.

It also needed to have facts checked and other related tasks. You would put together an activity around the journal article that would invite you, your fellow authors, a corporate attorney or two, and researchers into the activity. In fact, the IBM Innovation Jam, put together from IBM employees, customers, partners, consultants, and even employee family members to figure out investment strategies, is a perfect example. They were an ad hoc group that was given access to a workspace that would monitor tags, persons involved, date/time stamp, revision history, file type, and so on—a mini-wiki environment that lasted about five months. What made this really amazing was its scale. In its first three days, in this environment, it generated and registered 46,000 ideas with 160,000 participants. But, it ended with the investments that emerged from this effort. The way this works is that as the new activity is carried out, an RSS feed drives knowledge of the activity to the participants—much as PBworks did for me when the CRM 2.0 wiki was edited. I was notified of the changes via e-mail.

When the activity is complete, the group is disbanded, permissions rescinded, and the results archived. Simple and rather neat, don't you think?

But this also leads to the unusual decision that IBM made to not include wikis in the components—or podcasting capabilities—though you can integrate with independent versions of either. While I do think this is easily the best social software suite out there, their use of rich media is a little limited. Luckily the integration capabilities make it less than a major problem.

IBM certainly gets it. Now they can ship it.

MINI-CONVERSATION WITH PAUL GILLIN: THREE KEY ELEMENTS OF A SOCIAL MEDIA STRATEGY

Paul Gillin is a writer, speaker, and online marketing consultant. He specializes in social media and the application of personal publishing to brand awareness and business marketing. Paul is a veteran technology journalist with more than 23 years of editorial leadership experience. His first book, *The New Influencers*, was published in 2007 and his second book, *Secrets of Social Media Marketing*, was released in the fall of 2008. His website is www.gillin.com and he blogs at www.paulgillin.com.

There are nearly a dozen different kinds of social media tools, ranging from blogs to social networks to shared bookmarking services to video podcasts. Chances are that your objectives require a combination of tools to address different audiences and situations. Here are three underlying principles that apply to all social media interactions.

> ▶ **Start with a strategy**   *Not every tool is appropriate for every purpose. For example, blogs are well-suited for delivering opinions, but not for brainstorming or customer support. Social networks are terrific for customer dialogue but are difficult to focus and control. Online video is a superb way to deliver some kinds of messages, but it lacks interactivity.*
>
> *Start with a strategy and then choose a combination of tools that fit your objective. For example, a product blog combined with a podcast and video series is a good way to introduce a new product. You can then hold a press conference in Second Life.*

> ▶ **Don't talk, listen**   *Customers are sick of being talked at and that's why they've embraced social media as a means to reach out to each other. If you view these tools as another way to force a message down people's throats, you will only make them mad. Social media is all about discussions between people, not messages from institutions. Invite feedback at every opportunity, respond to both compliments and complaints, and demonstrate that you care about what customers think.*

> ▶ **Make the experience personal**   *Designate people from all parts of your organization to engage in social media interactions. Set guidelines and policies but give them freedom to use their own voices. Let them speak in the first person, tell their own stories, and share their own opinions. Show your customers and prospects that there are human beings working at your company. Your customers will form tighter bonds with people than they will with corporations.*✦

Wait! We don't end here. Thomas Vander Wal, the father of folksonomies, has just entered the room and there is a three-takeaway mini-conversation coming along right now.

MINI-CONVERSATION WITH THOMAS VANDER WAL: SOCIAL TAGGING – OLD CONCEPT, NEW SERVICE

Social tagging is not exactly new as a concept, but in practice the focus and modifications to it in the past few years have really twisted it into a service that finally provides good value. In the past, many services included tagging (including free tagging—not just focused on preconceived keywords and categories). The services did not provide for holding onto or account for individual's perspectives and contexts. Tools like del.icio.us started changing this model and providing what many individuals had been asking for for years: their own tagging tools as part of the whole (it was a regular request for CompuServe forum file sharing in the 1990s).

Focus on Letting People Tag as They Need, Manage What They Tag

The change in social tagging that has occurred in the last few years that needs to be adhered to and retained is putting and keeping the focus on the people who are doing the tagging and letting each person who wishes to tag have that opportunity. Each person must have the ability to see and manage what they have tagged. Based on organization priorities and guidelines, what the company shows to others may not be what all the taggers have tagged. Too often tagging is being limited to what is allowed, rather than what the individual needs.

The key is people are putting tags on objects like photos or other products and related information, that help put that object and their relationship to it in their own context, which then provides someone reading the individual's tags a look at the natural perspective of the tagger. This allows the tagger the ability to identify alternate uses, get value, use their own vocabulary and create emergent terms, as well as providing their own bond to the object. This personal bond in their context can help them more easily find the object again when they want and need to so do. This freedom of association provides a great value to the person tagging, but also to those who own, manage, and share the object.

Listening Has Incredible Value

Many social media and social web services encourage engaging the customer. Social tagging has its best value in listening. Not only listening, but really hearing what is being said and learning to embrace the differences of understanding, context, and perspectives. While engagement is good, listening provides the ability to connect on the customer's terms. Listening allows the provider of the documents to learn broader contexts rather than just identifying fans and hoping the people will echo a message and marketing pitch. Listening means being able to read the tags and understand the context in which the tags were produced. If you do that, it's insight into the minds of the taggers.

Understand and Embrace Many Perspectives and Contexts

Listening and hearing from this perspective provides a foundation for deeper and broader understanding as potentially embracing a wider variety of perspectives and contexts. The terms and uses expressed in the tags may be positive, connective (means to tie in external ideas and alternate uses), or highlighting a need for improvement (as well as market segments that will not be happy with the offering *no matter what is done). The various perspectives provide the means to modify and extend the product in the near term as well as in future iterations.*

There is a broad array of social web and social computing options that allow for organizations with products to interact with their customers (current, potential, and future), but few allow for the ability to easily and deeply gain access to customer's thinking around the product that social tagging provides. This perspective insight and ability to capture broad context is really valuable if you can provide some framework around how the tagging will be done.◗

We are done with this chapter, and I suspect you now are conversant with at least your friends if not your business unit when it comes to how social media fits into customer engagement strategies—a.k.a. Social CRM. If you're not, remember, I'm going to cry.

7

Love Your Customers Publicly: Blogs and Podcasts

I know what you're going to say about blogs before you say it. That's because I'm a mentalist—I did *not* say mental case—I said mentalist. It's also because I've heard it a lot: "Blogs? Sure, there are a lot of them, but most of them are junk. They're just kids spewing about something, or they're pictures of postcards or vacations, or they're infantile and meaningless. They aren't any good."

True in part, but utterly irrelevant when it comes to the business response you must have if you're mounting a strategy for customer engagement. Blogs affect you because of the way that customers apportion trust—with very little of it going to your company. That could be due to your past behavior as a company, general distrust of corporate institutions, or simply bad days the customers had that weren't your fault but impacted you.

By the way, I'm starting with the assumption that you know what a blog is—another indication of its commonplace acceptance.

Before we get into how to think about blogs, what to do with them, and what tools are there for you, let's start with some raw numbers.

The Blogosphere

It's impossible to count the precise number of blogs that exist, there are so many. In 2007, which is the last "State of the Blogosphere Report" before blogging got so big that the report didn't matter anymore, David Sifry, former CEO of Technorati, mentioned 112.8 million blogs that Technorati, the blog indexing service, tracks (mine ranked around 61,000 on the list). But that doesn't include, for example, the 72.9 million blogs reported in China, or at least not all of them. We can estimate that there are more than 200 million active blogs out there. According to Technorati, in the same 2007 report, blogs are being created at the rate of 1.4 per second—or 120,000 per day if you like big numbers.

All in all, what these sweeping numbers prove is that not only are there a lot of blogs out there, but they are not a phenomenon. They are a mainstream activity. They are accepted as a legitimate channel of discourse and journalism, with bloggers being credentialed at conferences that were previously the domain of only traditional journalists and trade writers. For example, Oracle now holds a regular blogger call with dozens of technology-related bloggers who are treated as if they were press and/or analysts—because they are.

But what about the, ahem, less good ones? You can't avoid asking that, can you? Let's put it to rest before we get into the meat of the chapter. It's true, there is a lot of wasted cyber real estate. Gartner estimated in late 2006 that the blogosphere was peaking at 100 million blogs and that there were 200 million other blogs not being updated at all, because the folks who started them got bored after the novelty wore off. But even with that wide Sargasso Sea of dead, floating blogs, there are a lot of serious bloggers out there—those who update their blog at least a few times a month. Forrester Research did a chart on blog activity in their 2007 Social Technographics report (see Table 7-1) that showed the ever increasing participation of consumers in the blogosphere that proves the point.

Table 7-1: How Online Consumers Are Using Blogs, Podcasts, and User-Generated Content (Source: Excerpted from "Groundswell: Winning in a World Transformed by Social Technologies," by Charlene Li and Josh Bernoff ©2008 Forrester Research, Inc.)

Percent of Online Consumers Using Blogs and User-Generated Content					
	United States	United Kingdom	France	Germany	Japan	South Korea
Read blogs	25%	10%	21%	10%	52%	31%
Comment on blogs	14%	4%	10%	4%	20%	21%
Write a blog	11%	3%	7%	2%	12%	18%
Watch user-generated video	29%	17%	15%	16%	20%	5%
Upload user-generated video	8%	4%	2%	2%	3%	4%
Listen to podcasts	11%	7%	6%	7%	4%	0%

I'm going to do the math. According to the Miniwatts Marketing Group's Internet world stats, in 2007 there were more than 219 million

Americans using the Internet. If the Forrester numbers are consistent, there are therefore roughly 55 million Americans reading blogs and 24.1 million writing blogs. Keep in mind, the blogs link to each other, so there is a powerful group of loosely connected lobbyists out there numbering in the millions that can be a great benefit to a business or a great headache, depending on how you write your blogs or respond to others.

Social CRM Includes Blogging (It Does)

Blogs are among the most important of the new tools at your service and among the most important of the vehicles for communicating with your customers outside your walls (see Figure 7-1). Intelligent companies are hiring people to monitor blogs or, in some cases, hiring a chief blogger, who functions typically at the level of middle management. Their sole purpose is to monitor or write blogs. They do nothing else, despite the fact that you can't exactly come up with a tangible ROI—though you can measure things like the level of activity through number of comments or the influencers who are making the comments and their reach, etc.

Why hire these people? Because the conversation goes on with you or without you, and consequently it is your call as a business to decide if you want to engage in the conversations or let them continue without your input at all. It is no longer just a matter of you carnivorously and unidirectionally gathering feedback from your customers' discussions—not that you did much of that either. But now you engage your customers and your detractors by proactively reaching out to them.

Here's an intriguing Fox Business News press release, dated April 3, 2008:

> Eastman Kodak Company . . . today announced that it has named Jennifer Cisney as the company's first Chief Blogger. Cisney will provide daily oversight and creative guidance for Kodak's two blogs—"A Thousand Words" and "A Thousand Nerds"—and will boost the company's social media presence. In addition, Cisney will serve as the company's eyes and ears online, listening to customer feedback and sharing ideas and tips related to Kodak's products and services.
>
> "Just over ten percent of Fortune 500 companies have public blogs. Fewer still have Chief Bloggers, and Kodak is among the first to name a female Chief Blogger," said Jeffrey Hayzlett, Chief Business Development Officer and Vice President, Eastman Kodak Company. "As Kodak continues to break new ground in the imaging industry with our innovative products and services, we are committed to staying on the cutting edge of social media by utilizing the talents of our people."

Figure 7-1: AMC blogs are sources of information and engender loyalty. (Source: Six Apart)

She is not the only chief blogger out there. Dell has one, triggered by a major problem they had—caused by an outside blogger. More on that later in this chapter. It doesn't all rest with the chief bloggers, though. There is more to do than just have one of those.

Blog Monitoring

Blog monitoring is the practice of tracking blogs. More and more, companies are seeing its value. More and more, they're debating how to handle it. Some of the benefits are apparent.

You can monitor feedback. There is nothing more valuable than seeing the raw customer conversations in blogs. They can be positive or negative, cool or heated, but they are there. *Eddie Murphy—RAW* is pretty tame by comparison. One good site to directly monitor for large companies is PlanetFeedback (www.planetfeedback.com), which has thousands of complaints that are not just organized but sent to the subjects of the complaints. There is more than that on this site. Figure 7-2 gives you an idea of their scope and Chapter 13 will elaborate even more on it.

However, there are a couple of traps to be aware of. This is by no means the extent of the kinds of venues you'll need to monitor. Not only are there sites dedicated to general consumer complaints, but it's entirely possible there is a site devoted to despising your company. While not the subject of this chapter (see Chapter 9), there is also chatter on social sites like Yelp (www.yelp.com), which rates businesses in communities (restaurants, hotels, etc.) or in environments like Twitter (see below), the conversation "channel" that's grown wildly popular.

We'll stick to blogs for now.

If that isn't enough, responsive customer service is another benefit if you do it right. This is simple and powerful. If you are aware of a complaint, you can deal with the complaint. There was a blog entitled IHateDirecTV that was created to be a single repository for all the complaints about DirecTV across all digital real estate. I'll be coming right back to it in a second to show you what can be done with blog monitoring. I'm going to reproduce the *one* blog entry that existed for the IHateDirecTV site, which was trumpeted by its owner in TiVo forums on the TiVo site. Here it is:

"Within 3 hours of starting this blog and communicating to DirecTV the experience I had, I received calls from the President of DirecTV and the Senior Vice President of Customer Service. These calls were not from the offices of these individuals, but from the actual executives themselves.

"While this probably shouldn't be as impressive as it is, rarely does a customer complaint warrant the attention and receive the prompt reply that mine did today.

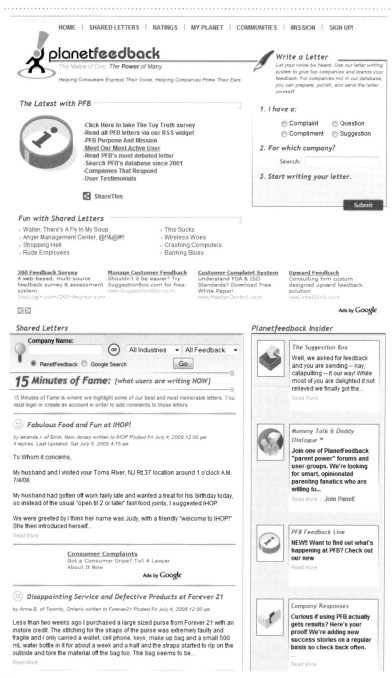

Figure 7-2: PlanetFeedback: The voice of one, the power of many. A consolidated site for customer complaints and questions.

"The executives I spoke with today resolved all issues and have convinced me to remain as a loyal customer of DirecTV. While I'm still not enthusiastic about the conversion from TiVo to the new R-15, I do believe I am a customer of the best digital television service available, 10 years and counting.

"I'll keep this post up for at least the next few days, just for those that have seen my other postings up recently, and want to know the results."

Boom. Problem solved and potential viral issue diffused. It also improves the reputation of the company when other complainants see the company's responsiveness to them. Additionally, the former complainant often becomes an evangelist for the company. Look at the note above: "While I'm still not enthusiastic about the conversion . . . I do believe I am a customer of the best digital television service available." This from a guy who went as far as to register IHateDirecTV so that he could attack them.

Blog Monitoring Tools

There are several ways to monitor blog traffic. One of the most recognizable is Technorati (www.technorati.com), a site that does nothing more than monitor the 112 million blogs not only for their web traffic statistics but for their content. There are widgets and search tools that can provide you with what you need to see what the blogosphere is saying about you. The scope is so large that there are often significant gaps in the blog updating that Technorati (theoretically) automatically does, so be aware of the lag time.

Google also has Google Blog Search, designed exclusively to find blog information. Set up a Google Alert for the web and blogs, and each day you can have the information you seek sent to you.

The downside is that because these are search tools, you have to know the search terms you want to use and to be pretty precise about it—first, to make sure you don't get a ton of extra detritus with the true nuggets of value, and second, to make sure you cover the things you need to cover, which may not be apparent in a searchable phrase.

A lot of companies get around all of this by using their public relations firm to monitor blogs for them. I would make sure that my PR firm, as a hiring criterion, was fully conversant in social media. They will not only be the branding agency for you but will be taking an important role—finding those whose who may be great prospects as customers but are still least likely to pay attention to you, and getting them to engage with you.

Business Blogs: Not Just Any Old Blogs

When you think "blog" (which if you say it out loud sounds really strange) you are not likely thinking business blog. It is most likely someone's personal blog, a technology blog like TechCrunch (www .techcrunch.com), or an entertainment blog or news blog with a political bias like *The Huffington Post* (www.huffingtonpost.com) or a purely political blog like *The Daily Kos* (www.dailykos.com). But rarely do you posit a business blog in your thinking. The reason for that is that businesses are still somewhat wary about blogs. There are clearly defined success stories, but there are also easily available stories of embarrassing failures.

Hopefully, we'll be able to give you some strategic direction on what to do to engage customers, at minimum prevent failure, and optimally be so successful that your results will be measurable. But remember that despite mainstream acceptance of blogging, we are still at the early stage for business blogs, and the rules, frameworks, constraints, and best practices are not fully realized yet. That (and myopia) is one of the reasons only 12 percent of the Fortune 500 have blogs in 2009, though those that do are often enthusiastically involved with hundreds and even thousands of blogs that are either customer-facing or internal. Those at the enthusiastic level include Dell, the aforementioned Kodak, IBM, Intel, and SAP. In fact, IBM purportedly has 3,600 internal blogs and 5,000 customer-facing blogs. I say "purported" because even though I've seen corroboration of this number several places, it's too staggering to get my arms around.

Customer Engagement, Trust, Transparency: How Does Blogging Help?

Blogs are tools. Perhaps they allow customers to access your corporate leadership or perhaps one of your key employee mavens is the designated voice to the customer community. They can also be the vessels for innovation from customers—such as MyStarbucks.com, which was designed to get input from Starbucks advocates on the new drinks and new possible services or amenities that Starbucks might offer—and the community had a chance to vote up the ones that they thought were the smartest, best, or just coolest.

Okay, you're in, I presume. You see blogging as one of the social tools that's needed for Social CRM. Now a brief look at the framework for a business blog and some dos and don'ts. How to actually write a blog is covered in many good books out there. It's worth going out and buying one.

Customer-Facing Business Blogging Rules and Regulations

The purpose of your blog is not to drive revenue. It is to increase the level of trust in your organization with those who may not have had it before and those who have lost it. That principle sustains your blog always. For those blog readers to trust you (and remember, this is just one part of a Social CRM strategy), you have to be authentic and be seen as a company that is willing to be criticized by its own if that is merited. This latter one is the toughest pill to swallow but one of the most important features of a blog. Honesty to the point of pain.

What to Do

1. Learn about the tools you're going to use. Spend time reading other blogs and understanding how they work.

2. Set the expectations for the blog, both internally and to the potential readers—with clear guidelines. For example, Fast Lane, the GM blog written by GM vice chairman Bob Lutz, and one of the first senior corporate blogs, made it clear from the beginning that he would be talking about products and not customer service issues. This set expectations and allowed the readers to be focused on the subject. They currently have 7,500 unique visitors per day. That would be well-focused visitors. (Except maybe me when I'm on it.)

3. Make sure that your chosen bloggers are able to write in a personable, passionate, and authentic way—and then give them the leeway to do just that. The worst thing you can do is stifle the bloggers you've given the pen to.

4. Make sure it is focused on the subject at hand. This is a corporate blog and your subject is what your company is about.

5. Make sure comments are turned on. You must allow readers of the blog to be able to say what they need to (within the bounds of decency, of course) whether it's good or bad.

6. Make sure that the bloggers, whether high or low on the corporate food chain, are accessible to the public reading them.

7. Make sure you have an honest authentic story to tell as a company that your bloggers are empowered to tell in their own way. The bloggers have a voice; the company has a purpose. Let the company's purpose be expressed in the blogger's voice.

8. Link to important resources, even if at times they might have a contradictory interest for you. This will improve the trustworthiness of the company. You've seen the ads for Progressive Insurance. If you can get a quote lower from another insurance company, they'll find it and you can go get it. They are trusted as not just shills but honest arbiters who care about the customer/reader, not just pushing the corporate message into the faces of the readers.

9. Let your bloggers out once in awhile—if they gain some fame, with the publicity that goes along with it, they can be important spokespeople for you because they are doing some of the "cool" and beneficial work for the company. Let them have the freedom to speak authentically. They'll get the constraints without heavy-handed approaches.

What Not to Do

1. The most important thing not to do: Do not be fake. Don't make your blogs into PR-run efforts or marketing campaigns. They are meant to be what I just described—authentic voices from the company engaging with customers and others interested in the company for whatever reason they choose.

2. Do not do let legal control the blog postings. Let legal work with you to set the ground rules for the blog and let marketing have a say in its formation. But once these are established, they have to step aside and let the bloggers blog. Legal should not be approving every entry. When it comes to blogs, their role changes from preventing fires to putting them out if they occur. But the bloggers need to be responsible enough to not create them in the first place.

3. Don't avoid difficult comments. Respond to them.

4. Don't post with mediocre material that reads like corporate bro-chures. Remember the words of the authors of *The Cluetrain Manifesto* (more on this in Chapter 12): "*We want access to your corporate information, to your plans and strategies, your best thinking, your genuine knowledge. We will not settle for the 4-color brochure, for web sites chock-a-block with eye candy but lacking any substance.*" Take this very seriously.

What Happens If You Screw Up? Dell Hell and Independent Bloggers

In June 2005, experienced blogger and communications pro Jeff Jarvis, a slight, almost white-haired, friendly guy, wrote about problems he had with Dell customer service in his influential blog *The Buzzmachine*. To characterize his problems with Dell, mostly having to do with Dell fail-ing to fix a broken laptop as their service agreement stated they would, he coined the term "Dell Hell." Shortly after he coined it, a Google search found 2.4 million references to Dell Hell, of which only 68 were Jeff's. This viral explosion of Dell references due to customer service problems caught the attention of traditional media like the *New York Times* and *Washington Post* and was picked up significantly by them. Besides Jeff's 68 entries, the *New York Times* was next with 40 mentions. The combi-nation of new media and traditional media was devastating to Dell because of the sheer volume of people reached by the blogosphere and by the accepted authority of the traditional press.

A research report done by Onanalytica entitled "Measuring the Influence of Bloggers on Corporate Reputation" (December 2005) found that the approaches used by the conventional media and by bloggers of influence such as Steve Rubel (now with Edelman but also the owner of the influential blog Micro Persuasion) were very dif-ferent. The traditional media were focused on Dell customer service issues. The bloggers focused on the problems that Jeff Jarvis had with Dell. It was personal and thus a "person like me" with "problems like me" was someone who was more authoritative than the company responsible for the screw-up.

The Dell Hell incident was exceptionally damaging yet invigorating for Dell. It hurt them badly enough to change the way they approach customer service and the way they deal with their customers. They hired a chief blogger who is highly regarded. Even though they are not all the way back, they are on the way back—largely catalyzed by Dell Hell and similar well-publicized instances.

Edelman, Wal-Mart, and Inauthentic Corporate Blogging

On September 27, 2006, Wal-Mart launched the company blog *Wal-marting Across America*. It purported to be the journal of the travels of two Wal-Mart customers who were traveling through the country in an RV and talking to other Wal-Mart customers about how wonderful Wal-Mart was for all kinds of reasons, goshdarnit. Well, it turned out to be a scam—those "customers" were hired to act the parts (one was a photographer and the other a relative of someone who worked at the Edelman PR firm). This was about as faked as it could get, short of hiring professional actors.

This was blasted from coast to coast as a fiasco. In fact, Media Post called it a "flog," which is either a crunched term for "fake blog" or a description of what happened to Wal-Mart's public image when it was exposed by *Business Week*, who outed them about two weeks after they started.

As a reader, wouldn't you be upset if one of the RV-tooling couple started the blog by saying this: "We are not bloggers, but since our lives have always been more journey than destination we are explorers at heart. . . . We figured we'd give it a go." Wal-Mart paid for the trip, so they were giving it a go at Wal-Mart's expense through the ad agency that ran the campaign, Edelman. In Wal-Mart's defense, it was Edelman that really screwed this one up. Wal-Mart suffered for it though—and they did go along with it, which is no defense either. Wal-Mart, after a period of extreme defensiveness, is now actually aggressively changing their stance on this with their blog, ElevenMoms, which have real mothers blogging about their Wal-Mart experiences. They also have a senior director of customer experience that is concerned with the interactions of Wal-Mart customers with the stores.

Business Blog Benefits: Customers

There are significant benefits for the relationships between you and your customers. which can range from marginal to profound.

Dell's response to Dell Hell was incredibly smart. They understood that their use of blogs was characterized by the customer's ownership of the conversation. Bob Pearson, vice president of communities at Dell, says, "Dell blogs [don't] differentiate between consumer and B to B customers." In other words, he understands that their impact is going to be on individuals.

If a blog is successful, it creates an authentic dialog between the company and its customers, especially through the comments.

That honesty breeds trust because the representatives of the company writing the blog are able to speak of the company honestly—something refreshing when you've lived in a world of marketspeak for a long epoch. The customers feel as if they have a direct pipeline to the company, which means they have the transparency they need to make intelligent decisions on how they will deal with the company and the means to resolve issues when they occur.

Think about it from a personal standpoint. Over the many years that you've spent developing your wisdom, how many times would a simple phone call have resolved a situation that instead escalated to be outright ugly? I'll bet you can point to more than one.

Business Blog Benefits: Employees

For the sake of brevity, I'm going to simply outline the benefits of blogging for employees:

▶ Employees feel a sense of participation when thinking about the customer is no longer just management's domain. If corporate policy allows employees to blog, then it is conceivable that they can engage customers directly, rather than going through management. In June 2008, Oracle started a Social CRM blog (http://blogs.oracle .com/socialcrm), which is for the members of their Social CRM product team to communicate with customers and developers.

▶ Project planning and execution can be done in real time or nearly so. IBM routinely uses blogs as tools for innovation jams that are designed to generate ideas in 72 hours.

▶ It generates remarkable ideas and improves employee morale. IBM had 3,600 internal blogs in 2006 (latest numbers I could get). Here is a comment from an interview with Christopher Barger, then head of IBM's blogging initiative, now at General Motors: *"We are no longer informers; we are influencers. It's a scary step, but we need to ride this. Inside the company, it's democratizing the process of innovating and collaborating. Both the executive and the intern can now be thought leaders—in this marketplace, it's the best idea and not the biggest title that wins out."*

How Do You Measure a Blog?

As I mentioned earlier, you won't learn how to write a blog here. But one aspect that does concern businesses greatly is the often dicey issue of measurement. This is at a toddler's level when it comes to blogs.

I'm not even going to advance the argument that if you don't measure the results of a press release or a feature article you write, why should you try to measure the results of a blog? I'm going to assume that you're interested in something to bring to your boss, or you are the boss looking to pull the trigger on doing it, and you'd like to at least feel there will be some metric accountability down the road.

Luckily, Eric Petersen, a web analytics maven, unveiled a set of blog metrics at the Web Analytics Association–sponsored eMetrics Conference in 2007. Here they are, for better or worse. Recognize them as guides, not definitive fixed answers with no alternatives. They are a good start.

1. Percent increase or decrease in unique visits

2. Change in page rank, i.e., a list of the top ten most popular areas and how it has changed in the last week

3. How many sessions represent more than five page views

4. In the past month, the percentage of all sessions representing more than five page views

5. Percent of sessions that are greater than five minutes in duration

6. Percent of visitors who come back for more than five sessions

7. Percent of sessions that arrive at your site from a Google search, or a direct link from your website or other site that is related to your brand

8. Percent of visitors who become subscribers

9. Percent of visitors who download something from the site

10. Percent of visitors who provide an e-mail address

Microblogging and More: Tweeting on Twitter

Those of you who either live under rocks or are traditionalists when it comes to CRM may never have heard of Twitter. Or, even if you have, you may be wondering why Twitter is in a chapter on blogging.

Twitter is, to many, a blogging tool—a microblogging tool. Those blogging entries, called "tweets," are a maximum of 140 characters, shared in real time with people who have chosen to follow you or whom you have chosen to follow. I don't mean stalking or being stalked, just to calm your already frazzled nerve-endings.

Figure 7-3 shows what a Twitter client and Twitter messages look like.

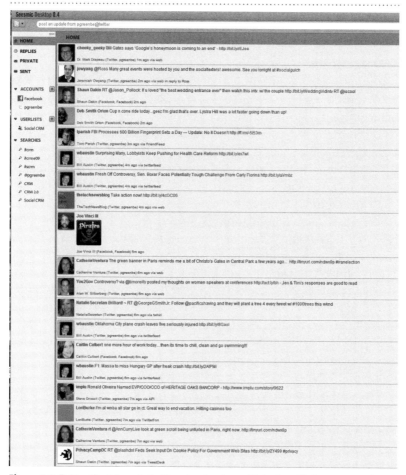

Figure 7-3: Twitter Client Seesmic Desktop showing the sophistication of Twitter conversations

It's usually at this point in a discussion on Twitter with corporate execs (which you very well might be or aspire to) that I hear the following regular lament (which by the way, exceeds my 140-character limit):

"I get blogs, and I get podcasts and wikis and we're trying to figure out this social networking 'thing' but I just don't get Twitter. I don't get it. I DON'T get it. I don't GET it. It seems like such a waste of time."

However, there are more than 23 million Twitter unique visitors in June 2009 and 11.5 million registered users as of July 2009, which tells you that there are more and more people getting it every day. The growth rate year over year from 2007 through 2009 is 2565 percent according to Technorati.

Okay, impressive numbers, but what possible business value is there?

A Few Twitter Tales

When Research In Motion and SAP jointly announced their SAP CRM 2007 mobile sales application for the BlackBerry, *CRM* magazine managing editor Josh Weinberger live-tweeted the event (for those of you techno-Neanderthals, that means using Twitter to cover something live, broadcasting it moment by moment to Twitter followers). Not only were the updates nearly instant—as fast as he could type 140 characters—but his commentary was incisive and he could take questions from his followers.

On April 24, 2008, IT Toolbox SaaS director Dennis Stevenson reported in his blog, *Original Thinking*, how SlideShare employees answered him via Twitter due to a tweet in which he expressed how slowly SlideShare was operating. SlideShare customer service used Twitter's own search service to track text strings with the word "Slide-Share" in them so they could respond to customer service issues and track SlideShare feedback across the Twitterverse. They informed him that SlideShare was under a denial-of-service attack, at least giving him a reason for the problem he was having, if not solving it at that moment.

The business value of Twitter is certainly being recognized by the CRM vendors. Everyone from SAP and Oracle to salesforce.com and Microsoft to many of the smaller claimants to the Social CRM throne have multiple Twitter accounts that they use to broadcast their events, interact with their customers, generate possible leads, and even just do some blabbing. Many of them participate in groups which are indicated by hashmarks. For example, one of the dominant Twitter presences in the Social CRM Twitter group (#scrm) is Prem Kumar, who runs the Social CRM initiative for the CRM practice for Cognizant, a system integrator and consulting firm with a large CRM practice. He has been able to establish a leadership presence effectively without being seen as an "intruding vendor," which is how vendors usually are seen when they try to participate. Twitter has given him the platform to present his very intelligent ideas without any suspicion around his motivations.

Business Benefits of Microblogging

I think you can see that marketing is a key application of Twitter—and by extension, microblogging—but there are some dangers inherent in it. One of them, perhaps the most dangerous, is pushing a corporate/personal agenda too hard without a return in value (as was going on with one unnamed person I used to follow). The equivalent is having your conversations constantly interrupted with "OMG! I'M AMAZING. I'M ON TV BIG TIME! HELP SELL ME! I'M TOO MUCH FOR WORDS—AT LEAST TOO MUCH FOR 140 CHARACTERS!!!" That can be particularly irritating because this is a highly personalized albeit short message communications platform. No one wants the ego of another in the way. Rather than classic, distrusted corporate marketing hype, the hype gets personal but is even more distrusted because of how blatant the offenders are. The conciseness needed for messaging in 140 characters or less can work both ways.

If used effectively, as Cognizant is doing, microblogging, which at the moment is pretty much totally represented by Twitter or the corporate versions like Yammer, allows individuals who represent companies to become participants in the environment, akin to a conversation among friends at the bazaar. References to events or useful articles are looked upon with curiosity and interest, and traffic goes to them through the hyperlink embedded in the tweet (most of the time in the form of a tinyurl—a shortened proxy URL for a long address that takes up too many of the allotted 140 characters). Twitter's potential is limitless as a marketing tool, microblogging tool, customer service tool, networking tool, and community participation tool.

Twitter's value has been noticed and applied by multiple large enterprises or innovative smaller companies. In 2007, Dell created a Twitter presence they called @DellOutlet to give product offers to their prospective customers. It generated $3 million between 2007 and June 2009—not bad for something with no business value. The only "no" is zero marketing cost.

Tony Hsieh, Zappos CEO (Chapter 4) uses Twitter to give away shoes, invite his 965,000 followers to happy hour at the company and for frequent interaction. They even encourage Twitter use through their customers and hookups (via Twitter, you nasty minded creatures, you) with their employees. Hundreds of Zappos employees are on Twitter and they even compete for friends. Fun—and good business.

But customer service is really where Twitter shines. Companies like Jet Blue, H&R Block, and especially Comcast have used it that way to great effect. @ComcastCares, a Twitter-based customer service effort, gets this always-maligned cable company major kudos for its conscientious efforts to reach customers with issues through the program. They are smart cookies. Why? Because not only are they solving customer service issues, they are doing it via a platform that is automatically viral and, thus, customers will talk about what they are doing. Check out Twitter search for @ComcastCares and see what I mean. Also check out Chapter 13 where I zero in on Twitter and customer service.

Superstah! Six Apart

Six Apart is a company I've had a bit of a love affair with (my wife knows) over the past few years. I use TypePad, their on-demand blogging platform, to host and update my blog every morning (yeah, right, every morning—who am I lying to here?). I'm not the only one either. They serve over 20 million bloggers worldwide. Their client list is a Fortune 500 A-list with companies like GM, Dell, and Boeing among them. A case can be made that they are the powerhouse platform in the blogging world, with their only real competition coming from Word-Press. But WordPress isn't the subject of this section because Movable Type proved better in my assessments. Plus Six Apart just has it all—coolness, 200 employees, venture backing, and a helluva product.

Their appeal is wide and they are constantly innovating in ways that are unique and genuinely interesting. For example they have released a mobile blogging tool that is specifically for the iPhone that is, I have to say, while a little awkward, pretty nice—though typing on an iPhone keyboard is always difficult.

But beyond just an iPhone app, we are talking about enterprise-ready technologies that are media for communications with customers, which must be part of your CRM strategy, and Six Apart hits a sweet spot with their offerings.

Movable Type has a vibrant community of developers and designers constantly working on the platform—some employees, some independent—but all in all numbering in the thousands. They have a vibrant wiki (http://wiki.movabletype.org) which is constantly being updated and refined so that whatever information you need from the nitty-gritty of installation to the granular nature of customization is openly and publicly available.

Mission 21st Century

Six Apart's mission was never a secret. Their home page (www .sixapart.com) has this brief little blurb: "Ever since Ben and Mena

Trott created Movable Type together so that Mena could blog and build a community. . . ." Building a social platform with blogging as the nucleus has been the aim from the beginning.

Anil Dash, their VP of Customer Evangelism, and a very articulate and active Web 2.0 advocate, always knew they'd do what they're doing:

> *Our original business plan was that in a couple of years, we'd have an enterprise product. We had several reasons for our confidence level in that. One was that we understood that this wasn't something that was going to be aimed at the past patterns of going to CIOs and CTOs. We knew that technology gets adopted because people want to use it and when it gets there, it can't be stopped.*

The Product: Movable Type: Enterprise

How can a blogging platform have an edition that can provide the features and functions needed to build user communities and at the same time provide the security, administrative functionality, and scalability that a large company might need, you might ask? Though I suspect this is not the question that springs immediately to mind after that first Starbucks venti doubleshot espresso gets you going.

On the one hand, doesn't Movable Type just create blogs, something like WordPress? Also, if it's at an enterprise level, can it really scale to the level that I need for my thousands of potential readers and dozens of bloggers—and how does this translate into the capacity to build integrated communities?

Thankfully, Anil answered that for you (and me):

> *Every blog is a social network. It's a long tail with community features. For example, each tag is a community because you find those of like interest when you access the tag. People and relationships are managed with profiles and they can rate and recommend and forward content to others. Links to Wikipedia, Craig's List, and Digg add to the social elements.*
>
> *If you want to take it deeper, the compatibility with both the Open Social and Facebook APIs makes it extensible immediately. It's not just a closed silo. It provides a context for where the minds of the customers are across the web.*
>
> *We also understood that in the Internet world, enterprise scaling could be seen as (for our purposes) lots of visitors to a single blog on a good day.*

That settles that. Almost. Here's the snapshot of their technology offering.

Basic Features

▶ **Global blog templates**   Even with multiple sites you can maintain consistent use of brand elements. If a change in an element is made in one place, it can be propagated across all the sites using the template. There is full administrative control over the use of the templates and their elements (see Figures 7-4 and 7-5).

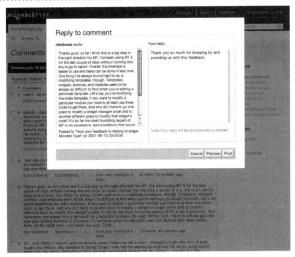

Figure 7-4: While this is a comment reply in Movable Type 4.2… (Source: Six Apart)

Figure 7-5: …This is what's going on behind the scenes (Source: Six Apart)

▶ **Multiple authors**   Each blog can have multiple authors individually authenticated.

▶ **Roles and permissions**   Administrators can control all permissions of all readers and authors and vary them by blog or by assigned role, such as designer, author, administrator.

▶ **Mobile Movable Type**   Both the BlackBerry and the iPhone can be used to post entries.

▶ **Rich media and asset manager**   The platform supports the use of rich media (video, audio, etc.) and also conduits to other services like YouTube or your own asset management. The native asset manager allows the reuse of assets across multiple properties.

▶ **Content aggregation/relationship links**   I'll explain this with an example. You have a specific topic that you want to investigate, such as CRM in financial services. You can create a microsite that can pull all the content on that subject into the site ranging from blog entries to embedded PowerPoint presentations. You can then incorporate the related links to this content. All of this is done by using the tags that are associated with CRM and financial services. Clear enough?

Enterprise Features

▶ **LDAP user and group management**   It provides administrative control of user accounts with inherited group privileges which are automatically applied to new users. The user accounts are managed internally.

▶ **User account synchronization**   Administrators can edit user profiles within the LDAP director and then sync them within Movable Type.

▶ **Automatic blog provisioning**   Administrators can quickly provision new personal blogs for new users.

▶ **Professional social network**   There are thousands of Movable Type developers, designers, and consultants available as a resource for the Movable Type community members, which includes customers.

Community Features

▶ **Community user profiles**   These are the equivalent of a Facebook profile. You can track the user profiles for changes to the profile, comments made by the owner of the profile, responses to the comments made by the owner, or owner recommendations of posts or comments.

▶ **Comment authentication**   The use of CAPTCHAs—those annoying and often unreadable combinations of letters and numbers that help minimize the spam that generates automatic comments.

▶ **Recommend This**   A voting mechanism and the ability to sort the recommendations by criteria—in other words, sift the postings that were best liked and have them organized from most to least.

▶ **User-controlled privacy**   The user controls who can comment and respond. Comments are publicly listed on profile page.

Six Apart doesn't think in terms of a "blog application" universe. It is a social publishing platform that integrates well with the other social media that it potentially has to live alongside or can be used to create blog-centered user communities, directly through its Community Edition, its newer Social Publishing edition, or its Vox platform (www .vox.com), which certainly is worth looking into. Part of their value is in their platform and much of the rest is in the vision of the company, which makes sure that you won't be left behind.

Podcasting: A Brief Look

By year end 2009, it's estimated that the total number of people who will have listened to a podcast in the U.S. alone will be 21.9 million. This is projected to grow to 37.4 million by 2013, according to eMarketer's senior analyst Paul Verna in his 2009 "Podcasting: Into the Mainstream" report. Yet, I'm not going to spend a lot of time on them in this book.

The reason is easy enough to fathom. They have a more limited though important benefit when it comes to engaging customers, but podcasting still remains somewhat alien to most of those people you are going to call your customers to begin with. I made a command decision to not incorporate a lot about podcasting in part due to a couple of salient pieces of information. Of those who are listening to podcasts, according to the Edison Group's 2008 Survey on Podcasting (1,857 respondents), 71 percent of those who listen still listen on their PC, which makes podcasts a sophisticated archived piece of recorded Internet radio. But even more telling, *63 percent of the respondents in both 2007 and 2008 never even heard of podcasts* even with the growth rates mentioned above.

The true value of a podcast is what our good buddy Beth Comstock of NBC Interactive called "timeshifting" and "placeshifting"—the ability to take the podcast from somewhere and put it on something else (placeshifting) and then listen to it when you want (timeshifting).

For those of you who are confused as to what a podcast is and are thinking it's what doctors put on the broken spores of the aliens from *Invasion of the Body Snatchers*, it's an audio file that is enclosed by a piece of XML code called an RSS feed. RSS stands for Really Simple Syndication. If you're technically conversant, it is really simple—it just isn't for those who aren't. So what facilities like iTunes (in particular) have done is make podcasts available via subscription, so that each time there is a new episode of your podcast, upon synchronization with either a podcast aggregator or with a site like iTunes directly, the podcast episode is updated. Then you can listen to it (or watch it if it's a video podcast) on your PC or set it to download to your MP3 player (I'd say iPod, but some of you anti-Apple people might be offended).

The Business Benefits: Podcasting, Mindshare, Branding

There is some direct revenue-producing benefit in podcasting. For example, the topical humor website *The Onion* (www.theonion.com) derives revenue from major company ads, because it has a wide listenership and an even bigger audience for its videocasts. Several "amateurs turned pro" like Cali Lewis on GeekBrief.TV get sponsorships and advertising because of audiences in the hundreds of thousands. But for the enterprise, this model is actually almost stupid unless you are a small business producing podcasts for a living.

The real value in podcasting is for establishments that are interested in capturing mindshare, which should always be part of your CRM or, if you still care to separate them, your corporate strategy. By providing you venues where you're able to either educate your customers or prospects or even those outside your obvious target market, or entertain them and put a human face on the company, you are able to capture the mindshare that can be your true differentiator—if that's what you're after.

For example, as part of its MIT OpenCourseWare project, MIT now has most of its courses available via podcast. Anyone has access to them free of charge. There are assignments and class notes and all of them are downloadable, so you can do all the timeshifting and place-shifting you want. You can even subscribe to an RSS feed to get updates on the classes as they are created.

While you won't earn your degree doing this, and there is some core material missing, the value for MIT is immense. You get to see the high quality of MIT offerings, and MIT itself is branded as a progressive school with a deep and abiding commitment to learning and providing knowledge. That reputation is what drives interest in becoming a student or making a donation or a bequest to MIT, rather than somewhere else.

So the real value of podcasting is thought leadership and branding. It has value as a medium because it's portable and convenient to listen to and update. Because the customer/listener consumes it the way they want to, they are in an optimum state for listening when they do, and they develop an intimacy with the information they wouldn't otherwise have. It's greatly engaging and entertaining for your customers.

There is a strong business-to-business (B2B) case to be made too, and this is leading to a growing audience for podcasts from companies like Cisco, General Motors, Wells Fargo, and IBM. There is also a upward trend in the number of listeners, as we saw earlier. That's the response to the "why do it if it's not well known" query on the lips of all.

Why the popularity of podcasts in the B2B space? As Paul Gillin (whom you'll remember from Chapter 6), put it, "They're a godsend for busy corporate executives."

But there is a simple downside. It takes a considerable amount of time to produce one. Podcasts are expected to have some real charm. There is a bit of an expectation that a podcast will be done either by a smart amateur or by someone stepping outside their corporate persona and being an authentic voice. But there is also an expectation, due to years of television watching, that the production values will be professional, regardless of the broadcast's authenticity or, at worst, truthiness. These are inescapable requirements—honest voice, professional production.

Thus, there is a cost to produce a podcast. The equipment costs—hardware, software, and so on—are dependent on how high a quality you are aiming at. A large enterprise is going to be expected to provide a serious, TV-quality show. That can means thousands invested. But, by the same token, a small business can get 85 percent of that professionalism for about $1,000 and a good quality show for half that or less. The real cost is labor time because you have to do a show consistently week after week or you can actually turn off your customers.

When developing a customer engagement strategy, a podcast can be a valuable tool but one that has to be approached with a good deal of care. Check 'em out for yourself. Go to either iTunes to subscribe to a few or go to Podcast Alley (www.podcastalley.com). Or listen to mine with Brent Leary called "CRM Playaz" (at http://www.crmplayaz .com). Then make your decisions. Be careful. It's a lot of fun, though.

Let's close this chapter with Shel Israel, who is one of the foremost bloggers in the world. We've got wikis to cover and miles to go before I sleep.

MINI-CONVERSATION WITH SHEL ISRAEL: THREE BLOGGING TAKEAWAYS

Shel Israel is an amazing guy. Even though he relentlessly investigates and reports on social media's impact on business and culture all over the world, he is also one of the nicest and most responsive people you'll meet in business. As a result of these varying traits, he has interviewed diverse people, ranging from Michael Dell, founder and CEO of Dell Computer, to Wael Abbas, who posts videos on YouTube about Egyptian police brutality. He's also famous in the world of social media, despite his humble protestations. He's the co-author (with Robert Scoble) of *Naked Conversations: How Blogs Are Changing the Way Businesses Talk with Customers*, the seminal book on business blogging. He also co-hosts (with Scoble) *WorkFast*, a weekly live video show for FastCompany. TV on the future of work. You need to be listening to what he's telling you here and visiting his blog, Global Neighbourhoods (http://redcouch.typepad. com/). He knows from whence he came. Very savvy dude.

We are moving from an Era of Broadcast into a new Conversational Era. This changes a great deal for the modern enterprise. During this transformation, there is a sense of discomfort caused by the disruption, but an increasing number of corporate thinkers are coming to understand that there are enormous efficiencies and advantages to the relentless advance of social media into corporate communications.

The three things that enterprise strategists need to keep in mind are:

▶ *There is revolution in conversation. For the past 50 to 60 years, companies have engaged in monologues. They sit in conference rooms and devise messages to insert into the foreheads of customers and prospects, primarily through marketing efforts. These days, most people do not want to be marketed to. While the expense of marketing programs continues to rise, the effectiveness is steadily decreasing. Through social media, people are now ignoring marketing and influencing their peers on what to buy and where to buy it, what to watch, listen to or visit. This is a fundamental change in how businesses interact with the markets they serve.*

▶ *The objective is to get closer. While marketing's objective has been to deliver messages and sell, social media's objective is to get closer to customers simply by having conversations. If you listen to your customers, chances are they will help you provide them with improved goods and services. By listening and responding you can increase sales and profits while decreasing marketing costs.*

▶ *Youth is the killer app. If you want to understand what your business will look like five, ten, and twenty years down the line, go talk to your kids or some young people you know. Watch their habits. They have a Teflon resistance to traditional sales techniques. They are getting their information not from newspapers or even broadcast TV, but online from each other. As time goes by, they will join the marketplace where social media will dominate the influences that impact them. The best and brightest of them will demand social media tools to do their jobs, and they will do their jobs better when they are afforded use of the tools they are accustomed to.*∎

8

Wikis Are a Weird Name for Collaboration, N'est Çe Pas?

Back in 2005, a columnist for the *New Yorker* not named Malcolm Gladwell, but instead, James Surowiecki took some of the stage for himself with the release of a book called *The Wisdom of the Crowds*. This book posited that, in the right circumstances and under the right conditions, groups can be potentially smarter than the smartest person in the group and can be exquisite problem solvers—better than any so-called expert in the problem. This collective wisdom has been proven often to be an accurate answer to questions that may not be solvable by individuals.

The necessary conditions for this to happen are threefold.

▶ **Diversity** People with different backgrounds, sources for knowledge, levels of knowledge.

▶ **Independent opinion** This means you aren't involved in a focus group and expressing the opinion that you think others want you to. This is the simultaneous delivery or at least the anonymous delivery of the decision, devoid of any kinds of group dynamics.

▶ **Information aggregation** Technology that captures and organizes the information.

There are countless examples that make this a reasonable proposition. I'm not going to get into the arcane instances, though there are so many examples of "crowd figures out number of stones in a jar" that I can't figure out the total number of those examples on my own. I'm going to meet about 400 people at the corner of Irony and Sarcasm, if you want to join us. We'll get the answer right.

Crowdsourcing

Over the past three years, the wisdom of the crowd added frameworks and structure and has become crowdsourcing. This is a business model that takes something that an expert was typically hired to do and outsources it to a group or the general population with the assumption that the cream will rise to the top. In effect, this is mass collaboration. I'll be bringing it back home in the discussions later on social networks (Chapter 9) and strategy (Chapter 18).

For example, in the past, high quality photographs were taken by professional photographers. They were very expensive to license—often thousands of dollars for key photos to keep them royalty free. Now you can go to iStockphoto.com. There you'll find hundreds of thousands of royalty-free photos uploaded by an amorphous mass of professional and amateur photographers who are adhering to the iStockphoto terms of service. The pix, which I've used for several presentations, are bought with prepaid credits. When a purchase is made, the photo's (or video's) owner gets a royalty. There are several ways to assure the quality of the photo, including downloading watermarked comps to see what they look like and, of course, standards that iStockphoto expects of their photographers, amateur or professional. What you have is a marketplace that is available to people who ordinarily wouldn't have had the chance to break into this kind of closed market. The quality of the photos is good because it's in the interest of the provider that they be good. Their price is cheap because of the incredibly large numbers—millions—of photos available. This is crowdsourcing the way it is supposed to work.

But we're going to concentrate on wikis. Prior to the invention of wikis, there were whiteboards—both digital and (with Sharpies) analog. But wikis are quite different and are built from the idea of ground-up crowdsourcing. Wikis answer the question of how to capture the wisdom of the masses. They are a social media tool that is based on collaboration, whether collaboration among total strangers (Wikipedia) or specifically designated communities (CRM 2.0 Wiki) or employee-based (Dresdner Kleinwort Wasserstein).

You all know the story of Wikipedia, so I'll just mention the numbers as of April 2008 so you can see how incredibly important wikis and crowdsourcing can be. Wikipedia attracts 683 million visitors annually. It has over 10 million articles in 253 languages, comprising a combined total of over 1.74 billion words combined.

Even more recently in August, 2009, the English Wikipedia had 2,982,662 articles. Staggering. The greatest compendium of human knowledge probably ever produced.

The first question that comes to mind for you tech-savvy older readers is, I presume, why wikis? What does a wiki do that makes it so important? The second question is how does a wiki workie with Social CRM? Finally, I'm sure you all want me to prove it with some stories.

One thing at a time.

Why Wikis? A Conversation with Ross Mayfield

Ross Mayfield, who, you will hear more from at the end of this chapter, had a chat with me that was exceptionally enlightening. He identified the larger trends that are leading to the success of wikis.

There are a lot of converging trends that make this a very good value proposition. The cost of forming new groups is falling to zero. Where it used to require expensive infrastructure, the tools that are available to consumers and, to some extent, the enterprise make the cost almost nothing. The cost of publishing is almost zero too.

But what makes this particularly cogent, is also a massive demographic shift. The Net Generation is already in the workforce for the last one to two years and the older generation is leaving the workforce. The Net Generation has consumer interests that border on activism. That makes these tools and their cost even more interesting.

This is leading to a transparency of customer thinking too. The quality of interactions is improving; the edge of this is the extranet of customer/partner. In fact we're seeing business development, vendor management and supply chain management being impacted by this transparency. Conversations turn into content and best practices.

Just Plain Wikis: Simplicity Is the Norm

The plainer the better when it comes to a wiki. Think of it this way. You have an editable digital white space with rules and edit tracking that can be accessed by anyone—or in the enterprise, by anyone you want to access it. You can do what you want on that white space. It's pretty much got a text editor with Word-like tools, though not nearly as deep. It's got the ability to embed rich media such as audio or video or photos. In the enterprise, the wiki can be controlled by administrators who can open it or limit it as they please and can integrate it with multiple systems, including CRM. Anyone who participates can, if permitted, edit the entries of anyone else who participates.

That's the easy way to look at it.

Here's what one looks like. This is my CRM 2.0 wiki that's been used by the industry to define Social CRM. It's powered by PBworks, an excellent hosted wiki service. A couple of screenshots should give you the flavor. Figure 8-1 is the home page.

Figure 8-1: The Social CRM wiki home page

Now a comment page that shows a bit of the ongoing discussion on Social CRM (Figure 8-2).

Now let's piece it all together and see a diagram, courtesy of Socialtext, that actually shows you what a wiki does with some actual explanation (Figure 8-3).

Social CRM + Wikis = Collaborative Knowledge, Customer Support

While wikis clearly have value when it comes to both internal and external collaboration and can lead to inventive solutions, how can they work in the more traditional realm of CRM? Ross Mayfield, who is not only the founder of Socialtext, our Superstah! winner in this chapter, but a true thought-leader in social media, didn't hesitate when

Figure 8-2: The CRM 2.0 wiki discussion on Social CRM: A comment page

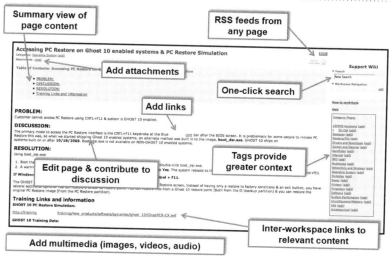

Figure 8-3: This is what you can actually do with a wiki (source: Socialtext)

he had to answer the question: "It can create a participatory knowledge base for service and support organizations."

For example, Microstrategy, one of the few surviving independent business intelligence vendors, uses their Angel.com site to showcase their IVR products. There is an IVR wiki on the site whose stated raison d'être is "When we set out to create a website to publish and share best practices it was high on our mind that **we don't have all the answers**. In fact, we're here to learn from others. So we decided to create this wiki, where each webpage can be modified by anybody. That way, we hope we can support the community of people involved with voice automation."

This means that creating IVR solutions or solving IVR-related problems is not just in the hands of technical support but involves the members of the community who might be partners, suppliers, vendors, representatives of the phone carriers, or, best of all, most of the time, customers.

By looking at Figure 8-4, you can see what's being worked on. Among the types of things that this wiki has been successful at incorporating are:

▶ Documents as works in progress

▶ Conversations among the various Angel.com IVR community members

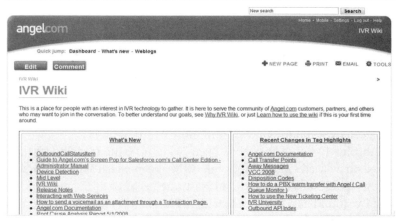

Figure 8-4: The Angel.com IVR wiki (Source: Socialtext)

► Meeting agendas

► Project plans

The value to Microstrategy is incredible because of the concrete and always dynamic information contributed by external resources who have some expertise in IVR or who have been involved in fixing a problem. Best practices are available to all comers. Additionally, it fosters a spirit of "we're working together to solve this," and that spirit goes a long way toward reducing the anxieties that customer service issues cause and increasing the bond among the participants.

This constitutes a social benefit for CRM strategy. But there are also some benefits to integrating the wiki information with your traditional CRM system applications and even your traditional CRM roles.

Ross Mayfield mentioned collaborative intelligence as a CRM benefit in our discussion, which means he really gets how wikis and CRM work: "Marketing gets the opportunity, when using a wiki, to communicate with field sales and get immediate feedback. This means that there is shared learning with customers and prospects. The field sales rep is the customer interface and the wiki captures the information."

But this isn't the only benefit that companies derive. When a business has an extensive customer support operation, wikis allow them to capture and integrate the approaches they've taken to solve customer problems. As a particular problem is solved and then as the solution is continually refined by multiple customer service representatives (CSRs), they are able to update and revise the solution without massive procedural, technical, or administrative issues in the way.

Integration with CRM Systems

While these are cool, very 2.0ish features, there are still a lot of traditional CRM systems around with a great deal of sunken investment. Does using a wiki mean that the operational CRM systems have to be replaced by something newer and more contemporary?

Absolutely not. There have been wiki and issue tracking systems based on wiki sites integrating with CRM systems such as Siebel, Oracle, NetSuite, salesforce.com, and at least one instance of SugarCRM. All that I've found have been done with Atlassian's Confluence wiki system and their JIRA issue tracking systems, which makes Atlassian a short-listed choice if you're looking at enterprise-grade wiki platforms.

In fact, Vtiger CRM (you meet it in Chapter 16) has a JIRA and Confluence plug-in that integrates the Vtiger (owned by the stalwart fellows at Zoho) CRM customer data and customer communications (such as e-mail, phone, and audio logs of the phone calls) with the various Atlassian products. It can pass the CRM data such as names, e-mail addresses, phone numbers, and titles—in other words the basic fields—to the wiki. While not highly sophisticated, it is a proof of concept that wikis and traditional CRM data can be integrated.

The Trouble with Wikis

That doesn't mean that wikis have no issues and are the ideal collaborative workspace all the time, always driven by innovation and good will. There are a significant number of human factors that have little to do with wiki technology and more to do with human resistance to change. Some of what constitutes trouble is just ordinary human behavior; some is unfamiliarity with the technology; some of it can be related to the corporate culture and this new form of collaboration.

Here are some of the typical problems that you run into with a wiki in a corporate environment—especially when you allow customers to participate in the project.

Participation Inequality

Jakob Nielsen, the web interface design guru, now a Microsoft UI lead, wrote an article in October 2006 entitled, "Participation Inequality: Encouraging More Users to Contribute" (www.useit.com/alertbox/

participation_inequality.html). Nielsen claimed that in studies done on multiuser communities and social networks, including wikis in this category, you consistently find a ratio that's now called the "90-9-1" ratio.

▶ 90% of users are lurkers—the ones who mostly read—you know, like you. Hey! I didn't say stalkers. We all lurk.

▶ 9% of users contribute from time to time, but other priorities dominate their time.

▶ 1% of users participate a lot and account for most contributions: The way Nielsen put it was, "It can seem as if they don't have lives because they often post just minutes after whatever event they're commenting on occurs." That's pretty much everyone on Twitter.

Needless to say, should this be entirely true, the wiki contributions are going to be disproportionately those of the 1 percent. Despite the numbers that seem to validate this, it's a somewhat flawed idea. For example, the most often quoted case is Wikipedia. Jimmy Wales, the creator of Wikipedia, once said that 50 percent of the edits were done by 0.7 percent of the people. But with a deeper dive, in his (wiki) article, "Who Writes Wikipedia?" Aaron Swartz writes:

When you put it all together, the story become clear: an outsider makes one edit to add a chunk of information, then insiders make several edits tweaking and reformatting it. In addition, insiders rack up thousands of edits doing things like changing the name of a category across the entire site—the kind of thing only insiders deeply care about. As a result, insiders account for the vast majority of the edits. But it's the outsiders who provide nearly all of the content.

So this shouldn't be taken at face value. While the rule of thumb does hold in a surprisingly large number of cases with social networks and user communities (which also define a wiki), it can be changed with a deeper knowledge of what you're doing and some smart adoption practices, which I'll go into below.

Always the Culture

Top-down cultures still predominate in the enterprise world. Wikis are truly bottom-up. The most enthusiastic users are usually not managers, but staff employees. This creates the issues that you would expect. Managers want control. Cowboys want to dominate the wiki use.

As we have stated throughout the book, we are seeing a Gen Y move into the workforce, and they are expecting collaboration tools like this to be part of what their employers are offering.

Technical Issues

Security always seems to be a concern if the wiki is offered over the corporate intranet. This is a particularly false concern since the enterprise wiki platforms like Socialtext, Atlassian Confluence, and so on offer strong security and administrative controls.

Where technical issues can be a little more difficult is when you invite your customers in, because they are likely to be using different technologies than you. It could be as simple as Firefox versus Internet Explorer versus Safari browser or more complex if you're capturing and integrating the information into your CRM system and you're getting some of that information from outside your own corporate framework.

Content Issues

This is always a problem for wikis—and has been highlighted by some of the early problems that Wikipedia had with inaccurate content that bordered on the libelous. But one of the marvelous things about enterprise wikis are that not only are editorial controls possible if needed, but, as in all wikis, the users of the wikis are vested in its accuracy and use and will almost always self-police. If something egregiously false is entered, someone is likely to edit it out. If something borderline is not supported, there is bound to be someone who asks for supporting proof. The success of the wiki depends on its members, and the authenticity of the information is vital.

Again, the place it gets more complex is when your customers are part of the collaboration. You have to rely on much more of the level of user investment in the information's accuracy than the document management or content management rules you impose. Your customers have every bit as much investment in the wiki collaboration working as you do, and the loyalty capital you gain by allowing them access is significant.

Wiki Adoption: As Hard as the Wiki Looks Easy

I'm going to spend some time going through a program for wiki adoption, not because I think that it is something that you have to follow step by step to make sure that your collaboration effort is adopted, but because it reflects the somewhat different adoption standards that Social CRM has in comparison to traditional CRM. While some of it overlaps, of course, there are a few differences well worth noting because they will impact Social CRM adoption, which we'll be discussing more in the strategy chapter (Chapter 18). The reason I'm using wikis to highlight the differences is that wikis have the most well-articulated adoption strategies of all the social media, and in fact, have a comprehensive site devoted to a deep understanding of the practices and cultural issues for wiki adoption—Wikipatterns (www.wikipatterns.com). Of course, it's in the form of a . . . one guess . . . right . . . wiki.

Organic Growth

This is the number one wiki adoption practice that tends to differ from the more traditional practices that we're all used to in CRM—though when something is available and freely encouraged, it tends to have an audience that's going to want to use it.

There certainly have been precursors to this one. York International, the HVAC provider, implemented Siebel Field Service in 2003. One of the features of this particular application was the ability to create a knowledge base that could be used to accumulate best practices, for example. When the technicians heard that it existed and that they could add to it, they organically (and virally) added 1,200 best practices within a week. These could be accessed by other field service technicians who used them in lieu of the manual.

This is carried forward into wiki adoption. For example, by rolling out tools and training and pre-populating the wiki with valuable content, the most-studied wiki, Dresdner Kleinwort Wasserstein (DrKW), was able to lure business professionals within the company to the wiki. Initially it was used for three things:

▶ **Managing meetings**   Coordinating times and dates, compiling agendas, updating status, distribution of meeting minutes.

▶ **Brainstorming**   Back and forth discussions on new ideas and the development of documentation to support those ideas. This is where order is created out of chaos. Usually it's a few comments and discussions that are random, but it self-organizes. It becomes a concrete document made available via the wiki to the members. Another example of this is the aforementioned Wiki-Patterns. The amount of discussion around wiki adoption and the practices and impediments became substantial enough to become a published book on wiki adoption. Additionally, the ideas generated by the CMR 2.0 wiki community (around 200 strong) are a major part of this edition of CRM at the Speed of Light.

▶ **Creating presentations**   The content was created on the wiki and then often made into a PowerPoint presentation, making for much more compelling content. More steak, less sizzle.

Dresdner Kleinwort Wasserstein peaked at around 2,500 users in 2007 and stabilized at that number—in a two-year adoption cycle.

Wiki Leadership

This is a tried and true principle—one that I advocate in my discussions on "natural leaders" for improving CRM adoption rates. When a team forms to collaborate via a wiki, there is often someone who is more interested than the rest in how the wiki works and he or she takes on the role of informal caretaker. Give that person administrative privileges. That way they can formalize their caretaking. Make sure that the teams working on the wiki trust that person before you do that, though. One alternate possibility is suggested by several wiki administrators. That would be to have any team about to start on a wiki nominate a champion who is their elected leader. On the one hand, this person is the support contact and the contact to management. On the other hand, he or she is the wiki evangelist beyond the team itself. This will support enterprise-wide adoption.

Simplicity, Simplicity, Simplicity

Simplicity is the rule of wiki-thumb. You don't need extensive guidelines on use. In fact, Figure 8-5 shows the (noncorporate) acceptable use terms from my CRM 2.0 Wiki, which could mirror a corporate acceptable use policy in the beginning of the wiki's life.

The best way to think about this is that it is content management's good twin. Wikis are focused on the content. Content management is focused on administration. That doesn't mean it shouldn't integrate into your content management system in time, but it doesn't have to on day one. Additionally, if you want it to integrate with your CRM system, that doesn't have to happen on day one either (see below). Make the creation of content easy for your teams or your wiki collaborators.

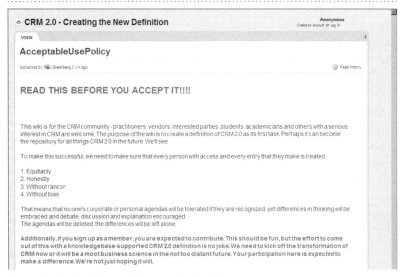

Figure 8-5: Social CRM acceptable use policy: simple but concrete

Engage Customers from the Beginning

Wikis are valuable tools for both improving the sales opportunities with your customers and for collaborating with them directly. If the latter is your goal, and there is a collaboration project that you think would be best served by working direct with your customers (see Chapter 11), then create a group for that project and invite the customers in at the beginning of the effort—not somewhere in between. Their input can be invaluable in helping you evolve the wiki policies and increasing wiki participation—and it engenders more loyal customers because they are participating in something of value to them and the company.

A Look at Wikis that Worked Well

There are hundreds of wiki case studies that show its value for CRM and interaction with constituents. Companies like IBM and SAP, salesforce .com, and others use them routinely to communicate with customers and, of course, with each other. I've chosen three short examples—two private sector, one public sector—each of which is a lesson unto itself.

Intellipedia

Intellipedia is not only one of the most famous U.S. government wikis, it is one of the most celebrated wikis, period. It was created after 9/11 by the director of national intelligence to share intelligence information as much as possible among the entire intelligence community, not just a single agency. Because there would be classified information involved and 16 agencies, it made the effort particularly complicated.

It is not only a place to coordinate and collect intelligence data, but also has become a best practices repository for the intelligence community. Because there are national security concerns, only cleared employees can participate in the wiki.

Intellipedia has been mindful of its public benefit too. They appointed, early on, Sean Dennehy as the Intellipedia Chief Evangelist, not exactly a typical government title. (I wonder how they handle his pay grade?) He has been speaking on Intellipedia at such venues as the Enterprise 2.0 conference, where he has been among the most well received. The idea of having someone who can handle public relations for your Social CRM programs is a good one and the title in any domain not a bad one at all.

One thing that has been notable about Intellipedia is their approach to its users. Organic growth is the route they've chosen and it has paid dividends. They've found that the contributors are not just the younger members of the intelligence community. In fact, as Doherty has often noted, the most active participant is a 68-year-old man.

Fachagentur Nachwachsende Rohstoffe (FNR)

In Germany, the agency responsible for maintaining awareness of renewable resources, the Fachagentur Nachwachsende Rohstoffe (FNR), is funding a three-year program to make sure that the German language version of Wikipedia, the best-known wiki/online encyclopedia, will be aimed at providing accurate entries on specialized renewable resources. The funding will not go to Wikipedia but to the Nova Institut, who are creating the entries and see that the information is accurate.

What's important here is the outreach. One of the core lessons of the entire social media environment is that there are activities going on outside your business that impact your business. You have to be diligent in monitoring them as well as creating your own activities within the corporate walls. Communication through this kind of outreach is of vital importance. It follows the dictum that we've discussed already several times in several ways—the conversation is going on out there. Not participating is a risky proposition.

Polycom

Anyone who's ever worked in a corporate office knows Polycom. If you've ever been on a conference call and were in a room with several people on that call, you probably noticed that you were talking to something resembling a black three-cornered hat. The three-cornered hat was a Polycom teleconference device—easily the best quality in their industry at their varying price points.

That quality matters a great deal to Polycom, and to assure that quality, they have a highly structured, need I say it, quality assurance program. One of the core requirements of that program is being able to track issues related to their equipment and then resolve them. They use the Atlassian JIRA program I mentioned a bit earlier around CRM integration.

They tracked the issues, and suggested solutions, routed it appropriately, and so on using the Atlassian JIRA program, but they also needed to make sure that this information was integrated into their help desk system—which was Siebel.

While this might have seemed easy, it really wasn't. One of the peculiar difficulties of this integration was that there were changes in data formats and types in the Siebel systems that needed to be replicated in the JIRA issue tracking system without the need for developers each time those changes occurred. Plus there was always the problem of how to handle the integration so that there were few issues if the data was bad or one or both of the systems were down.

A Polycom service provider, Customware solved the integration puzzles by creating a plug-in for JIRA that allowed a dynamic definition of messages from Siebel to JIRA—thus solving the changes in data types and formats in a real-time environment, without those pesky developers having to get involved.

Wikis are among the more mature collaboration tools available for Social CRM deployments, and the industrial strength versions like Atlassian and Socialtext can be integrated into transactional CRM systems as well. There is little excuse even for you traditionalists to not incorporate them into your Social CRM strategy.

Superstah! Socialtext

It's funny, but there are a lot of Web 2.0 social media outfits that aren't really businesses. They are playpens with a business veneer. They've developed their tools out of altruism, mischief, passionate interest in technology, wanting to be the best first or the first to the dance, but they have no business plan, no idea how to make money, and are not driven by capitalist mores.

This is definitely not the case with Socialtext and particularly its founder, Ross Mayfield. He's a true thought-leader in the social media playground, but he also understands that he's in business to make money—not just great tools—and this perception has served him and his company very well.

For example, they are easily the most important enterprise wiki platform, with few competitors anywhere near their level. Their primary enterprise competitor is Atlassian Confluence, a formidable package and one that has more CRM connectors than Socialtext, but none have the depth of functionality or are as forward thinking.

Socialtext is the crème de la crème of wiki suppliers. Their 4,000 plus customers include companies like Symantec, Humana, Nokia, the *Washington Post*—even Oracle and SAP use them rather than native tools. Even more to their credit, SAP Ventures is one of their financial backers.

They are recognized by most of the analysts as the leaders in their industry, with Gartner in their October 2008 Team Collaboration and Social Software Magic Quadrant making them among the most visionary—ahead of Microsoft, BEA, and even IBM. That says something, especially in the latter case.

Mission 21st Century

Ross Mayfield on Socialtext over the next few years:

Socialtext will continue to innovate around its wiki-centric platform to increase ease-of-use and simplicity of operations, as well as continuing to integrate more closely with core enterprise infrastructure. Socialtext introduced its spreadsheet-in-a-wiki, SocialCalc, and sees this opening up a new category of enterprise software. Socialtext will leverage marketing, sales, and co-development efforts by working with partners in adjacent areas such as blogging, RSS readers/servers, and other social software and networking tools. Socialtext expects to see the collaboration and social software market increasingly converge around Web 2.0 technologies plus social networking tools. Socialtext is going to continue to grow to integrate these tools with core enterprise infrastructures, other applications, as well as traditional collaboration tools for unified communications.

I'd like you to note the sentences that I bolded—because that reflects the thinking that drives Social CRM as well as the social software and social media markets.

The Product: Socialtext 3.0

This is an industrial strength enterprise-level product. While it can appeal to small business with its hosted edition, it is built for midsized and large corporations and has the administrative functions needed for that scale. But it is also a remarkably resilient product platform. It has pretty much all that you would expect of a wiki that needs to be integrated with other data sources. From my standpoint—which, of course, means Social CRM—the only thing that it lacks is a large group of prebuilt connectors for salesforce.com, Oracle, and other major CRM vendors, but the tools are there to build them if you're so inclined.

Individual Features

► Personalized, customizable dashboard that shows internal and external social activity

► Dashboard templates for business solution areas

► Profiles and user directory allow you to tap expertise and subscribe to activities of people you work with

► Draw profile information from directories and enterprise applications

► Easy to create group workspaces and invite team members

► Manage user permissions and remove users; this can be done at the administrative level or the team level with a team leader with administrative permissions

► Collaborative document editing

► Integrated team blogs within the wiki framework

► Comments and ratings

► Full revision history with rollback and complete audit trail; the audit trail can be very important

► WYSIWYG editor that has Word-like functionality but is easy to use

► One-way or two-way links to a page, workspace, section, file, or image; access is controlled by the administrator

► Personalized watch list to track pages, tags, people, search results

► Subscribe to changes via e-mail or RSS, so even if you are still primitive and want to use e-mail, you can monitor wiki changes or project developments

► Device-ready mobile access; it will auto-recognize your device

► Offline version, allows you to read and write wiki content when disconnected and will provide you with the ability to sync with a server

► Powerful search engine; you can find wiki pages, documents, or individuals through Boolean or metadata queries, and only those the user has permission to access

► Tagging lets you find common areas of interest or expertise/ practice and organize content

► Reusable content by including pages; can be shared through widgets for searches or RSS subscription feeds

Enterprise Features

This is what distinguishes Socialtext from its rivals. The range of administrative functions is truly staggering. This allows them to provide the levels of security, policy management, privacy management, and integration that make them one of the few in social software that can be called world class. They have both an SaaS and an on-premise edition. They can be run on VMware—which means, for those of you not in the world of the terribly geeky, virtually. Uniquely, they have an offline edition too and an open source version, which gives them the benefit of thousands of developers working on their product in the true spirit of the collaborative value chain (see Chapter 11).

They understand market opportunity with the enterprise. As you might remember, in Chapter 6 I mentioned the odd decision of Lotus Connections to not include a wiki component—instead they replaced it with what they call activities, which are outcome-based team collaboration, not wikis. Socialtext recognized the market opportunity and built a connector for Lotus Connections—smart, very smart.

Here we go with the enterprise features:

► Integrate with LDAP/Active Directory and single sign-on systems

► SSL-protected browser access

► Password-protected RSS feeds

► REST and SOAP APIs

► RSS and Atom feed format standards

► Convert content from other wikis and data sources

► Widgets support OpenSocial gadget standard

► Detailed reports on adoption and usage

► Web-based administrative console (Figure 8-6)

► Centrally view and manage users and workspace configuration

► Granular access control for groups and users

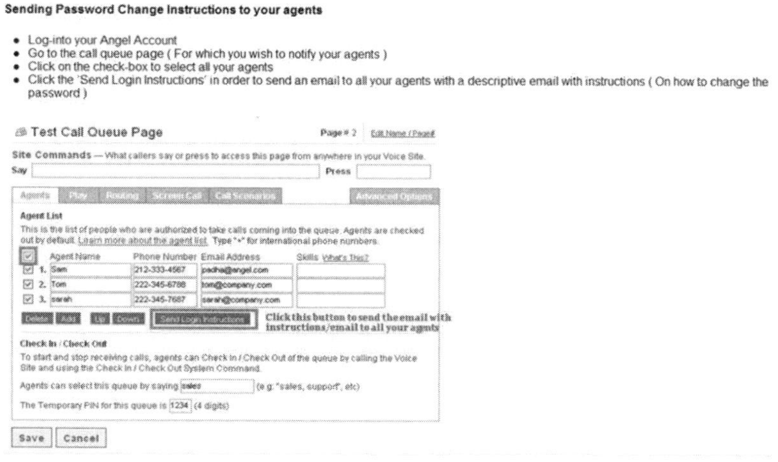

Figure 8-6: A Socialtext administrative screen (Source: Socialtext)

Actually, this is very much a culled feature and function list. The total amount is apparently infinite—or close to it—all philosophical implications of that statement aside. What I have listed are the ones that I find the most important to a CRM audience on either side of usage and that I can vouch for through experience with the application during the vetting process. This one is world class and deserves some consideration in your vendor selection process.

Socialtext continues to innovate when it comes to the product with their 2009 introduction of a free full-featured version for 50 users or less and an actual hardware appliance that comes with Socialtext built in. In late 2009, a mobile edition was introduced that works in any smartphone environment.

Wiki Wrap-Up

Just one final thought before I drop you off at your meeting with Ross.

You've probably noticed that I've spent a good deal of time in the last two chapters on blogs and wikis in particular, and before that, on social media as a whole. The reason is that they are the contemporary tools for customer engagement. They give your company the means to converse with your customers (blogs), to work with them (wikis, blogs), and to educate them (podcasts) and through this, to enhance your brand, create loyalty where it wasn't before, and to tap the intelligence of your actual base. That's why there is so much emphasis on the social tools so far. They are a part of customer engagement strategy that can't be ignored.

But now we move on to the vessels for this—social networks and user communities. This is the hottest topic and the most difficult because of the misconceptions out there due to the innumerable discussions of consumer social networks like Facebook and MySpace. Rest assured, we'll be clearing that up and . . . oh, we're here. Meet Ross Mayfield.

Ross Mayfield is a man who knows his business—and knows business. He is not only the chairman, president, and co-founder of Socialtext, but he's also a noted blogger, thought-leader, and by his own admission a serial and social entrepreneur. Ross partnered with Dan Bricklin, the creator of the first spreadsheet program, VisiCalc, to co-develop and distribute SocialCalc, the first wiki-based social spreadsheet in addition to the better known Socialtext wiki products. Always the innovator, that guy. Now let's listen to what a genuine thought-leader in the world of wikis has to say about what you should be thinking when you leave this chapter.

MINI-CONVERSATION WITH ROSS MAYFIELD: UNDERSTAND WHAT IS DIFFERENT ABOUT SOCIAL SOFTWARE

Traditional enterprise software is top-down, highly structured, run by business rules, and serves the goal of automating business process to drive down cost. The problem is your people don't spend most of their time executing business process. Most of their time is spent handling exceptions to process. An exception happens not just when a design is flawed, but when the design or process is outdated because of a change in the environment. Resolving exceptions at speed is not the only opportunity. When the edge of an organization can sense and respond to change while learning, exceptions are the greatest recurring source of innovation.

The structure of a social software application emerges as a by-product of people using it. For example, a major consumer electronics manufacturer deployed Socialtext as an after-marketing product support knowledge base. Previously, their 5,000 reps were using a traditional structured knowledge base. But the structure became crufty, lacked contribution outside of the primary known issues with known solutions and rigid troubleshooting steps—and 17-point solutions were created by teams around it. In three months, using Socialtext, not only were reps generating thousands of pages, but 99 percent of the pages were tagged, allowing a new structure to unfold. Answers could be found through unstructured search and browsing through tags, but also added with the click of the edit button, often while on a call. Time to resolution gained recurring improvement, and employee anecdotes expressed increased satisfaction—also, by their measures, the average call time was reduced by 30 percent.

I should highlight one of our latest innovations, SocialCalc, the social spreadsheet we have developed with Dan Bricklin who invented VisiCalc, the first computer spreadsheet. The unique combination of wiki and spreadsheet not only enables easy linking, tagging, revision and authoring that you would expect from a wiki foundation, but lets people work with structured data in an unstructured way.

Successful Implementation Requires Focusing on People

Over the last five years, we have seen the use cases evolve for social software. In 2002, it was project communication and lightweight documentation for technical groups. In 2004, the software became easy to use, so the use case shifted to business people using it as an alternative to e-mail for workgroup collaboration. In 2006, it shifted to mass collaboration, building "Wikipedia inside" knowledge sharing communities. The latest shift is to process-specific implementations, such as participatory knowledge bases for service and support. The latest shift can be described as from "above-the-flow" sharing to "in-the-flow" collaboration, where sharing is the by-product of getting work done. Our VP of professional services, Michael

Idinopolus, who used to run McKinsey's Knowledge Management practice, makes this distinction. While we have learned how to foster adoption for above-the-flow sharing, building sustainable communities is a challenge in many corporate cultures and the value proposition is more intangible. In-the-flow process-specific implementations are where we've found the greatest customer success.

The first metric that matters in a social software deployment is adoption. What is the rate of adoption and how fast are novices becoming experts? And the important investment that can be made is at the outset of the implementation, an investment in people. There is no such thing as collaboration without a goal. Defining the goal and getting a shared belief in it may require working with outside consultants. But at the very least, a small investment in training and coaching your people significantly increases the rate of return.

Partner Line of Business with IT

Considering that adoption is the critical success factor, people add value to the application and generate its structure, and the goals and outcomes are driven by line of business—organizations need to treat social software differently. This isn't like previous bottom-up technology like e-mail or IM that IT can simply provision as a communication utility. It is a new form of collaboration software. This isn't like traditional enterprise software, where IT can add value by hard-coding workflow and process automation, and users fill in forms to be able to go to the next step. This isn't like something you push out to the desktop model and provide training for individuals, because the productivity isn't personal.

Don't take it personally, but IT deployments of social software have high rates of failure. What's the point of 1,000 dead wikis that may have satiated bottom-up and buzzword demand? Pick a pilot and partner IT with line of business. Iterate together, focus on adoption toward a business goal, and learn.⬥

9

Social Networks, User Communities: Who Loves Ya, Baby?

O kay, by now you've read enough about the components of the new customer-centered enterprise and the social media tools that you can use, but what about the places the customers hang out? Where do they congregate? What are they saying (about you)? What do companies do to engage those assembled customers? How do they retain the information from those conversations? When will these questions stop?

When I answer them—but let me explain, please.

I'm a social network party guy. I have 900-plus connections on LinkedIn, more than 500 on Facebook, over 1,400 followers on Twitter, and hundreds of others on dozens of other social networks. I understand how each of them works. I use the applications that many of them provide to me. On Facebook, I poke you. On Twitter, I tweet you. On LinkedIn, I link to people who were two or three degrees from me just yesterday.

None of that qualifies me to develop, manage, or even understand the value of a social network or a user community in business. But it does qualify me to understand the thinking of the customer and how they might be interested in engaging with your business. Maybe. However, please have no misconceptions. Facebook and LinkedIn may be sites where you can create a social network for engaging your customer, but they are not meant to be the ideal enterprise social network. We'll see why over the course of this chapter.

The business value of community and collaboration in the new world of the social customer can't be underestimated—or if you do, it's at your own risk. Thus, while I recognize the value of Facebook, I'm not going to concentrate on the business uses of Facebook, though I will cover it. Remember, this is a book about Social CRM. We have to look at communities and social networks that you can develop from the standpoint of your enterprise, what the guidelines are for setting the rules, and some of the best practices for community management. These are tricky but navigable waters. They are waters that you pretty much have to dive into to at least remain competitive now. Put on your bathing suits, brothers and sisters, time to jump in.

The Conversation Can't Be Avoided

I'm realizing that there's an irony in what those of us who spend our time shouting our "outlooks" to the rafters about the customer experience are doing. For the most part, we're commenting on and chronicling what has been going on since the dawn of man. It's called conversation. Most importantly, conversations at specific locations.

Of course, to belabor an obvious point, in the past, present, and future, those locations were, are, and will be marketplaces, homes, on the street, inside of other buildings—almost any place that humans get together. When humans banded into groups of like interest or practice they formed organizations that effectively localized or focused conversation around those interests. So we saw (and see) investment clubs or book review groups or veterans halls or even stadia where people of mostly like mind get together for a short time. Think about it. The investment clubs are communities of interest—those who are interested in figuring out what's the best way to invest. The veterans' halls are communities of practice—those who fought in foreign wars. The stadia, which might host a baseball game for your community team (the Yankees, of course), are outcome-based communities. When the event is over, people of like mind disengage and go home. But they congregate for that time to achieve or observe that outcome.

In other words, what we're going to discuss here was physical and "analog" long before it was web-based and digital. The conversations that go on in all these places are actually that: interactions and communications between people for some reason at a tangible location.

The online communities are dramatically transforming what defines a location, but they are also impacting the physical locations where we congregate. Where those Gen Cers we chatted about in Chapter 1 now congregate, and how they connect to each other and to other locations, directly affects your business.

Check it out.

Just So Ba-NAL, Dahling—All You Dahlings

If this was 1990, and you made the oft-repeated comment, "This does *nothing* for me," that would have been a statement of purely personal expression. You would have gotten a nod of the head or perhaps a disgusted stare from one or two people who felt it did something for them and that's pretty much it.

However, in the year you're reading this (or 2525, according to Zagar and Evans), "does nothing for me" is social commentary that sets off alarms everywhere. Why? Because the customer is possibly telling that to thousands of people who actually listen to him.

In the present, the customer is willing to talk to people they don't know without a second thought because the tools are so available. What makes this even more powerful and potentially dangerous is that they can easily find online locations teeming with citizens who might have generally similar interests and views or identical specific out-looks. For example, there are sites devoted to satellite TV with forums like Satellite TV Forum (www.satellitetvforum.com) where you can vent about DirecTV or Dish Network.

You need to know what these things are, how the network works, who the influencers are within the network, and what you as a corporate mogul can do to involve your company and maybe even yourself in this conversation going on outside your corporate walls. That's where the enterprise social network comes in for one part of the solution.

What Are Social Networks and Communities, for Real?

To get some idea of the definition of community, we're heading back to the 1950s. So go buy yourself a chocolate malt, flip on some Elvis, slip on those white bucks, and pay attention.

In 1955, George Hillery, Jr., a professor of sociology at Virginia Polytechnic Institute, took 94 sociological definitions of the term "community" and analyzed them. He found 16 common concepts within the 94 different characterizations. Interestingly, he found only one concept that was common among all 94 and that was the most obvious: they all involve people. That said, he found that "69 are in accord that social interaction, area, and a common tie or ties are commonly found in community life."

Those common areas define communities today too. Most online communities are built around a location that gives a like-minded group of people a place to interact around their common interest. That would be a 95th definition. For the sake of easy sailing, I'm going to use "social networks" and "communities" more or less interchangeably.

Social networks exist indigenously. The primary difference between the current social networks and the traditional ones are that you don't have to physically be in the presence of the other members or the key intersection points of the network (called nodes) to have an impact on the network. The new digital versions have other advantages. You can capture the data that is provided by the members' conversations. With the right tools, you can respond to the members' concerns, fears, disgust, or love, even if you had no idea that the member was conversing about it that day. You can uncover and analyze the conversation a lot easier than in the past. It's no longer an issue of someone going behind other members' or the network facilitator's backs. All the information is right there for the picking. Transparency is the order of the day.

Social Network Styles: What Models Can You Choose From?

There is no one form or style of social network. Kids use social networks through Club Penguin and Webkinz by the hundreds of thousands (see Figure 9-1). Baby boomers and seniors can use TeeBeeDee to meet their generational needs. Members of the real estate industry (not just agents) use ActiveRain (www.activerain.com), which had more than 150,000 members in July 2009. SAP has SDN, run by the talented Marco ten Vaanholt, with over 1.3 million SAP software developers. There is even a social network ensconced on Facebook for Victoria's Secret PINK line of clothing that went from 390,000 fans in June 2008 to 1,252,714 fans in June 2009—the increase presumably mostly male who got a glimpse at the photo gallery.

Figure 9-1: Kids use social networks like Club Penguin and Webkinz (Source: Morgane Murawiec, Hannah Hartley, Jenna Hartley)

The use of social networks is mainstream—time to get used to it. According to the Pew Internet Study on American Life, as of December 2008, over 35 percent of all adults had a profile associated with one or another social networking site. More germane, Nielsen Online in their March 2009 study "Global Faces on Networked Places" found:

1. The fastest growing sector for Internet use is communities and blog sites, with a 5.4 percent increase in a single year, more than any other category.

2. Member communities reach more Internet users (66.8 percent) than e-mail (65.1 percent).

That's remarkably important data because, though still a primarily young-generation phenomenon, this reflects how we are experiencing the transformation of how we converse, with a profound impact on business communications with customers.

As I'll show you posthaste, there are several classifiable types of social networks you should be aware of when contemplating a CRM strategy. Some are for dealing with customer issues, some are for marketing or the creation of sticky loyal customers, and others drive revenue directly. Each of them is potentially worthy of inclusion in someone's business model—possibly yours. But don't just assume any are worthy. Decide whether or not a social network is in your interest and which ones work for you, given your strategy.

"Participating in the Community of the Consumer"

I love that phrase. That's the way Jim Keyes, Blockbuster CEO, described their Facebook group, which is, for the most part, the kind of community that you see most commonly right now. There are dozens of businesses using the most popular social networks to create groups, or pages, or fan sites to develop an external (beyond their own firewall) community. They are going to where the customer lives, but not necessarily where they shop. E-commerce is not Facebook's strong suit.

In creating a Facebook group for your organization, you're banking on a number of things:

▶ That your customers actually use Facebook

▶ That they can be informed via the Facebook tools of the existence of your group, in addition to your own normal communications channels

▶ That they will find what you are providing to be of enough interest to make your community a regular stop when they are logged in to Facebook

▶ That they will opt in to being updated about the continuing activities of your community

▶ That they have no objection to Facebook owning the knowledge of their activities in your group as an asset and as part of their Facebook "customer record," also known as their profile

The benefits of these external community pages can be well worth it if you are willing to accept that you don't control the source—in this case, Facebook. Marketing and loyalty are areas that profit from this kind of external community. Customer service can be served by these communities, though Facebook pages are not necessarily the best vehicle for that. There are sites like GetSatisfaction that provide external customer service communities created by either the customer or employees of the company. Additionally, companies like TiVo have seen the value in Facebook as a supplementary site for garnering and capturing customer service issues and data (see Chapter 13 for a little more on that).

Things Go Better with Facebook: Coca-Cola's Fan Club

Coca-Cola established their Facebook fan page in September 2008 and as of July 2009 they have recruited 3.4 million fans. Actually, this isn't entirely accurate. What they did was find a page that had been created by a couple of 29-year-old Coca-Cola fans and, rather than sue them (which is what one of the youngsters feared), instead worked with the two fans to build the page up. But this wasn't a case of buying the page. The creators became an intimate part of the continued development of the page. Coca-Cola had a savvy understanding of the benefits and the limitations of a Facebook group. They understood that Facebook was a site that their customers used, not one that the company owned. Coke wanted to be unobtrusive and leave it as a "fan club." While I'd say that they aren't unobtrusive any longer, they have been entirely successful because of their understanding of how Facebook works and their intelligence when it comes to collaborating with their fans.

While the founding fans still use the pages, Coca-Cola has a wide range of interactions on the page. They use it for promotions. They track the conversations of their customers through the postings to the

Facebook wall and to the discussion groups. They give fans "exclusive sneak peeks" at things like the Coca-Cola iPhone Facebook app, which makes those fans feel like they are on the inside of something.

When it comes to the visual arts, they don't just have generic or random photo uploads. They wield photos like artists use brushes. One album is an archive of historic Coke photos evoking nostalgia. Another is an album of Coca-Cola employees celebrating a birthday—Coca-Cola's—but as informal shots at a beach. They also allow fans to upload their own Coke-related photos to the site.

Think of what kind of brand image is projected in just the way the photo archives are used. In essence, it says, "We are a company with an immensely proud tradition that not only can stay current with the contemporary trends, but are also personable and intimate with you, our customers. We want you to know us and we want to know you."

The brilliance of the fan page doesn't stop with photos. If you look at the Wall updates, they are in Italian, French, English, Spanish, two or three languages I can't figure out, and even when in English, reference Coke in Macedonia, Thailand, Romania, and France. "I'd like to teach the world to sing, in perfect harmony. . . ." (I know you know that one.)

What the brand leaders at Coca-Cola, particularly the director of worldwide interactive marketing, Michael Donnelly, realized is that if you let the fans control their own conversation and support it, you can build something substantial and engender advocacy in ways that weren't even a glimmer several years ago. What that translates to is 3.4 million fans, the second largest fan "club" on Facebook, second only to President Obama with over 6.4 million.

Facilitated User Communities

These are managed communities. The setup, administration, and facilitation are done by a third party. They are private. The membership is mostly invited. These are not the "damn the torpedoes, full speed ahead" kinds of sites that many of the others are. Even those behind the enterprise walls are often open and public, just administratively controlled by the company that created them. These aren't those. These are planned neighborhoods, often whose primary purpose is to gain insight into customers.

Typically, they are organized around a specific topic. They can be communities that exist for an explicit time and delimited purpose or communities of interest for a longer duration. Their differentiator is that these private communities are carefully managed. Some of the characteristics:

▶ The size of the membership is restricted.

▶ The members are specifically chosen according to segmentation or other demographic or even psychographic information.

▶ The community is moderated by experienced facilitators who, while not intrusive, are still managing and directing the conversation, though not to any particular conclusion because that would taint the purpose.

▶ The community's owner can be visible or not. The moderators always are visible.

Facilitated communities can be expensive because of the labor time involved in moderation of the community. The upside is that they are remarkably good for either providing long-term support for networks that need the interaction and some direction on how that interaction should occur or for short-term insights into particular areas or problems. The latter use facilitated discussions to capture the data they need to make key product or services decisions.

But that's also where the most significant downside comes in. Pharmaceutical companies have been known to create these facilitated private social networks around a disease they have some drug treatment for or around the drug itself. But rather than let it be known that they own the community, they instead stay in the background observing, something like using one-way glass in an interrogation. The question arises, is that ethical? Would you want to be watched and your discourse harvested without knowing that there is an interested company behind that one-way glass? Not me.

That said, don't rule this form of community out—either as a long-term option or an outcome-based social network. The ethical issues aren't applicable to the bulk of them. The value is clear if they meet strategic needs.

National Comprehensive Cancer Network

The National Comprehensive Cancer Network (NCCN), an alliance of 21 cancer care centers, initially collaborated with premier facilitated community builder, Communispace, to build a private network that was for first-time cancer patients at all stages. The idea was to provide a mutually beneficial environment—a community—where cancer patients could express their worries, concerns, and ideas without fear and without being judged, while also providing a place where the care centers could learn how to improve their care to the patients. There were 350 patients chosen for this private network, based on studies that identified what it would take to optimize the discussion and provide the strongest mutual support.

The community was designed to calm—the colors of the site being soothing, for instance—and to develop intimacy between the caregivers and the patients, and the patients with each other. There was 24/7 access, so no one was ever alone. At first, the site itself was administered and facilitated by Communispace, which is what Communispace does.

Insights gained from the caregiver-patient and patient-patient discussions led to dramatic changes at the 21 centers. The range of improved patient experiences go from preadmission testing to clinical trial participation to oral therapy compliance and on to psychosocial programs. This was so successful that NCCN launched two more communities, one for late-stage cancer patients and another for early-stage cancer patients.

NCCN is important because the success was based on mutually derived value, the hallmark of Social CRM strategy and purpose of an enterprise social network. The patients were supported by each other, and they had access 24/7 to experts so that they were never unsupported. As someone who has been through the process with my wife's successful fight against breast cancer in 2004–2005, the value of access to information and support is an almost incalculable benefit in the fight to beat that horrible disease. The more you know, the better the chance to beat it.

This is a somewhat dramatic but important example of how communities can provide value to both sides—even when they aren't Facebook or LinkedIn.

Community-Based Businesses

The growth of communities and social networks has been instrumental in supporting the development of new business models that have objectives based on the growth and evolution of the communities rather than the more traditional numbers that you see from accounting departments. The concept is directly in line with Social CRM's fundamental tenet: value and values are given, and value and values are received. The scions of the new social networks have often had trouble figuring out what kind of business model will yield them revenue and profits. Witness Facebook's constant struggle for revenue. However, community-based businesses, such as community-based retailing, have no such issue. They have proven to be immensely successful, as we can see in the case of Karmaloop.

Karmaloop

Karmaloop is one of the most innovative clothing retailers in the world. Founded in 2005 by Greg Selkoe, they have grown to well in excess of $20 million for reasons that will become apparent. Rather than an e-commerce site, they call themselves, rightfully, a "community of style."

More of the data first. They have their own clothing line called the Sons of Liberty. They have only one store that I think, given the name of the clothing line, you can make a reasonable guess as to its location. No, not Philly. Boston. They have a community of nearly a million members as of 2009. Their community is skewed toward young, hip Gen Yers who are web-savvy and love to buy stuff—which is just about all of them.

Karmaloop gets community-based business. They are masters of how to implement community retailing with enough success to be the poster child for a contemporary Social CRM success story—without using any CRM software, though they do use software, obviously.

Karmaloop engages their community. They provide a location to get the hippest big brands like Adidas and Nike, and they also use a significant amount of their web real estate to give independent designers a place to hawk their ideas and their wares. In June 2006, they created the Kazbah, a mini-mall of 45 "stores" chosen by Karmaloop that gave their customers a place to sell their independent brands (see Figure 9-2). Selected customers can peddle their wares, and Karmaloop provides an e-zine that highlights the independent vendors to the Karmaloop community.

If that's all there was, it would be cool, but it goes *so* much further. They have KarmaloopTV, a web TV show devoted to fashion trends. In 2008, they created an invitation-only network for trendsetters in fashion, Jungle Life. While I think they could have done better with the name, the idea is spot on. You become a trendsetter in a private social network within a community. Acceptance into Jungle Life guarantees you reputation and influence as a trendsetter (at least within Karmaloop), which of course was the plan from the get go.

Figure 9-2: Karmaloop community-based retailing

But the *ne plus ultra* for Karmaloop is their street teams. Street teams are usually teenaged kids who get paid for slapping up posters for concerts or other events all over town. But Karmaloop has taken the idea of street teams to another realm entirely. Their street teams are 1 percent of their community members, roughly 8,000 young souls, who function not just as evangelists/advocates but as part of an extended sales force.

When a community member becomes part of the street team, they are given a unique identifier that they will use for all transactions, including purchases they make, or purchases they convince others to make, or uploading a video. Not only does the street team member help sell, they are providing rich user-generated content for the Karmaloop site and adding to the discussion by uploading those videos, pix, and comments on the styles, techniques for selling, great stories of their street team work, and questions they need answered. In other words, they have an unadulterated sense of community which has been translated into rewards for both company and customer. Interestingly, in this model, the company and the customer are symbiotic extensions of one another.

In return for this yeoman work, they get discounts and points that can be redeemed for cash and clothes. They don't only get them for the sales, but also for recruitment to the community and community participation.

The street teams, the 1 percent of the community who actively participate in Karmaloop sales and recruitment, have been an enormously important part of Karmaloop success. If you include what the street team members buy themselves in combination with the sales they generate, the 1 percent generates 15 percent of all Karmaloop revenue. That's eye-opening stuff.

You'll note that, so far, I haven't mentioned software. However, that isn't to say that they don't use software to support this new business model. After all, what would Social CRM be without software? Karmaloop uses MyBuys, which generates personalized offers based on customer preferences and browsing behaviors. For example, if you indicate a preference for Adidas, personalized offers will be sent to you via e-mail or RSS. If you're on the site and you (thank you, cookie) come in from Canada and have spent time looking around at T-shirts, you might see personalized offers and panels on the right side of the screen for Canadian T-shirt companies' offerings. There was an increase in successful e-mail conversion of 220 percent in 2007 and according to Greg Selkoe, a lift uptick of 3 percent. Software can help.

Community retailing isn't only done by Karmaloop. It's done with a great deal of success by like-minded T-shirt company Threadless, skewed to the same Gen Y demographic and similar in concept. What it proves is that communities and social networks are not only about marketing and customer service; they can be part of a successful sales and revenue model if you think outside of the box.

DIY, No Not DUI, Communities

I'm not going to dwell on this kind of community. They are the do-it-yourself communities best exemplified by Ning. Their idea is simple. Come in, sign up, and you have the tools made available to create a community/social network according to your heart's or business's desire. Ning in particular, headed up by the extraordinary Gina Bianchini, had, by March 2009, over 200,000 active social networks (out of 700,000 total created networks), with 2.4 million members. Other numbers that just make Ning's success all the more obvious: also by March 2009, each day 2.6 million individual pieces of content—photos, blog posts, etc.—are added. The site had 2.7 billion page views that month and nearly 3,500 new social networks were created each day. They had 83 social networks using the keyword "CRM" alone. However, most of them had between 15 and 50 members.

Ning itself wasn't that immediately profitable. In early 2009, they were making $55 per month from each of the 12,000 social networks who bought premium feature access. While they have enough data to make it very interesting to advertisers, they don't discuss much about their financial model or their plans.

Is this where you'd want your enterprise social network to reside? Probably not. Ning lacks the administrative and security features and the controls you'd need to establish a truly robust social network for your customers or for internal collaboration. But this model can have business value. Jay Dunn, the VP of marketing at Lane Bryant, created a Ning social network that he calls SuperGroup with roughly 200 approved members. While it isn't an official corporate social network, (Lane Bryant has Inside Curve) the members who represent retail industry leaders and other key parties can converse, link to other sites, push their feeds into the community, track each other's activities if they want to, see what each other are reading, blog—you name it. While this is Jay's network, what makes it valuable to Lane Bryant is the ability of the members of that network to get to know a member of the senior management of Lane Bryant and to provide an informal channel to Lane Bryant on preferences in clothing, for example, or issues of marketing in the retail industry or to just break down formality. What makes it valuable to Jay is that there is a forum for retail leaders to discuss how to improve their businesses that provides an informal channel where there is no competitive stress to talk over the ideas and to get to know each other. Lane Bryant by inference becomes known as a leading edge company and Jay as a cutting edge thinker. All in all, a win-win for Jay and Lane Bryant.

By the way, there is a *CRM at the Speed of Light 4* social network on Ning if you want to participate in the discussion, currently by invitation only, though I may open it up soon. E-mail me at paulgreenberg3@comcast.net or go to the McGraw-Hill site for the book and let me know you want to be a part of it and I'll send you the invite you need. Access is everything, isn't it?

Outcome-Based Social Networks

Even though the name outcome-based social networks (OSN) is of my own creation, I have to give credit for the concept and inspiration to Anthony Lye, Oracle's CRM SVP, whom you met in the electronic chapter on CRM leaders and will see more of in the chapter on Sales and Marketing. I had a conversation with him on the phone in 2008 and he said something very close to this:

> We shouldn't distinguish between corporate and consumer social networks. Social networks are containers for a series of activities by people—a container across social, geographic, company, and other boundaries. They can exist for years, or for a few minutes, hours, or days. It can be around a marketing event, a service request. Basically, a social network is a container that drives meaningful outcomes.

This is a really important concept. Most people see social networks as something that has permanence and at the same time involves investing in long-term efforts to add to content or to increase membership. But that isn't necessarily the way they always work. Motivations for the creation of the social networks are different, and the benefits derived by business from the social networks can vary widely.

Outcome-based social networks are often organized around an opportunity in sales, an engagement, or a particular transaction or interaction that has a limited lifespan. Lotus Connections (see Chapter 6) provides their wiki-like functionality around what they call activities, which are not wikis with permanence but outcome-based social networks that are used for a project and, when done, archived.

Don't underestimate the value of this kind of network. Bad thinking about how you are going to engage your employees—or more germane to this book, your customers—leads to communities in a dead zone. For example, Ning has 700,000 communities of which 200,000 are active, which means 500,000 are either whimsical or unsustainable. I've built communities that had a specific purpose using wikis as the vehicle; one was for the definition of Social CRM. When that's defined to the community's satisfaction, the planned outcome will have been accomplished and the community members will disperse.

It's really no different from an audience at an event. I spent 72 hours at Woodstock in 1969 and listened to all 28 concerts. I suffered the rain, loved the music, didn't sleep (even without drugs) for a second, met all kinds of people, had excited discussions around the music being played, offered undying fealty to my new friends and vows of permanent friendship after the festival were made. Then when it ended, I went home, slept for 14 hours, and never again saw anyone from there I didn't already know before. The outcome-based social network of 600,000 at Max Yasgur's farm was archived in my memory.

These networks are very valuable to business if conceived strategically. They should be used to support a specific time-delimited occurrence that needs to have intensive structured conversations to improve the possibilities of the success of the outcome. The value of the network is that the data from the conversation becomes part of the permanent knowledge base in addition to its efficacy while active. Plus it is part of a lasting record that can be pointed to as an example of best practices and success.

YouTube Symphony

One extraordinary example of an outcome-based social network was the YouTube Symphony Orchestra (www.youtube.com/symphony). This was an effort sponsored by Google, which worked with the San Francisco Symphony's music director, Michael Tilson Thomas, and the London Symphony Orchestra. Composer Tan Dun wrote an original piece to be performed for the occasion. The idea was to create an orchestra that would not only perform live at Carnegie Hall in New York, but also on YouTube. The orchestra would be wholly recruited through YouTube auditions. Using a channel on YouTube for the aggregate community, videos of the potential members performing were uploaded; comments on everything from musical styles and technical aspects to the performance selections were posted. YTSO artistic coordinator Bill Williams, one of the critical on-the-ground drivers of this outcome-based social network and a principal trumpeter with ensembles such as the San Francisco Symphony and Santa Fe Opera, pointed out that until they did the physical dress rehearsals at Carnegie Hall in April 2009, they had never played together. One unique feature of this OSN was a mash-up of selected video entries of Tan Dun's musical piece into a single video ensemble piece, which resides on the landing page of the symphony.

By June 2009, there were over 8.8 million views on the channel and nearly 40,000 subscribers. The interaction among the orchestra members and the subscriber/members was incredible and deep. One of the flautists, Nina Perlove, wrote, along with a video, "Nina Perlove looks at some of the places music was heard during the YouTube Symphony Summit . . . even after 8 hours of rehearsals! Please rate and subscribe and visit me at www.realfluteproject.com." She had 3,300 views and dozens of comments. Also note that this is linked to her own site/ network. It uses rating tools and RSS feeds to expand the connectivity of this social network. Often when you click on a subscriber's picture it takes you to the individual member's own YouTube channel or MySpace page.

Even though the community continues to exist, its short-term outcome was the April 2009 concert at Carnegie Hall. Its longer-term strategy was to use contemporary tools to introduce an audience not predisposed to classical music to that music. On all fronts it has succeeded.

Now do you see the benefit of outcome-based communities? These need to be a part of your strategic arsenal when it comes to a customer engagement strategy. The proof is in the strings, the winds, and the brass.

Communities of Interest

These kinds of communities pepper the socnet landscape. For the most part, they're dedicated sites organized around a common interest. Television shows such as HGTV's *Rate My Space* user community are representative. *Rate My Space* is a TV show run by Home and Garden TV that does makeovers for rooms in chosen homes. The *Rate My Space* community provides the forum for members to upload the photos of a room in their house they are proud of or not so fond of. The rooms are rated by members and commented on by members. Low rated rooms are chosen to be given a major makeover on the *Rate My Space* TV show. Members then can rate the makeover.

These communities can be as simple as a threaded forum, which, while missing a lot of the new social capabilities, are still places where customers congregate around a specific interest, whether it's a social issue or a car they love or a service they hate or a team they root for. They can be as complex as HGTV's community, which not only rates rooms but also provides tools to design and buy a kitchen or bathroom as part of "my space." This is very much in the same vein as the innovative work done by Kohler for kitchens and bathrooms, designing, building, and financing a room—with Kohler products, of course.

These can be immensely successful communities if managed well. They can provide you with customers who want to congregate at your site and who will provide you with substantial data to enhance your knowledge of those customers.

KLM Clubs China and Africa have figured out how to make communities of interest work on behalf of their business.

KLM Club China and Club Africa

I haven't had any occasion to fly on KLM, but they've been on my radar for a few years now. They've become one of my favorite airlines without having ever been on them, because of their award-winning communities of interest, Club China and Club Africa.

Clubs China and Africa go well beyond the ordinary service club that many airlines have. Typically, a service club will provide concierge services for VIP fliers. So, for example, if you're a 1K flyer for United, you get increased miles for flying, priority check-in, complimentary upgrades, and so on. If you've flown 1 million miles over your life on United, then you get other things. But what you don't have is access to communities of interest, which is precisely what Clubs China/Africa are.

What makes these clubs unique is that they appeal to a specific group of travelers who fly KLM to a specific location, and give the travelers the means to interact with each other in multiple ways. Take a look at Figure 9-3.

Figure 9-3: KLM Club China provides value to and from the members

The benefit to the customer is wide and deep. Besides traditional services and free stuff, they rely heavily on the customers interacting with each other. As a member:

▶ You can subscribe to their Twitter feed, which has over 2,300 followers. What makes Twitter interesting is how KLM uses it, broadcasting Club China events (or Club Africa) on their Twitter feed, as well as information from other members such as "seeking employment" or "seeking local partner to do business."

▶ You can learn from the best practices on doing business in China that are posted to the club by other members.

▶ You can look at the calendar and see what members are going to be where in China when.

▶ You can arrange meet-ups in China or at any other locations where more than one member is congregating.

▶ You can share your experiences on doing business in China by posting stories.

The business benefits for the members are obvious. KLM has benefited as well. The numbers support that. They now have over 15,300 members from 100 countries in the two clubs combined. Their traffic is steady and consistent and, most important, sticky. For example in May 2009, Club China had 7,000 unique visitors accessing 36,500 pages and spending 3 to 5 minutes on the site each. KLM didn't stop with this kind of success, though. The next month, they implemented video chat on the site. The customer's and KLM's mutual benefit was highlighted by a comment from one of the Club Africa members that said pretty much all that needed to be said, "I really appreciate it. It is beneficial to the airline and the travelers, has made Africans feel recognized as important to the KLM strategy and has helped businesses get new worthwhile contacts. Getting to know a person you would have not have had an opportunity to meet." This is mutually beneficial business from a community of like-interested people. Social CRM indeed.

That's the bulk of your community options. But that's only about half of what you need to know. What else? How about what practices work to manage the community once you've realized that it is an important part of your Social CRM strategy?

Managing the Community

The management of your community is as important as the recruitment of your customers and experts to the community. Companies like Communispace have experienced moderators and facilitators to help you manage your social network. However, if you're looking for your own community manager, there is a now substantial body of practice to draw on in trying to figure out how to do just that. Ultimately, you're providing value by exposing your company and information to your customer, derived through the company itself, discourse between customers, or discourse between customers and company employees or outside experts. In return, you're getting valuable data, building the brand and reputation of the company, and creating the kinds of advocates that Karmaloop has turned into part of its extended sales force.

Community Management: Valuing the Customers

The purpose of this community endeavor is the ongoing engagement of your customers. You have to provide them with a reason to keep coming back until they do it without a second thought. What can you do?

1. Make sure there is a clear purpose and common interest for the community. For example, Sage Software has their ACT! community, a social network that supports ACT! users around the globe. Because the community has become the location for ACT! it has been incredibly successful, with 8.9 million page views and 266,000 searches in its first 12 months. The community has also served as a catalyst for a 15 percent increase in ACT! Net Promoter Score. The ACT! community is powered by Lithium, a community building platform well worth investigating if you're considering that sort of thing.

2. Make sure you have a great community manager and team. Remember this is a full-time job or at least takes up a *dedicated* part of a day. Don't be shy in recruiting volunteer moderators to support your effort or to recruit clearly influential members of the community who are "natural leaders" to help you support the community. Great community managers can materially affect the success of a social network. For example, Lawrence Liu, at Telligent Systems and blogger supreme (LLiu's *Community Zen Master Blog*), realized that there is a 90 percent reduction in cost if an incident is solved within a community rather than via the phone. So being smart, he incentivized community members to help him with incident response—which he was able to track—and thus save a lot of money as well as adding to the knowledge base.

3. Identify and work with the community leaders. This is the 1 percent that are identified in the 90-9-1 rule, called "participant inequality" by its creator Jakob Nielsen, now of Microsoft. It's considered the rule of thumb for online communities.

Ninety percent of the members don't participate; they read but are invisible. Nine percent will respond to various activities from time to time. One percent are creators who are responsible for most of the activity. Find that 1 percent because they have the community influence and reputation to affect how others respond to the community.

4. But don't discount the nonparticipants—the lurkers. Lurkers can become active, so don't make like they don't exist. Give them something to do—a short poll, a contest with something that might have value to the winners, and so on.

5. Community managers need to gather the requirements of the community and engage the appropriate parts of the company to meet those requirements. That means always being alert to the requests of the customer members but at the same time being cognizant of company limitations. While you're an advocate for the members, you're also managing to the corporate strategy.

6. Practice moderation by exception. Set the rules for the community up front, involve your legal and other departments in the beginning to create the regulations, the ethics code, and the protocols of conduct. Then all of them should step aside and only intervene when there are violations. Don't try to micromanage the activities of the community, even if they veer to the negative.

7. However, respond to the negative immediately. The rule of thumb is: make the negative at least neutral (though preferably positive), make the neutral positive, and reinforce the already positive.

8. Content rules. Seed the site with expert content until it is self-generating. This is easier said than done. You have to be as provocative as you can with the content you provide. I mean that in a nice way. Give them content that reflects the interests of the site. For example, if you are an Xbox 360–related community, provide the members with information on tips and tricks to benefit their gaming; product announcements that are leaked in advance to the members before the general public; contests they can participate in for prizes of some sort; chats with top

experts in the field, which, in the case of a gaming console, might be a star player or someone within the community with a high reputation for the platform; beta programs for the members. Content isn't only in the form of articles or blog postings.

9. Encourage peer-to-peer interactions within the borders of the social network. This takes #8 even further. Ultimately you want the community to be self-seeding content. That means giving them the ability to upload content, possibly have their own blog, comment on content, link to each other's sites and back to their own sites. Establish forums for discussions around a particular thread, and make sure members can initiate threads in those forums, even though you are moderating the forums inside the community.

10. Members should be encouraged to collaborate with the company. Collaboration can be as elaborate as the development of a new product or as simple as giving the members the ability to help you solve a customer service issue. If you want to get a little bit sophisticated about it, provide the members with the ability to rank the solutions if it's a customer service issue, for example, or suggested features and functions if it's product development. Since the most active collaborators will be the creators in the 90-9-1 rule, by providing the ranking tool, you're giving the 9 percent some active means to collaborate with you.

11. Members need to feel valued continuously. Reputation models are the foundation for the tools that can help members feel valued. They need to be valued by not just you but by other members of the community. Use TRIP (trust, reputation, influence, and persuasion) as the social characteristics that enhance members' sense of value. If you can, give them formal tools or informal means to allow them to enhance their own reputation, such as ranking (see #10) or tools that score their activity and provide rewards for high scores.

12. Don't just reward sales-related activity, though. Provide rewards for community participation. The more active the member, the better the reward, the more committed the member becomes. Remember, value and values are given, and in return, value and values are received.

13. Members need to sculpt their own experience—that is, self-direct. Though facilitation will always be necessary, the less interference by you and your managers, the better. The members want to personalize their experience as members. When it comes to Social CRM, the best thing you can do for a member is let them.

14. Feel free to have some expectations of your members too. It's a two-way street. Members of the social network shouldn't expect total privacy. This is a *social network*, not a private cabana on the beach. Social implies people, not solitary individuals. Network implies the same. As a business, you have the right to expect certain things from the members. The ability to gather data from them and use it is one thing. Another might be civil behavior. What's most important is that the members need to know what you expect from them from the beginning and that should be laid out clearly for them prior to their registration. They need to know what they are getting into. While they can't really have a terribly deep expectation of privacy, given the nature of what they are participating in, they can have an expectation of trust, meaning that what you've told them to expect they can expect. For more on this, see the web chapter entitled "Honestly, I Want This Chapter to Be on Privacy, But If I Wrote It, I'd Have to Blog About You."

Community Management: Doing It Wrong

So far I've been laying out the hunky-dory "be good" stuff when it comes to handling a community. The results are some guidelines on what kind of social network might fit your business and some practices for managing the community too. Would that life were that easy. Unfortunately, even though in principle there are companies that seem to be committed to building enterprise social networks or at least communities that use external platforms like Facebook, that doesn't mean they are doing them right.

So, be forewarned, newbies or even seemingly experienced social network mavens. There are things you *don't* do too. Here are four of them:

1. **The community is not just a site for harvesting information.** The business model and principles that govern a community/social network are not traditional principles. They are based on co-creation and collaboration with the members.

The business model is designed for *mutual* value. Don't think of the site as acreage that's available for data harvesting only. Congress actually has done that in the past with e-mail. According to participants at an Institute for Politics, Democracy and the Internet (IPDI) CRM Conference in 2007, one rather heinous practice in more than one congressional office was to send out a survey that ostensibly asked constituents for their opinions on some relevant policy issue. The results were ignored, but the e-mails were harvested for future congressional mailings. Draw a lesson from that. While you should harvest the information, you have to continually provide reasons for the members to come back. Which takes far more effort than Congress expended in caring about the survey results.

2. **Do not underfund the community effort.**   There is an incredible amount of partially misleading discussion about the inexpensive tools available for social media and social networks. While the low cost may be true in part, there are two things to remember. First, if you are an enterprise trying to provide a robust community, the tools will not be inexpensive. From the SaaS platform provided by Neighborhood America to the facilitated communities run by Communispace, there is a substantial possible cost. You're paying for the technology that secures the community and the information, that maintains, administers, and sometimes facilitates that community, and for the vast array of self-managing technological choices that you're giving the members of the community. You're paying for ease of use. That's just the technology. The costs of sustaining the content on the site are going to be even higher because that involves personnel and research. It also involves the site moderators and managers having relationships with the members. Forrester Research's in 2008 did a report entitled "Vendors: Prepare for Falling Prices for Enterprise Web 2.0 Collaboration and Productivity Apps," which predicted the commoditization of social networking (and social media) applications over 2008–2013. They claim that the drop will be due to the extensive use of Microsoft SharePoint, their long-standing entry into collaboration applications, which puzzles me, given the weaknesses of SharePoint. I'm in complete agreement with the ReadWriteWeb analysis: "The one thing we'd caution here is that SharePoint so far has proven to be a complex

and difficult-to-use beast, so we're not so sure that easy-to-use alternatives will be commoditized by SharePoint. In theory it sounds sensible, but in practice how many people actually use SharePoint to network." ReadWriteWeb's skepticism is justified. What I would do if I were committed to developing a social network is plan for an incremental rollout. I would make sure that I implement some predetermined baseline features and functions selected through research and through "voice of the customer" discussions with your customers. That way I would have a handle on what will launch most cost-effectively and at the same time provide what the likely members would want to start the community. Just don't do it all at once. You may not be able to get it on the cheap, but you can control how much you spend and what you spend it for.

3. **This is an ongoing commitment, not short-term, unless it has an explicit short-term purpose (OSN).** This is obvious and self-explanatory, but how do you actually explain that only 200,000 of the 700,000 social networks on Ning are active if that is so obvious? They aren't all outcome-based social networks. They just aren't sustained.

4. **Never forget the individual member has a *personal* stake in this.** The second principle of Social CRM is "all human beings are self-interested." This doesn't mean selfish, just that each of us has a life we want to lead, and we pursue that life in the ways we want to pursue it, even if it's not perfectly executed. If I'm a member of a social network, it's because there is something about that social network that appeals to my individual interest. I'm not a member for altruistic purposes unless altruism is part of my makeup. That cannot be emphasized enough. I'm not a member because I love your company. I'm a member because your company satisfies something of my personal agenda and I see this community as a way of effectively accomplishing that. All too often, corporations get so caught up in their own ROIs and their own cultures that the member/customer is viewed as the "object of information," another variation on "object of a sale" (see Chapter 12), rather than the subject of a self-crafted experience. President Obama's campaign staff made this mistake once with his MyBarackObama.com site (see Chapter 14 for that) and it hurt him, but didn't cost him.

The IT Landscape

Now that you've figured out what kind of social network(s) you want to commit to and you've learned something about how to manage and not manage that community, what about the technology you need to actually implement it? Not so easy. The number of white label social networking platforms out there is mind numbing. Jeremiah Owyang, a partner at the Altimeter Group and wildly popular social tools guru, estimates as of January 2009, there were more than 100 white label platforms. ("White label" means that you can rebrand the platform under your own name if you purchase it.) I'm not going to cover all of them here. That's a huge undertaking. My concerns for this book are how they impact CRM systems and the social customer.

In order to understand the business impact of social networking technology, I've enlisted Harvey Koeppel, the executive director of the CIO Leadership Council. Harvey has been the CIO for the Citigroup Consumer Banking Group and a consultant for an incredible number of companies, and, of course, their CIOs. He truly gets it—and I mean that in a social customer-focused kind of way. His insights will help you do the same.

CONVERSATION WITH HARVEY KOEPPEL:

ENTERPRISE ADOPTION OF SOCIAL NETWORKING: A CIO'S PERSPECTIVE

As recently as a couple of years ago, if you were to say words like "Facebook," "MySpace," or "YouTube" to a typical CIO (assuming that you could find a typical CIO), their general reaction would be to first shudder as if an icy wind had just blown through the room, then fold their arms across their chest—in part to protect themselves from the cold and in part to protect themselves from the emotional pain associated with even thinking about the topic. Then, once they gathered their composure, typical responses might have been:

"Yeah, cool stuff. My teenage kids are on Facebook all the time . . ."

"Okay for personal communications but that type of technology has no relevant use in a big company like mine . . ."

And then there would be the inevitable conversation annihilator:

"No competent information security officer would ever allow that kind of transparent and immature technology to be implemented here. It's a compliance nightmare—we have standards . . ."

During the past couple of years, I have spoken about these issues with hundreds of CIOs and CxOs from just about every industry, large, medium, and

small companies, private and public sector on just about every continent on the globe. I am pleased to report that, just two years later, both attitudes and behaviors have changed. Please don't misunderstand—I am not envisioning the next great Cultural Revolution, but rather, lots of small points of light which are beginning to connect businesses to customers and businesses to businesses in some new and very exciting ways. An undeniable shift in enterprise thinking (and doing) has begun and will likely continue to progress through the four stages, from:

1. *Banishment* ➔ *Acceptance*

2. *Fear* ➔ *Curiosity*

3. *Cynicism* ➔ *Inquisitiveness*

4. *Status Quo* ➔ *New Business Model Adoption*

While, for years to come, anthropologists, sociologists, and psychologists will likely be talking about and writing about the first three shifts noted above, from an enterprise perspective it is the Fourth Dynamic *(likely a whole other book) that presents significant challenges and even bigger opportunities for CIOs. Let's look at both.*

A Few of the Challenges

Lines are getting blurred between personal and business data. Corporate information is prevalent across personal networking sites, and personal information is increasingly being populated across business networking sites such as LinkedIn, Twitter, Ning, Plaxo, and so on. Wikipedia lists a couple hundred of these sites with the caveat, "Please note the list is not exhaustive, and is limited to some notable, well-known sites."

The volume of business, customer, and personal information has expanded exponentially and is likely to continue to do so for the foreseeable future. Social networking sites often contain business information in unstructured text or images (still or video), which are hard to find and even harder to analyze when found.

Messaging, blogging, and discussion threads are significantly impacting (reducing) e-mail traffic among community members. A new global language has emerged (LOL) in this context which will likely surpass Esperanto as the new universal tongue for business and for personal use. The infrastructure that supports this form of intra-community communication (and inter-community in the more advanced form) is not managed by the enterprise but rather by community managers. Traditional phishing, pharming, spam, and corporate information leakage filters don't work in that environment.

Social networking sites are at the same time both ubiquitous (everywhere) and ephemeral (here today, gone tomorrow). Enterprise adoption of these sites is therefore risky business because there will likely not be a very good continuity of business plan to rely upon. Whether a particular site is online or defunct, there is no accountability around the information that was captured, stored, and/or propagated and/or replicated across other websites. Once information has been put onto the grid, it is almost impossible to take back or delete. Companies cannot yet control what their employees are saying and doing within social networks. In enterprise-speak, not in control is generally the same as not in compliance.

Such sites also belie the concept of "authoritative source" of information since, in cyberspace, everyone is an authority and the onus is on the user to validate what they read, believe in it, or not. Again, a significant compliance nightmare.

Social networking has enabled customers to communicate among themselves (C to C) in the context of a commercial (B to C) transaction, which tends to pass control of company and product identity from the marketing department to the town hall. Access to customer-generated publicly available ratings and opinions of companies, products, and services has become part of the typical online buying experience. The power of the Brand is slowly and surely giving way to the power of the Customer Rating.

The Opportunities

As daunting as some of these challenges appear to be, the commercial opportunities presented by the practical use of social networks are enormous, likely beyond our wildest imagination. Here are a few examples.

Reach (the number of people you can touch) and frequency (the number of exposures to an ad) have long been held as the cornerstones of any marketing/ advertising campaign. Both are constrained by the number and expense of channels utilized, such as TV, radio, magazine, direct mail, and so on. There is a science associated with which channels and with what frequency ads should be run (at a cost) based upon a particular product and its intended customer base. Leveraging social networking tools and techniques has the potential to both fine tune specific messages targeted to specific customers and at the same time broadcast both specific and generic messages in a viral manner across the Web in a matter of minutes or hours compared with traditional campaigns, which could take weeks or months to run their course.

Customer information is available and will continue to proliferate in quantities and of a quality not even conceived of within most of today's most modern CRM applications. And enterprises are not limited to capturing information about customers and prospects solely based upon their own experience or research. Simple tools can very quickly provide marketing and sales staff with knowledge of things like what books you read, what music you listen to, what shoes you buy, pictures of you and your fraternity pals at the annual beer blast (maybe that one is for HR), and on and on. Clearly there needs to be a proper balance struck between information availability and its use versus the customer's right to privacy although, in general, it is now widely accepted that if you put something onto the grid, unless it is explicitly protected by the host—for example, credit card or health information—it is there as public domain. Customer usage of RSS feeds provides enterprises with mountains of information about an individual's areas of specific interests and propensities.

Perhaps the most profound opportunity presented by the prudent use of social networking within an enterprise context is the enablement of new and significantly more effective business models, those which can be driven by massively parallel collaboration. Enterprises are already discovering that they can effectively leverage broad communities of otherwise unrelated individuals, often who don't even work for the company, to help solve technical problems, supply chain problems and even help to define and popularize new products and services. Both costs and time to market are reduced to fractions of what would be expended using more traditional methodologies.

Enterprise examples of this emerging trend can be found in companies such as IBM, which runs Innovation Jams where, on a prescheduled and structured basis, usually during a one- or two-day period, literally hundreds of thousands of employees and customers come to a virtual community to discuss innovative new product ideas, exchange thoughts about new uses for existing products and, in general, both provide and obtain massive amounts of market information with stakeholders.

Innocentive is an enterprise-strength social networking platform that allows Solution Seekers to post rewards ranging from $5,000 to $1,000,000 for solutions posed by Problem Solvers, who may or may not be employees of the firm posting the challenge. SAP, for example, has recently created Polestar OnDemand—a cloud version of their current BusinessObjects Polestar technology. Within the framework of the Innocentive community, SAP will pay the winning developer(s) $20,000 for creating novel ways of leveraging the Polestar OnDemand product.

From the examples above, it is clear that social networks and the communities they spawn are transforming the way in which the traditional enterprise works by enabling and nurturing collaborative innovation throughout the ecosystems within which forward-thinking enterprises live, work, and play. ✒

The Vendor Picture

Vendors in the enterprise social networking platform space abound, but there are, as always, standouts. I've got a Superstah! for this chapter, but there are several that deserve at least a mention. The criteria for selection is how effective they will be in a large enterprise environment. That means an open architecture that eases the path to integration with legacy systems, including existing CRM systems. It also means the security and administrative functionality for managing large customer communities. It means scalability. It means powerful programming and configuration tools. But it doesn't stop with that. The vendors should be able to offer professional services for installing, administering, and/or managing the communities. Because of the newness of this area, an experienced vendor with a large customer base—like Jive, with 2,500 customers, many of whom are Fortune 1000—would be a real plus. I'm not saying rule out the smaller or newer vendors. Just take experience into account when establishing your criteria for selection of an enterprise social networking platform.

Forrester Research issued a WAVE report on enterprise social networking platform vendors in January 2009 in which they established weighted criteria such as breadth of offering (the most important at 30 percent), data, platform features, company leadership, financial viability, and so on. Because of the particular concerns of this book, I have some differences. The biggest difference is in the assignment of importance to integration. Where Forrester gives it a weight of 10 percent (meaning that it is one-tenth of the overall consideration), I'd have to up that to around 20 percent. The ability to capture the conversations and then populate CRM databases—and to provide some preconfigured integration APIs or tools that make integration at least less difficult—is particularly important. That said, the two that Forrester chose as their market leaders are Telligent and Jive Software, both of which I also highly recommend.

Integrating with CRM

I've prepared a couple of charts that I think are reasonably complete when it comes to how well CRM and enterprise social networking platforms have prebuilt integration. Check it out in Table 9-1 using the Forrester Top Nine as the study group.

Table 9-1: Social Networking Platforms Integrate (Sparingly) with CRM Systems

Forrester Top Nine Enterprise Social Networking Platforms	Forrester WAVE Status	Integration with:
Jive	Leader	salesforce.com, Remedy, Omniture, open architecture
Telligent	Leader	Microsoft SharePoint
Mzinga	Strong performer, close to leader	Nothing apparent
Pluck	Strong performer	Open architecture
KickApps	Strong performer	JavaScript Event API
Awareness	Strong performer	Uniform Web Services APIs
Lithium	Strong performer	RightNow, Omniture, salesforce.com
LiveWorld	Strong performer	Open architecture, XML support for integration into CRM
Leverage	Contender	APIs

Table 9-2 shows the reverse chart: CRM companies that integrate with various social network platforms. Please note I didn't include the integrations with sources for unstructured or open source data, such as Radian6, InsideView, or Jigsaw. There are loads of those.

Table 9-2: CRM Companies Integrate (Sparsely) with Social Networking Platforms

CRM Company	Integration with:	Notes
salesforce.com	Facebook, Neighborhood America, Helpstream, Twitter, Lithium	
Microsoft Dynamics CRM	Neighborhood America, Helpstream, SharePoint (obviously)	
RightNow	Lithium, Twitter, YouTube	Facebook and LinkedIn are on their horizon
SugarCRM	Helpstream	Specialized communities like Slashdot and Lifehacker through Cloud Connectors
SAP	Twitter	APIs are available for other integration
Oracle	Helpstream; Oracle Connect, a co-creation/collaboration platform	

A couple of quick observations. The scarcity of prebuilt integrations isn't necessarily a flaw or a bad thing, though it would be nice if there were more. It does indicate two things, though. First, that the idea of integrating CRM with social networking platforms (not social media—a different and more easily attainable breed as you already saw) is new and not that comfortable an option yet. Additionally, with the improvements in the quality-of-service oriented architectures over the last several years (Chapter 15), and the growth of cloud computing, SaaS (see Chapter 16) and web services in general, integration is becoming more and more seamless and, as Martin Schneider, director of product marketing at SugarCRM, puts it, "snap in." Here's a description from Martin on the rationale, which certainly makes sense:

> *(SugarCRM's) Cloud Connectors also come with (in the admin panel) a Cloud Connector framework, so instead of us picking and choosing, all a user needs to do is point the connector and BAM!—you're bringing in that data as a view or through a data merge into your CRM records. We don't want to decide what networks get chosen, rather have every network a potential connector and let the community/user base do it with ease. . . . We open sourced the tools, instead of hoarding the connector as an offering.*

So I wouldn't view this as a bad thing, just as a nascent industry segment. However, you should account for it in planning out your Social CRM strategy.

But there is a social network platform that embraces CRM like a brother, which is one of the reasons they are my Superstah! chosen from all enterprise social networking platforms. Give a warm welcome to Neighborhood America.

Superstah! Neighborhood America

For the most part, I love Neighborhood America. I think they have a strong platform that can use some work when it comes to social media tools, but all in all, they are the best out there. I've thought this since 2006 and will probably continue to think so until someone else proves me wrong—which would take a lot.

Apparently, I'm not the only one who thinks highly of this Naples, Florida–based company. They won the Software and Information Industry Association (SIIA) Codie Award for best Enterprise Social Networking Platform in 2008 and 2009. The finalists are chosen by judges, but the winner is based on the SIIA members' votes. This is the equivalent of the Academy Awards—the members of the industry voted them up.

What makes them stand out isn't just their high caliber platform that's been put to the test by NASCAR, HGTV, CNN, CBS, Fox, Adidas, and Kodak, among many others. It's also their constant innovation, their CRM integration, and their interest in doing something more than providing a hosted enterprise social networking solution—a.k.a. doing some good in the public arena.

Kim Kobza, their CEO and a co-founder of the company, along with David Bankston, their CTO, embrace the applicability of technology to satisfy their curiosity about how networks work, about how influence and persuasion affect public discourse, and how they might make a difference in business by solving those problems. Personally, I'd call David Bankston a technological prodigy and Kim a fervent evangelist when it comes to social software, how it gets used, and what Neighborhood America sees as its ongoing mission in the 21st century.

Mission 21st Century

Here's Kim Kobza, CEO, on Neighborhood America's mission in the upcoming years:

> Neighborhood America believes that every organization and every process within every organization in the world will benefit from the value that networks create—networks of customers, partners, employees, and in the case of government, citizens. Organizations that understand this disruptive transformation, what Yochai Benkler describes as the "networked information economy," increasingly will embrace what we think of as "a network perspective."
>
> Having a network perspective means that by listening to customers, partners, employees, and citizens, and making them a part of business process, organizations gain a competitive advantage. Neighborhood America believes that having a network perspective will be a strategic imperative to the competitive survival of virtually every organization.
>
> Organizational ecosystems embody many forms of networked behaviors. Therefore they require technology models that support networked behaviors that solve many unique business problems. Neighborhood America's technology model reflects this vision. It is built on a construct of "business services" that serve the many unique network requirements of virtually any business or government organization. As business and government move from the experimental stage of social media to a more advanced understanding of how to drive value from

multiple networks, they will increasingly require that social media technologies be delivered with a platform that provides utility class benefits, security, and scalability. They also will require discrete analytics.

Reflecting today's trends, the dominant technology model of the future will be in the cloud—a highly scalable "software as a service" offering—that enables every business and government agency to share common learning and experience. These enterprise models also will clearly have to enable multiple integration points to existing technologies such as CRM, ERP, and BI applications.

Over the next three years, Neighborhood America will continue to build our catalogue of business services, engineering, and analytics engines. We will especially focus on integration and distribution relationships that enable organizations to leverage existing investment in networks of customers, partners, employees, and citizens as well as the software and technology systems that support those relationships.

The Product

Neighborhood America's products and services are based on the idea of platform as a service. They host their business services on an exceptionally robust SOA they call ELAvate, which stands for Engage-Listen-Act . . . uh, vate. It is a highly flexible, easily configurable architecture and, as of 2009, has added strong analytics functions and data warehousing. (See Figure 9-4.)

Here's CTO David Bankston's informative statement on the value of analytics in a social networking environment:

It's becoming clear that much of the true value of networks lies in the understanding of the "network behavior" inherent in patterns of use. These patterns unlock the key to understanding how to match the network purpose to the business needs.

Organizations demand a return from all investments, including social media. ROI comes from business intelligence, yet this has been a long-standing gap in our industry. Network data analytics provide customers with the intelligence they need to really understand their business, their customers, and the interaction taking place within their community. With these insights, they can then make changes that will drive ROI.

We're also finding that as enterprises embrace social media, they discover multiple ways in which it can add value throughout their organization. They launch multiple communities—both internal and external

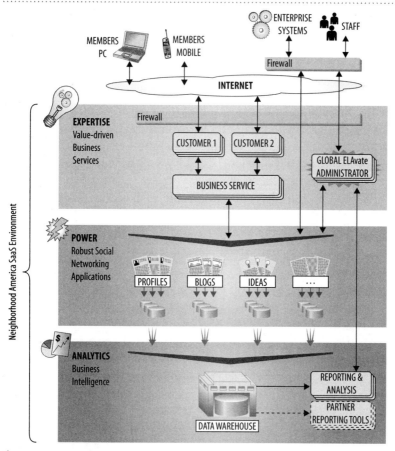

Figure 9-4: ELAvate three-tiered architecture (source: Neighborhood America)

networks—and need the ability to analyze and report results with enterprise-wide consistency. Our analytics provide this capability.

One more important point is that all of our data and analytics are served in a dedicated data warehouse environment, separate from the social network or CRM system that it may integrate with. Data in its raw form can be reported and analyzed in any way that adds value to the customer—or integrated into existing reporting systems.

Data can also be "anonymized" so that only the patterns across multiple communities can be extracted and studied. This model also creates an entirely new business model. A proper data warehouse can now host key community preference/behavioral data in aggregate, across all of its customer communities.

One thing Neighborhood America does very well and didn't ignore like many of their counterparts in this category is integration with CRM. They currently integrate with salesforce.com, NetSuite, and Microsoft Dynamics CRM, and there are more preconfigured CRM integrations in their future.

Their software solution, REVEAL, which sits on top of ELAvate, has a wide-ranging set of features. Some are what you would expect, such as threaded forums, ranking tools, a robust tagging system, channel creation, profile building, and idea generation programs. Others are just in the "too cool for school" category, such as video chats for up to six participants in a single channel.

REVEAL is completely customizable so an easily navigable user interface is not hard to develop with the provided tools. Take a look at Figure 9-5, which is the Grand-Am racing site they build, and you'll see the clean and easy-to-understand interface.

Figure 9-5: Grand-Am social network home page (Source: Neighborhood America)

If I have any problem with them, it's that their social media tools (such as their blogging platform) are not that strong and need to be enhanced. However, this does not extend to their resources for integrating user-generated content like videos, audio, social tags, ratings, and comments.

REVEAL has nonpareil administrative functionality too, allowing you to own and control your social network. The administration is so robust that you can control several communities from a single dashboard without a whole of sweating. They don't leave you twisting in the wind either. If you are a little unsure of how you want to set up your community management, no problem—Neighborhood America provides you with several templates for community management (see Figure 9-6).

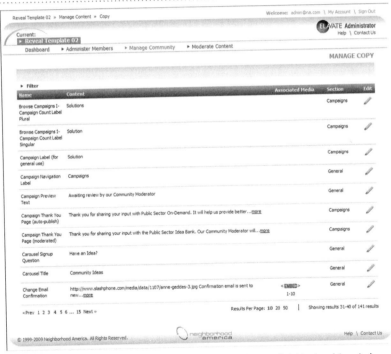

Figure 9-6: REVEAL template for community management (Source: Neighborhood America)

Neighborhood America claims some pretty serious ROI too. For example, they built an Idea Center to supplement the Kodak Gallery, a photo-sharing site that reaches 55 million Kodak users. Registration was done through the Kodak Gallery. The purpose of the Idea Center was to share ideas on the use of Kodak products—such as creating photo albums, photography methods, and other resources. It was instantly popular. In six weeks, 25 percent of the site members were buying products through the site, and the Idea Center was a trusted source for sharing and exchange among its community.

All in all, we are looking at a scalable, secure, manageable world-class enterprise social networking solution that also gives customers the ability to manage their own experiences. Unlike many of their competitors, they see the value in not just harvesting the data that those customers provide, but also in analyzing it so that the most valuable data then populates your CRM system. That's what I call complete.

What a great segue into the next section. We've completed the entire section on the social tools and strategies for their deployment. Now let's see how all of this Social CRM talk affects the more recognized CRM pillars—sales, marketing, and customer service. Please remember, you're taking your traditional CRM 1.0 outlook into your own hands.

10

Movin' and Groovin': The Use of Mobile Devices

I'm untethered. No, I said untethered, not unhinged. When I'm on the road, I take my 3G (S) iPhone with me and I use it like a sub-microcomputer. I make phone calls, I get my e-mail "fetched," I watch movies and TV shows and video podcasts; I listen to music and audio podcasts; I read blogs, watch the news and read it too; I take pictures of the exotic cities I'm in; I play games; I track my expenses; I text my colleagues and friends; I monitor my Twitter "tweets." I can actually go on for another 10 minutes telling you what I can do with the iPhone—all G-rated. Well, mostly G-rated.

That's just me. Multiply the potential to do that by the number of hand-sets on the planet and you've got 1.5 *billion* me's making 3.2 billion connections (source: www.gsmworld.com).

Granted, that's currently not a fair statement because I'm working off the most advanced smartphone in the world and most of the handsets out there are regular old cellphones. But keep in mind what the millennial variety of cellphone is. That's a phone that can make phone calls, take pictures, watch videos, and surf the Internet. All for $49.99 or maybe even free.

What's this got to do with CRM? As Babur Ozden, CEO of Berggi, a mobile video provider, said at the 2008 Stanford AlwaysOn Summit, "This is the most intimate device anyone has." It's the one device you are engaged with—and in the right mood, would be engaged to if you could and you were single.

Think not? Let's make it really easy to discount your doubt. How do (or would) you feel if you lose your cellphone? Immediate stomach clutch. I know because (I bow my head) it happened to me. Intimate indeed.

But that's not the reason that mobile CRM is a topic for this book per se. Mobile CRM is a subject because it is increasingly important that the traveling professional whatever has their information with them at all times in all ways. If done well, mobile CRM can provide, if not a competitive advantage, an improved chance of a successful closing of a sale and a connection to the office that can't happen otherwise. With the increasing interest in mobile use of social media and in carrying on community activities via mobile devices, Social CRM is a prime subject for those little machines so close to your heart.

Traditionally, mobile CRM has been used in two areas, sales and field service. With the spike up in social networking, the integration of GPS and thus the availability of location-based services, the always increasing bandwidth and speed combined with the improvements in available device storage and processing power, the opportunity to do so much more is there—now. We'll look at that at the end of the chapter.

I'm going to call you in just a sec and we can roll.

A Needy Market

The sheer magnitude of the mobile market is staggering. In January 2008, IDC predicted that by 2011 there would be 1 billion workers who would be mobile. The U.S. workforce, who in 2006 was 45 percent mobile, is projected by the same IDC study to be at 75 percent by 2011. Whether that's true or not obviously remains to be seen, but it is at least a good anecdotal indication that there is a tremendous optimism and recognition of the need for mobile applications. Historically, CRM has been the enterprise application that has been applied first and most successfully. Companies like Vaultus and iEnterprises have developed mobile CRM applications for SugarCRM, Microsoft Dynamics CRM, and NetSuite, among others. There are mobile versions of salesforce.com and, most recently, an excellent mobile version of SAP CRM 2007 sales that was developed by RIM and SAP conjointly. SAP even carried their mobile CRM activity further with a 2009 alliance with Sybase so that Sybase's iAnywhere framework allows communication on the fly in real time with any mobile device regardless of operating system. Oracle has its own Mobile Sales Assistant, a sales-related BlackBerry-compliant device with an iPhone version in the works. Not only that, Maximizer has organized its entire CRM suite around mobile devices.

This is just the tip of the iceberg. The desire for mobile CRM—an untethered version—is not transient. Sheryl Kingstone, who is one of

the most respected analysts in mobile, wrote a piece in June 2008 entitled "The Mobile CRM Tipping Point" in which she declared:

> Today, mobile CRM projects have evolved from nice-to-have to need-
> to-have. As businesses continue to transform into Anywhere Enter-
> prises, anywhere applications become strategic priorities. According to
> the Yankee Group Anywhere Enterprise–2007: U.S. Mobility and Busi-
> ness Applications Surveys, CRM remains one of the most important
> strategic mobile applications. Although the primary driver is customer
> responsiveness, plenty of other reasons indicate that mobile CRM has
> finally reached its tipping point.

I couldn't agree more.

If you have mobile salespeople or field service technicians, this
should be a part of your Social CRM strategy, without reservation.
Note I didn't say without consideration. There are lots of considerations when developing a mobile CRM capability for your enterprise.
I'll get to a good deal of them soon enough.

Why the Growth?

Sheryl Kingstone is making a powerful and unequivocal statement.
But she has good reason. Some of the issues that mobile CRM had,
from processor power to bandwidth issues to poor user experience on
a small screen, have been eradicated or are close to annihilation.

One of the most important factors is, oddly, the energy crisis. You
would think this was just the opposite. High oil and gas prices means
less travel, thus less mobile, thus less need for mobile CRM. But we
do live in Bizarroworld where logic often is turned on its head. As a
result of the energy problems, more workers are working from home
and need to be available via their cellphone as they do their local things
while working. There is an important integration of home and work
life going on in combination with employers recognizing that their
employees are happier when they can work at home. Companies
like Rearden Commerce are successful because of their knowledge
of this.

Mobile services have become increasingly comfortable for the bulk
of the population. For example, according to the Pew Internet and
American Life April 2009 survey on wireless activity in the U.S.
56 percent of Americans have accessed the Internet wirelessly.

Thirty-two percent of those did it via a smartphone like the BlackBerry or iPhone or via their cell phone. What makes this even more telling is that 50 percent of the respondents said they are dependent on wireless access to stay in touch with friends and to get information.

Technology advances are moving lightning fast and the ones that matter to mobile users are the ones that increase data transmission speeds. The 3G top data transmission speed was reached on May 8, 2008, by mobilkom austria using Internet High Speed Packet Data Access (I-HSPDA), which reached 10.1 megabits per second—a super 3G rate.

But that's a piker of a rate when you realize that Samsung is experimenting with a pipe that reaches 100 megabits per second wirelessly in a car moving at 35 mph, which is the equivalent of being able to watch six TV stations simultaneously. Even more staggering, in a fixed location, in the same project, they reached 1000 megabits per second—10 times that rate! On a more earthly plane, after fits and starts, Sprint has been investing in 4G WiMax technology, which will bring high speed wireless connectivity.

Mobile Enterprise Adoption Accelerates

There is confidence in mobile growth especially for business reasons among almost all layers of the population. This extends from the largest enterprises to small and medium businesses (SMBs) to even government agencies. In fact, the government agencies in several surveys are the fastest adopters.

Back in 2005, Forrester Group, in "Mobile Application Adoption Leaps Forward," made the following surprising statement: "Large enterprises are adopting mobile applications faster than planned." They went on to say that 39 percent of the largest enterprises planned to adopt wireless e-mail or the BlackBerry and 51 percent actually did. This was the forerunner of what Forrester analyst Ellen Tracy called an adoption rate starting in 2008 of "ubiquitous technologies," like mobile enterprise applications and devices, as one moving into the mainstream.

But by 2008–2009, mobile adoption had superceded even Tracy's optimistic picture. Forrester's related 2008 survey of small and medium business adoption shows that the SMBs are adopting mobile applications at the rate of 38 percent all in all. What's even more interesting is that they are adopting sales force automation (SFA) mobile applications and field service mobile applications at the rate of 16 percent—which is a healthy and better than expected chunk. Further proof has been the staggering number of iPhones that have been bought by an adoring global public. From their third quarter 2007 release to third quarter 2009, Apple sold 26,378,000 iPhones of the 2G, 3G, and 3G (S) varieties. Yet RIM and the BlackBerry still hold the lion's share of the market with 55.4 percent of the market as of first quarter 2009, according to IDC's Mobile Market Tracker, which shows you how mainstream mobile adoption has become.

So there is a predisposition toward mobile CRM applications and the adoption rates are serious enough to merit a real look at the new applications and the future ways that mobile Social CRM can be deployed. But there still are some concerns. Listen to industry veteran and president of w-Systems, a mobile CRM development company, Christian Wittig. He makes some seriously good points here.

Mobile CRM is undergoing a first generation product trial. Buyers are extremely interested to evaluate and identify products that will allow them to expand their CRM deployments to mobile users but are uncertain of which mobile CRM product characteristics to look for. Buyers do not have the benefit of previous mobile CRM experience and thus do not have the benchmark of previous product failures or successes to guide their evaluations. Since it is such a first time buying experience it is very likely that history will repeat itself and that we will see many failed initial mobile CRM deployments just as we saw many failed first time CRM deployments. Mobile CRM buyers should remind their CRM vendors of this situation and press for detailed product demonstrations, proofs of concept, and other risk reduction elements.

When considering mobile CRM solutions the buyer is faced with evaluating applications on a completely new platform (the mobile phone) which has unique and somewhat extreme usability characteristics (small screen, small keyboard). Both buyers and vendors are attempting to arrive at the tipping point of requested and offered functionality where mobile CRM emerges as a natural and expected component of an organization's CRM software portfolio.

What's It Look Like? Mobile Technology

So what are we talking about when we talk about mobile CRM applications? What kind of functionality is considered endemic? Is there a difference between, say, a mobile sales application and mobile personal information management? What should you be looking for?

Let me be unequivocal. Mobile versions of ACT! are not mobile CRM applications, nor is any mobile contact management, because none of their full-sized versions are CRM either. That's not to denigrate any of them. They are good for what they do.

That said, let me describe the features and functions of a mobile CRM application. I'll start with the current version of mobile SalesLogix for the BlackBerry. This is both a representative mobile CRM application and a well-constructed one.

▶ **Account and contact management**   This is where the ACT!s and Goldmines of the world start and stop. You can view accounts and contacts, add them, or take notes related to account activity.

▶ **Integrated calendar and activity management**   Here you can schedule activities and mark them complete.

▶ **Sales opportunity management**   This gives you the capability to create opportunities, upgrade a lead to an opportunity, or check on existing opportunities, including finding product pricing information.

▶ **Customer service ticket management**   If your customers have open support tickets, they will be shown here. Additionally, they will show up on the account record.

▶ **Lookups and groups**   Create specific groups so that you can organize your contacts the way you want. Do lookups of the key people in an account or activities associated with an opportunity.

▶ **One-click dialing and e-mail**   These are the most BlackBerry-specific features. They use the WAP interface for BlackBerry with the tabbed access and automatic one-click dialing of numbers that appear on the screen. Plus, of course, the famous push e-mail from your BlackBerry.

▶ **Familiar experience**   The same experience but different interface for the mobile application.

▶ **Fully customizable**   You can customize your own dashboard view, graphs, and charts.

▶ **Built on a solid mobile platform**   In this case the Corum platform.

▶ **BlackBerry reporting dashboards**   Drill down from the dashboard to the granular reports on revenue, opportunity, time to close, and so on.

Note what isn't in this application that you will see in the mainline versions: pipeline management. Mobile CRM is aimed squarely at the user—the salesperson or field service technician—not their management. However, because of synchronization and over-the-air data updates, management will be dancing in the aisles with joy, given the ROI that mobile CRM provides (see below).

Considerations in Mobile Enterprise Planning

I'm assuming that, since you're reading this chapter, you're pretty jacked up about the possibilities of mobile CRM. Let's assume so or else this is going to be a really short chapter.

What do you have to consider for a mobile CRM deployment? Most of it is no different than preparing for a normal CRM implementation. But there are some different considerations and that's what I'm going to concentrate on here. If you want to see what's the same, go to Chapter 18 on strategy and Chapter 20 on implementation.

Here are some of the technical and operational considerations:

▶ **Form factor**   This is the most overlooked and yet, because style matters, this is a serious consideration. Remember in Chapter 3, the clunky versus sleek BlackBerry comparison? You remember which one interested you, don't you? Well, having an iPhone or a cool BlackBerry is actually an important facet of your choice. If you give your sales reps a cool smartphone, they'll literally be happier. Form factor is not just shape and weight but size.

▶ **Service providers/carriers**   There are geographical considerations. Coverage is often spotty. For example, T-Mobile just started building its 3G network in 2008. The 3G HSDPA networks of AT&T are fairly well covered, but there are spotty locations where signal strength fluctuates between HSPDA and the slower 2G EDGE. Verizon and Sprint 3G EV-DO networks are ubiquitous. Be alert to the geographies that your wandering roadies are going be traveling to and the kind of networks that are available from the carriers.

▶ **IT**   What kind of architecture do the devices have? What kinds of applications are available? What kinds of interfaces are available for those applications? Are the applications device-agnostic, meaning they can be used on any device? Are the applications device-aware, meaning they can dynamically adjust to the specific device with the right screens and the right functionality according to the device and operating system? Do they have over-the-air synchronization?

▶ **Security issues**   Data needs to be protected and made available to those who need to see it. There should be administrative controls over configuration, security, sensitive data, and so on.

▶ **Cost**   As obvious as this is, make sure that you build in the costs of the work/home integration—for example, service costs.

▶ **Application vendors**   This really is no different from choosing a vendor in a standard CRM program.

▶ **Platform considerations**   What kind of processor power does the device have? How strong is the platform to build applications or re-engineer existing apps? What about the operating system? Can the applications read and show docs/presentations in multiple formats? Does the application have an offline edition? What about device interoperability—can the devices talk to each other? This is becoming easier with the evolution of standardized web services.

Untethered Benefits

There are management benefits of mobile CRM that are undeniable—more than 50 percent annualized return, according to Gartner Group vice president William Clark—but the real benefits are for the road warriors themselves.

The workday of a salesperson on the road is considerably longer than eight hours. Because they're on the road, they also carry out their personal business. For example, the National Basketball Association issues BlackBerrys to the players so they can call home and send e-mail while traveling from game to game. Of course, interestingly enough, with the rise of Twitter and mobile clients for Twitter that pretty much exist for every device, the problems with providing those devices are beginning to show with guys like Charlie Villaneuva of the Milwaukee Bucks being slammed by Bucks management because he tweeted during halftime of a Bucks-Celtics game in March 2009.

Because the salespersons are dependent on the devices they use, what device it is will directly impact their productivity. Studies done by Richard Hill of PowerHomeBiz.com found that the impact is so great that 82 percent of the managers surveyed believe that handheld access will drive field usage of CRM, and even more (91 percent) believe that mobile SFA will be really important. Other known benefits:

▶ **Improves relationships with customers**   What the customer needs to know is there in real time certainly, but an iPhone or BlackBerry Bold can break the ice and start some "coolness" discussions. Don't underestimate the value of that.

▶ **Order management**   If done right, you can create new orders and get status on existing ones. Often can be tied to catalogs.

▶ **Sales information for customers**   Pricing, available quantities, discounts, order status all available to customers.

▶ **Competitive intelligence**   This doesn't appear in most mobile CRM apps at this stage as more than web-based surfing. But the near future will bring that from some important companies.

▶ **Customer intelligence**   Creating reports on the device that outline customer account activities; or with the use of GPS, customer availability, or, with the ascension of the social web technologies, a look at the customer's profile which includes their likes and dislikes. All those things needed for greater customer insight.

But let's not ignore management. Aberdeen Group did a 2008 study and came up with these numbers:

▶ Seventy-nine percent experience year-over-year improvement in revenue per sales rep.

▶ Ninety-two percent achieve a bid-to-win ratio better than 20 percent.

▶ Sixty-nine percent achieve better than 60 percent rates of sales performance.

One thing about mobile CRM is that the ROI is actually tangible. That's great for now. What about the future?

The Future: Social CRM Gets Down and Wireless

The war for cellular hegemony in the enterprise is underway. It became serious when the iPhone became compatible with 3G networks in 2008. The press started to talk about the enterprise features of the iPhone, its ability to access Microsoft Exchange, and its "push" (more like "fetch") e-mail. What made it most exciting was the App Store—the exchange for iPhone developers who used the SDK to create applications. Thousands of applications appeared as if by magic, but of course really through the largesse of Apple.

Among those thousands of early applications were an interesting twosome, one from salesforce.com that linked directly to your salesforce.com account, and another from Oracle, which linked the Oracle business intelligence applications to the iPhone. Mobile CRM came to the iPhone. As of August 2009, all the major CRM players had one or more iPhone applications.

This wasn't the first time, though. There had been an attempt back in the days of the 2G iPhone where browser-based CRM applications were optimized for the iPhone. They included NetSuite, Etelos CRM for Google, and EBSuite and HEAP, two small business CRM applications. After a complete review of all of them, my conclusion was, when it comes to CRM, stick to the BlackBerry. The reason was simple. The EDGE network was too slow to wirelessly handle the robust CRM functionality that was normally required. Load times for a page could be over a minute in length and sometimes considerably longer. But that's changing. RIM's BlackBerry is still the CRM platform of choice, but the iPhone's greater speeds, especially with the release of the optimized 3G (S), make it a platform worth looking at. Oracle, SAP, salesforce.com, and NetSuite, among others, are looking to the iPhone as a development platform for CRM. The Palm Pre, which is premised on Sprint's forthcoming 4G transmission belt, is a promising mobile CRM platform.

But this is just the present. There is a much more robust future as data transmission speeds increase and CRM becomes an increasingly flexible set of services. That means mobile social CRM.

Mobile Social CRM: True Dat

Take a look at Figure 10-1. That's the mobile adaptation of the blogging tool Typepad—the on-demand version of Six Apart's Movable Type (see Chapter 7). You can read or post to a blog directly from the device.

Figure 10-1: Blogging from the iPhone (Source: Six Apart)

But this is only the beginning. The social CRM mobile applications will be more commonly available by the end of 2009 and into 2010.

People, Place, Time

True mobile Social CRM will be driven by the addition of features associated with what Kamar Shah, Nokia's head of industry marketing, calls "people, place, and time."

This isn't particular new or surprising. Time shifting—meaning the ability to download, say, a podcast anytime and play it anytime you want—is a long-standing practice. Place shifting—taking that same podcast and playing it on any device anywhere you want—is also quite common. But Kamar Shah means more presence and location-based services that would be focused around business. The interest in this reflects the incorporation of consumer thinking into business strategies, processes, and technology.

PRESENCE- AND LOCATION-BASED MOBILITY

Presence- and location-based mobility is the near-term future for mobile CRM. For those of you who just aren't cool technophiles, the combination of presence and location on a mobile device means that, if it's yours, the mobile device can identify accurately where you are and, if it's a friend of yours, they will receive a transmission from that mobile device letting them know where you are. ABI Research predicts that by 2012, 335 million North American consumers will subscribe to some sort of location-based services.

Many consumer mobile devices have GPS chips embedded, which are a prerequisite for presence- and location-based services. As a result, knowing where your children are is a family service offered by a number of the carriers and their cellphone manufacturers. The 3G iPhone, still primarily a consumer device, has dozens of applications based on location services.

One of the most intriguing of the consumer apps is the Yelp iPhone application. Yelp (www.yelp.com) is a social network of people who review retail stores, restaurants, hotels—all brick-and-mortar businesses in local geographical areas—and is one of the most popular and incredibly powerful.

One day, a friend and I decided to find a good restaurant in Manassas, Virginia (where I live). That wasn't something obvious in this town, where most of the restaurants are at best so-so. I went to the Yelp application on my 3G iPhone. It used the GPS locator to find restaurants in my vicinity. I narrowed the search to Thai food. I found a restaurant I never heard of, Siam Classic, which had five-star reviews from everyone reviewing it. I clicked on the button in the application that took me to Google Maps. The GPS chip identified my current immediate location. I filled in directions to the restaurant according to the address in Yelp. We went there. The food was outstanding.

Think about this. I've lived in Manassas for 17 years and never heard of this place, but the use of location-based services and a social network that identified it gave me confidence in the choice and guided me there. That's quite cool now, and in a few years, this will be ordinary.

But that's the consumer side. What about the business side? What about mobile CRM? Since we've already identified field service and sales as the easiest entry points for mobile CRM, it stands to reason that presence- and location-based business services are most advanced there.

In field service, location-based services have been used to optimize the schedules of technicians in the field. By tracking the location of the field service personnel (yes, they can be tracked in real time), not only is the use of each technician's time optimized but if an appointment falls through, the dispatchers are able to one-click another nearby service ticket and send the technician over there instead.

It works the same way for sales, but its utility at this stage is a little dicey. For example, SalesLogix for the BlackBerry has a button on a sales screen that says "Nearby Accounts." Click on it and based on your location, it will find those clients that are nearby so that you can maximize your effectiveness when out on client calls.

But it gets really interesting when presence is added. NEC has unified communications services that not only will find the closest technician when they have a problem to solve, but will find the closest *available* technician—the addition of presence functions allows you to not just broadcast where you are, but what you're doing. In the NEC version, there is a profile of the technician that immediately shows how they prefer to be contacted and then a one-click contact accomplishes the connection in the manner the technician prefers.

PEOPLE TOO

From Social CRM's lofty perch, the most exciting part of the future of mobile lies with the on-the-go participation in social networks and the use of social media. This is only possible because of the growth of 3G and because of the capacity for incredible amounts (though by future standards, I'm sure, minuscule) of processing power crammed on the mobile unit.

This isn't something we have to look forward to someday; it's happening now. A study released in July 2008 from Informa Teleca said that 50,000,000—2.3 percent of all mobile users—were already using social networking, and this is expected to rise to 12.5 percent by 2013.

Helio was an early failure in this area. It was a mobile virtual network operator (MVNO). That meant it provided services and devices but didn't provide bandwidth, which it leased from Sprint. In 2006, they announced a partnership with MySpace and developed a custom portal for their devices, but they rose and fell with the popularity of MySpace and since have receded into the background, quietly absorbed by one of the parent companies, SK Telecom.

However, companies like Movo, which was acquired by Neighborhood America in 2006, the enterprise social networking platform I awarded the Chapter 9 Superstah!, are able to carry out large-scale community creation with the use of texting and mashups with Google maps and of course presence and location services. For example, one nonprofit was interested in creating communities of interest around social issues. Over 1 million opt-in SMS messages were sent out with requests for the recipients' interests. Then another SMS opt-in message was sent to those who responded, with a few more requests to deepen the profile that was being created.

All in all, the result was a geographically based set of different communities of interest based on the social issues that concerned the members. If there was the need, let's say, for some action in Seattle over Darfur or global warming or the financial crisis, then it was easy to find the people in Seattle who were in the appropriate communities of interest. There was a call to action via text message. The actions were taken. All mobile.

The business value of this is immeasurable. The information about customers, the ability to segment them organically, and their participation in the discussions going on about the interests or practices that fascinate them—this is an emotional connection. This engenders advocacy, and this is the future of mobile CRM.

Superstah! Research in Motion, SAP, and CRM 2007 for the BlackBerry

This is a joint Superstah! award to both SAP and RIM. They collaborated on what I think is, to date, the best release of a mobile CRM application I've seen. The interface is excellent—especially given the BlackBerry's somewhat historically ugly but functional UI. The functionality is solid with both easy navigation to any function for the salesperson and rich salesperson-level management capabilities, which I'll briefly outline below. There are also several cool and useful features.

But what makes this particularly interesting is that RIM developed the actual application using the sales side of SAP's CRM 2007. Not SAP. RIM. This collaboration was unprecedented in SAP's history because they had always developed their own applications in the past. It was a significant cultural milestone as well as a technological one.

Mission 21st Century

From Paul Briggs, RIM's CRM product marketing manager:

> To assess what's ahead first we must acknowledge the year that was 2008 in mobile CRM as a tipping point. All the major players in CRM—SAP, Oracle, salesforce.com, Sage Software—made significant moves to bolster their mobile offerings. BlackBerry's launch of a range of more powerful devices in 2008 enables a truly enhanced mobile CRM experience. What's the BlackBerry mission for the future? More of the same. Innovative handsets and a continually enhanced platform for extending CRM from the desktop to the fingertips of the mobile workforce."

Features and Functions

What makes this not only cool, but also important is that the mobile SFA application that SAP and BlackBerry acolytes and others will love is actually functionally complete and useful.

It has what you would expect of a substantial SFA application. Contact, account, lead, opportunity, and pipeline management. Location services that help you figure out how to get to your clients offices. The ability to do account-level (meaning multiple contacts) e-mails and to access your calendar to see what you're doing on any given day at a given time. It all shows up in a convenient opening dashboard on the BlackBerry (see Figure 10-2). Keep in mind that this stuff is in your pocket. Not on your laptop. Not on your desktop. But in your pocket, either being used the way it's supposed to—as a valuable business tool—or gathering lint on the screens that show the pipeline.

Figure 10-2: SAP/RIM BlackBerry application: your sales force automation-driven day begins (Source: RIM/SAP)

This is good stuff. Is it missing anything? Nothing fundamental. Profile access would be a good thing. Links to Facebook and Twitter associated with the contact and the account would be good. Even the ability to gather sales intelligence associated with the account would be good. But that, I'm sure we'll see in due time. What is amazing is that this is one of the first mobile SFA tools that I've seen that is simply and easily attractive—and useful.

MINI-CONVERSATION WITH PAUL BRIGGS

Paul Briggs is one of the coolest industry guys I know. Not only was he an industry journalist and thought-leader during his tenure when he was editor-in-chief of a national Canadian magazine focused on supply chain management, but he now is the leader of the CRM marketing at RIM's Business Solutions Group. In fact, he's been doing that with a great deal of success since 2005. Paul truly gets what's going on in both the mobile world and social CRM world and that is a powerful combination, indeed. In fact, the only fault I can find with Paul is that he is an ardent Toronto Blue Jays fan. Beyond that, at least in my eyes, the dude is flawless—and he knows what he's talking about when it comes to mobile CRM.

With that resounding intro, I'm going to let Paul give you a picture of what you have to consider when it comes to mobile CRM.

RIM's been working in the mobile CRM space since the early 2000s when browser-based solutions were first made available. Since then, our customers have taught us a lot about what they need in a mobile solution and what are the best practices for a successful deployment. Here are the top three:

▶ *Go local   While handset browsers were a popular first generation attempt to extend CRM to mobile workers, the limitations were quite clear early on. Browser solutions rely on effective wireless connectivity for the speed and quality of the mobile CRM experience. Out of coverage scenarios and date rate speed limitations at each navigation point in the application compromise the overall efficacy of a mobile application. Best practice is clearly the deployment of a client application that operates locally on the handheld and integrates tightly with other native Black-Berry apps like e-mail, PIM, GPS, and calendar. This enables a snappy user experience, a superior user interface, and an "always on" experience no matter whether the user is in coverage or not.*

▶ *Baby steps   Most first generation mobile CRM projects languished due to over-ambitious deployments that tried to mimic the desktop user experience. Attempting to extend all of a CRM package's functionality to a* mobile device is not practical and technically suboptimal. It's not practical because a mobile user's requirements are different than a desktop user's requirements. Technically, porting multitudes of features and large volumes of customer data puts undue strain on processing power and memory. Best approach here is to identify two or three CRM functions to make available for the mobile user (e.g., start with leads and account records only) and phase in more features over time.

▶ **Users rule**   The most common cause of CRM failure is lack of user adoption and the same is absolutely true for mobile CRM. A good process for securing end-user support is to get them involved early and truly value their feedback. A good way to achieve this is through a pilot, involving a subset of users for a period of at least 30 days. This will allow IT to assess deployment challenges and enable users to provide feedback based on actual usage in the field and in front of customers. Mobile CRM will succeed when the system becomes an indispensable sales tool rather than an administrative burden.◆

PART III
Baby Stays, Bathwater Goes—
CRM Still Needs the Operational

11

The Collaborative Value Chain

If this were the previous edition of this book, I'd be lauding the virtues of your enterprise value chain—you, your suppliers, vendors, and partners working together to do things that would impact your customers. I'd be saying hosannas if you could show me a case where the entire value chain cooperated to provide real value to customers.

But this isn't the previous edition. Cooperation among the principals in the vast conspiracy of business entities is not the notion du jour. Collaboration, ah, now that's what we're talkin' about.

The new ecosystem demands a collaborative strategy, both internally and externally. Where one company could John Wayne it in the past to reach and satisfy their paying clients, that is no longer possible. In reality, it was never possible, but the idea of strategizing with competitors or suppliers or customers was not really top of mind in the 1950s through the late 1980s except in rare instances. There was some inkling things were changing in 1994. Adam Brandenburger, a professor at the Harvard Business School, and Adam Nalebuff, the Milton Steinbach professor at the Yale School of Management, wrote a valuable book called *Co-opetition*. *Co-opetition* stressed the changes that were driving the marketplace into the arms of the customer. This demanded that competitors with complementary offerings begin to cooperate without guilt. Here's how the professors put it:

> If business is a game, who are the players and what are their roles? There are customers and suppliers, of course; you wouldn't be in business without them. And, naturally, there are competitors. Is that it? No, not quite. There's one more, often overlooked but equally important group of players—those who provide complementary rather than competing products and services.

While Brandenburger and Nalebuff put the entire book in the context of game theory and game players, the principle was sound and reflected something emergent. The idea that suppliers and vendors and partners—and as a trailer of things to come, customers—could work together, much less competitors who provided complementary services and products, was a new one. But the rate of acceleration from the mid-1990s to now is far more rapid than the preceding era. We've already rocketed through the need to create an extended value chain (EVC) to a new and actually pretty exciting version—the evolution from the EVC to the CVC—a collaborative value chain. This supersedes the idea of mere integration among CRM, supply chain management (SCM), and enterprise resource planning (ERP) applications. It is a network that extends beyond the corporation per se and into the world of all of those other businesses, agencies, and even customers who provide the complementary goods and services and can trigger the insights that make the value proposition of a company exceptionally interesting to a customer. That would be the kind of integrated effort among all the parties that is a necessary condition of modern business.

The last generation, the one that I covered in the third edition, was one where you could put together the EVC that would then reach out and touch customers to keep them in the fold. But using a corporate extended value chain isn't sufficient any longer to meet the customers' escalated demands. Their expectations require their engagement in this new way that intersects both the company's extended value chain and the customer's personal value chain.

That adds up to a collaborative value chain. With one additional element to be mixed into the brew—transparency. Let's start with that because it permeates the entire collaborative value chain.

Transparency

Transparency has a lot of currency as a term because it's usually used in the world of GRC—governance, risk, and compliance. But that's not what I mean. Transparency when it comes to the world of customers is their ability to get the kinds of information they need to make intelligent decisions. It also means that as a company, you're willing to own up to mistakes and let the customer know honestly what they can expect, whether or not they are going to like the answer. It means that as a company you are willing to provide continuous avenues of communication from your customers to your decision makers or at least to the appropriate parties to meet the specific customer needs. Since that's normally on the fly, you have to provide the pipelines and the spigots and just make sure the customers have a means to turn them on.

That transparency can be of enormous value or its lack can be quite damaging. Sandvik, a 47,000-employee-strong Swedish engineering and tool provider, has operations in 130 countries and a revenue of 86 billion Swedish kroner (roughly $14.25 billion U.S.). They also have an operating profit that ranges between 15 and 17 percent year after year. All in all, a very successful B2B company and one of the world's best companies, period.

One of the core reasons for their continued success is the corporate value statement they call "The Power of Sandvik," a three-pronged program that promotes openness, fair play, and social responsibility. As a company, they demand the participation of all 47,000 employees in the program—and make it a part of their relationships with suppliers and partners—and almost all the company activities are transparent, offering deep visibility into operations. For example, they not only expose the corporate senior management bonuses, they also show how they accrued them. These kinds of actions make them among the most profitable and trusted companies in the world.

Once transparency is added to the mixture, we need to look at the systems that make that mixture as delicious to customers and companies as we think it can be.

The Systems

Let's start by sauntering down memory lane for a bit. I want to take an evolutionary walk through the types of value chains that have been both popular and useful in the enterprise and, then, take a brief look at the kinds of business and application integration they fostered. Each of these has evolved to something more contemporary and appropriate, but each still is beneficial to a company, either in isolation or in conjunction with the more contemporary approaches.

The Enterprise Value Chain: The Back Office Met the Front Office

Way, way back when CRM was CRM in a manly way—big, beefy, and flabby—and the business ecosystem was a customer-focused corporate ecology, integration usually meant application integration. How did you conjoin those data-driven CRM applications with the legacy systems that your company had invested gazillions in and the third-party applications that you just didn't want to give up? As the corporate ecosystem reached its end of days, it evolved past the data and applications integration it so loved and became something better. It was the front and back offices, the supply and demand chains interlocking as a unified customer-centric business effort. That included the traditional CRM departments like sales and marketing or support. It included the old ERP functions like finance and human resources. It even included those inevitably boring supply chain activities like inventory management, scheduling, sourcing, delivery, and logistics. They all worked together for a common cause—a grab at customer insight, and even more important, a shot at customer "pleasure." In other words, it was not just application integration, it was process integration geared toward the customer's wants. Applications communicated with applications, processes communicated with rules, and applications tied themselves to processes. Web services were the interface between those applications, processes, and rules.

Not all that clear? If this were purely application integration, we'd be looking at how to make salesforce.com's sales application talk to an AppExchange application like Studentforce, or we would see how it integrated with SAP financials and supplier relationship management—using the interfaces of either application. Business integration is interested in also making them communicate but more along of the lines of having someone enter closed deal information in the sales application. This will generate an order, which will then be booked in the financial system. This order will be applied to a compensation program that is part of the human resources system tailored specifically to the individual salesperson who closed the deal. Additionally, the order management system will generate a lookup of the available product inventory and send the information to the logistics team. That team will pack and ship the product, while an e-mail is being generated to the buyer on the expected ship date and delivery date, based on how the buyer chose to handle the shipping. None of the specific application integration points are of interest, nor will it be apparent to the salesperson doing the entry or the buyer receiving the e-mail. It is an application-agnostic approach, though the specific applications that will be engaged will matter.

Back and Front Offices Integrate—and It Works

As far back as 2003, in the Yankee Group's Edge of the Enterprise end-user survey, 71 percent of the companies polled (an admittedly small

78-company sample) increased spending on applications to improve interactions with customers, suppliers, and service providers. While we hadn't entered the Era of the Social Customer and weren't too far from the Age of Aquarius, I still can't imagine that most of them were hoping with Zen-like desire to get in harmony with the customer ecosystem, since it wasn't truly there yet. But it indicated a growing knowledge in the business world that the orientation of their technology buys and the way they sculpted their processes had to be focused around an increasingly predominant customer. META Group (now integrated into Gartner Group), in fact, was foresighted enough to detail the coming of this change back in 2001 in their report, "Integration: Critical Issues for Implementation of CRM Solutions." This report identified an enterprise ecosystem that linked supply chain management, enterprise resource planning, and CRM beneath the transactions and collaboration layer. They saw it from the standpoint of a customer-driven *corporate* ecosystem, though. Even before that, in 2000, the very smart META Group analyst Steve Bonadio, in his short piece, "Exposing the CRM/ERM/SCM Intersection," wrote "Organizations can no longer afford to view customer relationship management (CRM), enterprise resource management (ERM), and supply chain management (SCM) initiatives as separate. Synchronizing front-office, back-office, and supply chain activities is critical to attracting/retaining customers, fulfilling demand, and improving cycle times." Bonadio was quite the oracle, wasn't he?

Back and Front Office Integration: Bad Story, Good Story

Even back in 2000, the integration of the back and front office was an apparent win-win. But that wasn't enough as the business ecosystem began to shift in 2004–05. The extended value chain was beginning to emerge from the cradle. Before we look at what came next, a couple of stories—a failure due to broken back office to front office technology, process, and culture—and a success because the customers came first in the back.

Lessons of Real Life Failure

In mid-2007, a friend of mine, we'll call him Steve, ordered something from a hardware chain that came with the wood cracked. He called their customer service department, was told that there was no problem, he had a lifetime guarantee and within two days the replacement was there, the offending original whisked out the door.

Great story, no?

No.

When Steve's credit card bill came, he found they had charged him for the replacement. Why? This was supposed to have a lifetime guarantee and was certainly replaced soon enough to be free under the warranty. It had nothing to do with bad customer service or deceptive policies. If it were that kind of story, it would be in Chapter 13.

When he got to the bottom of it, Steve found out that this company didn't have any processes or even technology in place to handle exchanges. They had a purchase and a refund for returns and that was it. The system treated the exchange as a new purchase and a return refund. Because of a glitch, he got dunned for the charge as a new purchase, but then wasn't credited back. This wouldn't be so horrible except for the incredibly antiquated system, but he was eventually charged (and sometimes credited) three times.

Steve spoke with a first-tier customer service representative initially. Then he upped the ante by speaking with the customer escalation manager. Each time he spoke with a new person, he had to re-explain the situation because even though there were transaction records on his customer history—purchases, charges, records of customer service calls—there were no interaction records.

Steve then went to the store where he bought the goods and spoke to the manager, asking him to cut a check to solve this issue with the multiple charges on his credit card. The manager was unable to give him that check even though he wanted to because he had no authority to do so. That was managed at customer service only. To add to the indignity, Steve had to explain the situation anew to this guy too, because the manager couldn't access the system even with the transaction records. Ultimately, the only thing the store manager could do was send a memo in support of Steve's case.

Procter & Gamble: The Customer-Centered Supply Chain

Procter & Gamble knows that they have to appeal to their customers. This has to permeate every experience, every product, every process, and every innovation that the company fosters. They even saw it as part of the permeable membrane of their supply chain.

They recognized that the customers' experiences came first and that they had to develop the metrics and build the supply chain processes around that. First, corporate leaders appointed a general manager of supply chain innovation whose sole job is to figure out how to make the supply chain work on behalf of the customer in both effective and efficient ways.

As far back as 2002, P&G key executives recognized that 60 percent of their sales were made based on what they called "events"—roughly equivalent to what I and others call "experiences." So, for example, Pringles had a Mac the Stack "event" that gave teens decoder cards at concerts and theme parks. Teens took the codes online and found out how much they won, from $3 to $50. Procter & Gamble used this event to create an adventurous experience—and discover a lot of people who then bought products.

Sixty percent of a company that makes tens of billions of dollars is a lot of dollars. This didn't exactly escape the notice of the P&G leadership. First and foremost, to bolster the idea of experience-driven sales, they appointed Jake Barr as the general manager of supply chain innovation and then put a plan into effect based on this idea: "If you can't drive sales and deliver product at the point of purchase, you lose." (*Procter & Gamble: Delivering Goods*, by Randy Barrett and Tom Steinert-Threlkeld, *Baseline*, July 1, 2004.) This led to P&G adopting a "pull," rather than "push," approach to inventory, which cut out excess inventory and was based on the idea the company would produce only what customers bought.

Second, the company reverse-engineered the products by looking directly at the cost components after it had surveyed customers to see what price point they were willing to pay for varying products. The idea was to manufacture the products profitably and still be able to set a price customers were happy with. It's called pricing from the shelf back, and it's a hugely important KPI when the customer-centered supply chain is where the focus is. The customers are effectively setting their own prices.

Third, company leaders put other KPIs in place designed to produce and deliver quickly according to purchases made. So, for example, besides the ones mentioned above, they look at:

▶ Total supply chain response time, from purchase at register to purchase of raw materials to replace product. Originally six months, it came down to two months.

▶ Shelf level quality—how many and what kind of damaged or unappealing packages are on the store shelves. Zero is the optimal number.

▶ Out-of-stock rates—a mission-critical KPI for the customer-centered supply chain. P&G research showed that 41 percent of the time an item is out of stock, the sale is lost; 28 percent of the time, a competitor gets the sale. Given that they were producing "on demand," the risks here seemed high, but I'll get to that.

Keep in mind, it wasn't just a matter of P&G doing this alone. The company has 5,000 key retailers and 30,000 key suppliers dealing with its 300 brands. They all had to buy in. The demands weren't only around impacting the customer but also convincing that incredible number of partners and suppliers that they should be part of this seemingly aberrant approach.

Needless to say, if they had failed in this unique customer-centered initiative, I wouldn't be using P&G as an example, but the plan has been wildly successful. Here are the numbers:

▶ Out-of-stock rates dropped from 16.3 percent to 7.6 percent between 2003 and 2004.

▶ Earnings growth went from 15 percent in 2002 to 20 percent in 2004.

▶ P&G saw annual supply chain cost savings of between $50 and $100 million.

▶ Sales increased from $40 billion in 2002 to $43.4 billion in 2004.

Getting help from the customers might actually work, don't you think?

Integrating the Back with the Front— Still Not Too Shabby

If we're in an era where engaging the customer with the company and its partners in a collaboration is becoming important, is there any value in cleaning up the supply chain in the way that P&G did? It seems so . . . incremental at this point.

The answer is "Yes, there is." According to Benchmarking Partners, inventory being held by retailers at any single moment is approximately $1 trillion. This is based on U.S. Department of Commerce data.

If planning, forecasting, and replenishment were improved, the inventory could be reduced by $150 to $200 billion (in other words, 15 to 20 percent). That's just for the SCM changes. Imagine if you were able to forecast customer demand and understand customer behavior, making far more sophisticated analyses. But the return doesn't stop there. CRM/SCM integration provides a measurable return on a number of key indicators that don't apply to just CRM or just SCM. AMR Research identified them in a report on the benefits of this integration in March 2003:

▶ Shorter order cycle times—decrease up to 65 percent

▶ Increased order accuracy—up to 100 percent improvement

▶ Incomplete orders—reduced by 20 percent

▶ Fewer order status calls weekly—up to 86 percent

▶ Inventory costs—10 percent reduction in sales inventory days

▶ Enterprise spend—5 to 10 percent savings on the cost of goods

There's something to be said with results that are this blatantly good. But there is something else that shouldn't be ignored. These numbers, from 2003, are the most recent numbers easily available. While the ROI is there, the conversation is starting to diminish around this because it's escalating about customer engagement. Yet, back and front office integration is something with an undeniable benefit.

The Next Step: Value Chain Integration

Back and front office integration is only one kind of integration with benefits available to an enterprise. Let's take it a step further (or deeper, depending on your metaphor inclination).

Value chain integration is the evolution from a series of linearly interlinked processes that had historically been isolated from each other, to a smoothly functioning integrated business model that is effectively a single link from multiple parts of the enterprise. CRM, SCM, ERP, and a strategy for product lifecycle management (not covered here) will provide a complete "system" for a refreshed look at the new enterprise and what it needs.

Imagine this scenario. You made a decision to take your company to new revenue heights. To do this, you decided that you had to move from a product-out-the-door sales plan to a voice-of-the-customer strategy. You formulated a CRM strategy and included all the right elements. To gain some early credence among your colleagues, and to solve some immediate issues, you took care of the first damaged area: sales. You developed new compensation plans based on customer satisfaction ratings for the salespeople. You implemented a new SFA solution that reduced administrative time and improved the real-time access to customer and competitive information. Pricing customization was now easier.

You had amazing results. Your product sales numbers improved by 45 percent. Your sales teams had 17 percent more time with customers, gratifying the customers, because administration and attention were that much more efficient. Things were going great, weren't they?

Sure. CRM strategy aimed at the front end alone worked wonderfully—for a little while. But where were those products to be delivered coming from? How fast were they getting out the door? Did you (and do you) have sufficient inventory to meet the demands of the increased sales? How were you going to schedule the delivery of those products so that customers who ordered them received them in a timely way? If the sales numbers were that improved, the strain on the supply chain had to be enormous, because it is likely you didn't make any fundamental changes to the organization of the supply chain. After all, this was a CRM sales force automation initiative, wasn't it? Backlogged orders needed to be entered into the financial system, but they were straining the staff because no new employees were hired to enter the data properly. Employees had to work overtime to meet the load created by the success of the CRM strategy and the application of the SFA tools. As time moved on, you began to fail to follow through on orders, delivery was routinely late for your items, and orders fell off precipitously as customer satisfaction with your company declined, even though the customers liked the salespeople personally and admired their effectiveness. Before long, the success kills you.

The lesson: Don't be successful! (Just kidding.)

The real lesson is that a CRM strategy in the new world customer ecosystem is merely the forward facing part of an encompassing collaborative enterprise strategy, whether you are a behemoth or a mosquito-sized company.

Integration Challenges

The challenges of linking the demand and supply chains are substantial, and the failure of any one segment can have catastrophic efforts on your customer. The most formidable problem comes when the supply chain and the demand chain are each seen (and thus organized) as a discrete set of processes and practices that are uniquely optimized. The relationship between them has been parallel at best, not integrated. For example, supply chain management has been touted as the organization and optimization of production and performance, including delivery and logistics. CRM has targeted the identification of and improvement in the customer experience, leading to improved top and bottom lines. Historically, SCM has been associated with efficiencies and cost controls; CRM traditionally has been associated with effectiveness and revenue increases.

The irony, of course, is that the supply chain's entire purpose is the efficient delivery of the products and services to *customers*, so how well that delivery is executed is vital to the pulse rate of those customers. Think of it this way. One of my clients is David's Bridal. As you may know, they sell all apparel and accoutrements related to weddings. Imagine if their supply chain success rate was *only* 98 percent. That would mean 2 percent of all brides they delivered to wouldn't have their gown ready on their wedding day (note: they do far better than that). Let's just say the expression "going postal" would become "going bridal." That's how important supply chain success can be to an integrated customer-centered initiative.

But we're talking about a lot more than just an internal set of operations, aren't we? What about the partners? They have their own value chains to deal with and their own systems they use and their own processes, yet they are part of a fully integrated extended value chain.

The Extended Value Chain: Meet the Partners

The customer ecosystem creates some serious complexity. Not only are customer demands more intense, and their need to use companies to not just purchase but attend to their personal agendas more important, but the levels of service that partners have to provide are more granular than ever before. This is particularly daunting for partners because they are often limited to areas that are far more specific than the range of their expertise would permit. But they have to be that specialized, even if it limits their markets to some extent, because as Sand Hill Group venture capitalist rock star M. R. Rangaswami noted at a 2006 conference, CIOs don't want to talk to startups, and startups usually are modeled to sell directly to users—not to CIOs.

This leaves small young companies in the arms of the largest vendors as a role player if they want to penetrate markets that those vendors are in. To a certain degree, the smaller partners—those that don't fit the designation "strategic"—are beholden to the big boys. Luckily, the vast majority of the large vendors don't treat their partners the way that Wal-Mart treats its suppliers—we're the behemoth, you're the mosquito, so you do what we say. Most vendors see the value that the smaller companies bring to their overall ecosystem and they work with them accordingly.

Microsoft is perhaps the paradigm for working with partners. They were in 2004, when the third edition of this book came out, and they are in 2009 with this edition. Microsoft has understood the business value of partner ecosystems for a long while. Historically, the best reflection of their ideas around building ecosystems has been their partner network. Think of these two numbers:

▶ As of 2009, they reached one million partners (including partner affiliates) globally

▶ Year after year, they get around 95 percent of their total revenue from partners

While those are numbers that could stop Tony Stewart cold in lap 50 of the Daytona 500, it's actually not enough to understand how contemporary ecosystems work. The partner ecosystem is a true ecosystem—not just a channel. Microsoft understands they can't do everything to meet the more demanding customer's imperative or even the business and consumer's separate demands to provide an adequate customer experience. They also can't acquire enough companies to do it without them running out of money. So they built, after all kinds of permutations and glitches, an extraordinary partner-driven ecosystem that covers what is perhaps every vertical and horizontal facet of a given individual's life.

Okay, back to the strategy. The partner ecosystem was built with a lot of problems along the way. At one point, Microsoft had 54 partner programs. They've consolidated to a single program that is chock-full of incentives for partners, including Microsoft handing over business. The way they focus their partner program is not only the revenue driver for the company, but each partner also fits into an appropriate place in the overall ecosystem they are utilizing to provide the level of personalized experience each of us craves. They also are quite generous with code, so there is a large community of developers dot-netting away, and that can only bear fruit for Microsoft's plan to create that unique environment—because they have outside innovators innovating toward that end.

At the Worldwide Partner Conference in Denver in August 2007, Kevin Turner, the excitable and articulate COO of Microsoft, nodded toward that idea when he announced to some 10,000 acolytes that "while Bill Gates's vision used to be a PC with a Windows operating system on every desktop, his new vision is for Microsoft to be the one company in the world connecting digital work style and personal lifestyle." Which will take a lot of partners, since the one thing that Microsoft gets above all else when it comes to partner ecosystems is that Microsoft can't do it alone. They actively solicit partners who can fill specific holes in a channel portfolio.

Brad Wilson, Microsoft's CRM general manager and the man responsible for their CRM strategy, put it well when he described the partner ecosystem for CRM:

> A lot of our perspective on partner ecosystems comes from a global view. We have thousands of partners in over 80 countries and we have to consider the pre-existing environments and the needs of the individual partners and the nations they reside in. This has an effect on our choice and how it's used.
>
> For example, an auto dealership in Turkey who might be serviced by a partner there differs from a bank in Latin America being serviced by a partner there. So the requirements vary accordingly. The technology platform used for such a widely diverse set of global partners needs to be highly flexible and allow the partners to tailor it accordingly.

This is why Microsoft is so effective. They understand the benefit of a laser-sliced view of the customer and are working to make sure that their partner ecosystem can meet those highly specific needs.

But the partners themselves are becoming as demanding as the customers and create an interesting conundrum for the brand-holding business they are associating with. They know they have a choice as to whom they partner with. They have no qualms whatever about leveraging that. The brandholders that understand that do well. For example in July 2009, Microsoft announced the revamped Partner Network which incorporated, among many other changes, a community feature that integrated partner communities and use of social media tools to enable the interactions among partners and between Microsoft and the partners and a partner "accelerator" that allows partners to manage sales leads more effectively.

Of course, those brandholders who don't get this, fail.

A Mini-Conference

I'd like to welcome all of you to the first *CRM at the Speed of Light* mini-conference. We have two distinguished analysts here today to discuss the often daunting business of partners and the channel, and how their needs and models are changing.

First, I'm going to ask Louis Columbus to step up. Louis is an analyst who now works happily at Cincom. He is one of smartest guys in our industry and has one of the kindest hearts. He has a strong set of bona fides, having worked as a senior analyst at the highly respected AMR Research. He's published 15 technology books (how he did that, I'll never know—I had enough trouble with this one). He knows the partner channel inside out, and I'll yield the floor to him so he can tell you what they are thinking and where they are going.

EXTENDED CONVERSATION WITH LOUIS COLUMBUS:

CHANNEL PARTNERS ARE NO LONGER THE SILENT MAJORITY

It's time to question the assumption that channel partners aren't interested in, and further, don't have the technical skill to be more connected with each other and the companies they resell for. Social networking is turning this assumption on its head, and with it, completely reordering distribution channels and value chains. Frankly, it's amazing this continues to be an assumption in so many companies, as social networking is serving as the catalyst for much more interactive and online learning going on—much more so that any given application vendors' learning module as part of their partner relationship management (PRM) system could deliver. Granted, there are Luddites out there who are afraid of even dial-up, but the vast majority of resellers have had to change or risk being driven out of business by competitors who embrace new technologies and use them to grow their businesses, and find new ways of delivering value to their customers. Watching Twitter traffic or blog entries scroll in any RSS reader that includes entries from resellers regarding the pros and cons of selling Microsoft CRM versus salesforce .com just makes this point even clearer. Channel partners definitely aren't the Silent Majority anymore; social networking continues to be the catalyst that is leading them to create new channel networks of their own.

Forget about the diagram showing channel management as a top-down hierarchy, or the rigid structure of a value chain. This isn't accurate anymore. Think of channel relationships as a series of interconnected networks, resembling more molecular structures and less command-and-control. Now intersperse in the many companies that even a single reseller interacts with, and the point becomes clear: the reseller's world has become infinitely more complex. Compounding all of this is the fact that there is more to learn than ever before; product lifecycles are increasing in many industries. Differentiation through using firmware, or electronics embedded in products, from refrigerators and appliances to cars and aircraft forces resellers to learn faster than their competitors, master specific product and sales knowledge, to gain a competitive advantage. It's not about winning the sale anymore by just having price and availability, it about earning the trust of customers with an exceptionally strong grasp of product, selling, integration, and use data. In essence, channel management and managing value chains is much more about knowledge and a lot less about products. It's enough to wake up even the quietest of a Silent Majority.

Time to Knowledge Now Critical

There are no doubt entire books written on how channel management strategies can be made more efficient by synchronizing them with supply chains, in effect re-engineering an entire value chain to be more efficient and customer-centric. Yet all this business process re-engineering misses the point: knowledge is the fuel that makes the entire channel management and value chain engine run. What's remarkable is the octane social networking has and continues to enrich knowledge with. Managing channels is now more about what any given company can contribute to these conversations and less about trying to restrict transactions, learning, or decisions. In a sense the essence of marketing and channel management is now laid bare in social networking; it truly is all about giving more than you get if you want to succeed. Paradoxically the command-and-control models of channel management and value chains, while still enforceable by market makers (Wal-Mart for one), are going by the wayside for more integrated and network-based models. Products themselves even become gradually incidental to the really valuable asset: knowledge of how to transact between partners and companies and trust that gets built over time.

In Search of the Perfect Refrigerator

If you've ever had to replace a major kitchen appliance and you're like me, you immediately dive into the manufacturers' websites you know of, scouring their selections, checking Consumer Reports *for reliability ratings, and thoroughly reading reviews on third-party sites. Armed with all that data, my wife and I headed out to see the models we'd settled on in person. From the high-end Expo store, a Home Depot spin-off that didn't know what a counter-depth refrigerator was yet wanted to sign us up immediately for a credit card, to big-box retailers Home Depot, Lowe's and Best Buy, to a Maytag store, we ran the gamut of channels refrigerator manufacturers sell through. Here's what we found out: up-sell and cross-sell techniques are drilled into the heads of sales reps in the Expo stores. Maytag stores are staffed by product experts who tend to want you to fit into their products' range and not vice versa. Big-box retailers in general stress price. Here's where my wife's and my expectations were changed, however. Our qualifying question at each big-box store was why there was such a variation in price between the websites and the store. The Lowe's sales rep immediately dismissed that with a commitment to beat the price online, and then proceeded to ask us about what we felt we needed in a refrigerator. This conversation went on for 45 minutes and in the end, we bought from them. The sales rep had been to these manufacturers' websites, and understood how each manufacturer does their energy efficiency ratings slightly differently. It was the sales rep's combining of knowledge and empathy that won the sale. In the end we bought from the sales rep who was the most informed and the most interested in helping us make the best decision. He was the most informed because he'd taken the time, online, to understand so many more nuances of these products than anyone else. Social networking's potential from this is clear; the more knowledge is seen as the most valuable part of managing channels, the more effective customer interactions become.*

Thank you, Louis.

Now, to drive this home, since I know a good number of the people who read this book are business people looking to partner, I'm going to turn over the podium to Mike Fauscette. You can see Mike's credentials below. I've known him 10 years and he is one of the few analysts who really got his chops on the street as a leader in industry. For example, before he went to IDC, he was the group vice president in charge of global professional services at Autodesk. Hands on.

He's going to give you three takeaways to consider for a new kind of partner model—one that fits quite nicely into the collaborative value chain, thank you very much.

The Partner Joins the New Ecosystem

Michael Fauscette is the group vice president of the Software Business Solutions Group at IDC. The group includes research and consulting in ERP, SCM, CRM, and PLM applications (and the associated business process that the software supports), small and medium business applications, partner and alliance ecosystems, open source software, software vendor business models (software as a service, or SaaS), and software pricing and licensing. Prior to joining IDC, Michael held senior consulting and services roles with seven software vendors, including Autodesk, Inc., PeopleSoft, Inc. and MRO, Inc. His software experience spans the entire enterprise lifecycle process and covers all facets of the global software business. A former U.S. naval officer, he began his technology career as a surface line engineering officer. Michael is a published author and accomplished public speaker on software and software services strategies.

MINI-CONVERSATION WITH MIKE FAUSCETTE: SOFTWARE PARTNERS IN EVOLUTION

As I look at partnering in the software industry, several factors have emerged over the last few years that are driving significant change. The software industry itself is in the midst of a change cycle that began post-Internet bubble and has continued for the last seven years with consolidation, new business models, and new use paradigms. Software partner models across all partner types are not exempt from the effect of these industry changes. There are three key partner issues around these changes: the emergence of software ecosystems, the effect of SaaS on traditional software partners, and the emergence of new partner types around the SaaS model.

The old model of point-to-point partnerships is not serving the software industry effectively. A new paradigm has emerged that is starting to create a networking effect that places the partners in a constantly evolving ecosystem of peer-to-peer networks. There are many factors driving this change from vendor strategy to customer needs. Software vendors are realizing that partner-to-partner networks have the potential to increase wallet share of their products and increase the overall satisfaction of their partner community by increasing partner revenue. Customers, who have increasingly demanded more complete and industry vertical specific solutions, are engaging more readily with these networked solutions. Partner ecosystems are developing into vendor mega-economies around a few large software vendors. This has accelerated because of the continuing consolidation in the overall software industry and has partners coalescing around Oracle, SAP, Microsoft, salesforce.com, and IBM because of their dominance in the marketplace.

As the SaaS on-demand business model becomes more mainstream, software vendors and their partners have struggled with the need for new partner models. Value-added resellers (VARs) and system integrators (SIs) are the most affected by this change but even the independent solutions vendors (ISVs) are contemplating the impact of SaaS on their businesses. Software vendors with traditional VAR distribution models seem to be perplexed about how to shift their current indirect distribution models to effectively distribute SaaS offerings in a volume model. Since SaaS software products are of particular interest to small and mid-market customers, the need for a volume distribution channel is even more critical. The problem with traditional VARs is a business model issue; on-premise software is often sold in a dealer model that is based on a one-time license revenue transaction (thus delivering margin in a single transaction). On-demand software does not have an up-front license fee, but instead is based on recurring subscription fees. The VAR could be engaged by the vendor in several ways— there could be an agency fee that is a percentage of the recurring subscription fee, or there could be influence fees that are paid at deal close. Neither delivers the large up-front revenue to the VAR or is a significant change in the cash flow and sales compensation models for the VAR. The commitment to shift the business from the old model to the new is large and can be very difficult for businesses that are often cash flow challenged anyway.

SIs also have to retool their businesses to meet the challenges of the SaaS business model. Customers will not accept long, complex software implementations. Instead SIs must offer similar value in their services that customers see in SaaS offerings: fast time to value, easy deployment, minimal hardware and infrastructure investment, and so on. In addition, many of the traditional skills that SIs have employed are not necessary for SaaS deployments, since there is no on-site infrastructure and minimal (or no) customizations. Instead the skills required are more oriented around business process, and the services must deliver value fast. Delivering small incremental service packages is much more palatable to customers.

The SaaS business model is also driving the emergence of new partner types, fueled by the need for industry-specific business process expertise. The new partners seem to fall into two types, business service providers and business domain specialists. Business service providers are often customers turned partner and offer a combination of business services on top of the SaaS software. Business domain specialists combine deep business process expertise applicable to specific micro-verticals. Their job is to assist others in the industry to apply business process around new software deployments.

Overall partner models are in transition. Today, traditional SIs often resell product like a VAR or develop add-on product like an ISV. VARs add revenue through the delivery of services and by adding custom product. ISVs also resell product and provide services around their solutions. P2P networks are taking hold and changing the way partners go to market. Vendors are working out new business models for SaaS distribution partners. The end result of these changes is still not obvious and should continue to play out over the next two to three years.

That's it for the conference. Please fill out your evaluation forms. When you hand them in at the back, you'll be getting a keychain with a clock and a pen with a light attached to it. I know it's a unique gift you've never seen anywhere—except every conference you've ever been to.

Now Meet the Customer: The Collaborative Value Chain

The extended value chain worked on the principle that all aspects of a company—from the internal processes that governed the corporate parent to the relationships that engaged the suppliers, vendors, and business partners—applied well to the more traditional CRM 1.0 notion of being able to manage the relationships of customers so that they had an optimal useful experience with the company. The company still played the central role.

But with the advent of the "era of the social customer" (see Chapter 1), the nature of the value chain altered. Because a significant segment of the customer base was demanding entrance into the company and participation in the planning of their experiences with the company, the customer's personal value chain (PVC) had to be accounted for. This meant the things that affected their lives individually, whether the company had control over it or not, became meaningful to the revenues and profitability of the company, because those personal occurrences and behaviors affected how the customer engaged the company. But, of course, there is no way for a company to control the personal value chains of the individual customers. Thus, engaging those customers in some form of collaborative activity became very important, actually a mission-critical imperative—and forward-thinking companies did just that. The customers' expectations were that the company would be transparent, trustworthy, and willing to provide them with what they needed to team up. This was a dramatic change, even though it seems to be not much more than a word shift from "extended" to "collaborative." After all, what's that? A gain of five letters? Piffle.

But to see that this is more than piffle, we have to understand the customer's role in the CVC before we can "know" the CVC itself.

Personal Value Chain

When I came up with the idea of a personal value chain, I struggled with a way to clearly explain it, falling into the "why explain something with a few words when a million will do" trap for quite a while. Well, damned if Patricia Seybold didn't answer it for me with an economy of language in her book (and blog) *Outside Innovation*:

> *We use Eric von Hippel's term, "lead users," to describe the somewhat larger group of customers and non-customers who are passionate about getting certain things accomplished. They may not know or care about the products and services you offer. But they do care about their project or need.*

Eureka! I get it now. The personal value chain is the institutions and individuals that I utilize each day, each hour, to both interact with other institutions and individuals and to help determine how I'm going to interact with them. It is solely under my personal control. It solely exists for my purposes. No institution or other person has any control over it. They can only control their own behavior and interactions with it. It is my personal agenda and what affects it and what it has an effect on.

Michael Gaylord, vice president at TV Land Digital:

> *It's much harder now to accurately mine the data and understand consumer behavior because there are so many touchpoints. The whole notion of "come to one website and one brand" is quickly eroding. Consumers aggregate their own content, on their own websites. Their experience with content providers is much more ephemeral.*

One story explains it all. About two years ago, I was using a Palm Treo. I wanted to trick it out, which shows you how lame I am—trick out a Palm Treo? To do that, I needed to accessorize. I ordered some things from two different Palm Treo focused sites. One was TreoCentral and the other was the Palm home site. I ordered on a Sunday and ordered two items—one from each site. The Palm home site sent their item by UPS, and TreoCentral used FedEx. The UPS package was sent ground, but only after I used that valuable little tool that estimates the cost and the travel time for the package based on zip codes. Two days. Federal Express was second-day air. My expectations, thus, for both packages to arrive on Wednesday.

Both sites were diligent in notification. I knew by Sunday night that both packages shipped that night. Still, Wednesday was my expectation for each of them. Wednesday was when UPS showed up. Tuesday was when FedEx showed up.

The result? FedEx had exceeded expectations. UPS met them perfectly. Also, since the originators were responsible for the couriers, both had provided me with an exceedingly painless and pleasant experience.

Would I use either of the sites again? No! I have an iPhone now. Why would I need them? C'mon! But if I still had a Treo, would I? Sure, without qualms. Would I use UPS again? Of course, they met expectations *perfectly*. But FedEx exceeded expectations, so they gained a slight edge in courier competitions when weighing the future—even though they weren't the central players in the experience stakes here. TreoCentral and Palm were.

That is how a personal value chain works. These two purchases and the experience associated with them met my "project" (the purchases to trick out the Treo) requirements. However, there were important personal decisions I made out of the control of the originators of the experience. Those decisions had a bearing on what influenced me and how it did so, *and* what my expectations were of the pending interactions. For example, if I paid for two-day shipping, I expected it in two days. If I paid for ground shipping with a two-day expected arrival, I expected it within a reasonable time frame close to two days. In other words, I had a nuanced difference in how I approached each carrier.

This personal value chain is the driver of the customer's activity, be they a B2B customer or a B2C customer. It is the set of events, memories, agendas, relationships, processes, rules, and experiences that the customer has that affects how they interact with you and/or your company.

One piece of advice. Since you can't control the customer's personal value chain—at all—all you can do is provide them with what they need to meet those agendas. Just be mindful that the effect of all the other parts of their value chain might impact you at any given time.

Co-creation of Value

The benefits of a collaborative value chain is almost what the name explicitly states—collaboration between internal corporate resources with external resources to innovate, and/or to create value in ways that would otherwise be either less effective or more expensive. The benefit is that some value (see Chapter 20 for more on customer value) is created for all the parties involved. There is an enormous volume of literature out there on the business models for co-creation of value. The rules and the infrastructure that allow customers to participate in the activities of the company are designed such that not only are the customers an integral part of the value proposition of the company but the customer's relationship to the company will also shift.

While examples abound throughout this book, I wanted to acquaint you with the concept. You'll see it implicitly and explicitly in every facet of Social CRM thinking, planning, and actions in this book. If you'd like to read more on it, I highly recommend C. K. Prahalad and Venkat Ramaswamy's *The Future of Competition: Co-creating Unique Value with Customers*. Their models are exceptionally clear and their examples, while limited, are really interesting—especially John Deere.

Ecosystems Begin to Rule

By the time you get to this chapter, I suspect you have realized that customers have become the dominant business force—so strong a controlling presence in the business environment that I think we should make customers a new species or at least a new genus. Ecosystems are beginning to rule the business planet and they demand value chains that incorporate all the elements.

By creating ecosystems, the business model shifts (see Chapter 5 for details):

▶ From the world of the corporation to the world of the customer

▶ From separation of business from personal to the unification of the two—at least at an emotional and intellectual value

▶ From value residing in the products produced and the services created to the customer themselves

▶ From looking at the return on investment to seeing a return on customer

As we saw in Chapter 5, the business model has evolved too—from a business model where the company was the producer of goods and services to a model where the company is an aggregator of the necessary components to optimize a customer's individual experience.

Take a look, for example, at a Microsoft acquisition reported in the *New York Times* on February 26, 2008. Microsoft acquired Medstory, which applies artificial intelligence to medical and health info in medical journals, government documents, and the unstructured Internet through a sophisticated search engine.

Why in hell would Microsoft do that? Well, let's do the math—in context that is. Probably addition. In 2006, they purchased (and this is the real name) Azyxxi—which is either Superman's old nemesis or a company that makes software that retrieves and displays patient information from multiple sources, including documents, x-rays, MRIs, and ultrasound images.

Then they added (note the math reference) Medstory in 2008. Why would software company Microsoft purchase a company that retrieved medical records and another one that retrieved medical information? Microsoft doesn't have a history of providing medical advice or physicians.

The *Times* article explains this "why":

> *"The Medstory purchase," said Peter Newpert, vice-president for health strategy at Microsoft, "was a first step in a broader company strategy to assemble technologies that would improve the consumer experience in health care."*
>
> *... these companies and others are seeking ways to build businesses on the Internet that profit from what is called consumer-driven health care. The notion is that shifts in demographics, economics, technology, and policy will inevitably mean that individuals will want to, and be forced to, make more health care decisions themselves. ... Aging baby boomers, accustomed to personal choice and to technology, tend to want a say in their treatment decisions.*

Now did it make some sense for Microsoft to acquire those companies? Actually, not if you leave it at that. Why health care? They already have the XBox 360, Windows 7, MSN Search, Office 2007 with 2010 on the way, CRM Dynamics 4.0 on premise and on demand, *ad infinitum*, and have penetrated both the personal and the work side of life. Do they need more than that?

It makes perfect sense if you are trying to create the all-encompassing environment that addresses all facets of business and everyday life. Health care attends to key portions of that personalized value chain— the individual's approach to gaining control over a hopefully rich and long life. In other words, with the availability of comprehensive sources of information previously only seen by health professionals, ranging from the ability to find how one drug interacts with another to your direct health records to references for experts in a particular health field, an opportunity to get some control over your health issues is now extant. How it gets handled is more under your control, because you have the mechanism to get whatever information you need to do that.

Okay, before all you *1984* readers and privacy paranoiacs get up into Microsoft's face about controlling your life and fulminate about the implications on privacy of this strategy, take a deep breath and remember a few things:

1. Microsoft provides tools—not ankle shackles, technology tools. These actually can help you.

2. You control your life, no one else. Not even Steve Ballmer or Larry Ellison.

3. Use reason, not hyperventilation.

Microsoft's acquisitions are wise moves for them because they provide a full-featured environment that aggregates the knowledge that you individually need for your health—making you want to use the one-shop-stop resources (at this phase, in principle) that are powered by Microsoft because of a powerful incentive—convenience. Aggregation is the model that's powered by convenience.

But all that we've looked at to date—the back and front office integrations, the partners and vendors, the acquisitions, the customer involvement—are the elements to build a collaborative value chain that drives customer engagement. How do you build it? Who is the best at it? That's what we're going to answer in the next episode of "Whom Do You Trust to Handle Your Agendas?"

Building the Collaborative Value Chain

I'm now presuming we're in agreement that we have to be willing to go beyond the "ordinary" extended value chain of company, partners, suppliers and to the CVC when appropriate. That means engaging customers and remembering that there are other experts who need to be a part of the effort.

If that's true and I'm not blowing smoke, then I'm going to outline the steps to prepare the way for a collaborative value chain—what has to be in place to make it happen.

Steps to the CVC

Step 1: Make sure that the internal processes, technologies, metrics, and corporate structure are aligned appropriately. If there is something that's internally broken, the effort will be doomed from the start.

But this isn't the typical alignment based on efficiencies. Many companies will use processes like Six Sigma or lean manufacturing to design their systems to reduce deficiencies and align based on purely internal criteria. Even though I'm speaking of internal alignment, it's in conjunction with customer-focused objectives so it isn't purely agnostic. For example, say you have an accounting process that is efficient and saving the company thousands of dollars a year, but it's impacting customers negatively. While this meets a possible Six Sigma objective, it doesn't meet a CRM objective—which is to provide positive impact to your customers, or at least not impact them negatively. Even if you lose the savings by changing or discarding and replacing the process to make it work in a more customer-positive way, it's worth it. The alignment of all internal objectives is painted with the brush of customer expectation.

Step 2: Make sure you have all the processes and technologies associated with external interactions working well. Typically, this is going to take the form of web-based activities. The communications media— blogs, wikis, podcasts, and the more "traditional" forms such as e-mail—have to be working effectively among the elements of the internal ecosystem and for the customer. You need to also have processes, procedures, and governance in place for how you and your customers or your partners will share intellectual property and information that ordinarily is considered competitive. Agreements need to be in place, and the rules of the game have to be defined clearly.

This is probably the most important single part of the first two steps. The reason is that you might be doing collaborative forecasting or joint scheduling with your partner, or you might be handing over product design documents. You might be sitting down with a customer who is reviewing the product that you and they just developed. There are clear hurdles that need to be overcome when it comes to how you participate with each other and what kind of legal considerations have to be given.

This isn't that unusual. Its Neanderthal manifestation was software companies providing customers with beta software for them to implement and test for free. In return for the participation in the beta program, the customers got to use a licensed version of the software prior to its release. But it wasn't just a matter of installing it and starting to use it. Since it was beta software and being put into a laboratory environment by a rather bold customer, liability had to be assessed; agreements that took that liability or lack thereof into account had to be signed. Nondisclosure agreements (NDAs) had to be executed so the nature of the new version wouldn't be leaked to the press or competitors. The software needed to be in a specific environment, which may have forced some investment by the company. In other words, the t's were crossed and the i's dotted before the program got underway.

Because the results of this collaboration could be a jointly held asset, how that manifests has to be worked out from the get-go. Who owns what for how long and what the expected uses are have to be considered in the preparation. Once these things are done, the final step can be taken.

Step 3: PricewaterhouseCoopers has a lovely description of the third step, though it's not *their* third step. This comes from Matt Porta in an article in *Cygnus Supply and Demand Chain* on what is a maturity model for the collaborative value chain:

> *They recognize the potential of the new business model enabled by the Internet and collaboration. They have a track record of applying new processes and using technologies in new ways. They are moving beyond collaboration with supply chain partners and are starting to include customers and the sales and marketing processes into their collaborative value chain. These companies seek to link the entire customer-driven value chain in a new way to improve their competitive position, to drive customer loyalty, and to improve profitability.*

Step 4: Make sure that you have clear management for the CVC—someone who will be the facilitator and have decision-making power. There are substantial and complex decisions that have to be made. The CIO is actually a good choice for this because of the impact on business rules, IT, and processes—in addition to the social aspects of the CVC. That's a first. I never thought I would see the CIO as a viable choice for anything in CRM. Regardless of who is chosen, he or she should be a champion for the idea.

Step 5: Remember that the CVC requires not just your customers, vendors, partners, and suppliers, but also industry and other expertise. As you'll see below, SAP has MyVenturePad.com as a place to access these industry experts so the benefit of third-party knowledge can be realized.

Needless to say, this isn't meant to be the exhaustive guide to creating a CVC—just an indicator of what it takes to bring together the internal and external resources that are necessary to align the processes, technologies, and social interactions in an exhaustive way so that innovation and collaboration are encouraged and customers in particular are engaged in creating what is important for them and other customers. I didn't really elaborate here on the cultural issues involved in this kind of effort. If interested, check out the online chapter "You Can't Handle the Truth—So You Have to Change," where I discuss how SAP, in particular, made those cultural changes—in fact more effectively than any other company that I can recall. Which is why they are the Superstah! for this chapter! I know you want to hear all about it, so let's take it to SAP.

Superstah! SAP

This is an unusual category for Superstah! Most of the Superstah! winners prior to and subsequent to this are focused on the companies that best represent the technologies that are appropriate to the chapters involved. In this particular one, about the best represented collaborative value chain, I could just as easily have chosen a practitioner like Procter & Gamble for their innovative approach, but I chose SAP.

Two reasons for that. First, they are a technology company and that maintains consistency. But that's the trivial reason, since I'm not wedded to technology companies. SAP is genuinely among the best practitioners of a highly evolved collaborative value chain that I've seen. Period. That is reason enough. Technology company aside, they give the Procter & Gambles a run for their money.

But I'm not going to follow the book's protocol here where I have the Mission 21st Century, etc. Instead, I'm going to let it hang out there and just talk.

Practice What You Preach (but Didn't Not That Long Ago)

If this were 2007, SAP is not the company I would have pegged to win the Superstah! designation in the collaborative value chain category. If this were five years ago, I would have laughed if it was suggested. That wouldn't have been because I had anything against SAP. On the contrary, I've been a very friendly critic—a "tough love" guy when it comes to this megalopolis-unto-itself.

But as you will see in the aforementioned online chapter, SAP has made the difficult but necessary culture changes that actually give them the basis for a true collaboration with their customers. Because of the processes and technologies (both internal and social) they have available to them, they are actually one of the companies that is defining the collaborative value chain, not just toying with the notion.

The reasons for their success are myriad, but ultimately simple. They are targeted to the needs of the individual. This could be the individual customer, the individual partner, the individual supplier, or the key expert. Any of these could be their customer at any given instance. As one SAP SVP told me, "The customer is our true north." (See the online chapter "You Can't Handle the Truth—So You Have to Change" to end the suspense on who that is.) SAP's interest is in how they contribute to the success of the individual in his or her day-to-day life.

They create their communities for their collaborative value chain accordingly. Once the individual needs are being served, they can group them into communities of interest or practice that will provide each individual with the forums for communication, the tools for increasing effectiveness, and the access to get collaboration done that will benefit all parties involved. For example, unbeknownst to you, I'm sure, they have multiple social networks. Each of them is targeted to a specific group. For thought leaders or insightful influencers who are not necessarily SAP employees, they have MyVenturePad.com, a social network built on the Social Media Today enterprise social network platform (www.socialmediatoday.com). For process analysts and other internal nondevelopment people, they have the BPX (Business Process Expert) community, a social network numbering 350,000 members. For developers, they have the somewhat boringly named SAP Developers Network (SDN), which has a far from boring 1.7 million members. They also have vertically focused communities called Industry Value Networks that are focused on multiple industries, among them aerospace and defense, automotive, banks, consumer products, oil and gas, and public sector.

But the numbers don't stop there. According to a July 2008 article on the SAP ecosystem on Businessweek.com:

> Roughly 25,000 new participants sign up for the latter each month, and from 2006 to 2007, its number of page views doubled, to more than 150 million. Participants contribute some 6,000 online posts per day and create better than 60,000 wikis to handle ongoing discussions, while at least 1,200 bloggers comment regularly on community topics. More than 3.5 million posts have accumulated in these forums, and the pace of activity is accelerating. It took three years to reach the first million forum posts, nine months to reach the second million, and only six months to reach the third million. In total, 100,000 members have contributed posts to the online forums.

The numbers get even more interesting when you realize that SAP's commitment to the individual is real. That same article identified the average response time for the SDN from the time a developer posted a question to the time he got his first response. Hold on to something so you don't fall over—it was 17 minutes.

I'm not going to catalog all the different communities SAP has, because that really isn't a collaborative value chain, but it is how the members of a CVC communicate and work together. But there is another facet of the collaborative value chain that SAP excels at—and that would be the most important one: creating value for all parties involved. SAP can point to successful efforts in this regard in multiple areas. For example, SAP and one of its strategic partners and several of its customers collaborated on creating an asset that the customers were asking for. The idea was that the joint creation of this asset would be of benefit to each of the parties involved in a specific noncompetitive way, and the joint collaboration was the most effective way to accomplish that.

Also recently, twelve hospitals in Germany and Austria joined an SAP-created Enterprise Services Community Definition Group and defined a universal key services interface for several vital business processes. This took less than six months. Well done, SAP.

Next, we're going to look at the internal business requirements of Social CRM. It's very similar to "classic CRM" with a couple of twists in how to think about it, plan it, and execute it.

12

Sales and Marketing: The Customer Is the Right Subject

Every other edition of this book has separate chapters for sales and marketing. When CRM jefe Denis Pombriant suggested that I combine the two chapters, I actually had to think about it for a while, because sales and marketing have been such distinct pillars of CRM for so many years. There was still some good reason to keep them separate. But when it came down to a decision, you see a single chapter. Of course, some of the reasoning was utilitarian—the book is big enough without an additional chapter. But that's not my primary motive for the single section. The alignment of sales and marketing is.

Sales and Marketing Are Now Integrated, Aren't They?

Well, not exactly, and the likelihood of their actual integration is not really that great for the present. But they can and should be aligned if you're going to deal with the world as it now is. At least as far as your strategy goes.

Before I explain why, I want to clarify something. Sales and marketing remain two distinct disciplines. Sales is the art and science of getting a customer to purchase something; marketing is the art and science of getting the attention of a prospective customer and keeping it until they buy something, and then after that. Marketing doesn't include the purchase, but if done well, it convinces the customer to go ahead and make the purchase. While the disciplines remain distinct, the two teams need to work as a single team to accomplish the objectives of a 21st century organization. That means they have to have a unified vision. They should know who the real customer is and whom they envision as the customer over the next few years. Their efforts from lead to cash, so to speak, need to be coordinated and working in conjunction as if they were a single department with the same objectives, not two departments with conflicting objectives.

I'm not trying to put salespeople or marketing people out of work by rationalizing the two departments. While there is no reason to consolidate and do what is now politely called a "reduction in force," since salespeople still have to sell and marketing people need to grab customers' attentions, there is a need to make sure they are working together as a coherent team while still discharging their individual functions.

Don Peppers, in a document co-developed by Peppers and Rogers Group and Microsoft Dynamics called "Sales and Marketing: The New Power Couple," points out that traditionally sales departments and marketing departments have been separate entities and even have different operating processes. Salespeople are focused around short-term results such as making their quarterly quotas. They are measured by number of sales calls or the number of presentations, so quantity in a short time anchors their KPIs. They get rewarded by commissions on sales, not long-term business development.

Marketing departments have both long-term and short-term objectives. They develop initiatives around brand building that take some time. But more often than not, when they spend their marketing dollars on something other than a campaign, they are told that their spending better generate leads. Brand building is fine when you have the luxury to do it.

I've seen the evidence of that and how marketing departments get around it too. I'm the co-owner of a training company called BPT Partners, LLC, along with Bruce Culbert, Jeff Tanner (see later in the chapter for more on JT), and Bill Howell—all contributors to this book. We certify those we train in CRM strategy and social media. Our business model is that we get sponsors to handle the venue, meal costs, transportation costs, and so on. Those sponsors are typically, but not always, CRM software companies. The marketing departments of those companies make a decision on what they are looking for. It is one of two things, or both. First, lead generation. They have access to the people attending the training, who often represent Fortune 1000 companies and are qualified by their attendance. The other is brand building by association. The trainers are CRM industry heavyweights.

There is a benefit to having an association with thought-leaders. Even if the only real benefit is their association with thought-leaders, the marketers still justify it by saying it is for "lead generation." As Don Peppers puts it in the "Power Couple" document, "In the long term, marketers are spending time on branding and positioning, which is valuable but can be perceived as 'the soft stuff' in a numbers-driven culture." That's why they say "lead generation" even if they're doing it more for branding. Lead generation is not soft stuff.

All in all, sales and marketing are driven by different imperatives but need to be aligned because ultimately company success is a product of mutual alignment for those two departments.

What should it look like? One final piece from Don Peppers, a chart (Table 12-1) that I think reflects exactly what aligned sales and marketing organizations need to be doing—with one modification on my part, which you can see in italics in the table. The rest is Don Peppers' take on it.

Table 12-1: The Alignment of Sales and Marketing (Source: "Sales and Marketing: The New Power Couple," from Peppers and Rogers Group and Microsoft Dynamics, 2008)

The Focus	The Goal	The Solution: What Do You Need to Get There?
Success criteria	Business profitability	Full visibility into results/KPIs; predictable pipeline and accurate forecast to allow earlier insight for adjustment
Vision of the ideal customer	Customer profitability	A joint definition of the ideal customer that looks at revenue and costs to serve over the lifetime of that relationship
Knowledge of the real customer	*Eliminate presumed knowledge of customer expectations and align with ideal customer*	*A jointly done granular mapping of the customer experience that identifies the actual interactions with the company and customer, not the perceived ones*
Relationship quality	Long-term	Needs-based and collaborative as a result of capturing knowledge over time
Process	Collaborative and easy to use	Joint planning, shared customer database, connects all users in a single customer lifecycle
Technology	Integrated CRM	Holistic view of the customer; best practice workflow is created and improved over time

But even the successful alignment of sales and marketing doesn't negate the reality that the customer has changed, as I've spent pretty much this entire book trying to get across. What does that mean to sales? What are Sales 2.0 and Marketing 2.0? (Man, I'm getting 2.0ed out and there are still quite a few chapters to go.) How do they differ from their predecessors? Ask and ye shall get response.

Sales 2.0: Customer Expectations Have Changed

If there's anything I hope I've gotten across so far in this work, it is that the expectations of customers have dramatically changed over the past several years. That is not only in regard to whom they trust and what kind of experience they are expecting from a company. They are also no longer expecting to be sold to. They are expecting to be partnered with. They want to be involved in the decisions the company makes that affect them, and consequently they need the information to make an informed decision about their interactions and transactions with the company.

Sales processes were and are the traditional method a salesperson uses to interact with the customer. But they tend to be product driven, which objectifies the way the customer is going to be approached. They are organized around the concepts of finding and qualifying a lead, identifying that lead as a prospect, creating an opportunity with that prospect, proposing a sale, and negotiating a deal with that prospect and closing the deal.

There is nothing inherently wrong with using sales processes, because they are best practices that have been validated over time.

Sold to: Sales Process Driven by Product

A sales process map looks like what you see in Figure 12-1.

Note all the elements present in the sales lead qualification steps:

1. Initial contact (receive application)

2. Application of initial fit criteria (info sufficient?)

3. Sales lead (qualified?)

4. Need identification (ask for permission to contact decision maker)

5. Qualified prospect (permission granted?)

6. Proposal

7. Negotiation

8. Closing

9. Deal transaction

This map doesn't go beyond step 5 because this is a process that stops at the qualified lead, but the fundamental elements are there as they need to be.

These elements are typically present in any sales process, though sales processes can vary from company to company and from industry to industry. Sales processes are traditionally created from the most successful practices of salespeople over a long period of time. Those practices have been organized and hardened into a methodology. The

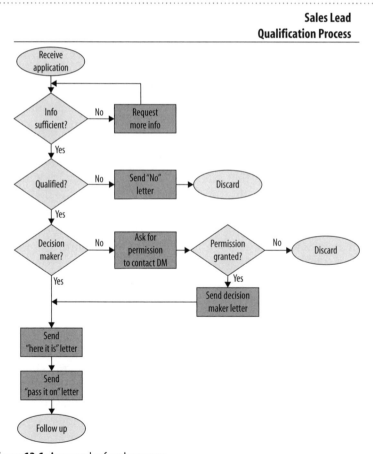

**Sales Lead
Qualification Process**

Figure 12-1: An example of a sales process

rigor with which sales processes are applied is often as much a product of the operational requirements of the company using the sales process as it is an approach designed to increase the chances of success in the sale. This means, of course, at times it can conflict with an actual relationship with the customer.

These kinds of sales processes are commonly available with sales force automation tools with the more standardized and popular selling methodologies like Miller-Heiman or Solution Selling often templated parts of the vendor's SFA software. Total Account Selling is embedded into Siebel Sales. Miller-Heiman is embedded into SalesLogix. The ability to tweak those processes or create your own set of sales processes is also a common part of the traditional CRM offerings. That functionality is one of the characteristic differences between sales force automation and contact management.

But is it enough to have an established sales methodology to sell to the social customer? These are best practices. They are useful to some. They are helpful to companies that have never had any sales processes before or to new salespeople who are just learning how to sell. But again, that is supporting the operational side of a business, which doesn't automatically make it the most effective way to sell to a newly empowered, peer-trusting, myth-busting, never-rusting social customer.

Selling with: Sales Driven by Experience and Relationship

Of course the problem that salespeople will have in spades with the social customer is that the social customer might not really give a youknowwhat about the sales processes that the salesperson is required to comply with so they can enter transactional data and customer information into "the system" and qualify for their commissions and bonuses. What the social customer is expecting is a human being who is not selling products at them or just following a particular path, but is providing them with a relationship that will be mutually beneficial to both.

For the salesperson, it will be the purchase of something by the customer. For the customer, it will be an experience that provides them with what they need to solve a part of their personal agenda—be it in a B2B environment (such as meeting an equipment need for the department the customer runs) or in a B2C environment (purchasing a vacation package that handles the needs of a father, mother, and two young children). That can and now does typically have to include much more than just the hotel, airfare, and trip to Disneyworld (I'm writing this part of the book on an airplane coming back from Orlando). But the expectation goes beyond that. The customer is looking to have a relationship with the company that the salesperson represents if a relationship with the salesperson isn't going to be possible.

This isn't unique or anything new either. A salesperson's self-proclaimed greatest asset isn't their looks or product catalog. Ask any salesperson the question and you'll get back something like "my contacts" or, more accurately, "my relationship to my accounts." One of the reasons that salespeople have had such a hard time (though less so now than a few years ago) adopting sales force automation, but loved contact management applications like ACT!, was that with ACT! they were able to sequester their contact files to their own desktop with no meddlesome interference from their managers who had no visibility into the flat file database that ACT! provided. With SFA, their contact file and accounts were no longer just their private fiefdom. Managers had complete access to the files, taking away what salespeople saw as their leverage should the need arise. It's no great secret, at least to me, that many salespeople keep a sequestered copy of their contact files offline or away from the office environment in the event they are let go or quit—even with a contractual obligation to "leave the file behind." Be real. They would be silly to do that.

But why so protective and secretive? Because they have actual relationships with their customers. It's not the company they work for taking the customers out to ballgames or drinking or dinner. It's the salesperson.

Companies that have half a brain recognize this and embrace it by having internal customer advocates tied to business development and sales. For example, SAP has what they call the Customer Value Network for some of their most strategic customers. One of the senior directors, Jim Goldfinger, is without question the best person I have ever seen in the role of interfacing with customers at any company—not just SAP, not just the software industry. He not only represents SAP well, he represents the interests of the customer within SAP.

But he takes it well beyond that. I attended a CVN cocktail party at an SAP conference in 2009 that had about 60 people, probably representing 40 enterprises there. Jim at one point went around the room and had people introduce themselves. In an incredible number of the intros to the intro, he mentioned some highly specific personal fact about almost all of the individuals who were there, which showed his deep and remarkable capacity to know them as people—and remember them as people. He even knows their skills in karaoke! This went on for one after another. He is legendary for throwing a party at his own house on his own nickel for roughly 200 customers. I can't vouch for the number, but I can vouch for the commitment he has to all these people. As a result, they and the companies they represent are committed to him and, by straight-line extension, to SAP.

Salespersons' relationships with customers are nothing new. But what is new is that the digital world has had an impact on how those relationships are ascertained and what it takes to have the relationship. Especially when it comes to how leads are generated and how opportunities are managed.

Leads and Opportunities: The Feeling Is Mutual

Clearly, personalizing leads is not exactly the easiest thing to do. If a salesperson tried to have a personal relationship with every potential lead and prospect that was deep and abiding, that sales rep would be a babbling idiot after two months.

But luckily, that isn't exactly what the B2C customer at least is looking for, and it can be mitigated for the B2B customer. What the customer is typically looking for is a bond with the company that the salesperson represents—not just the bond with the individual. So the feeling of closeness—sometimes without a human relationship—is there. It's expressed with the statement "I just feel that they know me."

Are you skeptical of that? Think about your own relationship to Amazon.com. Why do you shop a lot at Amazon, if you do?

▶ **They are convenient.**   You can usually find what you want. Your order is delivered to your door (without you standing up until you have to get it from your front porch), and there are valuable tools that make it even more convenient such as Amazon Prime, which costs about $80 per year and guarantees second-day air on all purchases directly from Amazon and many of their third-party merchants—and discounts next-day air. They even will on occasion upgrade, without asking, the delivery of a preordered product on the same day it is released to the stores. I ordered the EA Sports Active, a strength training program using the Nintendo Wii that was to be released to stores on May 19, 2009. It showed up at my door on May 19, 2009. Not the next day. The same day.

▶ **They "know" you.**   Because of the complex algorithms and analytic programs that Amazon uses for their recommendation engine and because of the incredibly deep toolset they give you such as blogs, reviews, video uploading, and so on for engagement on the site, customers feel that Amazon knows them—in a personal sense. This of course is not the case unless there are Amazon rogue neural networks seizing the site as we speak. That feeling is perhaps the most important piece of the success of Amazon. They have engaged the customer, primarily through self-service tools, in a way that makes the customer bond to the company and the site without knowing a single human being. This doesn't just create fiercely loyal repeat customers, but, as I've seen time and time again in formal and informal surveys that I conduct, it creates a large group of advocates. I would say, anecdotally, they have now surpassed Starbucks (who have fallen back pretty badly) as the most memorable company in the eyes of at least the U.S. attendees to the conferences I speak at.

The most important lesson for sales? Customers are now looking to be involved in the process, not just sold to. There is little a salesperson can do about a customer's state of mind on a given day, so they are best served by figuring out how to do what the customer almost always wants—especially on larger sales or repeated repurchasing. Customers want to be engaged and they want to feel "known." They don't just want to be the subjected to the multiple steps of Miller-Heiman because of the operational requirements of the company. Amazon engages and knows the customer by giving them tools, not by voices over a phone. You know I'm right. Just look at your credit card bill.

Special Circumstances Include the New Norm

What is undeniable is that someone somewhere wants to figure out how to sell to empowered customers in special circumstances. That could be a B2B environment or during an economic downturn. The question that generally applies is pretty much the same. Does customer behavior change and thus how you sell to customers change in different environments? The answer is yes and no. That helps, I'm sure.

What About Business-to-Business (B2B), Buddy Boy?

The only way I know how to start this is by telling you what I tell every audience member who raises this issue.

At the end of B2B is a C. An end customer.

Is that vague enough for you? That means that while you, salesperson, represent a B2B organization, they may be a B2C organization, and no matter how many B2B2B2B2B transactions and interactions there are, ultimately it rests with a C.

Let me give you an example. In 2005, I spoke in beautiful Zagreb, Croatia, at their first ever CRM conference. After I did my bit, there was a panel discussion. On that panel was the nation's largest retail grocer, who also had some wholesale food distribution business, and the largest national wholesaler—which did food wholesaling in part. These were two companies that epitomized the idea of coopetition—competitors cooperating. What they decided to do was that when it came to food, they would share forecasts, distribution, channels, and other pertinent data because they both agreed that their job was to ultimately please the person shopping at the retail grocer's store when it came to food. Transparency became critical to delight the customer—so they did it. Not easy for two competitive institutions. But they got it when they realized that the individual consumer was the ultimate customer.

By the way, visit Croatia. The food and wine are great, the people wonderful, the land beautiful. Don't miss it.

That said, there is no doubt that the B2B selling cycle is longer and more complex than a pure consumer-driven purchase. More often than not, the sales organization could do with a more complete knowledge of the organization they are selling to. That means broad knowledge such as how this publicly traded or privately held company is doing when it comes to its stockholders. How are they being affected by market conditions—either generally, or things specifically that might affect them?

But it also means intimate knowledge of who's who in the organization. Because of the way corporations are impacted by the cultural transformations going on everywhere, it's now no longer enough to know who the decision makers are. It's almost imperative to know who influences those decision makers, both formally, meaning in the organizational chain of command, and informally, meaning their buds at the workplace.

As we'll see in both the discussion on social media monitoring and on Oracle Social CRM, the tools are out there to help figure out these intricacies.

What About the Recession Then?

We humans tend to be wholesalers in our approach to life—or at least I am and thus, I project it onto everyone. What I mean by that is if something is and there is a change, then there is a new "is" and what "was" isn't any longer. In practical terms, that means, with Social CRM for example, there is a constant chattering going on about how the social strategies and tools *replace* the operational and transactional strategies and tools. That's not true. The social tools and strategies *extend* traditional CRM.

I've heard similar blabbering about the recession. "Oh, now that we're in an economic downturn, the social customer reverts to the same customer he or she was back in 2001 when price and utility ruled the roost as much or more than experience." Right? Once again, the operant principle is wholesale replacement.

Except that's not what happens. The recession doesn't erase the social customer, it solidifies the resolve of that customer. They still want what they wanted back in Chapters 1 through 3, but they want even more than that. In addition to the experience, tools, products, and services to specification, they want a great price or a big old value-add even more than they did prior to the recession.

What makes this almost unreasonable demand dangerous for businesses is that they have to consider ways of giving it to them. Why? Because the customer's opportunity to buy what they need elsewhere is greater than ever before; plus the tools to make that buying experience simple, short, and sweet are also easily available to the customer— either consumer or organization.

Additionally, the inclination to spend is down considerably during depressed economic periods. It's not only that people will not spend, but if they finally decide to make a purchase, they are interested in spending cheaper.

Here are a few items from April 30, 2009 from multiple sources:

▶ Procter and Gamble reported a drop in quarterly profit—almost 4 percent—the first time in eight years. They forecast a drop in full-year sales with sales down already 8 percent.

► Kellogg said sales were down for the quarter 3 percent.

► Colgate Palmolive saw a 6 percent revenue drop.

► Grocer Safeway, Inc. saw revenue drop 8 percent.

► A 2009 American Heart Association survey found that 29 percent of their respondents had cut back on fresh fruit, vegetables, and other essentials due to financial considerations.

What makes this particularly significant is that these companies sell staples like soap and food. Yet, regardless of the need for these items, people are buying less and cheaper because of their uncertainty about their economic future. A lot of customers are taking the "wait and see" approach, letting inertia rule. Where in the past they might have made that impulse buy, now the impulse is more "Nah, I'll wait."

For salespeople, this reluctance is piled on top of the increased competition for attention and competition from smaller companies than those that could have competed in the past. Add the demands of the customer created prior to the downturn—such as participation in the process, and real-time communication—and you have a difficult, highly competitive, increasingly angst-producing situation for many companies.

Fearing fear is not exactly the way out either. Concerns are solved by doing what was just as important before the downturn—listening to the customers, providing them with what they need if you can do it according to your own business plan, and then differentiating yourself through an experience that involves those customers in your activity.

To do that, of course, you have to find those customers and, once you do, maintain a relationship with them, but they are reluctant to act or become visible. So how do you generate leads and successfully manage opportunities to conclusion in a tough environment? Or a good one, for that matter?

Not Your Predecessor's Lead Generation

If you were to look at a definition of lead generation, it's typically placed in the context of marketing, which for the most part is a fair characterization. For example, here's the general Wikipedia definition:

> **Lead generation** (*commonly abbreviated as **lead-gen**) is a marketing term that refers to the creation or generation of prospective consumer interest or inquiry into a business's products or services.*

The definition goes on to distinguish between marketing leads and sales leads, but both are generated from a marketing effort. However, there is no rule that says salespeople can't generate leads through both traditional lead generation methods and more contemporary approaches.

What makes this a unique time for salespeople, recession or not, is that we have vast digital properties available on the Web that are locations for their prospects depending on what their company produces or sells. That means that there is, to some degree, a process of self-qualification of a lead going on in a community of interest or practice.

Additionally, it's entirely possible to build a community to draw those potential leads to you by having the right location, the right mix of tools, and the right content to attract the right folks.

But I need to be clear on something. Social media doesn't close business. There is no way that anything but consistent follow-up and good human interplay, plus of course a viable proposal, will close the deal. What social media can do, as we'll see, is to generate a richer relationship with your existing contacts and give you the opportunity to spawn leads.

Being Practical About Lead Generation

Traditional lead generation was facilitated by such marketing techniques and methods as broadcast advertising, or direct mail, event marketing, content provision (e.g., white papers) through registration, e-mail marketing, and a dozen other approaches. Traditional approaches can work and will continue to. But due to the cost-effective nature of social media there are a remarkable number of available tools that will, for free or a very reasonable price, support lead generation for salespeople.

Here are some things you can do with some of the protocols for the specific environments/channels.

▶ Participate in expert discussions within communities that are in the realm of the solutions or products you sell. But do it as a discussion participant, rather than a sales guy pushing product. You will be flamed if you try the latter. They're looking to see you as "someone like them" and the more like them you actually are (not pretend to be) the more likely they will come to you when they need what you have.

▶ Participate in threaded discussion forums where you use your expertise to answer questions that you can. They can be questions about your product or questions about something in the field that your product or service is part of.

▶ Use tools, such as social media monitoring tools, to scope possible leads. The best social media monitoring tools, such as Radian6, which you'll hear about in the marketing section here, are not only monitoring the more traditional sources like Reuters or Hoovers, or online newspapers and journals, but follow the blogosphere, social networks, and threaded forums—in other words, the conversations, not just the formal content. This is a rich source of locations for leads and, if the monitoring is sophisticated enough, it will identify the influencers of the conversation—who might be your leads.

▶ Comment on blogs when appropriate, again, without being too salesy.

▶ Write a blog covering sales expertise that you have—perhaps on sales optimization, the use of sales intelligence, the way to build relationships, handling sales data. Whatever topic floats your boat works here. Make sure that you create an RSS feed so it can be subscribed to and that you open up posts for comments. Stay free of sales pitches, though it can be okay to talk about your products in an informal way. Let your sales prospects or your account contacts write guest posts. Encourage them to comment and participate in discussions. Link back to the appropriate on-topic blogs of your customers or prospects.

▶ Create videos and podcasts to highlight your expertise and then provide them for free via your own website or upload them to YouTube or Vimeo or other key video sites. Show your personality and, if you're up for it, your humor in audio or video casts. The more you show your personality, the more you appear as "someone like me." They can be and if possible should be informative, fun, and humanizing. Plus, salesperson, you are who you are, aren't you?

▶ Create a couple of Twitter accounts, one personal—you as an individual—and one corporate. The personal one should be just that—a Twitter stream that integrates your outlook with your company activity, including what you're doing and saying about whatever is interesting to you. The corporate one can be a notification of a discount or an event—work with marketing on this. But don't go overboard on pushing the sales information.

▶ Upload your most public presentations to the Slideshare.net community, a site with millions of PowerPoints. (I call it You-Tube for Old People.) Just put them out there to be watched, used, and embedded. They are in the public domain, so be careful about which ones you release. Great for thought-leadership and generating interest in what you do. Make sure that the topics are educational—not product pitches, though you certainly can mention your company. Salesforce.com, Oracle, and many others use the site to also show their presentations from events, which do have a more product-focused purpose. Be sparing.

▶ Create a social network or community of interest or practice (see Chapter 9). Bring in experts to enhance the content and value of the community. Find the advocates in the community who can operate as a personal sales support team—selling your products for and with you for compensation—if the sale isn't complex.

If you combine these suggestions with traditional approaches, it should improve your ability to generate qualified leads. Keep in mind, by going to the sites that are specific to your expertise and company's solutions, you're entering a somewhat self-qualified location. There can't be much better than that by the pound—or for the dollar for that matter.

Case Study: Social Before It Was Called That

In 1993, I worked for a company that required me to do the business development and the staff recruitment for the projects I landed. The projects were highly complex Lotus Notes projects that were for major companies that we were doing partnered with Lotus Consulting.

I could have taken the ordinary route and gone to recruiting firms and asked for résumés or, using what passed for job boards, put up the requirements for the developers or administrators I needed. But I took a different approach. I went to Usenet. For those of you who don't remember this, shame on you for reminding me of my age. Usenet was a community of user groups around particular interests and practices that used their online presence to carry out discussions. I went to the Lotus Notes user groups and monitored the questions being asked by various parties. I read each and every answer that was freely given by the members of the group. I also made my presence known in the group. Then, based on the answers I read, I contacted the providers of the answers so that I could start the recruitment of those people. As a result, I was able to hire some of the best Notes people in the world. This approach, which was based on the idea that those providing answers were generally passionate enough about the subject to do so, and that the best answers were the sign of a highly experienced or highly innovative individual, led to an actual ROI that was measurable. Our developers and administrators were so prized by Lotus Consulting that they did more business with our little company than any of their other 17,500 partners in the world. In 1994, we did 14 percent of the global partner business with Lotus Consulting, twice the second place—7 percent—which was Software Spectrum.

This is the exact same process that a salesperson can use to generate leads, which is what I was effectively doing. Think of the steps in the process.

1. I found the forums that were of specific interest to my business concerns.

2. I monitored the conversations going on among those I was interested in possibly having a conversation with.

3. I stayed visible in the forums myself, adding to the content value of the user group where I felt I could.

4. I then contacted (via e-mail, not the user group) the individuals it made sense for me to contact. This was the hardest part since their e-mails weren't readily available. But I managed.

These steps are as applicable today as they were in 1993.

Handling Opportunities Better and Way Cooler

What happens once you've generated this lead and made it into some sort of opportunity, you hip, way cool Sales 2.0 guy?

Then comes the need to optimize your chances of closing the deal, and there are Sales 2.0 tools for collaboration in the enterprise and for richer insights on your possible customer. Companies like InsideView provide you with the sales intelligence tools and the Superstah! winner, Oracle, with the Sales 2.0 collaboration tools that can improve your chances of effectively concluding the sale.

There are two important social capabilities for the Sales 2.0 professional. First is the ability to engage the human resources and knowledge of your entire company, not just your sales team member. That means that the collective knowledge of the staff can be put to good use helping you determine what resources you need to bring to bear to help you with your opportunity.

The second is the use of tools to scour the Web for information that will give you a competitive edge, a.k.a. sales intelligence.

Collaboration: Sales 2.0 for the Enterprise

In 1380, "Pearl," an alliterative poem written by the same guy who wrote Sir Gawain and the Green Knight (you read that, right?), referred to *"The mo the myryer, so God me blesse."* This was the first known reference to "the more the merrier," which has achieved the exalted status of a trite cliché. However, in the case of successful sales, it's the truth.

Engaging other employees—say, in the marketing department—who know the companies or people involved in your opportunities, who have legal expertise you might need, who are on other sales teams that might have sold a similar deal, has become something that can make or break a closing. That doesn't mean you have to walk department to department to find the individuals who might know a snippet or a chunk of information. It doesn't mean you have to send out an e-mail query in the hope of response.

What it does mean is that, using contemporary digital tools, you can actually improve your chances to win a deal.

As we saw in Chapters 9 and 11, IBM Lotus Connections has an outcome-based social software module called "activities"—a temporary wiki built around a specific time-constrained event that is retired to an archive when the activity is completed. Salespeople use it to create an opportunity-focused collaboration space where all the possible experts or knowledgeable individuals in regard to the opportunity can aggregate that knowledge.

For the longer term, sales organizations use wikis, not just the activities, to do things like fine tune sales "scripts" or develop field sales guides that cover all components of selling at a particular company or to a particular customer segment. What makes these collaborations particularly valuable is the addition of comments on the different facets of selling that enhance the skills of the salesperson. To put it simply, shared content rules.

Salesforce.com is one company that is providing a platform for aggregating content for the benefit of salespeople. In 2007, they acquired an AppExchange startup called Koral and rebranded their social content management system as part of salesforce.com's platform. It was renamed Salesforce ContentExchange. It provides a capability to incorporate any content and then comment on it, tag it, create RSS feeds, rate it, rank it—all those things needed to make it a genuine conversation that draws on actual knowledge.

That is just one of the tools that sales can use—especially when aligned with marketing. All the tools that companies use for their Enterprise 2.0 efforts (see Chapter 4) can be organized to benefit sales departments.

That's the perfect segue to introduce our Superstah! for this chapter: Oracle Social CRM.

Superstah! Oracle Social CRM

There is no question that Oracle has come a long way since 2007 with the announcement of their Social CRM applications. Since then, they've become a leading contender when it comes to market leadership in CRM. They've got a visionary leader in the personage of Anthony Lye, their SVP of CRM and a long-time CRM industry veteran. They have a number of Enterprise 2.0 based sales tools that are both unique and valuable to the industry. They've embraced to a large extent the on-demand model and have a genuinely good product with Oracle CRM On Demand (previously known as Siebel On Demand, previously known as Upshot). Coming from me, this is high praise indeed, since prior to 2007, I can't exactly say that I was a fan of the company. But with Anthony Lye at the helm, it all makes sense now.

Mission 21st Century

I asked Anthony Lye directly what the future holds for Oracle Social CRM. Here's what he said:

> Social CRM will separate winners from losers. Oracle will drive Social CRM to be solutions where the consumer Internet meets the corporate intranet. A platform for conversation for customers to connect with each other, with companies, all in the context of a campaign, a sale, or a service request.

As if to prove Anthony right, Oracle hasn't stopped with the Sales 2.0 apps (see the following section) they call Social CRM. They have working with L'Oreal to develop an iPhone application for marketing and selling L'Oreal products (that can be generalized to any products) that would access the social reviews of the products in addition to the company materials and allow you to rate and comment on those products via your iPhone. They are working around the clock to incorporate cloud-based applications that would be appropriate to CRM—though at the time of this writing, we still have no idea how things are going to shake out after their acquisition of Sun.

The Products: Social CRM by Any Other Name

Perhaps their CRM-related crown jewels are their Social CRM threesome. They go by the name of Sales Prospector, Sales Library, and Sales Campaign Manager. Collaboration is the common thread for their applications. While each has a set of unique features, the one thing that stands out is the ability of the salesperson to build a collaborative network—an outcome-based social network—around existing opportunities to optimize the chances of the sale to succeed.

The premise that underlies these applications is best explained by Anthony Lye:

Complete CRM is now a combination of three main solutions: transactional CRM, analytical CRM, and Social CRM. Social CRM leverages social media, social networking, and social metadata to support new relationship structures, C2C, C2B, and new processes as control of the relationship shifts from vendor to customer to community. As we saw with the introduction of analytical CRM eight years ago, companies who embrace Social CRM will do better than those who do not!

Sales Prospector

Sales Prospector is premised on its ability, using the "like me" model, to forecast the rate of success of an opportunity. It uses sophisticated algorithms to predict the likelihood of the deal closing, the time it is likely to close, and the likely amount of the deal. It's based on the idea that the history of prior deals like it in combination with externally captured knowledge can generate a reasonably accurate map of the possibility of success. It uses the historic customer data of deals past to see which product mix would engender the best rate of success—in other words, an enterprise version of a recommendation engine. The purpose is to use history and social sources (external sources) to increase the likelihood of success—or, if you take the glass half empty approach, decrease the likelihood of failure.

Not only does Sales Prospector have this very useful purpose, but it looks pretty damned good too—with a UI that a salesperson can actually use (see Figure 12-2). Nice and clean. Even I almost understood it, which means that a regular Joe can figure it out in a heartbeat.

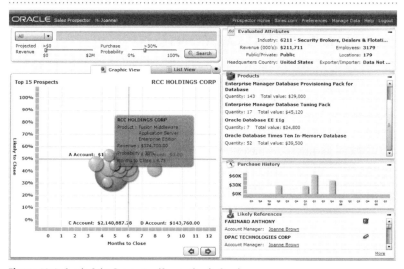

Figure 12-2: Oracle Sales Prospector (Source: Oracle Corp.)

As good an idea as this is, it is a bold move for Oracle. Its accuracy makes or breaks it. If the forecast for likelihood of closure, time of closure, and size of opportunity is close to accurate (100 percent would be a bit much to ask for anything made of digital pieces), then Oracle has a real winner that looks good too.

Sales Library

Sales Library is an important product in the Oracle portfolio and one that can be a huge factor in the success of a salesperson's efforts at closing an opportunity. It is wisely set as an SaaS-based application, which will allow it to integrate with any Oracle on-premise or on-demand CRM capability.

Oracle's description of what it does is pretty good, but undersells what it's capable of. They call it a "collection of shared content, which users can rate, tag, comment on, and leverage to build the best presentations for advancing their sales opportunities."

Which it is. But it is more than that.

The library—the shared content—is, in its own right, actually an outcome-based community, what has been called an activity in prior parts of this book, that exists to improve the chances for that sales opportunity to succeed. It gives the particular salespeople and those in the company who need it access to presentations that can be rated, tagged, and commented on. Those presentations are being discussed via these tools by a community of interest built around the opportunity. The content can be broken out by slide or by presentation. If any participant sees a particular presentation as valuable they can promote that presentation so it can be included in the discussion.

Check out Figure 12-3 for the visual you need.

Figure 12-3: Oracle Sales Library—aggregate, tag, rate, and comment (Source: Oracle Corp.)

Sales Campaign

This application borders on being a marketing application, but the beauty of the application is that a salesperson can create an HTML or e-mail campaign and track the results with or without the marketing mavens' involvement. That has a potentially big upside with the ability to develop a campaign quickly that is both professional and can track its own results. The downside is that marketing might get upset that your unaligned sales self is doing that. But it is a very important part, though the least sexy, of the Oracle Social CRM suite.

More Products to Come

In March 2009, they announced several substantial additions to the Oracle CRM On Demand portfolio, including:

► Oracle Self Service E-Billing On Demand

► Oracle CRM On Demand Deal Management

► Oracle CRM On Demand Enterprise Disaster Recovery

► Oracle AIA integration between On Demand and JD Edwards EnterpriseOne

They aren't stopping for anything.

They are champs and deserve to be recognized for their pioneering efforts for Sales 2.0 for the enterprise. So I will.

Sales Intelligence: Mo' Better, Richer, Deeper

Community knowledge and collaboration aren't the only things that Sales 2.0 provides. Predictability and direction through improved forecasting need to be part of the equation too. Does that mean better algorithms? Not necessarily, though that would help, wouldn't it? What it does mean is improved intelligence, gathered from a much wider range of resources that gets fed into the algorithmic furnace, so that "I told you so" is actually something more than infantile. To get that information and then put it in a useful format constitutes sales intelligence.

Jim Dickie, one of the principals at CSO Insights and one of the leading sales analysts and consultants in the world, put it well when he said, "The information salespeople really need is often not accessible." In the contemporary world, that would mean "not easily visible." But it can be made visible with the uses of sales intelligence tools. When done well, not only does it provide greater insight into customers—an intangible with substance so to speak—it has measurable benefits that go to the heart of a business (revenue) and to the hearts of salespeople everywhere (achieving quota).

In Early 2009, Aberdeen Group analyst Alex Jeffries released a study on the use of sales intelligence as a best practice called "Sales Intelligence: The Secret to Sales Nirvana." Best-in-class companies, which Aberdeen Group defined as those that aggregated in the top 20 percent, were seeing year over year improvement in:

1. The time sales reps spend searching for relevant intelligence/contact information. It was noticeably less.

2. The rate of lead conversion, i.e., what it took to identify a lead that could become an opportunity was decreased.

3. Sales cycle time decreased, meaning that the amount of time from the inception of the possibility to the closing of the deal was noticeably less.

4. The percentage of sales reps achieving quota was increased.

What Aberdeen also found was that the best in class companies had distinctive knowledge of not only how to get sales intelligence but were clear on the criteria they needed to define the intelligence they wanted to get. They found that the best in class:

1. 79 percent understood prospect's business challenges (+13 percent better than the norm). This meant that they had a clear picture of what the potential customer needed to solve to make their business better.

2. 73 percent understood how to map offerings to those business challenges (14 percent over the norm). This meant that they also understood what offerings they could provide made sense when it came to solving the business challenges.

3. 73 percent had intelligent knowledge of competitive differences (18 percent over the norm). This meant that they knew what the offerings of their competitors were relative to their own.

What exactly does that mean, all in all, for us innocents? What kind of sales intelligence tools are we talking about using here? What do they do?

Before we get into that, there are some things we need to remember. Sales intelligence supports customer insights. The garnering of that information provides the salesperson with a richer, more thorough profile of the accounts, and the people and the competitive landscape that gives the sales team what they need to beat their competitors, if you're into that kind of thing.

But what distinguishes great sales intelligence tools from the lesser ones is the ability to integrate with CRM systems data so that there are rich customer profiles that will mean a greater chance to exert a more significant influence over the possible success of an opportunity.

That means grabbing data from traditional sources and from all the relevant conversations going on via the Web—and from nontraditional data sources. Note by the way, I said "relevant" conversations, not just conversations. The tools you use need to be able to distinguish what's important to your company from the ambient noise that might be critical to Mom or the federal government, but meaningless to you.

Probably the best way to get a feel for how sales intelligence is both derived and used is to look at our sales intelligence Superstah! for this chapter, InsideView's SalesView tool.

Superstah! InsideView

I ran across these guys by accident, if you call an e-mail from a public relations person an accident. When I received the e-mail in mid-2008, it told me a tale of a product called SalesView that was being released by a company called InsideView. I have to admit before I was halfway through the e-mail I was skeptical because as soon as I see a company that uses the word "sales" as an adjective in a product name, I zone out.

But something, perhaps divine intervention, compelled me to keep reading and to this day, I'm glad I did. Because what they did was anything but uncreative.

SalesView, their flagship product, does one thing and does it very well. It accesses resources across the Web and ties the appropriate resulting information to internally acquired customer data. That data is then usable to dynamically identify potential opportunities or even prospects. Not only that, it can provide rich information, integrated directly into the CRM data source that will give you what you need for a competitive edge. That means that it can grab data from external resources like blogs, social networks such as Facebook, LinkedIn and Zoominfo, from data aggregations like Jigsaw's Open Data Initiative (ODI) data, from more traditional sources like business news wires and company profilers such as Hoovers, Reuters, and Dun and Bradstreet. It then can tie that to the internal data related to account or customer records within varying CRM systems.

Currently, they are integrated with salesforce.com and, interestingly, wisely, with Oracle CRM On Demand, Microsoft Dynamics

CRM, SugarCRM, NetSuite, and with social application Landslide. While you can use the application as a standalone, it actually has an enterprise mash-up that appears as a screen within your internal CRM application so you don't have to access SalesView separately. Your information is at your fingertips.

This product has to be seen in context. While it monitors 20,000 selective sources and in mid-2009 added Twitter and Google Blog and Compete.com monitoring functionality, what makes this an important product is the unique scope of integration with CRM products. Once they integrate with SAP, they will pretty much have run the gamut of major CRM players. No one else can make that claim at this time. They are optimized to be able to integrate their results into CRM databases.

To understand how it works, take a look at Figure 12-4, which shows the NetSuite integration dashboard.

Figure 2-4: SalesView integration with NetSuite (Source: InsideView)

They're analyzing masses of unstructured data through a series of what they call "connectors" which then organize that data by "target" (for example, a particular company). They are able to look at the target and get information on things like:

▶ Key events related to the target

▶ Key selling triggers such as organizational changes

▶ Connections between the users you're speaking with and the decision makers in an account

▶ How relevant a piece of information is based on its context and the timing

▶ Figuring out who the best bet is as the prospect

The key, which I'm never unhappy to repeat, is that this data is integrated into whatever CRM system you happen to be using—and it pops up via a widget native to the system.

Important. Très important.

Mission 21st Century

Everything that InsideView does is based around their concept of the socialprise—a business that they describe as:

Socialprise is the natural convergence of social media and enterprise applications, emerging as a mash-up of both the information and user experience of these previously separate universes.

Everything they do is motivated by this. Their roadmap reflects it well. As Rand Schulman, chief marketing officer of InsideView and an industry old-timer who truly gets it—all with a major dose of sense of humor—said in an interview:

We are going to continue to legitimize and accelerate the adoption of social media and social networks within the enterprise—by way of not only CRM integration but other enterprise applications as well such as LinkedIn, Facebook, blogs, and Twitter, for example.

They ain't stopping there either. Continuing their drive for CRM ubiquity, they will be integrating with the other major CRM platforms and even going beyond CRM in the enterprise and beyond sales and marketing by expanding their integration with other business processes. I would have to presume supply chain processes are among their targets. To do this, they've built a robust set of APIs that they are using internally and farming out to a growing partner community.

Socialprise? Not surprised. These guys just get it.

The Sales 2.0 Value Proposition

Okay, time to get down to the aligned companion discipline—marketing. But before we do, let's do a quick review on why Sales 2.0 is the currency of contemporary business.

▶ **Increased potential for success**   If you make a collaborative effort, have better forecasting tools, and know more about your customer, your odds of success are that much greater.

▶ **Increased customer insight**   This is customer insight based on data that goes far beyond the transactions, but it gets to the personal profiles, the influencer relationships, the state of a particular company or account, and, to top it off, some of it is based on insights from other customers and employees who in the past you had no idea had that insight.

▶ **Mitigated risk**   The better the chances of success, the lower the risk (duh).

▶ **Collaborative environment**   The benefits of working well with co-workers on projects are long established.

▶ **Improved engagement with customers**   The more you know them, the better your relationship, the more likelihood the deal closes. See the SAP Customer Value Network discussion earlier in the chapter.

▶ **Portability increased**   Many of the Sales 2.0 applications are delivered as SaaS applications or on mobile devices.

▶ **Competitive differentiation**   You're able to target more precisely than in the past.

▶ **Reputation, influence, persuasion**   It's not who you know, but who you know who knows who you need to know. Those "loose connections" can be more powerful than the more direct connections. Validation is a powerful need among human beings. Abraham Maslow's Hierarchy of Needs identifies one level of the hierarchy as the need for love, affection, and belongingness, and another as the need for esteem. Validation by one's peers satisfies that. Knowing who has the power to validate or having that ability is entirely helped by understanding of how the connections among people are organized and who can influence who.

Now to the other peak.

Marketing, uh, 2.0: New Mindset, New Tools

What I'm about to say may be obvious, but doing what I'm about to say just isn't easy. In order for you to sell to someone, they have to care enough to know who you are, know what you sell, and see some reason to buy what you sell. They also have to see the reason why they should buy what you sell from you since they can probably get something similar from someone else.

That's the essence of marketing, but to achieve that customer advocacy nirvana takes a lot. It takes a strategy, the use of tools and systems, and a completely new view of what marketing today is.

Listen Up! The New Competition Is Attention

When you go to Whole Foods, you see heirloom tomatoes, regular red tomatoes, plum tomatoes, cherry tomatoes, grape tomatoes, locally grown tomatoes from a variety of different local farms, and organic versions of all of them. Which do you buy? Oh, you don't shop at Whole Foods? Oh. Well, the point is that there are some 20 or 30 different varieties and types and sizes and farm-specific versions to choose from. If you're confused about which to buy, you tend toward the familiar. You buy regular or organic regular tomatoes. If you're decorating a salad with something other than slices or chunks, you might use heirloom tomatoes for their riot of color. But if you're making a sauce, you know it most likely calls for plum tomatoes— sometimes in another section of the store where you can get canned versions of the same. If you're someone who supports local farmers as a principle, you get a locally grown version.

In other words, your choices are specific to you. The person next to you buying the exact same tomatoes might be buying them for different reasons entirely.

Now, multiply that by some number that reflects all the other vegetables calling out to you from the produce department—and then the fruits in the same area. If you're not planning on buying tomatoes, the rest of the produce might make you skip them entirely. There is so much to see and choose from that the choices become bewildering.

The tendency when confronted with too much is inertia—to simply not make a choice. This creates a major problem for marketers, as we'll see in just a moment.

The Attention "Economy"

If 20 or 30 choices of tomatoes are blindingly difficult to decide about, imagine what it takes to do something when you're besieged by 3,000 messages per day or roughly one million per year. That means via the Web, direct mail, on television, when you see a billboard or an ad in a store or in a newspaper or magazine and in a video game.

Think that you're immune to it as a consumer? Here's test that I do when I'm lecturing and the subject of capturing the attention of someone comes up. I ask the crowd (and you can ask yourself):

1. How many of you get direct mail? (Of course, everyone raises his or her hand.)

2. How many of you read all the direct mail you get? (Almost no one raises his or her hand.)

3. How many just throw out most of or all of the ads? (Almost everyone raises his or her hand.)

I have no doubt that the vast majority of you follow the crowd when it comes to answering those three questions. If you don't, you win a prize. Let me know your address and I'll put it in the mail. Just remember, don't throw it out when you get it.

As marketing guru Seth Godin put it in an interview with William C. Taylor of Fast Company at the end of 2007:

Marketing is a contest for people's attention. Thirty years ago, people gave you their attention if you simply asked for it. You'd interrupt their TV program, and they'd listen to what you had to say. You'd put a billboard on the highway, and they'd look at it. That's not true any-more. This year, the average consumer will see or hear 1 million marketing messages—that's almost 3,000 per day. No human being can pay attention to 3,000 messages every day.

This is called, as you might be able to guess, interruption marketing—your attention is captured because your routine activity is interrupted. But with 1 million messages a year, this doesn't work the way it did in the 1960s. You do what I said above—you just zone out.

This isn't just some construct that is there to move things in this book forward a bit. While you might think that your business competes with other companies who put out like products and provide like services, the stark reality is that you compete with every single message being thrown at your prospective customers. You can't even start a smart legitimate marketing campaign aimed at lead generation without capturing the attention of your prospects first.

This is a recognized problem. Howard Handler, the chief marketing officer of Virgin Mobile USA, understood it in 2008 when he said, "To cut through with a message or a brand or a piece of content is more challenging than ever." The underlying idea in Handler's comment is that because the amount of attention a consumer can give a product or service or company or idea is finite and increasingly more difficult due to both bad information like spam and rich information sources available everywhere, the competition for that attention is increasing and attention is becoming a commodity.

Customers are so tired of being bombarded (aren't you?) with this constant barrage of messages that they simply zone out and don't want to give their time or consideration to companies they might otherwise be interested in. What they actually want and are beginning to accomplish is control over what messages they consider "taking" and what brands they allow into their homes. Attention is given so little at this time that it's been commoditized by its scarcity.

Evidence of this commoditization of attention is pretty easy to find. It shows in the compensation that is often given if you'll just watch something. For example, when you watch a TV show that you've had queued in Hulu (the web-based service that's either owned by NBC, Disney, and News Corp. or by aliens who look like Alec Baldwin and Dennis Leary), you will often get a choice of watching commercials that run at regular interludes through the web broadcast or seeing a single one-minute commercial at the top of the show. For your attention to the commercial in the form that you want, you are being compensated by being allowed to watch the show for free. This is a very different model than Apple's iTunes, which sells the content commercial free for between $1.99 and $2.99 per episode. What the Hulu model is doing is buying your attention. They know your name through the registration on the site, but they recognize that having your name and you watching a commercial doesn't mean that you're a qualified lead. It means you gave them consideration. Period.

Compensation for attention is something that is not only being considered, but has to be considered. The rather old-fashioned idea of "pay them for their time" is becoming "pay them for their attention." There are companies that will give you free things—cell phone minutes, ad-free music—if you view their ads for X amount of time. There is a model for online revenue sharing that even Microsoft is looking into. There is a service called Scoopt Words that operates as a "blogger agent" that will get companies to buy what bloggers are saying for commercial use and then split the revenue stream, which sounds kind of nice for bloggers, but not exactly in the spirit of the blogosphere.

The music industry has had an ongoing discussion (which may go nowhere) around attention compensation, driven by music piracy. The idea would be that rather than trying to prosecute or scare or harass someone who downloads a music file illegally, give them the music in return for them viewing a 30- or 60-second ad. Once the ad has been completely viewed, they get the music. While that may never go anywhere, it points to how serious the competition for attention really is.

There are nascent metrics to measure the attention too. They're called engagement ratings and they're primarily focused around TV at the moment. Not exactly a big surprise. They're being used to figure out what programs to advertise on. Also not a big surprise—and sadly typical of the TV world—new metrics, old reasons.

Engagement ratings are the equivalent of "stickiness" on a website. It's not just whether you have a large audience; it's whether that audience is willing to continue to lavish its attention on you and your advertisers.

Myers' Emotional Connections research in 2007 showed that Fox News Channel topped the "viewer engagement ratings" with positive engagement ratings in four categories by 80 percent of its viewers. But it dropped to 21st place and 30 percent (for two categories) when it came to advertising engagement. What this can be interpreted to mean is that the audience was riveted to Bill O'Reilly and made a sandwich during the ads. (I'd be the other way around.)

Despite the particulars here, what's important about the Myers work is that they're doing some of the first research and measurement of level of attention and what it takes to gain that attention—which precedes even lead generation.

But attention-getting can go overboard. There are devotees of what is called the attention economy. They actually think that attention capture can literally replace money. Meaning that you will spend your "attention time" (in a manner of speaking) instead of your national currency in return for goods and services.

You heard me. Yes, really.

Lead generation from the marketing side comes when you have gained and kept the attention of your potential customers—but I wouldn't go overboard with this either.

Hard Times for Tradition

Marketing never gets respect (we miss you, Rodney Dangerfield). Never ever. Never ever ever. Know why? Because marketing is viewed by the company as an expenditure with no immediate tangible return. Marketers are viewed by the customer as a nuisance. They are viewed by people like me as a department that presumes for the customer and doesn't really know what the customer is actually thinking, which is often true.

It's even truer now because the stakes are higher, the expectations and demands of the customer have increased and their hunger for being contacted in multiple ways—the ones of their own choosing—is greater than ever.

But that doesn't negate the value of traditional marketing—especially when it's used in combination with new marketing approaches. For example, the conversion rates in e-mail marketing are still between 2 and 5 percent. Good numbers there. A study in May 2009 done by Internet marketing small-business legend Hubspot took a look at the effectiveness of traditional press releases as opposed to social media press releases. It found that the traditional media releases were considerably more effective in syndicating. The typical ratio was about 5:4 in favor of the traditional press release when it came to the number of places it was syndicated. The only time the ratio was favorable to the social media releases was with online properties. Not exactly a surprise. But what that indicates is that you shouldn't stick with a single kind of release or a single approach. Do what makes sense for the location, channel, and people you're trying to reach. Social media marketing, search engine marketing, and the like are becoming the centerpiece of many organizations' marketing efforts.

If I had to speculate (or maybe pontificate is the right word here), marketing is up for the most comprehensive and dramatic overhaul of any of the three traditional pillars of CRM. Marketing professionals are aware of this and those that aren't panicking are remodeling the way they do what they do

I'm only here to help. I come to praise Caesar, not to bury him.

If you don't believe me, maybe you'll believe this statement from someone with a lot of street cred on what constitutes successful contemporary marketing. Anil Dash, Six Apart's Chief Evangelist, who you met in Chapter 7, says, "Ultimately, successful marketing results lead to people relating to brands as culture. They will be part of a cultural, emotional and entertainment bubble."

You know he's right, don't you? So remember, traditional isn't dead, but the old marketing logic is.

Getting on the *Cluetrain Manifesto*

What does this new marketing do? Most importantly, it moves from being the brand messenger of the company pushing messages at the customer to becoming the first line of conversation for the customer with the company.

The premise for this was established back in 2001 with the publication of the seminal, though mildly hyperbolic, *The Cluetrain Manifesto: The End of Business as Usual*, a joint effort by authors David Weinberger, Christopher Locke, Doc Searls, and Rick Levine. This work, called just *Cluetrain* by its devotees, is considered one of the drivers behind the understanding of the social customer's identity.

I've converted some of the central principles of the book to a table with the *Cluetrain* concept on the left and my notes on it on the right. The gist of the book is in these particular notions, and they are fundamental to how marketers should be thinking about the social customer.

The *Cluetrain Manifesto* Principles	Notes
Markets are conversations.	Human interactions drive business activities.
Markets consist of human beings, not demographic sectors.	Each individual is self-interested with a personal agenda, regardless of whether or not they are in the same customer segment or micro-segment.
Networked conversations are enabling powerful new forms of social organization and knowledge exchange to emerge.	The emergence of the Web and tools to communicate via the Web and cell phones has given rise to new kinds of institutions.
There are no secrets. The networked market knows more than companies do about their own products. And whether the news is good or bad, they tell everyone.	This reflects what is now prevalent with review sites where customers provide better, honest reviews for all to see. They are the users of the products, where the company doesn't necessarily eat its own dog food. Especially if the company makes dog food.
Already companies that speak in the language of the pitch . . . are no longer speaking to anyone.	The "pitch" is like marketing collateral that is aimed at pushing a product. It's in the metaphor of the company, not the customer.
Most marketing programs are based on the fear that the market might see what's really going on in the company.	Transparency is the new norm. Opacity is the tradition. Spinning something (public relations) is the perfect example of this problem. Mask a problem by the way you speak of it.
Markets do not want to talk to flacks and hucksters. They want to participate in the conversations going on behind the corporate wall.	Customers are interested in conversations that are honest and revealing with real people—whether in person or online.
We want access to your corporate information, to your plans and strategies, your best thinking, your genuine knowledge. We will not settle for the 4-color brochure, for websites chock-a-block with eye candy but lacking any substance.	Let customers know what's actually happening. Be transparent in ways that provide knowledge to customers that they can use. They're immune to collateral because they know it just pushes product—not value.
We've got some ideas for you too; some new tools we need, some better service. Stuff we'd be willing to pay for. Got a minute?	There is no question that customers are willing to pay a premium for something they want. Think Starbucks, extended warranties on large expensive items, Amazon Prime. Ask them what they want and they will pay the premiums if you provide it for them.
We want you to take 50 million of us as seriously as you take one reporter from the *Wall Street Journal*.	While traditional media are still and will continue to be important, there is something to be said for the "wisdom of the crowd" and its purchasing power.

Authenticity Trumps Consistency

The *Cluetrain* model—marketing for the social customer—is built on the overall experience of the company and how that experience is transmitted to the customer and other interested parties. Transparency, which we'll discuss in the electronic chapter called "Honestly, I Want This Chapter to Be on Privacy, But If I Wrote It, I'd Have to Blog About You," and authenticity are the cornerstones of the establishment of trust in a company by its customers.

From marketing's standpoint, that means that the human side of the company and its individuals has to be obvious and that multichannel honesty is the actual best policy when it comes to things ranging from service issues to product availability to messaging. To be authentic, what a marketing or public relations maven has to provide is something that is not scripted and not necessarily perfect.

Authenticity doesn't mean that you can't be fake. You can. Look at the world-class blog *The Secret Diary of Steve Jobs*, written by Fake Steve Jobs. This blog got a ton of national attention because it was written as if it was Apple's CEO Steve Jobs writing it, and it was intentionally hilarious. For a long time, it was known it was a fake Steve Jobs, but no one knew who the real writer was. It turned out to be Dan Lyons, a technology columnist at *Newsweek*. No one attacked him for his "inauthenticity" because his intent was clear. He was an authentic fake.

But being authentic isn't as easy as it sounds. It's often a matter of a culture that is used to micromanage messages. While they are aiming for what has passed for marketing nirvana for years—consistency of messages across all channels—they are missing what customers are now looking for: an actual conversation about the company with the representatives of the company.

For example, there is a large technology company that has managed its messages so tightly that every executive presents in the exact same fashion with the exact same phrasing and even on occasion with the same slides from speech to speech or presentation to conversation. While their messages are absolutely consistent and well aligned, they sound so identical that it rings untrue—scripted and faked.

The way to actually deal with consistency isn't to provide the same message in the same way. It's to establish the content of the message and then when that's clear, let those who are presenting that message do it in the way that reflects who they are. In their own voices.

Think of these two mantras:

▶ Consistent messaging doesn't mean identical messaging.

▶ Authenticity trumps consistency every time.

If you establish that authenticity and make sure that it reflects in the culture of the company and the way that you sell and market, you'll have a company that is trusted by its customers—even if it makes a mistake. Because the model is built on trust, the reputation of the company, not the message, becomes the brand. If that is the initial intent of the branding and marketing, then authenticity becomes an embedded part of the company culture and all its activities. But to get to that state, using tools for it can be something that validates your corporate honesty. Two things you can try:

First, quantify an assessment of your marketing practices by certifying them through credible third parties like TRUSTe. That way you can authenticate your product or other marketing claims which are validated by that third party.

Second, do what SAP did with its release of sustainability tools in 2009. They are able to guarantee that a product in a store is the environmentally best of its class because they've developed tools that measure the claim based on government standards for sustainability of products.

Use the tools to support a culture of authenticity. They, in effect, prove the point—verification of authenticity across all channels and in all conversations. But to be able to use the tools effectively, you have to have some idea of what the conversation that's going on is about and who's saying what to whom.

The Marketing Model: Old vs. New

The historic components of traditional marketing thought have been the so-called 4 Ps—product, price, promotion, and placement. While it's probably needless to say that these are still to be considered as part of a philosophical marketing portfolio, what has to be said so that old school marketers hear it is that there is little value in thinking in those terms any longer. They are part of a world where value was based on products produced and services provided—the world that I outlined in Chapter 1, so many years ago. With the 4 Ps as the predominant marketing logic, the perceptions of marketing campaigns immediately calls up to a customer words like hype, buzz, spin, b.s., corporate shills and . . . you get the message.

There are three competing logics that need to be clearly distinguished so that marketing departments can get on with their new roles as the entry point for conversation. I'm going to briefly go through each so there is no longer any excuse except all the excuses that are being used to not do what's necessary now.

Broken: Product-Centric Marketing Logic

Product-centric marketing was based on the communication of tangible value through the attributes of a product. Remember this one? "Winston tastes good, like a cigarette should." The idea behind this thinking is that companies win by producing superior products and enhancing those products' features over time. The success is measured by how well they are able to communicate these features to customers to get the response they are looking for—which of course is the purchase of the product.

However, in an era where international commerce is increasingly easy and e-commerce a norm for business, this differentiation is increasingly more difficult. Where a "good tasting cigarette" might have been a reason for success, now, because cigarettes can cause cancer and because "good" is not enough of a product differentiator to stimulate any response with an increasingly sophisticated customer, these kinds of pitches, even for health-friendly products, don't carry any weight.

As Robert F. Lusch and Steven Vargo point out in their seminal work, *The Service-Dominant Logic of Marketing*:

> *Products are merely means to an end. To help customers achieve their ultimate goals and outcomes, products and services need to be integrated into customer solutions that solve the complete customer problem. [Author's note: the personal agenda of the customer] This move toward solutions demands a different mindset.*

Broken: Company-Centric Marketing Logic

This always looks better than a product-centric approach to marketing but isn't really at all. The basis for this thinking rests with the idea that the company is more important than the customer. Where it differs from product-centric marketing, it attempts to satisfy the customer by utilizing the firm's resources to get across the message that the company feels the customer wants to hear. This is more brand than customer focused. The brand isn't based on the relationship that the company has with the customer, it's based on the presentation of the corporate message with the customer viewed as the passive recipient of that message. The communications are one-way and en masse. There is no differentiation for the customer, except as defined by customer segments. But the logic is not a service-dominant one. The customer is not served, except on a branded platter.

The supposed value of this kind of logic rests in brand propagation and the identification of the consumer with the brand. But it sadly ignores the customer's need for value. The brand is still built around the products or solutions that the company provides, rather than the kind of equity built around the trust in the company.

New Marketing Logic: Customer-Centric

The 21st century demands a new, more workable customer-centric marketing logic. Rather than focus on the product offering or the brand per se, it emphasizes those interactions that assist the customer in achieving multiple desired outcomes. These would vary according to unique customer needs and specific contexts. That assistance would take the form of offerings that create a personalized value for the customer.

What makes this different from the other two approaches is that the skills, knowledge made available, and the processes available to the customer are part of the engagement of that customer. They are no longer just a product of internal operations—they are a value-add to the customers who need them.

All in all, the new marketing logic follows what I've deemed since 2006 as principle number one of CRM: "Value and values are given and in return, value and values are received." The new marketing needs to be a long-term commitment that involves the customer, especially influential ones (more on that later) with the company. The company needs to be proactive about this too. The customer is moved into the sphere of "value-in-use." Marketing doesn't just engage in the old logic of product pushes and brand messages, but becomes an agency that helps customers derive value from multiple, ongoing interactions with the firm and its products and services. Marketing becomes a department that not only makes sure the customer is aware of products and services that are available but becomes the source of content that is of value to the customer.

For example, Kohler and Company has an interactive website where you are able to design a kitchen or bathroom using the product catalog. But rather than just doing that, they provide content to the prospect who is interested in the design. Content that covers latest trends in kitchen appliances or financing options so that you can afford that astonishingly expensive remodeling of your kitchen that staggers your imagination and life savings. The content is part of how marketing engages the customer. They are providing knowledge, a source of competitive advantage. I know that if I want to get the details on the creative and practical side of designing these Kohler specialty rooms, I can set up my own MyKohler.com "space" and I can get all the content I need to understand my options and think through my plan.

By making knowledge instead of product the source of competitive advantage, the customer's willingness to engage is increased. But keep in mind this is still only one-way communication. There is so much more to be thinking about.

In the new marketing model, sales and marketing are not the only aligned departments. There has to be a commonly constructed purpose that makes mutual sense for a relationship between marketing and customer service.

Before you get all twisted about this, think about it this way. Part of marketing's responsibility, forced by this social change, is engaging the customer in a conversation. One way they can do that is to figure out what the customer is saying outside the company's four walls. That means monitoring and listening to the conversation going on about the company. Once they're able to hear it, they will, with the right tools, be able to figure out who are the most influential people doing the talking. This will affect how those particular garrulous customers are treated by the company. That will impact customer service, marketing offers, and all in all the relationship that the mini-lord of conversation has with the company.

If I know that the influencer is someone who is negatively impacting others because of a wrong that the company committed, I can perhaps fix it and, if it's timely enough, can turn it around, as did one clothing apparel company. One of their customers was a strong negative influencer located by the marketing department folks monitoring Facebook for possible problems. She was head of a small but growing group of gripers on Facebook. Because marketing found her, they were able to recruit her to a customer advisory council, reversing her stance and impacting her membership in a much better way as a result.

The new model is always aligned around the ongoing experience that the customer has in his or her interactions with the company. Marketing becomes the seeker of conversation, the teller of stories, the purveyor of content, and the one at the door shaking the customer's hand before anyone else. They not only talk to the customer, they listen to them and act accordingly. Marketing moves from being the pusher of product, or the brand protector, to the initial contact for customer engagement and value creation.

What are the best ways to take this new marketing model and run with it? As they said in the Broadway musical *The Wiz*, time to "ease on down the road."

Social Media and Marketing: More than Just *du Jour*

Dissecting marketing types is a Herculean effort that actually makes the trials of Hercules pale by comparison. There are search engine marketing, relationship marketing, database marketing, emotional marketing, trust-based marketing, direct mail marketing, e-mail marketing, mobile marketing, social media marketing, product marketing, solution-based marketing, and well, let's just make *ad nauseum* the punctuation.

I deliberately left out word-of-mouth marketing because though you can make a case for it as marketing—which the Word of Mouth Marketing Association (WOMMA) does—it is more than that. It's how we communicate with each other, and it is the most potent influence in what we purchase. To illustrate this, BigResearch did a 2007 study on purchasing influences in varying industries, and word of mouth came out on top in most of them. For example, in consumer electronics, word of mouth had a 39 percent mindshare with nothing else particularly close.

But the one that has captured the imagination of marketers, primarily because customers are responding to it, is social media marketing or, more properly, using social media tools as part of a marketing strategy. The numbers are there to justify it. A 2008 study by Cone on business in social media found that 60 percent of Americans are using social media, with half of those using it more than twice a week. The numbers have skyrocketed since 2008 according to other studies to between 74 percent and 84 percent, depending on who you feel like believing this morning. But what is incontrovertible is that a majority of Americans are engaged in using some form of social media from the more passive blog reading to the more active creation of blogs, podcasts, and participation in social networks.

I was one of the speakers at the 2009 Global Retail Marketers Association (GRMA) event in Florida. The audience there, a mélange of senior marketing officers with many years of experience in their respective industries and positions, were not only blown away by the new customer-centric marketing logic referenced in this chapter, but were found to not be all that participant in the social media either personally or at the companies that they worked for. I had a significant number of the attendees (more than two hands worth) come up to me and ask for the presentation notes because they wanted to bring back the ideas to their very substantially sized companies. These were extraordinary people, with deep expertise, who were just beginning to see the power of social media, both from cost and reach.

The lack of experience isn't stopping the likely spending on social marketing. In April 2009, Forrester released a survey on online advertising that forecast a growth in all areas of interactive marketing from 2009 to 2014, but the growth in each of social media marketing (34 percent) and mobile marketing (27 percent) was twice the growth or more of almost any other category over that time span. The figure that they throw out for social media spending is $716 million in 2009 to $3.1 billion in 2014. Gulp.

These numbers or the equivalent commitments are repeated almost across the board as spending in more traditional ways decreases. But that doesn't mean that there is a long or deep cultural adoption of social media marketing. To do that would be a change in culture that would portend the discarding of the product-centric or company-centric previous models. That ain't an easy task, princes and princesses.

Avanade, the odd couple alliance between Microsoft and Accenture, released a study they hired Coleman Parkes Research to do in late 2008 called "CRM and Social Media: Maximizing Deeper Customer Relationships." In a nutshell, they found there is no doubt that companies see the value of social media. Apropos of marketing in particular, 64 percent of the respondents saw an improved reputation in the marketplace. Substantial numbers indeed. Two in five claim that they can associate an increase in sales to the move to use social media. While I'm a little skeptical of that one, who am I to argue with the numbers?

But the problems are manifest too. Between fears of security (76 percent), senior management apathy (57 percent), fear of using unknown technology (58 percent) and, biggest myth of all, a fear of a negative impact on productivity (50 percent), the level of actual adoption was low, with over 60 percent of the respondents saying that adoption of social media was not on the agenda. While marketers may be intrigued by social media, they haven't planned on what to do with it. In fact, only 18 percent had any kind of social media strategy at all.

Yet social media marketing value has an ROI that can be benchmarked. Aberdeen Group did a study in early 2009 on the ROI of social media marketing that found those same concerns over investment, with 59 percent of the respondents concerned about the difficulty in getting buy-in for it. But what Aberdeen is able to do in this study is show that the best in class companies figured out how to use it well and got value:

▶ 68 percent had a social media monitoring process

▶ 58 percent had dedicated social media marketing resources

▶ A surprising 61 percent were hosting online communities

Needless to say, this was far higher than the normal or mediocre performers.

So the contradictions are stark here. Companies are willing to spend the bucks, there is a proven good result, but once the technologies and the processes and protocols are put in place, adoption isn't certain by a long shot, either at the top or at the grassroots.

What's terribly sad about all of this is that there is no doubt about the promise of social media, beyond the shiny new toy part of it. Over 50 percent of the companies feel that companies that don't adopt it will be left behind, but 60 percent of the same don't plan to adopt it. Sixty-one percent see it as a key way of communicating with the customer. Interestingly, 78 percent see it as an effective way to communicate given the cost reductions of a downturn. But they are going to fail unless they can discard the broken marketing logics that tend to predominate in their corporate lives.

We are a cheery bunch with a rosy outlook, aren't we? I'm presuming that you're plowing through this opus because you want to find out about how CRM is changing, how the customer is communicating and what they are demanding, and what you have to do to deal with that. So I'm going to presume that these corporate barriers are not there for the remaining part of this chapter.

Marketing = Monitoring—In Part

What do you do to track the conversation? Is the conversation all you track? What do you do with it when you find it? Actually, you're monitoring two things as a marketing person who, incidentally, is aligned perfectly with sales as far as my sunny self is concerned here.

First, you are monitoring information—news sources or analyst pieces, for example. You are also monitoring conversation—in the blogosphere, on social review sites, on Twitter, or Facebook and LinkedIn or in threaded forums or specialized social networks. That means what the crowd and distinct personalities in the crowd are talking about. The reason I separate the two is that you need to see the results somewhat differently.

We've already discussed monitoring information in the sales section and that is in part what SalesView does. But they are information focused—getting intelligence on the prospects you have, finding prospects from intelligence. What is more germane to this section is the conversation.

What Does the Conversation Sound Like?

One of the upsides of social media monitoring tools is that not only can they make coherent sense out of what is otherwise an apparent constant indistinguishable buzz, but they can capture the data and then integrate it, if they're really good, into traditional CRM data stores. Later, we'll take a brief look at one particular tool, Radian6, that is probably the premier tool at doing just this.

But before we go there, it pays to figure out what components are actually part of the noise. In a very important 2008 work called "How Consumer Conversation Will Transform Business," Pricewaterhouse Coopers identified four things to listen for. The notes are mine here.

▶ **Volume**   This is a look at the historic patterns of a particular topic of conversation versus the current amount of discussion going on. Take a look at the screen in Figure 12-5. This is a representation of what's trending in real time with Twitter. If you look at the tag cloud, the largest words are the "loudest" conversations—the ones with the most volume—a click on the term will get you to the tweets that reference the term.

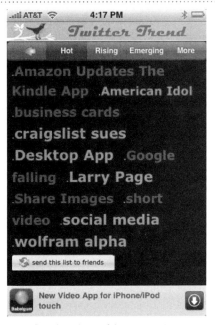

Figure 12-5: Twitter trends reflect the volume of the conversation

▶ **Tone**   If you're Craig Newmark of craigslist, you might be interested in the reasonably high volume conversation going on about craigslist suing the South Carolina attorney general. What you don't know from the volume is what the tonality is. This is the positive, negative, or neutral discussion. Let's say you see a prevalent thread in the conversation using the words stupid or jerk when it comes to the South Carolina attorney general— you'd get a good sense of the positive view of craigslist in this tiff, in addition to the obviously negative view of the attorney general. If it just simply reported on the same thing without any emotional phrasing around it, you'd get the idea that this was of topical interest only and would not be buzz for very long.

▶ **Coverage**   This is based on the number of sources who are generating the conversation. If the large tag in the trend cloud around "craigslist sues" is the result of 20 people talking a lot about the subject, it would have a decidedly different context than if it were about 200 people who made 300 comments.

▶ **Authoritativeness**   This one is far more important than it might seem—it is a qualitative ranking of the sources. Are they influential? Are they not? For example, if you found that much of the negative commentary about the attorney general not only emanated from some citizens of South Carolina but came from a key opponent of the attorney general who barely lost to him in an election race (this is all fictional speculation for the purposes of this discussion), that might have a huge impact on a lot more people than if it were random members of the crowd on Twitter.

This is what you need to take into account each time you begin to monitor and then distinguish the conversation. As we'll see in the chapter on customer service, up next, there are conversations being monitored on Twitter that are evaluated via sentiment analysis. For example, the Business Objects Insight tool uses text analysis on specific conversations that garner the attention of the program because of rules and filters that are preset, e.g., "find anything that says product sucks," and then according to preset business rules, alerts whoever needs to be alerted based on the sentiment involved, how it's ranked, and the intensity of the language involved. For example, "horrible" is worse than "not very good" is worse than "so so."

One caveat when it comes to social media monitoring. It is monitoring, not interaction. It's also not strategic action either. What you're getting is data that you need to make an effective decision on how you're going to approach your customer, prospects, and those who influence them—or how you're going to capitalize on an emerging trend. But once you know that, you still have to actively engage customers with a strategy that's appropriate to the ongoing interactions—not just the interaction based on the conversation. It could be a service issue to be resolved or a trend that you want to actually capture so that you can derive revenue.

Listen to PwC again:

One of the major challenges for companies today is not only understanding how to hear whispers but also having the processes in place to react quickly enough to verify them with other slower-moving data streams (e.g., customer surveys or financial projections), and finally to change strategy quickly enough to take advantage of a trend before it wanes.

That is the difference between just using social media monitoring to garner information or using Social CRM to figure out how to move to action. It's always how you use data, not the fact that you have it.

A Brief Note on Influencers

Influencers aren't only people with mass followings. Just because someone has 500,000 Twitter followers doesn't make them influential. Actually, there's a member of the Twitterverse with the handle Sockamillion who has more than 1.1 million followers at this writing. He's not an influencer. He's a cat. Ashton Kutcher who has more than 3.4 million followers is not a real influencer except as a celebrity within the Twitterverse—and he doesn't personally correspond with his followers either. So what he says has little gravitas, which I'm sure is fine with him, but you shouldn't waste time on his pronouncements. You're not being punk'd.

However, there are people who are influential within an industry that may affect you who have perhaps 1,000 followers on Twitter, or a blog or two read by those who should be reading it. If your offerings are in and around that industry, even with 1/10,000 the audience of Ashton Kutcher, you are going to want to meet and converse with that person—get them involved with you. Their weak ties—meaning the folks within their network with two or three degrees of separation—may be your future clients. Don't underestimate that. Make sure you connect with them.

As Paul Gillin, in his 2009 brilliant "how-to" book, *The Secrets of Social Media Marketing*, puts it:

> *One of the most common mistakes that public relations professionals make is to contact the media only when they have something to promote. That's not a relationship. That's a transaction. It's easy to keep track of what influencers are saying. Subscribe to their RSS feed and keep an eye on new activity. Send e-mails or leave comments on their site every so often to show them that you are engaged. You won't believe how rarely this is done and it will pay huge dividends for you.*

If you know your target audience and know who and what influences them, what can you do to succeed at this? Let's look at Procter and Gamble, who under the stewardship of CEO A. J. Lafley just seems to keep doing it right.

Case Study: Procter and Gamble Get It Right ... with a Few Glitches

In February 2005, Procter and Gamble (P&G) began what was an innovative marketing campaign. For a company with over 300 brands and 26 of them worth more than $1 billion, it was radical. They announced an antiperspirant called Secret Sparkle Body Spray that was geared to a preteen and early teen market. No, that wasn't what was radical. Listen up. Don't be so impatient.

What made this a transformational marketing initiative was the use of social tools aimed at that young girl market. They started by using some traditional means such as TV advertising and print media, but they fell afoul of CARU—the Children's Advertising Review Unit—which monitors advertising for inappropriate ads. In the case of P&G, they were advertising a product on TV and in print that clearly stated "please keep away from children" on the label, which they were not supposed to do. They withdrew the TV and print ads right away to comply.

Much more appropriate was the May 2005 launch of the blog sparklebodyspray.com—a website that centered around blogs associated with the four antiperspirant scents: Vanilla, Peach, Rose, and Tropical. Each blog had a color scheme, a series of contests, and interactive activities to cement kid communities. These could include building a dream date with an ideal guy and then e-mailing the "date" to your girlfriends. Additionally, there were active discussions and expert advice for these kids on music, fashion, parties, and sports.

Blogs that are associated with a culture or a product but are not truly individual are called "character blogs." The bloggers, who might be professional writers, are reflecting the character of the site. For example, entries on the Tropical blog, a shade of yellow (like the sun I suppose), would talk about days at the beach or the use of sun block. These blogs often come under fire because they aren't an "authentic" individual's singular voice or even a group of voices. But there is nothing wrong with them if their intent is stated and the idea clear. It's only when they are deceptive that there's a problem. In the case of P&G, it was meant to be more engaging to their target audience.

It was and it worked. By July 2005, mostly through digital word of mouth, there were 12,000 unique visitors per week who spent an average of *25 minutes* per visit! While the stickiness factor of 25 minutes is amazing, what's even more astounding is the ROI. By the end of July 2005, Secret Sparkle Body Spray had 0.8 percent of the entire antiperspirant market. That amounts to $83 million in revenue. That's the entire market, not just the preteen and early teen girl market. I would guess they had 100 percent of that.

Ah, but the story doesn't stop there, my friends and colleagues. In 2007, recognizing their audience had grown older, sparklebodyspray .com grew up with it. Instead of dream dates with 12- to 14-year-olds in mind, they figured on what the 17- to 18-year-old girl might want. The contest? Upload a video to becauseyourehot.com with you bustin' your best dance moves—if you are a 17- to 18-year-old girl with parents' permission. This was a nationwide contest with road shows in Chicago, Los Angeles, and several other American cities. The winner got to dance in a JLo video—that's Jennifer Lopez for those who were cryogenically frozen for the last decade or so. If you're still not sure who she was, I can't help you.

Listen and learn from P&G. They are innovative and they run throughout the whole book because of that. If you're Fortune 100, you have a lot to learn here. Even if you're a little guy, you can learn from them. Their marketing department thinks out of the box that results in something that marketing doesn't often do—they drive revenue directly. That should get and keep your attention.

CRM Vendors Have a Problem Here: Poor Apps, but Improving

This would all be wonderful if it could be organized into something other than an operational *mishegoss* (mess). But most of the CRM applications and even the standalone marketing automation applications are traditional in their functionality and aren't that great at it either. Even the new breed CRM marketing automation applications like Marketo and Infusionsoft are built along traditional lines, though they are good.

But there are some changes afoot. In particular, enterprise-strength industry leader Eloqua, e-mail marketing star Silverpop, and newcomer Loyalty Lab are all beginning to incorporate contemporary feature sets that will matter to the customer.

Short and Sweet: Social Media/Marketing Automation— A Match Made in Technology

Want to hear about a trend that you're not going to find on Twitter? Marketing automation applications are increasingly incorporating social features and, while doing that, strengthening their more traditional CRM-ish functionality. In the meantime, social media monitoring applications are increasingly adding CRM-level functionality or integrating with CRM applications to bring their data into the CRM databases and to make their data usefully actionable.

Marketing Automation Adds Social Features

The marketing automation, analytics, and e-mail marketing companies in particular are feeling the pinch of the social customer. ExactTarget, one of the foremost e-mail marketing applications, second to Silverpop in my thinking, did joint research with Ball State and found that more than 46 percent of the e-mail marketing campaigns in 2009 planned on using some social media in tandem with the campaign—up from 13 percent in 2008. Rather than sit on their duffs with this information, ExactTarget went and did something about it. In mid-2009 they launched their Social Forward solution. This allows subscribers to share e-mail content with Facebook, LinkedIn, and other communities and then tracks what the subscribers do. The subscribers can do it with a click of a button, so it's easy. Since it's already integrated with salesforce, Microsoft Dynamics, and Omniture, among others, this data becomes an invaluable addition to the arsenal for customer insight.

Other companies aren't sitting still either, a hard thing to do in a world of ADD. Omniture, an open source provider of web analytics, added new capabilities that allow it to track video shared across the social web. So, if I embedded a YouTube video in my blog, it would distinguish between someone who viewed it on my blog, someone else's blog, or at the YouTube site.

I want to point out two companies that I think provide what is perhaps the best in their respective class—the grander marketing automation application—the enterprise powerhouse Eloqua and the e-mail marketing innovative leader, Silverpop. The profiles are brief, but the kudos loud.

Enterprise Giant: Eloqua

There is no doubt in pretty much anyone's mind that Eloqua is the industry leader when it comes to marketing automation. They are scalable, secure, can handle complex campaigns, and have pretty much a complete portfolio of products ranging from demand generation and lead scoring to varying marketing types and event management. They are an on-demand application with a target audience that is large enterprise. They have the client list to prove that too. Think Nokia, Dow Jones, and a huge segment of the software industry. They integrate well with CRM applications in a wide variety of environments. In the web chapter called "Get Down! Right to the Vertical Nitty-Gritty," look at the story of salesforce.com and Eloqua with the NHL's Philadelphia Flyers. In Chapter 14, check out the same combo with the Washington, D.C., leading think tank, the Center for American Progress. They are everywhere.

They don't only stop with salesforce either. They integrate with Microsoft Dynamics CRM, SalesLogix, and Oracle CRM On Demand. They innovate too. Their chief technology officer, Steven Woods, wrote a book in 2009 called *Digital Body Language* that describes those things you can measure and identify that can indicate a propensity to buy online. It is an insightful smart book that isn't mundane in any way, and to Eloqua's credit they've developed a solution around it called Digital Body Language (surprise!) that gives you the toolsets you need to make those measurements.

They don't have a lot of social features baked into their product as of 2009, but they are as complete and smart a marketing application as you're going to get without them. Just put aside the bucks. They ain't cheap, but they are worth it.

Silverpop

Even though their primary message delivery solution is via e-mail, they don't call themselves an e-mail marketing firm. They provide engagement marketing to B2C and B2B customers. In fact, their commitment to this concept is so strong the product is called Silverpop Engage, with B2B added to the product of the same persuasion.

What makes these dudes unique is that they have an incredibly rich functional array that they provide from analytics that measure almost every facet of the e-mail "engagement" from when it gets opened to when it gets discarded and all those actions in between. They have a powerful business rules and workflow engine. Using it, a highly personalized e-mail can be sent very quickly to a customer who has just spent time on a website. Very quickly, as in seconds after the visit.

But they do even more than that. In 2008, they were the first e-mail marketing company to my knowledge to add a share-to-social feature, which allows e-mail recipients to share content with others in their social circles on social networks like Facebook and MySpace, among others.

This is a tiny portion of the feature set of the products that this company provides. They do such good work that the Engage B2B product was a finalist for a 2009 Codie Award for Best of Breed business software.

Social Media Monitoring Adds CRM Features

There was a point in 2009, the exact date escapes me, when a flurry of discussion around "Is Twitter Social CRM?" became a hot topic—at least among the social media mavens and CRM gurus. The discussion, which I jumped into big time because of the claim that it was from some of the mavens, reminded me of *West Side Story* and the Jets and the Sharks squaring off, though I don't know which side was which. We quashed it pretty quickly, establishing that Twitter was a channel, not Social CRM, but what emerged from the rubble, in a phoenix-like sort of way, was that there also was this effort by social media monitoring companies to either add CRM functionality or integrate CRM applications with their monitoring capabilities. This was a smart move for companies in this realm because it allowed the data that they were accumulating and reporting on to become actionable based on the criteria set by the company using the monitoring tools.

This is no small thing. There are, according to SMM analyst Nathan Gilliat, 170 social media monitoring products out there. They are now one of the hottest industries, but most of the companies were (and are) small. The CRM market is a mature multibillion dollar market that is a natural fit for the integration of the two capabilities. This is a way for the product providers to drive revenue and the practitioners to get additional content for their forays into customer insight. A true win-win.

The Crème de la Crème: Radian6

I'm married to a Newfie—for you mainlanders, that's someone from Newfoundland. As a result I have an interest in all things Canadian Maritime Provinces. That's why when I began hearing buzz about a social media monitoring company in New Brunswick, Canada, my ears perked up. Turned out they should have, for all kinds of reasons.

The company is Radian6, what I think is the premier social media monitoring company in the world today. They have the capability to monitor not only 100 million blogs (not exaggerating) but also social review sites, videos, photo sites, twitter streams, pretty much you name it, they monitor it.

They also measure it. They can measure volume, coverage, authority, and most recently, sentiment, a.k.a. tone. They allow you to slice and dice results in ways that tell you what you need to hear to make decisions. For example, who spread news about your company that you wanted spread? Where did it go? What languages was it in? Who spread news you didn't want heard? Who heard it?

But they don't stop there. They are integrated with CRM applications like salesforce.com. They have a client list that anyone would love, with companies like Dell drinking their Kool-Aid.

The only shortcoming they have is that alerts and triggers aren't automated yet. They will have the workflow and business rules engine they need to truly scale by the end of 2009, according to CTO Chris Newton. You need to go with an SMM tool. This is the one. I say that even without the effects of my love of the Maritimes.

Oh, yeah. One more. There is one other company that stands out when it comes to a new framework for marketing and that's Loyalty Lab.

Up and Coming: Loyalty Lab

Loyalty Lab, a company I knew next to nothing about, released version 3.0 of its integrated marketing platform in 2008, which they cutely called "Ready-Aim-Engage." While releases of software or platforms or services are hardly earth shattering—in fact, hardly glass shattering—this one caught my eye because of what the platform purports to do, especially in the world of marketing. Here it is in short order.

Marketers can track responses wherever customers purchase or interact, providing what the company calls "a more accurate view of response rates and performance." The standalone e-mail marketing product provides data integration with "Ready-Aim-Engage." It enables marketers to link e-mail to transactional (of course) and *nontransactional* behaviors, so messaging can be relevant to social networks.

Up to this point, it sounds interesting for its nontransactional promise, but not real interesting, right? But then you see it recording customer activities that go beyond simple transactional behavior, including:

▶ Interacting with social media applications

▶ Recording important dates

▶ Reading or posting to blogs

▶ Referring friends

Now *that* should get your attention.

Why? you might ask in a puzzled way, with your brow furrowed and your finger (depends on which one) up in the air—all the while thinking that Paul is nuts.

The former features are ways of integrating traditional tools such as customer segmentation, the operational kind of CRM, and a nontraditional tool or two (like actions on nontransactional behaviors) to a traditional channel, e-mail in particular. Nice, but not dramatically different than a number of things out there.

BUT.

Their tools for recording, interacting, reading, and referring are the foundation for a platform that truly believes that, as *The Cluetrain Manifesto* says, "marketing is a conversation." Which makes it completely unlike all the marketing apps tied to CRM suites or best-of-breed approaches, which, with some exceptions mentioned above, remain remarkably traditional given the times.

There is a unique value in this approach that has a double edge. First, this is allowing a company to create an actual dialogue with its customers and informing the company as to when the dialogue advances. That is beyond merely important—that is mission-critical to interacting with customers who control the business ecosystem.

The second side bears a little more explanation.

In her "Social Technographics" white paper of April 2008, when she worked for Forrester Research, current Altimeter CEO and author of "Groundswell" social computing whiz Charlene Li found that companies (1) don't know how their customers use social technologies and (2) are inexperienced with what works, when it works, and where it works. Plus (not from the paper) it's hard to measure and, because much of the behaviors generated are emotional (nontransactional in this case), the value is hard to understand. What makes R-A-E 3.0 important is that it gives the enterprise social mavens the ability to capture interactions that involve the social media—blogs, social networks, and so on. This is not something that has been easily available—especially in a framework. It seems that part of the technology solution is that they have prebuilt bridges to social networks like Facebook and APIs to customize the connections between the social networks and the enterprise or to build internal social network applications. Plus, they provide social network analysis tools which allow you to discover which customers are influencing your "database," as they put it in their promotional materials.

And all of this is on demand.

While trolling around the website, I found that they had a modestly interesting and certainly informally (entertainingly) written blog called Loyalty Dogs that basically covers topical areas like customer experience, loyalty (duh!), program analytics, technology trends, and "interesting stuff." Additionally, they have a Loyalty Lab Library, which is a compendium of recent articles drawn from the industry standard sources (such as they are) such as *DestinationCRM* and *1to1 Magazine*, again on topical subjects. What is glaringly missing in their library are the blog resources that could add a lot to their library or wiki resources or podcast links. But that can be a niggling or painful omission, depending on your requirements.

This is something worth looking into further. I'm not sure how well executed it is. I've never seen it in a production environment so I don't know if R-A-E 3.0 even works. But I have to say that Loyalty Lab at least seems to be not just paying attention to the customer that is now running the ecosystem, but also trying to capture what that customer is doing. And that is attention-getting.

That's enough technology, I think. Given that I started this whole thing with the idea of aligning sales and marketing, what better way to close the chapter than a pair of mini-conversations, one with senior marketing whiz John Cass, and the other with CRM and sales superstar Dr. John Tanner, a.k.a Jeff Tanner.

John Cass is someone I've personally known since 2008, but knew of for his work at Forrester Research Group for years before. He is one of the foremost experts in marketing in the United States and is not only a savant, but a genuinely good guy. He is currently the director of marketing at ideaLaunch, a content marketing services company. He also is smart enough to be part of the brain trust at the Society for New Communications Research, a leading think tank in figuring out what the new paradigm for communications actually is. So he's well worth listening to. Which is why he's leading this conversation.

MINI-CONVERSATION WITH JOHN CASS

Marketing is dead. Social media has swept the need for promotion, advertising, and sales, and instead conversation, dialogue, and engagement have replaced traditional marketing techniques.

VRM is all about ordinary customers managing their vendors with tools, typically web based. Those companies that can help enable customers to manage vendors will have more success in the future. At least that's my understanding of the concept.

That's the story some social media evangelists would propose. In reality, web 2.0 does not mean that marketing has ended but rather the Web and consumers' new powers of creation and participation mean that it has never been easier to fulfill the real meaning of marketing.

"Creating, communicating, delivering, and exchanging offerings that have value for customers" and "identifying, anticipating, and satisfying customer requirements" are two descriptions at the core of both the American Marketing Association's and Chartered Institute of Marketing's definitions of marketing.

Both descriptions represent that marketing is and always has been about listening, observing customers to make something of value for customers. The rise of social media does not mean the strategy of marketing has changed marketing, just the tools available to understand, anticipate, and innovate based upon customer needs.

Customers coming together on the Web are able to create their own content about products, brands, and ideas, on their own sites, blogs, or in social networking sites such as Facebook. That ability to easily connect and create content changes the relationship between customers and companies. Consumers have more power to discuss and influence other consumers without having to go through mainstream media. Companies also have the ability to connect with customers for customer service, innovation, and customer evangelism.

For marketers steeped in the tradition of push marketing, the new Web is a challenge; you can push your message, but be prepared for customers to interact with your company and push back, sometimes with a louder voice than your company! Learning how to engage the community using social media for customer service, though leadership and innovation management, is something every company will have to learn eventually.

Three Considerations

1) Business intelligence about the product and service delivery is dramatically affected by social media. The difficulty in identifying relevant conversations gave semantic technology tool vendors the opportunity to develop monitoring technologies using natural language processing. Once companies wanted to respond, the question became who in the organization should respond? As a result, semantic technologies are being integrated with CRM so that companies can respond.

Monitoring the Web, triaging opportunities, and responding can all be conducted using manual tools and processes. The volume of content online means that companies need filters to find the most relevant conversations. Natural language processing can provide an automatic review of online content by filtering compliant conversations for useful analysis.

Natural language processing is the process of analyzing content found on the Web for meaning. Sophisticated linguistic technologies source content by issues and content, then determine key metrics associated with the content. First, large volumes of content are collected into a database, then identifying information will be tagged, perhaps by the source or author of the content. All of the data is standardized into one relational database. Lastly, key metrics are drawn from the raw data. The metrics might include the specific issues being discussed, or the sentiment of the posting. Sentiment determines if a discussion was favorable or not.

Semantic technologies enable companies to understand the meaning of content, and in the process enable companies to automatically determine how people feel about a brand. Natural language processing can help to determine the volume of conversation about issues, the importance of issues, and the rate of growth about new issues as they arise. NPL can help to determine who is influential on a topic, or if a company's marketing communications efforts engage and resonate with customers.

As the sophistication of companies about what it means to engage customers has grown, so has the understanding that the entire organization should be involved in the process of engaging customers and community online. Semantic web technology vendors have developed workflow processes that copy the manual systems developed by companies to triage online opportunities. These workflow processes are CRM tools. In the process, semantic technologies have moved from just business intelligence or monitoring tools to engagement tools that allow sophisticated response management across the enterprise.

2) Personal referral and customer feedback continue to be the most important facets of how sales occur. Social networking and social media give ordinary people the ability to efficiently refer products and services to their peers. Companies that facilitate such referrals and listen to customer feedback will accelerate the process of referral.

Doc Searls, one of the authors of The Cluetrain Manifesto, *proposes that companies help facilitate the development of VRM—vendor relationship management systems. VRM is all about ordinary customers managing their vendors with web-based tools. Those companies that can help enable customers to manage vendors will produce more referrals because they are helping consumers to find the best vendor. By facilitating the exchange, the chances of referral increase.*

3) Company responses to private citizens are no longer private. Whether public, if they occur in social media, or recorded by consumers, companies have to develop a strategy for handling both customer support online and the publicity that can surround their response.

Managing the volume of content in social media is difficult. Not only does monitoring take a lot of time to understand what is being said about a company and their brands, but it takes time to respond to the community. Customer service in the world of social media is outside such existing channels of communication as e-mail and the telephone.

Because any company response takes place in the public realm, companies are unsure as to which part of a company should respond to a customer support opportunity. Public relations professionals are more adept at understanding how to navigate the process of responding to questions in the media, while customer service has the infrastructure and the answers. Companies have to understand the new reality and build a new infrastructure that can deal with how social media works. This new infrastructure will be different for every company, different people drawn from different disciplines and with different workflow processes.▰

Now we move on to Jeff Tanner, who is as brilliant and laconic a person as I've ever met. He is not only one of the most accomplished academicians in the United States in marketing, sales, and CRM, he is the author of more than a dozen books, including leading texts in sales (*Selling: Building Partnerships*) and B2B marketing (*Business Marketing: Connecting Strategy, Relationships, and Learning*).

He holds a unique position in academia as a professor of marketing at Baylor University, where he also serves as associate dean in the business school. He also is the head of the only CRM M.B.A. degree program in the United States, and maybe, though I don't know this, the world.

He is a great friend, truly one of my favorite people, and a cofounder of BPT Partners with me and Bruce Culbert. With all this, he also actively consults and trains, working with the likes of JCPenney, Teradata, and IBM. But you know what's coolest? He owns and races thoroughbred horses, including one he used to have called Thunkin' Theodore, who owned my horse-loving heart for a long time.

Your classroom, Jeff.

MINI-CONVERSATION WITH JEFF TANNER

Marketing is no longer about the 4 Ps. As Hiram Barkdale, one of my professors said over 20 years ago, "We've been P-ed on long enough." Marketing is now about creating offerings that deliver value, then communicating and delivering that value.

But when the sales force is the lead go-to-market channel, marketing's role is often vilified while sales is glorified. Marketing's contribution to creating, communicating, and delivering value is hindered, in part by marketing's own assumption that it has responsibility and control over customer strategy. Questions over who owns the customer take over the conversation, and everyone's ability to deliver value is diminished. Since this book is more likely to be read by marketing types, here's how to play nice with salespeople:

1. *In all situations, the one closest to the customer should own the relationship. So if you have salespeople who call regularly on customers, they own the customer.*

2. *That means they own the data. You might own the CRM system, but until and unless they put data in your system, you got bupkes.*

3. *Prove your value to salespeople first. Then ask for the data. That means you have to buy data, make do with less, try a test case, whatever; prove your value first.*

4. *Automate data capture. There are many others who touch customers who can contribute valuable data to your dataset. Salespeople can also add data without pain if you can think of ways to make it easier. Don't forget that customers can add data, too. If you have self-serve options for customers, use those touchpoints as an opportunity to gather information.*

5. *Never underestimate the value of a smile and a little flattery, as well as asking. Qualitative data from salespeople can be even more valuable than hard data if gathered in a scientific and formal manner. For example, trade shows may be "old school," but they are still a great opportunity to meet and gather information from customers. Yet, when creating your messaging for the show, consider asking salespeople what messaging they*

use that opens doors for them. If they can open a door with a certain phrase, use it to bring folks into the booth. Use it to get prospects to open an e-mail. You can't get that kind of knowledge from a database.

Salespeople engage customers in conversations. Yes, they are directed conversations, meaning the salesperson is attempting to direct the customer toward a specific action most of the time, but they are conversations nonetheless. Take a lesson from sales and treat data gathering as a conversation, beginning by asking to listen in and learn.❧

This may have been an overly ambitious chapter, but I think it was necessary. Sales and marketing, at this point, necessarily need alignment and at some point might even be integrated. We'll cross that bridge when we come to it.

But there is one other traditional pillar of CRM that we have to look at. Perhaps more than any other, it is undergoing the most dramatic, if not the biggest transformation and has the most viral implications. That is customer service and, after you catch your breath, we'll head over to the customer service department.

13

Customer Service Is Our Name—and Our Game

In 2006, Vincent Ferrari had an agonizing exchange with an AOL representative when he attempted to cancel the account. He taped it and it went viral. The employee was fired.

In 2007, Sprint "fired" 1,000 customers because they were unprofitable. It was later discovered by intrepid web reporters that 200 of those customers were deployed military in Iraq and Afghanistan so they were in areas where roaming had to go on. Sprint was embarrassed and the accounts reinstated, as were many of the other 800, who were cut off due to excessive calls about Sprint's billing mistakes.

In 2009, when I go to clients and begin to examine their customer service models, I almost always hear from them that they "already have great customer service representatives." This is true—to some extent. There are some customer service representatives whom the customers love and, even more germane, trust.

Do you see what these stories all have in common? Each of them demonstrates an immediate fix—firing employees or reinstating customers or relying on individually excellent customer service representatives—but none of them deals with or even considers the actual issue. How do you institutionalize the kinds of practices, processes, and engagement models for customer service that will prevent the problem from happening ever again? Keyword once again: *institutionalize.*

This is not a trivial issue. Engaging customers to get reciprocal value because they're happy with you is one thing. Dealing with those same engaged customers at their most upset is quite another. What makes it worse than just going head to head with someone who's ready to smack you upside that head is that in our lovely, connected, peer-trusting world, that attempt can spiral out of control a lot faster than you can ever imagine and you'll end up smacked by thousands of people, including many you can't afford to be smacked by.

That said, great resolutions to customer service problems can turn passionate detractors into ardent advocates when done well and consistently.

Emily Yellin, in her superb 2009 book on customer service, *Your Call Is (not that) Important to Us*, quotes Bob Garfield, *Advertising Age* columnist:

> *"Now we can aggregate to have our voices heard and to put pressure on these people. Customer service and customer relations management is going to be so critical to all corporate futures. . . . It's going to be all about cultivating, exploiting and collaborating with consumers. And you can't do that if they hate you."*

I couldn't have said it better, so I didn't.

Customer Complaints Go Viral—and You Love It

Human beings as a species have a dirty little secret. We love to complain. You know that's true. How many times have you ignored a complaint someone shared with you about bad service they got somewhere? "Never" would be the right answer here. In fact, you eagerly scarfed up the venom and then what did you do? You used that as a jumping-off point to hurl poison at some other company who offended you with their level of service. Didn't you?

Want some scientific proof so you can have some numbers to prove what you already know? The United Kingdom, which regularly studies the culture and behaviors associated with complaints, is happy to provide you with that data. RightNow (more about them later in this chapter) commissioned a study of 2,800 British consumers back in 2007 that was done by YouGov. The study found that 69 percent of the respondents had actively registered a complaint with a company, and 79 percent of those complained about their treatment between one and five times over a 12-month period.

One of the more interesting results of this particular survey was the snapshot of customer expectations. Sixty percent of Britons surveyed expected that the problem would be fixed to their satisfaction. Twenty-seven percent said the problem was actually fixed to their satisfaction.

Thirty-four percent said the company took absolutely *no* action after the complaint had been made. You might think that the most interesting part of these results is the gap between expectations and results. Granted, that's interesting. But one thing that might escape you— thank goodness you have me to tell you this—is that *only 60 percent even expected the problem to be resolved.* That means that fully two-fifths of the population didn't expect the problem to get solved to their satisfaction to begin with. Whoa!

That points to what I'm going to repeat. The measure of a successful customer service strategy is the institutionalization of best practices that actually work, technologies that have value, and, most importantly, a service culture that is defined by well-trained, empowered customer service representatives (CSRs) who can be replaced with other well-trained, empowered CSRs when some leave—no individual disrespect intended.

There are problems to overcome, but there are also models to adopt, both enhanced traditional models and newer models geared toward Social CRM.

The Definition of Customer Service

First, let's decide what we're talking about when we say customer service in the context of Social CRM. It is the customer care activities that surround the purchase of a product or services. That is an aggregate definition that pretty well encompasses the average and median definition of customer service, derived from several dozen.

This definition extends customer service to something well beyond just handling complaints. It also includes, for example, inquiries and questions that require a non-urgent answer, but are still expected to be answered on the first contact.

But even just this example can get dicey when you have to figure out who carries out this function and what channels are used for it in a company.

For example, is field service part of customer service? Is the call center the primary way that customer care should be carried out? For the purposes of the fourth edition, field service is not going to be covered—please see the third edition if you want to a detailed and still appropriate look at field service. But we are going to look at the state of the call center to see how (and if) it fits into a contemporary customer care strategy.

The Contact Center: The Illusion of Successful Efficiency

John Ragsdale, who is the vice president of technology research at the Service and Support Professionals Association (SSPA), did a study on service technology spend between 2008 and 2009 and found that there was one big winner and one big loser. The big winner was multichannel and e-services, which went from 22 percent in 2008 to 30 percent in 2009 of all service tech budgets. The big loser? Contact centers, which dropped from 39 percent to 27 percent in those two years—and pretty well funded all the increases in other categories.

Why? Because it is increasingly apparent that not only are alternate service channels becoming a more important part of service execution strategies, but customers would rather rely on themselves than a CSR, given the level of frustration and the expectation of failure they already have for that traditional environment. That doesn't mean they don't want to talk to someone. They just don't trust that the "someone" will solve their problem.

You can't blame this shift—if blame is the right word—on the empowerment of customers, their Internet savvy, and their desire to resolve their own problems on their own time. It is a strong factor in this move toward multichannel customer service. But equally important is the failure of contact centers to recognize that the processes they use, their sadly misaligned cultures, and the metrics they measure by are part of why customers don't expect to get their problems solved despite their calls. It's an institutional failure. In 2008, Forrester Research queried 5,000 respondents and released a report called "Why Talking to Customers Is Ruining Your Business," which outlined why customers felt this way. The primary reasons were:

▶ **Routing calls to the wrong customer service agent**   Fifty-seven percent felt that the routing failed to get to the person who could actually solve their particular problem.

▶ **Horrible knowledge management capabilities**   Sixty-two percent felt the knowledge bases were average or worse. You know this to be true. How many times have you gone to a knowledge base to find an answer, entered a search phrase, and come up with about 10 answers that had absolutely nothing to do with the search phrase you entered?

▶ **Poor customer data access**   Sixty percent felt that agents didn't have the ability to successfully review the customer records needed to respond to customer queries. This might not be true, but it's the perception. That's all that's needed to reduce trust.

The problem isn't the problems themselves. The way that call centers are organized and customer service reps are measured militates against successful interactions with customers. Customer service reps are measured by the speed with which they clear the call queues—one way or another. Customers are looking for a resolution to their problem or answer to their question and an experience that at least meets their standards. These are diametrically opposed expectations.

If you look at traditional call center metrics, they include how many calls per hour are answered, how long it takes for a call to be answered (average speed of answer, or ASA), how long a call takes (average handle time, or AHT), how many calls have been abandoned, the mean time to resolve tickets, and so on. These are all KPIs that are aimed at efficiencies in the call center, not the actual solution to the customer's problem or the answers to their queries. This is the precise difference between a corporate culture and a customer-centric culture. The former tries to resolve things to the satisfaction of management, the latter to the expectations of the customers. The most significant call center metric that aligns with the customers' actual requirements is first contact resolution, not first call resolution. This is a multichannel world now.

This is an endemic problem spanning multiple industries. Here are a couple of very typical snippets of discussions about call center KPIs that go on in a number of forums:

▶ "We are a state government owned utility company. As far as our owner is concerned our only KPI is Grade of Service (70 percent of all calls answered in 30 seconds). To them nothing else counts." (CallCenterOps.com, 2007)

▶ "Total incoming calls; average wait time before call abandonment; abandoned calls; average speed to answer; average calls per agent in an eight-hour shift. . ." (KPIfix.com, 2008)

Efficiency rules. The question is why? According to Natalie Petouhoff, a senior analyst at Forrester Research, who runs their customer service research practice and whom you will hear from quite a bit in this chapter:

> *Twenty years ago when customer service strategies and the resulting technologies were first adopted, without meaning to, they set customer service up to fail. How? The primary goal was to make the corporation more efficient. Cost-cutting strategies defined customers' questions and concerns as a nuisance to be dealt with in the most minimal way possible. In response, technology vendors focused on the automation of customer complaints. Businesses then weren't attuned to concepts like "customer experience" or "customer lifetime value."*
>
> *The resulting customer disdain combined with rapid rise in adoption and use of social media by consumers have today formed a "perfect storm" that is driving the change in the world of customer service.*

But unfortunately, as Fred Reichheld pointed out in his book *The Ultimate Question: Driving Good Profits and True Growth*, there is an 80/8 gap. When it comes to customer experience, 80 percent of the companies think they are doing a good job, but only 8 percent of the customers think they are. When it comes to call centers, the delusion of success is there, because, as frequently as not, they perform well according to their KPIs. They reduce handle time; they meet the SLA basic terms; they reduce abandonment rates. But they don't improve the customers' experience or resolve their issues to the customers' satisfaction.

Can Traditional Contact Centers Still Work?

The traditional contact center is not going to go away. So the question is, can they work using traditional approaches and efficiency-based metrics? They can, but not without a significant organizational process transformation and cultural change. What that involves is what CRM initiatives always involve.

▶ **Executive sponsorship and commitment**   Not only does there have to be cooperation between all the customer-facing and back office departments to make sure that customer service has the data and cooperation they need to deal with customer contact, senior management needs to understand that customer service improvements—including the right training, technology, and the actual interactions with customers—will cost money over time. They need to commit to increased budgets based on improved customer experience, not cut budgets for operational efficiency improvements. The latter are marginal, the former are dramatic.

▶ **New training fosters new skills**   It's no longer a matter of just following agent scripts, though that can help to some degree. Agents need to be able to connect with customers. Aside from product knowledge and technical skills, soft skills need to be equal partners in the training mix. Rosanne D'Ausilio, CEO of Human Technologies Global, did research that proves soft skills training shows "measurable reductions in job stress, improvements in job performance (including benefits such as reduced average call duration), better customer service scores, and reduced turnover."

▶ **New metrics combined with old**   While few are suggesting that all efficiency-based metrics are eliminated, customer-centric metrics such as first contact resolution (FCR) need to gain in importance. In 2007, the SQM Group did research on first call (not contact) resolution and found that customer satisfaction drops an average of 15 percent with each customer call past their first. But on the positive side, for every 1 percent improvement in FCR, you get a 1 percent improvement in customer satisfaction. Other customer-centric metrics could include self-service accessibility, which shows not only how many customers begin self-service transactions but complete them.

▶ **Appropriate use of multichannel and voice technologies**   It's no longer about just the use of IVR technologies to increase efficiency by reducing human interactions. There are dozens of other channels, both internal and external, that customers converse on. Judicious use of technologies and allowing the customers to choose which channels they are contacted through can improve the customer experience dramatically.

▶ **Culture change**   The agent environment should be changed so that agents are encouraged to listen to customers and initiate discussions, not just up-sell, cross-sell, and answer questions. As a major part of this change, agents should be incentivized to actually be customer-centric, which means their KPIs would include customer comments and thoughts about the individual agents. The idea is for agents to converse with the customers—reactively or proactively—and be accountable for the results.

Building a New Customer Service Model

But what if those changes to the traditional model aren't enough? (Which they shouldn't be.) What would be a new customer service model that can meet the needs of the social customer and still be viable to the business?

The new model starts with a very old model.

Bruce Katz is a man you should pay attention to. Aside from being articulate, with a lightning-fast intelligence and a great sense of humor, he has been a business success in a remarkably disparate number of ways. He was the founder of Rockport Shoes, which drove the "casual shoe revolution." He provided the seed capital for the wildly successful The Republic of Tea, whose products make up roughly 90 percent of all the teas in this house of tea drinkers. He also owned the first online virtual community, The WELL, from 1994–1999. His range is amazing. I asked him what his principles of customer service were since Rockport and The Republic of Tea have been known for that for an incredible amount of time. His answer:

> First it starts with the golden rule: do unto others as you would have them do unto you. Would you like to be on hold? Would you like to be sent to voicemail? Would you like to hit 27 different keys to navigate menus and get hung up on? Would you like to wait 45 minutes? No.
>
> There's this interest in efficiency. Go to the website and talk to a robot. Is that a real savings? It frustrates customers. Customers want to talk to a real person.

This isn't some old-school thing that no longer applies. This is the single most important observation when it comes to a new customer service model. These precise observations were supported by data released by Forrester Research with their "North American Technographics Retail, Marketing, Customer Experience, and Service Benchmark Survey" during the fourth quarter of 2007. They found that regardless of generation the most important channel was a direct call to a customer service representative on the phone. Even Gen Y preferred that over going to a store or sending an e-mail (41 percent to 35 percent and 6 percent, respectively). Only seniors (age 63 and up) preferred going to a store more than making a phone call. A phone call won with older and younger boomers, Gens X and Y.

Bruce again:

It's the same reason that people used to love to shop. The salesperson would make you feel like the most important person in the world, even for just a little while.

You have to want all the calls that you are getting regardless of why they call. If they are calling to buy something or to complain or just ask a question, it doesn't matter. All those calls are important. I wouldn't want to outsource the call because I want to be able to deal with all the calls myself. For example, I remember back in the earlier days of Rockport Shoes that one caller mentioned that if the shoes were made in white, she, a nurse, would wear them in the operating room. We launched a whole line of shoes for nurses that was highly successful.

The foundation of any successful customer service model is going to be actual human interactions—not IVR, not VoIP services, not high-speed Internet connectivity. It will have to do with how quickly a human being can provide a meaningful experience to a customer who has engaged them.

But what does that mean when social communications have transformed the world? Jeff Bezos, CEO of Amazon, being interviewed by *Business Week* in March 2009, nails a customer service model that should be emulated by companies:

Internally, customer service is a component of customer experience. Customer experience includes having the lowest price, having the fastest delivery, having it reliable enough so you don't have to contact anyone. Then you save customer service for those truly unusual situations.

This is the core of any real customer service: how to minimize problems and optimize the customer experience an individual customer is having. It also means that when there is a problem there needs to be a resolution of that problem immediately. That implies a first contact resolution.

The new model also anticipates the social customer's multichannel preferences to communicate. It recognizes your customer service problems won't only be discovered at your site, but will be lurking in the cyber world via social media channels and social networks/communities.

However, unlike the preferences of some of the more naïve sorts out there, this customer service model builds on the traditional. There are still operational business requirements, cases still need to be opened and closed, data has to be captured, the customer record needs more than just transaction data, and agents need to be human beings who can warmly respond to what could be an irate other human being. The more knowledge that agent has about that individual customer, the smarter they are and the better experience they can provide.

Keep in mind, there are different sets of expectations when a customer complains as opposed to when they request something, and each of them has to be handled. But if you handle them well, whether they are complaints or simply queries, and you provide a customer service that can exceed expectations—which are low to begin with—there is a distinct benefit. In 2009, J. D. Power and Associates did their annual ranking, published in *Business Week*, of Customer Service Champs. Over half of the top 25 percent of the brands had improved their customer service, despite the recession. Conversely, of the bottom 25, most of the customer service scores had fallen. The willingness to invest in improvements paid off with improvements in commitments of customers to the brand.

Tenets and Principles of the New Model

There are broad tenets that govern the new customer service model.

1. **Golden Pillar**   Customer service is becoming the most important of the Social CRM pillars because it is where the most highly charged customer interacts most directly with the company.

2. **The experience dominates**   Customer experience is the core of customer service, not efficiency.

3. **At least one step forward, no steps back**   The thrust is to take the negative reaction and either neutralize it or make it positive, take the neutral and make it positive, and take the positive and reinforce it. This should be a proactive effort.

4. **Inbound, outreach**   The complaints come from outside the firewall as well as inside so there needs to be outreach as well as an internal effort to resolve issues or answer questions.

5. **Community-based care**   Customers are always willing to help other customers with similar problems or unanswered questions. This kind of customer-to-customer interaction should be encouraged and brought under the aegis of the company through the use of communities.

6. **Listen and learn**   The conversation outside your firewall that goes on about your issues is as valuable if not more so than the concerns directly raised to you by the customers. But don't underestimate the value of the information that may be contained not in a complaint, but in praise such as a 3- or 4-star review of what you do. Knowing what your advocates don't like may be the best way to solve the customer service issues of the future or preventing them by solving the problem in advance.

7. **Value in collaboration**   No longer is customer service solved only by the company but also by other employees in different divisions. Through the use of the tools of Enterprise 2.0 (see Chapter 4), such as wikis, the wisdom of the crowds can be drawn out by empowering employees to add to the knowledge base.

8. **Value in anticipation**   If you've listened well, you'll be able to anticipate problems. Be predictive and prevent problems. As Smokey the Bear says, "Only you can prevent forest fires." When it comes to customer service issues, only you can put out the fire, but it's far better to prevent it, though it may not have the dramatic impact of putting one out.

9. **Measuring the experience**   The metrics of customer service need to move from pure efficiencies to experiences. Rather than the number of calls taken in some time period, first call resolution should be given increased weight as one of those metrics that are most important to the customers themselves. Spend the time to figure out the benchmarks and the KPIs for customer experience in a call center environment.

Community-Based Customer Service

It's very expensive to get technical support for a significant software product for a large company (hear me, Microsoft?). Over the past five years or so, I've come to rely on Google search and threaded forums to get the answers to my technical questions. Recently, I had a problem with QuickTime, which kept giving me an error message even though there was nothing wrong. I did a search for the problem and found a number of answers on Mac forums. I tried them, one worked, problem solved in about half an hour. I had nothing to do with Apple. It was Apple customers who solved it freely and easily.

If you're able to bring that in-house and form a community that your business owns but is for your customers—and you give the customers the freedom to identify and fix problems on the site—there is not only some quant loving ROI associated with it, there is also an incredible amount of good will generated from your customers about you.

Why? Because you're willing to air the problems, get your customers involved in helping solve them, and at the same time make sure that you're involved in that too. You begin to see an ROI as fewer service tickets that have to be opened, saving you money. There are more first resolution solutions, which means you have direct cost efficiencies. ServiceXRG did a study that shows that in a typical call center, a first call resolution will cost $49 on the average. But if it reaches 24 hours it goes up to $61 and at two days is $155. *Ad infinitum.*

Think about it. If the problem is solved by your customers, it doesn't even reach the status of a first call. Helpstream, one of our two Superstahs! in this chapter, found that implementing their solution, which is organized around customer service communities, led to their customers seeing 20 percent of all customer service issues solved by the community, with 20 percent solved by the knowledge base articles, 30 percent by forum threads, and 30 percent by the agents. This is a very significant cost savings. Seventy percent of the customer service problems never needed to be solved by an agent.

In general, the ROI of online service communities is very high. Natalie Petouhoff finds that there is a generic ROI of 99 percent in less than 12 months.

Community-based customer service is not a new idea at all. Threaded forums and user groups did that independently of any company and continue to do it. Now you can find customer service threads in discussion groups on Facebook. What is new and important to the new customer service business model is the creation of these specifically customer service focused communities behind the corporate firewall and the collaboration encouraged by the company with its customers—even if the company has to be transparent about its problems. That leads to customer-developed solutions, often not thought of by even the help staff.

What is technologically new about it is the means to capture the conversation—those customer-provided solutions—and making them part of the knowledge base. Also new is adding the business rules and workflow in combination with sentiment analysis that can alert a company employee to a problem within the community automatically.

But that's only one part of the equation. Developing alternate service channels is the other.

Alternate Customer Service Channels: Time to Use the Remote

This new business model has ramifications that are already being felt. The idea of community-driven customer service (see Helpstream later in this chapter) and alternate customer service channels is a direct result of the realization by many companies that they have to create a new model for their customer service interactions.

The customers' ownership of the conversation that we all have so glibly spoken about here and many other places is vehemently reflected by the social websites that focus on customer/company interaction and others that reflect those service interactions. Let's take a gander at the growing group of alternate channels that you will have to concern yourself with when developing the customer service part of your Social CRM strategy, and broadly, what the protocol for dealing each channel should be. The caveat here is that handling each channel isn't necessarily the right thing to do for your company and that how you handle them can vary by company. These protocols are recommended guidelines.

Customer Service Social Sites

These are sites that you can guarantee will be talking about your company, though not necessarily in a nice way. The two most prominent are the Consumerist (www.consumerist.com) and PlanetFeedback (www.planetfeedback.com). Each has a somewhat different take. The Consumerist operates as an aggregator of bad corporate mistakes or mishaps being reported by news and consumers. Typically, there will be a report on something like "Mattel Will Pay $2.3 Million Penalty for All Those Lead Toys," which will generate about 2,000 views and 30 comments or thereabouts.

The PlanetFeedback model is different, as you can see in Figure 13-1. They are a site for customer complaints and compliments too—though, take my word for it, complaints far outweigh compliments. One apparel company showed up on the 15 minutes of fame section (which should be "shame," really) and within about 20 minutes had generated 167 comments on what seemed to be their egregious error. Even though after an investigation it turned out to be the problem of the complainant, it didn't really matter. The damage was done.

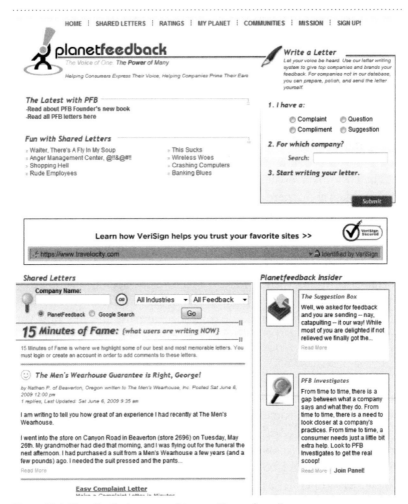

Figure 13-1: PlanetFeedback.com: complaints outside your firewall

What makes the PlanetFeedback model even more sensitive for a company is that they will become advocates and investigate the complaints by trying to contact the company. Woe to the company who has an "ignore the inquiry" policy.

The existence of this kind of channel for customers' angry conversations requires a protocol for response, because the damage can be great. Keep in mind the reason that people are on the site is because they are already most likely very angry to begin with. So they are prone to go viral on something if they sense they can.

PROTOCOL

Outreach program should include not only monitoring the sites, either via the use of social media monitoring applications or direct daily human monitoring, but there should also be an immediate response to the issue raised by someone who is authorized to do it.

Additionally, if contacted by the site, openly respond to them. Make sure there are clear rules for the authorized responders on what they can offer and what they can say, but not how they can say it. Do not try to do any up-selling or cross-selling here, which may sound obvious but, believe me, given the silliness that I run across at sales-driven companies, bears mentioning.

Review Sites

This is the type of site we've discussed in prior chapters, review sites like Yelp or CitySearch.com or Epinions.com. These are a much trickier proposition. The primary reason that people write on review sites tends to be positive (see Figure 13-2). For example, on Yelp, the first 1,210 restaurants listed get 4 or 5 stars before a 3.5-star review shows up, though there are higher ratings after that again. Don't get me wrong. There are 1-star reviews, which are complaints in a different format. But what makes this kind of site interesting is that there is valuable customer service data buried in even good reviews that should be monitored and gathered.

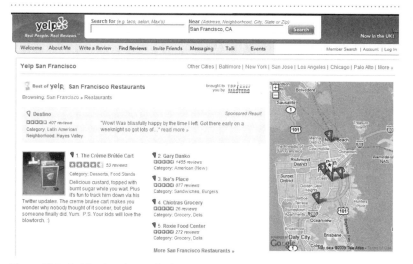

Figure 13-2: Social review sites tend to be positive.

Here are an example of a customer service matter (not issue) that is buried in reviews of San Francisco's Crème Brûlée Cart:

▶ **3-star review**   "It took us 30 minutes to find this place after receiving updates from Twitter and calling our friends to find out where this phantom cart was heading. It was like trying to nail a fly with chopsticks."

▶ **5-star review**   "Yes, I totally stalked CBC on Twitter, and yes, I left work early to get it, and yes, I couldn't find the damn cart until I saw a swarm of people running towards a small garage! And yes, I finally ate it!! And must I say I ate the damn crème brûlées within 10.5 seconds!!!"

These are positive reviews—the last one very positive. But there is a customer service "problem" that runs throughout them: how do you even find the cart? That's something that needs to be addressed not by responding to a comment, but by listening to the customers.

Protocol

First, when it comes to egregious customer problems that are creating bad reviews, you need to do what you would expect here: resolve them. But this isn't necessarily the value proposition for dealing with review sites. For example, the two positive reviews above indicate how difficult it is to locate the cart. This can be resolved by changing the location—a cart can move with a new permit.

On the other hand, there are often problems to address in the 1-star reviews. While there are typically ways of directly addressing them, they can be tedious and awkward. For example, Yelp forces you to sign up for a business account which then allows you, as the owner of the business reviewed, to comment directly on a review. But that has limited value because the comment is isolated to the single review, not to a thread. That means that if there are 30 reviews that point out the same problem and you as the authorized respondent want to reply, you'd have to reply to each and all of the 30. Which you might have to.

However, these sites still need to be monitored for customer service. Start by handling problems that require an individual response. Actually by doing that, you can gather valuable customer service data on improvements that can be made, which provide action items that speak louder than a comment if you proceed to fix the concern.

Threaded Forums

The threaded forums I'm speaking of here are not the ones that are on customer communities (which I covered in Chapter 9), but the ones that are externally owned and run. The forums are typically organized around products like Windows 7 or areas of interest like astronomy or specific groups like the Enterprise Irregulars, of which I am a proud member, who cover the enterprise software industry. What makes them valuable is that they carry out organized conversations with a thread that someone starts, then a response to the thread, then either a response to the response or another response to the thread. In other words, they can group substantial conversations and make them easily accessible.

An example of a customer service issue in a discussion that is outside the company is this one from the everythingiCafe (www.everythingicafe.com) on one forum member's iPhone 3G:

my iPhone stopped working! WTF?

Yeah so I think the touchscreen went out for like no reason at all the phone has never been dropped and it's never seen water. I bought the phone end of February will apple cover this? What will ATT tell me if I take into their store? Also there is an apple store about 30 mins from my house at the local mall will I possibly have to make an appt out there to go and get it fixed or do I just send it in to apple and they will send me a new one? I've never had a iPhone that crapped out on me so any suggestions would be greatly appreciated.

The response from another forum member, Europa, not an employee of Apple.

What happens when you connect to iTunes?

Put it in DFU mode and restore to factory settings. If the problem persists after a restore, you'll have to have to take it to the Genius Bar. You could also send it to Apple, but I'd say just take it in since you have one fairly close. That way, you don't have to go without a phone all week. It will certainly be covered as long as there is no visible damage or water damage. Just be sure not to take it in jail-broken, if it is jailbroken.

This forum response is the typical way the new service model—community-driven customer service—is actually working, though that has other implications as we shall see. The members of the community solve the issues or at least suggest solutions.

PROTOCOL

It is entirely smart to monitor and respond to threaded forum issues that are buried in the thousands of threads and hundreds of thousands of views that some of these forums get. First, to show that you are as responsive as customers are now expecting. Second, for the invaluable answers that you maybe haven't thought of yet. Third, for quality control, since there is no guarantee the answers that your customers are getting from other customers are good.

Responding as an authorized company representative in one of the forums outside your firewall is the way to go. Your authorized representatives should identify themselves as such. They don't promise an answer, they answer the question. "I'll get back to you on this" doesn't wash in this situation. Threaded forum members are looking for answers—period. If your reps see an incorrect solution being proposed, they should *respectfully* point out that there is an official solution that will work. The customer may always be right (not), but the solution provider may not be.

Blogs

The blogosphere of course gets the most PR when it comes to flaming because there are more than 100 million blogs. Plus the nastiness of the bloggers when it comes to customer service issues can be clear, and their projected power is frightening, especially because the mainstream press is now committed to not only blogging but covering blogs. The Dell Hell incident mentioned earlier in the book is a perfect example of how damaging this channel can be on the one hand, but how beneficial it can be if you don't just react to your detractors but actually listen to them. That also means, don't just solve the immediate problem, but actually see if what they are complaining about has merit in the bigger sense.

PROTOCOL

This is simple. Presuming you are being flamed on the site, and that comments are open, respond as an authorized representative immediately, before the thread gets out of hand. If you have to follow up and you don't have an immediate answer, this is a place where you can speak to the raucous crowd, calm them, and tell them you'll get back to them. Then get the answer you need and respond to them publicly and privately. Depending on the problem, your public response can be "I responded to you with the answer via e-mail" or it can be entirely public—your call. But follow up and respond as soon as possible.

Twitter

Ah, Twitter. We discussed it back in Chapter 7 under microblogging. It's also been called Social CRM by some of the social media mavens. Suffice it to say, if it takes me 800 pages to write about Social CRM, and Twitter is maybe 5 of those, then it isn't. What it can be is an effective rapid response channel for customer service. What makes Twitter important is that the complainant's conversation can be picked up quickly and responded to in real time. The existing Twitter third-party tools are sophisticated enough to find the problems and to provide a mechanism to respond quickly, even if multiple customer service representatives are involved. For example, CoTweet is a young but good enterprise-oriented Twitter tool that allows internal staff groups to communicate and collaborate via Twitter so that they not only can identify and broadcast a customer service issue but can notify the appropriate group members to respond and handle the response.

Twitter can also function as a proactive customer service channel. For example, DirecTV has its own group (which is characterized with a # mark prior to the group name) that you can "tweet" with your problem (i.e., bring it to their attention). But the company is monitoring you in real time too. They are using Tweet Deck and other free clients with strong search capabilities to find as many problems as possible to respond to as quickly as possible, with the knowledge that this rapid response is so refreshing in comparison to ordinary response time, it can easily go viral—a huge plus for your organization. You'll see what the rock star of Twitter customer service, Frank Eliason, is doing with #ComcastCares on Twitter later in this chapter.

PROTOCOL

The second you complete this paragraph go to www.twitter.com and register the group names or the twitter IDs that you are going to need to reflect your company's presence, because if it's not already too late, it will be soon. For example, AT&T is simply @AT&T. Their customer service group is #AT&T. Then make sure you have at least one authorized representative using Twitter search capabilities to see what people are saying about you. When you run across a problem, respond to their tweet publicly (in 140 characters or less, remember?) by asking them to elaborate or contact you. Then solve their problem. But also make sure that your authorized representative is empowered to do random acts of kindness. That means that if you find something that someone wishes could happen, make it happen. I've seen one apparel company who saw someone who wished for a particular clothing item, in the "just a thought I've tweeted" category. The company surprised them and gave it to them. The result? An advocate for life for less than $100.

Facebook and Other Social Locations

This is very different than all the other channels. Remember, we are talking about external social networks here—locations that are not specific to your company or behind your firewall, nor are they focused around a particular interest or practice. For those of you who have just returned from the 1977 version of the Dharma Initiative, Facebook is easily the premier location for social gathering on the Web as of today. It's also the most complicated. It's used far more often for branding and marketing than for customer service, yet at the same time is a repository for a lot of "hate groups" for companies that already have customer service issues. Communication on Facebook is via private messages or on The Wall, which are public messages. Additionally, the nexus for a lot of the frustrated customers are groups they've created—rather easily I might add. For example, in mid-2009 there are 11 Facebook groups called "I Hate Bank of America" ranging from 164 members to one member. There are also 16 "Bank of America Sucks" groups and 15 "Boycott Bank of America" groups. Don't think because a group has only a single member that it's not a potential magnet for a customer service disaster. On the other side of the equation are a large number of neutral or positive Bank of America organizations that number in the hundreds all told. One of the problems for customer service when it comes to social locations is that monitoring the content isn't simple.

PROTOCOL

This is somewhat complex. Not only do you have to monitor the groups that hate you, but also the groups that love you or are related to you in a neutral sense. Additionally, you need to create your own group(s). But what complicates this even more is that you have to distinguish your group from the other groups.

TiVo is an instructive example. In mid-2009, they had over 15,000 members in their Facebook group. They built a discussion board within the group—a threaded forum, really—where any issue can be raised by a member, including "TiVo customer service is terrible," which had about ten people venting and a few more supportive. TiVo deserves a big thumbs up for being transparent and providing a forum that unblinkingly allows irate customers to have their say. They have a couple of thumbs down though—they don't respond at all to their angry customers, leaving it for their more supportive customers to respond. This is not wise. Response from the company is still necessary. Additionally, monitoring the other groups and responding to concerns there also matters.

Case Study: @ComcastCares: Now They Really Do

I've been a Comcast customer for well over a decade. When they were just starting to provide Internet service in the Manassas, Virginia, area, I was a beta customer. I've used their high-speed Internet service ever since and pay a bloody fortune monthly for it, but it is a genuinely high speed Internet service, not just one that claims it is.

Over the years, I've had a lot of problems with Comcast, though bunched at the front end of my passage with them, including a two-week downtime and an errant customer service representative who wiped out my entire customer history. Even though the history remained buried in their records, they had to rebuild the account from scratch rather than just simply reuse it. In fact, that accounts for my e-mail address of paul-greenberg3@comcast.net. I used to have paul-greenberg@comcast.net. Know why I don't anymore and have to use the one with the 3? Because someone else had the paul-greenberg@comcast.net after my account got wiped out. Know who that was? Me. So I couldn't get paul-greenberg@comcast.net back after the slaughter of my account, because I had the address already, which I couldn't use.

You see what I mean? Unfortunately, this was not unique for Comcast. Their customer service reputation was so bad that it drove one Manassas resident (not me—an elderly lady by the name of Mona Shaw) to take a hammer to the Comcast office here, which got her a suspended sentence and national headlines.

But then along came Twitter—and Frank Eliason. Frank is the customer care poster....man of the 21st century. By developing a Twitter channel to respond to Comcast customer concerns, he changed the way that the company and companies in general do customer service.

It didn't start that way exactly. In late 2007, Comcast had a reactive and somewhat random customer service policy. They would find blogs that mentioned Comcast and then pick up a phone and call the bloggers who did negative posts. The strategy was "apologize and fix." They didn't respond to all briefings, just the ones that made sense to them—not necessarily for them. They really weren't solving customer problems, they were marketing, attempting to create some buzz around Comcast doing "good things."

In December 2007, public relations asked Frank to address negative criticism somewhat more systematically and write on websites. Note it was PR that asked him to do that, not the customer care department. Frank turned that opportunity into a successful venture and within two months, Comcast realized that this was more than just a PR effort and decided to create a Digital Customer Care department that Frank would direct.

What Frank was then able to do was to develop a serious customer service strategy for the digital channels that were available. "Customers don't change because of numbers," he says. "Analytics don't drive change. The story drives changes." But he saw the unprecedented opportunity that the Web provided to a customer care department like his. "Finding stories is easy. The blogosphere is nothing but stories."

By 2008, he realized that it wasn't just the blogosphere that represented a viable channel for his digital care operations. Twitter was growing rapidly. It had reached the 1 million members mark in March 2008. So on April 5, 2008, Frank Eliason, under the TwitterID of @ComcastCares, began tweeting—an effort noted by the powerful influencer site TechCrunch and its owner Michael Arrington almost immediately. What made it notable was that it was among the very first efforts by a large enterprise to break down the formal communications barriers around customer service. It not only directly engaged the customer, but attempted to solve their problems as immediately as they were discovered and provide the customer with a place to go to deal with those problems.

Was it perfect at first? No. As a result Frank began to see critiques of the approach he took on blogs. Rather than ignore them or react to them, he listened to them and made changes where appropriate, which proved to be valuable in how he approached the Twitterverse and customer service generally. Some of the points raised were as simple as "Is your picture there?" or "Make sure that you are personal in how you deal with your customers with something like 'Hi, this is Frank speaking. How can I help?'"

Frank initially had three members on his team to handle Comcast customer queries and complaints. He had to make sure that while they were all associated with @ComcastCares (the group) each of them had their own TwitterID. The success rate was astounding. In their first five months, they had already reached out to over 1,000 customers who were having problems or who were about to.

Brian Solis, who not only runs FutureWorks, a social media focused public relations firm, but also writes the ubërpopular PR 2.0 blog, said, "Companies like Comcast are taking what was an inbound call center and turning it into an outbound form of customer relations, which can spot problems before they occur."

But the customers were not all that Frank had to concern himself with. He knew that Comcast management had to be on board and Comcast culture had to be aligned with the initiative in order to make it succeed. So he did something that is both simple and exceptionally smart simultaneously. He started an internal newsletter.

The newsletter, which goes out internally to 2,000 of their "closest and dearest friends" at Comcast every business day, covers the customer conversation about Comcast. They find 7,000 mentions a day for Comcast one way or the other (to be fair, including references to the e-mail domain comcast.net). But the most important ones are on the sites like the Consumerist or ZDNet—the highly trafficked sites. To add to the conversational spice, each day they highlight a different channel or feature. For example, Monday is YouTube; Tuesday is "Compliment Tuesday," which draws attention to the good things being said; Wednesday is executive complaints day, and so on. The circulation of this internal newsletter keeps the staff and management engaged with the Comcast customer crowd out in the ether that they otherwise would have no connection to.

What does @ComcastCares look like today? There are 11 members immediately responding via Twitter to the customers who are having problems. They have garnered praise for their innovative approach to customer service. They are considered one of the paradigms for the alternate service channel—one for businesses to emulate.

Have they stopped receiving complaints? Hardly. Problems still occur and there are still plenty of customers who are frustrated and hate Comcast. But @ComcastCares provides not only a great success story, but a model to learn from. So, spend the time, talk to Frank, read this, learn lessons.

Technology Finds 21st Century Customer Service

The call center vendor world hasn't changed terribly much in the last several years, though what they are offering has. You'll still see Siebel Call Center in a dominant role in large enterprises carrying out the more traditional call center approaches because it remains a solid product, though cumbersome. Companies like KANA have moved from their more traditional customer service offering to something they are calling service experience management and interaction management, becoming the largest of the web self-service vendors in the process. Avaya and Genesys still lead the market when it comes to voice-related technology and large enterprise contact center infrastructure, and they work with a lot of the other contact center vendors to fill out their portfolio.

But it goes much further. Salesforce.com, known historically for their SFA, brought in ServiceCloud in 2009, which gave them a robust, cloud-based, on-demand customer service offering that was fully integrated with Facebook and Twitter, to do what salesforce.com does best, provide innovation in their solutions. SAP was first to the block to integrate sentiment analysis through their Business Objects Insight product and Twitter actions to be able to monitor customer conversations and then alert the appropriate parties about potential issues based on the virulence of the emotions surrounding the issue. Parature, a small player just a few years ago, used their odd vertical, the interactive gaming space, to grow to a much broader group of 750 customers by mid-2009.

In other words, customer service technology exploded in 2009 and this was just the tip of the iceberg. There were too many specialists in areas like contact center search or workforce optimization (used a lot in field service) to even begin to discuss.

But the two that stand out to me for Social CRM offerings—the ones that matter to the social customer's business ecosystem—are Right-Now, a long-established early SaaS player in CRM, and Helpstream, a newcomer making a major play for the technology implementation of a new customer service model.

Superstah! RightNow: Building Beyond the Traditional

I've known Bozeman, Montana–based SaaS solution RightNow and especially its CEO Greg Gianforte for many years and have been tracking them for as long as I have known them. They have always been a company that provided a solid SaaS-based customer service application suite that just did the trick for service agents and management when it came to doing what was traditional call center and helpdesk work.

For a while they toyed with the idea of a full-service CRM suite, buying the deep process focused CRM SaaS application SalesNet for a bargain basement $9 million in May 2006. But that wasn't their forte. They were an ace customer service application and they quickly realized that. They still offer the full suite—sales, marketing, and customer service—but customer service remains what they are ubermensches at.

RightNow also pioneered the selective upgrade that is now standard throughout the on-demand world. They were the first who didn't just push the upgrade automatically, but allowed the customer to select whether or not they wanted to upgrade and the parts of the upgrade they wanted.

In 2007, they took a turn that has vaulted them into a position that gets them my Superstah! rating because they added the customer to their product and service configuration, not just in word, but in deed. Greg, a highly successful, articulate businessperson, author of several books, and a forward thinker, realized that not only was the customer experience the paramount "feature" of customer service, but that all the products that RightNow made needed to be able to engage customers in ways that satisfied the experience they were looking for. He began looking into the idea of customer communities and worked out an alliance with Lithium, one of the premier community-building services in the high tech world. In September 2009, he bought Hive-Live, a good enterprise social networking platform to enhance his social CRM offering even more. He began to incorporate experience-based metrics into the analytics he was providing, such as customer satisfaction KPIs. In conjunction with that, Greg released "Eight Steps to Improve Customer Experiences" in both print and digital formats.

But RightNow is also doing things that might be deemed more traditional very well. They have a large vertical presence in multiple industries, including the public sector, where they are very strong with clients like the Environmental Protection Agency and Social Security Administration, and the financial services industry; with a strong presence in software and services and consumer electronics. This is no mean feat. Establishing a foothold in one vertical is hard enough, multiple verticals a huge task—yet they've done it. As they've done many smart things.

Mission 21st Century

The factors that will affect RightNow for the next several years were defined by Greg Gianforte in a discussion he and I had:

The need for speed   *Instant messaging, texting, and Twitter have all contributed to make consumers expect immediate responses to their questions. Consequently, companies need strategies to address these rising expectations without driving up costs. The pace will continue to accelerate. Consumer care organizations will need to react immediately to most inquiries received from multiple channels.*

Collaboration everywhere   *Consumer care organizations are shifting from an "answer the consumers' questions" mentality to a "consumer empowerment" mentality. Empowering consumers means that consumers can resolve their own issues—without humans. This trend will be at the heart of most consumer care strategies going forward. We are seeing communities arise everywhere; Facebook, LinkedIn, MySpace are just a few examples. Companies must develop methods to monitor and participate in these open communities. Plus, creating company-specific communities presents an opportunity to build loyalty with consumers and leverage loyal enthusiasts to reduce consumer care costs if your consumers find them useful. You will need to empower consumers to self-serve 99 percent of all their inquiries.*

Work-at-home agents   *Most of RightNow's largest customers are either using work-at-home agents or investigating their use. Work-at-home agents often have lower turnover, deliver higher consumer satisfaction, and may lower operating costs as well. Plan for it. Most of your care agents will probably not be in traditional contact centers.*

Mobile   *Assume 75 percent of your consumers will be contacting you via mobile devices; consider how you will answer questions from online, SMS, IM, chat, or something else not invented yet.*

Proactive care   *Advanced consumer care automation will look at trends and predict when things will go wrong for consumers. Some companies are already experimenting with these predictive technologies. Consequently companies who adopt these methods will be able to solve problems before consumers even realize they have them. Where would you be if your competitors could predict problems with your consumers, but you can't?*

The Product

What makes Greg's Mission 21st Century statement particularly interesting is that his current products are a direct reflection of this exact thinking. He is absolutely right in his look at how communities and self-service are going to affect customer care, and anticipation of the issues is becoming increasingly important. His customer service products released in May 2009 reflect these trends. RightNow has all the traditional features and functions you want in this kind of solution, among them:

▶ **Agent desktop**   This is the most essential part of any call center–based technology solution. It provides the agent with all the contact and case information in addition to the knowledge base info the agent needs to resolve the customer's problems or answer their inquiries. The RightNow desktop provides agent scripting and guided assistance for specific problems.

▶ **Up-sell and cross-sell**   There is a Best Offer engine that provides the agent with the best possible "other products" based on the profile of the customer. Additionally, the agent is able to show the products to the customer through the Co-browse feature, which enables the agent to take temporary control of the customer's browser.

▶ **Feedback**   The customer service solution can gather data from the customer across all service interaction channels—phone, web, e-mail, and chat. You can incorporate surveys for the agents to give through the Feedback by Proxy feature.

▶ **Self-service**   This is self service via web or phone. When a customer logs onto the portal, the agent sees the customer's activity through pop-up screens and can communicate with the customer using the live chat function. But this is also how customers can use self-service to handle their own efforts such as registration or searching a knowledge base. One major benefit is that customer data is captured as they use the self-service portal. The RightNow system is so robust that iRobot, the company that makes that cute little robot vacuum cleaner the Roomba, now has 97 percent of its customers taking care of themselves. This led to a 30 percent reduction in calls to their call centers.

Using those features of RightNow ordinarily makes you successful, if you've done your due diligence and implemented correctly. What makes the user stand out is the focus RightNow is giving to the social customer's world. There are three major components that deserve highlighting:

▶ **Cloud Monitor**   While not unique, Cloud Monitor is innovative, intelligent, and sorely needed in customer service. This is integrated social media monitoring that not only goes out to the crowd conversation and finds the customer service concerns, but uses what they call their SmartSense Emotion Detector to separate the emotional substance from the noise. This is a sentiment analysis tool (see Chapter 19) that can identify and prioritize the unhappy campers to the top of the monitoring results. While it doesn't automate the business rules and workflow to send red flags to selected role players in the company, the dangerous issues are clearly delineated so the agent can take action. The agent gets a choice of what action to take, whether it is creating a service ticket, ignoring the issue, directly calling the customer, or kicking it upstairs if need be. It also provides a dashboard that indicates the search monitoring results and the agent actions associated with each of them. The record stems from the point of origination in the cloud so where the incident comes from is identified. My only beef with this is that they started with monitoring only two sources, Twitter and YouTube, though by the time of publication of this book, they'll have Facebook and multiple other sources. I'd have started with blogs and Facebook too. But that's a tiny beef, given the benefits of this incredible functionality, which you can see in Figure 14-3.

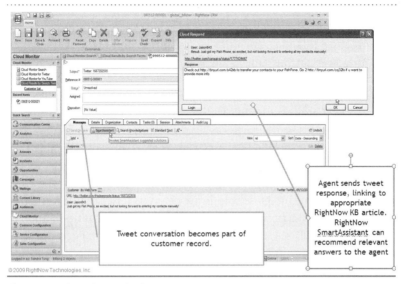

Figure 13-3: The RightNow Cloud Monitor

▶ **Customer communities** The RightNow alliance with Lithium puts RightNow in the forefront of community-driven customer service, which I've already explained.

▶ **Enterprise analytics** RightNow's enterprise analytics, built around an SaaS-based data warehouse, integrates CRM, call switch, telephony, RMA, and order management data and then runs its industrial-strength algorithms. The strong reporting function gives managers and agents a good look at the data in the format they need, from scorecards to performance management data.

These are merely snapshots of RightNow's rather robust offerings. But what is right about RightNow is they've figured out that there is an actual benefit to solving customers' problems, even if those customers morph into something more demanding and more social. They get the picture.

Superstah! Helpstream: Community-Driven Customer Service

I met Tony Nemelka, at the time, CEO of Helpstream (author's note: he has since moved on) and an industry veteran, for breakfast at IHOP in mid 2009, the same IHOP I started the third edition of *CRM at the Speed of Light* with back in 2004. Over a calorie-conscious garden scramble, we talked over outlooks and philosophies. But that's not what they were at the time. They were (and still are) a nearly perfect Social CRM solution—for their niche.

How? They incorporate the social functionality needed to involve the customer community in solving customer service issues and also to monitor and capture the feedback they get from the customers. But to make it truly a Social CRM application, they incorporate analytics, business rules, and workflow to make sure that customer service activity in the community is not only monitored and analyzed (in a left- *and* right-brained—whole-brained—way), but that the responsible company staff members are notified when situations appear. Those situational responses are triggered and then flagged due to a business rule, workflow routes the flagged occurrence to the selected authority, and that person is notified to take action in some way. Perfecto. Besides their well-executed apps, they have a smart strategy. Their plan is for Helpstream to morph from a platform for community-driven customer service to something much bigger. They are going to be filling in the gaps between the community and the traditional pillars of CRM—sales, marketing, and support—this is their vision down the road. They won't have a full CRM suite, but by partnering with companies like Oracle they will be able to provide the glue that welds external customer engagement processes to business operations.

These guys have 150 customers and run communities with their on-demand offerings that total over 250,000 members. Interestingly, they have a number of marketing automation vendors as their clients, including Marketo, Eloqua, and Infusionsoft.

They are what Social CRM *is*.

Mission 21st Century

About halfway through one of the two buttermilk pancakes at that IHOP (with sugar-free syrup), Tony Nemelka outlined the rationale for that transformation of the company as it goes forward into the 21st century.

> *Customer service has focused too long on solving problems instead of engaging and developing relationships with customers. Huge*

investments have been made in systems designed primarily to deflect customers and reduce the costs of resolving problems. But customers don't tolerate that anymore. The Web has provided a venue for customers to vent their experiences and frustrations. Other customers listen and respond, so companies have started listening too. In a word, business has become social.

Social business is not about problems and solutions; it's about people, expertise, and getting value. Companies are wasting incredibly valuable resources in their customers by not empowering them to have a voice or not listening to them when they do; not enabling them to talk to one another; taking too long to solve their problem. They miss a huge opportunity to leverage customer passion for the brand or helping other customers.

For most companies, customers are the most under-utilized asset they have, a terrible waste for company and customer alike. Customers who have already spent money with you are very likely to spend more money with you. Customers have experience using your product and they know what works, what doesn't, what needs to be improved. Customers are a tremendous source of ideas for new products and innovations you might not uncover otherwise. Customers will refer you to other customers if they are happy with you.

Helpstream's mission is to lead a new wave in customer service, one that is focused on engaging and leveraging customers. Helpstream provides social, community-aware business solutions that turn customer service into the most strategic activity in the company. We believe the next-generation of customer service professionals will be focused on helping companies leverage their customers to build community, solve problems, and increase the value customers receive from the company's products and services. Our job is to provide the technology platform to make that task easy and rewarding for everyone involved.

The Product

Helpstream's product remains true to the mission and vision. It integrates social customer service with business rules and workflow to create a tight connection between business operations and the external customer. The feature set reflects a progressive business culture, something that Helpstream itself has and encourages with the evolution of its product lines.

▶ **Integrated self-service portal**   Through the portal, authorized users can browse or search for information, interact in the community, or submit, update, and check the status of a case. End users have permission-based access to the same information available to service representatives.

▶ **Federated search**   This allows users to simultaneously find matching content across all areas, including Q&A threads, discussions, and ideas in the community, FAQs, checklists, and content-rich articles in the knowledge base, open and closed case histories from the service desk, and matching content from external sources.

▶ **Community**   This is Helpstream's true differentiator. As members, customers can ask and answer questions, mark best answers, open discussions, post comments, and maintain a public profile. A user generated content-based feature, Idea Brainstorming enables users to submit improvement suggestions that can be voted and commented on by other users. Electronic subscriptions enable users to receive automatic notifications of new posts in areas of their interest. In all cases, service representatives retain full editorial control and can determine what is published for public and private viewing. ActivityStream enables users to subscribe to other users and follow their stream of activity to see what others are working on in the community.

▶ **Service desk**   This is where your inner quant gets satisfied. Helpstream case management routes, queues, and manages cases for resolution, depending on the SLA. Using customizable workflow, user-definable fields, and rules-based escalation, case assignment can be automated or controlled manually via drag and drop. Agent-assignable wizards can be used to communicate step-by-step procedures to customers, who can switch to agent mode if they get stuck on something in self-service. E-mail integration allows end users to create, update, close, and rate cases via e-mail. The Service Waterfall graphically shows how and who resolves cases (see Figure 13-4).

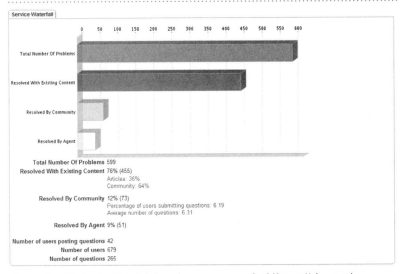

Figure 13-4: The Service Waterfall shows how cases are resolved (Source: Helpstream)

▶ **Knowledge base**   The knowledge base can store and manage any type of file, each with publishing rights, version controls, and usage tracking. It includes authoring tools and permission controls so that useful community posts or case histories can be converted into wiki articles where they can be specifically formatted, tagged for search, and then kept up-to-date by subsequent users.

Not bad, eh? That's Helpstream. They are more than just an alternative. They are what mainstream customer service technology needs to become.

Closing It Out

I've been talking about Natalie Petouhoff from Forrester Research and customer care rock star Frank Eliason of Comcast throughout this chapter. So rather than talk just about them, I set it up so you can talk with them. First we're going to listen to Natalie to see what she has to say about customer service best practices and then we'll hear Frank on the same thing.

MINI-CONVERSATION WITH NATALIE PETOUHOFF

Dr. Natalie Petouhoff, Senior Analyst, Forrester Research

I've known Dr. Nat for several years and am always amazed at her knowledge and articulate expression of that knowledge. She is able to stay ahead of trends in her work at Forrester and was one of the first analysts to see the value of social media and community in customer service. She focuses on the quality of the customer experience and the effect that has on brand equity, revenue, and profits.

Prior to Forrester, she spent years in management consulting and at systems integration firms, including Hitachi Consulting, PricewaterhouseCoopers, and BenchmarkPortal as well as working at GE, GM, and Hughes Electronics. She has been on network television and radio espousing her innovative ideas for customer service and is no slouch at writing, having written articles in many industry publications and co-authored four books, including Reinventing Your Contact Center: A Manager's Guide to Successful Multi-Channel CRM *and* Customer Relationship Management: The Bottom Line to Optimizing Your ROI.

Talking to Your Customers Is Ruining Your Business

Forrester Research surveyed nearly 5,000 consumers. While 45 percent still want to talk to a customer service agent, 55 percent are disillusioned and disappointed—at least enough to take their business elsewhere. Self-service rated worse. And because self-service channel interactions are so dismal at helping customers complete their goal, customers often pick up the phone expecting the agent to make up for the poor self-service experience. Angry customers are generally difficult and lead to agent frustration, stress, and attrition.

To determine why the experiences were so poor, Forrester also surveyed business and IT leaders. Fifty-seven percent of the companies reported that their adoption of customer service best practices was poor/below average. This flies in the face of the fact that Forrester Research also shows companies that provide better consumer experiences are more financially successful. So why don't more executives understand how not adopting customer service best practices is risking their company's bottom line? And what can they do about it?

1. *Get relevant* *Get ready to hang up your company's "going out of business" sign. Forrester predicts that companies that understand the new paradigm—that customer service experiences, expectations, and thus loyalty are the future growth and revenue drivers—may still be in business in ten years. Companies that don't put customers first, won't be. No customers, no business; it's that simple. Executives must drive the* *adoption of customer service best practices as a corporate-wide financial strategy. And these customer service experiences should be part of a broader effort to adopt Experience-Based Differentiation (EBD), which Forrester defines as a systematic approach to interacting with customers that consistently builds loyalty. To make customer service experience initiatives relevant, measure, measure, measure. How to get started?*

2. **Get data** *Tap (or develop) your Voice of the Customer (VoC) program and customer service analytics data to rate actual customer service interactions against best practices. Successful measuring initiatives include: 1) a repeatable process for collecting insights and data, 2) a process for taking the information and making changes to the business, and 3) a champion with executive level power, for instance a chief customer service/ experience officer, to remove roadblocks, provide resources, and budget. Create a business case for change and a customer service improvement plan and schedule. Continuously engage the CEO, COO, CFO, and CIO or CTO in the progress. If the changes are going to stick, these executives will need to lead cultural attitude changes toward people, process, and technology. Otherwise the initiative may be perceived as another "management improvement initiative du jour" and lead to dissension and low employee moral. Worse yet, resources are wasted on an initiative that never reaches the customer.*

3. **Get real** *Get to the root causes of what stresses out agents and customers. Customers get frustrated when they can't complete their goal in one interaction with a company. Obviously, agent performance, which affects the customers, is affected in turn by stress and often the stress leads to agent attrition. Some of the not always obvious factors include ineffective agent-assisted service and self-service technologies, and poorly mapped out company-customer interaction strategies. But it can go further than that and even be part of human capital leadership issues such as:*

▶ *Poorly defined hiring processes*

▶ *Inappropriate job assignments*

▶ *Unclear or confusing performance goals and career paths*

▶ *Poor supervisor-to-agent staffing ratios*

▶ *Poor teaming and leadership capabilities of managers*

▶ *Inconsistent quality monitoring /coaching programs*

▶ *The lack of a formal process to escalate calls to experts*

Conversely, empowered agents can become brand ambassadors. Spend some time and train agents on the impact their attitude has on customers. Show them how one bad experience can cause bad word of mouth and be detrimental to the company's brand—and how poor experiences lead to customers going elsewhere. Agents will begin to understand that without customers, agents won't have a job. Impress on them the value they provide to the company, the brand, and to creating lifetime customers. Then support them with organizational structures, processes, and technology best practices required to create great customer service experiences. Make "once and done" an actuality, not a slogan.

From a customer-centric point of view, providing contact centers with the right people, processes, and technology is critical for great customer experiences and avoiding unnecessary frustration for both agents and customers. And from a company-centric view, adapting customer service best practices (both agent and self-service) will not only increase "first contact resolution," a major driver of customer loyalty and repurchase probability, but also provide the foundation for customer experiences that generate higher revenue and profits.❧

Thanks, Dr. Nat. Frank, it's your turn.

Frank Eliason is an innovator when it comes to customer service. The resulting effect was viral and buzzworthy. But this guy doesn't let it go to his head. As director of Digital Care at Comcast, he is constantly looking for ways to continue the innovations he started. He's not into the glory, but he is into his customers. Comcast (and we) are lucky to have him at the Digital Care helm.

Mini-Conversation with Frank Eliason: Customer Service 3.0

As we all know, customers are talking. This is nothing new, but since the start of customer reviews on place like Amazon, customers have gained a much larger voice. This continues to grow with places like Facebook, Twitter, and many others. Companies have long debated the best approach. At first marketers decided that they wanted to go out and sell to the community. Judging on click-through rates for ads, especially on websites like Facebook, this was not a strong approach. Next up on the hit parade was PR. What was missing from both of these approaches was a two-way dialogue. Customers did not want to be told a position or sold—what they really want is an opportunity to have a conversation. This brings us to Customer Service 3.0. Although I must say calling something 3.0 feels so '90s at this point. It is really the natural progression of customer service.

Customer service done publicly on the Web is no different from how customer service professionals coach how to handle calls, chat, or e-mail. The first step is hiring the right people for the positions. I always have found that passionate people make for the best customer service representatives. You know the type: if you're a manager they are coming to your desk regularly because they disagree with a policy or procedure that has a negative impact for the customer. I know they can be tough to manage, but they are always striving to do what is right and customers love them for it. It is also easier to coach as to why the policy is in place than to coach about when people should have brought concerns to your attention. The next step is to define your goals within the space. Our goals were easy: listen and learn from our customers, and offer assistance when possible. It was really an effort to meet the customer where they already are. Since starting this initiative we have learned a lot. Here are a few things that may help:

1. ***Listen first***   *Do not jump into a space because it is the "hot" trend or the CEO or someone in the organization says we need to be there. First listen and understand the space. Are your customers or prospective customers there? If not, it may not add value. It is also important to understand the dynamic of the space to determine the best approach. For example, we reach out to customers in many spaces on the Web and we take different approaches depending on the space. In forums on the Web, we typically use private messaging instead of posting to the website. This is so we do not interfere with the peer-to-peer relationship. On Twitter, we respond to someone needing assistance with simple words like "Can we help?" This allows the customer to decide if they would like our assistance or not.*

2. ***Personal connection***   *We know on some of the best calls there is a personal connection that develops between the representative and the customer. Sometimes it is the way the representative empathizes with the customer's experience. The same holds true in social media. This is about relationships and connections. This is why the brands most recognized for their work are clear about the person on the account. We strive to humanize in many ways. On Twitter, each of my team members has their own account. We also use our own avatar (pictures representing us). Some on my team use a symbol, while others, like me, use a picture of themselves. On my Twitter page you will see Comcast links, but also links to my personal blog and family website. You can think of it this way: when someone calls, you always provide your name in the introduction, and you should do the same here.*

3. *Keep it real*   In this space, it is important to be as open and honest as possible. If you do not know the answer, you need to say that. Avoid spin on topics and be accepting of all feedback. Another way to keep it real is to add transparency to things that are being worked on. As an example, if you are working on customer statements, let your customers know in social media and ask their feedback. They would love to have a say on what you are working on.

4. *Only sell when appropriate*   Nothing is more frustrating to a customer than when someone strives to sell something and did not even resolve the reason for the call. Also selling for the sake of selling never goes well. We all coach to "earn the right to sell by resolving the reason for the call." Also we teach representatives not to throw something against the wall to see if it sticks. Make sure in social media spaces the same holds true.

An effort to meet your customers where they already are does take planning, knowledge, and the ability to get things done. It is also important to partner with many areas of the organization, including PR and marketing. We actually define the roles for PR and service. PR handles corporate positioning and press-related blogs. My team handles customer-specific related concerns. Social media engagement can be a very rewarding space for companies, but it is important to plan and do it right. People that represent your company need to have access to different parts of the company to resolve concerns in a timely manner and share feedback. As we look through the historical aspect of service, it all started with in-person service and through the years we added in mail, phones, e-mail, and chat. And now the next evolution is the social media frontier.

One last thing. There is one thing that customer service isn't.

Maybe you remember the *Twilight Zone* episode about aliens who come to Earth in peace and start to set up tourism to their planet. The Earthlings who go there send back postcards on how wonderful it is on the aliens' world and how everyone should come visit.

One day, one of the aliens drops a book that those who can translate the alien lingo find out is titled *How to Serve Man*. You'd think that it was a wonderful guide on Earthling treatment and customer service, wouldn't you?

It wasn't. It was a cookbook.

Okay. Let's get cooking, in a much nicer way, and get on to the next chapter.

14

The Difference:
CRM, the Public Sector, and Politics

If we make the assumption that all of us truly do believe that we each should control our own lives to the greatest extent possible, then the idea of a government would seem to be anathema, wouldn't it? But not only isn't it, the idea of no government is much more of a frightening idea than the rule of laws and men are.

Why is that? Because as rational beings, we understand there must be organized sets of rules with people and institutions that facilitate them. It is truly the only way we can support the delicate balance between the freedom to act as you choose and the freedom others have to act as they choose *and* the common good that is necessary for all.

These are not academic commitments. The support for or condemnation of government institutions is something never taken lightly by its citizens. It is something embedded deeply into their psyches, as is their willingness to respond in some way—either through unbroken and faithful involvement in the processes of government and governing, or intermittently, perhaps through voting in elections that have some meaning to that individual. Almost all citizens of any nation see that nation's institutions as something that means something to them—whether for practical purposes such as getting a license or for more altruistic purposes such as participating in a campaign that supports something they believe in passionately.

But these citizens also have expectations of how the institutions of their government will perform. Some of these standards are based on a comparison to history—in the United States many look with reverence on the administration of John F. Kennedy, even though his assassination made his presidency less than a single term. Though I will point to statistical validation for the reverence, much of it is nostalgic and emotional. In retrospect, it was "Camelot" when a young vibrant president with a talent for stirring a population understood the dynamics of the profound social change going on during his term. He spoke to those changes memorably and reached the hearts of the citizens in an era where economic growth was strong and the massive social upheaval had already begun. "The energy, the faith, the devotion which we bring to this endeavor will light our country and all who serve it, and the glow from that fire can truly light the world." He backed up his soaring oratory with policies that actually cohered with the expectations of his constituents—and the government institutions that were under his command responded to the population. There were results. In 1961, multiple polls showed that nearly three-quarters of the American population trusted the institutions of government to do the right thing. Prior to President Obama's accession to the White House, the contemporary polls run by CNN/Time put the number at 32 percent. This isn't a matter of a lack of faith in a sitting president or the desire to believe in an incoming one. This is the institution of day-to-day government—executive, legislative, and administrative. This means bodies that supersede individuals and that outlast any one administrator. It also means governments beyond just the United States.

But how we act as constituents toward government is based on so much more than just the effective utility of the institutions. From the time we are children, even in the casual world we now live in, we are taught the history of our country, the arc of its beliefs, and the purpose of its existence. (I am speaking here of the United States, of course, because that is my experience, so international readers please forgive me.) We are taught to believe, whether we choose to or not, in the idea that we are a nation "conceived in liberty and dedicated to the proposition that all men are created equal." And we are taught to represent those beliefs as beacons for them.

What is implied in everything we learn is that we are all equal in the eyes of both human and divine law and that equality when acted on is a profound manifestation of humanity operating at its best. Philo Judaeus, a Greek philosopher who doubled as the head librarian of the library at Alexandria, said in his work *On the Creation According to Moses*, "each man is a miniature heaven"—something that not only do I truly believe but that is also imbued in the best interactions between government and constituents.

The best interactions are what we have to be concerned about here because the best interactions in *any* government are when its administrative institutions are responsive to the needs of and meet the expectations of its various constituents and, simultaneously, when its political institutions and movements reflect the embedded profound beliefs and ideals of their adherents.

You wonder what Social CRM has to do with this? I'm going to make the same claim I made in the last edition of the book but, as you will see, in a different light. Social CRM, in the case of public service and the public sector, in the domains of government and politics, has the capability to ennoble a population. Its coarser value is to restore the faith of a population in the institutions of the government that serves them.

This isn't a small issue or an aberrant chapter because it goes to the heart of Social CRM executed well. It also is an indication of how much things have changed from 2004 to 2009. Time for us to learn something about what it all means.

From 2004 to Now—Wow, What a Difference

In October 2002, the then Office of Management and Budget's associate director of information and e-government czar, Mark Forman, wrote an article for *Washington Technology* magazine that had a profound effect on the thinking of government institutions. He called for a federal CRM program. "We need industry to be a catalyst," Forman said. "As consumers, citizens have become accustomed to high levels of service that, in the past, government hasn't been able to provide. The president has made it clear that the federal government has to become more focused on better serving its citizens."

There was an influx of private sector companies into public sector CRM after Forman's declaration. A substantial number of government institutions such as the General Services Administration (GSA), the U.S. Postal Service (USPS), the Defense Logistics Agency (DLA), and others brought in consulting companies such as Accenture, SAIC, and Bearing Point; CRM technology companies like Siebel (now Oracle), Oracle, and SAP; and on the SaaS side, RightNow, to improve the transactional and operational capabilities of government agencies. The programs in the aforementioned federal agencies were highly successful at the time. In the case of DLA and USPS, they continue to be successful.

By 2005, there had been some noticeable successes and "bring in the private sector to advise us" became a mantra for the public sector. This mantra continues to be chanted to this day but it's starting to lose its "Ohm." Flash forward to mid-2008.

I'm at the Center for American Progress (CAP), an organization that provides policy direction and initiatives to movements and institutions, primarily progressive ones. The head of CAP, John Podesta, was not only President Clinton's chief of staff, but ran the Obama transition team. I'm on a panel with a number of technology experts representing various both Democratic and Republican political leaders. For example, Justin Hamilton, the deputy chief of staff of George Miller, one of the smartest young people I've met in a while. There were members of the staff of Speaker of the House Nancy Pelosi and Senate Majority Whip Harry Reid, among others. We were speaking to roughly 70 advocacy organization reps on how to effect constituency engagement utilizing social media tools. One of the tech staffers said, "We need to bring the private sector in to help us. They're five years ahead of us."

I jumped in and said, "No! That's wrong. That's a mantra that has outlived its usefulness. The change that's been occurring is social. It's not led by business. They've been caught as flatfooted as you by the demands of their customers who are also your constituents. They know what you know and you could help them as well as or more than they can help you."

Why did I say that? Because there is a new constituent who's nothing like the constituent of even four years ago. Isn't that a familiar refrain throughout this book?

The New Constituent

The new constituent, 2009 version, is not the constituent of 2004. As we saw through the Barack Obama and Ron Paul campaigns particularly, but interspersed throughout all the primary candidates' campaigns, there has been an incredible transformation of demand—the constituents no longer want just institutional efficiencies that provide them with a service level that works, they are looking to engage in the way that they want, using the means they want, and at the time they want, very much like the commercial sector customers. Do you know why constituents and customers are making similar demands of the institutions they are involving in their respective lives?

It's because it's we're not talking about two different groups of people! The constituent and the customer *are the same person*. This is an individual with an expectation of performance and sensitivity by all institutions—whatever and wherever they are. In a commercial environment, that individual acts as a customer in how he or she relates to a business. In an environment dominated by government organizations, this individual acts as a citizen or as part of a constituent agency. The person who spent money on that Starbucks coffee before they visited the Environmental Protection Agency local office to get some issues around hazardous materials dumping taken care of is both the customer and constituent.

Meritalk, an online community of government technology specialists, released a study in mid-2008 that queried 2,000 Gen Yers—in this case born between 1977 and 1990, so the youngest was 18. They found that 88 percent of the respondents would get their news online in the next 12 months, 85 percent wanted the next president (the one who turned out to be President Obama) to reach out online to the public at least once a month, and 74 percent wanted more information online on government programs and spending.

The relationship between the government and its constituents is changing because the relationship among peers is changing and how we communicate and the tools available to us to communicate are changing. The Meritalk survey tells you that the level of demand and expectation of the very people who have been responsible for the movement that made Barack Obama the name he is are demanding a new way of dealing with that change which involves every institution they interact with. This is where Social CRM does come into the public sector.

Because of the way that the change has affected the United States and much of the world, this chapter takes on a deep significance for the entire book. To make it whole, we're going to be doing a few things. First, we'll look at multiple government agencies, because all facets of government have been profoundly affected and the new models outlined in Chapter 4 are particularly appropriate. Second, you're going to meet experts—four to be exact. In alphabetical order:

▶ Frank DiGiammarino, a leading thinker in the realm of using Social CRM for government agencies

▶ Julie Germany, a rising young star in the public sector CRM pantheon because of her commitment to public discourse and constituent engagement

▶ Bob Greenberg, my own wonderful brother, who by the sheer luck of it all is also one of the leading experts in the impact of social tools on government, especially in high-security situations

▶ Alan Rosenblatt, an established thought-leader and writer who will outline how social technologies are affecting political campaigns

Third, you'll hear several stories about a political campaign, and the role that the citizenry and government employees are playing in the transformation of government to a true Social CRM perspective. We'll then head around the globe to see how Singapore made constituent engagement a national imperative over the past several years. Finally, I'll ship you off to an appendix in this book written by my brother, Bob Greenberg, with a discussion of Virtual Alabama and its outgrowth, Virtual USA, and a look at the New Zealand Police Department.

This is exciting stuff, with the potential to be inspiring. At a minimum, there are lessons to be learned by your business—or your agency—or your campaign. So learn away.

Constituent, Not Citizen, Relationship Management

This may be the only time you ever hear me say this, but this is where the meaning of the acronym CRM is actually important. You may be wondering, though I doubt it, why I didn't say "citizen relationship management" here. I say instead "constituent relationship management." If you don't care, skip ahead. If you are at least curious, listen up.

There is a lot more complexity to the public sector than just its relationship to the citizenry. The citizenry-agency relationship is the most important one for the reasons stated above. The purpose of government agencies is to serve the citizens of the nation they represent. But to do that there is a complex chain of relationships that are, in theory, designed to serve that ultimate citizen-to-institution interaction.

For example, the General Services Administration (GSA) is defined by Wikipedia as:

. . . an independent agency of the United States government, established in 1949 to help manage and support the basic functioning of federal agencies. The GSA supplies products and communications for U.S. government offices, provides transportation and office space to federal employees, and develops government-wide cost-minimizing policies, among other management tasks.

The GSA's constituents are both the citizens who directly contact the GSA and the various federal agencies they support. Just limiting their strategy to the citizenry would be a serious error. Luckily they don't. The National Academy of Public Administration (NAPA) exists to define the creation and execution of special initiatives on innovative approaches to government management challenges. They don't deal with the citizens directly. As a result of their inter-agency efforts, they created a collaborative library of federal government Web 2.0 initiatives and case studies for all government institutions to access. This is not for directly interacting with citizens.

You could characterize the GSA and NAPA efforts as G2G, not G2C.

Perry Keating, a long-time CRM industry veteran and public sector expert, and currently managing director for Global Public Sector at Avaya, has this to say about constituent versus citizen:

> Public sector has some unique aspects as it relates to CRM because it must deal with so many different Cs. In addition to the traditional customer or consumer there is also the many different constituents that come into play (voters, media, specific government agency, lawmakers, etc.).
>
> If we just focus on the different constituents, what becomes interesting is that each wants very different things from their relationship with the public sector.
>
> ▶ Some want information about the individual public sector servant (how did you vote on certain issues).
>
> ▶ Some want information about the public sector function itself (where is the nearest IRS office to my house).
>
> ▶ While others want to be able to actually perform a transaction with that public sector function (renew my license plate decals or file my taxes).
>
> Because of this need to serve so many Cs in so many ways, in some cases public sector has done more with CRM and the Internet than many of their commercial counterparts.
>
> ▶ If you look at many commercial company websites there are some basic functions: the leadership of the company and its locations, some information about its product or services, and in some cases the ability to acquire some of its product or services.

▶ *If you look at many public sector websites, there is a vast array of information about the leadership and that agency's functions as well as connections to a tremendous amount of information about that agency's functions and the ability to perform virtually any transaction or inquiry with that particular public sector entity.*

If we look at the latest social networking tools (Facebook, Twitter, LinkedIn, etc.) again public sector is pushing the use of this technology faster than its commercial counterparts.

▶ *In some commercial companies the use of these social networking tools is limited or nonexistent. In fact, in some cases employees are prohibited from using such tools.*

▶ *In the public sector, many are viewing this as another effective set of tools to interact with the many Cs.*

Because of the complex matrix of government agency to government agency to citizen at federal, state, and local levels, and between branches of government too, calling CRM citizen relationship management is severely limiting. So do me a favor, and don't. Constituent relationship management works.

In Re: Engagement by the Administration

The salient point to remember about the administration of government is that it actually has to be administrated. The administration of government often can conflict with the requirements of the citizens that the institutions service. The expectations of those citizens were heightened significantly by the Obama campaign because of the successful use of digital communities and community organizing principles.

The Obama campaign's use of innovative approaches was crafted to get partisans engaged (see below) in donating, volunteering, or building events that would drive the campaign's visibility and success. That was marketing. It was "What can we do for Obama?" Now, as the administration, "it" goes from marketing to customer service—meaning, "What can the Obama administration do for us?" A very different issue demanding a very different set of processes, methodologies, and strategies, though some of the same technologies can be applied.

The Obama transition team was acutely aware of this. On top of citizenry's elevated expectations of receptive constituent services, there was the continued issue of dealing with a government that was saddled by an antiquated approach to these same highly charged, newly empowered groups of constituents.

Consequently, in late December 2008, the Obama transition team announced the formation of TIGR—the Technology, Innovation and Government Reform Working Policy Group. The group consisted of industry veterans from Google and Microsoft among others and technology leaders like Aneesh Chopra, CIO of the state of Virginia, now the CTO of the United States, and new federal CIO Vivek Kundra, then the CTO of Washington, D.C. Kundra, in a video released on the website Change.gov., succinctly identified not only the problems inherited from past administrations, but the core of the technology transformation they were tasked to lead:

Process has trumped outcome. And the biggest reason for that is that everyone is focused on compliance, no one is thinking about innovation and how to drive change in government.

Kundra went to the heart of the difficulties that government institutions have had for decades. It's why you hear the word "bureaucracy" thrown around in conversations about the U.S. government. It's why you hear "nonresponsive" in the same conversations—often as the companion adjective for bureaucracy. This is no small problem because the mandate for the current U.S. government is defined by transparency, collaboration, and innovation—the opposite of the mindset of many government agencies.

For example, the Government Accountability Office (GAO) noted in testimony in September 2008 that "While some progress has been made in recent years, agencies still, all too often, lack the basic management capabilities needed to address current and emerging demands. As a result, any new administration will face challenges in implementing its policy and program agendas because of shortcomings in agencies' management capabilities."

This is particularly relevant to the IT budgets and projects of the federal government that will be a cornerstone of the new engagement strategies. If the technology backbone can't be updated, changed, and upgraded, then the ability of constituents to actually reach the agencies or elected representatives will be severely constrained. That would be a big problem—a really big problem.

That big problem translates to big dollars. According to the Industry Advisory Council (IAC) Transition Study Group's 2008 report,

"Returning Innovation to the Federal Government with Information Technology," "There are nearly 500 major IT programs on the list of high-risk projects, each averaging more than $30 million. . . . Eighty-five percent of these projects are at risk of failing because of poor planning, according to OMB and GAO." By the way, do the math and you come up with $15 billion worth of high-risk IT projects.

The management problems aren't only related to bad management style. They're indicative of the entrenched mindset that Kundra alluded to. Kundra's correlation of processes to compliance and ingrained thinking is important, though it isn't a dig at processes.

Processes can be invaluable for improved efficiency, cost reduction, and increased effectiveness if they are done well (see Chapter 16). But "done well" means that the processes make the work of the employees who use them easier to meet the needs of customers/constituents when interacting with those constituents. Their success is not the purpose of the federal government. Significant positives outcomes are the purpose.

Though nascent, we are seeing many programs spanning an enormous range of government agencies that are providing greater avenues for those significant outcomes, meaning successful constituent inputs with results. For example, the Air Force, not exactly what you'd think of as a bastion of progressive change, created the Air Force Knowledge Now community in 2002. There are now 294,000 registered members including (as of April 2009) every single colonel and 80 percent of the AF master sergeants. Notably, most of them are *not* Gen Y.

More germane to the credo of participatory democracy put forth by the Obama administration was an outreach site put up by the transition team called "The Citizen Briefing Book." The idea of the site was to get the input of the citizenry on what issues they wanted the Obama administration to concern itself with. The site went up January 12, 2009, and was closed on inauguration day, so it had about a one-week shelf life. A citizen could present, vote, or comment on a single idea or as many as they cared to. The site was created using salesforce.com's Ideaforce platform, one of the smartest pieces of their "platform as a service" (PaaS) offering they've developed to date. It wasn't unlike other saleforce.com-generated sites such as MyStarbucksidea.com or Dell's IdeaStorm. The 10 most popular ideas, based on inputs from the site visitors, would be presented directly to President Obama during his first day in office. On January 21, 2009, President Obama received the list and the supporting materials.

The response to the Citizen Briefing Book was excellent. According to Michael Strautmanis, director of public liaison and intergovernmental affairs for the transition, over 70,000 people participated, there were tens of thousands of ideas, and over a half million votes.

The Citizen Briefing Book is representative of the desire, intent in the early stages of a Social C(onstituent)RM 2.0 strategy, that is designed to encourage participation and provide transparency—a contradistinction to compliance as a strategy. The ultimate broad benefit for the government in making this transformation is the restoration of belief in government institutions that has been missing for so many decades.

Think that's pie in the sky? That the Obama administration is too early on to really have this constituent engagement thing down? That there is no definitive proof that it works beyond gross numbers of hits or page views or questions asked? Think that I'd do well at fantasy baseball, since I'm clearly good at fantasizing? Let's take a look then, oh doubters, at the government of Singapore, which has been doing this for several years. They have the hard numbers to support exactly what I'm saying above about trust in the institutions of government. But first, the story.

The Case of Singapore: Social CRM in Action

The impact of President Obama's election campaign on the world fabric was profound, because it broke new ground in how social tools and constituent engagement strategies are applied. But applying it to administrative efforts through federal (and let's not forget state and local) agencies is very different than how it's used in a campaign. The campaign was marketing, so to speak, and the use of constituent engagement strategies and tools is customer service—also so to speak. It's easy to want to make the linear transition, but it's not a linear transition.

The transition to constituent engagement built around either a customer service model or a contemporary collaborative version of what's called the public-private partnership is a lot more strenuous and actually a lot harder because its purpose is a continuous engagement of a diverse set of constituencies at the individual level that does not have an election day end date. The social constituent doesn't just want transparency—which allows them to make more intelligent decisions on how they are going to engage with an institution—they want to actually engage with that institution. This is not the human partici-pant of even five years ago. They expect that transparency, honesty, and the means to engage will be made available from *every single insti-tution* they potentially interact with.

This is no mean feat when it comes to the government. To put it bluntly, no one trusts the government—at least in the U.S.—to do what it's expected to. In fact, the Edelman Trust Barometer 2008 points out that trust in government institutions across the 18-country board is at 39 percent—a pathetic level of trust. The numbers are staggering: United States at 39 percent; Europe at 29 to 37 (except Sweden and the Netherlands at 63 percent); Asia (India, Japan, South Korea) at 40 to 49 percent. China is an anomalous 79 percent. In other words, in 15 of 18 countries trust in government ranges from 29 to 49 percent.

The remedy is already on the table. Oddly, a government that gets somewhat maligned in the U.S. from time to time is easily the most responsive in the world. It's a place I've visited several times and writ-ten about on occasion: Singapore. I am not alone in these findings. As I'll show you in a bit, Accenture published a study in early 2009 that verifies my claims.

We begin in 2005.

2005

In August 2005, Singapore Prime Minister Lee Hsien Loong delivered what was a landmark speech in which he declared a "National Service Excellence Initiative" that would create a service environment along the lines of the Ritz-Carlton—"ladies and gentlemen serving ladies and gentlemen." What made this ground-breaking was that this was the first time (at least that I could find) that a government stood entirely behind an initiative that was based on creating an extraordi-nary customer experience that extended from every employee of gov-ernment or business to the employers to the individuals who touched the shores. Some of it was to encourage international investment in this tiny city-state, but for the most part it was to provide the kind of experience for its citizens that would make them loyal to the institu-tions that ran the country. It started with the retail industry but extended far beyond that.

I experienced this firsthand when I landed at the Singapore airport a month after the declaration of the initiative and they had someone who greeted me and took me through customs without a hitch. A few days later when I had neglected to get an issue of the *Singapore Business Times* that carried an interview with me and couldn't find it the next day anywhere, my hotel—a five-star called the Sheraton Towers Singapore—made an unsolicited effort to get me the paper by sending someone to the offices of the *Singapore Business Times* and delivering it to me in my room on a Saturday. The stuff legends are made of—and a direct result of the National Service Excellence Initiative.

2007

But Singapore didn't stop at just creating a high-caliber service environment. They have actually created feedback programs that would be classified by Trendwatching.com (sister site to Springwise) if they had "in-between" grades, something like Feedback 2.5.

About Feedback 2.0 (which is now being superseded by Feedback 3.0) according to Springwise:

. . . about these rants—and some raves—having gone "mass" (no, make that MASS!). The long-predicted conversation is finally taking place, albeit amongst consumers and not, as intended, between corporations and consumers. Companies have started to take note, but to a large degree still choose to listen, not talk back, trying to "learn" from the for-all-to-see review revolution. Which is surprising, to say the least, since a quick and honest reply or solution can defuse even the most damaging complaint.

Now look at the definition of Feedback 3.0:

Feedback 3.0 (which is building as we speak) will be all about companies joining the conversation, if only to get their side of the story in front of the mass audience that now scans reviews. Expect smart companies to be increasingly able (and to increasingly demand) to post their apologies and solutions, preferably directly alongside reviews from unhappy customers. Expect the same for candid rebuttals by companies who feel (and can prove) that a particular review is unfair or inaccurate, and want to share their side of the story.

Singapore probably falls somewhere in between that, around 2.5—as a country! Whoa! They actually have an annual National Feedback Day, which is designed to capture feedback from interested citizens so that they can input government policy and budgets. In 2007, I attended National Feedback Day with about 6,000 Singaporean citizens and watched with astounded fascination the mostly intelligent and passionate discussions on varying government reports with proposals in different areas such as housing, transportation, and education. Citizens flocked to general and proposal-specific sessions to discuss their thinking on the different proposals and present their counterproposals or support for the existing recommendations. The actual committees that wrote the report were on stage and available to be grilled. The back and forth about housing or education policy based on the proposal was amazingly detailed. Each committee had a scrivener who took notes on the citizens' comments.

If you couldn't attend, they had all of the reports available online and you could provide them with feedback there. All the in-person and online feedback was aggregated and then incorporated into the revisions discussion. Recommendations were made and policies changed accordingly. But it didn't stop there.

2008

While national feedback efforts were embedded into the political, governmental, and social fabric of Singapore, they remained on top of the transformation going on in communications too. So, in mid-June 2007, at the Arts House New Media Forum, Dr. Lee Boon Yang, minister for information, communications and the arts, gave a really amazing speech that showed the level of Singapore's commitment to contemporary communication. In the course of his wide-ranging discussion on the importance and potential dangers of "interactive digital media (IDM)" as he styled it, he announced a number of initiatives through the Media Development Authority and other agencies of the Singaporean government as part of the IN2015 program. Perhaps the largest and most significant was the S$500 million investment in IDM through the universities in conjunction with a review of the Media21 framework that would incorporate significant changes to include IDM for making Singapore a state-of-the-art media city-state.

By June 2008, this investment paid off, with the announcement that 82.5 percent of Singaporean households now had broadband, though their objective was 100 percent. In conjunction with that saturation point, the Infocomm Development Authority (IDA) and the Media Development Authority (MDA) began a series of initiatives to institutionalize an effort to create a truly digital engagement capacity and business model. These included making Singapore—the entire country—a hub to "manage distribute and trade digital media assets such as movies, video programmes, music, and mobile content" (this latter one is *really important*) through the creation of a "national authentication framework" for access to next generation services— meaning all those social media and social networking initiatives that we spend so much time riffing on. Phase 1 was a six-month $20 million Singapore investment that ended December 31, 2008.

For National Day Rally 2008, they decided that because feedback is so critical, they would conduct a feedback exercise that comprised "SMS, online polls, discussion forums, and blogs. We have also recently added Facebook as a new channel to solicit feedback from Singaporeans."

The ROI (If You Continue to Use that Archaic Measure)

In early 2009, Accenture put out its "2008 Leadership in Customer Service: Creating Shared Responsibility for Better Outcomes," a report that makes up in substance what it lacks in title mojo. This is one that they've annually done and, despite its abstraction of a title, looks at what best practices can be extracted from public sector institutions. This year, the four best practices are:

"Better service starts with better understanding."

"Engage. Listen. Respond."

"Harness all available resources."

"Be transparent. Be accountable. Ask for and act on feedback."

All in all, the report is well worth reading, which is saying a lot for me, given my historic (though softening) antipathy toward Accenture. Despite that, this is really good work. You can get it at http://newsroom .accenture.com/article_display.cfm?article_id=4783. Take a look at Singapore's resultant ROI by comparison to other nations who did well:

Accenture's Question	Result (Positive Responses)
How good do you think your government is at delivering a better quality of life for you and your family?	1: Singapore (59 percent) 2: Ireland (55 percent)
How good or bad is the government at providing equal access?	1: Singapore (67 percent) 2: Ireland, Australia (56 percent)
How good or bad is the government at targeting resources?	1: Singapore (59 percent) 2: Malaysia (48 percent)
How good or bad is the government at tailoring services?	1: Singapore (51 percent) 2: Canada (45 percent)

Accenture's Question	Result (Positive Responses)
How good or bad do you think your government is at seeking the opinions of its citizens?	1: Singapore (50 percent) 2: Ireland (45 percent)
How effective or not do you think the different government departments and services are at working together to meet the needs of citizens?	1: Singapore (69 percent) 2: Ireland (60 percent)
How effective do you think the government is at working with non-government organizations, such as businesses and voluntary/non-profit organizations, to improve the quality of your life?	1: Malaysia (61 percent) 2: Singapore (56 percent)
Overall trust in government to improve quality of life (worked on a mean score)	1: Singapore (3.5) 2: Malaysia (3.2)
Source: Aggregated from Accenture's "2008 Leadership in Customer Service Report"	

What is completely noticeable is that in all but one area *the government of Singapore comes in first in the world* when it comes to constituents who trust them to be transparent, provide a quality of life that is personally valuable to individual constituents, do the right thing, and at the same time, continuously engage their citizenry.

A meaningful ROI.

The core of Social CRM has always been engagement, whether the engaged individual is in the shoes of the customer, the constituent, or the game player—whatever role they play in and with the institution they are interacting with. Follow the right path around practices and strategy, implement the right programs, support it with money, listen to the changes that your constituents ask for, act on the ones that you are able to. That will net you a contented and involved citizenry—which is what it's all about, ain't it?

This is not a lesson lost even on long-standing government success stories. If you read the third edition of this book, I touted the GSA's FirstGov.gov as a paradigm for personalization when it came to specific constituencies. That was back in 2004. But Bev Godwin, director of USA.gov, and Casey Coleman, CIO of the GSA, recognized that what was good for 2004 wasn't necessarily good for 2008 or 2009. So they added blogs, RSS feeds, e-mail alerts, social bookmarking, and a presence on Facebook and YouTube so that they could improve content delivery. Rather than let a good program stultify, they understood the new demands of constituents and responded.

These efforts can be generalized to all public sector agencies. In order to draw the lessons from efforts like those of FirstGov.gov and USA .gov, I'd like to initiate my first mini-conversation of the chapter with Frank DiGiammarino, who will provide guidelines to consider when using tools for collaboration and engagement in the public sector.

Take heed.

MINI-CONVERSATION WITH FRANK DIGIAMMARINO

Frank DiGiammarino is currently the Deputy Coordinator for Recovery Implementation at Executive Office of the President, having handed over his position recently as the vice president of strategic initiatives of the National Academy of Public Administration (NAPA) after the inauguration of Barack Obama. When he was at NAPA, his mission was to find contemporary approaches to government management. He did it so well he was named one of the 2009 Federal Computer Week Federal 100—an elite group of innovators and leaders in the federal government who are paving the path to new ways of dealing with citizens and agencies.

This man truly gets it and knows how to spread the gospel too.

The rise of Web 2.0 and emerging technologies is transforming the way we all work, socialize, and create. This new era is defined by the value it places on transparency, diverse thought, and the knowledge that "the smartest guy in the room" can't beat the wisdom of the crowd. These trends are both exhilarating and scary, particularly because they are not questions of "if," but of how, and how fast, to take advantage of this unique—and inevitable—opportunity.

The National Academy of Public Administration sees strong evidence that leaders are harnessing collaboration to drive proactive change at all levels of government. The Collaboration Project, an independent forum founded by the National Academy, has already compiled more than 40 cases of government leaders using these tools to bring about fundamental changes in how government works. Examining these cases and talking with these leaders offers a few clear lessons.

1. This Isn't a "Field of Dreams"

Today, many public leaders see blogs, wikis, and other collaborative platforms, and feel immense pressure to do . . . something. But it is still fundamentally true that people only show up when you give them a reason. Simply deploying collaborative technologies doesn't mean that people will use them.

There are three key success factors that make a collaborative platform or tool an attractive proposition to potential users: It must solve a clear problem, target a specific audience, and provide a real value exchange. Lacking any of these three is usually the difference between experimentation with "cool" technology, and collaboration that truly adds value.

2. Do What's Right

Mass collaboration isn't a panacea, but it does give leaders an opportunity to bring data and people together in new ways. Today's most effective leaders are focused not on how they can solve a problem, but on who to pull into the problem-solving process. Leaders like Molly O'Neil at the Environment Protection Agency and Kip Hawley at the Transportation Security Agency effectively deployed collaboration in their agencies by realizing that bringing a wider array of stakeholders into the process wasn't just a neat idea; it was also the right thing to do. The technology simply enabled tapping everyone from employees to stakeholder groups to the citizenry to change the game and get results.

3. Embrace the Opportunity

Increasingly, it seems like the only thing easier than finding a reason to deploy collaborative technology is finding a reason not to. In an era that demands massive change we consistently call on our "inner lawyer" to slow innovation and empower the status quo.

The very attributes that make collaboration a powerful catalyst for change—low cost and complexity, widespread availability of data—also make it easy for normal citizens to bring about extraordinary change. This is a paradox of collaboration: Any technology that allows government to "go around" its normal bureaucratic constraints also has the potential to let citizens "go around" government itself. Inaction by government, in the face of a desire for change, contributes to public disenchantment with the formal mechanisms of public governance. Government must understand that mass collaboration represents not just an exciting opportunity to engage citizens, but also a responsibility to draw the public into the process and ensure that public deliberation is fueled by accurate data and realistic expectations about what government can and cannot achieve.✎

Politics No Longer Poker—Bluffing Don't Woik

Government administration is not the only place that the "new constituencies" have been active nor is it the sole domain that needs to respond in new ways. The same goes for elected officials and the executive branch of the government. The Obama campaign is a good starting point.

The Obama campaign was brilliant. It appreciated that people were communicating in new ways and that those same people were involved in his campaign because they were fulfilling self-interested agendas—not following him in a cult-like way (though there was some of that too). In fact, the only real slip-up of the campaign (which luckily had little ultimate impact) was when the Obama camp changed the rewards system (the "loyalty program") from volunteers acquiring individual points (e.g., 4,571 points) to volunteers achieving a certain rank (e.g., 0–10). That removed the individual accomplishment each volunteer had. For example, if you were the number 1 volunteer and had 5,000 points, that was better than the number 7 volunteer with 4,194 points, don't you think? But if you had 5,000 points and got a 10 ranking score and 4,194 points also earned you a 10, what's the benefit to you? The points didn't get the volunteers "stuff," but it did get them reputation, influence, and validation—three things high on the customer experience value chart. The idea of being high in the standings as numero uno volunteer among all volunteers is far more self-satisfying than just being one of a gazillion hard-working 10s (unless you're Bo Derek). As the number 1 volunteer said when the point system was eliminated, "They can't do that. It's my points!" Which is precisely the, ahem, point. The participation of the individuals in a political campaign is a result of their personal interest in doing so and because it satisfies an aspect of their personal agenda.

But through the use of social media and the idea that community organizing principles could be applied to the cyberworld in conjunction with technology, they carried out the most effective campaign in the history of at least American, if not global, politics. The results were staggering. Let me overwhelm you with numbers. There were more than 2 million profiles created on MyBarackObama.com. There were 35,000 volunteer groups created. There were 200,000 real-world events planned and carried out. Over 400,000 blog entries were posted. $30 million of the campaign's funds were raised by 70,000 micro-bundlers—individuals who had their own fundraising pages.

I don't want to dwell on the campaign, since many have written well about it. There are a number of great articles and several books on how President Obama's crew pulled this off. Many of them cover its applicability to business. For how the Obama campaign worked their magic,

I recommend two articles. First, check out this *Wired* magazine blog October 2008 posting by Sarah Lai Stirland, called "Obama's Secret Weapons: Internet, Databases and Psychology" (http://blog.wired .com/27bstroke6/2008/10/obamas-secret-w.html). Then check out "Barack Obama: How Content Management and Web 2.0 Won the White House" on the AIIM website (www.aiim.org/Infonomics/ Obama-How-Web2.0-Helped-Win-Whitehouse.aspx). For a more substantial look and the applicability of the campaign to business, go buy Brent Leary and David Bullock's book, *Barack 2.0: Barack Obama's Social Media Lessons for Business* (www.lulu.com/content/5508095). All are well worth reading for more on the campaign.

But campaigns end. The winners of those campaigns have to govern, they have to involve their constituents. That means that not only do they have to respond quickly, but they have to know something about those constituents to provide an effective response. Elected officials can respond the way many of them do, with a cynical outlook that I can only call "constituent avoidance," or they can respond by using CRM-related methods and techniques. This isn't a partisan thing either. There are Democrats and Republicans out there who are engaging their constituents via Twitter and . . . know what? I'm going to let this conversation continue with Julie Germany while I go take care of a different chapter for a few minutes. Julie is going to give you some real insight into how elected officials are using new means to communicate with their voters and what happens when they don't.

MINI-CONVERSATION WITH JULIE GERMANY

Julie Germany is one of the up-and-coming movers and shakers in the new Washington, D.C., landscape. She is the director of the George Washington University think-tank the Institute for Politics Democracy and the Internet (IPDI), an organization devoted to contemporary communications policy, especially around constituent engagement. She drives the annual Politics Online conference, which is the place to be if you want to deal with all issues of digital politics pre-campaign, during the campaign, and during the term of office. She's a sharp one.

The stage is yours, Julie.

Constituent Relationship Management by the Numbers

Elected officials at all levels (federal, state, and local) lose the opportunity to engage constituents positively when they handle constituent communications poorly—such as not answering constituent e-mails, handling constituent requests in a disorganized way, sending form letter responses by e-mail or snail mail, or delaying a response by weeks or even months. If you are interested in engaging constituents as an elected official or political staffer, here are a few things to keep in mind.

First, look at the numbers:

▶ *Americans are turning to the Internet as a first source for political information and communications. A June 2008 report by Pew Internet and American Life found that almost half (46 percent) of Americans use the Internet to receive political news and information.[1] And more Americans than ever are engaging in politics and political debate through online tools like e-mail, web video, blogs, social networking applications, and instant messaging. As more Americans use the Internet to communicate about politics, they begin to expect that same kind of experience when they communicate online with elected officials.*

▶ *Americans who communicate with their elected officials, particularly through electronic means, tend to have a multiplier effect in their communities. According to two studies released by the Institute for Politics, Democracy, and the Internet, "Poli-fluentials: The New Political King-makers" (2007) and "Political Influentials Online in the 2004 Campaign" (2004), people who take political actions online, such as sending e-mail to their elected officials, tend to be what people in the marketing world call "word-of-mouth opinion leaders." According to the research presented in "Poli-fluentials: The New Political Kingmakers," 63 percent of the people surveyed in this influential population sent a prewritten e-mail to an elected official.[2] When they have a good (or bad) experience they share it with their friends.*

▶ *Americans are becoming dissatisfied with the kinds of responses they receive when they contact their elected officials. According to a 2008 report by the Congressional Management Foundation called "Communicating with Congress: How the Internet Has Changed Citizen Engagement," almost half (46 percent) of those of who contact Congress are dissatisfied with the response. More than half (64 percent) said the response did not address their concerns and that the response was too*

---

[1] Aaron Smith and Lee Rainie, "The Internet and the Election," Pew Internet and American Life Project, June 15, 2008.

[2] Carol Darr, editor, "Poli-fluentials: The New Political Kingmakers, Institute for Politics, Democracy and the Internet," October 2007.

politically biased.[3] When you combine this level of dissatisfaction with the multiplier effect that many of these people exert in their communities, then that dissatisfaction can spread.

Second, evaluate your philosophy towards constituent communications.

▶ *Make responsiveness to constituent requests and e-mails a core value in your office or organization.*

▶ *Build an environment that encourages constituent interaction, rather than inhibiting it.*

▶ *Learn about your constituents—figure out the* why *behind their inquiries, not just the* what.

Third, find the right tools, tactics, and practices to help you act on your constituent communications philosophy in an effective, efficient way. This includes:

▶ ***A data plan*** *How will you collect and store constituent communications and data? A data plan can help your office determine what CRM tools and applications will fit best into your strategic plan.*

▶ ***An actionable database*** *Find a database or CRM solution that will function as the CRM backbone of your office. The ideal database will receive and store all communications (both electronic and offline), help you create and send outgoing communications, store constituent data, and manage casework.*

▶ ***Proactive online communications tools*** *Many elected officials, such as Congressman Tim Ryan and Congressman John Culberson, go beyond just sending e-mail communications to reach their constituents. They incorporate social media tools, such as micro-blogging on sites like Twitter, and multimedia tools, such as web video, to communicate in real time with their constituents about the issues they are working on and the bills they support.*◄

Concepts, processes, activities, plans, and strategies need support. Technology is perhaps the most significant part of that support—as much in the public sector as the private sector. There are thousands of companies large and small providing a complicated soup of services

---

[3] Kathy Goldschmidt and Leslie Ochreiter, "Communicating with Congress: How the Internet Has Changed Citizen Engagement," Congressional Management Foundation, June 2008.

and products to the federal, state, and local governments out there—even just in the world of CRM. Some stand out. Not all of them are highlighted here. Others I could have included are Oracle, SAP, Right-Now, IBM, and Aplicor when it comes to CRM-related services. But there are three in particular I want to talk about because of their innovative approaches and because of the diverse uses of their offerings. One in particular, Blue State Digital, is the choice for Superstah! in this chapter. You'll see why.

The Technology Champs

I've always said that technology isn't a driver, but an enabler when it comes to CRM and the strategies associated with it. The public sector is one place where it comes as close to being a driver as is possible. Technology never gets to driver status—not even designated driver, but it plays a huge role in the transformation that's going on right now.

There are many companies that are involved in CRM when it comes to the public sector. Companies like salesforce.com, Oracle, SAP, Aplicor, and RightNow have been involved in the public sector for many years at state, federal, and local levels. For example, RightNow has more than 135 federal agencies as clients including USA.gov, GSA, Social Security Administration, U.S. Postal Service, U.S. Census Bureau, Health and Humans Services, EPA, USDA, HUD, and a host of other three-letter institutions. In fact, as of 2008, the public sector was responsible for 20 percent of all of RightNow's revenues.

But there's also a new posse in town—in fact, a new sheriff. Companies like Blue State Digital (BSD), which has had a meteoric rise from 2004 when they were the company responsible for Howard Dean's Internet backbone on through 2008 and beyond because of their technology architecture for the incredibly successful efforts of the Obama campaign through MyBarackObama.com. Companies like BSD are beginning to incorporate the social technologies that are being used in the Social CRM constituent interaction strategies that seem to win things these days.

Not only that, the general trend toward technology integration is reaching into this same realm. Companies with CRM products are now developing the application programming interfaces (APIs) or using middleware like Websphere to integrate with social applications. In the public sector, the first integration well done is Microsoft and Neighborhood America's joint effort.

Integrating Social with CRM: Microsoft Dynamics CRM and Neighborhood America ELAvate

One of the paradigmatic and, also, puzzling issues of a Social CRM technology plan is, how do you develop a solution that combines the more traditional CRM applications that are geared toward operations and transactions and the social applications that are built more for external customer/constituent participation and engagement—meaning involving interactions? They aren't necessarily on the same platform, nor are they necessarily an obviously workable combination.

On the one hand, you're dealing with activities that are primarily data- or process-driven. They are centered in a corporate environment and their purpose is more about improving efficiencies and effectiveness than anything else. That would be traditional CRM activities in case you're either a newbie or tired—that's sleepy tired or tired of this book.

In the public sector, it gets even more complicated due to the existence of multiple legacy systems, which can get in the way of even the most comprehensive software and services solutions. The standards for those software and services solutions have changed over the years, too. Traditional mainframe architectures are now being replaced by service-oriented architectures and web services–based messaging. That means revamping much of the information technology that exists at many federal agencies, which still have to handle terabytes and maybe even petabytes of information quickly and effectively because real-time response is what the constituent is expecting.

So the subject of integration in the public sector is complex. The results move a lot slower than many companies or individuals want, but one of our public sector tech rock stars is a two-man band that uses service-oriented architecture and their own products to provide something that is the first CRM and social network platform integration in the public sector. Note, I didn't say the first platform to use CRM and social tools. I said integration.

That would be Microsoft and Neighborhood America, whom you were introduced to in Chapter 9. In March 2009, at the 2009 Microsoft Convergence conference, they released the integration between Microsoft Dynamics CRM for the Public Sector and the Neighborhood America ELAvate platform (again, see Chapter 9).

Amir Capiles, the public sector industry manager for Microsoft Business Solutions, and a key player in making this happen—besides being a really nice guy—had this to say about it:

While the technological foundation of this integration is based on MS CRM, the potentially transformational element of our approach lies in the fusion of MS CRM with the social networking community. Its first result, the Idea Bank Community, enables pretty much all constituents who want to share ideas, provide feedback, and propose new solutions to become part of a public sector–driven community while being linked to a myriad of social networking sites. This is empowering. It combines technology and social networking community engagement to realize a level of transparency, communication, and collaboration that gives a forum to the ideas of the citizens it serves.

Figure 14-1 provides a view of its technology services. Two things are notable. First, the ability of the citizen to use a single ID to access all the different services provided by the different agencies in different states or cities (or nationally) that use the system. Second, the ability to track the interactions between the citizens and the agencies.

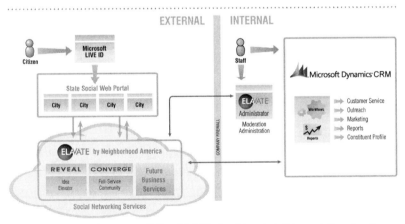

Figure 14-1: Microsoft Dynamics CRM and Neighborhood America's ELAvate platform together at last

The first actual instance of this integration was announced in March 2009 with the release of the Public Sector Idea Bank (www.publicsectorondemand.com). The idea was a community that would be a collaborative site for Microsoft Public Sector and its partners to interact so that they could improve the overall offerings to the public sector. While this is by no means a realization of the potential of this integrated platform, it is a useful first effort. One feature I want to point out is on the right in Figure 14-2. Latest Community Ideas is a place where there is discussion of public service–based events and the community scores them for their value and importance. The best ideas, like commercial sites that are using UGC-like rankings or ratings, bubble to the top.

Figure 14-2: The first results of the integration: the Idea Bank Community

All in all, this is an important step toward a public sector version of Social CRM. I expect there will be others, but Microsoft and Neighborhood America are first to the table with this and because of that are one of the technology champs in the Social CRM world.

Salesforce.com

Salesforce.com uncharacteristically has had very few big marketing moments when it comes to government business. Probably their biggest splash was the Citizen Briefing Book discussed earlier in the chapter. But that doesn't mean they aren't involved in either the government or with elections. They have an active presence in the cutting edge of government both from SaaS and social strategies.

Kaveh Vessali, vice president of public sector for salesforce.com, told me their strategy:

> For us, cloud computing as a delivery model enables connection and communication in ways that other delivery models can't. While it's okay to use the Web as a technology for efficiency, that isn't what it's about. It isn't about the software either. It's about the locations that exist because of the Internet.

What this leads to is a public sector technology model that is based on three "layers." The top layer is the outreach services. The second layer is the business processes that are needed to succeed with the outreach. The third layer, according to Kaveh, is the infrastructure, technology, communities, and the interactions among the agencies regardless of the level of the institutions.

Salesforce.com attempts to unify all three layers. They also have a wide range of services that they can cover because of the flexibility of their Force.com platform and the maturity of their CRM platform and the innovative uses of their technology as we see below.

Campaignforce

Campaignforce is a product of the fertile minds at salesforce.com. I came across it at a salesforce.com launch of something else I went to in San Francisco in 2007 that has a back story that I'll tell you if you ask (it involves wine). I was impressed and I saw its power both because it was something that you could quickly get up and running and because someone had put the kind of thought into it that made it more than a mere port of its salesforce automation application. Plus it had some very cool mash-ups using the always popular Google maps.

What it does is what campaigns have to do. It manages the volunteers and the donors for a given campaign. It provides visibility to budgets and their use, it organizes and tracks the donors by issues they are interested in or by geographical location (thus the use of Google maps). It can pull in data from national polls and compare results to the other candidates.

Probably the most important single feature is who it synchronizes with and how. It will actually synchronize via NetFile (in the states that NetFile is available) with the Federal Election Commission (FEC) to report donations. It then syncs FEC donation verification with the candidate's donor list so that the candidate has a true record of the donation levels of each donor. It can do this with some state election commissions too.

As with all salesforce.com applications and services, there are strong APIs and web services and the Force.com platform so that you can build mash-ups to pull in unstructured data like the status of Barack Obama's Facebook organization or the number of Twitter tweets about John McCain. By Super Tuesday 2008, 30 campaigns were using it, including Mitt Romney and Ron Paul. Not bad.

You're In the Army Now: On Demand

In February 2009, the U.S. Army announced that it was using salesforce .com in a pilot recruitment program. That itself isn't all that interesting, frankly. Just sounds like another customer. But in this case, it's being used in conjunction with the Army Experience Center, a recruitment center that includes simulations, video games, and interactive career tools. It is spacious, casual, and in a mall in Philadelphia.

The use of salesforce.com in this environment is for its ease of implementation and its ability to capture data and create a single "customer" record. When the prospective recruit registers, they provide basic demographic and contact info—age, education, and family military history, among other things. The idea is that the recruiter will be able to see the individual's likely level of interest and recruit more effectively.

What also made this valuable to the army was that it took only four months to implement. The army called the cost "inconsequential." Which might or might not be a good thing for salesforce.com.

The State of Virginia: Pilot One Stop

Get this one. There was a time not too long ago when if you wanted to register a business in Virginia you might have to fill out up to 28 forms that would be sent to four separate agencies at three separate levels—state, county, and city. Some of the forms were paper, others were either digital or paper. But none were connected to each other.

According to Kaveh Vessali, that meant registering a business in Virginia would require the registrant to enter their name, address, and Social Security number 19 times.

Salesforce.com was deployed in Pilot One Stop—a program using salesforce.com to create a wizard that would allow the registrant to enter data once which would autopopulate the forms and then send the forms themselves to the appropriate state, city, and county agencies. Any changes were updated automatically on all forms.

Note the uses of salesforce.com in campaigns, at a federal level, and at the state level, and, of course, with the Citizen Briefing Book, in the new administration. Maybe not lots of headlines, again, a salesforce.com anomaly there, but there are lots of uses in the public sector—both traditionally and contemporarily, which in this case, *is* a good thing.

Superstah! Blue State Digital

Blue State Digital (BSD) is something like the Kanye West or Mick Jagger or Madonna (all depends on your era) of political technology—hardcore rock star. They were the technology backbone for Howard Dean when he ran the first successful Internet campaign in 2004 and, even more importantly, they built the technology infrastructure for MyBarackObama.com, thus achieving the status of gods of rock. They only work on campaigns that, shall we say, "lean to the left." Note the company name, people.

Their historic success rests on their BSD Online tools, which are a technology suite and infrastructure that, coupled with design services, led to the creation of MyBarackObama.com's (from now on called MyBO.com) location. But that's hardly their only success. They've had clients like the late Senator Edward Kennedy, the Communications Workers of America, London Mayor Ken Livingstone, and AT&T. In other words, they are hardly a one-trick pony.

Mission 21st Century

Their mission is simple, but not what you'd expect. Here it is from Thomas Gensemer, who is the managing director of BSD:

> *Blue State Digital is the leader in online fundraising, advocacy, social networking, and constituency development programs for nonprofit organizations, political candidates and causes, and corporations. We*

strive to provide extreme value to our clients by providing the most current, creative, and results-focused strategic advice along with the best tools in the business for online engagement. These tools can be used by anyone, from politicians wanting to engage the public to help their election, to corporations wanting to engage their customers to affect their profits.

While this might sound a little formal in tone, there is one thing the company isn't and that's formal. While they build technology backbones and have a strong set of technology tools, their mission for 2009 and beyond doesn't sound like a high tech company, does it? That's because it's strategic. Technology for BSD is a set of tools and infrastructure they need to make sure that what they do is effective for their clients. This is not a company of geeks. This is a business-driven company focused on blue state efforts that is now also moving into the commercial realm.

Their Work/Product

When they took on the Communication Workers of America (CWA) as a client, they had a plan in mind. They were going to build a program that would support the union's legislative objectives, which included equal access to broadband and advanced telco services. The idea wasn't just to win the objective but for the CWA to emerge as the leader in the fight for equal access—and as the leaders in getting Congress and state legislatures to pass legislation in support of it.

The result of this was the Speed Matters program. Speed Matters (www.speedmatters.org) was launched in 2006 as an interactive site aimed at recruiting support for the legislative action through CWA. By 2008, there were close to 100,000 members of the constituency who could be mobilized through action alerts throughout the country. The hook was a Speed Matters Internet speed test (taken by 200,000 in two years) that showed how fast your Internet speed was, driving home why access to high-speed connectivity was so important.

But don't get me wrong. They are and have hardcore technologists there. In addition to providing what sources other than them call a "robust" online toolset for content creation and social interaction, they work on the back end of technology too.

When they built MyBO.com, they had to create something that has been fundamental to all CRM since CRM's version of time immemorial—about a decade and a half. That was a single database for a consolidated view of the individual "customer." While this has been done by 38 percent of the corporations out there in the Fortune 1000, a woeful number, it had never been done for a presidential campaign. The scope was massive because it was going to be at least terabytes of data. BSD, through Jascha Franklin-Hodge, the BSD CTO, learned what not to do from the Dean campaign's failure to consolidate data with their six disparate databases.

BSD, with 20 people devoted full time to infrastructure throughout the campaign, chose to use MySQL, an open source database for their data, PhP for scripting, and Movable Type to build blogs, websites, and social networks—plus good ol' HTML too. Of course, they didn't ignore their own tools either. The result was that they succeeded for the first time in campaign history, allowing the Obama campaign to see consolidated information on his donors, volunteers, campaign workers, and any other constituents—who often overlapped in roles (for example, volunteers gave money). We know the outcome.

It's victories like this, successful outcomes that they are intimately involved with and their incredible versatility, that gets them the coveted Superstah! designation for this chapter. Watch their work in the commercial sector as they begin to move to it. They are well worth it.

Okay, we're heading to the end of this chapter though there is more throughout the book on this important "vertical" when it comes to Social CRM. I'd like to close with another mini-conversation with you and my good friend, Alan Rosenblatt, who will take you through the way constituent engagement is working on the social web via advocacy.

MINI-CONVERSATION WITH ALAN ROSENBLATT

Alan Rosenblatt, Ph.D., is the associate director of online advocacy at the Center for American Progress Action Fund; founder of the Internet Advocacy Roundtable; a Fellow at the Institute for Politics, Democracy, and the Internet; an adjunct professor at Johns Hopkins, Georgetown, and American Universities; blogs at TechPresident.com and DrDigiPol.com; and is on the board of directors for E-Democracy.org. If all that isn't enough, he's the guy who taught the world's first Internet politics course at George Mason University in 1995.

Impressed? Let 'er rip, Alan.

Total Social Engagement: Constituent Engagement on the Social Web

Add one part freedom to petition your government with grievances, one part e-mail, and one part social networks and you come up with a concoction that is sure to overwhelm congressional staff as they try to keep up with the onslaught of constituent communications. In the past dozen or so years, constituent communication has grown from about 50 million messages to Congress a year to over 300 million (with more than 90 percent via e-mail), according to the Congressional Management Foundation (CMF). Even if most of these e-mails are spam that can be automatically filtered, staffers are still faced with triple the workload of their counterparts in the late 1990s. Meanwhile, the budget for staff and technology in Congress has not increased in over 20 years.

From a constituent relations management perspective, this is a recipe for disaster. Workload is increasing at breakneck speeds, capacity remains stagnant, and the Constitution guarantees the rights of citizens to keep sending their grievances. Throw in the fact that the vast majority of the e-mails are form letter campaigns organized by advocacy groups with large memberships and you can understand why, in the face of way too much work, congressional staff have developed a healthy skepticism about the legitimacy of these e-mails, with 50 percent believing they are fake and another 25 percent unsure, according to CMF (www.cmfweb.org/index.php?option=com_content&task=view&id=62& Itemid=109).

But, as I have said often and loudly, the First Amendment guarantees the rights of citizens to petition the government with grievances. So, regardless of the difficulties, congressional offices have a constitutional obligation to figure this stuff out. And with the availability of CRM and now social networking tools, the solutions are not that hard to imagine. The key is to change the paradigm from one that combines top-down broadcast message delivery with a reactive constituent communication management to one that is proactive and interactive.

Leaving aside the technical issues for processing large amounts of constituent e-mail, a problem being addressed by CMF, advocacy groups, software vendors, and individuals with deep knowledge of the congressional e-mail system like Daniel Bennett (www.advocatehope.org), a shift in strategy can go a long way toward solving this problem. If congressional offices become more proactive in their communications with constituents, using their websites, e-newsletters, and other e-mail to anticipate constituent questions and concerns by providing substantive answers in advance of the questions, they can better steer the engagement with their constituents into a relationship that serves everyone's needs.

This new paradigm would use new social engagement software like wikis, blogs, and social networks to allow congressional offices to move policy discussions to public, interactive venues. Once shifted to a public forum, the burden for responding to individual e-mails is alleviated. Congressional offices can publicly respond to thousands of inquiries simultaneously, rather than one at a time in isolation. And since the engagement is in a public forum where anyone can chime in, often offices will discover that other constituents in the discussion community will handle the answers for them. All the office has to do is monitor and correct any mistakes in those answers.

Further, by creating an interactive community for discussing policy, one that includes the active participation of the member and his/her staff, the relationship with constituents will deepen with potentially less workload. In political science research, we talk about internal and external political efficacy as an indicator of political engagement between citizens and government. External efficacy is the degree to which a person believes the government responds to the people. Internal efficacy is the degree to which a person believes the government responds to him/herself.

In a world where all constituent communications with Congress are private and one-to-one, the number of people who get direct responses is inherently limited and there is no opportunity to see how other people interact with lawmakers. If offices engage in public discussions with constituents using social applications like wikis, then both internal and external efficacy can improve, leading directly to greater trust in government.

Interestingly, according to Edelman's Trust Barometer (2008), younger citizens, those most likely to use the social web, are more trusting of government. The key is to increase the personal connection between communicators, whether it be between citizen and government official, or between citizen and citizen in the presence of the government official.

Integrating these social engagement technologies into the congressional constituent relationship management process is a challenge. Arcane technology rules crafted before the Internet, as well as those crafted in the early days of the Internet, limit the ability of offices to use much of this technology behind the firewall. That is slowly changing, but we still have a ways to go. A few offices are using open source servers that allow installation of wikis, but cultural biases continue to confound implementation. Still, some offices are pushing the limit, offices like Representative George Miller of California and Senator Dick Durbin of Illinois, which have been experimenting with wikis.

Moving outside the firewall, a few members are venturing into the social web on sites like YouTube and Facebook. George Miller has Miller TV, which starts with a YouTube channel (www.youtube.com/user/RepGeorgeMiller) and feeds the videos to his official congressional website (http://georgemiller.house.gov/millertv.html). Those watching the videos on YouTube are able to post comments and video replies. Other members have ventured into the social networking world. Many have created groups, pages, and profiles on Facebook, but aside from Congressman Ron Paul's presidential campaign group, the most successful only have a few hundred friends or members.

Clearly this is a brave new world for elected officials. When in candidate mode, they totally get the interacting with voters on a personal level thing, but once in office they tend to lose that sense. And even in campaign mode, few really tap into new social web technology to create a total social engagement with the voters (Barack Obama's presidential campaign being the primary exception).

A few years back I wrote a blog post about an upstart Senate campaign in Utah. Pete Ashdown, founder of Utah's first ISP, ran against the incumbent Orrin Hatch. Faced with a much better funded opponent, Ashdown created a policy wiki on his website and invited the voters to help him refine his platform. Meanwhile, Senator Hatch's website included a blog with the comments turned off. So while Ashdown was using technology to deepen his relationship with the voters in a truly meaningful way, Hatch was using technology as a vehicle for talking at the voters. This reminded me of the old 1770s debate driven by Edmund Burke about the proper role of an elected representative. Should they be a delegate, implementing the will of the constituents or a trustee, exercising judgment on behalf of constituents? Ashdown was clearly a delegate and Hatch looked a lot like a trustee.

In the emerging world of total social engagement, demands for delegates to replace trustees are inevitable. The more people can engage with government and their peers in public spaces, the less inclined they will be to blindly follow a trustee. The people have tools in their hands for learning about policy that rival the tools in the hands of congressional staff. This evening of the playing field changes the game completely. The old adage "knowledge is power" used to explain why the elite opinion leaders were powerful—knowledge was a scarce resource. But today, knowledge is no longer scarce.

In a market where knowledge is abundant, power is more evenly distributed. Those in elected office no longer have control over knowledge, thus they have less power relative to their constituents. And with social technologies at the disposal of a knowledgeable citizenry, giving them the ability to spread information, build networks, and mobilize them to action, power is now distributed in a manner that will make it harder and harder for elected officials to continue doing "business as usual." In a world of total social engagement, the game has truly changed.✎

That's just about it. Go get something to drink or eat. Then, when you've swallowed and digested, head over to the appendix for the final piece of this chapter, a piece written by my brother and expert in the social web and Social CRM when it comes to government administration and enforcement. That appendix is on an amazing project (among others) called Virtual Alabama, which uses Google Enterprise. It's been so successful that it's now spawning regional pilots throughout the U.S. under the name Virtual USA.

After that, we move on. We're heading into some big small territory next—how social CRM impacts small business and what small business can do with it. Very cool stuff following very noble stuff.

15

SOA for Poets

I'm hoping that if you're reading this chapter, you are not merely of the "I'm not technical" mind, but also travel on the "I'm the next Percy Bysshe Shelley" or at least "I'm the next Mary J. Blige" spiritual plane. Technical stuff is not only not part of your ordinary sensibilities but actually makes you feel like hyperventilating. If so, you're in the right place, because this chapter is written for you. If not, because you are deeply technical and not terribly poetic or just really don't care about what underlies the CRM system you're using, skip past this one.

There are two related architectural masterpieces that underlie contemporary CRM applications and social software. They are service-oriented architecture (SOA) and RESTful architectures (REST). Before you get into conniptions about this, stop here, take that series of deep breaths your doctor told you to take to prevent hyperventilation, and I'll explain.

Evaluating Architecture

Honestly, I'd have my IT department doing this if I were you. But I'm not you, so I'm going to give you just enough information on evaluating a customer-driven architecture to make you want the IT department to do it.

Web Services

CRM initiatives can be technically complex. Architecturally, they are based on web services and standards that are interoperable—and frameworks that incorporate those web services in some way. When it comes to architecture, there are competing platforms, such as .NET and J2EE. There are also various ways to address the services through different architectures, such as the service-oriented architectures and RESTful architectures mentioned above. But before we get to the architectures and the differences, let's talk about web services.

The World Wide Web Consortium (W3C), the official standards body for web services, defines a web service as:

> *...a software system designed to support interoperable machine-to-machine interaction over a network. It has an interface described in a machine-processable format (specifically WSDL). Other systems interact with the Web service in a manner prescribed by its description using SOAP-messages, typically conveyed using HTTP with an XML serialization in conjunction with other Web-related standards.*

What in the name of nomenclature does that even mean? In English, that means that web services provide a common way of "speaking" between computers via a network so that the action of one can be understood by the other and a response to the action can be sent that is understood by all concerned. Most important, it uses standards that are interchangeable between competing systems. For example, I send a request to the system to generate a form that will be used to enter a pricing quote for a client. To do that quote, I need to draw on the product catalog to get the most current pricing and to check inventory. My order management system is Oracle, my product catalog is in salesforce.com, and my inventory is SAP. Theoretically, because all of these use web services that are based on the same standards, it should be no problem to do that quote. Theoretically.

In order for that theoretically seamless communication to occur between competing systems, the web services need to meet certain criteria. There are certain components that are important for them to work effectively. Five of them to be specific.

Those five pillars:

▶ **Extensible Markup Language (XML)** XML is a "meta language"—a generalized markup language with which you can write other more customized markup languages. It provides a set of specifications and basic syntax that is stored in plaintext format, which is hardware, software, and platform independent, making it interoperable, easy to use, and future-proof. It also supports Unicode, which means that any human spoken language is usable with XML. While it allows machines and processes to talk to each other, it doesn't provide a way to actually display the information, so it has to be tied to more traditional approaches to display, such as cascading style sheets (CSS). Its flexibility—also known as extensibility—in creating custom languages is also a disadvantage because there are so many custom languages it gets hard to "hear" the appropriate one. There are XMLs for chemistry, cooking, and real estate descriptions, and ten separate custom XMLs for biology alone. There are even two XML standards, 1.0 and 1.1. But it does work.

▶ **Simple Object Access Protocol (SOAP)**   SOAP (most current version 1.1) is a series of procedures written in XML to allow objects and procedures to pass through from one operating system to another using HTTP as the transport mechanism. That way, system administrators don't have to take down firewalls so other ports can be accessed beyond the standard port 80 that is commonly used. Even though reusable objects are ordinarily platform specific, SOAP allows them to call and respond to each other regardless of platform, port, or firewall. This is not used in RESTful architectures.

▶ **Web Services Definition Language (WSDL)**   This XML language is used to describe the interfaces between web services (the endpoints between the services). The most current W3C recommended version is 2.0, formerly 1.2. (I love numbering and naming conventions.) One thing germane to this book is that 2.0 offers better support for RESTful web services.

▶ **Universal Description, Discovery, and Integration (UDDI)**   The UDDI is a registry that an enterprise uses to publish its web services descriptions so that other parts of the enterprise can discover and use those web services due to the common descriptors. This allows different enterprises to communicate via those web services. It provides information such as contact info, industrial categories, and the exposed technical specifications for web services from the specific enterprise. It sits between (in a manner of speaking) SOAP and WSDL, allowing SOAP to interrogate it and access the descriptors provided by WDSL. The current version is UDDI v.2.0.

▶ **Business Process Execution Language for Web Services (BPEL4WS)**   BPEL4WS, also known as BPEL, defines both business processes that use web services and business processes that externalize their functionality as web services. It is usually a tagged XML message that is sent between partners or links partner to activity. This standard was created by a lot of the CRM-related vendors—Microsoft, IBM, Siebel Systems, BEA, and SAP. The current version is 1.1. It superseded the WSDL extension called XLANG, which used business processes to orchestrate applications and web services.

But web services alone do not an architecture make. They are just the brokers for moving messages and actions within the overall framework.

The Architectures

If I were writing this book in 2008—oh, wait, I was—I would pretty much have left the architecture to only SOAs. Why? Because I saw RESTful architecture as something that was peripheral to the growth of CRM-related technologies. But the more I investigated and tracked it, the more REST—which stands for representational state transfer, BTW (which stands for by the way)—began making sense as an option. It also began to gain a lot of ground with me because of its adoption as a core technology by companies like Sage. Then I began seeing a series of RESTful application programming interfaces (APIs) showing up on the scene. Notably, Twitter was using them; Neighborhood America was using them to integrate social features into Microsoft Dynamics CRM; and SAP acquired the assets of Coghead, a "platform as a service" (PaaS) provider based on RESTful architecture and APIs. My thinking went from "hmm" to "whoa!"

So we'll look at both service-oriented and RESTful architectures, because both are important to the architectures that optimize CRM systems. First, let's glance at the current standard: service-oriented architecture.

Enterprise Service-Oriented Architecture

When I wrote the third edition of this august volume back in 2004, service-oriented architectures were not fully realized yet. They were the dream of a number of companies that had started to use them in conjunction primarily with business services. At that time, Rearden Commerce had what I would call the only complete SOA. Now there are many companies that claim they've completely developed enterprise SOA, among them SAP with NetWeaver, Microsoft, Oracle, and countless others. Do I know that they are complete? No, I don't, and, thus, I can't really say they are either. You'll have to take the vendor's word, for what it's worth.

What Is SOA?

First, a simple definition:

SOA is a series of loosely joined services that communicate with each other regardless of the underlying platform. It restructures applications from a single large module to a series of smaller modules—services—that can be used and reused and recombined into applications that are specific to a situation or location. What complexity it has is primarily due to how a company cares to call and use the service or combinations of services.

A service-oriented architecture's great strength is that it supports a common set of technology standards, particularly web services, as well as corporate (and beyond) processes and business rules. The services, data, rules, and processes can be shared, but the interfaces and even the workflows can be specific to the applications that are using them. Within the framework of an SOA, though, the shared components can be used (and reused) in any applications that fall within the framework and at any company using the reusable parts.

For example, let's say you have a process that covers a customer service process from initial contact to service solution. That means:

1. Receiving the request for the communication via any of a number of selectable channels.

2. Responding to the request via the appropriate channel.

3. Entering the information provided by the requestor.

4. Opening a ticket that might be solved immediately or routed to a higher level of technician or to a supervisor, or it might send a request to a central scheduling authority to provide an onsite visit to the customer by a field service technician.

5. Having the appropriate customer service representative resolve the issue.

6. Entering the data for the resolution of the issue.

7. Contacting the requestor to inform them of the solution or the suggested course of action.

8. Closing the ticket if it is positively resolved or, if not, routing it further until it is resolved and the ticket is closed.

9. Updating the knowledge base if necessary.

10. Tracking the quality of the customer service support.

Note the complexity of this process, especially in item 4 where there are multiple directions for the process to go. It might go to a supervisor, which would send it on one path, or be routed to a field service technician, which would direct it through an entirely different series of steps to get there and to execute the instruction.

That same field service call can also get complex. It is often through a selected partner in a geographical location who has multiple calls to do in that location, adding scheduling optimization and territory management to the mix of how the process works. It is conceivable that the web services and/or the SOA the partner uses are somewhat different from the ones the parent company uses.

Never fear, those of you who are faint of heart. As Rick Merrifield et al. pointed out in their *Harvard Business Review* article "The Next Revolution in Productivity" in June 2008 (thanks to my dear friend and CRM business analyst Hatrice Basak Yildrim for pointing me to this one):

> *The beauty of SOA is that it allows activities—or processes built from such activities—to be accessed using the now-ubiquitous Internet in a standardized fashion. . . . This transformation makes it vastly easier to share discrete activities and entire processes internally, to buy or sell them externally, to delegate their execution to suppliers or customers, and to update and maintain IT systems.*

The benefit of an SOA is that all these processes—which intersect the customer service department, the field service agents (even if outsourced), the supervisors, the level 2 technicians, the aggrieved customers, and likely the IVR and CTI systems and those responsible for them—can interchangeably use the standardized services to appropriately communicate with the right facilities at the right time. Even more valuable, SOAs allow automatic access to the web services associated with specific business rules, allowing for sophisticated communications that trigger workflow actions based on pre-established conditions—without you having to do anything! Except respond when it's you it's notifying.

With the increasing complexity of traditional CRM technological models, the levels of customization, configuration, and integration have increased to something that could befuddle even the most razor-sharp IT architect—especially when the models are proprietary. But there has been a sea change over the past several years that allowed SOA to gain enormous ground at enormous speed. Why? It's a more flexible architecture with an enterprise-wide scope that can manage ongoing business change.

To take it to the next level, a slightly more complicated definition:

An SOA is a collection of decoupled business services and IT functions that are constantly evolving along with business require-ments. These services communicate with each other. The communi-cation can involve something as simple as data passing from a sales force automation system to an order management system. It could also involve two or more services coordinating some activity. For example, you are providing a just completed, authenticated docu-ment compiled automatically as an Adobe Acrobat file (.PDF) to a person registering on the website for the first time. His registration, when completed and submitted, extracts the document from a data store somewhere on the system and then time and date stamps the extraction and e-mails the document to the new registrant. The data from the new registrant populates multiple data sources. Some means of connecting these services to each other is needed, most often through provided connectors or customized code. Each com-ponent involved is interoperable without being dependent on the other components.

One other remark on SOA before I forget. Remember that SOA is outcome-based, not activity or methodology focused. What that means in plain Yiddish is *oy*, how hard is this, really, to understand? What this means in ordinary English is that SOA architecture is designed to achieve desired outcomes, not to organize work in a par-ticular way. That's why the components are reusable. They can be plugged in to systems to achieve a result. They don't force any par-ticular methodology into the system, nor do they require a particular activity or process to function according to "SOA rules." The outcome desired as the outcome achieved, no matter which approach was taken to achieve it, is what SOA lives for.

The SOA Marketplace

Commensurate with the evolution of this technology is the hype surrounding it. Back in 2003, ZapThink, an all-things-SOA company, blissfully forecast a $43 billion market in 2007, which I benignly accepted. It was *way* off. If the market is seen as a middleware-driven market, it was $2 billion in 2007, with IBM, through its Websphere product, owning 64 percent according to a considerably more conservative 2008 *Research and Markets* report on the sizing of the SOA market. The anticipated market is roughly $9.3 billion by 2014. Given my track record on guessing this—or at least agreeing with those guessing—well, take it for what it's worth. Not much, but at least an indication that SOA is important.

There are a dozen other players in the market including BEA, now owned by Oracle, and Web Methods, now owned by Software AG. (I'm owned by my five cats.)

Building and Maintaining an Enterprise SOA

Once you know what SOA is, the question becomes, is it right for my business? How should you evaluate this architecture? Here is a brief checklist of what you might want to ask vendors—and ask yourself—to see if SOA or SOA-based applications make sense for your company.

Traditionally, when assessing enterprise architectures, you are considering the:

▶ **Environment**   What platforms and databases might be of value?

▶ **Organization**   Should the architecture be the now nearly defunct two-tier client/server or the n-tier architecture that is so favorable to web architectures?

▶ **Infrastructure**   Should your architecture be object-oriented with reusable assets? What standards are applicable to your architecture? What measures for authentication and security are appropriate?

▶ **Applications**   What applications should be used to execute your business rules or to implement web services?

▶ **Need for customization**   How much customization will be necessary? What kinds of tools are available to do the customization? Should you, for example, standardize on Oracle and customize using Oracle's authoring and development tools? Or find a universal tool for best-of-breed implementations?

▶ **Integration**   How many third-party and legacy systems must the applications integrate with—internally and externally? Will you use middleware, web services, or something else to integrate data, business processes, and workflow?

Once you've asked the questions, if you've come to the conclusion that SOA works for you, then how to build the SOA becomes the next concern.

One of the considerations you will probably have is how to handle dynamically changing business processes and the shifting IT structure. Well, "interenterprise on the move" is probably the right mantra to chant. Massive overhauls aren't necessary for IT to begin implementing an SOA. What is most important is developing architecture flexible enough to handle changes in IT functions and business processes as they occur, not all at once.

Build and Maintain a Platform-Independent SOA

The SOA is built around a strategic business initiative and appropriate business processes and services. IT functions interface with the business functions, so as the business processes evolve and change, so do the services and the IT environment. What makes this interesting is that you will be able to ascertain the state of IT services and functions through the business actions being taken by the system. While maintaining platform independence, recognize that you will be running across multiple platforms in multiple environments as you develop this architectural model.

Develop in Increments and Use the Reusable

Iterative methodologies are often effective because they are prototype-dependent and always involve the user in each completed production cycle. That allows changes "on the fly," so to speak. When developing your prototype SOA, remember that the idea of a reusable asset is to use it again. That means you don't have to throw out code that didn't absolutely apply in a particular instance. As you are developing the pieces of the architecture and testing them, you can use the assets in more appropriate places or even rework the code so it can be used elsewhere.

Encapsulate Existing/Legacy Functionality

Rather than create connectors and adapters or use middleware per se to integrate legacy and third-party systems with the newer system, develop web services interfaces to meet that requirement. Those web services will be available even as the functions and processes change over time.

Shoot for Standards-Based Interoperability

Historically, I've been a fan of enterprise suites and less a fan of best-of-breed approaches. But I have to admit, the advent of web services and the tsunami of interest in developing standards for data and messaging interchanges have me more convinced than ever that best of breed is a viable approach. Best of breed makes sense as an option if the BOB applications can speak a common language. I know I can reach an audience in English, but when I have to wait for simultaneous translation, the flow is badly interrupted, and I lose time and momentum. If XML-compliant applications can speak to each other in "XMLese," then who cares who makes the applications, as long as they work well together? SOAs can create the framework for this level of interoperability.

Functionality vs. Usability

The more things change, the more they remain the same. One of the timeless arguments in the world of CRM vendors is functionality versus usability. While customers often buy their applications based on the coolness of the functions and features, they only use roughly 10 to 40 percent of the available functionality. The same argument goes for the SOA and web services. While it is good to have an SOA with web services of varying stripes and hues, they are only clutter unless someone is using them. So that means the SOA has to be designed with the ever-popular user in mind.

Business Rules

Business rules are not business processes. They are constraints that are placed on a business that might trigger processes. They will ordinarily reflect some business policy or practice that is institutionalized in the rule. In the world of Business Process Management (BPM), they become variables or key points within the process. For example, there could be a business rule that triggers a second monthly meter reading for a utility company when the number of cycles used reaches a particular threshold or triggers a different price structure for a high volume of usage that is then distributed to the various systems engaged. Or there could be a human business rule that constrains the way a salesperson goes about his work. For example, at York International, a Pennsylvania-housed HVAC company, they were having a problem with the profitability of their highly complex service level agreements with some of their customers. Extensive analysis found that they were losing money on many service level agreements (SLAs). They created a business rule that was embedded in their sales process (through a Siebel sales application) that would not let the SLA proceed unless it met a profitability threshold.

Of course, embedding a business rule in a process can complicate matters. There are often multiple rules embedded in the large BPM processes and they have to be ferreted out in order to make the changes appropriately. They aren't necessary so easy to catch. That's why there are dozens of vendors on the market that are attempting to create business rule technologies that can handle the ferreting and embedding as needed. With the technology, business rules can be implemented in a repeatable and consistent fashion, and integrated with BPM and other applications that are being used by the company. As process management and change become increasingly real time, the ability to extract and change or re-embed or develop the business rules associated with those processes becomes increasingly important. BPM solutions will have to factor that kind of activity into their solutions. If they don't, embed the following rule into your purchasing processes: "If the BPM applications don't have business rule capabilities, don't buy."

In the technology you will likely deal with when it comes to SOA, the business rules are part of a business logic that assumes constraints or changes in the state of the data. It also constrains the use of data by individuals—an authorization constraint—and will trigger when an action on the data occurs. For example, take the rule mentioned above for the utility company. If you add the ability for managerial override of the percentage price changes due to volume, the technology could automatically trigger the workflow rules that allow the override request to be routed to the appropriate manager. By being able to see and steer the business rules that are in specific processes, you will be able to modify, subtract, or add rules to each process or even do a universal change to all the rules by some parameter or other criterion. Sleep will come easier if you can. Imagine doing it all manually? To err is human; to have business rules capabilities is, uh, good. Divine is stretching it.

SOA and Integration

Okay, SOA promises a beautiful world of applications that work together seamlessly, but that world is theoretical at best and ridiculously optimistic at worst. Since anyone reading this chapter is not likely to be an IT guy (because you don't need to be reading "SOA for Poets" if you are, or if you do need to, you shouldn't be an IT guy), you may think, as the business whiz you are, that you don't have to concern yourself with how this all works.

To some degree, you're right. But the reality is that when you are using applications that should be having a lovely coordinated conversation with each other and they instead spew disconnected invective back at you—meaning you can't get the information, data, services, functions, or results you want—you will need to know how to tell the IT guy what is wrong. If you don't, your customers are going to get upset.

Think of it this way. When you look at a Fortune 1000 company, the average number of applications it has working is between 400 and 3,000. Do you have a clue how to integrate that? Not only does integrating an SOA have extensive hardware requirements so that applications run seamlessly, you must also consider:

▶ Incompatible data formats between applications

▶ Legacy systems that don't have the necessary APIs natively so they have to be built—say, to foster the integration between the supply chain and CRM systems

▶ Licensing, control, and asset management issues that legacy systems create

▶ The evolution of on-demand (SaaS) as a viable delivery architecture—which means that it needs to be tied to legacy on-premises applications

But it goes further than that because even if you solve the problems created by the somewhat static conditions here, there are more dynamic elements that need to be accounted for in the integration strategy:

▶ Changes in business rules due to new management, changed business conditions, or new processes

▶ Changes in business models due to new products, corporate rollups or other acquisitions or mergers, new customer expectations, or new compliance and governance issues

> ▶ Changing IT infrastructure due to new protocols and standards or simply growth (or cutbacks) at the company

> ▶ Issues of external connectivity to partners, customers, or external agencies

All in all, these are not easy issues to deal with, but they are real—the cold water dashed on SOA users' faces. Be alert to possible problems with integration and you will be able to solve them a little more readily.

Superstah!

You know what? I've been through Oracle/BEA, IBM, SAP NetWeaver, Microsoft, Rearden Commerce, Sword-Ciboodle, and a multiplicity of other choices, and I can't come up with a winner. This is the first time in the history of *CRM at the Speed of Light* that I can't really distinguish a best-in-class vendor for SOA architecture.

I'm sure that I'll get a "What? Are you kidding?" from a few of the vendors; the other ones won't notice at all. But think about it. This is a good thing. It means that the standards, as of 2009, are so well established and are so . . . standard, that there is no winner because they all work pretty much in the same way. Pretty much.

It means that interoperability and communication between enterprises is achievable and that the SOA industry is mature.

So, as Crosby, Stills, Nash, and Young once warbled, "Rejoice, rejoice, you have no choice." There is no winner because SOA wins.

REST/WOA

Interestingly enough, there is another architecture that hearkens back to a simpler day when men were hunters and women tended to the fields and wash . . . oh, wait, that's the Neanderthals of the Middle Paleolithic Era, not IT architecture. Wrong tool set.

Actually, I'm talking about representational state transfer (REST), also interchangeably (if not accurately) called web-oriented architecture (WOA). There is one major CRM—actually enterprise applications—vendor who uses it really well. That would be Sage Software (see below) who has always varied from the norm when it came to architectures. REST is an interesting and important choice, and, I would venture to say, might even be the architecture of choice if you're a small or lower-end midsized business. It's worth more than a look—it's worth an investigation.

What Is REST?

REST is what I'd like to be doing at the moment I'm writing this. I can't because I'm too busy, but I can tell you about the value and the pitfalls of REST architecture.

Simply stated, REST is a web services architecture that has one and only one interface—one that is based on HTTP, meaning a classic web browser. Application-specific interfaces are taboo, which is, of course, where it differs from SOA. There are only four command states that apply—Get, Post, Put, Delete. Essentially, it's the same architecture that runs the Internet, and the one you use when you fire up Internet Explorer (or Firefox or Safari or any browser you use), type in a URL, and hit Enter. By the way, that would be Get in REST command lingo.

Representational State Transfer (REST)

REST emerged from what is now a geek-legendary doctoral thesis called "Architectural Styles and the Design of Network-Based Software Architectures," by Roy Fielding, at the University of California, Irvine, in 2000. Fielding, now the chief scientist at Day Software, figured out how to use the standard Internet protocols to interact with data.

There were only four basic commands (Get, Post, Put, and Delete) and one basic interface—a web browser—and that was the extent of it. The idea was that the URL was the equivalent of a noun, as Ryan Tomayko explained it in his posting, "How I Explained REST to My Wife."

Tomayko's explanation, as gender uncomfortable as it might be, is actually pretty good, whether you're female or male. HTTP is a protocol that is used to "describe the location of something anywhere in the world from anywhere in the world." That location is the URL. What Get, Post, Put, and Delete provide are the verbs in this schema. These are the universally possible actions that can be read by any machine in any format from any operating system. For example, if you wanted to read my ZDNET blog, you would type in the URL http://blogs.zdnet.com/crm and hit the Enter key on your PC or Blackberry and up would pop my blog's latest entry, which is a representation of the web page. The reason that it's a representation is because the web page is being reproduced in multiple other locations at the same time. If there was only the "original," no one would see it but the first person to access the URL. But there really is no original resource. There are only representations of the resource. That would be, according to Tomayko, the noun.

Got that so far?

Then there are the four Tomayko-labeled verbs. Get, Post, Put, and Delete are universally applicable to any machine. They represent the same thing regardless of platform, operating system, or hardware used—a condition called stateless. This is very much like SOA, also stateless. But, unlike SOA, those four commands are the only ones REST uses when it does something. So if you wanted to access a small section of a web page, there would be HTTP GETs going on until all the necessary representations to identify that web page segment were made available to you.

REST is secure with SSL (Secure Sockets Layer) and HTTPS, so there is no question of its ability to protect necessarily private information.

What makes it powerful is that it's simple. And because it is a well-known standard already adopted by anyone who writes for or uses the Internet, it gives developers more control over how they create access to its functions. In fact, according to a 2008 tutorial on REST from SearchCRM, when comparing SOAP to REST (no, not bathing to sleeping), 80 percent of developers preferred REST.

REST, CRM, API
Let's take a look at REST in a CRM system (Figure 15-1) (thanks to Sage Software for this diagram).

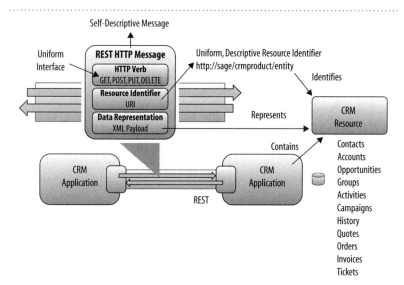

Figure 15-1: REST as applied to a CRM system (Source: SageCRM Solutions, 2009)

REST, in this figure, consists of three layers: the interface with its URL, the four verbs, and (when it comes to interacting with data) the XML payload—the same XML that SOA uses. This makes interoperability with SOA possible.

In fact, there are vendors who have come out with RESTful APIs that are normally designed to pass messages back and forth between REST and SOA architectures. Table 15-1 outlines a few of them.

Table 15-1: A Sampling of Vendors with RESTful APIs

Vendor	What RESTful API Does
Sage	SageCRM and SalesLogix work on REST architecture; APIs for integration in general
Twitter	Designed for general communication between services
Neighborhood America	Integration with SOA-based Microsoft Dynamics CRM
SAP/Coghead	SAP acquired Coghead RESTful APIs and development tools
BroadSoft Xtended Services Interface	Integrates VoIP into social networks

Data-Centric vs. Remote Procedure Call

One major difference between REST and SOA is that REST is data-centric while SOA is dependent on remote procedure calls (RPCs). What that means in nearly practical terms is that REST is data-centric and SOAP, which relies on RPCs, is process-centric.

What *that* means in totally practical terms is that the developer who uses SOA and SOAP for remote procedure calls is building an interface onto a specific application that does specific things. He then is giving the user access to the interface and the associated commands so that the user can use the application in the way it was created. For this, there are an unlimited number of verbs.

REST, with its data-centric model, is emulating the Web. So the four verbs that apply to the Web and its interface are what REST uses for information gathering and passing. By passing an XML document, the URL does the work to get the information that provides the variability of the applications.

So who does REST well in CRM? Time for the envelope, please.

Superstah! Sage Software

I've known Sage Software through countless incarnations, starting back in 1997 when it was not Sage per se but the standalone CRM on-premises application, SalesLogix. But they were bought by Best Software, which was swallowed up by Sage Software, a U.K.-based enterprise applications vendor that not only had the back office accounting packages but even their own CRM application— SageCRM—which to some extent actually competed with SalesLogix, owned through the varying rollups by . . . ta-da . . . Sage Software.

Oddly, even with their acquisition strategy, which is daunting, they've done just fine, thank you, with more than 56,000 customers for their CRM applications and more than 5 million customers in total. The vast majority are small companies and the lower end of midmarket businesses who appreciate the simplicity of Sage's offerings and easy to use interfaces.

Sage wins this category hands down. Not just because they use REST architecture, because others do that. But because they use it well. They understand the market they attack—small and lower-end midsized business—and they understand the value of REST to that market. They innovate using REST in ways that show the power of the architecture for the market they address. You just can't get much better than that.

SageCRM and SalesLogix: RESTful 2010

Sage has moved its focus to a more contemporary CRM model than they have had in the past, largely due to the visionary influence of Dave Van Toor, former general manager of Sage's CRM practice, now responsible for the companywide customer experience. Van Toor, in combination with some sound thinking from senior staff and serious investment in overhauling a model that in the past was often a half-step behind, has created a highly competitive, smart product.

The three pillars they are setting the building on are all based on REST:

▶ Interoperability and migration

▶ Anywhere workforce experience

▶ Connected front and back office

Interoperability and Migration

This sounds buzz-ridden but actually isn't. There is a pretty smart, very user-friendly strategy behind this. Figure it this way. Sage has two CRM and one contact management—CRMish—product. These are SageCRM, SalesLogix, and ACT! (though I wish they'd get rid of the exclamation point). ACT! has 2.8 million users scattered across 43,000 companies.

The key here is that companies grow. ACT! runs into its limitations when small companies get larger and even go to midsized. So how do you deal with that and keep the ACT!-using companies in the stable? Make SageCRM, SalesLogix, and ACT! interoperable by using the same data store and the same architecture—that would be REST for those of you who miraculously skipped to this part of the chapter without reading what came before.

This creates endless possibilities. A company can use ACT! in some departments and one of the CRM applications in other places without worrying about them reading each other.

This is a change from Sage's (pre-Sage, actually) somewhat checkered past when ACT! databases and SalesLogix databases were not the same at all. What this does is increase the likelihood of successful user adoption.

Is it as seamless as claimed? Never. There are technical issues that will crop up and cultural issues that will interfere. But it's an improvement by orders of magnitude.

Anywhere Workforce Experience

This is the sexiest Social CRM part of their strategy. It starts from the standpoint of the anywhere, anytime, any way workforce experience that has been popularized—to the extent it has any popularity—by analyst firm Yankee Group's Anywhere Enterprise. Declan Lonergan, vice president of the Yankee Group's Anywhere practice, found in early 2009 that by 2012, the combination of consumer broadband wired and consumer mobile—the two rocks of the Anywhere Network—would amount to a $962,000,000 business. That may be an exaggeration, but who knows? What is important is that the Anywhere Enterprise is becoming something that has both meaning and value.

This is where Sage differentiates themselves from the pack for now. The core offering is "customer choice." First, the customer gets a choice of on-premises or on-demand (their SageCRM product has a hosted version, SageCRM.com). Then the customer gets the choice of additional functionality that can be plugged into the out-of-the-box capabilities. The range is wide. The customer can choose a hybrid delivery model (on-premises mixed with on-demand) and can pick from connected, disconnected, or mobile.

But that's just the selection of models. Context Aware Services, which provide device awareness, user awareness, and network awareness, are something that Sage proudly presents as a critical differentiator, though they are not the only company providing it with their applications. SalesLogix 7.5 is the flagship here. For example, the UI for their web client is very, very good. It is the second best one I've seen in current generation CRM products (after SAP's CRM 7.0 user interface), which makes it the best in the SMB world. Additionally, like many other vendors (notably, SAP, Oracle, and salesforce.com), they have integrated enterprise mashups and useful ones at that. For example, SalesLogix 7.5 provides a scrolling Google newsfeed that was created through specific search criteria and RESTful calls. The unstructured data can be captured from the newsfeed (RSS enabled) and downloaded.

Another area that has a good deal of promise, though I still think is not being used to the fullest potential, is their addition of Timeline Visualization. This is a timeline of all account-specific or opportunity-specific activity, coupled with external data such as market conditions, which is organized around a strong, though not particularly pretty, visual timeline. It can give you a comprehensive view of what account activity occurred when. You can drill all the way into the single activity or event if you care to. By having the data from the newsfeeds populating the timeline, you can see what happened to the company/account on the day that you lost or won the deal and if there was any reason for the result that was external to your actions. What is missing so far is the ability to use the workflow to provide a color-coded result of good or bad. For example, if there was a setback you could see part of the timeline being red at the point of the setback while the good stuff was blue and the okay stuff was brown (or green, fuchsia, teal, whatever). Right now you can color code each line separately but not line segments. I hope that it shows up in the 7.6 release (hint, hint). But even without that, this is a valuable differentiator for Sage that accounts for how people use applications and how they navigate through them.

Mobile Is Part of Any Way and Anywhere

Since I'm not really covering ACT!, suffice it to say that there is an ACT! for the iPhone under development.

However, what is germane is SalesLogix Mobile for the BlackBerry. Their most interesting capability is the SalesLogix Mobile context awareness via location awareness for mobile devices with GPS. Aside from access to SalesLogix data from a very simple interface, it finds "Accounts Near Me." This directly ties BlackBerry's embedded GPS and voice recognition systems. If you hit the Accounts Near Me button, the following occurs:

1. The system locates you.

2. It accesses your customer list (based on your preferences) and finds the customers nearest you.

3. It speaks to you with a message like this: "You have eight customers within five miles. Three [of the five] have alerts."

4. You can view the alerts or call a customer.

5. You can use the BlackBerry GPS service (currently TelNav) and get directions to the customer's site.

Cool and useful—especially in the less likely event that the customer is willing to take an ad hoc meeting.

Connected Front and Back Office

Sage has done well with this one, probably as much for self-interested reasons as for the customer—which, if you think about it, is actually something that should be pretty much symbiotic.

They have products for both the front and back office. For example, Sage is the proud owner of the Accpac accounting product and the MAS90 ERP product, and vertically specific products such as Community Banking and HealthPro XL, as well as their flagship CRM products. Integrating them all is a naturally smart thing to do. Better than selling a product to a customer is selling products continuously to a customer. When products integrate, they benefit both the customer and the company. For the company, the benefits are opportunities for upselling and cross-selling and increased customer retention. For the customer, it's a better user experience with cost simplification and reduction. It pays to have common components, common and open standards, suite integration, and common interfaces. Plus the internal user impact on the front and back offices along with the customer impact on the two "offices" become preeminent features of the overall business experience in the new environment. End of story.

Okay, time to move ahead, now that you've become the SOA and REST maven you've always wanted to be. These are architectures that matter to your business and to your customers. So spend the time and the dime, and the result will be worth it.

16

At Home or in the Clouds—and in Open Spaces Between

I love arguments. I love them when it comes to sports and to . . . actually, anything. In the CRM world, *the* argument has been and will continue to be the argument over what's better, software as a service, which is evolving into computing in the cloud—or is it; or the on-premise deployment of CRM, which means the deployment of CRM for you by you at your business. The simplest part of the argument has always been around the "who owns the data" controversy—though it is driven by the vendors who have a bit of "nyah nyah nyah" embedded in the ongoing battle. Should it be you who will license the software, provide the servers, and supply the remaining necessary hardware, software, and personnel to maintain the system so that your business can control the data directly? Or should it be allowed to fall into the hands of a host who will provide all that hardware, software, and personnel overhead to install and maintain the system for the price of a subscription—but, horrors, in their own environment—meaning the data is in their hands, with, of course, potentially nefarious results.

Ah, if it were truly that simple. There is a simple answer to the on-premise versus on-demand (another name for it) contention—it depends. But that, of course, is what makes it more complicated.

There is another factor that makes this even more interesting. The development of open source CRM showcased by the ubiquitous presence of SugarCRM. While a seemingly additional headache, it actually is a very important part of the discussion as we move to Social CRM.

Just to set some expectations, I'm not going to jabber much about on-premise or on-demand—at least, not as much as I have in the past editions—since they are now well-established models that don't need me to explain them over and over again. I'm just going to provide some basics and a comparative checklist for you on the criteria to consider for selection of one or the other. I will dwell a bit on cloud computing because it is new and becoming important and is still a source of confusion for most people. I'm also going to clarify the relationship between open source and on-premise/on-demand/cloud computing, which is something like peaches to peach pits. Open source isn't competitive with the delivery models above. It isn't a delivery model and, in fact, as we'll see, open source CRM (or any) applications can be delivered many different ways.

Okay. Now that I've managed your expectations, let's rock.

On-Premise

Rather than bore the living hell out of you with a long technical discourse on the differences between the varieties of on-premise software and on-demand services, let's take a look at the basic definition of on-premise to start. By the way, technically, the actual term for this is "on-premises," not "on-premise." I'm going to leave it as on-premise because, as wrong as this phrasing might be, it's what most people already call it. I'm going to stand by it due to the Common Law Usage Rule, which says that even if it's wrong but in common use, it's right. By the way, I just made that up.

What Is It?

On-premise is the traditional model for software installation and administration that you probably already know something about. You license the software from a software vendor. You run an instance of the software or multiple instances at your site and store the data associated with that application on servers physically located at your site with your administration and your security. You control the data. You also hire someone to install and customize the software and then stick around to get that licensed software working, since the odds of you being able to do it yourself are about the same as the odds of the software vendors liking each other. Astronomical. Over roughly a three-year period, you tweak the system, handle downtime yourself, and at the end of the three-year cycle, you upgrade the software to meet the requirements you've developed over that time.

This model has advantages for large enterprises in particular because it provides optimal control over your own feature/function/ process/data destiny and it scales better than the on-demand versions. This doesn't mean that SaaS doesn't scale. As we'll see, it most certainly does. But most on-premise versions that scale are built specifically for the size of the enterprise that they were built for.

A complaint about on-premise that you often hear is that implementation can take months. While this is still true for the most part, there is some potential relief in sight. For example, late in 2008, I watched a demonstration by a Microsoft Certified Partner, AlfaPeople, which can provision an on-premise or on-demand Microsoft Dynamics CRM 4.0 system so that it is up and running in 10 minutes—without customization, of course. Even so, that indicates how incredibly quickly these systems can be set up. It actually took two seconds to install and provision a Microsoft Dynamics CRM system in the demonstration I saw. While long on-premise installations are hardly a thing of the past, there is progress toward the future.

Advantages and Disadvantages

These have been talked about so frequently in the technology press that it's reached something of a blah blah blah status. I'm listing them here so you can start asking the questions you're going to need to ask of vendors when the time comes for you to implement some sort of CRM technology. Table 16-1 has a brief description of the advantages and disadvantages of on-premise purely on its own merits, not in comparison to SaaS.

The Players

While there is no need for me to highlight any one vendor in the on-premise world, there are several who have notable products. They are, in no particular order:

▶ **Oracle**   With both Siebel and PeopleSoft, Oracle stands out for the depth of the suite. When the long-awaited Oracle Fusion products emerge, there will probably be a new CRM product to contend with, but the release date for that is still fuzzy. Target market: Large enterprises.

Table 16-1: Advantages and Disadvantages: On-Premise Applications

Advantages	Disadvantages
Tight integration between applications	Can be expensive to implement and maintain
Control over data	Licensing plans are inflexible
Control over the system by in-house administration	Doesn't integrate well with SaaS though that is constantly improving with evolution of SOA and RESTful architectures
Long established, mostly successful track record with complex configurations	Implementations can take months and occasionally even more
Highly scalable	Adoption is more often difficult than SaaS due to different audiences and interfaces for those audiences
Well-established security protocols and procedures	
Still has the vast majority of the market and thus the maturity and ecosystem	

▶ **SAP** With the release this year of SAP CRM 7.0, SAP moved into contention with a truly integrated enterprise suite. They added an enormous number of new features and functions to every part of their CRM suite—much of which was built in conjunction with their customers' advice. For example, they've added Pipeline Performance Management and Territory Management to the sales force automation module. It is fully integrated with all aspects of SAP's Business Suite. Target market: Large enterprises.

▶ **Microsoft** Dynamics CRM 4.0 has a common code base for both the on-premise and on-demand versions, making a genuinely hybrid application. It is priced to sell, as they say in the retail world. It is also a functional platform with open source components being made available by Microsoft to developers—a marked change in strategy for this rather big company. Target market: Small and midsized companies, departments of large enterprises.

▶ **Sage CRM** Sage is the multibillion European software empire that has a back and front office focused suite. While not much for supply chain management, they are focused on financials on the back end and CRM on the front end, with two products that are deliverable in on-premise and on-demand versions, though they are moving more and more to the latter. SalesLogix and SageCRM are both based on RESTful architectures, as you probably saw in "SOA for Poets" (Chapter 15). Target market: Small and the lower end of midsized businesses.

Needless to say, this is not an exhaustive list. It simply is meant to convey the news that on-premise is far from dead. In fact, Gartner Group, in a SaaS market study they released at the end of 2008, estimated that by 2011, SaaS will control roughly 25 percent of the market—which means on-premise will continue to control roughly three-fourths of it—so it's hardly buried yet. So if you see it walking around, it's not a zombie, it's alive.

On-Demand

Before I really get going on this chapter, I need to say something.

Sometimes all credulity is challenged. That happens to me most frequently when I'm watching episodes of *Heroes* (which I don't like) or *Lost* (which I love). But in second place as a category is listening to CEOs of major technology companies spout what I think I really couldn't possibly be hearing. For example, even with the enormous success of SaaS, there are still arguments deriding the SaaS model. Take a look at the following comment from Harry Debes, CEO of Lawson Software, in mid-2008:

> *This "on-demand," SaaS phenomenon is something I've lived through three times in my career now. The first time, it was called "service bureaus." The second time, it was "application service providers," and now it's called SaaS.*
>
> *But it's pretty much the same thing. And my prediction is that it'll go the same way as the other two have gone—nowhere.*
>
> *SaaS is not God's gift to the software industry or customer community. The hype is based on one company in the software industry having modest success. Salesforce.com just has average to below-average profitability.*
>
> *People will realize the hype about SaaS companies has been overblown within the next two years.*

Needless to say, this is a silly comment coming from someone who you think would know better. If he doesn't, perhaps the rest of the marketplace can set him straight. In December 2008, Gartner released "User Survey Analysis: Software as a Service, Enterprise Application Markets, Worldwide, 2008." The survey found that out of 258 executives worldwide, 90 percent of them intended to maintain or increase their investment in SaaS in 2009.

Okay, I feel better now that I've gotten Mr. Debes's rant out of the way. He may be a wonderful guy; I don't know him personally. But he shouldn't speak on matters he knows nothing of—apparently.

What Is It?

As I mentioned somewhere else in this book (it's too big for me to remember where), back when I wrote the third edition, what we now call software as a service (SaaS) vendors were called application service providers (ASPs) or the much sexier "net natives." In 2004, this was a pretty new category that was doing something that was still seen as radical. It provided software to you for the price of a subscription based on the number of users who used it. That would be paid monthly or annually, or whatever deal you could squeeze from the overeager salesperson trying to earn their keep. In return for that repeatable payment, you received financial comfort and the gift of no overhead costs and no maintenance by you. It made all the sense in the world.

At the time it was aimed primarily at small business, with even the "disruptive innovator" salesforce.com, the true pioneer of this new model, aimed at not much more than that. But from 2004 through now, something happened. The model worked so well that salesforce .com changed the customer paradigm. First, they won a large enterprise deal with SunTrust Bank. Then, back when Merrill Lynch was still Merrill Lynch, they won a 25,000-seat deal. It became apparent that one of the prevailing myths, that on-demand was for small companies or departments of larger ones only, was nothing more than that—a myth. On-demand was proven to scale to tens of thousands of seats. Shortly thereafter, Workday, an on-demand human resources services company run by PeopleSoft founder David Duffield, won a contract to deploy 200,000 seats at Flextronics, putting this story to rest for good.

SaaS's popularity continued to grow. It may have begun its current incarnation back in 1999 as a curiosity, but it is easily the fastest growing delivery method for enterprise software, led by SaaS-based CRM, especially in sales force automation.

But the sophistication of its use has grown too, so that some of the more complex or high volume CRM-related functions are now provided as hosted solutions. For example, SAP's Business Objects has a product called Business Intelligence on Demand (BIOD) that supplies complex business intelligence algorithms as a hosted service. SAS has the customer experience analytics product it offers that I introduced you to in Chapter 3. If you remember, in Chapter 12 you learned of sales intelligence product SalesView and the social media monitoring tool Radian6, and in Chapter 13 the customer service applications like Right-Now and Helpstream—all SaaS based. The list is nearly endless and covers the gamut of enterprise software, from back office to front office, from CRM to financial applications to the supply chain and logistics.

Advantages and Disadvantages

Having all these application services available doesn't guarantee the success of SaaS—though it is indicative of its adoption as a platform and delivery model. There are some well-defined and well-documented benefits that SaaS users tout. There are also some seriously funky disadvantages.

Information Week did a survey in June 2008 with 471 major IT users. Roughly 25 percent used SaaS as their platform. The respondents liked SaaS for reliability, upgradeability, and ease of use. They saw it as problematic for its costs, inability to customize, poor integration, and difficulty in switching vendors. For the most part, the value and the problems with SaaS are seen early on in the process, so the practitioners have very little gauze over their eyes throughout the life of the deployment

Matt Prise, a manager at Lifetime Fitness, which is using HR SaaS vendor Workday's services to the tune of 17,000 seats, offers an almost perfect reflection of the SaaS paradigm: "Workday is extremely configurable but not customizable at all." He mentioned its user friendliness and good user interface. He also mentioned that Workday is great on getting customer input for new features and functions. But he also knows its limitations. However, even customization issues are becoming moot with the release of Platform-as-a-Service products like salesforce.com's force.com.

Okay, table time. Put away your forks. I don't mean the dinner table. As I did with the on-premise section, Table 16-2 shows a breakdown of SaaS advantages and disadvantages on its own, not against on-premise.

Table 16-2: Advantages and Disadvantages: SaaS

Advantages	Disadvantages
Fast deployment time	Data controlled outside your company firewall
Few upfront costs beyond configuration	Can be reasonably expensive as users scale up; no economy of scale
Vendors usually have strong service level agreements	Even with strong SLA, downtime happens and you don't control getting services back up
Problems handled by the host	Complex customizations are not easy, though tools are getting better
Controllable, repeatable costs; lower cost of ownership	Not built for environments where significant data security required, e.g., classified materials
Upgrades are easy and can be incremental; you control the features you want to implement (this method was pioneered by RightNow)	Myths about "bad stuff" persist, which color perception, which colors buying decisions and adoption

Giving the Myths Back to Edith Hamilton

Enough with the myths, already.

In 1942, Edith Hamilton, known as the greatest woman classicist, wrote a classic of her own, called *Mythology*. This book became the go-to book in high schools and colleges and in general for anything to do with the study of Greek mythology. While not updated since 1942, the book is still revered within academic circles. With all the hubbub about the "problems' with SaaS, I think it's time to summon the spirit of Edith Hamilton, so she can update the book to append a section on SaaS mythology—or perhaps add a new chapter entitled "SaaS Problems: New Mythologies for the 21st Century."

There are quite a few myths, which have achieved at least the status of urban legend, if not full-blown status on Mt. Olympus. You'll note that even though I'm myth busting, you'll see one or two of these in the disadvantage column—primarily because the severity of the problem is the myth, not the problem itself.

Myth 1: Security Is a Major Problem

In the Gartner survey mentioned above, 62 percent of the respondents said they worried about their data being behind someone else's firewall. That worry is not that well-founded though there is always some risk in an environment not controlled by the data owner. But the fears are generally groundless because of the totality of the security schema that companies like salesforce.com use. For example, salesforce.com has:

▶ **Data center security**   That means onsite security guards 24/7; private "cages" for their hardware; security cameras inside and outside; access screens via photo IDs and biometrics; escorts to go to machines.

▶ **Internet security**   128-bit SSL encryption for all Internet traffic ensured via step-up certificates for any country in the world; VeriSign certification.

▶ **Network security**   Hardware firewalls; minimal routable IP addresses; Network Address Translation (NAT) for all servers; separate subnets for corporate websites and applications servers; centralized proactive log monitoring using algorithms for intrusion detection; historic log storage that is monitored for violations of multitenant security design or nonstandard URL access (something like what Google Feedburner does on blog monitoring).

▶ **Operating system security**   Hardened OS with all unnecessary ports and services shut down; untouchable root services; avoidance of native code to prevent hackers from exploiting security holes.

▶ **Application level security**   MD-5 hash encryption for all password storage; more advanced password options such as password reuse prevention; invalid password lockout; restricted access by role or profile; annual security audit; multifactor authentication.

That's blanket security enough to provide a security blanket.

That doesn't mean there aren't any security issues to be concerned with. There are. For example, in the on-premise world, because of potential security bugs, there were pretty frequent security checks run between alpha, beta, release candidate, and final versions of a product, to thwart any possible intruder. But because SaaS is a set of application services, the changes are continuous and incremental, so the frequency necessary to check for security problems goes up considerably.

All in all, though, your data is safe at the host's site—perhaps, depending on your own security schema, safer than it would be on yours. So while that might not bring you peace of mind, it will protect your data—which should bring you peace of mind.

Myth 2: Integration Is Difficult

This is a constantly debated issue that is truly a non-issue. Most SaaS providers use standard web services to communicate. The on-premise providers are increasingly using service-oriented architectures, which use standardized web services to communicate. Many vendors also use RESTful architecture. It uses a subset of standardized web services to communicate. All in all, these systems are interoperable. They can communicate with each other. Here is a case in point. Ingres is a roughly 350-person open source database management company. In 2007, they decided to go to an SaaS-based model that would apply to every single application they used. Their approach wasn't to use a single suite. They made the decision to go best of breed. So they used Intaact for financials, salesforce.com for SFA, Xactly for sales compensation, and ADP for human resources—every one of them an on-demand service. It has worked so well that they are going to expand to SaaS-based professional services automation, on-demand vendor Silverpop B2B for marketing, and something unknown as yet for contract management. Their rationale is the pricing model: its pricing structure is the same as a utility, a.k.a. pay as you go. They didn't see on-demand as any harder than on-premise to integrate. They also used Force.com to build custom screens, tables, and fields.

So integration is hard—how exactly?

Myth 3: The Amount of Downtime for SaaS Proves the Unreliability

On January 6, 2009, salesforce.com had a 38-minute outage. If you were to believe some of the pundits, this 38-minute outage was responsible for furthering the recession, if not the decline of civilization as we know it. My personal favorites all came from a pretty sleazy journal, the *Register*. They went like this:

▶ "Salesforce.com . . . was unreachable for the better part of an hour." (That would be 38 minutes—which technically is the better part of an hour—but it isn't 59 minutes, which, when a system is out, is a notable time difference.)

▶ "A single disruption paralyzes a small fraction of the world's economy as a whole." (As a result of the outage, the *Register* questioned the validity of cloud computing—not even the same thing. I'm sure it's a small fraction of the world's economy— a very, very, very, very, very, very, very to the nth small fraction. A recession is a bigger disruption I would think.)

▶ "Nearly a million customers" were affected. Actually 900,000 customers were affected, but by saying nearly a million, you could imagine up to 999,999 customers being affected. That's a 10 percent difference. "Nearly a million" is technically not false, but stated that way for dramatic panic-mongering effect.

Aside from the general hack job that the *Register* was doing, it is indicative of the fear that downtime induces. The reality is that not only is downtime at a minimum in hosted environments, with the vast majority of the vendor-hosts having closer to 99.99 percent uptime than not, but more recent studies have found that there is far more downtime in environments that are on-premise.

In June 2007, Managed Objects, a business management-consulting firm with something to gain most likely by these results, found in a survey of 200 IT managers that the bulk of downtime in major corporate environments is as a result of on-premise home-grown or custom applications. In fact, 61 percent said downtime was due to applications and 82 percent said the cost of downtime, estimated at $10,000 per hour, was significant enough to impact their business. Their estimated downtime *per instance* was three to four hours.

To make it more direct: Google hired Radicati to do a study of Gmail downtime versus the on-premise Outlook or Groupwise e-mail downtime and found out that in 2008, Gmail averaged an aggregate 10 to 15 minutes a month downtime, with the on-premise e-mail averaging 30 to 45 minutes a month.

Part of the problem with the downtime is that perception is far worse than the reality. Think about your Internet service provider (ISP). How much time in a given year do you lose when your connectivity is lost, either for a moment or several hours? I estimated from my own provider, Comcast, I lost about eight hours all in all last year, in increments of a few minutes to about four hours. I managed to not only live through it, but my business continues to prosper. Yet, the SaaS downtime "events" bring out the critics who attempt to mold public opinion, such as the *Register* did in January 2009.

Really, it's the difference between cars and airplanes. Airplanes are among the safest modes of transportation—much safer than automobiles. But the problems are more spectacular and affect larger groups of people, so they are perceived as a more dangerous way to travel. Because on-demand outages affect multiple companies and are public, while the on-premise outages usually just affect a single company and are private, the perception of the on-demand outages is worse despite the shorter time periods.

The best way to deal with this—the only way to deal with it—is to have a strong guarantee for uptime in the SLA that you have with your host. This won't prevent downtime, but it will provide penalties for it, which means at least you won't pay for it.

The Players

While there are an inordinate number of key players, because they are the pioneers and the innovation leaders, salesforce.com is the clear market leader. But that doesn't mean there aren't others whose track record isn't worthy of an award or two. That would include RightNow, Aplicor, all the companies I mentioned in the earlier part of this chapter, and, most of all, NetSuite.

The reason that I'm singling out NetSuite as the Superstah! for this chapter is because it is the only SaaS suite that is end to end, covering the gamut of back and front office applications—something like SAP on-demand.

Superstah! NetSuite

NetSuite has had a consistent strategy that is unlike any other of its ilk in the industry. Led by the charismatic and definitely hip CEO Zach Nelson, and the uberbrilliant co-founder and CTO Evan Goldberg, NetSuite hasn't attacked the market with social features or been focused around innovation as its core. Its basic strategy has been to continuously improve functionality so that you can do enterprise-related operational work anywhere in the world in an on-demand environment. Even though they are focused on consistent improvement, they will add major pieces to the suite when merited. In April 2008, they developed their One World edition, which handles globalization and localization in one fell swoop in a rather effective way with a single interface. Also in 2008, they jumped into the business platform pool, as have many of their competitors. But unlike their competitors, their platform, NS-BOS, is narrowly focused around developing industry-specific applications. It isn't just a generally applicable PaaS.

What this points to is a solidly practical strategy that permeates everything they do. They were founded around an order management system that focused in the back office, hence their original name,

NetLedger. But they didn't scrap this just to be "new." They kept this order management core and built their CRM applications, NetSuite CRM+, around the same idea. For a good look at how this actually works, see Figure 16-1.

Figure 16-1: NetSuite CRM+ Sales Dashboard (Source: NetSuite)

Mission 21st Century

What's in store for NetSuite? Let Zach Nelson tell you the 2010 plan.

The business case for SaaS will only get stronger, as advances in networks, virtualization, and computing power make running your business "in the cloud" an increasingly natural choice. That in turn will lure in new vendors seeking to replicate our success in providing an ERP-driven suite of applications designed to run a global business.

In NetSuite's second decade we will remain focused on responding to customer demand, which increasingly revolves around building industry-specific solutions delivered from the cloud. That means expanding our own functionality as well as creating a partner ecosystem that leverages NetSuite as a platform to extend our core ERP, CRM, and e-commerce functionality with their business-specific domain expertise.

The Product and Strategy

NetSuite is aimed at the upper end of the midmarket. Throughout their history, they have not hidden their desire to go after parts of the market that SAP covets too. For example, in 2008, they announced a Business ByNetSuite program for SAP customers to capture those customers who are exposed by SAP's lack of an SaaS offering. They spent too much time, to my thinking, in going after their competition publicly and not enough on the merits of their actual solid successful functional applications services.

In April 2009, they seemed to have a change of heart. They redirected their competitive strategy to something that reminded me of the U.S. cold war strategy when Khrushchev was Soviet jefe. It was called "peaceful coexistence."

What NetSuite did was announce SuiteCloud Connect, too confusing a name, but it was the name of a smart idea. Using their partners Pervasive, Cast Iron, Boomi, and Celigo, they released a set of tools and APIs that would allow customers to integrate salesforce.com CRM applications with NetSuite's ERP applications. Very shortly thereafter, NetSuite released a new version of OneWorld, which added a Suite-Cloud Connector for SAP so that companies with large investments in SAP on-premise systems could retain their investments and still run divisions or a "local" entity in another nation on NetSuite. This is ERP-to-ERP, unlike the salesforce.com connector, which is ERP-to-CRM.

In other words, they took advantage of their greatest asset, the broad capabilities that their suite provided, and instead of aggressively attacking their competition, created "coopetition" by using their offerings to fill the holes of their competition's offerings.

Finally, this is a company that knows how to market and communicate with the analyst community and press exceptionally well. Zach Nelson is a terrific speaker and a marvelous spokesperson in general for NetSuite and a very, very cool, good-natured guy. Mei Li, their SVP of corporate communications, is not only known throughout the industry but also extraordinarily well liked throughout the industry—not easy when it comes to cynical analysts and press. She keeps the press and analysts well informed.

There are a few weaknesses, which they are aware of and addressing. They have some customer service issues that they need to fix. They are doing that as this book goes to press. Their partner ecosystem needs some work yet—it is a bit thin. They are now addressing that though there is still a ways to go.

But this is a company that can easily be called Superstah! for their offerings' breadth, its CRM applications' deep integration with the rest of the suite, the management team, and, now, their intelligence when it comes to integrating with other players in the SaaS and on-premise space.

Choosing SaaS vs. On-Premise: Comparative Checklist

Rather than the usual kind of comparative junk that skews either toward SaaS or toward on-premise and does nothing to help, I've kept the comparisons of good and bad for each separate.

But now, without skewing anything—though maybe skewering me—I pulled in Mitch Lieberman, a true Social CRM intellect (via Twitter, in fact), to put together Table 16-3, a valuable chart on how to view SaaS and on-premise as a choice for your company. Mitch, who is the VP of strategic solutions for SugarCRM, has no vested interest in either SaaS or on-premise. SugarCRM delivers their product both ways—in fact, three ways, as we'll see in a bit. So he instead analyzed company characteristics and indicated which one would likely be better based on your corporate characteristics. The checklist goes a bit further because it identifies some permutations of the corporate characteristics that are less certain aids to making a decision, but still significant considerations when it comes to your choice.

We couldn't have a better segue than this. Before I get into cloud computing, I'm going to pause to inject a discussion of open source so that there is no confusion about it. It is often wrongly equated with SaaS or on-premise computing. It doesn't compare. Do you want find out why?

I *knew* it! Hence the section.

Open Source: Not Quite Any of Them

When "open source" is thrown into a discussion, it tends to be translated from "culture" to "software." The definition that's most often heard is that it is the mostly unrestricted sharing of code and programs with developers to use the code for purposes that benefit both the code owner and the developer. Typically, whatever restrictions exist are under a Creative Commons license (www.creativecommons.org), which allows them to modify the code for, depending on which of the

Table 16-3: SaaS versus On-Premise Selection (Source: Mitch Lieberman, VP of Strategic Solutions, SugarCRM)

Topic	SaaS is better suited to your needs if:	On-premise is better suited to your needs if:	Answers that carry less weight
With respect to non-hardware related technology, how do we view ourselves as a company?	We do not consider ourselves a technology company, and prefer to stay focused.	We consider ourselves a technology-focused company, and CRM is just another component of our core operations.	We are technology focused, but we get distracted easily.
From a hardware perspective, we are perfectly comfortable providing uptime guarantees to our business users within our own data center.	This statement does not accurately represent our company. We would prefer to make this someone else's concern.	We perform this function for many other systems, and we are perfectly comfortable adding another system to the mix.	We have a managed data center, so it would be someone else's headache anyway.
With respect to the core software technology platform of the CRM system we plan to deploy:	The application itself provides most (if not all) of the necessary options and extensions for us to run our business.	We are likely to find ourselves diving into code, in order to extend the application, and we are often frustrated by forced boundaries.	We plan to outsource the initial deployment and upgrades.
The data to be housed within (and owned by) the CRM application is:	Generally innocuous from a pure compliance perspective, and as long as the provider is SAS 70 and has documented security protocols, we are comfortable.	Extremely sensitive (either by law or corporate policy). This may be a country-specific issue/concern.	Sensitive, but the SaaS provider meets the specific criteria to be considered safe. This does not push a decision one way or the other.
There is important data, which the CRM application may require access to (via API, SOA or REST is) in order to present the user with a complete picture.	We are confident, based both on the location of the data and the communication-protocol (secure) used to access the data, to provide the CRM application with the data upon request.	We have concerns, based either on the location of the data and/or the communication-protocol (secure) used to access the data, about our willingness to allow access to the data if it is not 100 percent secure.	This issue is at the core of the most complex part of the decision, it should not be taken lightly, and you may decide to address this first.
The CRM project is a strategic initiative, and absolute control over all technological aspects of the solution:	Is not required. Everyone is on board, from the CEO on down, with releasing a bit of control over certain aspects of the solution.	May be necessary in order to succeed. History shows that fighting IT often results in internal tensions and in-fighting.	Leadership is strong enough so that everyone is on board with doing what is best for the company, and this is a message from the C-level on down.

Table 16-3: SaaS versus On-Premise Selection (Source: Mitch Lieberman, VP of Strategic Solutions, SugarCRM) (Continued)

Topic	SaaS is better suited to your needs if:	On-premise is better suited to your needs if:	Answers that carry less weight
From a purely financial perspective, the financial gurus prefer:	Operational expenditures that are more predictable, consistent, and look better on the balance sheet.	Capital expenditures, which are typically heavy up front, but fit just fine within the financial planning.	While the CFO is important, this is a "what is the best for the business" decision, not a finance decision.
With respect to the number of users:	We are likely to start off with fewer than 50 users and will grow beyond that if we are successful with the initial roll-out.	We need to get off the inadequate current system within a year; more than 250 users at the get-go is going to be the case.	If the user count is in between 50 and 250, this question is a toss-up and should not carry significant weight.
Load to the system is likely to be:	Very dynamic and unpredictable. The fluctuations might be in user count, customers accessing a portal, e-mails (campaign), or other transaction types.	Static. There will be little change and predictable customer activity. The user counts are not likely to change often, or impact the system load.	Not sure. User count likely to stay static, but end customers might access the system often. Not sure the corporate network can handle it.
We are _____ adopters of technology.	Early. Early adopters will also like taking advantage of the ability to quickly and easily use new features.	Majority are late adopters. We will build the needs of our system according the specifications and not add unless the business screams at us to do so.	It depends on the technology we are talking about. The sales force likes new and cool, the call center hates it when we change.
Our employees are great:	But they do not seem to hang around very long.	And they will be with us for 20 years.	The SaaS-supported answer is more relevant than the on-premise answer. Employee turnover influences lost knowledge, but should not discount an SaaS strategy.
Time to market for this system is:	Crucial, critical, and we need it yesterday.	Really important, but we can take our time to do it at a reasonable pace.	Again, the SaaS answer is more relevant than the on-premise answer. Time to market can be achieved more quickly with SaaS, but if you have time, that does not make SaaS a poor choice.

permutations you use, commercial or noncommercial purposes. When the technology is shared in this way, it can expose bugs, it can speed adoption, and it promotes interoperability—all of which has value for the company owning the code. For the developer, it gives them a means to create an asset for themselves. What makes this so valuable is that not only can they create an asset, but there are distribution networks available—either through an independent developer's community or through a marketplace that the code owners provide, such as Sugar-Forge from SugarCRM or AppExchange from salesforce.com or App-store from Apple for the iPhone. By the way, SugarForge is easily the best named of the bunch.

I'm including open source in this particular chapter because, frankly, a lot of people confuse it with either "on-demand" or "free." It isn't either, though it can involve both. To clarify, it overlaps all computing delivery models, and all enterprise software has open source versions ranging from SugarCRM in the world that we're concerned with to Compiere in ERP to Drupal in social software platforms. Its scope is staggering, its range wide. But it isn't on-demand, cloud computing, or on-premise—and any comparison to them is wrong.

Open source means considerably more than just providing code and tools and distribution channels to developers. So . . .

What Is It?

Open source isn't four things and is three things. It is not fundamentally a new application architecture. It's not a new delivery model. It's not the source of free software—though a lot of open source software is free. It's not aimed at proprietary nonstandards based code or services.

It is a license and a culture. It's also freely available source code for applications that can be tweaked, overhauled, or created if it's an open source platform, like Drupal. However, the ability to do that doesn't give you the freedom to use the code in any way you want. It just allows you to use it in ways that the intellectual property owner allows you to, meaning you have a license to lease the code—and that license carries restrictions.

The license approval body is called the Open Source Initiative (OSI) (www.opensource.org) and they have some 70 versions of licenses that can be used. In CRM, according to SugarCRM's analyst relations director, Martin Schneider, they use an unmodified version of a General Public License (GPL) version 3. I don't want to bore you with the entirety of the license—being open source doesn't make it any less boring. But in a nutshell, the license allows you to convey a verbatim or modified (with note that it has been modified) version of a source code. If you modify the code, it must be made available to the relevant community. What makes this interesting is that open source code components are frequently used by historically proprietary vendors who aren't conveying the modified code to anyone. What will make this really interesting is that Gartner Group, in September 2008, projected that by 2011, 80 percent of commercial software will be using some form of open source code components in their applications—creating a potentially very dicey situation.

The licensing of open source has widely varying conditions. For example, there are different versions of the open source Creative Commons licenses for music, which you will hear a little bit more of in the electronic chapter "Honestly, I Want This Chapter to Be on Privacy...". Depending on the license chosen, they allow a musical piece under a license to be shared with attribution by someone other than the artist according to the following combinations:

1. The work as is

2. Derivatives of the work

3. The work in full

4. Parts of the work

5. In a noncommercial environment

6. In a commercial environment

Take any combination above and mix and match and there is a license or sublicense to meet the artist's requirements. You must be very careful which one is chosen or it can bite you in the . . . you know. The aforementioned electronic chapter will tell you quite a story about it.

It also means something that has been antithetical to most companies for the life of those companies—it means shared intellectual property (IP).

Shared IP: Proctor and Gamble Gamble with Sharing Secrets

Proctor and Gamble (P&G) are not horribly beholden to the past of "everything a trade secret and all exposure a lawsuit." Their patents are exposed when it makes sense to P&G to share them. Their Connect and Develop program (www.pgconnectanddevelop.com) is designed to involve anyone who holds their own intellectual property (e.g., a patent) and P&G in a joint venture to develop technologies and products that can be brought to market.

It stems from the desire that A.G. Lafley, the visionary P&G CEO, had to find 50 percent of all its ideas and technologies from outside the company by 2010. They reached 35 percent in 2008, with their eyes on the prize of that 50 percent.

Connect and Develop is unique in many ways. It provides an opportunity for people who in the past would have no chance at penetrating the inner sanctum of a company like Proctor and Gamble. The specific projects that P&G has on the table are identified, with some real exposure of the patents that are associated with the opportunities. For example, a quick look at the P&G Connect and Develop website brings up this opportunity posted as of February 2008:

> *We are looking for an auto-foaming technology that is more cost and space effective to incorporate in a powder laundry detergent.*
>
> *Description of the Need:*
>
> *A technology that produces self-fizzing on contact with water to enhance foam in a powder laundry detergent for hand wash geographies. The product must dissolve without agitation and quickly deliver rich/creamy foam, yet rinse easily. The cost of the foaming system should be less than 1/2 cent per use.*

It then goes on to list what they are specifically looking for and what they aren't looking for. Why is this important? Hey, how could self-fizzing auto-foam *not* be important? Besides that, though, P&G is publicly listing something that in the past would function as a part of a product road map and would be a closely guarded secret, punishable by death by unwashed hands. Now it is being publicly exposed with collaboration openly invited and any patents or other intellectual property that P&G deems important to provide, they do.

But it even goes further when it comes to the open IP that we're talking about and the cultural environment that open source and open IP propagates. Heed the words of Jeff LeRoy, part of the External Business Development (EBD) group at P&G, in a podcast he did on the P&G home site:

> *If we think your idea, your product, your intellectual property, isn't necessarily a good fit for us, but it is for somebody else who we have a relationship with, we'll forward you on to those people, even if it's another company or a competitor, because we want to be known as the partner of choice, and we want you to call us back next time.*

This is an ideal example of how open source isn't just a developer's dream world but a true culture shift that makes collaboration a much more viable option between companies and customers.

Open Source Culture

That cultural difference is the antithesis of a company trying to protect nonstandards-based proprietary source code. Source code or IP is not to be protected by the full force of the law. It is to be distributed to those who want to use it in a way that makes sense to the owner. They continue to own the source code. They choose to provide it and allow its alteration as long as it's redistributed democratically.

What makes open source an option for CRM buyers is that it is often a bit cheaper, though don't assume it has a noncommercial purpose. SugarCRM, the paradigm open source CRM application and platform, has an incredibly simple table of prices. Table 16-4 shows you their options as of mid-2009.

Table 16-4: Open Source CRM Leader SugarCRM Delivery Options (Source: SugarCRM, April 2009)

Product	Pricing
Sugar Express (1–5 users) (hosted)	$9 per user per month
Sugar Express (6–10 users) (hosted)	$30 per user per month
Sugar Professional (on-premise or SaaS)	$30 per user per month
Sugar Enterprise (on-premise or SaaS)	$50 per user per month
SugarCube 1005 Internet Appliance (5–100 users)	$4495 for box plus license costs

What you may notice is that they have three ways of delivering the applications: SaaS, on-premise, and a turnkey solution through an Internet appliance. In other words, open source does *not* compete with SaaS, or on-premise, or the cloud—it uses them.

It also costs money.

The benefit of using an open source CRM application is that pricing is favorable to the customer. For example, SugarCRM's pricing in this new model is inexpensive whether you use the on-premise or on-demand version. Another benefit is that there is usually a wide array of add-ins, extensions, and additional applications that go with the original product because of the robust developers' communities that are attached to most open source applications. For example, Sugar-CRM has over 18,000 registered developers, out of a community of nearly 100,000 that write additions to SugarCRM and at times even write entirely new applications or vertical versions of CRM. There is a product called Carousel CRM that actually competes with Sugar-CRM that was written on the SugarCRM platform.

But this creates some risks too. How do you achieve a measure of quality control over 18,000 developers who are having their way with your code? The licenses don't restrict what modifications are made, they restrict or constrain the distribution of the modified code. So the variety and quality of the modified offerings are endless.

SugarCRM's workaround is to have paid employees developing the core code for the SugarCRM platform and products, while the developers' community does ancillary work.

Superstah! SugarCRM

This is the company that is so hands down the winner of the open source Superstah! that I can't actually put my hands down far enough to show you how much they won this by. They are the company that revolutionized the CRM industry, probably just a bit short of a disruptive innovation, by showing how CRM could be a collaborative effort and by not freaking out when their code was "hijacked" because they actually invited the "hijackers" in to take it and use it. They also moved the entire open source movement forward a bit by showing that the open source movement wasn't just a geek's sandbox. SugarCRM proved it was a viable alternate—now mainstream—approach to developing commercial enterprise-grade applications that had the power and the scalability of comparable, in this case CRM, applications and possibly even more flexibility.

Another factor, underestimated, but equally important, is their corporate culture, which is refreshingly open and yet highly professional.

Mission 21st Century

Larry Augustin, the SugarCRM CEO, is a savvy gentleman. Here's where he sees SugarCRM going over the next few years:

> SugarCRM is positioned at the nexus of three converging technology waves—open source, software as a service, and Social CRM. Our focus is on combining the flexibility delivered through open source, the ease

of use of on-demand technology, and the emerging social web to make CRM software more useful and intuitive.

Short and, of course, sweet.

SugarCRM: The Business

SugarCRM has a smart business model, utilizing 18,000 developers (amidst a community of 100,000) called the Sugar Network to develop on the core platform. They have a very business experienced CEO in Larry Augustin who has been on the investment side as well as management. They've made some excellent hires, for example, Martin Schneider, a former analyst for The 451 Group and a brilliant one at that, who ostensibly handles analyst relations for them but does so much more (and is a damn good rock guitar player).

When they released SugarCRM version 5.2 in late 2008, they overcame their glaring lack of social features by adding a small set of social feeds and what they call Portal Dashlets, which is basically a treacly name for enterprise mash-ups, a.k.a. widgets—something, of course, being offered by SAP, Microsoft, and many other vendors too. What's most germane to this chapter is that this open source CRM leader is offering cloud connectors, which are hooks to any feeds of a LinkedIn, Jigsaw, or Hoovers nature—in other words, external data sources to provide what would be a richer look at competitive intelligence. These are the technical links, not the actual feeds to any one of them. Finally, they've added Sugar Feeds, an enterprise-level Twitter-like way of interacting inside SugarCRM applications, which provides status, alerts, and notifications. In other words, not only are they a successful traditional CRM open source series of products, but they've brought their product into the 21st century with social capabilities too.

Because they function as a platform and a serious CRM application suite, their marketing messages get mixed sometimes. They lean to the CRM application suite side more than not. But what makes them interesting is that they are able to operate as a platform or as a flexible CRM suite.

Their sales model shifted in early 2009 from direct sales to channel sales—which is a major shift for any company. Their partner program, as 2009 progresses, is undergoing a major revamping and education so that they can successfully transform their sales model into what is already the most successful open source CRM model by about 10 earth circumferences.

The Product SugarCRM Data Center Edition

SugarCRM has innumerable editions that are every bit as extensive a feature factory as the largest CRM applications out there. They differ from most of the on-demand delivery models in that their SaaS offering is multi-instance, whereas everyone else's but Oracle's is single instance, a.k.a. multi-tenant. However, they've also done something that, while not unique exactly, plays with the big boys directly and at the same time, distinguishes them from their competitors in the small and midsized company market. That would be SugarCRM Data Center Edition (Sugar DCE) (see Figure 19-2).

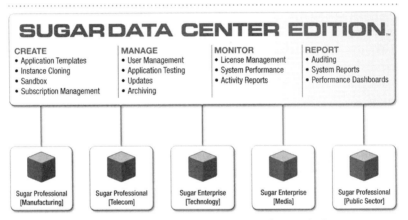

Figure 16-2: Configuration of the SugarCRM Data Center Edition by Vertical Industry (Source: SugarCRM)

Think of it this way. If you had multiple instances of SugarCRM running with multiple editions of SugarCRM, this would provide you with the systems management, provisioning, and monitoring tools and a centralized management console to handle those deployments.

I thought a portion of former CEO's John Roberts's take on the DCE in their official press release was very interesting: "...the single view of the customer for large companies is dead. Enterprises need the ability to create and manage multiple CRM instances to serve the differing needs of business units. Sugar DCE addresses these needs."

Even though not by a long stretch do I buy into the single view of the customer for large companies being dead, he's right that how the single view of the customer is viewed varies according to business units.

For this chapter's purposes, the Sugar DCE for Partners is particularly interesting. It provides a single console for value-added resellers to provision new SugarCRM applications at the click of a button. It does what you would expect a systems management console to do—manage licenses and monitor the system and the use of the licenses, all in an SaaS environment. What makes it most compelling is the sandbox environment that is innate to the DCE for Partners, which allows for the developers to come up with new functionality, including vertical functions and complex customizations in a way that doesn't affect any other instances managed by the console yet can be deployed to others if that's needed.

This is great stuff and does so much for the anecdotes that prove the case—open source environments can be highly successful commercially. SugarCRM leads the way in every facet of that. No sweet jokes. Please.

Vtiger

While I think SugarCRM has no real competition as of yet, Vtiger is worth taking a peek. They have over 1.5 million downloads of their CRM suite as of the end of 2008, far eclipsing all the other non-SugarCRM open source CRM vendors. In fact, they may eclipse them all *combined*. They are owned by Zoho. They've even added an iPhone app so that "sexy" can be added as a descriptor.

That's it. Time for a 15-minute break. Go out and get something to drink and maybe a snack and bring it back. We're going to clear up the mystery of cloud computing now that we've gotten on-premise and SaaS delivery models and open source out of the way. We'll head over to a new catwalk where the new season's most fashionable models are on display: cloud computing from the collection of EMC, Oracle/Sun, Microsoft, Amazon, and many other nouveau technology designers and architects.

Cloud Computing: Wispy or Real?

This one is going to be fun. Partly because this is such a hot topic and partly because there is an inordinate amount of confusion as to exactly what cloud computing is. In an April 2009 report that was otherwise maligned by a lot of competing parties, McKinsey identified 22 definitions of cloud computing and that was only the formal ones. As of July

2009, there are roughly 22,200,000 results for cloud computing when you do a Google search. So you can imagine the interest in it. This is now even higher with the purchase of Sun Microsystems by Oracle in late April 2009. Sun Microsystems is one of the key players in cloud computing.

There is a certain irony in that acquisition because of a statement made by Oracle CEO Larry Ellison at the 2008 Oracle Open World:

> *The interesting thing about cloud computing is that we've redefined cloud computing to include everything that we already do. I can't think of anything that isn't cloud computing with all of these announcements. The computer industry is the only industry that is more fashion-driven than women's fashion. Maybe I'm an idiot, but I have no idea what anyone is talking about. What is it? It's complete gibberish. It's insane. When is this idiocy going to stop?*
>
> *We'll make cloud computing announcements. I'm not going to fight this thing. But I don't understand what we would do differently in the light of cloud.*

You'll note that Larry Ellison isn't planning on rowing into the tsunami. What he says is, I don't know if this cloud computing thing is anything new or different, but it seems to have some serious mojo. I won't buck it so I can make a buck on it.

This isn't all that Oracle has done when it comes to the cloud. They also struck a deal with Google in March 2009 to create Google Gadgets and to use the Secure Data Connector (SDC) so that the gadgets they create can live in the cloud.

More irony in all this talk about the cloud is that consumers who use technology have been living in the cloud for a long time. The Pew Internet and American Life Project released a September 2008 report on "The Use of Cloud Computing Applications and Services" and found that 69 percent of the respondents use web-based word processing, storage, and e-mail services such as Gmail and like the convenience of having access from any device anywhere. The social customer is not hung up on the issues of data and so forth, but at the same time, to be fair, they aren't an enterprise either. There is a familiarity with cloud services among the population who have been using them, even though they don't necessarily know them as cloud services.

What does all this "living in the cloud" actually mean? Why is it important?

What Is It?

The contemporary lore as to how cloud computing got its name is that the way that Internet networks are represented in those awful technology diagrams you can't avoid is by a cloud. Is that true or urban legend? I don't know, but it certainly is within the realm of possibility. More germane is to figure out what exactly cloud computing is—and what it isn't.

First, here is the Wikipedia definition, which isn't bad:

Cloud computing is a style of computing in which dynamically scalable and often virtualized resources are provided as a service over the Internet. Users need not have knowledge of, expertise in, or control over the technology infrastructure "in the cloud" that supports them.

The concept incorporates infrastructure as a service (IaaS), platform as a service (PaaS), and software as a service (SaaS) as well as Web 2.0 and other recent (ca. 2007–2009) technology trends that have the common theme of reliance on the Internet for satisfying the computing needs of the users.

Next, here is a definition that I'm aggregating given the many other definitions I've read, the research I've done for this book and elsewhere, and factoring in the consulting I'm involved with that crosses the path of cloud computing:

The use of a pervasively connected Internet-based computing platform to source services, applications, and infrastructure employing a consumption-based (pay-for-what-you-use) pricing model. It is the deployment of your business workload on the Internet.

The Components of Cloud Computing

I trust that definition is satisfactory? If not, I can't do much about it, but continue to read on regardless. Cloud computing isn't as vaporous as a real cloud is. There are specific components and services that it encompasses and specific benefits that it has. Before we get into the benefits, let's peruse the components.

Infrastructure as a Service (IaaS)

This is perhaps the greatest differentiator between SaaS and cloud computing. What cloud computing provides under the aegis of IaaS *cloud infrastructure* is to deliver a connected grid, either real or virtual, combined with a utility- or subscription-based billing environment. The most intriguing permutation of IaaS is the deployment of a virtual server environment, rather than a physical server. Where SaaS-hosted models provide a physical server carrying multiple (or single at times) clients on a single instance of the application, the cloud computing model often provides a virtual server such as those provided by EMC's VMWare, that allow resources to be dynamically reconfigured based on the scale of the workloads at any given time. That said, no matter how much you "virtualize" the server environment, there is going to be a physical server somewhere. It just doesn't matter geographically where it is.

The Amazon Elastic Computer Cloud (EC2) is an excellent example of how this works. To use it, you create what Amazon calls an AMI (Amazon Machine Image) that includes your existing applications, libraries, data, and configuration settings. This is loaded into their Amazon Simple Storage System (S3) repository, which consists of redundant servers in multiple data centers across the world. This is a virtual version of your business workload stored in a virtual storage area that is created by redundant connected physical servers in many locations.

Platform as a Service

Platform as a service (PaaS) in the cloud is designed for the facilitation of the development and subsequent deployment of applications without the physical hardware and software. The obvious benefit here is that it eliminates the overhead costs of that development and deployment, such as operating system maintenance or network connectivity. Most of all, you don't have to buy software or hardware.

Salesforce.com's Force.com is an ideal example of this kind of platform, though it uses Apex, which is a proprietary development language. Another example would be the .NET platform from Microsoft as it has been reconfigured for Microsoft's cloud computing effort, Azure.

Cloud Services

This component is perhaps the most difficult to truly define because of conflicting ideas on what cloud services are. For example, in that controversial McKinsey report, they distinguish between "the cloud" and "cloud services." To them, "the cloud" has to comply with three requirements:

1. Hardware management is highly abstracted from the buyer.

2. Buyers incur infrastructure costs as variable OPEX (operating expenses).

3. Infrastructure capacity is highly elastic (up or down).

The "true cloud," as McKinsey calls it, has to meet all three requirements. Cloud services only need to meet numbers 1 and 3. They identify Amazon EC2, Microsoft Azure, and Google as "true clouds," with Zoho, salesforce.com, and Gmail as "cloud services." I think that McKinsey might be overcomplicating it though I agree that Zoho and Gmail are cloud services. salesforce.com is more than that.

A cloud service is a product, service, or solution that is consumed via the Internet. Interoperable web services that communicate from machine to machine in a distributed environment (as we discussed in Chapter 15) are cloud services when they are available through the use of web-based software. Rearden Commerce using web services to provide business services like airport car rental or Zoho providing sales force automation via the Web and not as a hosted service would be ideal examples of how a cloud service works. It is characterized by an interface that is directly accessed via a browser from wherever you are.

Storage

This is an important distinguishing characteristic when it comes to understanding the difference between SaaS and cloud computing. In the cloud, data is stored online as a service—meaning that you pay for the amount of data you store at a rate typically based on gigabytes per month. This is not based on the purchase of a hard drive. In effect, you're not paying for the real estate or the storage locker, you're paying for the weight or volume of what you're storing. Of course, data is stored in the data centers of SaaS-based hosts, but you aren't typically charged for use of the physical storage as long as you keep within reasonable limits. The basic storage cost is built into the subscription price.

One of the simplest examples, though hardly a paradigm of how to do it well, is Apple's MobileMe. You can upload files to the Web in the MobileMe storage space—up to 10GB—and then synchronize it with your data on your PC or, more likely, Mac. Amazon's S3 is also a web services–based cloud storage capability. That's where the AMI is stored, as you saw above.

Applications

The easiest way to think about cloud-based applications is to just think about Zoho. Zoho is a cloud-based collaboration suite that provides dozens of products, all run through your browser. Zoho has 29 applications, add-ins, and plug-ins accessed from a web browser. Take a look at Figure 16-3 for the home page, which is not only a listing for the applications but a portal for accessing them.

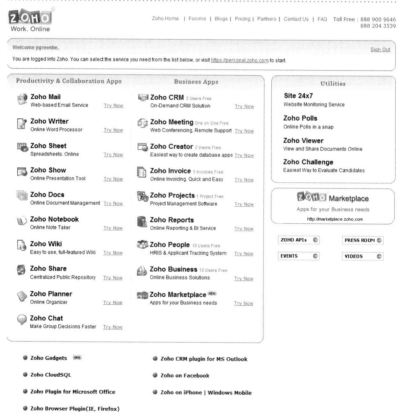

Figure 16-3: Zoho applications—a list and a portal (Source: Zoho website)

Theoretically, all the Zoho applications could be accessed through a single computer in any location from anywhere—or a single application could be delivered via a grid of distributed computers. The user has no idea how it is being delivered or accessed and most likely doesn't really care.

Web 2.0 Characteristics

While the majority of cloud computing players have social features built in, it isn't a mandatory component for cloud computing environments. However, this hasn't stopped some of the vendors from developing social cloud services. For example, IBM launched a collaboration and social networking cloud service called LotusLive Engage, which links LotusLive applications like Live Meeting or Live Activity—their cloud apps—to more traditional on-premise Lotus applications like Notes, Domino, or Lotus Connections. They call it, somewhat cutely, "Click to Cloud." The idea is that it allows employees to bridge the firewall by rolling all applications into the cloud whether they are on-premise or on-demand. It even provides an application called Content Collector that manages e-mail and instant messaging in the cloud, something like managing Gmail and MSN Messenger.

Utility Consumption Pricing

Just to be clear, this is not just a subscription model. Subscription or even traditional pricing is an option that can be provided to the users. But the idea behind the pricing model is pay-for-use. What you use is what you pay for—no more, no less. For example, Amazon EC2 pricing works like this:

- ▶ **On-Demand Instances**   This is pricing by the hour to run your AMI. It varies depending on geography (U.S. and Europe); size of the "instance" from small to very large; whether the instance is running on Linux or Windows, with special pricing for an instance running on a virtual SQL server, Microsoft server, or IBM.

- ▶ **Reserved Instances**   This is an option that lets you make a one-time payment with a one- or three-year commitment that significantly reduces your usage (hourly) cost. Same variances apply.

- ▶ **Internet Data Transfer**   There is additional cost for data transferred into the system or out of the system. There is a single price for data transferring into the system. Outgoing data pricing varies based on estimated amounts of data, from 10 terabytes to 150 terabytes per month. There can be variations based on region and zone.

▶ **Elastic Block Storage (EBS)**   This is the persistent storage that exists for the life of the instance. When the instance ends, so does the provided storage. The charges vary by location (U.S. and Europe). They are for the amount of gigabytes used per month and for each million I/O requests. They also charge for the number of EBS snapshots made per month that are stored on Amazon S3—their storage "backup" for EC2 in this case—though it does more than that.

▶ **Elastic IP Addresses**   This has nothing to do with what holds up your pants. It is a static IP address that's assigned to your account and that you can use to remap your instance in case of failure. The charge is a bit unusual. You're charged for non-use. When you are using it there is no charge. However, if you're remapping it to your instance—you're charged a "remapping fee" in effect.

Well, that was easy.

Actually, if you distill the pricing, you pay for use of storage, bandwidth, volume, location, and AMI activity. All in all, even though I didn't specify the numbers, it is quite small per unit, though since we are dealing with an enterprise, you could end up paying a fair chunk of change. But it still is less than the costs of your own environment.

Benefits of Cloud Computing

To look at the benefits of cloud computing, we're not going to do something so mundane as another chart. This time, we're going to take a case study, examine it, and break out the benefits based on the results of the case study. If you have any questions, please just blurt them out.

Case Study: DISA RACE. What?

The Defense Information Systems Agency (DISA) is responsible for the management of IT for the Department of Defense (DoD). Historically, the DoD had a problem with buying expensive equipment for product development and testing. When the effort was completed, the equipment remained on the books depreciating with only roughly 15 percent of its capacity having been used. A huge, wasteful, but still necessary expenditure.

In 2009, to deal with this problem, in the name of efficiencies, DISA launched RACE—the Rapid Access Computing Environment. It was aimed at creating a development environment that could be accessed from the cloud through a portal for only $500 a month. Because of the low subscription price, the users could charge the cost on a government agency's credit card—which allows purchases under $2,500 without too much paperwork.

What made RACE so attractive was that it was a complete development environment, providing all the tools, services, and infrastructure that were needed. Capacity planning wasn't necessary. Spending ungodly amounts of taxpayer dollars wasn't necessary. Rather than spending months to set up the physical servers and install the software and then watch much of it go to waste when the testing was complete, it took no more than 24 hours and usually considerably less to provision the entirety of the infrastructure and applications needed.

When the effort was underway, the environment could be accessed at the office or at home, on whatever device it needed to be accessed from. When it was done, the environment just retreated to the cloud—no muss, no fuss, no wasted capacity.

Breaking Down the Benefits

The benefits of cloud computing become apparent when you start to analyze RACE.

1. The RACE environment is provisioned in no more than 24 hours and typically well under that. This means that there is no vendor selection process, no technology implementation period, no capacity planning necessary.

2. The $500 per month subscription fee for unlimited use is a controllable cost that can be easily charged to a government credit card, bypassing what can often be an onerous procurement process.

3. Since the RACE environment is based on economies of scale, when the customer base grows, the price will decrease.

4. The development environment is complete and custom fit to the requirements of the agency that needs it. Since the environment actually resides in the cloud, there are no maintenance

costs that concern the agency—they are covered in the monthly subscription fee. There is no overhead, keeping costs down.

5. It is accessible anywhere through a web portal. That means that the users will be able to work in optimal environments of their (and the agency's) choosing.

6. Finally, when the development and testing are complete, the environment is just rolled back into the cloud so there is no underutilized capacity—utilization is a theoretical 100 percent. Additionally there is no cleanup necessary on the part of the agency when done.

Potential Problems with Cloud Computing

This doesn't mean that cloud computing is perfect. There are definitely problems, though they tend to fall into the category of "immature," not "horrible breakage." Even in that regard, there aren't that many egregious ones.

First, economies of scale, which is a very professional sounding phrase, are pretty much theoretical at this point since most companies are not working in the cloud. Additionally, the cloud hosts each have unique cloud infrastructures so there isn't exactly easy interoperability in the cloud.

Some of the concerns are the same concerns that people have had about SaaS: data security and control, downtime, and so on. In fact, McKinsey took a look at the uptime of cloud hosts and found it ranged from 99.5 percent to 99.9 percent, which led to concerns about the lack of availability of cloud-vendor service level agreements.

Most of the issues are due to an immature model trying to find its way. But cloud computing seems to be growing up fast. Gartner Group issued its annual technology forecast at the end of March 2009 and, despite what they saw as a major slowdown in IT growth (3.9 percent), one of the few areas where growth was on fire was cloud computing. Expenditures on cloud computing were projected to grow 21.3 percent from 2008's $46.4 billion to 2009's $56.3 billion.

Case Study: Cloud Computing Does It All

BrandSCAN is an interesting company that focuses on using contemporary media for market intelligence and brand insight. What makes them interesting is not their product, which is interesting unto itself, but their development model. What they've done is take the entire production process from concept to product and combine outsourcing services with the cloud. Bruce Culbert, industry thought-leader and managing partner of BPT Partners, LLC, will take it from here:

> BrandSCAN's founders hired a U.S.-based development company who had their programming operations offshore. The founders of the company created concept, design, and user interface documents, which were then given to the development company to turn into a product. The product idea was straightforward. Collect actionable insight, information, and conversations from the Web and social media. Then create a functional easy UI that integrates with key CRM solutions like salesforce.com. The back end is run by a .NET architecture and a SQL database.
>
> The idea was to take this configuration and, using Force.com, create a framework that not only used salesforce.com but also could integrate various products via AppExchange. The back end application would use SOA and be hosted on Amazon's EC2 cloud. What BrandSCAN was able to do was to start with a concept and go to product release without any investment in fixed IT costs or in infrastructure. Because it runs in the cloud, the scalability is very flexible, meaning it can be deployed starting small and scaling higher—and still be priced based on usage.

Similar to RACE but in a commercial cloud environment, Brand-SCAN is a good example of a small company that simply figured out how to be cost-effective and remarkably efficient. Not a bad combo.

The Players

It's very hard to detail the players in this space. You've seen a lot of Amazon in this chapter because they were one of the first vendors who figured out that the cloud was a good place to be. They had a lot of unused capacity—and voilà, EC2 and S3 were born.

But there are several other players. EMC, which owns the virtualization powerhouse VMWare, recently introduced VSphere4. That gives companies the opportunity to create a private cloud environment behind their firewall—which might beg the point of the cloud but is still a viable idea. salesforce.com uses its PaaS framework Force.com to provide its cloud infrastructure. Google has been providing consumer cloud services like Gmail for a long time and is moving into the enterprise, though exactly what direction they are taking to do that remains to be seen.

Perhaps most intriguing is the April 2009 acquisition of Sun Microsystems by Oracle. Even though Oracle probably didn't buy them just for their cloud services, it is a part of what Sun provides. Given the comments of Larry Ellison earlier in this chapter, it will be fascinating to see what Oracle does with Sun's cloud capabilities.

Microsoft released its Azure cloud infrastructure, which they describe as a "cloud services platform" in late 2009 after announcing it in late 2008. This one has a lot of promise because it has been released in "flavors" such as Azure for web developers, corporate developers, system integrators, independent software developers, and business. They've already thought through who was going to use their platform and created the environments and toolsets to meet the requirements.

There are others—companies like IBM, 3Tera, and Hewlett-Packard. In fact, a list compiled by John M. Willis, in his *IT Management and Cloud* blog, found 48 companies in 2008 that had some relationship to the cloud as a server or a service provider or who had an application that lived in the cloud. We can expect to see lots more vendors in the near future. Take note here. The cloud is not only here to stay, but in a few years (I'm hedging a little) might be the way to go.

As Jim Carrey used to say, all righty then. We've laid the groundwork over the past 15 chapters with a description of the social customers, what kind of experience the customer has and needs to have, and the tools and the infrastructure and architectural choices that are available.

But it's time for the good stuff—the strategies that you might choose for Social CRM. Ready to go? On to Chapter 17.

17

Big Picture, Big Strategies

As of now, you have enough to start piecing together a Social CRM strategy. There are some questions that have to be answered to do that, including "What's a Social CRM strategy?" Incidentally, that would be a fair question. So I'm going to answer it with a caveat. That caveat is that while these are the components of a Social CRM strategy, I would not use this book to define my strategy if I were you. I would use it to guide my strategy. I'd use it as a reference for my strategy. I would even use it to help me decide how my strategy would look—at the 1,000 foot level or so. But I wouldn't do what a shall-remain-nameless internationally based company did several years ago with the first edition of this book. They sent me a note saying, "We have developed our CRM strategy directly from your book and have become stuck. Can you answer some questions?"

Know what my first somewhat more vehement than represented here response was to them? "Stop! This book wasn't written about your company. It was written as a guidepost to how to do something—not what to do specifically for your enterprise. This can't be taken as literal gospel." Each company is individual, and each strategy has to be appropriate to that individuality, taking into account culture, existing personnel, existing technology, future plans, the current state of the economy, and the needs of the sector that the company is in, and . . . I'm getting ahead of myself.

Just suffice to say that "Stop!" still holds even with the fourth edition. The approach to strategy discussed here is nonspecific to any one company and should be seen as a set of best practices and suggested approaches that then have to be tailored to whatever it is your company does and is.

This is a *big picture* chapter. I need to set some expectations here. Don't expect tons of granularity—this is the overview of the elements of strategy and a case study that is meaningful. The details will be in Chapters 18 through 21, so bear with me. Please. And thank you.

Introducing Strategy

At its broadest, a Social CRM strategy is one focused around customer engagement. It differs from more traditional CRM strategies because the primary concern is not managing relationships that are based on understanding a customer's transaction history and behavior, but instead is founded on treating the customer as a partner who will, in return for benefits of some kind, provide value to your company.

CRM 1.0 strategy was operational and tactical but was at its core a strategy for actually managing corporate transactions with customers— and at its best a strategy for managing the interactions with customers. The software associated with it was based on process efficiencies and interaction effectiveness. Pretty much the best you could expect from it was a greater knowledge of a customer via the 360-degree view of the single customer—which still is in woeful short supply at the companies that claimed CRM in their portfolios. A McKinsey study placed it at 38 percent. On the other hand, the February 2009 Speed Trap/ Econsultancy Social CRM study (a slideshow summary is available at www.slideshare.net/econsultancy/speedtrap-crm-20-survey) found that 70 percent of their respondents had at least centralized storage for customer data—which isn't the same as a single customer record but at least shows some promise of progress.

But that was CRM 1.0. Social CRM is widely recognized as a strategy for encouraging the customer to participate with your company in making decisions that affect the particular customer. What it does is take CRM 1.0 and extend it far beyond its original bounds.

Social CRM *as a strategy* (less so as a technology) is actually maturing as more and more companies are adopting at least some facets of it. But to do it successfully, the implications need to be clearly recognized by the companies embarking on developing the strategy. For example, it assumes the existence of a social customer who controls their own interactions with other customers and with the company, which CRM 1.0 strategy did not. In fact, the fundamental idea behind Social CRM strategy is that the customer will engage with the company in a way that provides mutually beneficial value, rather than a strategy for the optimal extraction of value from a customer in exchange for, at best, a delightful experience. Not that there's anything wrong with that—it just limits what the customer and the company can do.

In a Social CRM strategy, the company's skin in the game is to be honest and straightforward with the customer (authenticity is the buzzword *du jour*), to be open with the customer and reveal more of the inner workings of the company to the customer so that they have the information they need to make intelligent decisions on how they are going to interact with the company—in the context of their personal agenda.

This doesn't mean giving away every secret the company has. Transparency doesn't mean slutty behavior. In the electronic chapter called "Honestly, I Want This Chapter to Be on Privacy, but if I Wrote It, I'd Have to Blog About You," there'll be more on transparency. Suffice it to say, what it means for strategy is at least an understanding that the customer needs to know more than they have traditionally in order to have a great enough personalized experience to want to continue to do business with you—at a minimum. Optimally, your KPIs will be around advocacy, not just retention. But we'll see about that, won't we?

The Social CRM definition from the CRM 2.0 wiki (http://crm20 .pbwiki.com) bears repeating:

> *Social CRM is a philosophy and a business strategy, supported by a technology platform, business rules, processes and social characteristics, designed to engage the customer in a collaborative conversation in order to provide mutually beneficial value in a trusted and transparent business environment. It's the company's response to the customer's ownership of the conversation.*

Increasingly, companies are incorporating customer engagement strategy into their efforts to develop customer value. There are an increasing number of companies, large, medium and small, using blogs, providing podcasts (both audio and video), developing communities, and participating in communities not built by them, such as Facebook or more specific communities that cater to the company's interests. What does that mean? It's recognition that the customer is now not only the owner of the business ecosystem but is controlling the chatter going on. What they don't control is the traffic flow—and that's where engagement comes in.

The Voice of the Customer Has a Larynx

The first element leading to true customer engagement is *always* identifying and integrating the voice of the customer. This does not mean making presumptions for those customers. This means actively involving them in helping you know them. Unfortunately, that's always in theory, since most companies don't do that.

In order to develop a customer strategy, knowledge of your customer is primo on the agenda. That's the way Social CRM rolls.

Who Is Your Customer?

Knowing who your customer is sounds like a piece of cake, doesn't it? But, in truth, it isn't. Who your customer is can change in a dynamic business environment. How you perceive your customer—even if it's the same people—can also change, which can complicate an already complicated matter.

For example, how many on the list below have you thought about as possible customers?

▶ Paying clients

▶ Sales consultants

▶ Management

▶ Suppliers

▶ Business partners

▶ Independent agents

C'mon, admit it. Most of them didn't even cross your mind as a customer that you had to serve. From your standpoint, the first one—the paying client—is what you ordinarily think of as your customer. But if you think it through, in a B2C environment that paying client, the individual consumer, is the customer that we're talking about. In a B2B environment, that paying client can be the senior management of another company. But you have to engage not only the senior management as customers but those who influence the senior management. In your own company, if you don't treat your sales consultants or suppliers as customers, it can cause damage that will impact your ability to sell to those potentially paying consumers.

But it doesn't stop with just the recognition of new categories of customers. It also means that your perception of customers can vary due to a variety of fluid conditions. For example, as we established early in this book, the social customer demands treatment as a partner, not just a paying customer, and that changes how you interact with that customer. There are a huge variety of factors that can affect your customers' interactions with you and your response to them. Among them:

▶ Business environment changes

▶ Customer behavior changes to the individual level

▶ Business model changes

▶ Product line changes

▶ Technology advances

▶ Social climate changes

▶ *Ad nauseam, ad infinitum*

You skeptical? Let's look at social climate changes. In Chapter 1, we established that peer trust became dominant in 2004. That was a change in the social climate that also triggered a change in individual expectations and the attitudes and behaviors associated with that change. This new direction for trust came simultaneously with advances in technology, particular web-based and particularly around personalized communication that gave peers the ability to interact with each other 24/7 and in real time.

That led to a very smart presidential candidate's staff tapping into a specific "customer group" that was particularly sensitive to both the new form of trust and the changes in technology that were dynamically being utilized following 2004. That group, Gen Y, and other web-savvy groups were a primary force responsible for Barack Obama's presidential victory in 2008. Yet, in 2005, did you even vaguely fathom that this was possible? I doubt it. Not only did you barely remember who Barack Obama was at all—unless you had seen him speak in 2004 at the Democratic convention—but you didn't know that this kind of customer could lead a social change that dramatically changed the perception of the United States once again.

Did you?

Developing a Strategic Map: The Elements

There are a few things different from 2004. First, it's years later! Second, you now need a customer engagement strategy, not just a strategy to manage customers around their transactions. Third, back in 2004, customer strategy was a significant and important of corporate strategy. Now, customer strategy *is* corporate strategy. That said, the elements of strategy I would have proposed in 2004 are pretty much the same as I'm about to provide to you here—with a few additions this time around.

There are some caveats and assumptions that you have to operate under when it comes to customer strategy. If the strategy doesn't benefit those executing it, you might as well chuck it. This may sound like a "duh" moment, but in fact, the primary reason that CRM fails, according to studies done by pretty much every 800-pound or less gorilla analyst firm, is because of the failure to involve users from the beginning. The most popular study, done by AMR Research as far back as 2004, claimed 47 percent of the failures are due to that lack of upfront involvement.

What that means is that when developing the strategy you have to consider personal values and concerns. They have to be part of the planning you're doing. *Don't underestimate the importance of this.* I put it in italics because it is a centerpiece for your strategic framework. Why? Because human beings are self-interested. This isn't a bad thing. Self-interested doesn't mean selfish. It simply means you have an agenda that you intend to fulfill to your satisfaction throughout your life—and that extends to your work, too. You matter. There may be no "I" in team, but there is an "I" in "I." Which is a good thing.

Personal benefits to the stakeholders who will be responsible for execution of the strategy or those who will be impacted by the strategy have to be considered when developing the business objectives. While ultimately you won't please everyone and will most likely lose even some highly valued employees to dissatisfaction, you can attempt to incorporate the idea that you are creating a "community of self interest."

On a practical level that can include:

▶ Incentives to make improvement in customer experience "worth it" to other customer groups

▶ Changes in compensation for employees who focus on customer satisfaction

▶ Supplier premiums for beating the baseline guarantees of SLAs

▶ Partner rewards for customer satisfaction to be applied for benefits

▶ Tools for the customer to not only manage but create their own experiences

But to include these things in your plans means to first be able to identify who those stakeholders are.

Choosing Stakeholders (Including Customers)

In retrospect, book burnings in the 15th century were a historic error. In retrospect, the strategy used by Vice Admiral Zinovi Rozhestvensky at the naval battle of Tsushima during the Russo-Japanese War of 1904–05 was an error of historic proportion. Choosing stakeholders solely from senior management is also a historic error, just of a lesser magnitude.

Stakeholders in a CRM strategy and program can be senior management, but may also encompass mid-level managers, senior staff, power users, some junior staff, business partners, suppliers, and customers. After all, who has more of a stake in this than the customers? But that said, choosing from all of these can be a bit unwieldy, and a stakeholders team of 5,000 is probably a bit much. Kidding. About the number, not the clumsiness.

Since other stakeholders are necessary for the success of CRM initiatives, it pays to be selective on who is recruited so that you can have a total group that can be effective, yet represents the important constituencies that exist.

NATURAL LEADERS

One group to ferret out and solicit has little to do with formal titles bestowed by the management hierarchies, but instead is those natural leaders who exist at every company regardless of size. You know them. They are the people who are the "mom" or "dad" of the department—always willing to listen to the troubles of their fellow employees. They are the power users you ask to fix your computer because you don't want to deal with IT and they know enough to do it—for the most part. They are Jack on the TV show *Lost*.

Essentially, these are peers who, for one reason or another, have risen through the ranks and are trusted by their fellow employees. Typically, while they hold no particular title within the company, they command the respect and the loyalty of specific groups of fellow employees. When developing a CRM initiative, it's important to find these natural leaders and select those who are able to serve on the CRM stakeholding team.

This serves two purposes. First, they are trusted peers who will ably represent the "constituency" that trusts them and the constituency will feel represented. Second, they are the best evangelists back to their constituents as the strategy evolves and is put into action.

CUSTOMER ADVISORY COMMITTEE (CAC)

The other ignored set of stakeholders is (he says, awash in a sea of irony) the customer. Needless to say, this is a stupid mistake that needs to be corrected before it ever gets made. Customers need to be involved in the development of the Social CRM strategy, since the strategy is being developed to optimize impact on them.

In order to hear their voice, creating a customer advisory committee is a must. Typically, customer advisory committees are in the world of B2B—because the customers are companies that are engaged in processes that are serviced by the company—and they have a stake in the creation of the tools and solutions that enhance those processes. It's corporate to corporate. That is typical. In fact, one B2C customer of mine attended a conference on customer advisory committees in 2008 that had about 100 attendees, and he was the only one from a B2C company there. He was looked at with a good deal of curiosity.

Don't shy away from a B2C customer advisory committee. The consumer knows what they want and recruiting them to help you figure out what that means strategically for you is something you should see as an imperative in your planning of the strategy.

Some considerations in recruiting a CAC:

▶ Consider doing a mailing to a selected segment of your customer lists that have shown something more than a passive interest in you. If possible, have the mailing give the customer a couple of options such as becoming a member of the CAC or being part of a community—to be planned—that would have less responsibilities than the CAC.

▶ Scour the Web for those customers who vocally love you or hate you and recruit them to the CAC. Yes, you heard me. Those who hate you too. They are passionate for a reason and if you can turn the frustration into a productive channel, it can be hugely beneficial because they are typically intelligent, savvy customers who have ideas. They also become great advocates—the passion transfers to the plus side of the equation.

▶ Make sure you have a well thought out (and spelled out in writing) purpose and make the amount and type of time commitment clear, such as one in-person meeting and a quarterly phone call.

▶ Make sure senior management is well represented during the actual CAC meetings.

▶ Make sure that the CAC suggestions are acted upon and reported back to the CAC.

▶ If you have an enterprise social network or community, give the CAC official visibility in that community. Reputation matters. Validation does too.

▶ Make sure the members of the CAC are compensated in some appropriate way. Their time is valuable.

Mission and Vision

Once you've chosen your stakeholders, putting together a corporate mission and vision statement is the next step. "But," you say with a puzzled look and a furrowed brow, "we have a mission and vision statement."

It doesn't matter. The idea is that you are developing a customer-centric corporate strategy focused around an objective of customer engagement, which is not the likely purpose that your original mission and vision statements were created for. Consequently, by developing new mission and vision statements, you'll be able to see the gaps that are in the older ones. Then you'll understand what you have to change at the company that much better.

The mission and vision statements are your anchors for the entire strategy. They are short versions of your entire strategy and programs. Marketing messages are aligned with the mission and vision statements. They aren't marketing messages.

MISSION STATEMENT

The mission statement is the "as is" declaration—the overarching objectives of your company as they are today. The Ritz-Carlton, perhaps the most famous hotel in the world, is defined by its level and quality of service. Their mission statement:

We Are Ladies and Gentlemen Serving Ladies and Gentlemen.

This is a poetic declaration (nothing wrong with poetry or creative metaphor when it comes to a mission or vision statement) of what the Ritz Carleton provides. It will offer elegant and perfect customer service, including the appointments in the room and throughout the halls, the training of the staff, the treatment of the customers, the quality of the food, and whatever else is involved in creating the experience of "ladies and gentlemen serving ladies and gentlemen."

VISION STATEMENT

Vision is the corporate grand strategic objective—the "to be"—also at its best poetic. Typically, it expresses your outlook for leadership, market position (of the future), and your value proposition.

One of the most famous vision statements in history was "An Apple on Every Desk," a clever visionary phrase by Apple which promoted their computers and used the old teacher/student metaphor to focus everyone on something that felt and sounded familiar but something that also was a future objective of the company. Notably, they didn't achieve this, but it was and might still be their vision.

Objectives/ROI

This is straightforward. What kind of return are you looking for? Are you looking for a strategic win (increased Net Promoter Scores across the company or 5 percent increase in market share over a two-year period) or a tactical victory (free up two hours per week per salesperson)?

The one thing that is tough here is that the objectives not only vary from company to company, so there's no real template, but they can be intangible or not all that easily measurable. For example, how do you measure what it takes to be more "engaged" with the customer?

Business Case Including Costs/TCO

This is the Episode Where You Justified Spending Money on CRM to the Boss.

Essentially, this is the "why" we are doing this. Because CRM can be hard to quantify, this particular segment has to be as crisp as an overcooked potato chip. In 2007, Gartner Group research vice president and analyst Michael Smith took an expansive view and at a high level defined eight elements of the business case:

1. Develop a CRM strategy to support your business strategy

2. Select business metrics to support your CRM strategy

3. Establish a baseline for these selected metrics before the project begins, and if possible, benchmark performance against industry peers

4. Describe the capabilities of the CRM application

5. Negotiate targeted improvements using the baseline metrics

6. Convert the targeted improvements into financial results

7. Develop the TCO

8. Calculate the ROI

You'll note that what Michael Smith defines as the business case encompasses everything that I've been (and will be) talking about within the context of a CRM strategy, including the strategy. Unless you want to be thrown into a Möbius-strip-like infinite loop, please don't think of the business case as a step in the strategy but as the documentation of the strategy and all its elements and the justification for the program in writing to the decision makers.

Risk Assessment

In 2005, I was speaking at the Financial Services User Group for analytics vendor SAS in New York. The setup was a stage not too high off the floor; there was a curtain across the stage from wall to wall. In front of the curtain was the screen; behind the curtain was a wall. This was a common setup that I had had several times before when speaking.

I'm a pretty demonstrative speaker. I move around a lot. At one point, I went back to make a point and use my hand to slap the screen. So, screen, curtain, but, oops—no wall. I went straight off the back of the stage and hit the ground. It was amazing to hear 100 senior execs from financial services companies simultaneously going "ooooooh." As a result of this, whenever I run across this setup, before I speak I go to the curtain and push at it to make sure there's a wall. No more assuming that there is.

What does this ridiculous story have to do with risk assessment and mitigation?

Everything.

Risk assessment and mitigation is not mysterious. They are what we do naturally with every step we take. Think of the story. I assessed risk incorrectly due to past patterns, which ordinarily had a wall behind the curtain. The wall wasn't there, so I fell off the stage. I mitigated future risk by hitting the curtain with my palms in all future similar situations and seeing if there was a wall.

Risk assessment and mitigation should be that little a deal when you're doing a CRM project. They have to be done because it's necessary to understand what might go wrong. It makes sense to then figure out what you might do to deal with a future problem.

If you're dealing with complex environments, you could do scenario planning (see the web chapter, "You Can't Handle the Truth, So You Have to Change"), but I wouldn't otherwise spend enormous amounts of time on risk assessment and risk mitigation. While this might sound flippant, it's not. What you plan for going wrong is often not what does go wrong. What you can be assured of is that something will go wrong. Be prepared with what you can, but more than that, be flexible and cooperative and you'll be able to get through a lot of the problems you run into.

Business Requirements: Processes

One commonly found problem in CRM strategies, when it gets to this granular a level, is that the technology tends to become the predominant factor in determining how the business is to be run. Several years ago, I had a client who called me in because their CRM strategy had gotten hopelessly ensnared in the features of the software they had purchased—leading them to a bloated implementation and to adding processes that were not needed by their business.

What we did was what should be done at a middle or late stage of the development of a CRM strategy. We reassessed every single process the company used and discarded those that were not valuable to the company and the customer. We modified those that could be saved, added those that were missing, and then decided which CRM applications were to be used based on the processes needed and the performance objectives of the company.

This was the methodology of York International, a multi-billion-dollar HVAC equipment provider in their award-winning implementation of Siebel Field Service CRM in 2003. They spent many months examining each and every process in the company—more than 250—and determining which made sense for the future of their business. Once they had a final process map, they were able to go to the CRM application vendors with this question: What can you do out of the box to meet these process and business requirements?

York International understood that some customization was going to be necessary. But by going into the selection process with a clear understanding of their business and process requirements, they were able to make the most cost-effective and best fit selection because the software had to be fit to the business, not the other way around.

There's a lot more on process in Chapter 19, so I'll hold off until we get there for a more detailed discussion on how to look at business processes when making these decisions for your Social CRM programs.

Metrics/Benchmarks/ROI

I'm going to spend a little time looking at the left-brained part of CRM, meaning metrics, including KPIs and benchmarks. Some of this is covered in more detail in other chapters. For example, ROI is covered not only here but in Chapter 21. Other discussions of metrics and measures are covered in Chapter 20.

While I'm always railing about the quants in CRM who substitute scales and numbers for human judgments and experiences, I do recognize that there has to be accountability for performance and also a way of determining whether you're doing "good" or "bad" against what you perceive to be the norm.

Those are served by developing metrics for your ROI, TCO, and benchmarks with key performance indicators for achievement, which means metrics and measurement and numbers—precisely the things that CRM left-brainers are always focusing on.

THE VALUE OF MEASUREMENT

Gartner Group did a study in 2007 of 251 clients who implemented CRM. They found that:

> ▶ 71 percent calculated effective total cost of ownership or estimated project costs

► 60 percent reported having measured the benefits

► 17 percent have performed an ROI analysis

► 5 percent have done a formal post-project review

The survey results indicated that the more measurement is done, the more successful a company is with its CRM implementation. For example, if the respondent indicated that they had done only a project plan, then they succeeded 50 percent of the time. If they added an ROI analysis to that, it rose an additional 10 percent. If they did a post-project review, it jumped to 70 percent—though I'm a little unclear how a review after the implementation is done can contribute to the success of the implementation, since it's done. However, the results are as indisputable as any survey results—the more you measure in CRM, the more you succeed.

KEY PERFORMANCE INDICATORS (KPIs)

KPIs are perhaps the best way to account for how a person or program or project or process is doing against expectations. They are what they sound like—a measurement that is designed to give someone a numerical standard to adhere to.

In order to establish KPIs, it's important to establish performance objectives for each department or sector of the business. Once those objectives are set, then the KPIs—which really are nothing more than the measurements of those objectives—can be established.

KPIs can be strategic or tactical. For example, a strategic KPI would be some rate of external innovation, such as Proctor & Gamble's intention that 50 percent of all technology the company develops will come from outside sources by 2010.

An example of a tactical KPI would be that the time of replacement of materials from the point of sale must be reduced to one day.

CRM-related KPIs that you might run across—both tactical and strategic—are:

► Revenue per salesperson or agency (sales)

► Ratio of administrative to street time for salesperson (sales)

► Customer lifetime value (CLV) (sales)

► Response rate percentage of increase for marketing campaigns (marketing)

▶ Queue time reduction (customer service)

▶ Increased up-selling and cross-selling opportunities over time (customer service, sales)

Culture and Communications

Communications in an environment receptive to a new outlook when it comes to customers are not only mission-critical but in fact symbiotic. Open communications on the nature of the strategy and its implementation to employees, customers, partners, and suppliers—in other words, those parties affected by the strategy—go a long way to making it much more adaptable than it would otherwise be.

By the same token, organizational change efforts are essential to CRM initiatives because how the company is going to function and the way that employees and customers interact will be successful only if the changes that become necessary are, by the end, not resisted. That means that open communications play a role in how well the organizational change goes.

I'm going to concentrate on the communications policy, both internal and external, as the CRM initiative moves ahead. The downloadable chapter "You Can't Handle the Truth—So You Have to Change" is entirely about organizational culture and transformation from the perspective of the customer-centric, so it doesn't bear repeating here. Suffice to say, culture change is one of the most important parts of an overall Social CRM effort.

INTERNAL COMMUNICATIONS

When the teams are in place, the customers are engaged in the creation of the strategy, and the effort is underway, it pays to make sure that the employees of the company are informed of the initiative by an announcement. How the announcement goes out will be indicative of what communications channels are used throughout the life of the program. They might include:

▶ E-mail

▶ Website posting

▶ Newsletter

▶ Twitter

▶ Instant Messenger

▶ Conference call via Skype or ordinary conference line

▶ Phone calls

▶ Party

▶ Flyer distribution

▶ Blog postings

▶ Podcasts

▶ Wiki entries

▶ Mobile/text messaging

These are just a few of the possible communications channels. Be alert to who at your company uses which of the channels. Like all other efforts, this announcement and the subsequent updates need to be *effectively* communicated, not just communicated. The Gen Yers at the company (see Chapter 4) will want to communicate via text messaging while the older generations will prefer e-mail.

Everyone loves a party.

Because communications about the strategy are widely disseminated, that doesn't mean they have to be entirely democratic. "Need to know" is certainly a good rule of thumb for the communications policy. For example, it isn't necessary to reveal the entire budget for the Social CRM initiative to every staff member. Some will resent it if they hear about it. Others will have no interest in it and consider the communication a nuisance. However, the finance department may need to know because they are responsible for allocation of the money, as are perhaps line of business (LOB) owners who will have their departmental funding affected.

The communications policies and the channels being used should be planned from the beginning of the endeavor. The reason? Communications are the lynchpin for the success of the effort.

You know I'm right about this. Just spend about two seconds to remember a time when communications with some company you were dealing with failed. What happened? You hated the company but you also thought "if only someone had just talked to me. . . ." Well, that happens all the time, and that's why internal and external communications about the status of the CRM initiative are so important. Don't under-estimate it.

ITERATIVE LEARNING

Training is going to be necessary. Not only is it necessary to get adoption of the system that you're using, it's important for the psyches of the staff who will be the system users. They want to participate in learning about the system and in shaping what they learn. That's standard operating procedure.

Iterative learning—training that incorporates the participation of the trainees in the evolution of the curriculum—is something that works in CRM technology and program training environments. That means interactive participation so that the training is modified as it is taught.

As part of my CRM "existence" I both co-own a CRM Training Certification company, BPT Partners, and I train on CRM strategy and social media implementation (two separate courses). We do a lot of interactive training and are constantly requesting feedback, including evaluations at the end of sessions and spot phone calls or e-mails to former students on what they'd like to see. We then incorporate the feedback into the future iterations of training and the process begins again. This is particularly effective when planning your CRM strategy. How you train is as important as who you train and what you are training them on.

To make sure the training is effective, the systems are adopted, and the communications continuous, it pays big time to train a superusers group who are trained to train. This is called, another "duh" moment, "train the trainer" and is something I can't stress enough. Often the superusers are the same people who function either as the natural leaders—those trusted on their personal authority by others at work—or even the stakeholders—the ones involved in creation of the CRM program. Because they are "someone like me," training them to train others is far more effective than even the professionals who might be doing the original training, simply because those taking the training trust its source.

Okay, that's internal communications. What about external communications with customers? Here, I'm turning over the mic to Marshall Lager.

Marshall Lager is the President of Third Idea Consulting and the former senior editor at CRM Magazine. His journalism and humor have both won him recognition in the form of APEX and Azbee awards. Additionally, he is a smart, insightful, and incisive analyst and consultant who knows the landscape. The combination of all these skills is wicked. I'm going to let this industry-leading journalist and dear friend speak for himself here.

Marshall is an insufferable know-it-all when it comes to customer-facing issues. He lives in New York, plays way too many computer games, and talks about himself in the third person.

External Communications Strategy

"What we have here is failure to communicate." Strother Martin's character in Cool Hand Luke *may have been talking about recalcitrant prisoner Paul Newman, but he also unwittingly described most companies' customer focus. Try as you might, you will not find a sane person who actually enjoys dealing with a business via any channel. What's more, despite a wealth of advice (like this book, natch) on how to fix customer communication problems, far too many are still making random efforts and hoping for good results. It is to them I address the following, in hopes of their eventual enlightenment: You're doing it wrong, and here's what needs to change.*

1. ***Unified channels.*** *Just because we call e-mail, phone, chat, SMS, and face-to-face conversation "channels" doesn't mean customers want to find something new each time they surf them. Contact centers aren't just call centers anymore—they are the nerve center of customer communication. Just because a customer calls in (by phone) doesn't mean the rep shouldn't have the e-mail history and purchase records. Clerks in a store should be able to see what a customer looked at online. If you text-message an offer to somebody, make damn sure the person in your organization who ends up fielding it can act on it. Sales, marketing, and service/support must have the same view of the customer at all points.*

2. ***Don't sell me; make me want to buy.*** *This may not sound like a communication strategy issue, but as contact center agents are increasingly called upon to cross-sell and up-sell, it becomes one. With the information you gather from a unified customer hub (you have one of those, right?) combined with real-time analytics, you can get a sense of what's on the customer's mind. Yes, you can predict what the customer is most likely to*

want to buy and then offer it—prepared scripts and must-push offers
have abysmal bite rates compared to what can be achieved this way. But
the real strength is in seeing the behavior of a customer who is frustrated
or planning to defect, and making that customer happy with whatever is
most likely to keep them with you. It can also reveal a customer who is
not worth keeping, so you don't subjugate your business trying to keep
them.

3. ***Be open.*** *Nothing turns a customer off like the impression that a com-*
pany is distant and clueless. A lack of unified communications will give
that impression, as will mindless cross-sell/up-sell attempts. But one of
the best ways to humanize a company is to make it act the way we want
our friends and family to act. Ask us what we think of what you're doing,
and be prepared to act on good advice—solicited or otherwise. If you
screw up, admit it and apologize—sincerely and with a minimum of
doublespeak, whether you lost a single order or designed a product that
is badly flawed. Then correct the error. Find out what we want, and
provide it the best way you know how. Remember, Strother's listening.

Thanks, man. Talk to you later—and always.

Vendor Selection Strategy

I'm only putting this in as a placeholder for Chapter 21, where you can
see how to go deep on vendor selection. Keep in mind a major caveat.
Vendor selection, which involves choosing the applications and the
company that provides the apps, is one of the later stages of the overall implementation of the strategy. You do it at the beginning and your
odds of success go down, though you might have the technology in
hand. You do it later, and you're doing it smarter. But I'll let Bruce
Culbert tell you about that in Chapter 21.

Model Project (Pilots)

Doing a pilot in the case of a CRM program doesn't mean a smaller
version of what will be a larger implementation. It means choosing a
specific tactical objective and then developing a strategy and implementing toward a solution for that tactical objective. For example,
several years ago, a client who was not prepared to do a CRM implementation because of cultural issues that were related to their

relationship to their sales force, which was independent agents, still needed a new marketing and sales management system because theirs was so badly broken. The implementation of that sales and marketing system was primarily to increase operational efficiencies, not make a change on how to deal with customers per se. We brought in NetSuite as an interim solution with the understanding that they would still have to bid with everyone else when this company was finally ready to develop a full-blown CRM strategy and implement a comprehensive system.

One of the effects of the effort was that the company and the agents got comfortable with the idea of a CRM technology, which will make the transition culturally a lot smoother when the time for the more comprehensive solution is at hand. The pilot fulfills a need and provides a quick "win" so there is acceptance of CRM at the senior level and among the staff. This isn't simply just a scaled-down test. It's a small tactical effort with a purpose.

Extending the Community

This is a new Social CRM element in the pantheon. Part of your planning now has to be on how you're going to engage your constituents— be they customers or voters or people with like interests. No longer are you implementing just the operational CRM programs that improve your business processes. You need to add a social component to your strategic thinking, which might include the use of social media, or monitoring external communities who are "conversing" (see Chapter 9) about you, or even creating a customer community that would be part of your ecosystem so that the conversation would at least be visible and available to you if not in your control.

But it goes even beyond the obvious. Part of this planning is how transparent and open you're going to be as a company—that is, what you are going to let your customers know that in the past you wouldn't. How are you going to treat your customers, as clients or as partners? What does that imply for your corporate culture? What kind of channel strategy does this mean? Are your partners a receptacle for your products or are they part of an integrated ecosystem that's organized around the enhancement of the customer's experience?

All in all, what you're planning for is how your customers will be participating in your business with you and what that means to your contemporary business environment.

The CRM Killing Fields

Okay, in a perfect world, the CRM . . . wait, there is no perfect world. Something is going to go wrong (remember risk assessment?). I guarantee that. Let me give you an idea of what could and how bad it can get, just so you don't get too giddy. These are the CRM killing fields.

Killing Fields	Explanation
Corporate politics	Vindictive, aggressive, selfish personal agendas for career advancement or damaging someone else's career.
Fragmented personal or departmental agendas	Siloed departmental agendas take precedence over the greater corporate good; interferes with CRM strategy due to selfish interest.
Stakeholders teams—wrong mix	Bad chemistry or wrong leadership positions can damage CRM programmatic development.
Misalignment of goals	Different stakeholders have different ideas on the result and there is no documentation that clearly defines the objectives or ROI.
Poor definition of objectives	Often seen by a badly done proposal that gives huge freedom to vendor without constraints.
Poor knowledge of terms	"Oh, I didn't know *that* was CRM!" This can be enormously damaging. A client of mine had a homegrown definition of CRM—took two years to overcome.
Not timely	"Just too busy to get to it right now."
Inflexibility	Assumption that what worked in the past works now. That never is the case.
Not vindictive, but shortsighted	Failure to involve users from the beginning or its permutation, no users as stakeholders.
Inability to identify self-interest	Personal objectives have to be clearly stated from the beginning and known among the stakeholders. "What do you get out of this?" Transparency is key.
One-way mandates	Stakeholders and executive sponsors can't order anyone to use the system or implement their piece of strategy. Imposing it is automatic failure.
Failure to be iterative/interactive	Learn as you go, and go and learn. This is user involvement in the training and in the selection of features and functions they need—for example, salespeople need order management.

Killing Fields	Explanation
Seeing it:	As a single project—it's a strategy and program.
	As a technology—it's a strategy, program, system, and technology, not just technology.
	As a system—see technology.
	With an endpoint—it's ongoing as long as you have customers, which would be always unless you go out of business.
	As a set of tactics—it is a long-term strategy that uses tactics, though winning small victories can be a strategic move.
Failure to involve customers from the beginning	The voice of the customer has to prevail. Social CRM demands early-on customer involvement.

A Case Study

We're heading into the home stretch now. I want to drive home the point on strategy by looking at a case of a successful Social CRMish strategy—even though it is still a work in progress and somewhat unconventional: David's Bridal.

David's Bridal: The Unconventional Social CRM Strategy

David's Bridal is a true American success story. In the late 1990's they were revolutionary and they built a dominance in the wedding apparel market that no one is near touching—with nearly 40 percent market share. But they are smart enough in some of their leadership quarters (including the CEO) to recognize that what an observer of the industry called a "disruptive force in the target sights of the rest of the bridal industry because their model created something that just creamed the rest of the industry" was no longer revolutionary. In fact, they understood that their extant model could be a brake on the progress toward their goals as the 21st century moved on.

Paul Greenberg Pretty Safe Harbor Nonfinancial Compliance and Full Disclosure Policy Statement

First, in the interests of full disclosure, David's Bridal has been my client for the last seven years, and they are simultaneously my favorite and most exasperating client. They drive me nuts and they make me *kvell* like a proud daddy. I've made friends there who will be my friends for life regardless of whether they or I have a continued relationship with the company. So what you're hearing here is their story, my story, and a story they know that I'm telling about them. In fact, the co-chairman of their Customer Value Review Committee (CVRC) (more about this in a minute) actually presented at the 2006 AAA CEO Conference with me because what they do is so out of the box and so compelling that it is a genuinely good story with lots of stuff worth hearing about, including the obstacles they overcome—and the rather unconventional approach that the CVRC represents. What they have in progress is something unique and, hopefully, repeatable as an idea—though I know they don't want it repeated in the wedding apparel industry. But it has a genuine practical value that goes far beyond just their $2.4 billion niche industry.

And Now, Back to Our Practitioner

So what's the story with David's Bridal? They are the world's largest wedding apparel and related accessories retailer. They have more than 300 retail stores in 46 states and Puerto Rico. Their business model is a massive selection of wedding apparel styles with multiple sizes on the rack from the Versaces and Vera Wangs of the world at unbeatable prices. Their stores are high volume retail outlets, not boutique service or one-on-one service providers. They are deeply sales driven. They have 3 percent of all the wedding apparel stores in the United States, but are so predominant that over 70 percent of all the brides who shop for gowns pass through their retail portals, though they don't necessarily buy. In the seven years I've been associated with them, I've seen their market share go from 20 percent to roughly 35 percent. They are immensely successful. Let's put it this way, while there have always been lots of issues to deal with (as there are with any company), I was by no means there to fix something broke. Their ROI is to take that nearly 40 percent market share and turn it into a 50 percent market share. They recognized that this was not going to be a short-term, one-shot effort, and wisely recognized that their business model and culture had to change for this to take place—from the CEO, Bob Huth, on down. But the statistics support the effort, thanks to research work done by senior director and CVRC co-chairman Scott Rogers. They found that if they just captured some of the business that walked in the door and then walked out and never purchased there, they could hit 50 percent market share without building a single additional store—just based on that 70 percent traffic volume and a greater conversion rate.

Eye-opening. Not store-opening.

Identifying the Problem

So step 1,001 was identifying the problem.

Huh?

Yeah, Metaphorical Step One Thousand and One (MSOTO). To get to the point of real breakthroughs took us (me and the forward thinkers at David's Bridal) two years with multiple missteps and let's just call them "misaligned" political agendas. It was painful, painstaking, and the constant pressures of the day-to-day jobs affected those evangelists trying to build an "outside-in culture" that had been intensely focused on "inside-out" sales—not customers.

Make no mistake about it. This was and still is an intensely sales-driven culture that aims at driving high volume traffic through its stores quickly and effectively. Their concern was how to develop a more customer-centric focus at the company. But to do that they had to answer the fundamental first question, "Who is the customer, really?"

Who Is the Real Customer?

Their customer for as long as they existed was perceived to be the obvious one—the bride. Not even the bridesmaids. That meant the customer lifecycle, which was defined by the length of time to the wedding date, was about as long as a very old fruit fly—say, seven months. (Please don't bother to look up the lifecycle of fruit flies. I'm sure that they're way shorter than seven months. Just grant me a literary license for the day. I'll pay whatever registration fees you want and fill out the paperwork.) That means from the time the bride was engaged to the time that the wedding was over and the bride was whisked off by the groom for all the after-hours stuff that grooms and brides do and probably had already been doing.

Yep, seven months and out. The running joke was that repeat customers at David's Bridal undermined the moral fiber of the United States.

Because the wedding was the end of the relationship, referrals, especially word of mouth referrals from the brides and bridesmaids to those with upcoming nuptials, were of major importance at David's

Bridal (henceforth DB). They measured 46 percent of their business as word of mouth referrals.

Their business model was based on the assumption that their value pricing and incredibly wide selection of high quality gowns on the racks was their critical differentiator, and if they provided good service they would get the referrals they needed. Thus one huge driver was their $99 wedding gown sale.

It sounds about right, doesn't it? It's a solid business model that earned them 40 percent of the market. But, as we found out quickly, there was a lot of work to be done.

Identifying the Problems? Ruthless

The first problem they discovered was that service improvements at the store level were in order. Imagine service complaints from people who are shopping for what might be the most important and certainly the most emotional day in their entire lives. The results of bad service in that environment could change the term from "going postal" to "going bridal."

Luckily, that didn't happen, but as their sales rose and the intensity of high volume activity increased without massive increases in sales consultants, the service complaints increased. But the selection of, among others, Versace and Ralph Lauren was so compelling and the idea of getting a super-perfect gown off the rack that day or shortly thereafter was just so powerful, sales growth continued.

There was another concern. The only person who got any attention in the store—for some of the reasons mentioned above—was the bride. The bride was the goddess of the purchase. The bridesmaids were essentially a coterie of clothing mannequins who tried on the bridesmaid dresses that the bride picked for them. So why pay attention? After all, this is event-driven sales. The centerpiece of the wedding is the same as the centerpiece of the wedding cake—the bride.

Concentrating on the bride pretty much exclusively got them to where they are.

Prior to my arrival, there had been a number of steps taken and systems put into place that affected the CRM strategy. One of the most interesting was the creation of a point-of-sale system that you'd think was a CRM system, except that data collection only occurred after the sale had been made—individual transactional customer data. Ordinarily, you'd think that this would be valuable because of the future purchasing patterns of the customer, but remember, they didn't expect to see the bride back after that fruit fly lifecycle ended. The relationship to the customer was event-driven (the wedding) and one-off ("happily ever after"). Thus the data was valuable only for historic reasons and market analysis, but nearly meaningless for the customer insights necessary to drive repeat business.

CVRC, Not CRM: The Right CRM Strategy

These were only a few of the specific issues that needed to be dealt with in conjunction with cultural mindsets that surfaced as the work continued. About two years into the process, I was sent about 300 pages of documents from different programs at David's Bridal to review to see if they were on a customer-centric track. They asked for my edgy New York style brutal assessment. After spending two weeks reading and then writing an extensive commentary, my conclusion was "no" despite the obviously good intentions built into the program. This sparked a series of meetings with senior executives and CRM-related team members, which uncovered something in retrospect that was not at all surprising. Like zillions of sales-focused companies before them, DB was presuming for the customer, as opposed to listening to the customer. So, because of the good nature of the people involved and the business value that the company could realize from a change, we decided to do something about it.

I went to the CEO, empowered by the David's Bridal evangelists, and laid out a plan to form a committee that I called the Customer Value Review Committee (CVRC). Here's how it was set up and what its purpose was:

1. **1.** Find the most customer-centric decision makers at the company and populate the committee with them. Keep in mind, this was *not* meant to equate to a classically cross-functional team that a CRM program typically demands. Fair departmental representation didn't matter. What mattered was that the members were strongly focused on the customer even if they ran the supply chain or the art department (so to speak). They also had to be decision makers who were empowered to decide on something at the meetings being held by the committee.

2. **2.** Recognition that this wasn't a CRM implementation and it wasn't a "project." It was a programmatic approach to changing the culture at David's Bridal from sales-driven to customer-driven, but not a full-blown CRM effort.

3. It would be publicly endorsed by the CEO and that endorsement would be known throughout the entire company so that its authority as an empowered committee would be clear.

4. It would do several things:

▶ Find out what the customers were actually saying and thinking—not presume for them at all.

▶ Find out what the store of the future would be like, as well as who the customer of the future would be.

▶ Do a high level process and program review to see which DB processes were customer-value friendly and which weren't. This was not a full look at each process, just an overview.

▶ Do deep customer mapping of customers who were selected by store, geography, and other characteristics and interviewed by the members of the committee—this was an absolute requirement. Committee members, as customer-centric as they were, had in several instances little or no interaction with the customers in their recent senior management job incarnations.

5. Once this process was completed—over about a year's time—expand the results to a pilot.

6. Keep the committee alive to act as the conscience of the customer inside of David's Bridal and to be the fount from which all customer-centric wisdom and projects would spring.

We got complete buy-in from the DB CEO and we were off to the races. There were seven committee members and me. We fought, laughed, loved, cried, got confused, lost focus, refocused, but at the end of it all, were able to say amen and hallelujah. There were several significant epiphanies on the committee, particularly after the customer mapping was done and the results supported by both anecdotal and metric evidence. All of a sudden what had been presumed for the customer was seen to be, simply, wrong. For example, the registration process at the front door was seen to be an event of major impact. It turned out the bride didn't even remember registering the vast majority of the time. Second, the assumption throughout DB history was that price and selection were their great differentiators. It turned out that price wasn't as important as selection.

Keep in mind that the mapping has topical and timely utility so, for example, in an economic downturn, pricing might become as important as it was previously presumed or even more important.

Critical to the mapping process was the questionnaire for DB customers, which was primarily designed by Scott with the help of members of the committee. This questionnaire, a model for customer experience mapping, was perfectly done, with questions designed to trigger a memory but not to direct the respondent customer to any preconceived conclusion. The breakthroughs were worth the effort.

From Fruit Fly to Human Being

One of the most significant things that we found, thanks to the brainstorming among the CVRC and the mapping, was that the customer of the present was nothing like the customer of the future. The bride was the customer of the present, with somewhat more than faint recognition that the bridesmaids were going to be brides one day. But the customer of the future wasn't the bridesmaid, though she certainly was a potential future DB customer. The future customer is, ta-da, the mother of the flower girl. Yes, *the mother of the flower girl*. Here's how it goes.

David's sells wedding gowns (and associated accessories, of course), bridesmaid dresses, flower girl dresses, junior bridesmaid dresses, quinceañera dresses for the 15-year-old Latina, prom dresses, sweet-sixteen outfits, and so on. After marriage, one of the things a bride often becomes is a mother. The bride becomes the mother of the flower girl, junior bridesmaid, bridesmaid, and bride (and some of those others in between), and then that bride becomes the mother of the flower girl, *ad infinitum*. What was a seven-month one-off relationship becomes a lifetime relationship with, admittedly, years between events. But nonetheless the nature of the customer and the lifetime value equation changes dramatically, as does how the company works with that customer.

There's still a long way to go at David's Bridal. The CVRC has expanded to a second circle of senior store management so that a social network/community pilot sanctioned by the CEO using Neighborhood America's technology can begin with some of the stores to see how the store of the future will work. This is very cool. I mean, think about it. I have no kids. This year marks our 28th anniversary, so a wedding isn't in my future, but I'm excited over wedding apparel!

This is exciting CRM strategy—an unconventional CRM strategy, but it points out one of the core lessons of CRM strategies. They are never the same from company to company. In some companies, conventional strategies work really well and the application of best practices is entirely appropriate. In others, conventional strategies and best practices applications will literally take the company down—which means creative thinking is in order. Don't worry about whether or not you are following the "right" steps when it comes to engaging customers. Just figure out, given the business model you have and aspire to, how your company is going to do it, even if it doesn't use conventional means. The key to Social CRM strategy is doing what you have to for collaborating and partnering with your customers, not looking good to someone because you followed the textbook and used the right buzzwords.

I don't mean to be harsh (well, maybe a bit), but strategic CRM methodologies are sometimes driven more by appearance and pleasing someone notable to a career than by substance and the customer. Delight your customer and your managers will be delighted. Take my word for it.

Okay, we're heading toward drill-down, not meltdown. Now that you have a broad picture of the elements of a CRM strategy, we're going to start digging into some aspects, somewhat more technical and functional, of what it takes to develop an organization that is engaged with customers. But before we do that, two things.

First, read the takeaways that Doug Leather, a highly respected consultant and business leader in the southern hemisphere, provides to you—free of charge—on developing a CRM strategy.

Second, take a deep breath, take a break, and get yourself a drink. Non-alcoholic? Orange juice might be a good choice. Alcoholic? Lagavulin 16-year-old single-malt scotch or a really good Manhattan. Either way, come back later and the trip through Social CRM land will continue.

Mini-Conversation with Doug Leather: On General Strategy

Doug Leather is the CEO of REAP Consulting, a group of global customer management experts specializing in the development and delivery of tools and programs that build business value. He's also someone that I know from having served on the CustomerThink Board of Advisors with him. I am glad that I did. He really knows his stuff with over 25 years in marketing and customer management. He is acknowledged as a leading expert and thought-leader in customer centricity. He is laser-focused, on providing a great CRM methodology and a detailed knowledge of best practices. He takes all that experience and knowledge and applies it to the practical application of customer management in different geographic territories, markets, and industries. The man is smart!

1. **Make sure that you're not solving the wrong problem really well!** *The delivery of an "intentional customer experience" is reliant upon an organization being suitably aligned and joined up so that everyone is clear about what the experience is to be, and any bottlenecks to the delivery of the experience have been identified and resolved. As such, to build appropriate customer management (CM) capability requires a clear understanding of end-to-end organizational capability to deliver the experience. Make use of an appropriate CM assessment framework (ideally with benchmark capability) to measure organizational customer management capability, as the first step. If you don't know how good (or bad) you are, how will you ever effectively bridge the gap (between your enterprise capability and global good practice) to become as good as you want to be? Heaven forbid you invest time and resource in an intervention, project, or program that doesn't enable you to get to the very foundation of what is required to be truly customer-centric.*

2. **If everybody has responsibility, then nobody has responsibility.** *Most businesses do not have somebody who is responsible for customer management. Appoint a customer management executive or a chief customer officer who is responsible for the integration of sales, service, marketing, and customer inputs, and accountable for maintaining and enhancing the value of the customer base, as a key company asset.*

3. **Customer management is change management.** *Customer management is not a temporary endeavor undertaken to deliver a unique product, service, or result. It is a set of related projects managed in a coordinated way to achieve benefits or synergy that cannot be achieved by managing them individually. If CM is business strategy, then it is the CEO who must principally sell this direction to the board, financial analysts, staff, and customers. Be crystal clear about what you're trying to accomplish and ensure that everyone understands the pressure for change, ensure that everyone understands the vision, ensure that organizational capacity for change exists, and ensure that a set of actionable first steps is in place.*

18

Mapping the Customer Experience

I don't think I need to establish the case for a highly personalized customer experience being the epicenter of a successful CRM engagement—for any company. If I do, I'm sorry. I thought I did that in Chapter 3.

But what I do have to establish is how to go about finding out what that customer experience actually is. It isn't so easy because of something quite fundamental. I am an individual and human and thus have "things" that appeal to me as an individual that simply might not be that appealing to any other individual in the way that they appeal to me. What floats my boat might sink yours.

This is a daunting problem for a business because while the company has a culture and offering that might or might not appeal to the customer, at least it is a consistent offering, at best customizable in a modular way. But that isn't necessarily how a customer wants to interact with the company. They interact with the company for multiple reasons. Customers don't only expect their demands to be met or exceeded. They expect them to be met or exceeded in a particular manner—particular to them, that is.

For example, here are two five-star reviews from Yelp (www.yelp.com) of San Francisco–based "My Trick Pony," where you can customize T-shirts and other apparel with your own images.

First Reviewer

"Have you ever said to yourself "I wish I had something like _____" and not been able to find it in the store because the images are off, or just too generic for your taste? Get out of the stores that make you feel like you're settling and wear what you want, whatever that may be!

"This store is so much fun. You can take any image and have it put on clothing you already own and love (and want to customize) or you can pick up something there and make it special from the start.

"There are a ton of books with prints for you to choose from, or you can bring in your own image and they can work with that. The cost is roughly $20 per square foot for the print screen and worth it. They can do it for you right there, so the wait time is about 10–15 minutes (I love the instant gratification of my purchases) . . ."

SECOND REVIEWER

"This place is great. I have walked by this place almost every day and until recently always wondered what it was . . . so I went to Yelp and realized I'd discovered a little piece of heaven. So I went in on a whim one day just to feel it out. Micah greeted me and he was extremely helpful. I had an idea so he searched around on the Internet for a similar photo to work with and did some quick Photoshop magic to give me a taste of what it could look like. I told him I would return with my own photo when ready.

"Next time in, Matteo was there and he was amazing. He seemed even more excited about my design than I did. He was very helpful, didn't mind that I looked over his shoulder while he worked, and genuinely took an interest in what I was trying to accomplish, who it was going for and why, and what kind of person I was. I feel that this kind of knowledge always enhances work and you know that real appreciation is going into it. He was also very helpful when I was trying to decide on color combinations. A great and talented man indeed.

"When I got the shirt I was so happy. I just gave it to my boyfriend yesterday and he loves it and it looks wonderful on him. And like other people have said, this place doesn't break the wallet. So go in and create something wonderful and unique!"

What's so different, you might be wondering? The desired end result is exactly the same, but what the customer finds important enough to lead to a five-star review is quite different in each case. What they expect is different, so how they respond is different.

The first reviewer saw the critical moment as "I love the instant gratification of my purchases" and the entire tone of the review is around the coolness of the product and the process. The second reviewer was entranced by the incredible helpfulness of the staff and the interest they took in working with her to provide her with the finished product. Though the result was the same, what was important to the customer was very different, and the knowledge of those differences is the difference between a single-time visitor and a committed vocal advocate.

So, because I try to always be helpful, I'm going to provide you with a great tool this chapter—a basic customer experience mapping methodology.

The Benefits of Your Customer's Lovely Experience

In a study released September 2008 by The Aberdeen Group, it was found that for companies that used best-in-class customer experience methodologies and programs, there was a 90 percent year over year increase in retention and a 68 percent year over year increase in customer profitability. What Aberdeen Group found was a series of common characteristics that drove those successes. These are reflected in Table 18-1.

Table 18-1: Best-in-Class Customer Experience Practices (Source: Aberdeen Group, 2008)

CEM Practice	Percentage
Regular customer surveys with results incorporated into management decision making	67 percent
Centralized repositories of sales and customer data	66 percent
Insight "repositories" gleaned from customer interactions	53 percent
Regular review of customer facing business processes	53 percent

In other words, constantly taking the pulse of the customer and then capturing the pulse rate are best-in-class practices that have material benefits for the companies that utilize these practices.

What does that entail, you might ask? Let's begin with why customer experience mapping is important, if you don't mind.

Why Customer Experience Mapping?

How many of your employees directly interact with your customers? How many of your senior management ever interact with customers by anything but accident? How many of your customers have demands that you think are probably outside what the company can do or ever has done? How many of you use the incredible amount of intelligence that customers provide even in normal conversations? How many of you presume you know your customer? By the way, "presume" is a precisely chosen word.

The answers: Many. Almost none. Several, but what can you do? Not too many. All of us, especially marketing people.

Here's how little you really know your customers. eMarketer reported on a 2008 study done by QCI International:

▶ 41 percent of the companies surveyed do not record customer contact channel preferences.

▶ In more than 90 percent of companies, the staff who are responsible for talking to customers could not articulate why customers should buy from them.

▶ Only 13 percent of senior management has regular contact with customers.

Truthfully, we don't know our customers all that well, despite their often easy willingness to be known. Put on your customer hat for a minute. About how many companies are you willing to say, "Damn. They seem to know just what I want!" A few . . . maybe. But what about this next statement, "They not only know what I want, but how I want it!"

Back in Chapter 3, I talked a lot about American Girl. I mentioned the options they had, each of which cost something. How each girl dresses her doll, which services she chooses (haircut, hot dog), and which associated media she sees or buys affects the revenue of Mattel. It's rarely a matter of price except as a consideration in a granular look at the customer experience.

The reason for all this variation is that each of us is self-interested. Even Mother Teresa was self-interested. Doing Good with a capital G was a way of satisfying her internal emotional "benchmarks." Self-interest is not selfishness. That individual interest can be a benefit to a company that understands what it is that drives that customer, but a major headache when it doesn't. The biggest "fail" is when someone at the company presumes they know what the customer's self-interest is, and they don't. Believe me, they don't.

There is a simple answer to that presumption failure, though, which I mentioned back in Chapter 3. It's worth repeating: *Ask the customer what it is they think and want!*

Mapping will be your first set of brushstrokes for your freshly painted customer portrait.

The Preparation

Customer mapping isn't merely a questionnaire that you get to ask a customer—via Survey Monkey or your internal e-mail system. However, preparation for customer mapping can be done using the traditional instruments for customer queries. But it doesn't start with that. Before a single question is even discussed, there are several strategic CRM elements that have to be in place.

Consistent Perception of CRM Mission and Vision

I established the importance of the mission and vision statements last chapter. *Nothing* proceeds without a clear mission and vision statement that provides the customer-facing cues the company needs to define how it will approach its interactions with the customers and what the future holds for that. This is a prerequisite for any sort of customer experience mapping you are preparing to do. The full evolution and development of a strategy isn't.

The reason it isn't is pretty straightforward. If successful, the mapping will help you define the strategy, helping you execute on your mission. As time goes on and you redo the mapping—yes, redo, this isn't a one-time-whew-we're-done—it will provide you with the insight to tweak the elements of the strategy going forward. That means that your vision can be realized.

Before you get to that, you have to make sure that the perception of the mission and vision is consistent across the company. What do I mean by that? Let me get literary.

In Shakespeare's *Julius Caesar*, Titinius returns home to find Cassius, of the lean and hungry look, dead. He says, "Alas, thou hast misconstrued everything." That is a state you have to make sure you avoid.

The only way to avoid it is to make sure the mission and vision that are the fundamental statements for the Social CRM strategy are not only clearly defined but clearly understood across the entire value chain. By having that mission and vision clear, the direction that the strategy has to be pointed will be obvious to all concerned, and that doesn't require the entire strategy to be complete.

The entire value chain includes the accounting department, your logistics organization, the warehouse managers, the human resources department, and all the others in the back of the company. The reason this encompasses the entire value chain is that with the increased customer demands and the heightened emotional sensitivity due to extreme economic fluctuations, among other things, how every part of the company performs will have an impact on the customer experience.

For example, several years ago, a client of mine called up with an odd dilemma. Their accounting department, a few years before the call, had developed a technique they used in accounting entries that saved their rather large department around $40,000 per year. However, they had added e-commerce to their portfolio of sales channels. As a result, this accounting technique created an online glitch that made the customer purchasing online enter some of the same data twice. Never mind how it got there—it's not germane to this. They wanted to know what to do.

My recommendation, since it wasn't technically fixable, was to jettison the technique despite its improved efficiency, because it was degrading the customer experience and thus irritating customers, who expected their online shopping to be seamless and easy.

They did just that. Which is great, but the true moral of this story is to note how even the back office can affect a customer experience that is expected to be something it turns out not to be—in other words, there is a failure to meet expectations. So what can you do to prevent that—and, hopefully, even exceed expectations?

The Traditional Approaches

There is nothing wrong with traditional approaches—though they work less and less. When I say "traditional" approaches, that includes focus groups, standard surveys, customer interviews that have directed questions, and attempts at customer segmentation. Each of them has a strength or two, but they tend to have an underlying flaw: the results tend to reflect the prejudices of the company, rather than the raw honesty of the individual customer. Even with analytics-driven customer segmentation, for example, your result is the assessment of people who are similar to you, not of "you" as an individual. While "someone like me" might be your customer's most trusted source, companies should remember that it isn't a good demographic in the eyes of that same individual customer. They may trust someone like them, but they want you to know *them* personally. To do that, you need to start by mapping the customer experience.

Now We Map

Mapping the customer experience is a granular process and one that encompasses all channels a customer uses to interact with you or vice versa. If you are a retail store, it encompasses every interaction starting with the moment the customer walks through the door and notices something to the moment that they leave the store and go home, and to the time they call up customer service or the sales rep who has to do follow-up on the purchase. It encompasses their web experience and how they interacted with you on the Web, ranging from how comfortable the site was when they were navigating to the effect that the 11 seconds of latency that you uncovered in your customer interview affected that customer behavior or marred their experience—or not.

But as important as the specific interaction is the expectation of the result of that interaction the customer brings to the table and what kind of importance the customer assigns to it. I'm going to start by breaking out the fundamental elements.

Interactions

An interaction, for the purposes of the customer experience, is any time a customer communicates with the company—regardless of the communications channel and regardless of whether it is a cyber-communication or a physical conversation.

Examples of good and bad interactions are in Table 18-2.

Table 18-2: Examples of Good and Bad Interactions via Different Channels

Communications Medium	Good Interaction	Bad Interaction
Retail store	Clean, well lit, friendly service from a store representative, and well-stocked	All the other good but a surly store representative
Web-based	Easy to navigate, no latency when ordering	Ten seconds or more wait for order to complete when Submit is clicked
Telephone-based	Immediate access to the right human being	Multiple IVR menus
E-mail	Rapid customer service turnaround in answering a support question	More than 24 hours' wait time to answer a support question
Customer service	Solving a problem—and adding a bonus such as "we're sorry"	Lack of knowledge or unsupportive CSR
Fax	Completion of a transaction	Unsolicited offer from a company you know

These are simply examples. What I'm sure is that as you read them, you were able to attach a real-life experience either specifically or that more generic, slightly ethereal feeling that you know what I mean, but you can't pinpoint it specifically. But "good" or "bad" can be attached to interactions only if there was an expectation of how that interaction was going to turn out. If it met or exceeded the expectation—*voilà*—good. If it fell below the expectation—*oy vey*—bad.

Expectations

Then what is a customer expectation? One definition, put forward by J. Olson and P. Dover in their 1979 piece, "Disconfirmation of Consumer Expectations through Product Trial" in the *Journal of Applied Psychology*, says, "Customer expectations are pretrial beliefs about a product that serve as standards or reference points against which product performance is judged." I don't know about you, but that's good enough for me.

There are at least six significant factors that customers incorporate when it comes to determining their expectations. What kind of result do I expect:

1. Given my past history with this company—especially my last interaction

2. Given what I've heard about this company—especially from my peers

3. Given what I expect of the industry this company is in (e.g., airlines)

4. Given what that kind of interaction, in my experience, typically results in

5. Given ordinary standards of human behavior when it comes to interactions

6. Given anything that might have happened to me the day (or so) that I'm interacting with you that could affect how I'm thinking about things (random and uncontrollable)

Each of them, and, usually, all of them, has an effect on what the customer thinks the outcome is going to be.

Weight

But not all expected outcomes and their actual results are the same. What makes understanding the customer's thinking even more difficult is that each expectation and how well or poorly it is met has a different importance in the eye of the particular customer.

But you already know that, don't you? For example, I have to assume that most of you reading this have used review sites like Yelp to find a restaurant you might want to eat at or Epinions to see about a camera or Amazon for the book reviews. When you go to the review, you use the ratings—say, 1 to 5 stars to filter how you want to read the reviews. Maybe you want to only read the bad reviews, not the good ones, so you can see how bad the negatives are on something you really want to buy. Or maybe you read all of them. What I think most of you don't do is to aggregate the stars and make your decisions based on the number of stars that a product has. Instead, you actually read the reviews. What you then do is to say, as you read them, "Oh, that reviewer says the delivery was a bad issue, but that doesn't matter to me, but they loved the look of the product, which matters to me a lot." Or "That reviewer says they think the duck at the restaurant is too dry but the tilapia is to die for." If you like duck, you tend to not go; if you like fish, you tend to go. You are weighing what is important to you—and not. But note that "if" is a key word here. Fish or duck? Your personal likes and dislikes will drive your expectations of the place whether or not the review might be 4/5 stars.

Want to further check how you weigh decision factors? Go back to the beginning of the chapter and read the descriptions from the review sites. What's important to you in each of the reviews? Was it what was important to one of the reviewers and not the other or a compilation of both, or did neither meet your standard for importance?

You get the picture now? This is a major facet of what can be uncovered when you do customer experience mapping.

Mapping: The Four Questions

Okay. Before I ask the four questions (not related to Passover), I'm going to show you a couple of diagrams. First, take a look at a high-level version of a customer experience map (Figure 18-1). Now, look at a portion of that map broken out and incorporating the use of RFID-related technologies for a part of the customer experience (Figure 18-2). Both of these are related to a shopper at a grocery store.

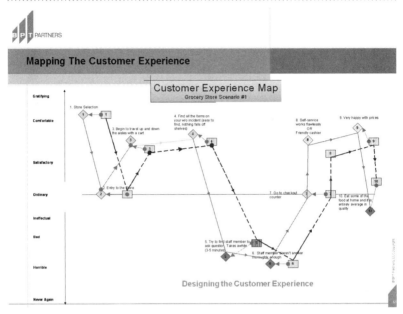

Figure 18-1: A high-level view of a customer experience map. Interaction in the boxes, expectations, and the results in the diamond (Source: BPT Partners, LLC)

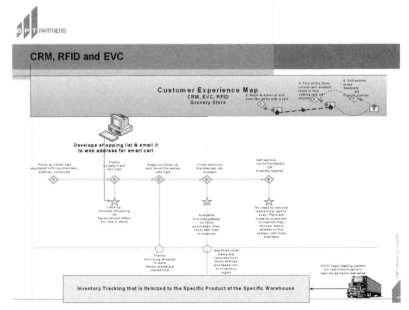

Figure 18-2: A view of a segment of the customer experience map in Figure 18-1 (Source: BPT Partners, LLC)

Now, the four questions.

1. What is the interaction?

2. What does the customer expect the outcome of that interaction to be?

3. What was the actual outcome?

4. What kind of importance did the customer place on the result?

Mapping: Prior to . . .

I have a standard rule for when I engage a client. If customer mapping is part of the engagement, then some of the customer interviews done have to be done by senior management. The reason is quite simple, really. Senior management has very little to do with actual interactions with customers. I don't blame them (I actually do blame them), but they need to get over it right at this point. I won't take the engagement if they don't agree that they'll do some of the interviews. Senior management needs to know how customers think. You know they don't. You saw the numbers earlier in this chapter—only 13 percent have regular contact with customers. Amazing—and bad. Senior management needs to engage, as a learning experience for them.

The other preliminary step is to agree that the customers will be compensated for their time. They need to know their time is valued. The compensation can be money—in one smaller sampling $100 to the interviewee was considered reasonable. In a larger sampling it can be a gift certificate or an outright gift, but one that makes sense to whom you are questioning. Give them a choice if gifts are options.

Mapping: Choosing the Customers

How large a sampling and from what segments you choose are pretty much up to you and your comfort zone. The number is the least relevant, though the smaller the number, the greater weight each of the respondents has in your thinking. I would recommend at least 100 customers interviewed for any sampling. What does require some serious thought is from what segment you get it. For example, you might not want to use just the traditional demographic segmenting. For one retailer, we looked at segments that were nowhere near what you would expect the norm to be such as:

▶ High-performance stores with maverick (rule-breaking) managers

▶ High-performance stores with traditional (rule-following) managers

▶ Low-performance stores with maverick managers

▶ High-performance stores with traditional managers

It was then broken out by geography as a subcategory. The idea was to see what the best (and worst) practices were when it came to processes that worked (or didn't) in store environments. The customers and the locales they came from, since regional preferences mattered in this case, became the arbiters of the store interactions. While not a normal segmentation, it was one that answered the questions that the mapping exercise was created to answer.

Mapping: The Questions

David's Bridal, one of my best clients and one that's done the customer mapping successfully, has graciously allowed me to use some of their questions to give you an idea of how to craft the questions you're going to use. Needless to say, the interactions you're going to be questioning and those of a highly emotional bride are not the same—so please don't do this at the chapel.

The questions have to be developed with two principles in mind:

1. They cannot direct the respondent in any way.

2. They cannot have an emotional tinge.

That means that they have to be agnostic and emotionally neutral. It's the difference between asking:

▶ What did you see when you came through the door? Did you enjoy (hate) that?

  and

▶ What did you see when you came through the door? How did you feel about that?

  and

▶ What did you see when you came through the door?

In the first example, you're directing their answer by asking them about the emotion they felt specifically, which will compel them to answer in the box you created for them.

In the second example, while you didn't ask them about the specific emotion, you are asking them to verbalize an emotional response, which might or might not be a truthful answer. Sometimes, in these situations, you should be prepared to read the emotional state that the memory puts them in. So if you see them crying while they declaim the blasé nature of it all, you know they aren't exactly being truthful. It's where your judgment has to come into play and not be tainted by an expectation of your own.

The final choice is the most pristine and the right question. Give them the guidance they need to note which interaction you're asking about and then let them respond freely from there.

GREETING AND REGISTRATION

▶ Were you greeted when you first came in? *If yes*, can you describe how you were greeted?

▶ How would you describe the mood/personality of the person who greeted you? Do you remember what he/she said? *If no*, where did you go, what did you do?

▶ Did any employees ask you if you needed help?

▶ How do you feel about not being greeted?

▶ Did you register? *If yes*, can you describe what happened?

▶ Did the greeter give you a registration form to fill out or did she fill out the form for you?

▶ What did you think of the length of the time it took to register?

▶ Were you given catalogs to look through?

▶ Was there a consultant called over immediately or were you given a realistic time of how long you would have to wait?

▶ How long did you have to wait for a consultant to come over and help you?

CONSULTATION AND PRODUCT SELECTION

▶ What did you think of the consultant you worked with? How would you describe the personality/mood of your consultant?

▶ Did your consultant listen well and show you gowns that were similar to what you requested?

► Was your consultant knowledgeable about the product/store policies?

► Can you describe your experience shopping for the gown? Did you pick out the dresses you wanted to try on or did your consultant pick for you?

► Did your consultant show you different styles and colors of wedding gowns? Did your consultant help you pick out coordinating accessories to go with your gown?

► How did you feel while trying on your gown?

► Did you visit the store more than once before deciding to buy your gown? If yes, how many times did your consultant spend adequate time helping you?

While this is by no means the complete "store experience," it is entirely representative of how questions need to be constructed. Note that none of the questions are either judgmental or point in any direction. They are designed explicitly to trigger the memory of the interaction in the sequence it is likely to have occurred through a particular channel.

Customer Mapping: The Interview

Once memory of the interaction is triggered, it's up to the interviewer to interpret the responses. That's why these interviews need to be one on one and live—over the phone at the very least and in person if it can be done. E-mail will not do. This isn't a survey nor is this a focus group.

Customer Mapping: Ten Cardinal Rules

That's about all I can fit in a single chapter. I hope that you find it at least useful. If not, my bad. Here are the summary rules for customer experience mapping

1. Never presume for the customer.

2. Make sure that your customer-centric mission and vision are consistent across the enterprise before you begin this process.

3. When developing the questions, remember that they need to be designed to trigger the memory of a specific interaction, not to guide the memory.

4. The interviews need to be live.

5. Remember each customer will consider different things important to them.

6. Let the customer have the freedom to react to your question.

7. You don't know why the customer remembers what they remember. Use these questions to find out.

8. Be prepared to read the customer's responses from the live interview—sometimes in contradistinction to what they are saying to you.

9. Senior management needs to do some of the interviews.

10. This is not a one-time effort. It must be done periodically.

Before we move on, I want you to have a conversation with Scott Rogers, the man responsible for those remarkable David's Bridal questions. He's a longtime friend, a guru in the retail CRM space, and the driver of David's Bridal Social CRM initiatives. He is also a delightful human being and someone I'm glad I know.

MINI-CONVERSATION WITH SCOTT ROGERS

I'm going to introduce you to Scott Rogers, a senior director at David's Bridal. Scott is a remarkably insightful, wonderful human being who knows his stuff when it comes to CRM, big time. He is an experienced practitioner, speaks at events in retail and other industries on CRM, and, frankly, could be a CRM consultant if he chose to—and a really good one. He's been a key leader in the CRM and social initiatives at David's Bridal since 2002.

Listen up.

By now, the reader should be well versed in why the customer experience matters, so let's dive into how to determine what the customer experience should be. As business people, we are probably familiar with, either directly or indirectly, Michael Hammer's process re-engineering, internally defining the current and optimal processes, and the steps necessary to close the gaps. In customer experience mapping, the difference is defining those processes from the customer's viewpoint.

Conceptually, the idea of customer experience mapping is to understand the experience the customer has from end to end, from before the interaction to after—from the identification of their desires and needs to information gathering, their expectations, the decision-making process, their attitudes toward the interaction and the products/services offered/purchased, the relative importance of each step in the process and minimal expectations for each, how well the company performed at each step, and any tipping points that occurred. The only way to accomplish this is to talk with your customers. After completing this process, the next step is to map the internal processes that support each step, and survey your internal people to identify how well your company perceives it performs, and finally to define the opportunities, costs, and ROIs from the improvements identified.

Before embarking upon this process, there are three critical points to keep in mind:

1. *Choose a representative sample of customers to talk to, whether that means your customer segments, or high value/frequency customers to low value/frequency customers. By limiting the sample to your best customers, you'll never know whether minor changes in the experience might increase the frequency/value of the lower tiers.*

2. *Engage members of senior management to participate in the surveying of customers. Often this is the best way to achieve customer-centric epiphanies and gain high-level support for future process changes.*

3. *Start the conversations with customers by listening and not leading. The points that customers initially talk about are the top-of-mind memories. These can be emotionally positive to neutral to negative, with the positives and negatives being the core of the word-of-mouth conversations customers have about you. The number of people you talk to depends on your budget—optimally, you want a large enough sample to clearly understand the breadth of experiences, expectations, and performance. If your budget is tight, follow up with quantitative research, based on the qualitative (and a conjoint analysis to get at the trade-offs we all make in any process requiring a decision).*

Be prepared to do this more than once in your lifetime. If the prospect of this frightens you, read (or reread) The Experience Economy, *by James H. Gilmore and B. Joseph Pine II. You will be surprised how many ventures that were leaders in customer-centric experiences in 1998 are either no longer around or exist as a shadow of their former glory. The world is not a static environment.* ❧

19

Process and Data Go Together Like...CRM Operations

Toward the end of 2008, Gartner Executive Programs conducted a survey of CIOs that encompassed 1,527 enterprises in 48 countries across 30 industries, both private and public sector. This survey looked at 2009 spending business and technology priorities of the CIOs. Know what the number one business priority was? Business process improvement. Know what the number two technology priority was? CRM.

Making this a very smart idea for a chapter.

But it isn't meant to be all that technical, certainly not as technical as the third edition. Data and process become valuable when they solve business problems or enhance customer knowledge. They don't really have value beyond that—though, admittedly, those two areas are so broad they can encompass anything in the known universe.

What I'm going to do with this chapter, to spare you business readers the agony of technical terms, is look at the most important parts of data and process—those that are related to customers.

In the house of data, that means the consolidated customer record and, especially, something that existed mostly in principle five years ago when universal masters became something to talk about. No, not masters of the universe, Klingon fool, I said universal masters. Now preeminent and *au courant*, we have master data management (MDM), which is a far more intelligent approach to handling customer data than we have had the benefit of over the past several years.

When it comes to process, I'll traverse the worlds of business process management (BPM) and call upon process expert Dick Lee to take us through a methodology that simplifies how to handle that BPM, and focus around customer-centered processes, rather than agnostic ones.

Why do it this way?

In 2008, Yankee Group conducted a global study for Amdocs on service providers in the wireless, wire line cable, and satellite markets. They found that over 50 percent of the respondents were unable to clarify what a worthwhile customer experience should be. The supposed reasons were that they lacked an integrated view of the customer and had segregated information jammed into what they called internal information silos—a data issue. They also blamed inconsistent business processes with disconnects across all business lines.

Even worse, they discovered that while 70 percent of the respondents felt that business processes have a direct impact on the customer experience, 28 percent said they didn't have the dedicated resources to either manage internal business processes or to meet customer experience–focused KPIs.

However, there is cause for optimism here, not pessimism. Forty-seven percent of the respondents said they were going to invest in customer experience–focused KPIs, and a majority said they were going to make MDM and unifying business processes a priority. That means they do get what they have to do when it comes to CRM and Social CRM.

That, once again, makes this a very smart idea for a chapter.

Not Just Your Transaction's Data Anymore

For so long, the single view or 360-degree view or unified view of the customer was the centerpiece of the quest for CRM's Holy Grail. That complete view or, in customer data lingo, the unified master—meaning a complete record in a single place of all transactions (sales) and operational interactions (marketing response or customer service tickets)—was what all companies drooled over.

The idea of that single customer record with the circular view was that it would provide a rich source of data when it came to making important decisions, especially around either optimized offers from the sales side or ticket resolution on the customer service side. Marketing folks could target the customer more specifically if they knew that not only was the customer a purchaser of full-length mirrors for their bathrooms to preen in front of, but called into customer service fairly regularly because they tended to break the mirrors because the mirrors didn't exactly see them as the fairest of them all.

Knowing all this, the companies could more easily sell them reinforced glass with steel backing for their future mirrors—up-selling the customer and decreasing their likelihood of calling in again to replace a broken mirror.

However, all this really turned out to be was a dusty perspective that didn't lead to an enormous amount of action beyond placement on wish lists. It's not that businesses don't recognize the value of a single customer record. They do. For example, in 2007, the Economist Intelligence Unit did a study called "Conquering Convergence: Focusing on the Customer" that found in the ICE industries—information, communications, entertainment—consumer pull is pushing convergence, meaning consolidated customer knowledge. They interviewed Peter Skarzynski, SVP for strategy at Samsung Telecommunications America, who said, "We are spending more and more time to understand the customer better. It's become a very competitive market."

This was bolstered in the study by 92 percent of the companies claiming they had a strategy for staying focused on their customers, though, frankly, I would doubt that, with most of them thinking that the strategy had been at least somewhat successful.

What makes it interesting, despite the skewing of the numbers toward highly successful, is that when the question was asked, "What are the main obstacles preventing your company from being as customer-centric as it would like to be?" (they could select three), the number one answer was "incomplete customer data" with 41 percent and then "lack of clarity about what customer data should be measured" with 32 percent. Fragmentation of customer data or inaccuracies of the same were the next two. In other words, it's hard to aggregate the accurate customer data that you need when you're not even sure what customer data you're looking for.

That confusion about what customer data to look for is compounded by the availability of much more individual customer data than ever before and also by which of that highly personal profile data is valuable to a business.

Historically the idea of the single customer record was encapsulated rather easily into the three traditional CRM buckets. The 360-degree view of the customer would incorporate sales transaction data, marketing response data, and customer service inquiry data. That was that. It would all be in a singular place and just oh so easy to deal with.

But that actually never became the case. Even with all this commitment to customer centricity, the idea of what comprised the 360-degree view was decidedly old school. Here's the way that EIU/Oracle framed the idea of that 360-degree customer record: "My company has a 360-degree view of customers, including purchases/contact history, preferences, and demographics." That's missing what we're going to see is important for the new customer record in just a few. But even that particular approach generated only a 33 percent "we do have that for sure" response, with the rest being either neutral or denying they have it.

Things are getting more complex for businesses when it comes to customer data, because the historic transactional and demographic information is no longer sufficient for getting you what you need to ascertain what to do with that individual customer clamoring for personalized relationships with your company.

The New Customer Record

What should the new customer record include? Before I go through what should be a part of the record, here's what the traditional customer record incorporated if it was considered complete:

- ▶ Account data

- ▶ Order data, including in-store (if such a thing existed), phone orders, e-commerce

- ▶ Billing information

- ▶ Credit information, including third party (Dun & Bradstreet rating, bank information, credit agencies inquiries)

- ▶ Customer cost allocations data

- ▶ Interactions data that involved communications with the customer, including e-mails, phone calls, online chats at the company website

- ▶ Service data, including open tickets, successful (and not) resolution of service requests, standard inquiries (overlap with interactions data)

- ▶ Marketing data, including campaign responses, promotions offered, successes and failures

- ▶ Segmentation data, including standard demographic data, household information

Obviously, there are a lot of overlaps among the kinds of information listed here, but you get the idea. The totality of this in a customer record about you would comprise everything a company traditionally could or would want to know about you.

But that isn't sufficient for a contemporary customer record. Just as we're defining Social CRM as an extension of traditional CRM, the 21st century customer record is an extension of the traditional. It includes all of the above, but then goes to the more informal unstructured channels and looks for:

▶ Records of unstructured individual customer conversations found via social media monitoring and text analysis (see Chapter 20), which might include comments, discussions in threaded forums, blog postings, etc.

▶ Profile information gleaned from Facebook, LinkedIn, MySpace, and a myriad of other social networks/communities

▶ Records of articles written by the individual influencer or customer

▶ Third-party information associated with an account, including competitive intelligence, or contemporary news

▶ If the customer is an influencer or decision maker within a business (in a B2B transaction) or in a community

All of this can be harvested and incorporated into the customer record through text analysis, among other things, which effectively aggregates unstructured data and structures so it can be integrated into more traditional databases. There are many tools out there, such as InsideView (see Chapter 12), that integrate the unstructured data directly into CRM systems data, which makes it even easier to incorporate the data into the 360 degrees that the customer record purports.

The challenge that the new customer record presents isn't so much in finding the data—with the proper tools, it's doable—but using the new data. As in all data harvesting, there are issues that involve privacy and transparency (see electronic content "I Want this Chapter to Be on Privacy, But If I Wrote It, I'd Have to Blog About You"). Are you "stealing" information that is easily available on the Web, but still owned by the provider? But even more than that, what benefit does it provide to you when it comes to developing insights into individual customers? Is it just more noise or is it really valuable?

What that means is that you have to make decisions beforehand on what data is going to be important, whether it's traditional or new. Ultimately, what data you use is based on how you want to use it. For example, if you merely need to know the transaction history of your customers, then don't monitor the blogosphere for their conversations. While I think that's insight suicide right now, you get the point. Use what's valuable.

One of the other dilemmas that data mavens face in this deep dive into personalized customer data and the 360-degree view is how to deal with all the issues that are created by pulling in data from disparate sources. That, my friends, is what customer data integration (CDI) is for.

CDI, Not Miami

This is exactly what it sounds like and truly is sans David Caruso. It is the use of technology, services, and best practices to consolidate customer data, including names, addresses, phone numbers, company names, and so on (often called entities in the analytics world) so that there is a single clean reference to a specific individual rather than a larger number of incorrect, duplicated, and possible but not certain references to that individual.

The process for doing this is straightforward. It works something like this:

1. Taking normal contact data and updating and cleansing it.

2. Consolidating customer records by purging the duplicates and linking those that can be clearly identified as belonging to the same customer but are sitting in multiple data sources.

3. Bringing in the third-party and external data once steps 1 and 2 are taken.

4. Ensuring that the records meet whatever standards, internal rules, and external regulations are required to keep the company on the right side of the law and respect the individuals who are named in the records.

As an example, let's presume that we have four records in four separate databases:

▶ Will Smith: Los Angeles, California, age 41, married to Jada Pinkett Smith

▶ Bill Smith: Detroit, Michigan, age 41, unmarried

▶ Willard C. Smith: Los Angeles, California, age 41, marriage status unknown

▶ William Smith: Los Angeles, California, age 38, married to Jada Pinkett Smith

Effective CDI would clean up these four records and come up with two individual records by first consolidating Will Smith and Willard C. Smith with the information it has. But then it would have to have rules set up to deal with the specific case of William Smith. Even though it's clear that he's from LA and married to Jada Pinkett Smith, which would indicate it was Will Smith, Will Smith is not 38, he's 41, and his name is Willard, not William. So what do you do?

There is a lot of ambiguity in customer records due to data input incorrectly at the beginning or from siloed databases with duplicate but slightly different information on the same person, such as a donor and a volunteer database for a nonprofit with the same person donating and volunteering. CDI becomes an important technology for cleaning all that data, since even exfoliating soaps won't do the trick. Once cleansed, then combined.

But is that enough? Just taking care of the data? What about the use of customer data by multiple sources? According to Ray Wang, one of the top enterprise analysts in the world, in his 2007 Forrester Research report "Wave on Customer Hubs," traditional CDI (wow, already a traditional version exists) is being superseded by what he calls customer hubs. These go beyond the traditional use of customer data integration and administer how the data is arranged for specific sources through the use of business rules and event management following the technical cleansing, deduplication, and structuring of the data. The customer hub takes the data and applies business rules that tell it how to organize the data according to the preferences of the systems that want to use it. There are a number of well-known vendors providing CDI services that are focused around the customer hub, such as Oracle with its Customer Data Hub, Siperian's HubXT, and IBM's Websphere Customer Center, among others.

What makes the customer hub valuable now? According to Wang, now a partner at Altimeter Group, in an article in *SearchCRM*, January 2007: "While everyone is moving toward [a master data management] solution in general, it's very hard to implement that kind of change across an organization. Starting with a smaller target like customer or product is a good way to make sure that you will ultimately succeed."

Master Data Management: Better Read than Dead

Ray Wang, of course, aside from being a convenient segue, raises another question or two. Why is everyone moving to master data management (MDM)? What is MDM? What does it have to do with CRM now? Actually, that's three questions, all of which I'm going to answer briefly before we get on to business processes.

What Is MDM?

MDM was a drug that was used illegally in the '60s and '70s. Oh, wait, that was PCP. Actually, MDM is an increasingly popular paradigm for taking all data in an enterprise, whether it is customer data, product data, or supplier data, and linking it to a single file that provides a common reference point. They call the single file a master file. Then, depending on what you need, you can access the data in the way that you need it.

On the surface, MDM's definition eerily mirrors the original definition of CRM. Aaron Zornes, perhaps the leading MDM guru, uses these definitions and subdefinitions at his MDM Institute.

Master Data Management (MDM): *The authoritative, reliable foundation for data used across many applications and constituencies with the goal to provide a single view of the truth no matter where it lies.*

These are his sub-definitions:

Operational MDM: *Definition, creation, and synchronization of master data required for transactional systems and delivered via service-oriented architecture (SOA); examples: near real-time customer data hubs and securities masters.*

Analytical MDM: *Definition, creation, and analysis of master data; examples: counterparty risk management applications and financial reporting such as global spend analysis or chart of accounts consolidation.*

Collaborative MDM: *Definition, creation, and synchronization of master reference data via workflow and check-in/check-out services; examples: product information management (PIM) data hubs and anti-money laundering (AML).*

If you remember the original MetaGroup definitions of CRM, they are based around three distinct "types" of CRM: operational, analytical, and collaborative. The master CRM definition focused around the single view of the customer as its centerpiece.

But reality points in another direction. If you reference Chapter 11 around the collaborative value chain, then master data management (MDM) makes a lot of sense when dealing with large or mid-sized data stores that might emanate from multiple sources and be of multiple types. The collaborative value chain is the core of a well-integrated enterprise value chain engaged with the personal value chains of individual customers. That means the customer is partnering with the company either to help them innovate or to receive information that allows the customer to make intelligent decisions on how they deal with that company. For that to work effectively, there have to be high degrees of data integration and the ability to call up that data in ways that allow companies to make their own operational decisions or to reach out to the customer with what the customer needs from them.

For example, the combination of product data, supplier data, and customer data allows you to tell a high-value customer with some precision that his shipment of equipment is in inventory, will be shipped on Thursday from a warehouse in Richmond, Virginia, to his location with an expected arrival of the following Monday, all units contained in a single package. You'll also be able to identify how much this will cost you, how much it will cost the customer, what kind of history you've had with this customer when it comes to on-time delivery, and whom to flag in the event that a problem surfaces. And now you can also see if the customer has been complaining to his peers about your company.

Why Is Everyone Moving Toward MDM?

The MDM industry is by no means gigantic yet, but the promise is. It's a new idea, which is why the market spend was only $730 million in 2007. It's projected by the MDM Institute to go to $6 billion for software and services by 2012, though, because the need for it is becoming more apparent as the amount of data available and the amount of work required to parse it and analyze it, and establish the relationships between different data points and types, increases by the day.

The value proposition is not all that difficult to grasp. A centralized master data source makes governance far easier, since it's far easier to comply with rules involving a single source than those involving multiple data sources.

Business process integration becomes a lot more efficient. With a data hub to work from, business rules can determine and direct where and how the data will be used—emanating from that central source rather than from a variety of different locations—which would mean different sets of business rules, which conceivably could conflict with each other. Rules that involve privacy preferences or pricing discounts are one kind that MDM serves; rules that involve results leading to action are another, such as a problem with delivery needs to be routed to a supervisor for a preemptive call.

There is another interesting wrinkle. All the data I've spoken about so far is structured data. What about the mass of unstructured data that's out there currently? How do you deal with that?

The Disruptive Nature of MDM

MDM seems to have an answer—at least fourth-generation MDM solutions do. First, they've centralized all data around process hubs, which allows the enterprise to manage the business rules and processes that are needed to use the data in specific and appropriate ways. Then they are integrating enterprise search. Zornes foresees the complete fourth-generation MDM solution looking like this (from his "Enterprise Master Data Management Market Review and Forecast for 2008–2012"):

> While the majority of contemporary [author's note: third generation] MDM solutions focus on the structured data held in CRM and ERP applications, the reality is that a plethora of valuable customer, product, supplier, employee, etc., information resides in what is characterized as "unstructured" information, e.g., emails, instant message log files, voicemails, etc. To provide a robust "universal customer view" . . . it is clearly desirable to incorporate these valuable information sources as part of the composite view.

While that is a lovely vision, is there anyone who's actually doing that now?

MDM Market Leaders

Not entirely. There are market-dominant MDM forces, which include a Big Four who are beginning to investigate the fourth generation of MDM, though still a long way from implementing that enterprise search capability: Oracle, SAP, Teradata, and IBM. However, they are still aimed at improving and have made some surprising efforts. In the second quarter, 2009 SAP and Teradata announced an MDM-like partnership to integrate SAP's NetWeaver and BW with varying Teradata solutions so they could actually satisfy the requests of their customers, rather than try to up their market ante. It seems that there was an 80 percent overlap between SAP and Teradata customers, according to Teradata EMEA CEO Herman Wimmer. Many of those customers, like Hershey's in Pennsylvania, welcomed the move.

As far as fourth generation capabilities like enterprise search, one of the more promising approaches has been the integration of Microsoft SharePoint with their MDM solution. Though I'm no fan at all of SharePoint, this at least points in the right direction for the future of MDM.

What in Heaven's Name Does MDM Have to Do with CRM, Except Sharing an M?

Even though technically you could call CDI a subset of MDM, the value of MDM is that it provides a complete and integrated view of *all* enterprise data, not just the customer data. It subjects that data to the expected analytics tools, and also to business rules and workflow so you can make the post-analysis results actionable and also direct them to the appropriate parties to take that action. Because it's SOA based, it integrates well with applications that would need to access it.

It has a potentially disruptive—good—effect on contemporary business models also. It supports Social CRM self-service efforts by making available the data that customers need to handle their own service requests or purchases, and then automates the transactions regardless of what systems are involved in the process. It gives both the company and the customer (with the permission of the company) visibility into what Zornes calls the "hyper-integrated 21st century chain," which means a supply chain that involves internal manufacturing, warehousing, distribution, logistics, and the outsourced pieces of that too.

At the early 2009 MDM Summit, Zornes (my man!) introduced three reasons for companies to consider MDM, especially as it evolves into the fourth generation of solutions:

> **1.** *Identify and provide differentiated service to its most valuable customers via their relationships (households, hierarchies); also cross-sell and up-sell additional products to these customers*

2. *Introduce new products and product bundles more quickly across more channels to reduce the cost of New Product Introduction (NPI)*

3. *Provide improved enterprise-wide transparency across customers, distributors, suppliers, and products to better support regulatory compliance processes*

For Social CRM, item 1 particularly concerns us, as it impacts customer lifetime value and how the social customer is identified, valued, and interacted/transacted with.

The ability to identify relationships using data that spans multiple locations and multiple data sources is a major leap forward, especially for the largest enterprises when it comes to their customers. This allows them a multidimensional look at their customers and those around them. It also provides them with the information they need to optimize the offers they are going to provide to those customers and determine what kind of investment the customer needs to get. This means that the transaction history is the supreme arbiter of net present value (NPV), the core metric in a customer lifetime value calculation. The relationships matter.

Before you get too complacent, this is only a beginning stab at how you measure the social customer—the technology that underpins the effort. There is much more to this, but you're going to have to wait until Chapter 20 to hear anything more on it. This chapter is on data and process. That chapter is on value.

So I think the benefit of MDM is apparent to you all. Yes? No? Let me know at the site that I've listed in the introduction or on my blogs. If there are any doubters among you, let me put your doubts to rest by introducing you to Jill Dyché, who's going to provide you with what you should see as the key benefits of MDM. Believe me, she knows.

MINI-CONVERSATION WITH JILL DYCHÉ

Jill Dyché is someone I've known for years. Her basic bio? She's a partner and co-founder of Baseline Consulting. She handles key client work and industry analysis in the areas of data governance, business intelligence, and master data management, and advises executives and boards on the strategic importance of investing in enterprise information. That's what she does for Baseline.

She's also written three books and contributed to a number of others. Her first book, *e-Data* (Addison Wesley, 2000), has been published in eight languages.

She is also the author of *The CRM Handbook* (Addison Wesley, 2002), which (even seven years later) is still the definitive guide to implementing CRM. Her latest book is *Customer Data Integration: Reaching a Single Version of the Truth* (Wiley, 2006), co-authored with Baseline partner Evan Levy.

Jill has been featured in major publications such as *Computerworld*, the *Wall Street Journal*, and *Newsweek.com*. She writes regularly as a columnist for Information Management magazine, is an Ask the Expert contributor for SearchDataManagement.com, a blogger on B-Eye-Network, and a judge on several industry best-practice awards. She writes the Inside the Biz blog on Baseline's website.

Jill is a player in both CRM and data management. Her knowledge of what to do with data exceeds the amount of total data I have in my head. To top it off, she is simply a good person who is a real pleasure to work with.

Ladies and gents, Jill.

Science fiction writer William Gibson once remarked that "the future is already here, it's just unevenly distributed." The same could be said of your company's customer data, which exists, to be sure, but in lots of different silos with many different uses. And if your company is like most, business and IT executives continue to grapple with how to invest the right funds and resources to manage enterprise data as a corporate asset.

Enter master data management (MDM). MDM isn't a new solution to an old problem, but rather a new solution to a new problem: the active correction and reconciliation of customer data, often in real time, to enable de facto data sharing among different systems. Put more simply: MDM lets the systems that process customer data play nicely together.

Someone in your company probably thinks you're already doing MDM. Chances are they're wrong about that. Why? Because of all the vendor noise. That's right. Your CRM, ERP, and data warehouse vendors all have their own MDM stories. MDM isn't a query system, it's not a fancy name for data quality, and it has a lot of functionality "baked in." Sometimes MDM's functional capabilities apply to your specific business problems, and sometimes they don't. It's up to you to figure out the various business use cases for reconciled master data, and apply the right MDM solution to those problems—and believe me, there is more than one problem out there that calls for reconciled customer data. Is your company focused on growth through acquisition? Think about all that incoming customer data and how to match that data against the data you already have about your customers. What about smarter target marketing? That's not going to happen as long as your customer mailing list is only as good as the individual silo you've pulled it from. And cross-selling at the time of purchase? Impossible without a comprehensive and updated customer record.

You get the idea. There are multiple justifications for integrated and accurate customer data. The trick is to know what yours is. You have at least one, you know, and it's screaming to get out. In the meantime, here are three takeaways— culled from my own work with Global 2000 companies in the throes of MDM development—that might help you not only liberate that business case, but ensure that MDM delivers significant return on investment.

Takeaway 1: Treat MDM as a Business Solution

It's fun to deconstruct the architectural styles of MDM. You'll hear the vendors spout them off: collaborative MDM, transactional MDM, registry-style, and so on, and your IT group might chime in, too. But business executives don't care whether your matching algorithm is deterministic or probabilistic, or whether the data model is fully attributized. What they care about is that MDM is going to save the company $30 million a year in compliance reporting fines, or that a single operational view of the customer across the company can save $50 million in development efficiencies over the next three years, or that your customer retention rates will rise a conservative 15 percent—when in reality the post-MDM measure doubles that figure.

My point here is that it's tempting to go down the "infrastructure" route. After all, who doesn't sound smarter talking about algorithms? But you'd do better to recognize the business value of MDM, and pitch it that way internally. That's how you get funding, and how you'll guarantee job security. These days, he—or she—who enables the information-driven enterprise wins the brass ring. And maybe even a stellar performance review!

Takeaway 2: Understand What Your Incumbent Technologies Can and Can't Deliver

Remember the days when the CRM vendors were all describing themselves as the 360-degree view of customer? And then we all tried getting non-native data into those systems and they barfed on us. CRM vendors wanted to be all things to all people. These days, as often as not, they've become legacy systems just like all the others.

I'm not knocking CRM software. Lord knows CRM's come a long way and much of the functionality is now "in the cloud." That's taken us off the hook for customizing and maintaining CRM. But the data's still there and we should be leveraging it beyond our CRM tool.

An MDM hub won't replace your CRM system. It won't manage your pipeline or recommend the next product a customer should buy. What it will do is ensure that the data about that individual customer matches on your company's proprietary billing system, in your data warehouse, and in your marketing automation system, and all those other systems that generate and use customer data, rendering a single version of the truth enterprise-wide.

After all, your CRM tool wasn't designed to manage B2B hierarchies or group business customers based on their relationships with one another. Your data warehouse doesn't automatically resolve customer identities. Your data quality tool doesn't necessarily link newly harmonized data back to the operational system from whence it originated. And your social networking tools don't automatically append new customer contact points and interactions to the customer's established profile.

Knowing the specific functional capabilities of MDM and how they map to your company's requirements (see Takeaway 1) can take you a long way in solving business problems that heretofore required a lot of manual work—or were considered unsolvable.

Takeaway 3: Know MDM's Role in Knowing Your Customers

If you're in financial services, how do you know whether to grant an applicant a home loan, or approve a credit card transaction? If you're in retail, how do you know product quantities to stock based on forecasted customer demand? In health care, can you track a patient across the continuum of care, certain of that patient's identity? In state government, are you continuing to give food stamps to deadbeat dads? In pharmaceutical, do you know that the doctor prescribing your medicine is affiliated with multiple hospitals?

Show me an industry and I'll show you at least one captivating MDM business case. There are general business needs for clean, streamlined customer master data; there are industry-specific needs as well. A gaming company we work with uses its data warehouse to send marketing offers to past customers. The data warehouse can generate a list of customers likely to make a return visit to the casino, and the marketing automation system can recommend the best offer combination—a free dinner, two show tickets, and two-night room comp— based on that customer's preferences. But the MDM hub can let the dealer know whether to make that offer on the spot when a player sits down at the blackjack table or whether to escort him off the property. See the difference? Historical behavior analysis versus real-time identification. Use cases like this can mean nothing less than first-mover advantage.

The extent to which we know our customers is the extent to which we can compete strategically, and differentiate ourselves competitively. The question is: Are you ready for MDM? Or, perhaps more aptly: When will you start?◼

Good stuff, huh?

I imagine you've noticed that in the case of both CDI and MDM, business process integration and management play a significant role in their usage and value. What about business processes and Social CRM? Is it different than last round? How should you view business processes in the customer ecosystem?

It's the Process, Man

Just because you've bought into the idea of integrating business processes into your data systems, or because you're investigating best practices for use in your business, doesn't mean that business processes just fall into place without any effort. They are not devoid of context. They are not universally applicable. You can incorporate the wrong business processes into your enterprise. You can add best practices for your industry that turn out to be the worst possible practices for your particular company and proceed to damage the company. Processes that make sense for one department might be affecting processes and damaging another department and possibly the company as a whole.

I had a mid-sized client with an accounting process they had developed that was saving them an estimated $40,000 per year. After a few years of self-satisfied tummy patting, they decided to incorporate e-commerce into their work. But because of the way the process had been created and because of the processes that had been incorporated into their e-commerce site, there was an "interdepartmental" glitch that caused the customers to enter some of their data twice into the system to satisfy the site. The company tried to technically correct it, but it didn't work without eliminating the accounting process—the one saving them $40,000 per year.

What would you have done here? (Play *Jeopardy* theme while answers are written down.)

You're right. That's what they did. They eliminated the process. Despite its monetary efficiency, they understood that it had a negative impact on the customers and that was worth a lot more than $40,000 per year to correct.

Processes may be nonspecific to customers, but they aren't agnostic. They are an integrated part of an enterprise that deals with customers, and therefore there will be some sort of impact. So identifying the efficiencies of a business process isn't necessarily the only way to think about it. Effectiveness and impact on the customer should be integral parts of your process design.

Customer-Centric Business Processes—Don't Be Agnostic

While not every business process is going to be customer-centric, all of them have to at least concern themselves with the impact they are going to have on the customer.

Here is what you should worry about when it concerns a modern business process for those of you who ordinarily couldn't care less but are now getting interested because your business or your job depends on having optimized practices that are focused around these incredibly demanding social customers of yours.

Managing Business Processes

Business process management (BPM) is now a mainstream methodology for designing which processes are going to be applied where inside your enterprise. It's an important part of strategic planning. Even with an economic downturn, redesign of the processes is an important way to improve the effectiveness of your CRM deployment without spending a lot of money. Gartner Group CRM vice president Scott Nelson, in a report released in May 2009, identified five cheap ways to improve your CRM program. Business process redesign was one of them. According to Nelson:

> Process is often an overlooked part of CRM, and in many cases all that CRM technologies have done is taken out old, broken processes and made them run more efficiently. Now is an excellent time to study customer processes with a view to redesigning them and creating a win/win situation for both the company—which gets greater efficiency—and the customer—who gets a "partner" that interacts with them in a meaningful way.

This is congruent with not just a recession, but also with changes in how the customers interact with you; resulting changes in your organizational structure and business model; and changes in your priorities in how you handle your customers. After all, if you are designing a CRM initiative or have one in place, and you have to change the way you do business, your processes will have to change.

This reflects the fundamental shift toward cross-functional processes (across multiple applications) that come with a business ecosystem dependent on a collaborative value chain. It is no longer useful to have packaged software silos in conflict with each other.

Luckily, from an architectural standpoint, web services provide a common language to bridge the operational gaps and the external interactions with the customers. They can provide seamless and standardized interactions between the process/business layers and the application layers and between multiple business layers. They make the task of evolving appropriate processes a lot easier than it used to be, whether internal or customer-facing. Changes to processes when made customer-friendly can have powerful benefits for a customer. Envision a mortgage company, a long time ago and far, far away, that saw its volume of work with loan origination increase by many times, because of the number of homes being refinanced to take advantage of the extraordinary low interest available. A seven-day decision-making cycle on loans was absolutely unacceptable, because of brutal competition for these home owners. By a thorough examination of the processes that were involved and a look at what benefited the customer for each step of the process, the mortgage company was able to reduce the cycle time to 48 hours, which in turn reduced the transaction cost from $250 to $60 per loan. This saved the company $50 million over a year, and the customer was thrilled with a 48-hour decision on the refinancing or financing of their house.

How do you identify these customer-friendly processes and manage them within your overall CRM strategy? I thought you'd never ask.

Trying to manage customer-based CRM processes is not the easiest task. Since it is not strictly an internal effort, all kinds of problems exist. Just dealing with efficiency improvements or deficiencies doesn't cut it in a CRM environment. When done well, customer-directed BPM links all of a process's internal and external participants—clients, employees, partners, suppliers, and vendors—through rules, workflow, processes, and hopefully, best practices. The payoffs are a smooth flow between all processes across departments and through applications. Manual and automated tasks work well together—at best, seamlessly. With the right framework, you can continually model new processes and test them easily, without disrupting workflow or the existing processes. You can measure how effectively the processes are working, using the analytics that are present in the best of the BPM frameworks. Customer-directed BPM can also:

▶ Standardize enterprise best process practices across all organizations

▶ Establish a powerful workflow that can move work to the appropriate next participant in the business process

▶ Gather, format, and present information applicable to each task activity in multiple formats

▶ Produce notices, correspondence, and communications to parties related to each process

▶ Manage service standard activity deadlines and constraints and automatically carry out the prescribed corrective actions when they have been exceeded

▶ Reduce process inefficiencies automatically by using business rules to eliminate valueless tasks, unique process by process

▶ Log, monitor, and report processing progress and logistics

▶ Automate and manage customer-specific process variations

Close Your Eyes and Visualize . . . Process Maps

It isn't just me who believes this. Michael Webb is a highly respected business process expert who, despite my general dislike of Six Sigma, has created a version of that efficiency-obsessed defect reduction methodology that is genuinely focused around improving customer effectiveness—meaning providing value to the customer by a well-functioning process at work inside a company.

In the course of his discussion on sales process in his book *Sales and Marketing the Six Sigma Way*, he looks at how mapping customer value at every integral place in your company is a mission-critical step in designing processes that will work for both the company and the customer. In fact, for a detailed look at how to go about mapping sales processes, I would highly recommend this book. Go get it.

When I look at a process map, I'm looking at owners and approvals—meaning which individual or group owns a particular process (e.g., a lead to cash owned by the VP of sales)—but not just that. I'm also examining what the objective is for the success of that process, how it is going to be measured, and what kind of interface is going to be used to execute that process. The most important component of the deconstruction of that process is what contribution it makes to the customer experience and value proposition. Or, by the same token, how does it detract from that customer experience and value proposition? For example, if I know that transparency has to be a part of the outlook for my company because of the newly significant demands of the social customer, I have to figure out the optimal processes to support transparency. When I decide how the company will be transparent, what assets we have to provide, and who will provide those assets to whom, then I have to build processes that work for that. Perhaps it's a process that provides documents to customers in a more simplified way than in the past or a process that allows customers to reach to higher levels of customer service more directly than in the past.

Customer value must always be assessed when considering the processes that I'm designing or redesigning for or eliminating from my business.

What kind of methodology should be used to make these assessments, to design these processes? Dick Lee, managing principal and founder of High-Yield Methods, is an expert in business process. He's developed a business process design methodology that takes BP design out of the realm of the super-uber-megaguru's hands and puts it in the hands of the people who are going to use it—and turns the development of those processes into a collaborative effort. It's called visual workflow, and here's Dick to discuss it.

DICK LEE ON PROCESS METHODOLOGY

Let's consider one of the most common Social CRM process problems—sending unfiltered web leads straight to sales. What happens as a result? Either sales resources wasted following up garbage inquiries, or marketing resources wasted because the sales force funnels all these inquiries into porcelain bowls, or both.

Going back to CRM 1.0, astonishingly few companies ever figured out the importance of pre-qualifying all advertising and direct mail inquiries before sending them to sales. CRM software was supposed to remedy the situation, but we all know where that went. But along with the move to the Web came a blind supposition that web inquiries are somehow inherently qualified. Hey, we just took our baggage with us when we went to the Web. Why? Because we staunchly resist fixing process problems if we catch even a whiff of potential organizational change. And as you'll see in a moment, "the fix" here requires far more than cosmetic process change.

However, the cost of not addressing sales lead management process defects far outweighs the cost of leaving the "as-is" as is—which you'll see explicated by Visual Workflow, a process analysis and design methodology that High-Yield Methods designed specifically for front and back office environments, as opposed to manufacturing.

Here's the VW drill and the outcomes it produces.

For starters, senior management must mandate that the lead management problem be addressed—and addressed cooperatively by all functions and individual roles involved. Because fixing the problem will require some uncomfortable if not outright painful concessions and responsibility shifting, without this imprimatur, the necessary process changes will almost never occur.

Next, management has to assemble a cross-functional team representing all participants, including customer-facing staff as well as managers. To knit the team together (and avoid bloodshed), management also has to engage a skilled, objective facilitator to guide the team through the assessment and redesign steps. Typically, companies select an outsider because finding internally the requisite level of objectivity and facilitation skills proves difficult.

Now management steps back, and the facilitator leads the team through a thorough assessment of "as-is" workflow and information flow. Tracking the movement of customer information everywhere in the company, from the time the company first becomes aware of a customer until the customer is dead and gone, provides excellent structure for this exercise.

What happens to this tracking info, which facilitators or assistants often capture in magic marker on easel pads? A little magic. Either you or the outsourcer converts these marker maps into "pictograph" maps that rely on representational clip art images to tell the story—and do they ever tell a story. The pictographs present what's happening now in an undeniable way so the *whole* team understands what's going on, rather than just one or two team members who can read symbology-laden process maps that are further obfuscated by terminology from unknown languages.

Everyone gets it, as you'll see by reviewing this sample "as-is" pictograph (Figure 19-1), which accurately portrays common lead management practices.

It's not a question of what's going wrong. It's a question of whether anything is going right. The download of inquiries into CRM looks

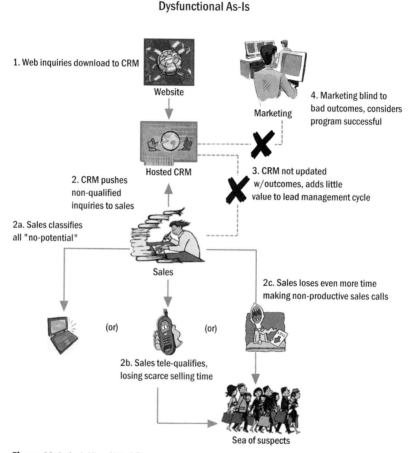

Figure 19-1: As-is Visual Workflow process

okay, but from there the whole thing goes to hell in a handbasket. Fortunately, when most companies come face to face with a mess like this, they understand they have to change. Especially the cross-functional team members.

On to the hard part. The team has to figure out how to make lead management work—which will require changing roles and responsibilities, requiring new accountabilities, and support from new and/or reconfigured technology, usually with an adult dose of data integration. Sometimes these sessions hurt. But everyone has already "pledged allegiance" to putting the customer's needs first, then the company's needs, but not introducing functional aspirations—a.k.a. turf issues. As a result, the peer pressure to "plan by the rules" can be immense.

The sample "to-be" pictograph shows (Figure 19-2) how much should change. Much of the lead management work is now outsourced—important because effective lead management requires time and skill sets rarely found internally. Every inquiry is tele-qualified, and only ready-to-buy prospects wind up assigned to field sales. And although not shown here for brevity, future potential prospects go into a nurturing queue for periodic contact by phone and/or e-mail until they are ready. Once the now-qualified leads show up on sales reps' task lists for follow-up, sales has to follow up in a set period or risk having the lead reassigned. Sales quickly develops the habit of reporting outcomes, because reporting compliance is now part of their

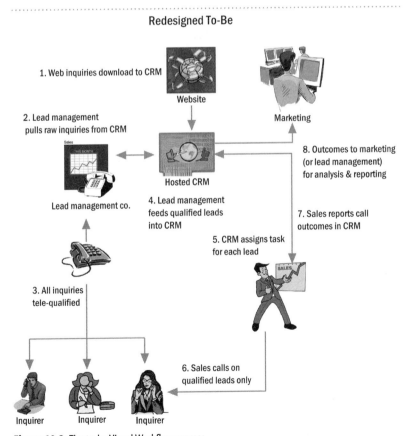

Redesigned To-Be

1. Web inquiries download to CRM

Website

2. Lead management pulls raw inquiries from CRM

Marketing

Hosted CRM

Lead management co.

8. Outcomes to marketing (or lead management) for analysis & reporting

4. Lead management feeds qualified leads into CRM

7. Sales reports call outcomes in CRM

5. CRM assigns task for each lead

3. All inquiries tele-qualified

6. Sales calls on qualified leads only

Inquirer   Inquirer   Inquirer

Figure 19-2: The to-be Visual Workflow process

comp plan (another key process outcome). And if reps fall off the wagon, the lead management company is right there with friendly "encouragement." Actually, many sales reps develop very positive, collaborative relationships with lead management account staff, much to the benefit of the lead program.

From here, it's on to selling management on change and implementing change, technically outside the process realm. However, companies with high-consequence work performed by individuals—banks, for example—may want to drill down to reengineer and map individual work processes that will support redesigned workflow, even going down to the keystroke level. This, by the way, is an excellent way to determine application software requirements.

Superstah! Process-Driven CRM: Sword Ciboodle

I have to admit, when I heard of Sword Ciboodle, I just thought, "Wow, is that a funny name." While researching them (a friend of mine, Ted Hartley, was in the running for the U.S. COO at the time—he got the job), I saw they put themselves in a category of CRM that I had never heard of, process-driven CRM. It was a legitimate category. They had been named the leader by Forrester Group in that category in the Forrester Wave for the fourth quarter, with competition including Chordiant, Pegasystems, and Consona Software, formerly Onyx. So clearly this was a category, and they were a significant CRM player.

But why hadn't I heard of them? I found the answer when I went to Chicago to do a webinar and meet with them. Yeah, you read right. I flew to Chicago to do a *webinar*. But obviously the meetings with COO Ted Hartley, CEO (for the U.S.) Paul White, and CTO Steven Thurlow and the U.S. staff were the reason I went to Chicago. Webinars are easy from anywhere.

I found out they were a Scottish company formerly called Graham Technology who had been purchased by the Sword Group in 2008. Graham Technology came to the table with a product named Ciboodle, hence Sword Ciboodle. They had dozens of major clients in Europe and were (and are) doing a huge implementation of their solution at Sears in the U.S. The Sword Group was not that small either. They are more than a quarter billion dollar company.

I got a chance to review their solution and the thing rocks. It does something that I think process-driven CRM is built for—if you remember what I called in the customer service chapter (Chapter 13) keeping the ordinary, ordinary. Process-driven CRM sees to it that nothing goes wrong when you make a query or a phone call, which is invaluable. Sword Ciboodle does it well enough to be the Superstah! for this chapter.

The Solution

The centerpiece of the Sword Ciboodle solution is their process-driven platform, which is organized around their J2EE architecture and run-time engine. The engine, built with common standards, is responsible for running customer configured processes and it handles all integrations, including external services, so that the customer experience can be seamless regardless of the channel that the customer interacts with the system from.

But it's in the modules that Sword Ciboodle begins to shine.

First, they are all built within what Sword calls the Business Process Management Suite. That suite gives you a plain vanilla out of the box set of agent- and customer-facing processes so immediately rich that French vanilla comes to mind. These processes are flexible enough to be entirely configurable—modified, replaceable, or used as-is.

Probably the most interesting and valuable for the user is the Intelligent Desktop module (see Figure 19-3), which organizes an entire agent work environment around a single point of access to all applications, native or integrated. This is coupled with a single view of customers, processes, and their interactions so that any employees who need to can see everything the customer did or is doing, and the possible answers to their problem, ticket, or inquiry. This is an "intelligent" desktop because of the embedded context-driven workflow.

There are dozens of modules that could arguably in combination provide one of the most powerful contact center solutions in the world. I wouldn't make the same case for their sales or self-described campaign management functionality, which, for the most part, just gives those other traditional CRM modules a passing wave. But the power of the solution is undeniable to provide agents with a true customer interaction so that when there is a problem, it gets resolved, and when there isn't a problem, it stays that way.

Figure 19-3: The Sword Ciboodle agent desktop shows everything (Source: Sword Ciboodle)

Another reason for that power is their customer management module, which does considerably more than similar systems. It's focused around real-time access to multiple systems so it can take fragmented data, whether it's personal information, relationship data, account data, or preferences, and provide an agent with structured data in a useful context. For example, if a customer has a serious complaint that is heading toward escalation, it can be flagged, so that if they call in again the flag will put the case history up front. But along with that, the service level agreement, the recent contact that the customer had with the company aside from the open complaint, and the purchase history (if it makes sense) will show up too.

Through out-of-the-box adaptors, Sword Ciboodle integrates with all the common telephony platforms—Cisco, Avaya, Genesys, and Nortel. The Sword Ciboodle eService component allows real-time agent/customer interaction.

Clearly this is an application that can handle highly complex processes at large customer service centers. But what truly distinguishes these guys is that they never forget that the customer is at the center of the experience—and all those processes.

Mission 21st Century

Paul White is the newly minted CEO for Sword Ciboodle Americas. He is a chipper, smart, and experienced CRM practitioner and has a solid vision of what a senior Ciboodler (their word) needs to see. Here's his view on what Sword Ciboodle is planning going forward.

We expect to see a substantial increase in "experience engineering" as a widely practiced discipline. The most customer-centric organizations are already designing the customer experience from the perspectives of consumers and partners as well as their own business operations and marketing goals.

This allows organizations to design the experience, rather than relying on mono-channel thinking and plain luck to govern if customers achieve their goals effectively.

His vision of experience engineering is a somewhat more technological version of the way that Pine and Gilmore, in their seminal work *The Experience Economy*, outlined the nature of experiences with a company. Pine and Gilmore saw commoditized experiences that would be created by the company. Paul White sees engineered experiences as a set of processes organized by a company that would be designed to enhance and contextualize the kinds of experiences that a company would provide to the customer in an multi-channel environment, though I noticed a strong emphasis on the agent when I reviewed the application.

White went on to outline what the going-forward strategy for Sword Ciboodle needs to be, given his vision of experience engineering. He sees their role as the ones who drive experience engineering. That means, in his view, they wouldn't just implement a CRM package, they'd reinvent the customer-business interface.

Their partnership strategy is curious, though understandable: "We will select only a few, choice delivery partners who will be accredited to deliver advanced, process-driven CRM."

This is a company that has it nailed when it comes to using process to enhance the customer experience. They are world class with a great leadership, a good outlook, and a deep solution that can handle the largest contact centers, which is their target market. Their name may be odd, but not their success.

I want to finish with Dick Lee again. He and Jill Dyché are a powerful duo when it comes to seeing how to use data and integrate processes into your customer engagement system. No reintroduction necessary.

Mini-Conversation with Dick Lee: Three Takeaways on Business Process

Many business-side people find office process design off-putting. They're not trained in process design. They have a full plate of work already. And many believe process is "someone else's job."

However, two factors are thrusting office process responsibility onto marketing, sales, service, and other points of front office and back office management. First, the word "process" turns out to be the closest connection between office process and manufacturing process. Skills on one side don't readily transfer to the other. And all the skills are currently on the manufacturing side. Second, senior managers are starting to sit up and take notice that the biggest process opportunities out there are right under their noses. Guess what's coming?

Office managers need to tune in rather than tune out to process—the office type. Here are three tips that will help you stay on the beam.

1. ***Don't ever let technology lead process.*** *Many companies approach office process by throwing technology at it, usually one function at a time. Reminds me of the "circular firing squad" image. No winners. Only dead bodies. Even the last guy standing shoots himself. You need to first redefine office process to add value to customers and streamline work—and then enable the new wok with technology. And don't let any software salesperson or IT guy tell you otherwise.*

2. ***Redesigning process is a process enabled by automation.*** *Forget about wrapping conference room walls with craft paper and writing indecipherable stuff all around. For workflow level mapping, use a charting tool. We like SmartDraw best because it has fewer idiosyncrasies than others. And Visio can't even print to Word—essential for wrapping flow charts in a narrative. For mapping finer, individual work process, we use ProCarta, which can draw 100 map pages with the click of a mouse.*

3. ***Don't redesign office process for cost-cutting purposes.*** *All you'll do is trim around the edges—whereas customer-centric design encourages structural changes that really help you accomplish more with fewer people. We usually see a 10 to 15 percent reduction in FTE requirements post–Visual Workflow—much more than you'd see taking the cost-cutting approach.*

That's it for this chapter. I combined process and data for the same reasons that I combined sales and marketing earlier. We've reached a nexus point. The best way for businesses in this part of the 21st century to operationalize how they are going to interact with customers is to not only have sufficient data, but business rules, workflow, and business processes in place that provide the means to make the data actionable and you much more intelligent about your customer. This demands a high degree of integration and interaction between those processes and the data. Hence, the two are as one.

There's an electronic chapter you can go get now, if you don't have it already, that provides a nice intermezzo to the next print chapter. The electronic chapter is on privacy and transparency—go to the site and find the one called, "I Want This Chapter to Be on Privacy, but If I Wrote It, I'd Have to Blog About You." We now have all the pieces of Social CRM in place but two—what comprises customer value and how to develop metrics and use analytics to determine that.

20

Value Given, Value Received: Analyzing the Return on CRM

*P*rinciple #1 of CRM: Value and values are given, and in return value and values are received.

—Paul Greenberg

One thing is certain about CRM. It's pretty much useless unless there is some sort of return for both your business and the customer. This is a science that encourages symbiotic relationships. That means that you have to define what value is to your business, and you also have to discover what value is to your customer. Then you have to figure out what are the things that you as a businessperson have to do to provide the value to your customer, which, as we saw in Chapter 3, are quite different from what businesses want. That's where analytics comes in. Then you have to figure out who's going to do those things and make them accountable for doing them. That's key performance indicators and benchmarks. Then you have to decide what you want from those customers. That's return on investment (ROI) or more appropriately, as Peppers and Rogers calls it, return on customer (ROC).

Data, of course, is not the subject matter here. We took care of that a few chapters ago. This chapter is about what we do to data. Step by step, inch by inch, we'll analyze, benchmark, and evaluate. Then we'll judge, which is what we of the human species do.

Analytics: Figuring Out Whassup

Note: I have to admit, I liked this section of the third edition so much, I'm reproducing a small amount of it here, though most of this chapter is new. Really.

Here it is, back by popular acclaim.

From true premises, it is not possible to draw a false conclusion; but a true conclusion may be drawn from false premises—true however only in respect to the fact, not to the reason.

—Prior Analytics, Aristotle

Since what is known without qualification cannot be otherwise, what is known by demonstrative knowledge will be necessary.

—Posterior Analytics, Aristotle

So, class, what conclusion can you draw from these two statements? No, it doesn't mean *that* posterior.

Aristotle is saying that from premise to knowledge takes demonstration. You may make a certain assumption, hoping it is true. You then have to create the proof of its truth. But it also can be that in the course of examining this premise, which conceivably might not be true, you still come up with a true conclusion because you uncovered facts that are incontrovertible. That is demonstrative knowledge. In order to develop a strategy or impact a group or make a point, you have to prove it.

For example, say your premise is that if you implement reduced prices during the recession to sell an item to a specific customer demographic, they will increase their purchases by some percentage. In the course of looking into that, you realize that this is a highly affluent group who isn't concerned about price, but they are concerned about style. So you improve the styling of the product and the purchases increase by some percentage. That's how this could work.

While those quotes (translated from Greek to English) may still be Greek to many of you reading this, the fundamental principles here are the governing principles of analytics. Use information that is examined in multiple ways and interpret it to come to a conclusion on how to make that information benefit, in this case, your business. In knowledge, there is power. But not just in information or data. Neither data nor analytics stands on its own.

What Are Analytics?

Analytics, in the realm of CRM at least, are the collection, extraction, modification, measurement, identification, and reporting of information designed to be useful to the party using the analytics. On the technical side, to chuck terms at you, this includes multidimensional online analytical processing (OLAP) techniques as well as calculations, logic, formulas, and analytic routines/algorithms against data extracted from operational (OLTP) systems (the "T" stands for "transactional," where the data is too granular to be useful for analysis). This means the slice and dice engine that is used to determine why you should be given a 10 percent discount on your next purchase of an Amtrak Acela ticket to New York from Washington, D.C., where you live. When you drill down from the offer you received for this, the analysis shows that you live in D.C., make 7 to 10 trips per year via train or plane to New York, are between 45 and 54 years old, have an income level over $150,000, and are a professional with a college education. That puts you in a segment likely to take Amtrak with some carefully offered incentive to do so. Especially the high-tech east coast corridor train Acela, which gets you where you want to go in two and a half hours.

What magnifies the value of analytics is the real-time nature of many of the products, such as those offered by our Superstah! winner this chapter, SAS, or the products that are offered by companies specializing in price, revenue, or offer optimization. Each of them is available to capture the moment almost literally. If you go online to buy something, you might get an offer for something else related that pops up on the screen while you are still in the web session. That is because of an optimization engine that is working to compare your customer history with your current online activity and then "thinking through" what would be the best possible up-sell or cross-sell opportunity on the spot. These real-time analytic engines are maturing now and can make a valuable difference in transforming customer behaviors or improving customer experiences.

But the social customer makes things more complex—as if you needed that headache. Now it is no longer good enough to have just transactional data for insight or to have an optimization engine making an offer they can't refuse. It's now necessary to be able to dissect conversations that might have nothing to do with their transactions with you. That could mean text and sentiment analysis. It's also no longer good enough to just analyze data that is stored in your internal databases. Web analytics become mission-critical since 74 percent of the U.S. population and comparable amounts in many places throughout the world have a social web presence. Old web measures like page views are no longer seen as the benchmark for that presence, creating such a dilemma that Nielsen Buzzmetrics changed their web benchmark from page views to time spent on the web page by unique visitors. Frankly, that's incredibly silly—especially with tabbed browsing being the norm for web visitors. Do me a favor. Open up copies of Google Chrome, Firefox, and IE8 and open up my blogs on ZDNet (http://blogs.zdnet .com/crm) and PGreenblog (www.the56group.typepad.com) on separate tabs in each. Then go on a two-week vacation.

See what I mean? Time spent on open web pages doesn't mean you're reading the web pages. Buzzmetrics hasn't exactly nailed it yet. But no one has a total handle on this, though there are some fair stabs out there.

But how to measure customer activity on the Web is not a trivial issue. So I've recruited Jim Sterne, president of the Web Analytics Association, to show you what the fairest of stabs actually is, later in the chapter.

Using analytics to assess customer value is an important part of your CRM portfolio, but there are hundreds of analytics products out there and picking one is like walking through a (data) minefield. The wrong one can destroy you, and the right one can support your efforts to actually *know* your customer. At the risk of sounding like a broken MP3 file, note I said *support* the effort. It doesn't substitute for the effort.

A Very Brief Primer on Analytics

To help you make the right choices, I'm going to do a very brief primer on analytics. It's brief because this edition is necessarily more right-brained than left. We'll cover analytics types just enough to give you some idea of what they are. We'll also look at some of the newer tools out there to help you figure out that elusive creature known as the social customer.

Analytic Types

There actually are analytic types. No, not psychologist, psychotherapist, and psychiatrist, though writing this book over the past year plus qualifies me for a few sessions with any one of the three. Those are analyst types. The analytic types are descriptive and predictive.

Descriptive Analytics

This is the analytics for "as is." It is a historic look at a customer's behavior, organization's performance, or customer segment's habits. For example, if you ran a marketing campaign, how effective was it? Have the CSRs been improving their call-to-resolution time? Since you completed the implementation of your SFA system, how has the sales team performed in each city that has it? If there are cities that don't have it, how do sales compare there? Are the logistics and delivery up to the task, now that sales have increased? These are some of the possible uses of descriptive analytics, also known as operational analytics.

Predictive Analytics

This is the analytics for the "could be if," rather than the "to be." This is where developing models of the possible and scoring the likelihood of achieving something that may be possible, identified down to the individual level, become an important part of the analysis. Predictive analytics take customer data and identify customer segments or individuals and forecast possible behaviors based on historic performance and other factors introduced into a model. They then try to figure out how to utilize the likely outcomes for the benefit of the company. For example, if you reduce the sales team's administrative time by 12 percent and provide them with the means to get information this much more quickly, what is the possible impact on cost and on your revenue? Or if you promote a specific price cut on a product to 18-year-olds with driver's licenses in Arkansas, what is the likely increase in responses and in sales based on that promotion? If you remember in Chapter 12, I spoke of Oracle's Sales Prospector. It uses predictive analytics to see what a deal's likelihood of successful closing is, what time frame it can optimally close in, and what the likely size of the deal will be.

Once you get past the types of analytics, there are a few analytics toolsets that need to be reviewed because of their importance to business. That would be business intelligence for the quant in you and text analytics for the softer side.

Business Intelligence (BI) Is a Separate Matter

Business intelligence remains one of the most important analytics applications linked to CRM. It was important enough that in the years from 2007 to 2009, every mega-giant business intelligence application provider was snapped up by an even larger company. So we saw Oracle snap up Hyperion, SAP snap up Business Objects, and IBM snap up Cognos. Yum. Why did they make these multi-billion dollar acquisitions? Because it made sense to them to take the most sophisticated BI purveyors with the largest customer portfolios and add their tools and customers to their own offerings. They were and are totally right about that.

To clarify what BI is, I'm going to answer some questions I've actually gotten and a few that I made up, thinking they might be important too.

What Is Business Intelligence?

Business intelligence is the use of an organization's disparate data to provide meaningful information and analysis to employees, customers, suppliers, and partners for more effective decision making. It is a critical component of a CRM strategy.

Is Business Intelligence Strictly a CRM Thing?

Customer intelligence is not the only BI that exists. Other BI that is frequently found includes product, services, supply chain, financial, and human resources intelligence. In fact, BI extends along the entire enterprise value chain and, even though that value chain is organized around customers, the BI can be broken down to specific links in the chain. The more information you have on each customer interaction throughout all steps of the value chain, the clearer and more innovative thinking you can do on how to treat those customers appropriately, either by segment or, if your information is granular enough, down to the individual.

Isn't BI the Same as Enterprise Reporting?

In a word, no. Enterprise reporting is the combination of multiple reports from multiple systems using a standard reporting tool and a common delivery platform. It reports the "as is" data that you want it to report from multiple places. It is an impartial information aggregator that grabs already analyzed and interpreted data from multiple sources, and neatly (if it's working well) ties the data together in a format that makes it readable. It's not more than that.

The analogy is sort of obvious. When you wrote a paper in college, you handed in a Word document or if you're as old as . . . my colleagues, a typewritten one. Are the actual physical pages the same as the thought and content? Nope. The physical pages are just the delivery vehicle. When I write a white paper, I usually have a clause in the contract with those hiring me that states that they own the work product, but I maintain my rights to use the ideas elsewhere. If I didn't, there are parts of this book that couldn't be written. The book, the white paper, the college term paper are all delivery formats to present the ideas. The ideas are not the reporting of them.

Is BI the Same as Predictive/Descriptive Analytics?

Not exactly. It uses both predictive and descriptive analytics, particularly the former, but isn't the same thing. The analytics features of business intelligence help present that actionable information and help you make decisions.

Business intelligence takes raw data and turns it into information. It uses complex algorithms on captured data in the "as is" state and makes some interpretive sense out of it. The information, once mapped, interpreted, and identified, is then presented through an enterprise reporting tool in a way that makes it intelligible to those of us with ordinary mathematical skills. That information provides tremendously valuable input for developing the innovations and approaches to improve customer experiences. Some of the general uses of business intelligence, according to the *OLAP Report*, are:

- ▶ Data warehouse reporting

- ▶ Sales and marketing analysis

- ▶ Planning and forecasting

- ▶ Financial consolidation

- ▶ Statutory reporting

- ▶ Budgeting

- ▶ Profitability analysis

Other possible BI benefits are to help you determine what you are going to sell to whom and when that sale is going to occur. For example, financial services companies might want to see what products will be appropriate for what segments during a certain time of year. You might be interested in creating a scholarship-related instrument that would be sold to 35- to 49-year-olds with children during a school year while their children were between 3 and 15 years old. The BI engine would help you decide whether or not this was a good time of year, a good segment, and/or a good product.

What Are BI's Challenges?

Implementing BI always has challenges. They fall into two categories, internal and technical. Internally, interdepartmental politics create fragmented, nonintegrated approaches. Simply put, the department wants what benefits *it*, not what benefits the company.

Ease of use is an issue. As far back as 2003, the OLAP 3 Report found that the inability to get users to agree on requirements is a common problem with BI implementations, and if the requirements are agreed upon, staying the course without changing the requirements proves difficult.

There are technical challenges too. The dispersion of the data sources, the "dirtiness" of the data and lack of standards for a common data format, the disparate technologies that are being used, the availability of web services—or not, the sufficiency of the hardware and software to do the job, the sheer size of the total data available—all provide significant challenges to the application of those pesky and complicated analytic algorithms.

For example, First Union has a 27-terabyte database with 16 million customers. Using SAS and Microstrategy, they determined what to up-sell and cross-sell to profitable customers. Technically, that meant 27 terabytes of centralized, normalized, and clean data just to make the data on 16 million customers useful. Then they needed to determine the relevant criteria for the data so the analytics engine could work. The data had to include the account information, sales and purchase data, demographic data, profile data, service/support records, shipping and fulfillment information, campaign responses, and finally, web and other touchpoint data. They did it and it worked, but imagine the effort involved in just readying things.

BI Well Done, Customer Value Received

If you meet the challenges that BI presents in a CRM environment, then the value of the customer intelligence returned can be immeasurable. It helps you identify four basic customer value categories:

▶ **Customers to retain**   These are the high value customers that should get the most attention because they will provide the highest profitability. However, as we'll shortly see, customer lifetime value is an adequate measure by itself.

▶ **Customers to acquire**   These are the customers that have high value potential based on their segments and the relevance of the products or services of the offering company.

▶ **Customers to grow**   These are the future high value customers that will become the company's and its partners' long-term investment. These are strategic accounts.

▶ **Customers to harvest** These are the low value, low margin customers or product/service offerings that can be gathered to the bosom of the company by optimized services or pricing with a minimum of effort and investment. Again, we've also discussed in prior chapters the risk associated with just letting these low value customers go because of their ability to socialize things.

Once you have this information, you have to plan to do something with it, not assume it is another notch in a belt or a thing to be catalogued and forgotten. Bells and whistles have to be rung and whistled. Use what you have received as valuable customer intelligence you now can act on. Other than that, it's just another way to look at data, hardly worth the million or two dollars you spent on it.

I ♥ Text Analytics, a.k.a. Text Mining

Text analysis is to unstructured data as business intelligence is to structured data. What I mean by unstructured data is the conversational data that is going on across the social web. For example, you might find some of it in a comments field beneath a YouTube video while at the same time will find the YouTube video embedded in a blog posting and comments on the video at the end of the blog posting that very same day. But it might be the posting on the wall of Facebook or a threaded forum discussion topic. It might be in the body of an e-mail or in the body of a presentation stored on SlideShare. It could be in a feedback form or from a survey. All in all, the information isn't exclusive to a single location; it has no standard format that can be easily identified. Most important, the information is freeform, not field delimited, and is without metadata.

But that's unstructured data. What we need to briefly see is what text analytics does to that unstructured data.

The Definition—of Text Analytics, Not ♥

My favorite definition (by someone other than me) comes from text analytics guru Seth Grimes in his Text Analytics Basics series of articles:

Text analytics:

▶ *Applies linguistic and/or statistical techniques to extract concepts and patterns that can be applied to categorize and classify documents, audio, video and images.*

▶ *Transforms "unstructured" information into data for application of traditional analysis techniques.*

▶ *Unlocks meaning and relationships in large volumes of information that were previously unprocessable by computer.*

What makes it a bit more than just another form of analytics is that most of the nontransactional data that you need to help you improve your individual customer insights and to determine what others are saying about you *is* unstructured and floating all over the social web.

What also makes this more difficult is that it is the combination of structured and unstructured data into a useful report that gives you the information you need to make intelligent judgments about your customers or on a course of action. Luckily, the tools exist to do this.

How Text Analysis Works

Text analysis, by and large, is relational. A tool extracts information from a source by isolating specific information. Wait. Let's do it by example.

You use a social media monitoring tool to compile a report that indicates there are 200 or so conversations going on about United Airlines across the Web throughout various channels. The SMM tool compiles the information, but the analysis it does is on the relevance of the piece of information to you, not the analysis of the content of that information. So the SMM tool will separate discussions of United Airlines from discussions of airlines uniting for some legislative action, for example.

When you launch your analytic tools, several actions are taken on the content of the information that you've aggregated. Natural language processing (NLP) is applied to structure the content, evaluate the content, extract distinct elements and define the relationships among those elements. Then the attributes associated with those elements are identified and abstracted. An example of this would be the use of sentiment analysis on sentences such as "I can't stand United Airlines"—you'll see why shortly. The data is then organized into an understandable and actionable report that helps you judge your strategy toward a group or even down to an individual customer.

If you want a detailed but understandable look at how text analytics works, I would head over to the following online pieces, both by Seth Grimes: "Text Analytics Basics, Part 1" (www.b-eye-network .com/view/8032) and, you won't believe this, "Text Analytics Basics,

Part 2" (www.b-eye-network.com/view/8339). They offer an excellent primer on text analytics, well worth the investment of time.

There are a number of pure play text mining specialist firms like Clarabridge, Attensity, and ClearForest that are worth looking into.

An Easy Case Study: Hewlett-Packard WaterCooler

WaterCooler is a text analysis tool used by Hewlett-Packard that indexes what employees say on internal and external blogs. The capability is there for workers to opt in or opt out. Even with the option to shield themselves from analysis, 11,000 HP employees have chosen to let all their musings be aggregated. This kind of analysis is more benign than therapy, I suppose. What happens is that the aggregate information then spits out tags that indicate what the 11,000 employees consider hot at the moment. So, if they are geeking out for the day, or week, you might see "server automation" as a hot topic, though, IMHO, that's really not very hot. However, if it is hot, that might indicate some course of action to a management team at HP. If the subject that's being discussed notably is "changeover in HP management team," it might indicate some frank discussion or damage control or support needs to go on.

This differs from trends tools such as Twitter Trends, which merely count search keyword instances and then make the tags larger based on the relative frequency with which the words appear. They don't use NLP or have any sophisticated reporting approach. They pretty much monitor volume only.

Love It or Hate It, It's Sentiment Analysis

Sentiment analysis is really a particular aspect of text analysis. It finds, evaluates, and processes attitudinal information. Unlike the "information extraction" segment of text analysis, this isn't just finding facts. It is aimed at customer and market knowledge based on customer behaviors and customer emotions. Do customers love or hate your company? What are they saying and how are they saying it?

If you remember, in early 2009, Domino's Pizza had a public relations disaster when two employees of a Domino's restaurant did something disgusting to pizzas that were going to be delivered, then filmed it and uploaded it to YouTube. If you were Domino's, you would want to know what customers were saying on Twitter, Facebook, in blogs, on the news, and so on. But not just where they said it or what they said as a fact, you'd also want to know what they felt about it and how vehement those feelings were—and how viral was the vehemence—good or bad. (In the case of Domino's, there was no good, trust me.) That's where sentiment analysis comes in.

Sentiment analysis measures factors such as expressive words—hate, disgusting, wonderful—words that identify tone, known in the world of sentiment analysis as polarity. It also looks at intensifying words—very, more—words that increase the strength of the tone. It not only looks at the negative or positive (or neutral) nature of a document, but looks at the same opinion state at the sentence level or the opinion associated with an entity—which could mean a word that relates to a human being—a name, a phone number, or an address, for example.

But it's more complicated than that. University of Illinois professor Bing Liu, a text analytics expert, points out that if a document has multiple entities within it, just deriving the "opinion" of the document isn't sufficient or even that useful. The multiple entities' opinions have to be ascertained.

If you look at the February 16, 2009, entry in my ZDNet *Social CRM: The Conversation* blog (http://blogs.zdnet.com/crm/?p=188) called "CRM and the Mac is Like Oranges to, uh Apple," you'll note there are 41 "TalkBacks," which means comments in ZDNet-ese. If you go through them, you'll find outraged Mac fan boys who call me an "arrogant imbecile," something that might be true but only my family's allowed to call me that. In the case of "arrogant imbecile," the entity it's associated with turns out to be me. The tone is obviously negative. That is sentence-level sentiment analysis. That one is easy.

But what do you do with a comment like this:

First of all, spell out terms like CRM first, before spouting them ad nauseam.

Secondly, FileMaker could very easily provide any sort of CRM you would ever need. There are paid consultants available. This is not a high powered database solution by any definition of the term.

Finally, learn to spell Mac. It's NOT an acronym.

On the one hand, there is nothing at the sentence level that is particularly negative. If viewed in that way, it sounds almost helpful. But at the document level, it's another story entirely. Then it becomes clear that the comment is written by an upset respondent to the blog posting.

So the factors that need to be taken into account here, aside from the respondent's nasty side, are context, the material that he's responding to, and the larger tone of the document, which is not that easy to identify as negative. The tip-off terms that would have to be prepopulated for the NLP to do what it's being paid to do would be words like:

▶ "spouting" (which would then have to be abstracted from whales)

▶ "NOT" in capital letters

▶ "ad nauseam"

None of them an obvious barn buster, but all together they indicate the document (comment) tone.

That comment is a perfect example of the difficulty of sentiment analysis. Yet, this is the moment in the history of business when text analysis in general and sentiment analysis in particular are becoming critical. The conversation needs to be heard and the data it provides needs to be captured if you hope to have any success with your customers.

Many companies are adding sentiment analysis to their products. In mid-2009, megamonster company SAP announced a product that uses sentiment analysis. SAP announced a customer service application that scores sentiment in Twitter feeds related to customer service. Using the Business Objects Insight product, they analyze Twitter feeds that indicate customer issues and the emotional intensity of the feeds. The product then looks at the potential for a viral outburst given the conversations going on around it. There are business rules that identify courses of action when the resulting sentiment scores come back in the context of what the problem is. Those rules are used to trigger an alert that gets sent to the parties who are given the responsibility to deal with problems of a particular type and intensity.

This isn't unique to enterprise companies either. Social media monitoring companies are now adding sentiment analysis so that they can not only track the relevance and frequency of whatever it is you want to track, but also the level of friendly or hostile activity.

Radian6, introduced to you in Chapter 12, added sentiment analysis to their product in late 2009 so that it not only aggregates the conversations around the subjects being listened to in real time, but also scores them for their emotion. This adds an entire dimension to listening. Radian6 uses the product to monitor anything ranging from customer service issues to consumer opinions on products. One use of the product is to see how the user of a company's services or products solves a problem. Rather than scouring forums for the results, the use of sentiment analysis can see how positively or negatively the community responded to the solution. If the solution is good and responded to with a thumbs up from the user community, then the company can integrate it into their own knowledge base. All of this is aggregated into a dashboard that the Radian6 user can see.

Structured + Unstructured = Home Run

Text analysis is one of the most important components of analytics introduced into the mix of available products. But the real power lies in integrating the unstructured data from the social web with the structured data inherent in operational CRM systems. While I've spoken frequently about integrating social media monitoring into CRM systems (see Chapter 12), this is another step entirely and far more powerful because of the rich customer knowledge it provides. The combination of transactions and conversation with personal details that have been harvested from the Web gives companies a very valuable look at either an individual customer or a trend that is moving in real time and its possible impact on your company.

The combination of historical record and real-time interaction is not without its problems. For structured and unstructured data integration, there has to be a default to some sort of structure so that the data can be combined in ways that are beneficial to the business.

Using XML as a bridge between the two data types is already a mainstream approach to this knotty issue. The idea is to take unstructured data, extract it, and then incorporate it into a standardized XML format. Structured data can already use an XML format, so XML becomes the common denominator for the integration of the two types of data.

The XML tags or the database table schema are predefined by the users. Then technology can be applied to tag the unstructured text. That can be a dictionary look-up, some sort of machine learning, or a rule-based pattern-matching application. These technologies identify and tag domain-specific information. Once all the data is "entered" into the XML schema, it needs to be cleaned and readied for whatever future reporting needs or slicing and dicing need to be done to create knowledge for insight from the data. The resultant XML file is in a form amenable to query, search, and integration with other structured data sources. Then all the data is imported to some centralized data store.

The value? You can see interactions and transactions of a single customer over time in ways that actually allow you to improve how you interact with that customer. Not only that, but since study after study shows roughly 80 percent of all data that an enterprise has access to is unstructured, the integration becomes invaluable to searching and finding the data to be used.

Slick stuff.

The Future of Analytics

I have to admit that analytics isn't necessarily the most exciting part of CRM to me—though sentiment analysis is kind of cool. As it's constituted now, it's a way of finding, capturing, and (duh) analyzing data so that there's organized useful information that becomes an important feature in making business judgments. Hey, if that's exciting to you—you know the old expression—whatever floats your boat.

But there is research going on with vendors and technology mavens right now that actually could make analytics not just utilitarian. This is the use case that you might be considering as a real story in just a very few months or maybe a year from when you read this (now that's a real trick . . .).

The Scenario: Old School

As things go now, you know that when you call customer service, most likely, a screen will pop up on the customer service representative's (CSR) side. The CSR will see what your history has been. If complete, that history will have your past purchases, your past complaints and their resolution, and any marketing data (such as campaign responses or literature requests). It will have what kind of contract or SLA you have with them and flag the appropriate level of service that you should be provided. It will identify if you are a customer who has to be prioritized. It will show what forms of media you use most frequently to interact with the company (e-mail, phone, etc.). If it's a sophisticated system, the CSR will have the ability to see how the problems had been resolved in the past and the links/screens with the potential solutions in front of them, given the probability of the same issues occurring. He or she will be able to quickly call up the possible answers to the problem due to an extensive knowledge base. The workflow is based on the SLA and scoring you as a customer based on your transactions, maybe even customer lifetime value or other metrics, to see how "important" you are to the company. The number and level of complaints in the past will drive whom you speak with, how quickly it escalates, and so forth. The trouble ticket is assigned and the dance begins.

The Scenario: New School

It starts the same way. You call customer service about problems with the company's product. This time, when your call is in and the complaint is generated, your customer record, the appropriate SLA level, and the potential solutions from the CSR's in-house knowledge base pop up. But now, information that has been captured from the unstructured social discussions about the product and customer-suggested solutions, and your conversations on Twitter, Facebook, and the Consumerist appear like lightning. The content of the unstructured information is automatically analyzed to see if it's about the same subject that you're calling about, and what your past relationship to the company is. Sentiment analysis is done on the spot on your external conversations to help the CSR determine how severe the issue is, what kind of complainant you are (chronic, one time, valid, whiner), whether you are an influencer, and so on. Based on the analysis, the CSR knows how to treat this case—a.k.a. you. It might mean sending you to a supervisor right away or working with you at a level that, in a prior era, couldn't have been determined.

If the problem is not solvable on the phone or whatever medium it's being addressed through, when the ticket is assigned, it's not just a specialist who gets the problem to solve, but a combination (potentially) of internal and external communities. Once they have used their combined intelligence to come up with an answer, then the answer is refined, enriched, brought in-house, and added to the knowledge base while your customer ticket is being punched as complete.

On a more disconnected scale, this is already going on. Companies like Samsung and Procter and Gamble are using external social networks (Chapter 9) to capture customer data and improve their product knowledge about everything. Remember Chapter 13's "Superstah! Helpstream" found that their clients who have customer communities get 17 percent of their customer service issues taken care of by the customers themselves. IT issues are often solved elegantly in the thousands of independent technical threaded discussion forums without any support of the company involved at all.

What isn't common is the aggregation of the unstructured external data, meaning the data extracted from the conversations going on in forums outside the company in a form that's usable by customer reps anywhere. However, the means of capturing structured and unstructured data into a useful report is becoming more easily available with companies like SAP and Oracle on the mega-side to much smaller companies like open source BI provider Omniture making them available through their applications.

Customer insights don't come free, but they do come if you interpret the data and make smart judgments.

Analytics in Service of Insight = Loyalty, Advocacy

Using the analytics tools can let you see the rich data you do have—the combination of transaction data, conversational data, and richer profile information—in ways that can help you make the kind of advantageous decisions that get you the value you're looking for from your customers. But in order to use these tools, you have to have a strategy that's geared toward what you want from your customers. Part of that has to be determined by your business imperatives—revenue goals, profitability objectives, cost efficiencies, and your longer term overall business strategy, including the present and future mixture of products, services, experiences, and tools that you want to provide to the customer.

Another significant factor is what kind of customer you're looking to "recruit." Are you happy with high customer satisfaction ratings? Is a loyal customer what you strive for? Are you measuring that satisfaction or loyalty by the number of products that you're selling the customer?

I've got a proposal for you.

Striving for Advocacy, Settling for Loyalty

The customer that you should be aiming toward is the advocate. You should settle for the loyal customer. Why? Because the advocate, also called a customer evangelist, is the same customer who feels vested in what you do as well as sees themselves, in part, as a good-will ambassador for the company. When this is harnessed by companies like clothier Karmaloop, their street teams, consisting of 8,000 of their 800,000-person community, make 15 percent of Karmaloop's annual revenue. These are the Harley hog owners who love their bikes and the company so much they tattoo "Harley-Davidson" all over their body. All . . . over. That commitment gives Harley-Davidson a 63 percent market share.

These are the people who will tell you how much they love Starbucks (or at least those who used to tell you that) or why they only shop at Zappos online for all their shoes. That grew Zappos to a billion dollars in eight years.

I'm sure you can name a company that you're passionate about, can't you? A restaurant you love, a theme park you've been to 30 times, a small barbershop that you've not only gone to but sent dozens of friends to get their locks shorn over the years.

What makes evangelism/advocacy even more powerful is now there are locations online for the advocates to go to and talk to thousands if not millions of others about their love of your company. Social networks like Yelp live for those passionate advocates. Your company needs to not only find and cultivate these advocates, but to put programs in place to provide value to the same customer.

Loyal Doesn't Mean Profitable

But, please don't confuse the customer advocate with a loyal customer. They are not the same and, often, confusing the two can lead to a potentially disastrous situation. Though loyal customers are nothing to sneeze at, they are not the optimal customer. One reason for that was discovered in a study by one of the true eminences in CRM value measurement, Dr. V. Kumar, professor of marketing at Georgia State University's Robinson School of Business and the executive director of the Center for Excellence in Brand and Customer Management at GSU. You'll hear much more about him later.

In 2003, Dr. Kumar and Werner Reinartz did a seminal study on the correlation between profitability and loyalty called "The Mismanagement of Customer Loyalty" in which they found that the correlation was "weak to moderate." The reason is that the loyal customer expects more from the company they are loyal to. They also are extremely well acquainted with the ins and outs of the company and know how to game the system when it comes to getting "stuff" from the company. For example, rather than simply resolving a customer complaint, loyal customers expect some compensation for their discomfiture.

This is isn't exactly a ringing endorsement of loyalty, though it does show there is some correlation with profitability—enough to not be ignored. But it also re-emphasizes the point—loyal customers are what you settle for, not what you aim at.

Advocacy Is Just So Much Better

How do the distinctions between loyal customers and advocates manifest themselves? Confusing the two can lead to a bad assessment of a customer—and a potential disaster in the relationship. Part of the problem exists because many loyalty marketers are focused on the quantification of loyalty, and advocacy is not something that is particularly easy to quantify.

To begin, I'll tell you a story that can sum this up considerably better than a lot of numerical machinations.

Lots of Frequent Flyer Miles + Rarely Flying Anyone Else/ United Airlines Company Culture = I Despise United Airlines

If you're a loyalty marketer and look at my United profile, you find something that would make you 4.5 on a scale of 5.0 when it comes to warm and fuzzy. You'd see hundreds of thousands of United Airlines frequent flier (FF) miles; a pattern that suggests that I fly United exclusively, including client bookings by their travel agencies on United for me. You'd see me signing up for dozens of promotions; you'd see me using hotel loyalty cards to get United FF miles in the place of hotel points; you'd see me flying United partners Star Alliance airlines whenever I can't fly United. I'd look like a very loyal United flyer.

I'd been Premier Executive for a few years, which means that I flew 50,000 miles or more each year. But in 2008, I had a horrible auto accident in August that limited my flying to virtually none for the rest of the year. As a result I flew 36,000 miles, which brought me down a notch to Premier. But by November 2008, I was okay and I had booked and paid for 26,000 more miles of flying from January 4 though February 15, 2009. That sets the stage. Oh, one other thing. United's time frame for determining FF status is from January 1 through December 31. Status privileges run from March 1 through February 28. In any case, as late November 2008 rolled around, I received a letter in the mail from United Airlines. In effect, it said: "Hey, we see that you only have 36,000 miles this year, which will make you a Premier rather than a Premier Executive flyer. Tell you what, you give us $2,300 and we will give you the additional 14,000 miles that you need to be Premier Executive. How about that?"

I swear. They wanted me to pay $2,300. I was incensed. How crass can a company be? But the real question is, what should have happened? If I were United's Vice President of Customer Experience (I believe that they've had four of those in five years, though don't hold me to that exact number), I would have an algorithm or two that would pretty much spit out the same info as they had. But then I would have had a plan to address the issue that wasn't "send us $2,300." It would go something like this: "Hey, we see that you only have 36,000 miles this year, which will make you a Premier rather than a Premier Executive flyer. We're concerned. What happened that caused you to fly so much less?" In other words, show me that you actually are wondering what caused the problem. In part because of a concern for the well being of the customer and in part because it would suggest a more intelligent course of action.

After I answered the question, should I choose to do that, if I were United, I would notice that Paul Greenberg had paid for 26,000 more miles for January and February *before his official Premier Executive privileges ran out.* Then I would send another note in this spirit: "Hey again. Since you've been a Premier Executive flyer for several years and you couldn't help your circumstances and you've already paid for 26,000 more miles, which would total 62,000 miles by the time your privileges run out, we'll take a chance on you and extend your Premier Executive flyer privileges another year. We're sorry about your accident."

They didn't do that but instead insulted me with their "offer" to let me pay. To clarify, and to make it clear I'm not a whiny premier flyer type, the smarter move was to show personal concern. The offer would be icing on the cake. They didn't do either. Rather than me moving a bit closer to being an advocate, I truly dislike United. Though my loyalty numbers don't show that, do they?

Measuring Advocacy: Is Net Promoter Score (NPS) Enough?

The industry standard, as nascent an industry as advocacy metrics is, is the Net Promoter Score (NPS) developed by Frederick Reichheld, Bain and Company, and Satmetrix in 2003. It was announced by Reichheld in a now famous *Harvard Business Review* article entitled "The One Number You Need to Grow." It was elaborated on by Reichheld (who is a great public speaker, by the way) in his important 2006 best-seller, *The Ultimate Question: Driving Good Profits and True Growth.*

The idea is incredibly simple. You ask one question: "How likely is it that you would recommend our company to a friend or colleague?" The key is not just would you recommend, but would you do that to someone you have a relationship with—meaning, because of their tight ties to you, they are going to trust what you say, and that is an increased emotional burden and factor in the willingness.

Recommending a company to a stranger is something like giving instructions to someone who asks you for directions to a place that you don't know. If you're a cad and you realize that you'll never see them again, to look good, you might give them instructions, knowing that you don't have a clue where you're sending them. But you look good and when they realize that you gave them phony instructions—well, out of sight, out of mind.

But to recommend to a family member or friend brings a number of other things to the fore:

1. You'll see them again and they'll see you.

2. They trust you. Duh, dude.

3. You have skin in this game because of your emotional tie to the person or because you're going to have to show up for work the next day.

4. If you're wrong, it matters to you that you'll look bad.

5. If you're right, it makes you happier because these people trust you and care about you—and vice versa. Plus, if it's a work-related colleague, office gossip counts.

The "how likely" solo question is rated by the respondents on a scale of 0 to 10. Based on the answer, the respondents are grouped into one of three categories: detractors (0–6), passives (7–8), and promoters (9–10). The percentage of detractors is subtracted from the percentage of promoters. With the resultant numbers in hand, the next step is to contact the respondents and see why they rated themselves as detractors or promoters, most typically. Dig in and get feedback.

A lot of companies have adopted NPS as a way of measuring their ability to create advocates. By the way, if you haven't figured it out, a promoter is an advocate, or, if you prefer, an evangelist.

While there are cases that show the value of NPS, its very simplicity brings it into question. A number of studies debunk at the least the underlying research assumptions as "biased." Notable in that regard is a study that came out in July 2007, entitled obtusely "A Longitudinal

Examination of Net Promoter and Firm Revenue Growth," which claims that there is *zero* correlation between NPS and revenue growth. That would be 0.0 correlation.

However, it's possible to find companies that have used it to benefit their top and bottom line growth. For example, by 2004, Schwab and Company was bleeding money. Their compound revenue had been dropping 5 percent per year starting in 2000. The company's Net Promoter Score by 2004 was negative 35 percent!

To deal with this alarming problem, Schwab set monthly NPS KPIs for each branch and held the branch manager accountable. They began interviewing the detractors to find out what made them so angry. Certain types of account fees turned out to be among the reasons, so 24 months later those particular account fees were gone. This conscientious approach to NPS seemed to reap some real dividends. By summer 2007, the Schwab NPS had jumped to a plus 23 percent. The stock price jumped too, and the company moved back into positive growth.

Clearly there is some benefit to NPS, but there is a long way to go in terms of the development of reliable advocacy metrics for the social customer. How does the advocate benefit the company as an individual? This kind of thinking is far outside the scope of NPS, which figures out a ratio of great guys to bad guys all in all. Its value lies in the reasons why people chose the number from 0 to 10.

But even that isn't enough. Feedback needs to become actionable, not just additional information to a numerical result. Unfortunately, apparently it isn't often used in the way it has to be, thus negating some of the value of a measure like NPS.

Jennifer Kirkby, one of the resident forward-thinking CRM gurus at the fabulous MyCustomer.com site, wrote an article in 2005 called "The Customer Experience: The Voice of the Customer" (http://www.mycustomer.com/item/131588). She quoted findings that made me want to cry—which I did just before I wrote this (in case your page is smeared).

"Although 95% of companies collect feedback only 50% brief staff on its contents, a mere 30% use it, and a paltry 5% bother to tell the customer what action they took. Prime causes of this sorry state are poor cross functional collaboration and lack of information culture. But the main culprit is the disparate sources of feedback with no overall owner, plan, or use. (See Squeezing more value from marketing information—by Professor Robert Shaw, City of London Business School.)"

Think about the irony in this statement. Companies spend all this time talking about the "voice of the customer"—giving it lip service, so to speak. Then when they collect the feedback that provides the voice of the customer information, they get laryngitis when it comes to feeding it back to the customers who gave them the insights—even though it is obviously useful for a customer to know what other customers think. Tell us all about yourself but don't expect to find out what we found out. The thinking must go like this, "Not only is that our proprietary information, but we reserve the right to not tell each other about it or use it."

Obviously, this lack of dissemination affects the value of methods like NPS, so what can you do?

I spoke with Syed Hasan, the CEO of ResponseTek (Chapter 3). They are, as you might guess, highly sensitive to engagement and feedback and advocacy measures. Of course, they've looked at NPS. They feel it's a bit simplistic but can be a useful measure. So they worked with one of their clients, Hong Kong Shanghai Bank Corporation, to create an interactive model that allows clients to use past/current customer experience feedback to better predict future NPS scores, which enhances the value of NPS as a model metric. Predictive analysis is done to help their clients assess where they should focus their resources and projects in order to obtain the largest return on investment, as defined by the largest increase in NPS scores. The model then creates a number of key drivers that are assessed with their likely impact on future NPS scores. The user/client can create scenarios that show the impact of specific investments in key drivers measured by their potential impact on future NPS scores. An inverse relationship can also be established whereby the model can help articulate how much decreases in the satisfaction with specific key drivers will negatively influence NPS scores. The model, used alongside existing data (financial metrics, operational metrics, etc.), can help turn the customer voice into actionable business intelligence to help drive strategic decision making.

But it has to be taken further than even this. NPS is useful, but there are social customers who are actively engaged with your company and their own peers. While knowing how you're doing generally is good, knowing the value the social customer as an individual provides is a way of pinpointing who your most ardent and valuable advocates are.

How do you measure a social customer when you can't get them to sit still long enough to join a focus group? Please realize I'm saying that ironically, okay? I don't mean it. I don't like focus groups.

Measuring the Social Customer's Value

The traditional way of looking at the value of a customer is customer lifetime value (CLV). That's the measure of how much a customer is worth to a company over the life of their relationship to the company. It's often couched in terms of net present value (NPV). In the last three editions of *CRM at the Speed of Light*, I've used the formulation that I still prefer—that of my colleague and friend and CRM pioneer, Mei Lin Fung.

But the same changes to the world that made me into a liar and fostered a fourth edition of *CRM at the Speed of Light* also impact how to measure the value of a customer who is now a social customer. Traditional CLV by itself is no longer sufficient.

Close your eyes and visualize this scenario: The customer you see in your mind's eye isn't very wealthy, so his "official" CLV doesn't add a lot to your corporate customer equity. He is, let's say, a low to lower-mid value customer. But this customer is an ardent advocate of your products, has considerable influence in his immediate circles, and is somewhat influential on the social web in some capacity—either as a blogger or reviewer on social sites. What does that make his *referral* value to you? How about his brand value to you?

Good questions so far? Let's throw another one into the mix.

I was speaking to the Association of Banks in Singapore in 2006. In the course of the discussion after the speech, I raised the specter of CLV in financial services with the immediate family as the core unit being measured. I was corrected by a bank mogul and told in Asia it was "household"—the extended family including employees and closest friends in addition to blood relatives and in-laws—being affected.

What does that mean to the measurement of the value of an individual customer? How do these considerations affect what you measure?

Frankly, if I were alone in all of this, I'd be scratching my head at about this point. However, I'm not and, thus, neither are you. There is a remarkable group of minds led by Dr. V. Kumar who are working on the more advanced, more extended (household) views of CLV, as well as developing the benchmarks, metrics, equations, and answers to how the social customer gets measured beyond their future purchase history.

Introducing Managing Customers for Profit and CLV, CBV, CRV

In his seminal 2008 work, *Managing Customers for Profit: Strategies to Increase Profits and Build Loyalty*, Dr. Kumar introduces a number of new equations and approaches to customer value. Chief among them is the extension of CLV through the addition of both customer brand value (CBV) and, for my purposes, most important, customer referral value (CRV). Coupled with CLV, these provide a well-rounded forecast of future customer behaviors and a quantifiable way of identifying real social value, not just their potential profitability—though that too.

What makes his value proposition even more interesting is that it begins to address the fundamental issues of creating or at least identifying advocates—something that NPS, despite its good intentions, doesn't do.

Customer Lifetime Value

Customer lifetime value is a measure that identifies the direct contribution a customer makes over a period of time toward a company's profitability. The most common definition is that this is the "net present value of future profit from the customer." It is a progressive (forward-looking) metric that uses expense, revenue derived, profit derived, and customer behavior to determine what the value of the particular customer is over time.

Its easy value is that it can identify on a curve what the growth of profitability is going to be for an individual customer. That means how you allocate resources to that customer is based on how profitable a customer is at either any given point or over the lifespan of his or her relationship to you. It allows you to determine what kind of customer strategy makes sense to increase customer equity on the one hand and, on the other, what management can do to optimize the individual customer experience based on an expected return.

I prefer to measure (though I'm not sure what it would entail) the CLV of households. This would incorporate the head of the household's future profitability, but also, for example, his direct relatives such as his wife, children, and sons-in-laws, and perhaps those he immediately affects, such as best friends or housekeeper. But is even the more robust CLV I'm proposing or the traditional CLV that's normally administered sufficient?

It isn't, because of the additional opportunities the social customer brings to the table.

Individual Brand Value (IBV) and CLV

Brand value has often been seen as something apart from the value that the customer brings. But brand loyalty, which is the customer's pattern of repurchasing from the same company, if not the same products, and brand advocacy, the customer's willingness to put the company forward to their friends, are part of the customer equity portfolio that is needed to know the 21st century customer.

To reiterate, the reputation of the company is the brand. Trust is the driver of that reputation. Thus attitudinal (long term) and behavioral (short term) commitment are part of the equation when it comes to determining the brand loyalty of the customer to the company. The company's establishment as a trusted resource to the customer is key to this determination. As Dr. Kumar rightfully puts it, "Hence, when evaluating a brand, it is not only the financial value generated by the brand that should be considered, but how the customers perceive the brand."

Perception of the brand stems from the brand knowledge, attitude, and behavior. Obviously, the more you trust a brand you are very familiar with, the more likely you're willing to spend the extra dollars on the brand that you trust. Harley-Davidson, because of those tattoos, owns 63 percent of the motorcycle market. The owners trust the brand and see its ubiquity, which gives them a sense of long-term awareness and comfort, which makes them say, I'll spend the few extra dollars for the Harley because it's going to be here for a while and they make great machines and they are really cool and they have a Harley Owners Group (HOG) that I can join for an experience of community. This factors into the CLV of the individual motorcycle owner.

But that still doesn't answer the measurement of the social customer and the advances of Dr. Kumar beyond NPS.

Customer Referral Value (CRV)

Forgive me if I'm oversimplifying, but this particular extension of CLV is the key differentiator as a measure and equation. This is where the value of the social customer over a fixed time period transcends the historic CLV metrics.

Dr. Kumar defines CRV as the ability of managers "to measure and manage each customer based on his ability to generate indirect profit to the firm." The impact comes from the recruitment of new customers by the referrers—the advocates, really—which reduces customer acquisition costs to nothing or nearly so. As community retailing companies like Karmaloop make it easy to see, it also increases the number of new customers and purchases by those customers due to the referral activity of the advocates.

What makes this part of Dr. Kumar's work particularly important is that while he goes as far as Reichheld in correlating the willingness to make a referral with the growth of a company's profit, he stops there and asks the most important question: Does the willingness to refer this company to someone you know mean that you actually make the referral?

Aha! Having the desire and carrying out that desire are two different things. We all know what the road to hell is paved with.

Dr. Kumar did a study of financial services firms and telecommunications companies asking the four questions that need to be asked—beyond the mere one of NPS. Pay very close attention to the questions and memorize them. Don't even read beyond Table 20-1 until you have.

I mean it. It's that important. Don't.

Table 20-1: The Four Questions: Customer Referral Value Goes Beyond NPS (Source: *Managing Customers for Profit*, V. Kumar, 2008)

Question Asked	Financial Services Industry (6,700 respondents)	Telecommunications Industry (9,900 respondents)
Do you intend to recommend this product or company to someone you know?	68 percent	81 percent
Did you actually refer this product or company?	33 percent	30 percent
Of those you referred, what percent became customers?	14 percent	12 percent
Of those new customers, how many were profitable customers?	11 percent	8 percent

There are two conclusions that can be drawn from this. Intent to refer and ultimate value are not strongly correlated, though there is some correlation. Even more importantly, the social customer's CRV is a major addition to the arsenal of measurement in contemporary Social CRM strategy development.

CLV, IBV, and CRV make a powerful combination in determining what kind of customer equity you have as a company and what kind of value your individual customers are capable of providing. That gives you a much better, but more complex and decidedly trickier, capability in determining what kind of investment you're going to make in your customer over time and what kind of offers you are going to provide. But what do you do with a customer who has a low traditional CLV but a high CRV, for example? If you proceed to invest in them, how do you keep them engaged, which will require a continual investment of something—time, money, both—so that their value is retained?

From Long Term to Real Time

Once you discover the long-term value of your customer, and you've made some investment decisions on what you're going to do with them, you still need to keep them engaged and then watch that engagement in real time if possible. That way, you're able to see if there are changes to the status of the customer (hear that, United Airlines?) or if there are things you can do for that customer. Any of those real-time or near-real-time customer activities can have an impact on the customer's long-term value, so interacting with the customer or monitoring their interactions becomes something that has to get done to protect the valuation and improve the situation.

The Web is where much of this plays out and, because of that, I'm bringing in the big gun to handle this part of the discussion.

CONVERSATION WITH JIM STERNE: ONLINE ENGAGEMENT

Meet Jim Sterne, an accomplished author, speaker, consultant, thought-leader . . . an accomplished everything. He's the author of eight books on Internet marketing, the founding president and current chairman of the Web Analytics Association (www.webanalyticsassociation.org), and the producer of the eMetrics Marketing Optimization Summit (www.emetrics.org) every year. The man just brings it. Your podium, man.

Will you hang on my every word? (Read my blog!) Will you see the world through my eyes? (See my photos!) Will you follow my every movement? (Watch my videos!) Will you follow along, absorbed while my thoughts flit from topic to topic? (Follow me on Twitter!)

I need to know if the effort of all my narcissistic outpouring is worth the pixels that give their all for me. I need to know how many times a day you think of me, write my name on a napkin, and sigh deeply while looking off into space. Because if I can't tell, I'm going to go back to standing in the middle of the street, tearing at my shirt and screaming, "Stella!"

Tortured, twisted pleas from the inner heart of teenage angst? No, this is the conversation that's happening where advertising meets web analytics meets social media. It's the discussion about the E word—engagement.

In the good old days, engagement was a promise between two people to marry. Today, it's measured in seconds and proven by clicks and posts. Did you watch my ad on TV? Did you see it again online? Did you go to my website? Did you rate my products? Did you post a comment on my blog? Did you e-mail my name to your friends? Has any of this had an impact on whether you'll buy my products?

As trifling as this sounds, brains with many more synapses than mine are digging deep into these issues. If this is where you are spending your money, or reaping your compensation, then you need to tune in to:

A. *The Association of National Advertisers (ANA), the American Association of Advertising Agencies (AAAA), and the Advertising Research Foundation (ARF), which provide a working definition:*

Engagement is turning on a prospect to a brand idea enhanced by the surrounding context

B. *Jeremiah Owyang, partner at the Altimeter Group and leading analyst (www.web-strategist.com), opines:*

Engagement indicates the level of authentic involvement, intensity, contribution, and ownership.

C. *Eric Peterson, CEO of Web Analytic Demystified, Inc. (www.webanalyticsdemystified.com), suggests:*

Engagement is an estimate of the degree and depth of visitor interaction on the site against a clearly defined set of goals

Eric goes on to posit the following formula at http http://blog.webanalyticsdemystified.com/weblog/2007/10/how-to-measure-visitor-engagement-redux.html:

$$\Sigma\,(C_i + R_i + D_i + L_i + B_i + F_i + I_i + S_i)$$

where

C_i = *percentage of sessions > 5 page views*
R_i = *percentage of C_i in last 3 weeks*
D_i = *percentage of sessions > 5:00 in duration*
L_i = *Visitor > 5 sessions total?*
B_i = *percentage of "brand driven" sessions*
F_i = *percentage of qualitative feedback sessions*
I_i = *percentage of sessions w/measured events*
S_i = *Visitor is a blog subscriber?*

Avinash Kaushik of Occam's Razor (http://www.kaushik.net/avinash/2007/10/ engagement-is-not-a-metric-its-an-excuse.html) suggests that things are not so cut and dried, "'Engagement' Is Not a Metric, It's an Excuse': An excuse for an unwillingness to sit down and identify why a site exists. An excuse for an unwillingness to identify real metrics that measure if your web presence is productive."

How you capture the right data elements in order to calculate a metric is the stuff of long, deep discussions. Follow the threads of the four listed above, and you'll come across several dozen people who have differing—and interesting— opinions. But they are determined to come up with a solid, universal definition.

While Eric goes to extraordinary lengths to calculate his own website's engagement factor, Charlene Li from Altimeter Group takes a more generic view that feels a lot more like that place where PR meets branding. In her report, back in her Forrester Group days, "The ROI of Blogging: The 'Why' and 'How' of External Blog Accountability," described on her blog (http://blogs.forrester.com/ groundswell/2007/01/new_roi_of_blog.html), Charlene discusses measuring the increase in brand visibility, the savings on customer insight, the reduced impact from negative user-generated content and increased sales efficiency.

I fear that engagement is a number that will only be useful for navel gazing. It's important to understand that I was born and raised in California, so I firmly believe that there is a valuable place for navel gazing, but one cannot compare one's navel to another's. There will never be a universal navel standard.

Eric Peterson got it right when he spoke of "a clearly defined set of goals." And ay, there's the rub. Goals are unique, once you get past the Big Three:

1. *Make more money*

2. *Spend less money*

3. *Increase customer satisfaction*

As an Internet marketing strategy consultant, I am constantly asked, "Jim, how do we make our website better?" My immediate response is always, "Better at what? What are you trying to accomplish?" That invariably kicks off days of political discussions exposing me as a corporate therapist who uses the Internet as the conversation starter.

Now that I am focused on online marketing optimization, my clients ask, "What should we measure?" My response is, "That depends. What are you trying to accomplish?" and we're right back to discussions about goals and priorities.

Eric's clearly defined goals are true for his site, and for sites that are very much like his. While some metrics seem appropriate for all (recency), others are very much in the "it depends" category.

If you spend a lot of time on a website designed for customer care, it may indicate that you are dazed and confused. Alternatively, you may be frequently interrupted by phone calls or friendly cube-farm visitors. A two-click stay for 17 seconds may have been a wildly successful visit if your prospect found the specification they were looking for.

Were they engaged? If depends on how they feel after the fact.

The number of clicks, the amount of comments, the frequency of visits, and many more hard numbers are subject to my favorite David Weinberger quote, "The universe is analog, messy, complex, and subject to many interpretations."

The hard-numbers people are due for a reunion with the fuzzy-numbers people. Branding folks have been at this a long time—it's called talking to your customers and listening to your marketplace. The goal is to ask people their opinions and measure how many of them feel one way or the other about your company and your offerings. These time-honored metrics include:

► *Unaided and aided awareness*

► *Message association*

► *Brand favorability*

► *Intent to purchase*

A poor web experience may have a larger impact on a company's brand than a poor telephone call, a disappointing stock-on-hand experience, or a bungled presentation by a field sales representative. These may be considered unfortunate incidents that can be remedied by the next call or visit. But a website visitor knows that the website has been planned, prepared, and produced by teams of smart people who were tasked with expecting the needs of each visitor. If, after years of development and testing, the website does not deliver on the promise, then visitors leave with a sharply diminished opinion about your company—your brand.

How your customers feel is central to whether a website is successful. You could say that all other metrics are simply there to drive customer satisfaction. Higher satisfaction will lower costs and increase revenues. It will encourage people to talk about you in a positive light and you will reap the benefits of a positive reputation.

How many times they look at your website does not reveal their level of engagement. It's all about how they feel about it.

The future of engagement as a metric is not to be found at a universal level, an industrial level, within a company, or even within a department. Engagement is to be codified at the project level, the campaign level, and useful only in comparing this project's progress to itself. Narcissistic, indeed.❦

Superstah! SAS and Customer Experience Analytics

What products are out there that do this well? I've already spoken of ResponseTek. I've mentioned SAP's flirtation with these new analytics using Business Objects Insight to analyze Twitter feeds for the emotional content of customer service tweets. But it's North Carolina–based SAS that wins the coveted Superstah! designation because of their superb customer experience analytics tool, which can quantify the interactions and engagement of the customers.

Mission 21st Century

Before we get into what the tool does, let's chat with Jeff Levitan, general manager, SAS Customer Intelligence, on their mission with this application:

> SAS' mission in the CRM arena is to enable organizations to deliver customer experience excellence. We're working to achieve this by providing organizations with solutions to improve their customer-focused, cross-channel marketing process. This process, which ensures a positive experience for an organization's customers, hinges on three core technology enablers, dubbed the three I's of marketing: Insight, Interact, and Improve.
>
> One key focus area will be to look beyond outbound marketing to a broader "intelligent decision management" platform within marketing and sales organizations. This encompasses not only traditional campaign management, but also more interactive marketing activities driven by analytics and optimization. These activities must be focused on providing a single, current "profile" view of every customer. The profile encompasses the decision support needs of not only marketing but also other parts of an organization that assess customers for various purposes (e.g., risk, fraud, customer service), and can provide the specific information needed for any given interaction in real time. Another quality of this kind of next-generation solution is a single point of control for synchronizing and managing to the "treatment profile" of every customer. Our most recent solution release marked a milestone in reaching this goal by providing a single point of control for inbound, outbound, and interactive marketing.
>
> A second key focus area will be a continual deepening of the ability for companies to transform online interactions into relevant customer insight and action. Ranging from capturing customer interactions with company web sites to mining blogs to understanding social networks,

SAS will help companies integrate this insight with other channel views to provide companies with a more complete picture of their customers. This approach allows organizations to more efficiently and effectively understand, model, and ultimately market to these same customers.

What Does It Do?

SAS for Customer Experience Analytics was developed because the SAS customer base insisted on a product that would help them get more out of their web channel. Companies that have invested heavily in the web channel and are becoming increasingly multi-channel were the targets for this application. Essentially, what it does is capture web-based customer interactions and integrate them with other channel views to provide a more complete view of their customers. Through the integration it allows the users to create new models of these customers. The integrated view is seen via the dashboard shown in Figure 20-1.

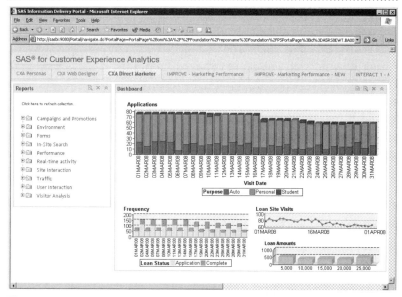

Figure 20-1: SAS Customer Experience Analytics Dashboard; useful and pretty too

Case Study

SAS told me of a case study for your perusal, though they couldn't tell me which global bank this was. But you'll get a great idea of what this product really does when you read the story.

The bank started by installing SAS for Customer Experience Analytics on their investment website. Up to that point, the information they captured from this site was limited to transaction insights, such as which pages received the most hits, which documents were downloaded the most, and so on. The bank had no knowledge of how specific customers or groups of customers used their site. Once the installation was completed, the bank began streaming web usage data to their data collection server. Next they converted the usage data into a data model for analysis and subsequent creation of a user history profile. As a result, for the first time ever, the bank could view profiles of specific investors visiting their investment site.

As a test to understand the impact of this technology, the bank started tracking an individual investor who had logged in that day. The data showed that the investor worked for JPMorgan Chase and that he had last visited their site three months before, downloading specific reports. The goal of this test was to illustrate that the technology could capture and measure the complete picture of the customer's web interaction. Ultimately, the test led to the idea of defining a scoring system on the site so that each individual customer record was scored based on their level of engagement. For example, if a customer downloaded one report, they got 3 points; if they came back multiple times, they got 10 points, and so on. In this way, the customer became the center of how the site activity was measured. With this information, the bank began asking questions like "Are we picking up return visits from investment bankers?" They could also begin distinguishing between prospects and actual customers coming to the site.

Because of this insight, the bank learned that advertising they thought was effective on a particular site, due to thousands of hits their web analytics package reported, had actually driven fewer than 10 "investors" to the site. The bank's quote on the ad effectiveness was that it "would have been more effective to hand out $100 bills on Wall Street" than to continue using this online ad. For the first time, the bank could understand the quality of the leads being sent to their site, and not just the raw number of people going to the site.

Armed with this new information, the bank was able to go back to their advertiser and renegotiate their contract based on the low number of quality leads that were being generated, saving enough money on future ads to pay for the cost of the software three times over. As a result of using the solution, the bank realized a 300 percent ROI in just three month and a 15 percent reduction in their annual online media spend by weeding out advertising initiatives that proved to be ineffective.

Pretty obvious why they win Superstah! isn't it?

I've spent a lot of time taking you through the measurements of social customer value, long term and real time. I've covered some of the analytics tools and the vendors that provide them. But all of this would be useless without discussing the return on investment. ROI is not immune to the transformation of the customer. Companies are being forced to re-evaluate how they measure value, results, and success.

Business gurus extraordinaire Martha Rogers and Don Peppers, long-time thought-leaders, took this head-on as a mission. Voilà, a book and concept called *Return on Customer*, which provides a much truer way of balancing shareholder and customer value to benefit everyone concerned.

Not only are they business leaders and prolific authors, but they are good human beings who have been tied at the hip for many years. They have made their mark on American business for the past two decades. Their latest book is *Rules to Break and Laws to Follow: How Your Business Can Beat the Crisis of Short-Termism.*

Without further ado, Martha Rogers and Don Peppers.

MINI-CONVERSATION WITH MARTHA ROGERS AND DON PEPPERS

Next December, your stockbroker will report to you what your dividends and interest payments were for the year, from your investments under his management. But dividends and interest payments won't give you a complete picture of your true investment results. You'll also need to know what happened to the underlying value of the stocks. Up or down? If your stockbroker refused to tell you this, insisting that you only need to know your "cash flow," you'd fire the stockbroker. And yet many companies content themselves with knowing how much they made from their customers in the current period, and never try to find out the underlying value of these customers, even though this value itself is constantly changing. Up and down.

The fact that a company cannot see or manage the value of its customer base often leads to inordinately risky and sometimes stupid or even illegal behavior. To avoid these mistakes, companies should be managing their customers as the financial assets that they really are, and Return on Customer, or ROC, is a metric designed to help them do this. It is based on three fundamental principles:

1. Customers create the value for an operating business.

2. The value customers create is realized in the current period (short-term value) and in future periods (long-term value).

3. Customers are scarce. You can manufacture more products, but you cannot manufacture more customers.

Given these three principles, a company should always try to create as much value as possible from every current and potential customer available to it.

Customer scarcity, and the conflict between short-term and long-term value, are universal marketing problems, especially now that interactive and computer technologies allow companies to treat different customers differently. You encounter these issues in a variety of situations:

1. What business rules should apply to your website or contact center to ensure that the right offers are communicated to the right customers, across several different product and service lines?

2. What is the right balance between customer acquisition and customer retention efforts, and how do you know?

3. What is the appropriate experience for a customer to have, across all different channels, in order to create the most value for the firm?

To address questions like these, you need to be able to measure the efficiency with which your customers are creating value for your firm in different situations, and this is the purpose of the Return on Customer metric. In the same way that return on investment (ROI) measures the efficiency with which a firm uses its money to create value, Return on Customer measures the efficiency with which a firm uses its customers to create value. Each metric provides important feedback, and they are easily understood, side by side.

For instance, suppose we have a stock that is worth $100, and over the course of a year the stock pays us a dividend of $5, while also appreciating in value to $110. The ROI on that stock investment for the year would therefore be 15 percent.

The same exact methodology applies to ROC. If we start with a customer who has a lifetime value (LTV) of $100, and during the course of the year we make a $5 profit on the customer, while by the end of the year we estimate that the customer's LTV has increased to $110, then our overall ROC on that customer would be 15 percent.

$$\text{So, ROC} = \frac{\text{Current profit from a customer } + \text{ Change in that customer's LTV}}{\text{Initial LTV}}$$

Note that the ROC metric includes both the short-term and long-term value created by a customer. The actions a company takes to achieve its marketing objectives often have conflicting effects and tradeoffs, requiring a balanced approach. For instance, a higher promotion budget might improve customer acquisition. But each new acquisition will be more expensive. It's possible to wind up spending more than an incremental new customer will ever be worth. Or a bigger variety of products might appeal to a wider group of customers, but represent a disproportionately high per piece production or distribution cost. Or an extra service might boost customer satisfaction, but at a cost that will be a drag on current earnings.

Clearly, creating value from customers is an optimization problem, which is something every business manager already knows. Often, however, the tradeoffs occur in terms of increased future cash flows at the expense of reduced current cash flows, or vice versa, and this creates a serious problem when a firm is focused exclusively on current-period sales. A short-term focus prevents a firm from making optimum decisions. If a company fires off a truckload of direct mail or e-mail to generate more current sales from its customers, for instance, it might also erode their willingness to buy in the future, or even to pay attention to future solicitations. Similarly, although a cost-cutting effort might not damage current customer cash flows, it could undermine future cash flows.

Reconciling the conflict between current profit and long-term value is one of the most serious difficulties facing business today. Failing to take a properly balanced approach not only penalizes good management practices but also undermines corporate ethics, by encouraging managers to "steal" from the future to fund the present.

Return on Customer can help a company optimize its marketing activities against a fixed supply of customers or prospective customers, and in a way that properly balances long-term and short-term value. ❧

21

When You Buy the Application, You Buy the Vendor, Though You Don't Implement Him

I have to admit a shortcoming. I also have to admit that parts of overall CRM program execution are not my favorite. So here goes.

My shortcoming: I am not very good at project management and I would be remiss if I didn't tell you that, since this chapter purports to be on how to select a vendor and how to implement CRM applications. That means project management is involved. Oy.

My least favorite CRM program execution phase: software implementation. This is either the cause for my lack of project management skills or vice versa. That said, I don't underestimate the importance of this exceptionally difficult phase of CRM, because business success can ride on the automation of processes and business rules.

Because it is important to implementation, I've been involved with many vendor selection processes and monitored or hovered over the successful implementation of CRM applications, which can be complex in a large or small company—or, considerably more rarely, a fairly simple tactical highly focused effort.

So what I've done for this chapter, so that you lovely people reading this book can actually get some real benefit from it, is to take advantage of something I can do—bring in a serious expert on CRM vendor selection and also give you a case study of a company that did a CRM implementation completely right—in fact, one of the most impressively well thought out implementations I've ever run across.

So, after a few opening remarks by me I'll make the introductions and let those who actually love the project show you what they do and how to do it right. I'm not so egocentric that I think I know everything. I just know how to be the expert when I am one and the author interviewing the experts when I'm not.

Despite Your Wishes, the Vendor Matters

One of the first mantras I ever chanted when I joined the ranks of CRM pundits was "when you buy the application, you buy the vendor." This came from a pretty simple logic and what was at that time a modicum of experience. The logic went something like this. CRM applications were functionally pretty much the same. For example, for sales force automation to be called sales force automation, for the most part it would include:

► Contact management

► Account management

► Lead management

► Opportunity management

► Pipeline management

► Integrated business rules, processes, and workflow

► A single customer record for all the individual customer data

Beyond that, the rest were what are ordinarily called "differentiators" but as often called "useless" or "overkill." But the above functions defined sales force automation whether Siebel, SAP, salesforce.com, NetSuite, or myriad other vendors offered it. You were sure to get those features for at least the vast majority of the SFA offerings.

So what distinguished the selection process for software applications? Why did it make a difference which application or vendor you chose if the features were commonplace? Several factors had to be considered—some technical, some operational, and some cultural.

Technical Factors

The most important technical factor is the architecture of the application you choose. This will affect how it integrates with your other systems (legacy or new), how you'll access it (Web or on the desktop), and how futureproofed it is.

CRM has come a long way when it comes to interoperability and integration. Web services have allowed CRM applications to talk to—meaning effectively exchange data with—other CRM applications and even a wide variety of back office applications. It is no longer uncommon to find ERP financial data being accessed by a sales force automation application so that you can see not only the orders and invoices outstanding but the payment status of an account.

As we saw in Chapter 15, there are several architectures to choose from—with the sexiest being enterprise SOA and RESTful architectures. While SAP CRM and Oracle's on-premise versions are based on enterprise SOA, SageCRM is based on a RESTful architectural model. Microsoft Dynamics CRM boasts of a single code base, which means its SaaS Live and its on-premise versions operate interchangeably.

But which architecture you choose will matter. If you have substantial legacy systems you are going to have to interact with, then you might not be able to use a system with an enterprise SOA. If you're still using client/server architecture, there will be a severe limit on which systems you can use—that might be none.

As of 2009, though, CRM applications from the mega like SAP to the micro like Zoho are all using similar web services and development tools that can create reusable code "objects." You'll see Java, .NET components for Microsofties amongst you, XML, AJAX, JavaScript, and several others routinely used in the development of platforms and operating systems, applications, and APIs.

Whatever architectural choice you make, make sure that you do make one.

Operational Factors

In the next section, Bruce Culbert mentions several of the operational factors that have to be considered when it comes to vendor selection and implementation. The total cost of ownership (TCO), which I'll leave to Bruce to discuss, is a mission-critical factor. The availability of resources to support the system once implemented is another important issue.

A concern that is not only becoming an overriding one, but something that's causing CIOs and CFOs to lose sleep, is related to both TCO and architecture—how you want the software delivered and, in line with that, how you are going to pay for it. While there is already an entire chapter devoted to the cloud and SaaS (see Chapter 16), if you're a C-level person, it still pays to pause, step back, and reflect for a moment on what you are about to embark on and how you are going to spend money.

For example, architecture aside, do you want to pay a monthly subscription fee that allows you to control costs? That shifts the overhead costs to the vendor, but puts your data on the other side of your firewall? Or do you want the feeling of safety and security (whether real or imagined) that comes from having your own data on your own servers with a licensed version of the software as a fixed cost? One-time payment plus maintenance and upgrades? Ongoing payment, but no maintenance and upgrade costs?

Cultural Considerations

Not just your culture either. The vendor's culture actually matters. Compatibility is the issue. This is by no means a trivial issue. Of course you have to do your due diligence when it comes to the vendor. Are they stable financially? What kind of track record do they have? What kind of references besides the ones that you've been given can you examine?

But they are your partners—not just a client. They are coming to your company and you are paying them to develop, install, and configure a system that can be the foundation for the growth—or the engine for the demise—of your business.

That's a big deal, isn't it? If you don't think it is, sell this book to someone, because you really don't get it and are not reading too carefully. If you've gotten this far, it's way too late to return it.

Think of it this way. There is a contract signed that is based on a statement of work that has been mutually agreed upon by you and your partner vendor. What if something goes wrong? Are you going to get into the "they did it" blame game to cover your butt? Maybe. But the reality is that it would be much better if the partner vendor and you were able to work together to solve the problem without pointing fingers—which get chopped off before they become property in lawsuits.

In order for you to trust the vendor to be a partner in a crisis, you need to trust them *before* the contract and statement of work are drawn up and agreed upon. How do you go about finding out if you and your partner-to-be are compatible? Here are a few steps:

1. Talk to customers who had implementation problems that worked with the prospective vendor.

2. Visit the prospective vendor's offices in the locales where you'll be working with them or their headquarters if they don't have a local office.

3. See how open they are about what they can and can't do, how they would deal with issues, and their financials. Find out if they are willing to admit mistakes.

The same characteristics that the social customer demands of you now—authenticity and trust—are exactly what you should be demanding of your prospective vendor.

I've just touched on the technical, operational, and cultural issues for vendor selection. I'm going to let Bruce Culbert give you the lowdown on how to go about it and give you a much deeper picture of what your concerns should be.

BRUCE CULBERT ON VENDOR SELECTION

Bruce Culbert is a major league thought-leader in CRM and an industry veteran with years of practical experience. He is also a wonderful guy and like a brother to me—and he is my business partner in the BPT Partners, LLC, CRM training venture. While near-brother is great for our personal friendship, it's not what got him to this chapter. Bruce is a heavy-hitting serious expert when it comes to leading CRM thinking and execution. He was the head of the BearingPoint CRM and Supply Chain practice and then went to salesforce.com where he was SVP of professional services. And before all of that, he was the founder of IBM's e-business practice. Now he's the Chief Strategy Officer at Pedowitz Associates. He's going to tell you about how to select a vendor and how the vendor thinks. This is an invaluable guide.

Knowing the Options

One of the critical parts of selecting a vendor, regardless of whether it is a technology or service provider, is to thoroughly understand what your options are. With so many developments in every aspect of the customer lifecycle, there are constant advancements in technology and approach that could potentially improve your company's ability to meet and exceed customer expectation while driving improved results for the business.

There are literally hundreds if not thousands of sources of information on CRM. To further your knowledge, I recommend you subscribe to more than one industry newsletter and research your specific topic of interest on the various industry and vendor websites. Here is a starter list of some of my favorite sources of credible information on the developments in the CRM industry.

- *1to1 Magazine* (www.1to1media.com)
- *CRM Magazine*/DestinationCRM.com
- CRM Talk Radio
- eCustomerServiceWorld.com
- SearchCRM.com
- InsideCRM
- Technology Evaluation Centers (www.technologyevaluation.com)
- Customer Relationship Management Association (crmassociation.org)
- CustomerThink
- GCCRM
- CRM Advocate
- Sales and Marketing Magazine
- American Marketing Association
- ISMGuide.com

Some analyst firms worth investing time (and money) in:

- Forrester Research
- The Altimeter Group
- Gartner Group
- Beagle Research
- Yankee Group
- IDC

Another good way to gain exposure to the myriad solutions and the companies behind them is to attend industry- or vendor-specific trade shows. These up-close and personal looks at technologies and companies are extremely helpful in making sure you get good alignment with your solution needs and your solution provider. There is only so much research you can do online and it is always useful to discuss the details of your specific needs and the vision for the solution so you can get a feel for how a particular solution and company's approach might best fit your needs.

Unfortunately, the breadth of open multivendor conferences has dwindled in the last several years and has been replaced by a very few large single-vendor events. Still, some important independent events happen around the globe. The annual Gartner CRM Conferences (typically one in Europe and one in the United States), the Forrester Conference on Social Computing, Enterprise 2.0, and O'Reilly Web 2.0 are all cutting-edge conferences on technology and customers. Other global events are sponsored by the national and regional chapters of the CRM Association. There are dozens of customer care, sales, and marketing conferences worth looking into.

The vendors also hold conferences, so if you are at the stage where you are selecting a small group of individuals and you have a bit of time, attending a vendor conference might be of some help. The largest of the conferences are:

▶ Oracle Open World

▶ SAP's Sapphire

▶ salesforce.com's Dreamforce

▶ SugarCRM's SugarCon

▶ Microsoft Convergence

And multiple other smaller conferences from specific vendors like NetSuite and RightNow are held throughout the year.

You can also subscribe to alerts and RSS feeds from all the sources above. There are many blogs out there that have been used by companies like yours to learn about the CRM industry. Those with a CRM slant include:

▶ **Paul Greenberg's two blogs**   PGreenblog (www.the56group .typepad.com) and ZDNet's Social CRM: The Conversation (http://blogs.zdnet.com/crm/)

▶ **Chris Carfi**   The Social Customer (www.socialcustomer.com)

▶ **Denis Pombriant**   Denis Pombriant (denispombriant.word-press.com)

▶ **Brent Leary**   Brent's Blog (www.crm2.typepad.com)

▶ **Dion Hinchcliffe**   ZDNet's Enterprise 2.0 (http:/blogs.zdnet .com/Hinchcliffe)

▶ **Vinnie Mirchandani**   deal architect (www.dealarchitect.type-pad.com)

▶ **Jim Dickie**   CSO Insights (www.customerthink.com/user/ jim_dickie)

▶ **Jeremiah Owyang**   Web Strategy (Jeremiah is an Altimeter Group analyst) (www.web-strategist.com/blog)

Plus the more general blogs and sites such as TechCrunch (www .techcrunch.com/), ReadWriteWeb (www.readwriteweb.com), Seth Godin's Blog (www.sethgodin.typepad.com), and the Church of the Customer (www.churchofthecustomer.com).

If you take some time to plug into the network of knowledge above, you should have enough information in 30 to 60 days to begin to zero in on what vendors and solution providers can help achieve your CRM goals.

The Pre-selection Checklist

Before we go too far down the path of evaluating technology and other solutions, let's pause to make sure you are ready to select, implement, deliver, and support your CRM investment. A solid understanding of the business, process, and customer experience goals is imperative prior to selecting any technology. If you have been generally following the guidance laid out in the other chapters of this book, you may be ready to move forward. To make sure that your organization is in the best position to maximize the return on investment in CRM, you should answer the following questions about your organization:

▶ Is there a commonly understood CRM strategy and vision for the organization?

▶ Have you determined how your CRM initiatives will add value to the overall customer experience?

▶ Is there buy-in for the strategy and approach by the people in the company most affected in sales, marketing, service, IT, and other areas?

▶ Do you have a clear definition of the results you are trying to achieve with your investment in CRM?

▶ Are the desired future business and customer processes identified and documented?

Answering these questions is an important step if you want to maximize your investment in something that supports the way you do business as opposed to making your business fit the way a particular solution works. This will allow for the conversion of business and customer engagement logic into technology and solution requirements that can be utilized in comparing potential solution providers and in subsequent discussions with your prospective choices. It should help ensure that what you are purchasing can meet your needs now and into the future. More questions to consider:

▶ Are the necessary budget and staffing available?

▶ Is there commitment from senior management in place to support the success of your CRM initiative?

If you answer no to one or both of these questions, you probably are not ready to begin to evaluate technology solution investments and your efforts will almost certainly be sub-optimized, if not a total failure.

If you are able to answer yes to most or all of the above questions, you should be ready to take the next step in evaluating and selecting a technology vendor, solution provider, or both. Sometimes you might need solutions or support from more than one company to accomplish your objective.

The First Big Step: Request for Information (RFI)

Using the RFI approach allows you to request information from multiple vendors in a structured way so you can begin to receive consistent and comparable information from the many solution providers that serve the CRM market. The general goal of the RFI process is to find out how the various solution providers and their technology and service offerings best enable and support your CRM requirements. When requesting information on solution offerings it is very useful to give the companies you are soliciting as much information about your needs as you practically can. Tell them about your business goals, your customer experience objectives, and budget and schedule requirements. After you issue the RFI, expect to hear back from the companies you sent it to.

Depending on the size and complexity of your requirements, the solution providers may have a number of questions. Do not shy away from these conversations. Answer their questions and let them do their job of educating you on how their solution can best meet your overall needs. Depending on how many companies receive the RFI, you may want to structure the feedback and dialogue by asking for questions to be submitted in writing and holding conference calls with all interested parties at once to make the process more manageable. This is the perfect time to engage in an exchange of information and begin to narrow the field of possibilities while building the foundations for potential relationships to come. It's highly likely one of these companies will become your business partner of sorts in the future, and this is a great way to begin to get to know them and build positive rapport. Generally you will want to have somewhere between three and ten companies on your RFI list. To get solid responses, allow at least 30 days for the submissions to come back and make yourself available to participate in dialogue about your needs with the companies interested in responding. In other words, don't issue the RFI to 10 companies and then go on vacation. The type of information to request in an RFI can vary, but I find the following information useful at this stage of the selection process:

▶ Overall company background and introduction

▶ General solution description and overview

▶ What is the solution to your specific needs as identified in the RFI, including timeline for implementation?

▶ What does it cost—one to three year total cost of ownership (TCO)?

▶ How will you be supported initially and over time? SLAs, training, ongoing user support, account management, customer support, etc.

▶ What technology is involved?

▶ What are the delivery options? On-demand, on-premise, both?

▶ What skills are required to use and support the solution?

▶ What other companies are successfully utilizing similar solutions?

▶ What other clients can be references if required?

▶ Future company and product roadmaps?

At this stage, as you can see by the categories and questions above, you want to be broader and less prescriptive than you will be later when you put together the final request for proposal (RFP). The goal is to get the most input possible so you can be exposed and educated to the possibilities in the market. This will help you gain momentum toward the final outcome of selecting a solution that maximizes your return on customer investment and a company to work with that is a good fit for your cultural, organizational, and business needs.

Interviews, Demonstrations, and Trials, Oh My…

After receiving back your RFI responses, it is usually obvious that there are some vendors that seem to be a better fit for your needs than others. Some companies may have realized that they don't based on the RFI requirements and disqualified themselves. You will want to understand all responses, including why any companies disqualified themselves, before moving forward. After the dust has settled and all initial responses are evaluated, it will be useful to select the top two to four companies that have a legitimate shot at meeting all or most of your needs and have further discussions with them.

Before finalizing a buying strategy, it is generally useful to conduct interviews or demonstrations with the top contenders to see the solution and the people behind the response. The best place to conduct these demonstrations and interviews is in your own office environment. That way you can potentially have others from your organization begin to be exposed early as well, and the vendor can see firsthand the type of company and environment their solution will be deployed in. While I highly encourage seeing the people and product in action prior to buying, I want to warn you about a sales tactic that is very popular with the vendors: the free trial offer. Many companies will recommend a free trial as a way of getting introduced to their solution. After all, it is free, so why not?

When Free Is Just Not Free

A typical trial or pilot period lasts between 30 and 90 days. The goal of a free trial is to get you hooked, make you do a lot of work, enter data, and use the product in a real business setting with your sales, marketing, or services team.

Most vendors know that once you have invested the time and effort to learn their system and have begun using it live . . . well, you get it, you're hooked and you won't want to consider any other solutions now that you have *invested* so much time and effort getting the *free* trial up and running. What's wrong with this picture?

Free trials are great, however, when you know what you want (solution) and who you want to work with (company). A free trial with a vendor that you know you are most likely to use can be a very beneficial thing. Doing your homework to make the best of this opportunity is critical.

Free trials can give an organization the time it needs to get its people exposed to the solution and make a game plan for moving forward without having the pressure of the meter running. On the other hand, using the trial opportunity indiscriminately can have a big negative impact on the organization. Too many "trials" and no "go live" plans will only serve to frustrate your customers and employees—not to mention you will be constantly hounded by the vendor sales staff in their attempt to convert the free trial into a sold deal. What is otherwise a very good e-newsletter solution has a whole business strategy premised on enticing people into taking their 30-day free trial and then working the sales process like crazy to get the prospective customer to convert to a paying contract by the conclusion of the trial.

Final Request for Proposal (RFP)

After receiving the RFI responses and engaging in dialogue with various companies as well as seeing the major contenders in action, you should have a pretty good idea of who will best meet your needs. At this point you must resist the urge to just select a vendor and run with them. Unless it is so obvious that there is a clear-cut choice or you are under severe time constraints, don't skip the formal RFP process. In the RFP, you will go back and address some of the things in the RFI but with different levels of precision and more specific intent to move forward with purchasing technology and or services to support your CRM program strategy and deployments. Through discussions with potential solution providers, you should have been able to further refine your requirements and be able to articulate them in more concrete terms so that the outcome of the RFP process is something that meets the specific needs of your business and that you can move forward with.

You should construct your RFP much like the RFI, but this time you want to give more precise guidance on your CRM strategy, expected customer experience and process details, and desired business outcomes.

Other details such as a specific timeline for implementation and results and specific budget expectations can and should be laid out in the RFP. This is the opportunity to clarify anything that came up in interviews and discussions during the RFI follow-up step. Other specifications or expectations as they relate to how you want to be serviced and supported by the vendor and its people should also be included in the RFP. The more detailed you can be about every aspect of your requirement, the better.

Perspectives on Pricing

There are many different solution options in the CRM market, and comparison shopping can be a bit tricky, especially when it comes to pricing. You need to do your best to level the playing field. You want to be able to compare the solution that can meet your needs and be sure you understand the pricing options specific to your situation—not necessarily the same as how the vendor prices and packages their solution to the general market. Therefore, I think it's important to mention a few tips when examining pricing and why it is never a good idea to rely on the pricing you get at the RFI stage. The pricing at that point usually has too many assumptions built in so that it is either unrealistically low or unrealistically high—for instance, if the vendor assumed the requirements would be more extensive than they actually are.

What matters most is that you are able to communicate as precisely as you can what you want now and in the foreseeable future so you can make the best decision based on total business and process fit along with best value in total cost of ownership (TCO) and return on customer investment (ROCI).

The CRM industry is the leader in SaaS options, and thus the pricing for SaaS offerings varies widely. There are also hidden costs and limits placed based on the pricing. As a result, the price quoted for a license for one use—or as it is sometimes referred to, a seat—is not always what it appears to be. Most vendors when advertising their seat price are quoting the lowest priced offering, and they try to make it sound like a no-brainer. After all, who wouldn't find value in an enterprise CRM solution for $25 to $40 a month?

A closer look reveals that these introductory or basic pricing options usually have significant limitations in functionality, number of users, scalability, and geographical deployment. Some may require significant custom development to meet your specific needs. The cost to add capability, either by adding more vendor modules or through customization, can add up very quickly and turn what looked like an inexpensive solution into a budget nightmare.

A thorough explanation and understanding of per-seat costs as well as total costs for your specific requirements need to be in place. You want to be able to calculate and compare six-month, one-year, and three-year total cost of ownership figures that have solid estimates for each element of cost. The total cost of ownership calculation should include the cost of the software license, any hardware or other software to support the CRM solution, customization/integration cost, ongoing support, internal resources required to develop, train, operate, and maintain the solution, external consultants and solution providers, and any incentives used to reward internal or customer adoption.

Competition is the key to getting the best price. The CRM solutions market is fiercely competitive, with more than 230 vendors in the space with solutions for all parts of the value chain. If you want the best pricing and therefore the best value in TCO for your CRM solution buys, be sure to explore more than one option. In the final RFP, have at least two or three companies (if possible) submit final, specific, and detailed solution and pricing proposals.

Some of the information you want to receive in the final RFP response:

▶ What is the solution to your specific needs as identified in the RFI, including timeline for implementation?

▶ What does it cost (six-month, one-year, and three-year detailed total cost of ownership)? Get firm, fixed price quotes if possible.

▶ How will you be supported initially and over time? SLAs, training, ongoing user support, account management, customer support, etc. Who in the vendor's organization are you specifically interfacing with in these areas?

▶ What technology is required (hardware, software, network, etc.)? How will the technology being proposed fit with your current IT investment and strategy?

▶ What are the delivery options? On-demand, on-premise, both?

▶ How will it be deployed?

▶ What skills are required to use and support the solution?

▶ What are the specific roles and responsibilities of the solution provider? What is expected of you in achieving solution implementation, training, rollout, and support?

▶ What other companies or business partners are required for solution deployment and support?

▶ What other companies are successfully utilizing similar solutions?

▶ Three references that can be contacted prior to final selection.

▶ What are the performance guarantees and warranties, if any?

The goal of the RFP process is to arrive at a best fit/best value solution that meets the specific needs of your business. Some tradeoffs might have to be made based on cost versus performance and capability, but if you follow the RFI and RFP process you will be down to some obvious choices and in a good position to select a solution provider that best fits your needs.

Selecting the Winner

By this time, you'll know pretty much who you want to be your vendor of choice. Once you've chosen that vendor, you'll enter negotiations with them to finalize the contract agreements, develop the statement of work, and identify the teams that will begin the implementation. Just remember a couple of things in closing. First, don't over-negotiate. You should know what the final terms will be by the time you've completed the selection process. Just make sure that the vendor adheres to them. Then start working closely with the vendor as your partner, not your arms-length suspicious predator who happens to be helping you. It's also in their interest that this implementation succeed—please take that into consideration. That will help you get off on the right foot, and the chances of the implementation succeeding will increase exponentially.

Thanks, Bruce.

Moving Forward: The Implementation Begins

In 2009, Gartner Group came out with a report that had the CRM success rate at 70 percent, the nearly polar opposite of their "famous" survey of 2001 that had the CRM failure rate at 55 to 70 percent.

The reason for this reversal to success is simple. The industry is mature. CRM vendors, service providers, and consultants learned from their mistakes. Practitioners have a huge body of knowledge to draw on given the tens of thousands of CRM implementations and programs that have been done in the last several years.

We are going to go to the well of practice we can draw on and come to some specific conclusions now that the CRM application vendor and services companies are in place, as, I have to assume, is your team. It's time to implement the sucker. Rather than just give you a generic look at the possible practices that may be effective, I present to you a case study for your viewing pleasure. This is the story of BigMachines, who did this nearly perfectly and have the results to prove it.

Executing Perfectly: BigMachines Does IT Right

If you roam the world jabbering about order systems and selling to customers, you've heard of BigMachines. They are perhaps the world's leading SaaS-based provider of product configuration, quoting, and proposal development and management systems. They integrate with salesforce.com, Oracle, SAP, and other significant industry players. Even in the midst of the post-declared 2008 recession, they grew their revenue by 75 percent and have seen a 287 percent three-year revenue growth. Plus they managed to increase staff size by 40 percent. Not bad for a recession.

But what is distinctly more impressive than even all their results is how they go about getting those results. BigMachines was one of the recipients of the 1to1 Marketing awards, jointly given by Gartner Group and Peppers and Rogers Group at the Gartner CRM Conference in 2008. They won the Bronze prize for CRM Enterprise Optimization. Deservedly so, because their CRM implementation was perfect—one of the best I've run across in more than a decade of CRM implementations. A lot more than a decade. Sigh. They are a perfect example of a set of best practices that garnered results when it came to implementation. Because of that, it behooves me to give you the complete rundown on their successful award-winning implementation so that you can have a solid guidepost for your own—with the caveat of course that if you're not BigMachines, you won't do it exactly this way, unless you're crazy. Here it is step by step. Much of the data was gleaned from the Gartner/1to1 Awards results with their and Big-Machines' permission and from a subsequent conversation with folks at BigMachines. The implementation took place from inception in 2006 to completion in 2008.

Identifying the Issues

BigMachines had been using a sales force automation application for what you would pretty much expect—managing customers rather than just prospects. All of a sudden there was a significant degree of increased complexity. Their customer lifecycle was software delivery, maintenance and support, asset upgrades and renewals, and, eventually, retirement. Not only did this add layers of complexity, it also required a good deal more information captured than they had currently. Because their original CRM requirements were around contact and account management, SFA sufficed. They had disconnected silos of knowledge and activity throughout the company. They used multiple applications that had no apparent relationship to each other. Look at this list:

▶ Quote generation—Microsoft Word

▶ Price lists—Excel spreadsheets

▶ Order entry—manual entry into accounting software package

▶ Use of sticky notes for a good deal of communication between departments. Sticky notes, rather than XML, were the IT standard at BigMachines. No joke.

Customer satisfaction was good despite these disconnects, but Big-Machines was aware of how much better it could be. Since there was no integrated customer information repository, the customer service reps had a fragmented view of the customer—as did all departments. Problems like this lead to poor process resolution and inefficiencies that affect the customer directly due to no real obvious responsiveness. One other red flag was that they were growing rapidly, which could lead to the magnification of the problem and interfere with their ability to scale.

The Strategic Objectives

BigMachines' primary objectives could be classed in the category "customer-centric." Service was the focus for the results. What this meant practically was the "classic" CRM holy grail—a repository for all singular customer records. On the one hand, each customer record would have all the customer information gleaned from multiple sources and channels. On the other hand, all of the records would be located in a single data store.

There were two other significant goals:

▶ They also wanted to incorporate a VoIP system with their existing CRM applications so that not only was complete customer information available, it was available quickly.

▶ They were expanding their solutions knowledge base, which had historically been used by their own internal staff. They wanted to give customers access to the knowledge base through a single point of entry to information and tools.

The final phases of their project involved the creation of a new department, Customer Success Management (they call it the Customer Success Management Team). What was interesting here was that the idea of customer success actually included the customer. Part of the implementation included the release of a new tool that allowed BigMachines customers to document and vote on new enhancements to BigMachines products. This captures customer ideas in their own words and incorporates those ideas into the knowledge base, which allows customers to collaborate and provides a huge amount of information for product management personnel as they plan product roadmaps.

The team itself was tasked to be proactively involved with their customers in a way that integrated customer participation into all facets of BigMachines work. Each member of the CSM Team manages customer communication, works to handle issues that go beyond helpdesk capabilities to resolve, manages renewals, and potentially even up-sells.

Finally, they began to look at some more advanced capabilities—some based on Social CRM, though they didn't call it that. As this book went to press, this was still in the earliest stages of implementation.

Planning the Implementation

In addition to the corporate strategic and tactical objectives, BigMachines' CRM team also began to identify which features and functions they needed to meet these objectives. They did this by looking at their business processes, identifying which were most important to them in reaching their objectives and which processes were of value to both BigMachines and BigMachines' customers.

Sales Support: The Process

The processes involved agglomerated prospect information that could be accessed by customer support when the prospect became a customer. The data from sales and support would be consolidated into a single record.

▶ Improving the existing leads to prospects to customer information (account contacts, status, customer status) process

▶ Improving existing customer contract repository (contract details, renewal dates, and documents linked to accounts)

▶ Improving existing hosting/operations new customer setup (access to contract information to ensure fast setup)

Customer Service: The Process

BigMachines looked at which processes would help the customer service department go wide and deep—wide by offering a greater variety of customer support services and deep by improving the quality of service from the helpdesk.

▶ Customer application profile (software versions, modules, customer status, special features, etc., to ensure the helpdesk can quickly access the most recent state of the customer's environment)

▶ Customer service case management (cases linked to user contacts, real-time dashboard reporting to ensure they track issues and performance in real-time)

▶ Phone-to-case integration (support calls linked to user contacts, visible to service agents to ensure fast access to all customer information and to automate data entry)

▶ E-mail-to-case integration (automatic creation of urgent care support cases from their urgent care escalation process for the most rapid responses)

▶ Proactive customer success management to monitor and resolve customer satisfaction issues before they become a crisis

Integrated Applications and Improved Technology Effectiveness: The Process

Because of the aforementioned customer lifecycle, they had to look at the CRM applications capability to integrate with their accounting programs, project management, asset management efforts, and employee systems access controls.

▶ Professional services project setup (data integration to project management tracking as new customers go live)

▶ Dashboards and metrics reporting (tracking and monitoring of helpdesk case load, gathering of information in support of their process and product improvement projects, including causes, volume and frequency of issues, and patterns and trends over time, to ensure continuous improvement)

▶ Access to all customer information (cross-functional access to consistent, up-to-date, real-time information)

Customer-Focused: The Process

For the first time, they consciously intended to make the solutions knowledge they had and all other appropriate information easily available to the customer—along with the tools to optimize the use of the information.

▶ Customer access to comprehensive solutions knowledge base, accessible online, real-time, and 24/7/365 (to ensure their customers can access the best practices and solutions that they use internally)

Vendor Selection: Before You Implement

I'm sure you've read Bruce's approach to vendor selection, so we can cut to the pre-implementation chase here. Vendor selection was probably less of a concern for BigMachines than was normally the case, because in 2005 they had begun using salesforce.com for highly focused sales force automation work around lead generation, lead and opportunity tracking, and prospect management. When 2007 rolled around and they needed to select the vendor they were going to use, since they had been successful with salesforce.com and saw the value-add of not having to maintain the hardware/software or manage the overhead by using an on-demand solution, it made sense to continue. What made this an interesting choice was that they were expanding the use of the salesforce.com platform for customer service.

Aside from the SFA successes with salesforce.com, they felt that salesforce.com integrated well with third-party applications, which in their case meant accounting applications, sales configuration tools, sales quotes, sales commission products, and project management applications. With the vendor selection obvious, preparing for the implementation was the next phase.

The Implementation: Phase 1, Preparation

Migrating customer-facing applications presents challenges in communicating and implementing a smooth transition plan. BigMachines worked long and hard at this, reviewing their plans from the customer's viewpoint. Having a pilot beta group allowed then to fine-tune their plans.

The BigMachines team realized they had to get executive buy-in for the implementation. They had a bit of a head start with the means to be able to point to the success of salesforce.com on the premises already. Getting executive buy-in was unusually easy. What made it easy was the culture of BigMachines, which is not just platitudes on customer success, but actually is aimed squarely at making things good for their customers. They were able to get buy-in at the highest levels of management and keep them engaged and updated. Of course, it didn't hurt that the executive champion was the CEO.

Preparation for the project was thorough. They developed a systematic plan to move their customers to the new system, with a phased rollout planned around a two-week migration time. They ignored nothing. They had a communications plan in place before the implementation began that involved multichannel communication with their customers via e-mail, web conferences, informational notices on the website, phone calls, and just informal channels—conversations in the hallway, so to speak. Training wasn't ignored either—both internal and customer training—for the new helpdesk platform. Once the plan was in place and the software selected, the implementation began.

Phase 2: The Implementation Begins

The implementation had step-by-step steps. Initially, given their legacy practices, BigMachines implemented leads and prospects management improvements to the sales process. When that was done, they migrated the legacy helpdesk application to the new VoIP-integrated helpdesk system. This had them particularly excited because there was an extensive upgrade in the capabilities of the helpdesk system, such as phone-to-case integration and e-mail-to-case integration. That done, they moved methodically to the next step, which included account information that encompassed application profiles—in other words the software they had, including the version, the customer's integrations, the customer's components. They then associated a comprehensive set of metrics with these software profiles, viewable via dashboard. They integrated their flagship quoting tool to the platform, giving them management of their internal quote-to-cash processes. They then integrated other third-party applications for project management and accounting with their legacy CRM systems.

As the implementation began, the teams didn't ignore what that meant to the culture of the company. Not only were they concerned with the implementation of the new systems, they had as great a concern for the adoption of the systems that were being implemented.

The Implementation: Changing the Culture

As noted earlier, BigMachines had a 40 percent growth rate in staff in 2008 as this implementation was going full blast. But for the most part they had to utilize their own existing operationally knowledgeable staff to set up new processes and customer migration plans. Because that staff had a lot of other things to do, it was something of a challenge. But fortunately for them, some of that 40 percent growth was for customer service and that allowed them to execute the transformation smoothly.

One reason is that they had a culture that would support the kind of transition they were attempting. Their company's philosophy and mission was "Customer Success Is Our Success." This notion permeates the company from top to bottom in a practical way so that it continuously reinforced and aligned employee expectations around the objectives of the implementation. Employees understood that one of the benefits of the implementation would be a set of real-time, granular metrics that would help drive the success of BigMachines' customers so that the acceptance of the transformation would go smoothly.

This kind of culture naturally encouraged cross-functional teams that draw on particular strengths in all departments as needed. Consequently, because the teams were already up and running, no new teams or task forces were created to "handle" the implementation. This minimized the politics and departmental concerns that often cripple CRM implementations.

The messages were consistent throughout the company too—BigMachines' customers would benefit. This was seen as a major plus for the implementation.

The Results: ROI Is King

Pretty amazing so far, isn't it? Hoping that yours will go so well, aren't you? Of course, there has to be a result that was worth the effort. There was—and is.

The Single Customer Record

The BigMachines customer support team now has all customer information at their fingertips whereas previously they had to look it up in multiple places and across multiple applications. When a customer calls on the phone, they now have phone-to-platform integration that launches their case data on a screen, which enables the CSR to be fully informed about a customer's status. This same information integrates with views for sales and marketing personnel.

What's important is that the customer service rep can see what the sales and marketing staff do, if, of course, they have the necessary permissions. So for example, a CSR can see:

▶ How many users for the customer have logged in and how many transactions they've made over the past month (i.e., how frequently they are using the system)

▶ When the customer was upgraded to the newest software release or if the upgrade is scheduled

▶ How often the customer has called with open issues, and how long it took customer support to solve these issues

▶ If they are waiting to make a decision on a new module or up-sell package from their sales team

▶ When their contract is coming up for renewal

▶ Their current customer satisfaction score

Significant Customer Service Benefits

There is now a comprehensive solutions knowledge base that is given to customers that has some of the best and brightest practices and answers from the BigMachines staff. It is accessible 24 hours a day,

7 days a week, and in real time. It is so substantial that customers often find answers to their questions without opening cases. But even if a case has to be opened, the level of knowledge and customer information available to the agent is substantially improved via the customer application profiles.

Real-time dashboards manage the helpdesk operational load, view specific customer statistics, and give BigMachines the means to gather data in support of their process and product improvement projects. Trend and pattern identification that aids in the successful solution to customer problems is considerably easier to see than in the past.

There were some side results that not only benefited customers but also provided some efficiencies of scale for BigMachines. For example, they were able to handle twice the amount of customers with no increase in staff. That's more efficient. They were able to meet their time to response of two hours for *all* cases and measure it where they couldn't before. That's more efficient.

They were able to improve their customer satisfaction scores significantly from 2007 to 2008. That's more effective. They had a nearly 100 percent customer renewal rate. That's way more effective.

Summing It All Up

The objectives and goals set out by senior management around being responsive to customers, improving operational efficiencies, and controlling the organizational scaling were met 100 percent. They did it on time and on budget—something rarely said of any implementation, CRM or otherwise.

What should you take away from this?

This was as close to a perfect implementation that I've seen, so see it as a paradigm, a model for you to use on what should go right. Without any doubt, things will go wrong in your implementation—no disrespect intended. But BigMachines provides a benchmark to start from and a useful example of how to go about things step by step, though your steps won't be identical.

Closing Up for the Night

That's about it for this chapter, dudes and dudesses. But there's one important final piece. It's what Peter Churchill tells you to take away from this chapter.

MINI-CONVERSATION WITH PETER CHURCHILL

Peter Churchill is president of Bridge Farm Consulting. He was formerly associate director of CRM and outreach technology at the Center for American Progress. He originally hails from the U.K., and he spent ten years working in Europe and the U.S. designing and implementing CRM solutions for the corporate sector. However, after gaining a master's degree in political management from GW's Graduate School of Political Management, Peter now focuses on implementing CRM solutions in the not-for-profit and political sectors in Washington, D.C. And he does it oh so bloody well.

Succeeding with CRM—For Real

The reasons for CRM projects failing are widely documented, from a lack of executive sponsorship to failing to address poor quality data. But the reasons why a project is successful often remain less easy to identify. But for me, beyond all the KPIs, "success factors," and revenue increases, a successful CRM implementation means the system is actually being used as intended. That may sound obvious, but it is all too easily forgotten. So these are my three suggestions for ensuring that having built the system, the users really will come and use it.

▶ ***Feel the users' pain***   *It is critical to remember that for your users, any new system means change, and as such, there is a good chance that it will actually make their life more difficult in some way or another. So when you are doing the initial analysis and requirements gathering and deciding what to prioritize, take some time to learn what would make a real positive difference for your users. Are there current ways of working that they know are inefficient, and if improved, would offer an easy win for the project when the new system goes live? When you can show the users how this new system will finally solve their problems, you are far more likely to ensure:*

  ▶ *They'll be more receptive to the new system.*

  ▶ *They'll feel like it is being implemented for them rather than for the benefit of big management, the consultants, etc.*

  ▶ *They'll be more willing to invest time and effort in working with you on future releases.*

▶ ***Start out simple***   *Just because you can implement a certain screen or workflow, it doesn't mean you should—at least not right away. I would argue that all developers/analysts want to try out new features and build clever code, because adding new fields or page layouts just isn't that much fun—I know, I've built a few! But for a new user, the more functionality that is available, the more intimidating the system is to learn and use, and* *without them being willing to do that, the implementation will never be successful (see above). I remember a global implementation of a large CRM system. The American version of the main contact screen was incredibly complex, with a huge array of fields and custom buttons, and lots of underlying code running behind the scenes that made the page very slow to work with. The version of the same contact screen for the Italian subsidiary was designed by an experienced sales director who knew his team and their limited interest in a new system. So his version just had the 10 most important fields to capture, plus the save button. The Italian version was much easier to demonstrate and got a far higher user adoption by the sales team, because they could use it on day one, with minimal training, and it was easy to understand. It was then possible for us to build on that success because the users were now bought in to the project.*

▶ **Train them up**   *Training is hard work, and always the first line item to suffer when projects are over budget, over time, and lacking resources. But without sufficient training and ongoing support, you can almost guarantee the implementation will fail, however well the final design meets the initial specifications. So remember:*

> ▶ **Start early in the process**   *Identify some potential power users, and test out some of the system with them. That way, you will have some ready-made advocates who can help train other people because they really know the system and understand why certain decisions were made.*

> ▶ **Make the training seem real**   *Telling a user "Sorry about that error—but in the proper system, x will happen" is not a good way to inspire confidence.*

> ▶ **Spend time with the users**   *Formal training sessions are important, but you won't get the real feedback you need. You have to spend time with the users in their normal working environment and see for yourself what they find difficult or frustrating. That sort of feedback is invaluable to ascertaining what additional training people need and what should be addressed in the next release.*

While implementation project management is not exactly *my* mad skill, I think that there's enough information here for you to take something useful back to your company. I actually feel like something's been accomplished. Wow. Cool.

I need some sleep before we hit Chapter 22. I'd suggest you do the same—unless you're reading this during the day.

22

Waving to the Future

I've been talking nonstop for about three weeks, I think. This is where the pressure gets really heavy. This is the end of the book and I have to keep my track record unsullied. Since the first edition, I've been making forecasts and I haven't been wrong yet. But there is always a first time, and what if this is it? I'm hyperventilating. Have to calm . . . down . . . now.

Before I get down to it, I'm going to say something that I think I have to. No fifth edition. This time it really is over, because Social CRM isn't going to morph into a 3.0 version of CRM any time in the near future—certainly not by the time you read this book. However, it will continue to mature. The acceptance of social characteristics and the use of social networks and media tools will be part of the way that CRM strategies, software, processes, and interactions are all simply done. Now it's still in its infancy.

But then the question is: What is the future of CRM? What's going to happen to it? What do businesses have to look forward to as they move farther into and past the first decade of the new millennium? We've seen the positive projections for CRM software from varying analysts throughout the book, despite the recession of 2008 and beyond. How accurate is this? What still needs to be improved and what's likely to happen? Let's close the book out with a bang, not a whimper, and go buck wild.

First, you're going to hear from Denis Pombriant. Then I'll close this opus with my outlook for the next several years in Social CRM. Then you can go home—if you've been reading this book somewhere other than home. If you are, hopefully you're reading a Kindle edition. Otherwise, this is really very heavy.

First, Denis Pombriant

I'm not going to reintroduce you to Denis. You already know him, unless you have serious short-term memory problems—or, given the length of this book, long-term memory problems. But there is one thing I want to remind you of so you can get your arms around his bonafides when it comes to prognostication. He was the guy—the only guy at the time, in fact—who said that salesforce.com was a "disruptive innovation" because of their delivery model, then called either application service provider (ASP) or "net native," now called SaaS or on-demand or cloud computing in its most recent morphing. He was right when no one else had figured it out yet.

Sustainability and CRM

Gasoline prices have flirted with and exceeded the cost of milk at times. Historic high fuel prices mitigated by a recession will rise again with global recovery. In short, there simply is not enough fuel to meet the expanding demand, and prices will necessarily increase. The high cost of fuel is a cause of economic worry and, I believe, a driver of innovation in CRM.

Fuel prices and CRM may seem like an odd coupling, and you would be supported for believing so, but as we think about where CRM has been and where the world may be going, it is worth pondering the relationship. As the cost of transportation goes up, it will cause a disruption in the economy and many front-office business processes will be adversely affected. The cost of fuel has a direct bearing on the cost of making a sales call. A spike in fuel costs might temporarily impact margins. A certain amount of dynamism in the cost of inputs is part of business life, and it can be overlooked.

But what if the overall trend in the cost of fuel is ever upward and, more significantly, what if prices begin to change dynamically so that customers have little left to budget for new products and services? Furthermore, how will a vendor (and we are all vendors) deal with the margin erosion that comes with unstable energy prices?

These and related questions are not idle curiosity. In the years ahead a relatively new term, peak oil, will infiltrate our lexicon and will become shorthand for the challenges all businesses face due to energy cost fluctuations. Briefly, peak oil refers to the maximum rate of oil extraction—how fast we can take oil out of the ground—regardless of demand.

When we reach that maximum, and some geologists say we have reached that point or will in the next few years, classic supply and demand will take over. Increasing demand for a fixed or even declining resource will produce the kinds of price spikes we have seen—and worse.

This piece is too short to provide a primer on peak oil. I recommend plugging the words into your favorite search engine and reviewing what comes back. In a peak oil scenario, travel will be one of the first casualties. Increasingly, conventional face-to-face sales calls will be scrutinized for their necessity and the salesperson's goals. And their outcomes will be analyzed and dissected before a sales manager authorizes any further investments.

In this world, the CRM software that business has come to rely on to market and sell to as well as to service customers will need to take on a greater role as a communication medium that begins to replace face-to-face contact. Some people might argue that the telephone was developed for just this purpose, and they would be right, but analogously, no one needed an abacus once the calculator was invented. In the arms race that is modern business, it is virtually certain that CRM will take on more of the characteristics of a contextual communications device and we will all be better off for it. Here are some innovations that I think will become necessary in the near future.

The Customer Module

CRM systems store a great deal of information about customers, but it's hardly the 360-degree view that we keep hearing about. We know who bought a solution, who uses it, and who pays the maintenance bills. Today. Will all of that information be the same in six months? Who will maintain it? Will sales be automatically notified when the person who made the original purchase leaves or gets promoted? Will some future sales representative find himself or herself pushing the same rock up the hill when it's time to upgrade? What about the customer—is there a systematized way for the vendor to capture relevant information about need, biases, modes of operation, lifestyles, and more? CRM still has some distance to travel, and I think placing these responsibilities into a central customer module makes some sense.

The customer module will need to incorporate several social networking techniques that have proven to be wildly popular and effective at enabling people to communicate more or less spontaneously. Social networking will enable customers to maintain their own contact information and control how and when it can be used. This much is beginning to happen. But social techniques will also play a role in enabling customers to get the assistance they need in using and troubleshooting products. Communities organized around business problems, products, and companies will stand on an equal footing with direct support from the vendor. Vendor-based service and support will diverge, with service equating more with those things that only the vendor can provide: a discount, an RMA number, or account service, for example. Support will be a community effort with peers providing an important dimension. Loyalty will be a natural outgrowth of using a robust customer module, and vendors will be able to develop superior metrics to support it.

Embedded Phone, Video Phone, Voice as a Data Type

If more people begin to work from home offices (a distinct possibility to save on the expense of commuting), they will need much better communications systems deployed over the Internet. Call center systems already have tightly integrated telecommunications, and sales could benefit from this capability too. Video phone is a natural extension of basic phone service, and if face-time is going to be reduced due to the cost of travel, video will transition quickly from a nice accessory to a necessary replacement.

While we're at it, the sooner we can use accurate voice transcription as data input, the sooner we can expand the role of the handheld device for the remote worker. Handheld devices with tiny keypads must give way to dictation as the preferred method of input. Not all input need be transcribed but, at least initially, we will need input that is recognizable by our current generation of applications.

Video Content

Content management has become a hot topic, and I think it is about to be taken to another level. No one has the time necessary to read all of the relevant content that vendors can produce. People are visual learners, and smart marketers will grasp this as the costs of video development come down. Developing full-motion video with actors and camera crews will always be expensive and largely out of the question for day-to-day marketing. But for CRM's purposes, what is needed to develop video content is practically on the desktop already. Think about the Ken Burns–style documentary format, which consists of stills artfully scanned and dissolved while a voiceover gives the essential information. You can do all of that today with a low-end Macintosh or Windows computer. I expect video development like this will be standard practice in less than five years, especially if transportation costs remain high.

Primetime for PRM

A great way to reduce a company's exposure to high travel costs is to outsource sales. Vendors have been doing this for a long time by recruiting partners that live closer to customers and understand their businesses. Expect PRM to get new life as transportation costs continue to rise, but also expect that, to make it all work, vendors will need a lot more from their analytics packages. Simple pipeline and forecast analytics are a great start, but to extend control and offer optimal help to partners, we will need analytics and metrics that dive into the heart of most PRM-focused business processes. It will be a two-way street as vendors also leverage their investments in video and video production, training, support, hiring, recruiting, and management.

Analytics, Analytics, Analytics

We need to become smarter about capturing data from interactions without slowing anyone down to ask them to fill out a form. Every action generates data that might mean nothing by itself but when aggregated can be a pixel in a big picture. You can tell a lot about how busy a salesperson or organization is by how long it takes to access a new lead and enter notes, and you can build a metric around it too. This is a simple example, but we need to be more proactive about this kind of frictionless data gathering and what we can do with the information it returns.

Final Thoughts

Sustainability is in the title of this section because I think the next move for CRM will be all about helping companies simplify and economize on their basic front-office business processes—in other words, CRM with an operational twist. No process and no business can afford to operate unprofitably for a long time (except airlines, for some reason), and the emerging energy market tightness is going to put the entire global economy through a wringer. The process will not be pleasant for anyone, but if we innovate, we can make our business processes more cost effective and begin to reach a level of sustainability that our survival demands. CRM ought to be the hub of innovation.

Now It's My Turn to Be a Fortuneteller, Err, Forecaster

Usually, from year to year, you'll see forecasts from Gartner, Forrester, IDC, Aberdeen, and the like for whatever area of technology interests you. You'll also see economic forecasts about the coming bust, bear, boom, bull market and complicated charts that prove that the human species is pretty much incalculable, despite the consistent and pretty peaks and troughs of the provided long-term cycles. Personally, I have a really complex formula when it comes to my forecasting, refined over years of research, observation, and algorithmic application. It goes something like $eu + gw \, (l*bl)/i = fw$, where eu = eye use; gw = guesswork; l=luck; bl=blind luck; i=intuition; and fw = forecast wisdom. Like most forecasts, these are based pretty much on observation and lucky or not so lucky guesses, and have as much chance of being wrong as being right.

But for now, let's dig into what else I have to say and you can kick my . . . no, slap my hand if I'm wrong. Actually, in case you try it, I'll invoke the "Pundit Immunity Clause," which states, "If I was completely wrong it was due to market conditions or you just heard it wrong or hey, are you crazy? No one can predict the future." This gives me immunity from neck chopping, hand slapping, nether part kicking, and whatever can be thrown at me, as one forecast or another falls by the wayside.

The Format

The format is going to be something like this. You'll see something called a Probability Rating followed by a number from 1 to 10 preceding my items. That represents what I think of the likelihood of what I'm writing actually occurring. A 10 means the feeling in my gut that whatever got the 10 is going to be right on point. A 1 means the feeling in my gut is probably indigestion. Let's get on with it.

The Future Will Come Back to Haunt Me

Mobile CRM will be in increasing demand by sales organizations in particular, and vendors will continue to invest in it, downturn and beyond. (Probability Rating: 8.0)

The investments in mobile CRM being made by Oracle, SAP, Sage, and, of course, RIM, among others, are going to start paying important dividends. There are several factors that point to this, even in the midst of economic decline:

► The increasing hardware power for BlackBerry

► The widespread availability of 3G and the beginning of the Clearwater-Sprint-Nextel rollout of the 4G WiMax

► The interest in making the iPhone a mobile enterprise platform, especially with CRM

► The purchase of Symbian by Nokia, converting it to open source

► The commitment of Microsoft partners to build Microsoft Dynamics CRM 4.0 Windows Mobile solutions

► The release (finally) in 2009 of SAP's kick-butt CRM 2007 Sales for the BlackBerry

► Oracle's commitment to the iPhone as a platform—a genuinely big deal

► Sage's release of SalesLogix Mobile CRM for the BlackBerry

► Maximizer's ambitious release of their CRM products on the iPhone, BlackBerry, *and* Windows Mobile

I'd pay close attention if I were a vendor behind this curve because the demand is on the increase and concerns about the economy only increase the desire for sales—and sales force automation and social networking have made the most significant progress as mobile applications. Not only were there iPhone-like lines for the BlackBerry Storm (their touchscreen device) but 400,000 enterprise-ready souls downloaded the BlackBerry MySpace application the first week it was made available. This highlights again what I've said all along: *consumer thinking is deeply penetrating the enterprise* and has to be considered in employee and customer strategies, even in a B2B environment. Mobile is beyond significant. It is critical to 2009 and beyond CRM strategy.

I'm not alone in this either. Gartner predicts a 40 to 60 percent increase in the use of mobile CRM from 2007 to 2010.

Integration between traditional CRM and Web 2.0 applications, features, functions, and characteristics will increase for the next several years. (Probability Rating: 9.5)

Even now, we're seeing CRM vendors like Oracle, SAP, Sage, Microsoft, RightNow, and salesforce.com integrate social applications as core CRM functionality. This is a major initiative for all the vendors and has repercussions throughout the entire suite offerings of the larger vendors. In early 2009, SAP announced that their Google-like user interface, first rolled out in SAP CRM 2007, is going to be the unified interface for all their applications, because of its great success. In Chapter 12, we discussed the release of Oracle Social CRM applications such as Sales Prospector and Sales Library, but it goes well beyond this. RightNow integrates its functionality for communities and unstructured search of community knowledge through an alliance with Lithium and their acquisition of enterprise social networking platform HiveLive in late 2009. SAP created both an enterprise-grade Twitter-like product called ESME and also developed a Twitter-trolling capability for their customer service application that analyzes customer tweets and then alerts the appropriate parties, depending on the business rules. Helpstream (Chapter 13) and InsideView (Chapter 12) have both formed alliances with companies like Oracle, salesforce. com, and SugarCRM with an eye to integration. On the other side, social media companies like Radian6 emphasize their integrations with CRM applications. There is also a continued effort to integrate external social networks like Facebook with more traditional CRM applications. This is a trend that will continue and is pretty much unstoppable as CRM vendors have finally figured out that they need to respond to customers by integrating what customers demand—in an ecosystem run by the customers. Amen to that.

Large enterprises will buy Social CRM tools; SMBs will look to simplicity in CRM and dabble in social tools. (Probability Rating: 6.5)

The interest in extending CRM applications and strategies into communities and social media will increase in the large enterprises as they begin to realize that to retain their customers they need to engage them in more valuable activities that will lead to continued purchases.

It will also be driven by a need to rely more on customers than ever before as part of an extended salesforce. It is also driven by internal pressures with the Millennials becoming significant parts of workforces both in size and influence. In fact, the Millennials go to workplaces expecting to use social media tools at the workplace. They don't care whether or not IT supports them. They intend to use them. According to a 2008 Accenture study, over 60 percent of them have no idea what the IT policies are for their company and they don't care. It's simple to understand. They are demanding at least internal use of the tools that they use as consumers, which helps drive changes in culture in the companies. (For a great study from McKinsey, go to www .mckinseyquarterly.com/PDFDownload.aspx?L2=13&L3=13&ar= 2174) However, the small business world is not looking at CRM this way. They are looking for low-cost ways to operate their businesses so they can keep their customers during economically challenged times. That means automating processes, not developing communities that have extensive overhead involved in their maintenance. Simplicity drives their CRM choices, and companies who understand that (like Zoho, Really Simple Systems, Maximizer, Sage, etc.), are working toward developing CRM products that make it easy for the small business to operate, not to engage customers, but to manage transactions with customers—in other words, traditional CRM approaches. Small businesses will certainly dabble in social media because the barriers and costs of entry are low and failure won't kill them. The interest is there, but the actual use of social media isn't widespread in the SMB world yet. Small business did not see an integrated Social CRM as a priority in 2009 and there is no reason to think they will in 2010 either. Their CRM choice will be driven by cost and ease of use for their operations, not social tools. Their use of social tools will be driven by their use of them as consumers.

Social software companies will increasingly integrate with CRM applications through APIs and plug-ins. (Probability Rating: 8.0)

From March 2009 on, for reasons unknown, the social software companies and social thinkers began to jump on the CRM bandwagon. There was a raging debate which is still going on about using things like Twitter as "social CRM" (incidentally, the answer to that is Twitter is a location and a channel, not Social CRM). The software companies began realizing that CRM was a lucrative area for them to go because it is an ideal mature industry. Consequently, over the next few years from 2009 on there is going to be an increased number of social software and CRM software integrations initiated by the social software companies. Typically they are developing APIs that work with CRM applications. Atlassian has been one of the leaders in this, integrating JIRA, their 2.0 project management tool, with SugarCRM, Siebel, Net-Suite and salesforce.com. Confluence, Atlassian's wiki application, is tied to salesforce.com and VTiger CRM, the latter an open source CRM poduct. IBM's Lotus Connections 2.0 announced its integration with iEnterprise CRM in September 2008—a curious choice of CRM applications, actually, but nonetheless indicative of the trend that's out there. Leverage, a leading community platform, has been integrated with salesforce.com for the last two years. Neighborhood America integrates with salesforce.com and has that very significant integration in the public sector with Microsoft that we discussed in Chapter 14.

There is a reason for the unfreezing of social software companies' relationships with CRM vendors. They are going where the money is. CRM is a mature market with high demand that seems to transcend economic downturns. Revenues may lag in the worst times, but they still grow all in all. Social software and social media monitoring firms recognize this and try to work with CRM.

Software as a service (SaaS) becomes the preeminent delivery platform for CRM and the cloud gains currency quickly. (Probability Rating: 9.0)

This one doesn't need Nostradamus to come up with it. It's almost too easy. For you left-brainers, it's bolstered by information released in early 2009 by Gartner Group that they've found that 90 percent of the survey respondents said they would maintain or increase their use of SaaS by 2010. The recession clearly affects SaaS purchases, with the number one reason cited for using SaaS being "cost effective." Interesting, when it came to new deployments of SaaS they mentioned "replacement of on-premise" as the number one reason for that. This isn't a surprise and the indications are everywhere that SaaS and (as we'll see in the broader sense in a minute) cloud computing aren't just trends du jour. SaaS is the preferred delivery vehicle for pretty much every practitioner except those with highly complex implementations or classified data that has to reside on a home-based server. While it's not recession-proof, enterprise SaaS sales were, even with the downturn, $6.4 billion in 2008 and are expected to jump to $14.8 billion in 2012. In other words, with CRM being its most visible application/service and with companies like Zuora doing other kinds of SaaS services that integrate with salesforce.com and other CRM applications, SaaS is nearly a lock for becoming the preeminent delivery mechanism for CRM (with the aforenoted exceptions). That said, the same caveat always applies: make sure, if you're considering a CRM solution, which of the varying delivery mechanisms—on-demand or on-premise—works for you. There. Consider yourself caveated.

When it comes to cloud computing, there is a tendency to confuse it with SaaS. Remember, it is not a delivery mechanism. It's more where you work and the impact it has on how you work. As we saw in Chapter 16, there is a difference. Cloud computing is web-based, massively scalable, technology-enabled solutions and storage. It is gaining ground and will continue to do so over the next five years. It has its detractors, but more and more companies are getting on board. With Microsoft joining the sky with its Azure cloud computing platform, we now have EMC, Google, Amazon, Sun, salesforce.com, and, of course, Microsoft among others moving to become the cloud computing king. No one is the king yet, but by 2011, cloud computing will be part of CRM, enterprise, and small business initiatives. Keep your eyes on it and consider it in your own deliberations about CRM.

Growth in the public sector for Social CRM continues in the face of recession. Use of social tools accelerates rapidly in the federal, state, and local government in the United States. (Probability Rating: 9.0)

I hope that you've known this since Chapter 14. I won't dwell on it. One of the primary ways that 2.5 million jobs are going to be saved or created is through federal programs that will build national infrastructure (this is of course the U.S. only I'm speaking of here—so once again, pardon my American-centric view on this one). We elected a president who was elected in part because of his sophisticated use of social technologies and is changing how government is going to work by unprecedented constituent access through social tools and sites like Facebook, MySpace, and Twitter. Additionally, because of the long-standing lack of confidence in U.S. government institutions, one of the core issues that administrative, legislative, and executive agencies in the government have to deal with is constituent engagement. But don't ignore constituent management either. The need for management is due to not just the high risk programs that already exist that were discussed in Chapter 14, but to multiple other issues, ranging from

congressional e-mail traffic to better tools for agencies to process millions of requests for information per day. Typically, agencies are looking into using social media and social networks on the one hand and
CRM tools on the other, though they don't see the connection. As
CRM vendors and social software/tool vendors begin to integrate their
offerings, the convenience will be obvious. In the meantime, the cob-
bled version will be what predominates until the federal frameworks
are actually built. Beyond 2009, the initiatives will be tactically separate
but strategically coherent, built around constituent engagement and
managing that engagement. The use of social media abounds throughout the federal government. We are also seeing a redefinition of the
idea of public/private partnerships with outreach between government agencies and existing social networks/communities, especially
advocacy communities, which have been historically at odds. So, for
example, in 2009, Care2, an Internet advocacy aggregator, with its
nearly 10 million members, linked up with the National Oceanic and
Atmospheric Agency (NOAA) in an initiative to save coral reefs in the
International Year of the Reef. On the CRM side, there is a somewhat
slower but continuing movement toward utilizing hard-core CRM or
sometimes case management solutions like those from Adfero as substitutes. But companies like salesforce.com, Oracle, RightNow, and
Aplicor have been making major progress with government agencies.
What this means is that you can look for interest by the public sector
in CRM and social initiatives to increase—the latter faster than the
former—but expect the connection between the two around constituent engagement strategies to remain hazy except for the most forward
thinking public sector officials or employees.

Social characteristics join features and functions as vital pieces of CRM applications: identity, actions, reputation, influence, and persuasion. (Probability Rating: 5.5)

My friend Thomas Vander Wal, a Web 2.0 legend, pioneer in social
tagging and folksonomies, and someone you heard from in this book,
has this important concept that he calls the "social stack." I call it
"social characteristics." These are things like identity, objects, and
actions in the biggest sense. The facets that matter the most (they all
matter one way or the other) to CRM are the social characteristics
identified (and grouped by me as a single group) as reputation, influence, and persuasion. It's easy to say that these have always mattered in

company/customer relationships, because they have. What makes now different from then is twofold. With a peer as the most trusted source, these characteristics are now being embedded into social applications and Social CRM applications via varying user-generated content features like comments, ratings, rankings, and so on.

But not just software. Salesforce.com's release of Ideaforce and its subsequent execution on MyStarbucksIdea.com or Dell's IdeaStorm are great examples of how this works. Oracle Sales Library uses "best guess" kind of algorithms to help figure out what documents and presentations will work for a particular deal and takes into account the thinking of the "crowd," a.k.a the internal sales and marketing teams' thinking, ranking, and comments around the materials available in the knowledge store of the company. Social network analysis tools are becoming more prevalent. They find the true influencers in a company or any sort of network through the use of rigorous algorithms. As far back as 2004, VisiblePath integrated social network analysis with CRM applications like salesforce.com. Batchtags created Tripledex, a web-based visualization tool that defines relationships (and the influencers and importance of the relationships) among people, products, events, and organizations in any combination, with a unique interface that actually allows the product to be used by a human. This is a new generation of applications and sites that embed the social characteristics. They are not some esoteric addition to features and functions of CRM or Social CRM. By 2012, these technologies will be an ordinary part of the considerations of those implementing Social CRM.

Authenticity and transparency will become strategically important to companies. (Probability Rating: 9.0)

Do you find it funny that I'm making some really right-brained forecasts about technology in this final chapter? Please don't. The reality is that the transformation of CRM is from a purely operations-focused, transaction-based system to a system that extends to interactions. CRM applications are now engagement toolsets as well as management tools. The transformation affects customer strategy in an era where the customer owns the business ecosystem. That means that there is a business model that is no longer just a theoretical nicety. It is one defined by authenticity and transparency. There's a lot of extant literature about these topics—authenticity is best defined by James H. Gilmore and B. Joseph Pine II's bestseller, *Authenticity: What*

Consumers Really Want—and there is an excellent article on transparency by Lauren McKay in *CRM* magazine's December 2008 issue (go here for that: www.destinationcrm.com/Articles/Editorial/Magazine-Features/Transparency-51725.aspx).

The trend itself couldn't be clearer than it is. Companies are being *required* by customers to be responsive and open. They want the companies they deal with on a regular basis to be straightforward about their problems, not push marketing hype or bad explanations at them. They require businesses to provide them with what they, as customers, need to make intelligent decisions about their transactions and interactions with the company. We are not only looking at a proactive social customer, one who is involved with his or her peers and wants to be involved with the company the same way, but also at the idea of the "customer as partner," not "object of sale." The way a company differentiates in the 21st century is not just products and services, but visibility into the information that customers need and having an honest, straightforward relationship with those customers. During a recession, this trend will only increase as companies who are honest with their customers and let them in will survive at least and prosper at best, while companies that don't won't. Watch for more and more customer strategies based on this in companies. This is the planning you have to do too, so learn from what you can find.

"Feedback 3.0" will become an intimate feature of most companies' customer strategy. (Probability Rating: 8.0)

I didn't invent the term "Feedback 3.0"; I took it from Trendwatching .com, who first identified it as a major trend in very early 2009. You can go to their site to read about what Feedback 1.0, 2.0, and 3.0 are to start this discussion (www.trendwatching.com/trends/halfdozentrends2009/#feedback). Their point is that companies have realized that the conversation is taking place en masse among consumers right now, and currently (Feedback 2.0) the companies have chosen to try to listen and learn. Feedback 3.0 is when they start to engage with the customers.

Feedback 3.0 and Social CRM have elements that overlap directly. The key place they overlap? Companies responding to the idea that conversations about them are already happening among the customers outside the corporate walls and they have to respond. This is hardly lost on the corporate universe. Companies like SAP have senior management people whose purpose is to engage the blogger community. Dell has a chief blogger and people on staff whose job it is to monitor blogs and review sites and then engage in the conversation going on about Dell (which is prodigious). Companies like Boeing and Starbucks are actively soliciting feedback from their customers and then responding through collaboration with them on new products. These trends are being reproduced in hundreds, perhaps thousands, of companies around the world. With the ongoing recession, the *need* to engage these customers, friends or enemies, becomes paramount. These customer partners-in-waiting are influential with their peers and could damage or improve the bottom lines of your company based on how your company participates in the conversations *they initiated*. Not an easy thing but a necessary one. While I see this as an imperative that companies are becoming increasingly aware of, the increase in financial pressures could conceivably make many of those companies shortsighted. Being prudent and curtailing investments to control expenses during the downturn may seem the wise thing to do, but the conversations are going on just the same. If you don't deal with them now, you'll have a much harder time dealing with them later. But my saying that doesn't prevent some companies from not investing. So that may hinder the growth of Feedback 3.0. I hope not.

In (Dim) Sum

So what does all this prognostication mean? Well, since I'm not doing a fifth edition, you can't catch me if I'm wrong. Oh, wait, I can be found on blogs, Twitter, as a participant in Facebook, LinkedIn, and a dozen other social networks, and aggregation sites. Oops. So I'd better be right.

What can be gleaned from all the specific details above is that, as I just spent several hundred pages outlining, CRM has changed. It has a new kind of customer to contend with, a business ecosystem no longer controlled by the very businesses that it represents, a new direction when it comes to its strategy, and a much more direct engagement between the company and customer necessary to extract any real value for either party.

That means that all of those forecasts above, right or wrong, are indicative of one thing (queue up the Traveling Wilburys' "End of the Line," one more time, please).

Wait, I don't mean it signals the end of the line for CRM. But it is the end of the line for this book. I hope you do think of me sometimes, but I actually have someone to love—if you read the dedication and acknowledgment you know that—and I think my life has worked out really well for that matter, but regardless, there is no need for a fifth edition. However, I will continue to love the Traveling Wilburys.

But while it's not the end of the line for CRM, it has changed. In the first edition's final chapter, I quoted Mike Hernandez from Microstrategy, who said, "Compre na Internet, e devolve para a loja. . . . Eu sou o mesmo cliente. Por que vocês não são a mesma loja? O system precisa se fechar nessa lacuna."

Of course, that was in the Portuguese edition. What it means in English is "Buy it on the Web and return it to the store is actually a very important concept. I am the same customer. Why aren't you the same store? The loop has to be closed here."

And since that was written in 2000–2001, that loop has been closed. Just take a look at Nordstroms.com, buy something online, and then go to any Nordstrom's in the country and return it. Or vice versa. The loop is closed.

In the second edition finale, of 2002, I wrote about the customer-centric convergence that was coming where I said I would "rename" the corporate ecosystem (presumptuous of me, wasn't it?) a customer ecosystem because the business ecosystem now revolved around the customer. How did CRM play a role in this as a technology? The systems were maturing and the ability of those systems to aggregate and organize data about transactions was leading to what Mike Hernandez said in 2000: buy on the Web, return to the store. A consistent experience for the customer across channels and locations was in transit, coming into the station. I put it this way, "If you've adopted CRM now or are thinking of it, chances are that you'll have been on the very exciting ride to the effectively ordinary. That's the way I like it. No trouble, just happy customers."

Effectiveness (not efficiency) was the purpose of CRM back in 2002 and even subsequently as we came out of the burst dot.com bubble and began more prosperous years. But of course, as I think has been made abundantly obvious, the stirrings of the social communications revolution changed the game and the customer's natural desires, demands, and expectations.

The third edition had an inkling of that when it came out in 2004. I closed the book with a discussion of why it had become necessary to not only have the 360-degree view of the customer and all the data associated with that, but a business model that was based on mutually derived value between the company and the customer. There needed to be a collaborative value chain among the corporation, its suppliers, and its channel—an extended corporate ecosystem—to meet the requirements of that customer. I even defined the business model as a "collaborative network," which sounds prescient if I want to lie about it. But what I meant was collaboration in that enterprise value chain, not between the company and the customer per se. I even said what has been consistent throughout this book too: customer strategy *is* corporate strategy.

But where this all comes home is here and now as we enter the second decade of the new millennium. CRM is no longer what it was in the first three editions of this book. The evolution of traditional CRM, the subject of the first three editions of *CRM at the Speed of Light*, has come to what has been called a manifold leap. It is changing its character because, since 2004, the customer has changed his or her character. The customer changed because of a revolution in communications driven by the easy and inexpensive accessibility of the Internet and the even easier accessibility of cellphones and smart devices. They live untethered, they live 24/7, and they require real-time response.

What I didn't anticipate fully is how much the customer wanted to participate in the institutions they were interested in. And that their peers would be their most trusted source of both information and conversation. Intimacy has a whole new meaning with the rise of online communities and social networks. Transparency is now a business requirement, not something you draw a slide on.

But what an amazing opportunity! Even though invisible technologies have made the communications among peers and companies and other institutions much easier, the emphasis is not on the technology. It's still on what has been consistent through all four editions of *CRM at the Speed of Light*. It's geared around the experience of the customer. Now the customer can craft their own experience and your business can provide the tools. That's a change in how experiences have been delivered. But what hasn't changed is that it still has to do with how to craft the most delightful or exhilarating customer experience at one level, and how to avoid bad interactions between your company and your customers at another.

When push comes to shove, despite the fact that there are millions of Google search results on CRM, CRM 2.0, and Social CRM, despite the fact that I've written nearly 2,000 pages on CRM just with these books and there are millions of other pages written by me and other industry folks, CRM still boils down to one premise:

If customers like you, they'll stay with you. If they don't, they won't.

Simple, isn't it?

And that's no lie.

APPENDIX

The Social Web and the Public Sector: From the World to the State

—by Robert Greenberg,
Founder and CEO G&H International Services, Inc.

In 2006, at a time when the New Zealand National Police was under a great deal of scrutiny, the New Zealand Parliament directed the Minister of Police to rewrite the 50-year-old Police Act. The task fell to New Zealand Police Superintendent Hamish McArdle, who immediately created a task force and asked them for their suggestions on how to accomplish the task.

Because of the spotlight they were under, the task force decided that the traditional methods of consultancy—which usually involved using a set of consultants who would write a document and then perhaps post it in the public library—would not suffice this time around. Instead, the superintendent asked his team, "How can we connect with people about what kind of policy they want to govern their police in the 21st century?" To answer that, the superintendent and his team determined that their effort would be driven by two criteria—transparency and engaging as many people as possible in the process.

An open and transparent process, they felt, would go a long way toward removing the suspicion and cynicism that the New Zealand public felt toward their police. In order to further build trust, they had to go beyond the usual experts they might consult on this matter and reach deep into the people they serve—including youth and minorities—to get their input and opinions.

They decided on a two-year phased approach using multiple methods to obtain the input they wanted and needed. In addition to traditional means of obtaining input, they decided to turn to the Web—especially the tools available through Web 2.0—as the key part of their strategy. After a great deal of experimentation, they succeeded in finding the right balance of tools to get the input they needed. In fact, it was during their final phase when they posted a wiki to help them write the act itself that they began to see the true value of the Web 2.0 tools they were using, as they began receiving as many as 10,000 inputs a day. And while that's not to say that all of the inputs were useful, McArdle believes that using Web 2.0 in the way they did was the key to the success of their initiative.

"One of the key outcomes," McArdle said during an interview, "was to help the parliamentarians know that our product was well consulted—that it had community buy-in." Another surprising result was the new ideas they received. "If this was a good process [the 1.5-year consulting effort] you would think we'd have heard all the ideas there could be. But the wiki brought in fresh ideas. While most of the ideas haven't been accepted this time around, they've introduced new ideas, ones we wouldn't have thought of, and brought a creative tension to the debate."

In other words, it accomplished precisely what they wanted it to accomplish and more. It wasn't easy. As McArdle freely admits, there were a lot of failures along the way—it wasn't a case of build it and they will come. In fact, as we will examine later when looking at best practices and lessons learned, they did build it and found that few were interested and no one came. But at the end of the day, the utilization of Web 2.0 tools for policy deliberation and development proved to be a major success and a model for what we might look forward to in the future.

Customer Relationship Management or Citizen Relationship Empowerment?

During and after the 2008 presidential election campaigns, there was a great deal written about how the candidates used—or didn't use—social media to reach out to supporters and potential supporters. Garrett Graff's book *The First Campaign* details how social media is beginning to transform politics in the United States. It does a good job of detailing the changes that have already occurred in presidential politics by using social media in fundraising, organizing meetings (using Meetup.com), communicating with voters (social networks like Facebook, MySpace, or YouTube), and in some cases directly interacting with voters (Hillary Clinton's campaign song, getting ideas on health care, and so on). Since then, there have been numerous articles and other books that reported on what was dubbed Obama 2.0.

The discussion has ratcheted up as the Obama administration has begun to look at how to bring the same tools that won the election into the business of government. While the posting of YouTube videos have begun to be an almost ubiquitous part of the White House efforts, most attention was given to what was dubbed the first-ever web-based interactive town meeting, held on March 26, 2009, where the president spoke to and took questions from the public via the Internet. According to the White House, 64,000 people tuned in, 92,000 people submitted questions, and over 3.6 million people voted on which questions should be asked. While it was not without some controversy, it is clearly only the beginning.

What is clear is that the use of social media in politics is changing the expectations of citizens as to how those vying for power or in power should interact with them. Increasingly, citizens no longer look at themselves as passive observers or at best consumers of information. The availability of social media tools and their use in the presidential campaign has created citizens' expectation of having a direct voice and a direct role. It is a short but critical step for them to want to go beyond simply organizing events to that of shaping policy.

But as the New Zealand example and others to be cited in this appendix demonstrate, Web 2.0 and social media can have a profound impact on the public sector far beyond just politics. In fact, they can have a transformational impact. These same tools can and are beginning to be used to significantly alter the way the business of government is conducted, including interaction with the citizenry, the ability to share information across government and with the populace, the way in which advocacy is conducted, and even the way in which policy is formulated.

The Critical Importance of Web 2.0 for the Public Sector

Suffice it to say that Web 2.0 is not a technology per se; instead, it is an approach to using technology to enable interoperability and collaboration. It is a means to engage what some have called mass collaboration. When most people think about Web 2.0, they are usually referring to tools and platforms such as YouTube, Twitter, Facebook, MySpace, and the hundreds of other capabilities that are being used on a daily basis. At the same time, it is equally important to understand how Web 2.0 provides both a new technology and a business model that enables those tools and platforms to work together to enable widespread information sharing and collaboration cross-platforms. As we shall see a little later in this appendix, it is the combination of both of these aspects that can create a truly profound change in the way in which citizens interact with their government.

In past presidential campaigns, even the best political websites were merely used to push information out and raise money. The 2008 campaign changed this forever. While the so-called "YouTube debates" were often maligned, they raised the specter of ordinary citizens being able to impact the direction of the presidential debates. They set the stage for the demand for every candidate to hold "virtual town meetings" in which local campaign events become opportunities for citizens all over the country to interact and interrogate candidates on a regular basis.

As important as the political impact is, the impact on formulating policy can be even more profound. During the primary campaign, both Hillary Clinton and Barack Obama took this one step further, soliciting input on policy such as health care. In Clinton's case, she received some 40,000 inputs. Shortly after the election, the Republican National Committee unveiled a new plan in which they declared their intention to have citizens help develop the Republican platform prior to the next convention.

Over the last a couple of decades there have been several initiatives designed to change the way in which the government provides information and services to the citizenry. Two of these initiatives—the National Performance Review and the E-Government Initiative—were largely efforts to use the Web to better serve citizens. While these had mixed results, even the best of them tended to be one-directional— providing information to the citizens. And if they involved any degree of interaction, they involved getting information from the citizens. What they didn't involve was any form of real interactivity where citizens and government were communicating and working with one another.

That is the next step. We are at a "perfect storm" where the technology, the business model, the expectations of the population, and the willingness of government are all coming together to create a true revolution in how the business of government can work.

This is not without its challenges. As the Obama administration moves the use of these technologies from the campaign to governing, they are finding numerous impediments. In an article in the January edition of *Fast Company* magazine entitled "The Wired Presidency: Can Obama Really Reboot the White House?" author Evan Ratcliff was one of many who outlined some of the basic obstacles that will have to be overcome in order to accomplish this.

First and foremost is the bureaucracy itself, which has fostered a culture that resists change. For example, according to *Fast Company*, the federal government has 24,000 different websites with each agency having its own rules of adoption, enterprise architecture, and the like. While one would think that agencies would welcome rationalizing these in some way, the opposite has often been the case, with each agency steadfastly defending its own approach. In addition to this are a number of mostly outdated rules and regulations that were implemented before anyone anticipated the potential for how Web 2.0 technology could help establish a truly transparent and interactive government. Among these are

▶ **The Paperwork Reduction Act**   Requires agencies to go through a painstaking process to do surveys of more than ten people. This could make obtaining input from citizens via the Web difficult.

▶ **The Presidential Records Act**   Requires preservation of all written communications from the White House. This could make maintaining a dynamic web presence difficult.

▶ **Security requirements**   Makes it difficult to link with non-government sites and difficult to use open source tools without going through a detailed certification and accreditation process. This also prevents government agencies from using many cloud computing capabilities, since they are required to protect their own data.

▶ **No endorsement rules**   This too makes it difficult for the government to link to external sites.

To the administration's credit, they began to tackle this problem almost immediately after assuming office. For example, the General Services Administration (GSA) negotiated arrangements with Flickr, YouTube, Vimeo, and blip.tv to allow government agencies to use tools that enable people to post, share, and comment on videos and photos on the Web. GSA has also been in ongoing negotiations with Google.

The appointment of former Washington, D.C., chief technology officer Vivek Kundra as the federal government's first chief information officer (CIO) is also an indication of the administration's commitment to change. Kundra is a leading advocate of government using these tools. Before joining the federal government, he created a "Virtual D.C." for the public using Google Earth, and he hosted a competition for the public to create mash-up tools for use by the D.C. government.

Finally, some government agencies are already beginning to use these tools to improve internal collaboration. The most well known of these is Intellipedia, a wiki created by the intelligence community for collaboration on various intelligence products. Less well known is the building of A-Space, a social network platform that is complementary to Intellipedia but provides a broader set of tools for collaboration purposes. In addition, there are literally dozens of federal agencies that have Twitter accounts and are now actively engaged in some form of blogging. A good source of information on some of this is the Collaboration Project of the National Academy of Public Administrators, a congressionally chartered organization that advocates the use of collaboration tools and has an archive of many of the federal, state, and local uses of these technologies.

The reality is that although the government is often an unwieldy and hard to move bureaucracy, change is inevitable. With that said, let's explore how it can profoundly change the way in which the public sector does its business. Interestingly, and perhaps fittingly, one of the most profound examples of this is how Web 2.0 will dramatically transform the way state and local public safety agencies conduct their business and how they will be using these tools to interact with the public in the future.

The Core Problems Facing Public Safety Today

One of the essential dilemmas we face in our effort to improve homeland security and public safety in general is one that arises from our system of government. Homeland security, like many of the public safety issues facing us today, is national in scope, if not international. Yet the "boots on the ground" that we have employed to tackle these issues largely exist at the state and local level. There are nearly 55,000 state and local public safety agencies spread throughout the 50 states and six territories, 3,000 counties, and 19,500 municipalities across the country.

In addition to being spread across the country, the majority of these agencies are small in size. Approximately 80 to 85 percent of the 18,000 law enforcement agencies have 24 or fewer sworn officers, with approximately 50 percent having 12 or fewer sworn personnel. Some 80 percent of the more than 30,000 fire departments are volunteer agencies. Others, such as emergency management and emergency medical, face similar issues. Yet these agencies—police, fire, emergency management, and emergency medical, which comprise some 3 million public safety officers—are the front line of our homeland security efforts as well as our battles against drugs and crime.

In the past, our state and local public safety agencies mainly concerned themselves with state and local issues, with federal agencies such as the FBI, DEA, ATF, and even the CIA focusing on the bigger national and transnational issues. That luxury doesn't exist today. In addition to the day-to-day local issues that public safety has to deal with, they also have to deal with issues that are regional or national in scope such as terrorism, organized crime, gang violence, and so on. In addition to handling manmade problems, these agencies are also the first responders when it comes to natural disasters and catastrophic events. Finally, the very nature of their jobs in today's world requires a level of capabilities and knowledge whose acquisition is difficult for a small, local agency.

While the ties of these agencies to the communities they serve are a large part of their strength, they have also proven to be an impediment to functioning in today's world. While collaboration, cooperation, coordination, compatibility, and interoperability are more vital than ever before, the fragmented and largely small nature of public safety has made that difficult to achieve.

Communications interoperability on a local, statewide, regional, and national basis has been consistently identified as one of the most critical needs facing the public safety community. Yet historically agencies have invested in communications systems that address their specific local needs. As a result, billions of dollars have been invested in legacy systems that, more often than not, cannot "talk" to one another.

Information/intelligence sharing has been cited by the 9/11 Commission as a top priority to enhance homeland security. While this issue has gained a high profile since 9/11, the reality is that it has been recognized as a critical need by law enforcement across the country for some time. Since crime doesn't recognize jurisdictional boundaries, law enforcement has long understood the need to share information, from intelligence information to being able to inform other jurisdictions of an unserved warrant. Unfortunately, similar to the problem with communications systems, state and local agencies have invested hundreds of millions of dollars in systems that addressed only their needs, creating "stovepiped" systems across the country. A critical element of the problem is that these systems are often proprietary, making it difficult to integrate their existing systems so they can communicate.

Responding effectively to a catastrophic event, whether manmade (terrorist) or a natural disaster, takes a high degree of coordination among all public safety agencies. In a large scale event, not only do local agencies need to coordinate among themselves, they need to coordinate on a statewide and regional basis. Doing this effectively requires that multiple agencies share a common operating picture, sharing information and being able to communicate with one another. This has proven to be difficult given that incident management systems have "grown up" in much the same way as communications and information systems, as fragmented and proprietary systems.

State and local agencies are increasingly required to implement national-level programs that they are often ill equipped to implement. Programs such as the National Incident Management System (NIMS) and the National Response Framework (NRF) developed by the Department of Homeland Security require a level of knowledge, capabilities, and training that often don't exist at the local level. The same is true of issues such as critical infrastructure protection and cybersecurity.

State and local agencies generally do not have the infrastructure and expertise to conduct due diligence on new products and technologies. (It is equally as difficult for vendors to get their products in front of public safety agencies in a cost-effective fashion.) As a result, smaller agencies often do not get information on new products or processes in a timely fashion. If they do, they often have to rely on the vendor who is attempting to sell them the product for their information—clearly an inherent conflict of interest. Finally, even if they can get the information they need, their small budgets often preclude them from procuring a new product. A case in point is that of software-based products where high license fees preclude agencies from taking advantage of a new technology.

While state and local public safety personnel are the "boots on the ground," the so-called first responders (and first preventers) dealing with national-level issues, they often have little or no say on the policies and procedures that are established to deal with these issues. At best, a limited number of state and local practitioners are consulted and asked for their input, often using the medium of temporary working groups or committees along with the occasionally advisory group. While it is easy to blame the federal government for this, the reality is that the fragmented nature of public safety makes it very costly and time consuming to reach out to the larger community. Regardless of who's at fault, the impact is the same—the lack of input leads to a lack of effectiveness due to lack of involvement and buy-in from the public safety community.

While there are programs that are focused on actively engaging the state and local public safety community such as SAFECOM, the Global Criminal Justice Information Advisory Committee (Global), and the National Law Enforcement and Corrections Technology Center system (NLECTC), even they have limited success. One of the main reasons for this is that the method used to get this input is often too expensive to maintain—on both sides. It is costly to bring significant numbers of practitioners together to discuss any issue. On the one hand, efforts to bring state and local practitioners to the table require paying for their travel and per diem expenses. On the other hand, even if all expenses are paid, it is often too costly to the local department to have their personnel out of the rotation for a period of two or three days. One result of this is that, despite best efforts, these programs have ended up relying on a limited number of practitioners—often finding themselves talking to the same people over and over again. In effect, the system has created a semiprofessional class of a limited number of subject matter experts who shuttle between projects, leaving the majority of public safety disenfranchised.

Breaking Down the Barriers

To understand the value that Web 2.0 brings to public safety, it's critical to first understand that homeland security and other public safety activities depend on making information actionable. At the end of the day, public safety depends on acquiring, managing, analyzing (including visualizing), sharing, and protecting information. As cited above, this requires a greater level of collaboration, cooperation, coordination, compatibility, and interoperability that has existed to date.

Until recently, technology—usually proprietary in nature and with a high license fee—has been yet another impediment in enabling agencies to work together seamlessly. Web 2.0 is about to change all that. The use of standards-based open source/open architecture systems will enable agencies to begin to break down the stovepipes created by the proprietary systems that have been imposed on them in the past. This should enable an unprecedented level of sharing information between and across jurisdictions and disciplines.

One of the biggest impediments to the use of advanced software tools by state and local practitioners is the high license fee that is usually charged for these tools. The open source approach to software tools implemented by Web 2.0 companies will enable state and local agencies to utilize these tools at minimal or no cost for a license. While the agencies will still have to pay for the operations and maintenance of these systems, that can be accommodated through their regular service providers or using their own internal IT organizations.

Web 2.0 interfaces such as those represented by Google will enable agencies to integrate diverse sets of data, no matter what the source, into a browser and visualization system. While this is not a complete integration of systems, it nonetheless enables agencies to make information that would otherwise be excluded from use, actionable in nearly real time.

A Real World Case Study: Virtual Alabama

Virtual Alabama was created by the Alabama Department of Homeland Security in response to the urgent necessity of gaining access to the large amounts of Alabama's geospatial data following Hurricane Katrina. What began as a situational awareness project designed to enable the governor of Alabama to visualize the damage done by the hurricane has rapidly evolved into a model of how Web 2.0 tools can dramatically transform the way in which public safety conducts operations and does business.

When Alabama Homeland Security director Jim Walker was given the task of obtaining and organizing all of the state's geospatial data in a usable format, he turned to the two people on his staff uniquely qualified to solve that problem. Norven Goddard, the deputy director of R&D for the Alabama Office of Homeland Security is, in the words of director Walker, "a true rocket scientist," as he is on loan from the U.S. Army's Space and Missile Command and has spent his entire career solving problems like this for the Department of Defense. Chris Johnson, the program manager of what became the Virtual Alabama project, on loan from the State Space and Rocket Center (the people who bring you the famous Huntsville-based space camp), is an expert in geospatial data and has worked in the area for over 15 years.

Before even looking at a technical solution, Goddard and Johnson developed a unique set of criteria for the solution they were to develop, breaking the usual practice of focusing on proprietary solutions. Instead, they decided that the solution would have to:

▶ Be able to integrate disparate GIS and other data sets into one platform

▶ Be intuitive to use, so it can be used with little training

▶ Be cost effective and sustainable

▶ Be scalable so it can be used by large numbers of people

▶ Be able to be "owned" by all kinds of government agencies

After looking at all available technologies, they settled on Google Earth Enterprise as their platform. Not only did Google Earth Enterprise meet all their criteria, the cost was only $150,000 for an enterprise-level license that they now owned in perpetuity, which gave director Walker the ability to provide a license to any dot-gov or dot-edu in the state and, in fact, across the country. Given what state and local agencies have been used to, this alone was a revolution. But the best was yet to come. In enacting Virtual Alabama, the Alabama OHS team achieved what Art Galinski (writing on February 11, 2009, for *Geospatial Solutions: Government and the Military*) called "the holy grail of geospatial systems." For the first time, one platform was able to seamlessly integrate GIS data from numerous GIS systems to create a common operating picture across the state. But that was just the beginning.

As the team spread out across the 67 counties in Alabama to convince county and city officials to provide their data for the system, they began to see the fundamental transformation they were enabling across their state. Their first step in convincing those officials to participate was to provide them with their own license—cost free. Their next step was to demonstrate the various uses that Virtual Alabama could provide them.

For example, they showed county sheriffs that overlaying publicly available information on sex offenders across their countywide maps and employing some simple tools would help them determine whether the offenders lived or worked within a specified distance from a school. They showed firefighters that by using the 3-D modeling tools that came with the software to model the interiors of key buildings and overlay data on hazardous and combustible materials they can better prepare firefighters in case they have to enter those buildings. They showed emergency planning officials how the tools in Virtual Alabama could be used to plan for disasters and enable cross-jurisdictional coordination if one should occur. The possibilities were endless.

Through overlaying GIS information with data showing the locations of utilities such as power lines and creating 3-D models, Virtual Alabama became a tool to map and assess the vulnerability of the state's critical infrastructure. By overlaying other information such as the location of critical assets (such as hospitals), they demonstrated the ability to use the tool to plan for disasters. Through including other tools such as plume modeling and traffic information, it became apparent how it could be used to respond to a disaster, including improving evacuation procedures, triage, and the like. Finally, the Virtual Alabama team has integrated a social networking–collaborative workspace tool into the system, enabling virtual real-time collaboration that can be used to plan, share best practices, or communicate during an incident.

Thinking more broadly by integrating communications into the system, Virtual Alabama could create a common operating platform not only for the state, but across multiple states. "Imagine," Walker has stated, "if we had a tool like this during Katrina. Anyone involved in the response and recovery could have shared the same operational picture of the situation, which would have vastly improved our efforts. And we could have used it virtually for staging, evacuations, and everything else we had to do." In other words, Walker is describing the ability to create a virtual national emergency operations platform that can be shared among and across state and local agencies as well as with the federal government.

Where Are They Now?

Just two years after launch, Walker and his team are now implementing Virtual Alabama 3.0. Far beyond simply a common operating picture, it is now a common operating platform for day-to-day and emergency use. They have successfully implemented it in all 67 counties across

Alabama and are now working with every state agency to use it as well. Currently, they have the capability to:

► Integrate thousands of data sets across the state

► Track moving objects in real time

► Get real-time video feeds

► Overlay information dynamically, as it develops

► Overlay numerous tools such as plume modeling

► Monitor sensor feeds

► Do 3-D modeling

► Do GPS-based asset tracking and management

► Create a social network and collaborative workspace to enable users to share best practices

This is not just a nice toy. After the tornados in the fall of 2008, Virtual Alabama enabled the state's emergency managers to rapidly determine the damage, resulting in filing their relief request with FEMA in record time—less than one week after the tornados ended. Moreover, they helped tornado-ravaged Greenburgh, Kansas, do the same.

Creating Virtual USA

Where is this going? According to Virtual Alabama program manager Chris Johnson, they haven't even realized 10 percent of the full capability of the system yet. (Interestingly, every time you talk to Chris the percentage seems to go down as she and her team are being surprised by the new uses that are found by the program's users every day.) Given their understanding of the value that this tool can provide the country, Walker and his team have been hitting the stump to preach the virtues of this Web 2.0 technology to anyone who will listen. In the spirit of Web 2.0, they are not doing it for any other reason than it is good public policy.

The success of Virtual Alabama, combined with other companies jumping on the bandwagon, has spurred the establishment of similar types of platform. For example, the Virginia Department of Emergency Management has created VIPER (Virginia Interoperability Picture for Emergency Response) using an ESRI platform.

Working with the Department of Homeland Security's Science and Technology Command Control and Interoperability Division (CCI), with the support for the First Responder Technology Program (R-Tech), Alabama, Virginia, and six other states are now taking this to the next step. They have established a regional pilot that will begin to vertically integrate new technology tools into these types of platforms as well as horizontally integrate the platforms across the states. In so doing they are looking to establish the capability imagined by Jim Walker where during an emergency these states can seamlessly share information of all types and dramatically improve their responsiveness to a critical incident.

In a February 25, 2009, article in *Federal Computer Week*, Dr. David Boyd, director of CCI, citing the importance of this technology to help create a virtual national capability: "It's not like we're going to build a national system. What we're looking to do here is to create a national system of systems, exactly as we have been doing with interoperable communications so that disparate systems can communicate with each other even though the basic application, the basic platform, may be different."

Making It Mobile

A next step is making these platforms mobile. Web 2.0 tools are not only available at the desktop or on a laptop, they are also available in a mobile environment. As the Apple iPhone, Google GPhone, and BlackBerry Storm demonstrate, many of these tools can be utilized in handheld devices that serve as mobile platforms, enabling practitioners to obtain information that they previously could have only received at their computer. This is of tremendous value to a practitioner community that performs the majority of its jobs in the field, where toting around a laptop is inconvenient.

Involving the Public

The states involved in these efforts are looking for ways to inform and involve the public. Alabama, Virginia, and others are already talking about and looking for ways to create a "public facing" version of their platforms to not only keep the public informed of what is occurring, but to directly communicate with the public during an emergency. This is critically important, as during emergencies it is often the citizens themselves who are most effective in alerting and helping their neighbors. Already the public is using Twitter to warn their neighbors during incidents like the recent California wildfires. Now public safety officials are examining ways to use platforms like Virtual Alabama and VIPER and tools like Twitter to enable better citizen/government coordination.

A Web 2.0 Success Story

By all measures, programs like Virtual Alabama and VIPER are great Web. 2. 0 success stories. Not surprisingly, as of this writing, Virtual Alabama has won six national awards in the innovative application of technology. That said, it is important to understand that what made it a success was the realization and insistence by the leadership team that the key was to engage all the local stakeholders. It is their use of this tool on a day-to-day basis that is ultimately responsible for the success of the program. After all, it is their data and their collective imagining of how to make that data actionable in a way that is meaningful to them that has rolled up to create the program called Virtual Alabama.

The leadership team also understood that in order to want to engage the stakeholders had to be given ownership of the system. What has made the program successful is that the thousands of users of Virtual Alabama feel that this is their system. Virtual Alabama took the opposite approach of most government programs where the government (at whatever level) creates a program and asks (or attempts to mandate) people to contribute.

In this case, the Virtual Alabama team took to the road to give the tool, free of charge, to over 1,100 agencies (including federal agencies) to use as they see fit. The only thing they asked was that the data be sent for inclusion into the Virtual Alabama platform. Even then they allowed the users (owners) to determine the policies by which the state and other users could "see" the information they sent. In other words, the stakeholders had true ownership of the system. It was after they saw the utility of the system for themselves, including the value of providing the information to the state, that the true value of Virtual Alabama emerged—complete with thousands of data sets and hundreds of tools. The ultimate mash-up.

What is important to note here is that it wasn't the technology per se that made or even was the enabler of Virtual Alabama's success. It was the process and business model inherent in the Web 2.0 approach taken by Google. If Google had taken the typical approach of providing a proprietary system that was licensed to the state of Alabama at high cost, none of this would have happened. Instead, it was the fact that the technology is based on an open source standard (KML, Keyhole Markup Language) and provided an enterprise-level license in perpetuity at such a low cost ($150,000 for such a license is, in the words of Walker, "something that every homeland security director can afford") that made it possible for Alabama to give ownership of the system to all the stakeholders.

Change Is Coming

Virtual Alabama is perhaps one of the clearest examples of how the application of Web 2.0 tools and philosophy can make a dramatic difference in implementing the business of government—in this case, at the local, state, and federal levels. But we are really only at the beginning of the dramatic transformation that the application of Web 2.0 will cause in the business of government.

As detailed in the Virtual Alabama example, people at all levels of government are beginning to wake up to the possibilities. There are also a number of initiatives going on at the local level. In a white paper entitled "Gov 2.0: Transforming Government and Governance for the Twenty-First Century," authors Don Tapscott, Anthony D. Williams, and Dan Herman discussed one such project, called Networked Knowledge Los Angeles (NKLA), which was established by the city of Los Angeles in collaboration with UCLA to provide citizens with the information and forum to improve their communities. NKLA accomplishes this by "mashing" together all kinds of public data and provides tools to enable citizens to explore how to address issues like substandard housing, crime, and social and economic problems facing their specific neighborhoods. In particular, it enables citizens to interact in a meaningful fashion with government officials, community organizations, and others to try and solve problems facing these communities. Moreover, the site enables communities to better address economic problems by empowering them to interact with the private sector by identifying potential investment opportunities, which can then help to redress community concerns.

It is a time-honored maxim that the federal government—with the possible exception of the Department of Defense—lags behind the private sector in the implementation of advanced technology.

In the case of Web 2.0 this is true not only for the traditional reason that government is risk adverse when it comes to adopting new technologies, but it would seem to be even more difficult because the adoption of these tools will mean a fundamental change in the way the federal government conducts the business of government.

Generally speaking, the federal government's approach to developing and implementing policy has been to rely on a (relatively) small handful of civil servants (sometimes referred to as bureaucrats) and internal subject matter experts. At their best they may rely on some outside organizations—think-tanks, not-for-profits, associations, and yes, the private sector—to provide input. But at the end of the day the government personnel make the decision as to what should be done and how it should be done. Often, those decisions are politically driven, and while many may bemoan that fact, it is the way our system works.

But Web 2.0 can—and will—change all that if for no other reason than, as described above, the citizenry will demand it. In other words, the cat is out of the bag. The implications of this are truly revolutionary— and that is likely to scare government officials who are not only not used to the kind of scrutiny this affords the average citizen, but who truly have no experience in being able to use mass collaboration to formulate and help implement policy.

The bottom line is that we are just at the beginning of transforming what has previously been called constituent relationship management to citizens relationship empowerment. Web 2.0 is making it possible— and inevitable—for ending the disenfranchisement of citizens in all walks of life by providing the tools that in turn will provide actionable information and enable them to take control of their own lives.

Index